Public Budgeting and Finance

Second Edition

Public Budgeting and Finance
Readings in Theory and Practice
2nd Edition

EDITED BY

ROBERT T. GOLEMBIEWSKI
University of Georgia

JACK RABIN
Auburn University

F. E. PEACOCK PUBLISHERS, INC.

ITASCA, ILLINOIS 60143

Contents

Preface to the First Edition

It is a useful administrative truism that where one sits often determines what one sees and how one reacts. Thus it was for me. I had long been concerned with the lack of useful teaching materials in Public Administration. Rather than doing much about this basic need, I indulged my own long-run romance with theoretical and applied behavioral analysis relevant to organizations. As Academic Director of the MPA Program at the University of Georgia for the last several years, however, I found the lack of teaching materials of far more immediate concern. At U. of G. we are attempting to provide up-to-date training—what I fancy as the training of "professional generalists" with broad and deep competencies—and we are providing that training for students at the university center and throughout the state. We see ourselves concerned not only with quality training, but also with training in large numbers. The ready availability of teaching materials is vital to achieving such ambitions.

Public Budgeting and Finance is one of several attempts to provide teaching materials for our use and, hopefully, for the use of others. There seems no question that the need exists. Consider only a single point. Derived from the same motivation as the present collection, a comprehensive set of readings suitable for graduate and undergraduate courses in Public Administration has already appeared.[1] The wide acceptance of that publication reinforces three beliefs underlying this volume. First, I feel Public Administration as an area of specialization gives every indication of rising beyond its "topping-out" point reached after World War II. Second, I feel that unparalleled demands for professional training in Public Administration will be increasingly made on those of us in our nation's colleges and universities. My friend, Dean Stephen Bailey of Syracuse, foresees at least a tenfold multiplier at work; I agree with his prediction. Third, I feel that conveniently available teaching materials can serve as a valuable catalyst for the present ferment affecting research and teaching in the arts and sciences of public management.

ix

At least two other aids to teaching in Public Administration will appear. A reader in public personnel is still some time off.[2] However, *Perspectives on Public Management: Cases and Learning Designs* will be published about the same time as the present volume.[3]

Such an effort patently rests on diverse research and publishing talents. It is at once humbling and challenging to attempt to give some pattern to the products of these many talents. I have tried to act as a cutter and setter of gems in this case, selecting among the richness of voluminous literatures and striving to bring out the particular features of individual pieces by providing appropriate settings.

However successful my efforts at craftmanship, meeting the present challenge was at least eased for me in several senses. Thus I took advantage of early conversations with my colleagues, Drs. Frank Gibson and Ira Sharkansky, in developing the general format and coverage of the volume. In addition, Mrs. Sigrid Saunders was an invaluable aid in giving tangible order and form to my editorial decisions. Carol Holcomb, Lane Howell, and Mrs. Jennie Rogers provided the massive clerical and typing skills necessary for any such effort. The efforts of Philip Rosenberg also deserve note.

Notes

1. Robert T. Golembiewski, Frank Gibson, and Geoffrey Y. Cornog (eds.), *Public Administration: Readings in Institutions, Processes, and Behavior* (Chicago: Rand McNally & Co., 1966).
2. The volume now has been published. Robert T. Golembiewski and Michael Cohen (eds.), *People in Public Service: A Reader in Public Personnel Administration* (Itasca, Ill.: F. E. Peacock Publishers, 1970).
3. Robert T. Golembiewski (ed.), *Perspectives on Public Management: Cases and Learning Designs* (Itasca, Ill.: F. E. Peacock Publishers, 1968).

Athens, Georgia   ROBERT T. GOLEMBIEWSKI
June 30, 1967

Preface to the Second Edition

It is pleasurable to see one's expectations being realized. And this second edition basically testifies to the soundness of the confidence in 1967 that training in Public Administration was about ready to increase in both quality and quantity. Without such a takeoff, simply, there would be no second edition.

This volume has three major motivations. First, the readings and the editorial introductions have been substantially updated and revised. As one measure of these changes, about one-half of the selections in this volume appeared after the publication date of the first edition. A number of classic pieces have been retained, so previous users of the volume no doubt also will see some old friends.

A number of classes and seminars contributed to this revision by evaluating the selections in the first edition. Drs. Augustus Turnbull, Jerry McCaffery, and Jack Rabin fielded these courses. Their efforts, and especially those of their students, are gratefully acknowledged.

Second, the focus of the second edition has been changed substantially. From one perspective, this volume reflects more concern with issues and techniques applicable at all levels of government. The first edition, while saying the same things, had a definite bias on federal institutions and practices.

Third, the present volume has an added emphasis on the description and evaluation of alternative techniques or approaches relevant to budgeting and finance activities.

Patently, such a volume rests on many talents and contributions, and our role as editors is minor among them. Especial thanks to Mrs. Sandra Daniel, an experienced hand in such matters, who managed the preparation and assembly of the finished effort.

May 1, 1974   ROBERT T. GOLEMBIEWSKI
                                            JACK RABIN

I

Some Conceptual Contexts

What is it? How well do we do it?

Public budgeting and finance patently encompass a wide range of phenomena, the breadth and diversity of which can only be suggested here. However inadequate the attempt must be, we cannot avoid trying to indicate in conceptual terms part of what is meant by the term "public finance and budgeting." The two focal questions in this attempt are: What is it? How well are we able to do what is required? The perspective here is intentionally broad. Subsequent chapters will add much detail.

The "what" of public budgeting and finance is given some initial content by two readings that focus on the possible uses of financial data. These contributions are drawn from Andrew C. Stedry and Herbert Simon and his associates. Reading 1 adds conceptual meaning to "budgeting," and Reading 2 microscopically details the uses of financial data.

Stedry's "Budgets: Definition and Scope" provides some important variations on the theme of budgets as an instrument of control as well as a plan of action. His discussion of "standards" and "standard costs" also is useful, for to "plan" and "control" require some estimate of how much of which resources are required for specific objectives. Thus budgets require commitment to some total figure as well as to their component standards. Standards or standard costs imply what is to be demanded in work for some sum of dollars. For example, a department in a university may have a large budget for salaries, but if the faculty-student ratio is high also, this implies a standard that many professors may find unattractive even though their salaries are quite pleasing. Directly, budgeting and finance must motivate individuals to strive to meet a total budget as well as induce them to accept its component standards.

The excerpts from Stedry, although brief, establish that the "what" of public budgeting and finance encompasses many phenomena at the heart of

1

the management of men and the coordination of cooperative behavior. Only a little interpretation will make the matter clear. The "plan" aspects of budgeting and finance require that their processes lean toward the future and embody and reflect some sense of things as they might be improved or as they would be at their best. The plan, however, cannot command total attention. The "control" aspects imply that the processes of public budgeting and finance also must rest upon a strong sense of things as they are, or as they might be at their worst. Avoiding the worst while attempting to permit the best—this is a human challenge of heroic dimensions. Just that challenge rests very near the central phenomena of public budgeting and finance.

Despite their value, the comments from Stedry certainly do not even begin to suggest the manifold characteristics of the "what" of public budgeting and finance. Simon and his associates provide some of the additional conceptual detail in an excerpt on "Management Uses of Figures" from their book *Centralization vs. Decentralization in Organizing the Controller's Department.* Basically, they argue that three types of questions must be considered by any comprehensive program of the "internal reporting" of financial data. According to Simon, these three types of questions are: (1) Score-Card Questions, that is, questions such as "Am I doing well or badly?"; (2) Attention-Directing Questions, that is, those such as "What problems should I look into?"; and (3) Problem-Solving Questions, that is, questions such as "Of the several ways of doing the job, which is the best?". These questions relate to both the planning and control aspects of financial reporting stressed by Stedry.

In their own way, the three types of questions isolated by Simon and his collaborators sharply indicate the centrality of the phenomena associated with public budgeting and finance. Score-Card Questions patently must play a crucial role in every organization. That is, organizations have as their basic purpose the effective utilization of collective resources. "Are we doing well or badly?" consequently must be of central organizational concern. Providing appropriate answers to Score-Card Questions is, however, not only a central need. Perhaps more important, the processes of providing those answers are very delicate ones indeed. Directly, budgeting and finance personnel could easily come to be seen as punitive because of their basic and traditional role. They provide answers to Score-Card Questions, and they thereby enable top management to control those at lower levels.

Hence the importance of giving extensive and successful attention to Attention-Directing Questions and Problem-Solving Questions. Two factors contribute to this importance. First, answers to these two types of questions can be helpful at many levels of organization. In providing such answers, and particularly in providing them directly to lower levels of organization, finance and budgeting officials can help compensate for the punitiveness inherent in some of their other activities, such as providing answers to Score-Card Questions. Second, financial and budgeting officials apparently are less active in seeking answers to the latter two types of questions, and particularly to Problem-Solving Questions. No doubt the traditional concern with Score-Card Questions helps explain this inactivity, implying as it does that internal financial reporters are less equipped and motivated to handle the other types of questions. In addition, answering Problem-Solving Questions requires working closely with officials at all levels, while budgeting and finance personnel typically identify more closely with top management. Finally, officials at various management levels who had been disciplined via answers to Score-Card Questions would be reticent to accept or ask for help, for to do so risks providing "inside information" to budgeting and finance officials which in turn might be used against the manager.

The main thrust of the excerpts from Simon can be summed up in this point: The three types of questions involving financial data highlight the breadth and diversity of public budgeting and finance. That significance extends from providing data about the effectiveness of performance all the way to providing these yardstick data in helpful and humane ways.

A substantially broader perspective on public budgeting and finance is provided by Arthur Smithies, who considers these two central functions in the contexts of the decision-making process. Smithies has two purposes in "Budgeting and the Decision-Making Process" (Reading 3). First, he seeks to establish some crucial linkages: All decisions involve the allocation of scarce resources among alternative uses; hence budgeting is a critical activity in decision-making, because it can help explicitly the choice between alternative uses, especially if the focus is on programs rather than on individual activities. Second, Smithies seeks to tie his discussion of budgeting and decision-making to the structure and procedures of a large organization. In this case, also, budgeting and finance can provide critical linkages. Specifically, Smithies notes that all large organizations tend to become fragmented, due to the basic need to specialize. The budget process is perceived as a critical one in integrating these fragmented parts of a large organization, in providing a sense of common thrust and direction to parts that have a tendency to go off in all directions.

Given the scope of the phenomena relevant to public budgeting and finance, and given the tendency of the parts of government to go their diverse ways, the underlying theory and its associated arts provide little comfort. We can only make one general point in this introductory chapter: that budgeting is at once a technical and a political matter, an issue of miniscule procedure as well as lofty policy and substance. This point has sometimes been lost sight of, with profound consequences. We refer the reader to Chapter VIII for a detailed analysis of the senses in which budgeting is both politics and techniques. Of particular relevance is James R. Schlesinger's "Uses and Abuses of Analysis" (Reading 35).

A brief review of Aaron Wildavsky's classic paper "Political Implications of Budgetary Reform"[1] will serve to alert the reader here to the subtle interplay of technique and substance in budgeting. Wildavsky notes that the insistent and long-standing demands for "better budgeting" involve far more than technical tinkering. The proposed reforms, he notes, "inevitably contain important implications for the political system, that is for the 'who gets what' of governmental decisions." At the same time, Wildavsky advises humility concerning claims about our present ability to design a budget system adequate to distribute the appropriate "whats" to the proper "whos," even if some reasonable agreement is possible about changes in "who gets what." About the "normative theory of budgeting," Wildavsky concludes that "we know very little about it." Even greater humility is in order about our capability to change the political system so that it will support the budget system of grand design.

Wildavsky goes even further: The "orthodox recommendations" for budget reform are to eliminate the "irrationalities" of budgeting, in sum, but Wildavsky emphasizes it is those very irrationalities that make our system work. That is, the recommended changes in budgetary processes will require changes in the underlying political system of which existing budget practices are but one reflection. For example, orthodox recommendations argue for a comprehensive review of the budget by a single person or by some small, cohesive group in a position to compare alternative uses of funds. However, our political institutions can be characterized as systems of fragmented power with numerous centers of influence, complex and shifting aggregations of which are required to get any policy adopted and implemented. Bargaining, swapping of favors, and kaleidoscopic coalitions tend to characterize our political system, with two basic results: only selected parts of the political system are energized from case to case; and the process of comparing policy alternatives is enormously simplified. On the whole, Wildavsky sees these "irrationalities" as not only existing but as more or less necessary, unless we drastically change our basic concepts of governance.

Given the major theoretical difficulties of coping with the phenomena of public budgeting and finance, control over public expenditures becomes an issue of enormous significance. This issue cannot be accorded just treatment in this chapter, and it will take the rest of this volume to sketch an approach to it. But, to simplify a little, it can be essentially posed as resting somewhere between the two positions exemplified by William Jump and Northcote Parkinson.

William Jump—a renowned financial officer who served in the Department of Agriculture—provides one view of the control of public expenditures.[2] Basically, Jump emphasizes certain inherent administrative features that limit the probability of padding or overstaffing. Overhead controls by financial officials in positions such as his have their place, he explains.

Eagle-eyed legislators can also make a major impact. But the most powerful forces toward efficient use of public funds inhere in the program drives of government executives. The active official has so many good ideas for programs that he necessarily utilizes men and money wisely. If anything, understaffing will be the crucial problem, for resources typically will be inadequate to do all of what the eager program official would like to have done. Moreover, the program official must justify his own demands for whatever resources are available in often-pointed competition with other program executives about who is likely to get the most mileage out of any funds. Thus part of the control over public expenditures comes from the individuals charged with spending them. This is a happy outcome indeed.

The tough-minded reader might be impressed only in part by Jump's thesis. Even if all program executives are as eager as Jump implies, his argument still applies only to spending whatever is made available. The control of the level of expenditures, of how much should be made available, is at least as important a matter. This implies no criticism of Jump, for control of the level of expenditures sorely challenges anyone's analysis. In his own way, indeed, Jump reflects the difficulty of controlling the level of expenditures. Thus he clearly notes his respect for the strong tendency of program executives to resist anyone—even Jump—who "meddles" with their budgets! In short, attempting to control the level of expenditures hits Administrative Man where he hurts. Financial decisions influence not only the size of the programs he supports but also help determine whether an organization is "dying" or "on the move," with implications ranging from doing today's job badly all the way to ineffective recruiting that implies long-run failure. The influence of decisions about the level of expenditures extends from what an agency can be today all the way to what it will be in the future.

However, if Northcote Parkinson's jaunty argument[3] has even a very approximate validity, concern about the level of expenditures is more or less pointless. Expenditures will rise as fast as income does, goes the central core of Parkinson's argument, and public expenditures may rise even faster than income. The point may be put otherwise. What goes up in this case, in sum, is not likely to come down. Wars encourage sharp rises in the level of public expenditures, and peacetime never quite seems capable of reversing the trend toward massive spending. Expenditures still chase after income, even if they do not surpass it. Individuals become accustomed to large public outlays, and perhaps to the inevitable wastefulness associated with warfare.

In contrast to Jump, Parkinson is a determined skeptic. Two Parkinsonian "laws" underlay his skepticism: (1) work expands to fill the time available, and (2) one multiplies subordinates but not superiors. Parkinson does acknowledge boundary conditions that can bring up short the reinforcing inevitabilities that balloon public expenditures, but he sees these boundary conditions only as "danger points" that presage "international disaster." His boundary conditions offer little hope this side of calamity, as he intends.

The remaining chapters of this volume will provide diverse evidence of the wisdom and limitations of these two contrasting positions on the control of public expenditures.

Notes

[1]Aaron Wildavsky, "Political Implications of Budgetary Reform," *Public Administration Review* 21 (Autumn 1961): 183–90.

[2]U.S., Congress, House, *Hearings before the Subcommittee of the Committee on Appropriations,* 2nd session on the Agriculture Department Appropriation Bill for 1947 (Washington, D.C.: U.S. Government Printing Office, 1946), pp. 69–81.

[3]Northcote Parkinson, *The Law and the Profits* (Boston: Houghton Mifflin Co., 1960), especially pp. 5–8, 150–53, and 218–22.

1

Budgets: Definition and Scope

Andrew C. Stedry

In an attempt to eradicate, or at least mitigate, some of the ambiguity which will result from the particular usage of the term "budget" in this thesis, it is necessary to relate it to the definitions in common use. The most comprehensive use of the term is exemplified by the following definition of "budget" by Eric Kohler as:

1. A financial plan serving as a pattern for and a control over future operations;
2. hence, any estimate of future costs;
3. a systematic plan for the utilization of man power, material or other resources.

Implicit in Kohler's definition is the existence of a multiplicity of purposes for which budgets are constructed.[1]

Two major functions are, however, immediately discernible. First, a budget may serve as a *plan,* indicating requirements of certain factors (e.g., cash, productive capacity) at some future date which serves the function of

From Andrew C. Stedry, *Budget Control and Cost Behavior* (Englewood Cliffs, N.J.: Prentice-Hall, Inc., 1960), pp. 3–12. Reprinted by permission of the author.

providing information for subsequent decisions and possibly guiding them. Second, a budget may serve as a *control,* containing criteria of cost or performance which will be compared with actual data on operations, thus facilitating evaluations and possibly encouraging or even enforcing some measure of efficiency.

As may be already apparent, these separate functions (i.e., planning and controlling) need not be mutually exclusive nor, in practice, is it unusual for both to be represented in a single document. That these functions are (rightly or wrongly) fused is aptly indicated by the following description of "production planning and control" by MacDonald:

> . . . one of the essential steps in the preparation of the production budget is the translation of sales estimates into specific production plans. While this activity is primarily the responsibility of the production executive, usually exercised through the head of planning or a production control department, it is so fundamental to practical budgetary control that it is essential that the budget executive at least be familiar with the essential features of it.[2]

There is certainly no doubt indicated in MacDonald's remarks about the advisability, or even necessity, of interlacing the planning and control functions to the point where they become indistinguishable. A question might be raised, however, as to whether the interrelationship described can, in fact, be achieved with only one set of budgeted figures—a set which would need to serve both planning and control functions at various tiers (and over various persons) in an organization. Consider, for instance, the impact of the following remark as quoted by two other authors: "A good plan (e.g., a budget or sales forecast) does not necessarily yield a good control."[3] Also, "Good planning data and good control data are not necessarily the same."[4] Therefore, it is evident that there is some room for disagreement as well as some need for clarification in these areas, planning and control.

In order to clarify this distinction, reference will be made to sales budgets where it is usual for distinctions of this kind to be recognized in the literature,[5] possibly because widespread divergencies between plans and actual operations are more frequent than in, say, production or financial budgeting. One type of sales budget (frequently termed a "quota") is designed specifically as a control device. Its aims are to effect the motivation and guide the judgment of the salesmen by comparison of budgeted and actual performance. This comparison may be (and sometimes is) re-enforced by connection with various rewards and penalties. On the other hand, the tie between these quotas and the planning of output is often extremely loose. The planned output is often based on "estimated" or "expected" sales, and the relations of these expectations to the quotas suggests an assumption that at least some of the quotas will not be achieved.[6] A question arises as to why the "quota" concept is generally not carried over into other areas of budgeting—e.g., production—as a control device. As far as may be discerned, the reasoning is somewhat as follows: the budget must serve as a coordination device. Hence production must be planned so that the needs emanating from "expected sales" will be met along with other criteria, such as the size or fluctuations in inventory, that are regarded as prudent. The assumption which is made in practice (or at least in descriptions of practice) is that the figures to be used for control purposes and the estimate of needs (i.e., the production plan) are the same.[7] It is an hypothesis of this thesis that the equality of the figures used for the control and planning budgets need not be assumed, but that its desirability is a testable proposition. Or, in other words, does some figure other than the planned amount, when used in the control budget, produce a performance which is actually closer to the planned amount?

The questions which arise regarding the disparity of plans and controls indicate that the "budget process" is actually not a homogeneous mechanism but rather a collection of processes with a variety of aims and procedures of application. . . .

BUDGETS: STANDARDS AND STANDARD COSTS

In order to convey the applicability of the treatment of "budgets" in this paper to control systems using "standards" and "standard costs" as elements of control, the similarity of these various elements will now be discussed. It will first be desirable to examine "standards" and "standard costs" to provide a framework for the discussion of similarities and differences.

Both "standards" and "standard costs" are so intimately related that the one is generally included with the other in any description of cost or profit control mechanisms. It is thus necessary, in order to maintain contact with the main body of accounting literature, to explain the context in which they (i.e., "standards" and "standard costs") will be used in this thesis.

In order to introduce these concepts as they will be used here, the definitions of Eric Kohler will be cited. He defines a *standard* as, "A desired attainment; a performance goal; a model."[8] It will be noted that Kohler views a standard as something to be striven for, and that although various types of schemes are used to set standards, the basic correspondence between standard and goal remains unaltered. Standards are frequently encountered in such specific contexts as "standard time," "standard material usage," etc. In contrast to standard, Kohler defines *standard cost* as, "A forecast or predetermination of what costs should be under projected conditions, serving as a basis for cost control, and as a measure of productive efficiency when ultimately compared with actual costs."[9]

Even with the fairly explicit definitions of Kohler, the problems of classification are not always straightforward. For example, items such as "standard labor costs" and "standard material costs" can be classified as "standard costs" and passed by without further discussion, since an absence of ambiguity in these classifications is usually assumed. But what about "standard overhead expense" and like items? Are these a "standard," or a "standard cost"? It is evident that there is some difference in the dimensions, at least as far as control is concerned. Whereas goals or levels used for control which are expressed in units other than dollars are necessarily classed as standards (or budgets, as will be explained later), those which are expressed in dollar terms are frequently classed as standard costs, but not invariably.

In practice, moreover, a "standard time" (expressed in hours) for a particular operation extended by a "standard rate" (cost per hour) for a worker employed on the operation is usually termed a "standard labor cost" for the operation. Any two out of the three figures in this case may serve as the basis for control; the particular pair chosen is a matter of convenience. Conceptually, there is little difference between controlling input or output in physical units as opposed to dollar terms, although they may require different procedures.[10]

From the above comments it may be inferred that the choice of a common denominator—a *numéraire*—is in reality fairly arbitrary, and hence the terms "standard" and "standard cost" can be used more or less interchangeably, at least in a theoretical document of this kind.

Another issue which requires clarification involves the difference between budgets and standards. The distinctions made in the literature vary considerably from author to author so that a concise summary is difficult to achieve. A view which is widely held, however, is that the difference is one of scope. This viewpoint is exemplified in the following remarks of S. Henrici.

> . . . Budgets are customarily set for all departments in the company, from sales to manufacturing. But standards are frequently set only for the manufacturing divisions and can, indeed, be confined to controllable costs in a limited number of cost centers . . . [11]

Similar statements may be found in Lang, McFarland, and Schiff,[12] and Heckert,[13] who consider scope the essential difference. Henrici, however, considers scope only one of the distinctions, and not the primary one. He states:

> The first distinction between standards and budgets is one of purpose. Budgets are statements of expected [sic] cost . . . Standards on the other hand, do not necessarily show what costs may be expected to be [sic] but rather what they might be if certain highly desirable performances are attained . . . [14]

On the other hand, I. Wayne Keller proposes a distinction which might well be considered dictated by (in the linguistic sense) "common usage." He writes:

... for control purposes the terms "standard" or "standard cost" are applied to the measurement and control of the costs of direct material, direct labor, and scrap [sic]. Expense is controlled through expense "budgets" rather than expense "standards."[15]

It is apparent from the foregoing conflicting distinctions that no common denominator exists upon which to base a single, well-defined criterion of separation between standards (including standard costs) and budgets. The situation is perhaps best explained by the following statement of the National Association of Accountants' (formerly N.A.C.A.) report, "A Re-Examination of Standard Costs." In relating standard costs to the "scientific management" movement, they note:

Historically, standard costs as we now know them and business budgeting developed at about the same time, but in the earlier years their development was largely separate. Standard costs developed in the factory while budgeting was applied first to the financial aspect of business. Later on it was realized [sic] that both were merely applications of the same management philosophy and that they were complementary parts of a complete programme of cost control.[16]

This view, which minimizes the difference between budgets and standards, would seem to be most sensible in light of the profusion of conflicting statements which may be found. It also seems, however, that planning and forecasting budgets might properly be differentiated from standards, although standards are frequently used in the determination of the plans and forecasts.

On the other hand, a control budget, as defined *supra,* carries with it the connotation of a "goal" or "desired attainment" which is noted in Kohler's definition of standard. It may thus be seen that "budgeted performance" and "standard performance" differ only in name if they are both goals or desired attainments.

Agreement among writers is more or less general only in the matter of the difference in scope exhibited by budgets and standards. It would not be contrary to this consensus if some distinction were made; e.g., a budget is a goal on a large scale, a standard a goal on a smaller scale. But even this distinction would appear to be artificial from the standpoint of classification by function since both a budget and a standard may, in this context, serve the same purpose.

In any case, in this thesis, the meaning of budget (as a control device) will be interpreted as a goal or desired attainment, and the foregoing discussion and quotations used should suffice to justify, to a first approximation, why findings from a study of "budgets" should also be applicable to "standards" or "standard costs" as one or the other (or all three) are used as part of a cost control system.

HOW A BUDGET CONTROLS

In the preceding sections of this chapter, it was noted that there is a control aspect of budgeting that is distinguishable, in some sense, from either planning or forecasting. Assume for the moment that this distinction is valid and can be sufficiently well demarcated; let it then be assumed that a mechanism has been created for the sole purpose of producing and administering a control budget. A question may then be asked as to just what the budget control system and the budget documents (which are an integral part of the system) should consist of in order to insure that the cost or performance elements budgeted are in fact being controlled.

It would seem reasonable that in order to insure some form of control, the process by which control is exercised should be analyzed. In other words, assurance of control would seem to require some answer to the question, "Just how do budgets control?" This issue is rarely addressed in the budgeting literature except by implication and by reference to "experience," "practice," and intuitive appeals that are more or less plausible (when stated).

A more than usually lucid treatment is presented by Henrici. He notes:

> The difference in a given period between actual cost and standard cost, known as the "variance," tells management to what extent costs can be controlled. The variance itself is not a control, for costs are not controlled by compiling statistics about them. The control consists of the steps that management takes to regulate or limit costs. And the effectiveness of these steps is gauged by the degree to which actual costs approach standard; in other words, by the size of the variance.[17]

An important feature to be noted in Henrici's remarks is the absence of the commonly held assumption that the means of reporting and controlling are the same.[18] A second unusual feature is the concept of an approach to standard as a criterion of effectiveness. It should be noted in this regard that Henrici's definition of standard involves a concept not far removed from the "technological optimum" of economics. He considers standards as emphasizing "what *should* be" and having a "primary purpose of establishing a 'sea level,' so to speak, from which to measure cost altitudes."[19] However, standards are frequently set by a criterion which is at best awkwardly paraphrased somewhat as follows: "Standards should be set so that they are 'attainable but not too loose.' "[20] If standards are interpreted in terms of this latter criterion, an "approach to standard" implies little more than an approach to a level of performance which was a priori assumed to be approachable, or perhaps more important, capable of betterment.

Returning to the problem of how this approach to standard is to be effected, Henrici's mechanism can be largely considered a search for cause. He assumes that, "Behind every variation from standard cost there is a reason in operating conditions—and very often an apparently good reason."[21] The size and trend of the variances direct supervisory attention to certain phases of activity and the causes of an unfavorable variance are ascertained. These causes are generally assumed to be remediable or non-remediable; "corrective action" is taken in the former case, whereas the latter is dismissed or excused in one form or another.

What has been described above is the essence of so-called "principle of exceptions" or "management by exception." It should be noted that a step has been taken in this thesis in the development of systematic search techniques for the finding and correcting of "remediable causes" of higher costs (or alternatively, lost profit) including the determination of priorities in the order of search. This work is described in Chapter 5. However, the process of "following up" unfavorable variances would seem to be only part of the gain which might be achieved from a system of budgets or standards.

The process of investigation per se places the burden of proof upon management to discover the cause of variances. This is partially transferred to the manager or department head within whose jurisdiction the unfavorable variance occurred; e.g., a report of explanation is required of him so that he must hunt for causes, or at least reasons, to enter in such a report. Often such reports are used to initiate or justify a requested change which, if granted or acceded to by "higher" management, will allow the department head to eliminate or reduce the reported causes of trouble. Alternatively, the report may focus on the existence of some "uncontrollable factor." In principle it may show inefficiency as one root of the difficulty, but here psychological (or economically rational) factors are likely to enter to cloud or obscure matters so that recourse must generally be had to other sources; e.g., bolstering of the controls by independent (internal) auditors, special studies, etc. Here again variations in report content as well as differing sources of information are utilized to achieve (or to attempt to achieve) "control."

Consider once more the problem of control as it depends on the motivation (or other psychological and organizational) factors as they affect the person who "causes costs to happen" in the first instance. The process of consideration may well commence with the setting or changing of a standard. The setting of the standard is not sufficient of itself to assure or even invite compliance. The problem of directing activity toward a goal is one of "motivation"; a problem which is ignored, by and large, in the cost accounting and budgeting, except insofar as it deals with issues such as understanding (or the lack thereof) of accounting reports by others. However, as the psychologist Ruch points out, motivation is an integral part of goal-striving activity:

In any activity there are certain internal conditions or forces *without which there would be no activity* [italics supplied]. These internal conditions [motives] serve to direct the organism toward certain *goals,* regardless of whether these goals are, at the time, present in the organism.[22]

This viewpoint (i.e., when there is no motivation there is no activity) is fundamental to much of psychology. To bring the matter somewhat closer to this thesis, it would appear that Ruch implies that a budget or goal, even if externally imposed, must receive some internal recognition if it is to be at all effective. The following quotation from H. J. Leavitt may be utilized to develop this line of thinking more fully. Professor Leavitt notes:

No matter how much power a changer may possess, no matter how "superior" he may be, it is the changee who controls the final change decision. It is the employee, even the lowest paid one, who ultimately decides whether to show up for work or not.[23]

It may be perceived from the foregoing remarks that a major area for investigation of the means of budget control involves the relationship between motivations and budgets and standards considered as goals.

Notes

[1]E. L. Kohler, *A Dictionary for Accountants* (Englewood Cliffs, N.J.: Prentice-Hall, Inc., 1956), p. 67.

[2]J. H. MacDonald, *Practical Budget Procedure* (Englewood Cliffs, N.J.: Prentice-Hall, Inc., 1939), p. 101.

[3]A. Charnes and W. W. Cooper, "Optimization in New Item Production," Third Annual George Washington University—ONR Logistic Conference, January 1952.

[4]*Ibid.*

[5]See, for example, J. B. Heckert, *Business Budgeting and Control,* chap. xi (New York: The Ronald Press Company, 1946).

[6]A third figure is sometimes apparent. A sales "forecast" emanating from the sales department may be adjusted downward (to compensate for anticipated optimistic bias) to obtain the sales expectation.

[7]This assumption is typified by some remarks of W. Rautenstrauch and R. Villers, *Budgetary Control* (New York: Funk and Wagnalls Company, 1950). They state:

The *yearly production budget* is not equal to the sales forecast, nor to the sales forecast less inventory on hand but to *sales forecasts plus (or minus) the increase (or reduction) of inventory required to bring the actual inventory to the level of budgeted inventory* (p. 114).

This budget is the only one which they propose for control purposes. Note that the distinction between what the budget *is not* and what it *is* is only one which (algebraically) assures that the estimates provide for a continuing enterprise. The possibility that estimated need and the need as stated in the control budget may not agree is not considered. It should be noted in this connection that Professors Rautenstrauch and Villers are industrial engineers. Their views, however, do not differ from those indicated in the citation of MacDonald, *op. cit.,* an executive, nor markedly from those of Heckert, *op. cit.,* chap. xviii, an accountant, on the subject of production budgets.

[8]Kohler, *op. cit.,* p. 389.

[9]*Ibid.* It should be noted that there are several types of standard costs in common use. Since these distinctions are not of prime interest here they will be discussed only briefly. A first classification may be made into two types: *basic standards* and *current standards.* The basic standard is essentially an index number. It is not used for control purposes, other than to

exhibit a trend, and frequently is an old standard or actual cost as of a given date, etc. On the other hand, current standards represent the type used in the ordinary context of standards for cost control. These may be set in a variety of ways and may be further subdivided on this basis into two classifications: estimates and standards. Both are expected to relate to current and future production and "the difference between the two is even conceptually a matter of degree. Estimated costs are the looser of the two." (A paraphrase of W. W. Cooper, "Historical and Alternative Costs: A Study of Some Relations between the Economic Theory of the Firm and the Accounting Control of Operations," Doctoral Dissertation, Columbia University, 1950, chap. v, pp. 18–19.)

Additional distinctions, often made, are *ideal (or perfection) standards* and *attainable standards.* These are both current standards, but the attainable standards are assumed to be able to be obtained under conditions of a reasonable degree of efficiency and effort. They may be either estimates based on past performance or *engineering standards.* The engineering standards are set by time study for labor cost or similar devices for other types of cost. These, too, are in reality estimates, since the standards are often subject to negotiation and there exists no reliable scientific basis upon which to justify an assumption of precision. So-called ideal standards are generally engineering standards, intended to describe the cost that could be attained under "optimum" efficiency. These are the closest to the concept of optimal cost in economic terms, but generally speaking each standard is set individually so that the factor interactions assumed in economic theory are not considered.

[10]Problems exist, of course, which may definitely indicate preference of one type of unit or the other. In the case of nondivisible joint costs, for example, dollar figures may be misleading. On the other hand, in the control of operations which involve large-scale aggregations of items with a multiplicity of physical units, dollar amounts may provide the only practicable solution.

[11]S. B. Henrici, *Standard Costs for Manufacturing* (New York: McGraw-Hill Book Company, 1947), p. 232. A quotation from this same author, to be given shortly, indicates, however, that issues of purpose may also be used to distinguish between "budgeted" and "standard" cost.

[12]Cf., for example, T. Lang, W. B. McFarland, and M. Schiff, *Cost Accounting* (New York: The Ronald Press Company, 1953), who state, "Control implies the desired objectives through the measurement of results, especially through comparative reports" (p. 435). I. W. Keller, in *Management Accounting for Profit Control* (New York: McGraw-Hill Book Company, 1957), likewise appears to overestimate the role of the accounting function. He notes:

> The first requisite for the control of material costs is organization, with responsibilities clearly established for all phases of the control problems. The accountant is the keystone in such an organization, for control will be no better than the accounting records and data which are established (p. 158).

Both of these authors depend upon the efficiency of their reporting schemes for control. It would seem, however, as though the best reporting scheme would be totally impotent as a control if there were no mechanism for translating reports into action. A *reductio ad absurdum* is sufficient to demonstrate the fallacy in both statements. If both supervisors and budgeted personnel were to ignore all reports—a possibility not excluded by the authors' statements—they would be valueless, regardless of how "good" they were as reports.

[13]Heckert, *op. cit.*

[14]Henrici, *op. cit.* It should be noted that this distinction is not consistent with the definition of Kohler, *supra,* which is used in this paper. (Henrici lists two other distinctions which also depend upon a definition of budget at variance with Kohler's.)

[15]Keller, *op. cit.*, p. 97.

[16]National Association of Accountants (formerly National Association of Cost Accountants), "A Re-Examination of Standard Costs," reprinted from N.A.C.A. *Bulletin,* Vol. 29, No. 11, Sec. 3, Research Series No. 11 (February 1, 1948), p. 438.

[17]Henrici, *op. cit.,* p. 154.

[18]Lang *et al., op. cit.*

[19]Henrici, *op. cit.,* p. 5. But note, however, that there is, within these broad directives, a problem of measurement of standards. Even in the area in which the most extensive work on standards has been performed—the calculation of standard time—the issues are not clear-cut.

J. G. March and H. A. Simon, *Organizations* (New York: John Wiley & Sons, Inc., 1958) point out that:

> ... Often it is unclear whether standard times reflect "average time using average skill and average effort," "minimum time" or "average time over a series of trials by individuals randomly selected from a pool of industrial workers" (p. 16).

It is thus apparent that, even with the best of intentions, a standard can be misleading.

[20]See R. H. Robnett, T. M. Hill, and J. A. Becket, *Accounting, A Management Approach,* p. 431 (Homewood, Ill.: Richard D. Irwin, Inc., 1954); Lang *et al., op. cit.,* chap. xvi, especially p. 320; and Heckert, *op. cit.,* p. 171, for only a few instances of the application of this criterion.

[21]Henrici, *op. cit.,* p. 154.

[22]F. Ruch, *Psychology and Life,* 4th ed. (Chicago: Scott, Foresman and Company, 1953), p. 105.

[23]H. J. Leavitt, *Managerial Psychology: An Introduction to Individuals, Pairs, and Groups in Organization* (Chicago: University of Chicago Press, 1958), p. 132.

========

2

Management Uses of Figures

Herbert Simon, George Kozmetsky, Harold Guetzkow, and Gordon Tyndall

In the seven companies studied,* accounting information is used at various executive levels to answer three different kinds of questions:

Score-card questions: "Am I doing well or badly?"
Attention-directing questions: "What problems should I look into?"
Problem-solving questions: "Of the several ways of doing the job, which is the best?"

The organizational problems of providing effective service to management in the score-card and attention-directing areas were usually quite different from those of providing services in the area of special studies. Different sets of operating executives are generally involved in the two areas; and the kinds of data and analyses used may be quite different. Because of these differences, a controller's department which is well orga-

---

From *Centralization vs. Decentralization in Organizing the Controller's Department* (New York: Controllership Foundation, Inc., 1954), pp. 2–4, 22–24, 26–27, 28–30, and 32–33. Reprinted with permission of authors and publisher.

*Editor's note: See Reading 28 for another extract from this work which gives some details of the study.

nized to provide the one type of service, may or may not be well organized to provide the other.

SCORE-CARD AND ATTENTION-DIRECTING USES

In a factory the total departmental variance from standard or from budget would be an example of an item of score-card significance and use for the supervisor of the department concerned.

To the factory manager, the cost variances of individual departments would be attention-directing items—they would be one of the pieces of information which would direct his attention to departments requiring more careful review.

Acceptance of standards and the constructive use of accounting data for score-card and attention-directing purposes requires that the operating executives have confidence in the standards and in the performance reports that go to their superiors. In all cases, a close and direct relationship between accounting personnel and operating personnel appeared to be the most important factor in producing this confidence. This relationship needed to be close in the standards-setting procedure so that the operating man might have an opportunity to negotiate a standard which he could regard as a reasonable and attainable forecast of his operations. The relationship needed to be close in the reporting process so that the operating man might have help in interpreting his variances, and might have a part in developing the explanations of off-standard performance that were presented to his superior. Hence, for effective attention-directing service, *it is essential for the controller's department to develop direct and active channels of communication with the operating executives at those points in the organization where operations are being measured.*

PROBLEM-SOLVING USES

When data are used for problem-solving purposes—to choose among alternative processes, to decide whether to buy new equipment, to help in policy decisions—a special study is usually required. This commonly draws upon engineering estimates and industrial engineering standards as well as accounting information and usually means going back into the basic records of the accounting system.

There are two principal ways in which accounting data may come into the problem-solving process:

Executives may turn to the regular accounting and statistical reports for help.

The controller's department may make special studies for particular problems.

In which of these directions does the greatest promise lie for improving this aspect of controllership service? In the direction of more elaborate periodic reports or in strengthening the special studies services? This study indicates that *further development of staff and facilities for special studies is a more promising direction of progress than elaboration of periodic accounting reports.*

In one company, an annual calculation is made for each factory of the ratio of profit earned by that factory to investment in factory facilities. For the plant manager this has a *score-card* value. If he earns a high percentage of profit, or if his profit goes up from one year to the next, he is likely to feel that he is doing a good job. If the profit is low or goes down, he is likely to be encouraged to additional effort. In some cases, the use of the accounting results as the basis for a supervisory bonus emphasizes the score-card function. Note that in these cases, the accounting figures act as a stimulus, but do not help the manager decide what can or should be done.

This very same figure, the factory's rate of return of investment, is used by top management in this company as an *attention director.* Those factories which consistently turn up with low or declining profit percentages are regarded as trouble spots requiring special attention from the company executives. In those factories where the rate of return is regarded as satisfactory, the manager is left rather free to run his own show. For the company management, therefore, the return figure is more than a score-card record. It also directs attention to operating units which need special analysis and review. Thus, the same item of information may be an attention director for one executive but primarily a score card for others, or it may have both score-card and attention-directing utility for the same person.

For example, take a factory general foreman or department head. His job consists in considerable part in "pushing" the work. He generally spends a large part of his time on the factory floor where he can actually observe the work being performed. He is concerned with seeing that jobs are filled, but that superfluous men are not on the payroll; that emergencies are met quickly and effectively, and delays minimized; that short-run, day-to-day problems of all sorts are handled promptly. His direct face-to-face contact with his subordinates and their work gives him many sources of information about what is going on, and he regards accounting information as only a supplement—and, in many instances, a not too important one—to the other sources. Accounting data are useful to him mainly in giving him a score card, summarizing for longer periods his day-to-day impressions. They also are useful in directing his attention to matters that are not visible and tangible—say, the rate of consumption of expendable tools, or of operating supplies.

In most of the companies, any appropriation for major new equipment has to be justified by an economy study or savings department. This is an example of the "problem-solving" uses of accounting data. These uses go beyond the case where out-of-line accounting figures call attention to a problem or show in what area the problem lies. In problem-solving uses, the actual accounting data are inserted in the equation, so to speak, in order to solve the problem. Apart from plant and equipment studies, the most common examples of the problem-solving use of accounting data are in the comparison of profitability of product lines as a basis for a selective selling program, and the use of accounting data to forecast working capital requirements.

At higher levels of management the problem-solving uses of accounting data appear more commonly. For the vice president for manufacturing there are policy problems—developing and putting into production new products, plant location decisions, installation of new equipment and replacement of old, make-or-buy decisions, and so on. In many of these areas of decision, accounting data are used for problem-solving purposes. Sometimes they apparently are not used where they *could* be. They are used in preparation of special analyses or studies usually prepared by the executive's own assistants or by "staff" departments.[1] An equipment study, for example, would be most often made by the industrial engineering department. Sometimes, special studies are assigned to the controller's department and, even more frequently, that department is called on by other special-study units to supply the accounting data or dollar statistics needed for an analysis. Hence, the extent to which accounting data are used for problem-solving purposes depends very much on the kinds of staff assistance available to the vice president and on how much he is accustomed to use them.

Another concern of the manufacturing vice president is the evaluation and development of men. He needs to learn how his subordinates are doing, their strengths and their weaknesses. Moreover, the vice president has far less opportunity than the factory department head to observe his subordinates on the job. Hence, he is more dependent on reports as a basis for evaluating their progress and problems. He often uses accounting data and reports of internal auditors as a score card for his subordinates, and as a means of directing his attention to the areas where he needs to apply pressure or raise questions.

Observations made on this survey indicate that the score-card and attention-directing uses are apt to be more frequent than the problem-solving uses at all levels of management. First-line supervisors tend to use such data primarily as a fill-in on aspects of the work that they cannot appraise from actual contact. At higher levels, the data are used as a means of judging subordinates and as an independent check on what is happening at the operating level. Problem-solving uses of accounting data occur primarily in administrative units (staff units) for making analyses or special studies, for use by general management.

SCORE-CARD AND ATTENTION-DIRECTING USES OF DATA

It has been pointed out that no sharp line can be drawn between the score-card and the attention-directing uses of accounting data. What is a score card for the factory manager may be an attention director for the vice president for manufacturing; what is a score card for the regional sales manager may be an attention director for the general sales manager.

Illustrations of Score-Card and Attention-Directing Uses of Data

Here are some typical interview replies that illustrate the relation of the two uses:

A general sales manager was asked: "How do you tell when your regional managers are doing a good job?"

"The main things are the sales figures. Then, we've got to watch their expenses. Let's look at our weekly summary statistics. I see that the sales of X product are low compared to the quota. I go back to the regional report and see that New England is the low region, also which of the sales branches in the region are low. Then I know to whom to write a letter to follow it up."

One of the regional sales managers in the same company was asked: "How do you tell when you are doing a good job?" He replied: "I have a sales quota and an expense budget. I try to operate my region so that I will meet the quota or surpass it; and at the same time, I try to do the job in the most economical manner."

.   .   .   .   .

Attention Directing and the "Principle of Exceptions"

The use of accounting data to call attention to problems is closely related to what is usually called "the principle of exceptions." For this procedure to work, the operating man must accept the validity of the standards for determining what is "out of line." Moreover, effective attention-directing uses of accounting data imply that it is through such data that problems are called to the attention of operating executives or general management.

Persons interviewed consistently reported that, in many instances where the production and sales executives *might* have had their attention directed to problems by accounting data, they had already learned of the problems from other sources before the accounting reports appeared. For example, delays due to equipment breakdown or material shortages are almost immediately brought to the attention of the foreman and usually the department head. If the problem is a serious one, the news travels upward rapidly, even to vice presidential and presidential levels. On these matters, accounting reports usually provide the supervisors with history but not with news.

On the other hand, in the course of his daily work even a first-line supervisor may find it difficult to learn that a particular machine logs excessive down-time because of mechanical failure. Here, a monthly summary of machine down-time with notation as to causes can be a valuable attention-directing report.

Interview data show conclusively that supervisors up to factory department heads use accounting reports for attention-directing purposes largely in areas that are not easily visible in the course of day-to-day supervision. The following comment of a factory department head is typical:

"Every day when I go out through the departments, I know the standard number of men who should be working on each operation. If I see more than the standard number working on a job, I check up to see why the extra people are there." "Couldn't you get that from the daily variance report?" "Yes, but I'd have to wait two days."

Operating supervisors were seldom able to cite other types of examples of the attention-directing services of the accounting system. On other items —direct labor, material usage, yield—the common reaction was: "We know all about that before the accounting reports come."

The following conclusions validly generalize survey information about attention-directing uses of accounting data by supervisors and executives who have direct contact with the factory floor or the sales market.

A large part of an operating executive's knowledge about his operation comes by direct observation and informal reports. These reports are frequently verbal and come to him through the regular supervisory channels. Accounting reports are only one, and not always the most important, of his sources of information, although they may be of considerable use in confirming his observations.

The operating executive has special needs for periodic accounting reports on items that are not "visible" from direct, day-to-day supervision. In manufacturing, machine performance and consumption of operating supplies are examples of such items.

For executives further removed from actual operations, the greatest significance of attention-directing accounting data lies in the information they transmit independently of operating supervisors. The existence of this independent source and channel of information has important consequences for the relations between executives at lower and higher levels.

.   .   .   .   .

THE ROLE OF STANDARDS[2]

When accounting data are used for score-card or for attention-directing purposes, a comparison of the actual data with some kind of standard or norm is always involved. This need not be a deliberately designed and established standard of the sort involved in a standard cost system, but may be any figure that is regarded as a "normal," "expected," "reasonable," or "satisfactory" value for the figure in question.

If an operating department head has become accustomed to "red" variances of $50,000 a month measured against the standard cost of his operation, then he is likely to regard a month in which his "red" variance is only $25,000 as a good one, even though the performance is still below standard. Similarly, a considerable number of executives were encountered whose real concern was not how they were making out with reference to the accounting standard, but how well they were doing in relation to historical records of past performance, or comparison with other plants in the same company.

Acceptance of Standards

Interview results show that a particular figure does not operate as a norm, in either a score-card or attention-directing sense, simply because the controller's department calls it a standard. It operates as a norm only to the extent that the executives and supervisors, whose activity it measures, accept it as a fair and attainable yardstick of their performance. Generally, operating executives were inclined to accept a standard to the extent that they were satisfied that the data were *accurately recorded,* that the standard level was *reasonably attainable,* and that the variables it measured were *controllable* by them. When there were doubts as to the accuracy of recording or classification of data, when the factors causing variances were thought to be beyond their own control, the executives simply did not believe that the standard validly measured their performance. Then they were influenced by it only to the extent that they were forced to think about the reactions of their superiors.

The degree of acceptance of standards was not the same, of course, in all the factories visited, nor even among different departments in the same factory. Some of the reasons for this are technical, and these will be discussed in the following paragraphs. In addition to the technical reasons, the length of time a cost system has been in operation has an important bearing on the validity and acceptability of standards. In all the companies studied, several years were required after the installation of a cost system before it was "shaken down" and a reasonably acceptable system of cost determinants arrived at. The same thing was observed in a case where a new processing department had recently been introduced in a factory which had a long-established cost system in its other departments.

It is not necessary to report on the degree to which standards were accepted in these various factories. As already mentioned, the range in level of acceptance was great. It is important, however, to learn what conditions have to be met so that accounting standards have a constructive influence upon operations, and how these conditions can be brought about through proper organizational relationships between the controller's department and the operating departments. For these reasons, the objections to existing accounting standards will be examined in some detail.

Two kinds of objections to standards were most frequently encountered. Some were criticisms of oversimplified determinants that failed to account for important external factors causing variability in costs. Thus, in several cases a cost that was only incurred during one season of the year received the same budget allowance per unit of output throughout the year. The fact that monthly variances in these cases were virtually meaningless tended to discredit the accounting standards and reports based on them.

In many instances the nature of the manufacturing operation practically precludes the establishment of adequate budget determinants. One problem frequently encountered is variation in the quality of raw materials. Food processing companies have continual difficulties of this kind, but similar troubles are found in other concerns. In companies like Westinghouse, where a standard cost often has to be estimated on each order, the task of arriving at acceptable and accepted standards is equally difficult.[3]

The recalculation of indirect costs was the second major source of distrust of accounting standards—and this on two scores. Almost all operating men stated their dislike at having on their statements items they did not regard as within their control. The objections were particularly strong when the items were not shown at standard, but caused variances on the statements.

Moreover, in the case of indirect items that were admitted to be partially controllable—maintenance expenditures, for example—doubts were frequently expressed as to the accuracy of the charges. In almost all companies there was a widespread belief (not entirely without foundation) that maintenance foremen inflated their time estimates to absorb idle time. As a matter of fact, at least one maintenance department head stated that he did just that: "Suppose the charges don't balance—there's $1,000 unallocated. Well, we know in X department they have some rough edges, so we shove that charge off on them." When clerical errors occur in charging supplies and maintenance to the proper accounts, they also feed this distrust.

In addition, there were frequent objections to the "lumpiness" of indirect charges. "You go along for months with favorable variances and then one month you'll take a licking." This sometimes led to the uneconomical ordering of small quantities of supplies, and pressure was often felt (and, fortunately, frequently resisted) to postpone necessary maintenance: "The machine was still not fixed and we were running out of our budget expense, but I didn't stop. They came around afterwards and said, 'You're way over your budget.' I said, 'Look out there. The machine is running, isn't it? Isn't that what the boss wants?' "

But a department head in another factory said, "I will sometimes pull back on some repairs when I think I can get along without them, especially toward the end of the month." Finally, supervisors could not always predict which month's budget would be charged with an expenditure. "When they throw charges in, they don't throw them in until the end of the month. I think I'm going along pretty well and then—bang—they hit me with some charges."

Reactions to Unacceptable Standards

Now, what occurs when an operating executive is placed in a situation where he fundamentally mistrusts the standards for any of the reasons discussed above, but where his superiors hold him responsible for unfavorable variances and expect explanations from him? There were frequent opportunities to observe how operating men reacted to such situations. The answer was always the same. When the operating man is placed in the position of justifying his performance in terms of a standard that he doesn't regard as fair he has two choices: to change the performance, or to change the measurement of it. And since he regards the measurement of his performance as unfair, he almost inevitably chooses the second alternative. The following two comments are typical of many made during the interviews:

"If you find a variance that's way out, it's either a poor budget or it's not set up properly."

"My boss comes around and asks me about my variance once in a while. This is often a good opportunity to point out things which are wrong with the accounting reports. If I say the standards are off, he should go back and see why the standards are off."

The first reaction of a supervisor who is confronted with an unfavorable variance in an account is to suspect that something has been charged to the account which should not have been charged. Hence, in a situation where the cost accounting is not completely trusted, a great deal of energy of accounting and operating personnel goes into discussion and debate about the correctness of the charges.

The second reaction of the operating man is to look for uncontrollable external circumstances that can explain the unfavorable variance. Thus, in the case of the seasonal item mentioned before, the operating man explains his unfavorable variances by pointing out that they will be balanced by favorable variances the next summer.

Distrust of standards coupled with pressure to eliminate variances leads to preoccupation with "wooden money" savings—to use a term that was current in one factory. When attention is directed by accounting data to an uneconomical operating practice and the practice is corrected, this leads to a real saving for the company that will ultimately be reflected in profits. When the concern with variances is centered on detecting wrong charges and getting these shifted to the proper account, only "wooden money" is saved and company profits are not increased. Here are typical reports by operating men of their use of accounting data to produce "wooden money" savings:

"The foreman keeps a running total of what he has spent. When the report comes back from accounting, he checks his total. It is important to analyze the charges slip by slip. We find that saves us five to six thousand dollars a month on incorrect charges by accounting or some other department."

"There's a good example of another reason why I think these reports are good. If I hadn't had that report, I would never have known this was charged against me."

In the interviews, the relative amount of emphasis on "wooden money" savings proved to be a sensitive index of distrust of standards. In situations where confidence in standards was lowest, the examples given by respondents of their use of accounting data almost all involved reclassification of charges, and not instances where accounting showed opportunities for improving operations.

Notes

[1] As is well known, "staff" is a slippery word that is perhaps best avoided altogether. In this publication the term is used simply as a shorthand way of referring to all the departments of a company other than manufacturing, sales, and engineering; and to all the departments of a factory other than the manufacturing and maintenance departments.

[2] Findings with respect to standards are in close agreement with other previous studies. See especially: John D. Glover and Fritz J. Roethlisberger, "Human Reactions to Standards and Controls," chap. viii in *Controllership in Modern Management*, T. F. Bradshaw and C. C. Hull (eds.), (Homewood, Ill.: Richard D. Irwin, Inc., 1949); and Chris Argyris, *The Impact of Budgets on People* (New York: Controllership Foundation, Inc., 1952).

[3] These problems, of course, go beyond the controller's department to the other departments, like industrial engineering, that establish the physical determinants of standards. Nevertheless, even when the controller's responsibility is limited to "dollarizing" physical standards established by other departments, the variances appear on accounting reports and the accounting personnel are the ones principally criticized for unacceptable standards.

3
Budgeting and the Decision-Making Process

Arthur Smithies

This chapter is designed to provide the analytic framework of this study —to bring out the relation of budgeting to the whole process of decision-making. Almost every governmental decision has budgetary implications since the process of decision-making almost invariably involves the allocation of scarce resources among alternative uses. Resources can be used privately or diverted by taxation or other methods to government use, and, if so diverted, they are allocated among a variety of government uses. A major thesis of this study is that the entire process of decision-making is improved to the extent that these choices are made explicitly and deliberately. Or if the Government desires to exempt a particular program from exposure to competition for funds, the decision to do so should be expressly made. The first purpose of this chapter is to elaborate this central argument.

The second purpose is to discuss the decision-making process, and the budgetary process in particular, from the viewpoint of the structure and procedures of a complicated organization. Although my concern is with the Federal Government, it is convenient at this stage to discuss the problem in more general terms and to work out principles of organization that can later be applied to the specific problem of the Federal budget. This chapter is thus designed merely to provide a basis for analysis. In no sense is it intended to provide a full description of the government decision-making process.[1]

STAGES IN THE DECISION-MAKING PROCESS

The process of decision-making by an organization can be represented as a continuing process consisting of six stages: determination of policy objectives, planning, programming, budget formulation, budget (or program) execution, budget (or program) review. These categories are reflected in varying degrees in an organization's structure and procedures. For instance, in the national defense organization each stage can be readily identified. At the opposite extreme, the proprietor of a business may carry out all the stages himself. In other instances the stages shade into each other. In any event, it is useful for analytical purposes to consider the decision-making process in these terms. These are first discussed on the assumption that each of them is carried out by the organization as a whole. Later the distribution of functions within the organization is considered.

The determination of policy objectives is a subject that is largely outside the scope of this study. The political and social processes of a country result in the adoption of national objectives with respect to national defense, resource development, social security, and payment of benefits to veterans. These objectives may be formally expressed in legislation, such as the G.I. Bill of Rights, or they may be expressed equally forcefully in the general political consciousness of the country—as is the case with major foreign-policy objectives. Policy objectives may be deeply rooted in a country's history and tradition; they may emerge as compromises among conflicting political forces; or they may result from general consideration of the national interest.

It is important to recognize, however, that governments as well as other organizations must frequently make decisions in an aura of great uncertainty, with respect both to the situations that have to be met and the results that different courses of action may produce. In the area of foreign policy, for instance, the Government may be unable to define its objectives precisely since the intentions and objectives of other countries are imperfectly known. Only after some course of action has been taken and has proved to be a move in the right or the wrong direction may it be possible to reduce uncertainty with respect to the future. Determination of policy objectives may therefore consist largely in extensions or reversals of what has been done in the past, based on the experience of the past. Consequently an effective review of past performance is an important factor in the determination of policy objectives.

Furthermore, objectives in the future may be changed as a result of actions taken in response to present attitudes. Social security, for instance, was adopted as a program in the 'thirties in response to the attitudes that then existed. But its operation for almost two decades has substantially altered national attitudes toward the program. If the consequent new decisions are to be well founded, this process of change in national attitudes should be based on as clear an understanding of past operation of the programs concerned as is feasible.

The adoption of a particular objective of policy inevitably implies a decision on the urgency or importance of that objective. When the Government decides that a change in defense policy is desirable, it must also form some notion of how desirable. And in that connection it forms some notion of how far it is prepared to sacrifice other objectives in order to attain its new objective. But such notions are vague and imprecise at the policy-formation stage. It is the purpose of the subsequent stage of the decision-making process to make them precise and thereby to formulate a unified program that will achieve the most satisfactory compromise among the various objectives of policy.

Planning, as the term is used here, means the preparation of alternative plans that will further particular policy objectives in varying measure and that are within the reasonable bounds of feasibility. Proposals to fortify the moon or to provide family allowances of $10,000 a year may be consistent with established policy objectives, insofar as those objectives have been made precise, but they may be generally considered to be so far outside the bounds of feasibility that they should be contemplated by visionaries rather than by planners.[2] As examples, military planners design an array of strategic plans to further foreign-policy objectives. City planners devise alternative methods of coping with a traffic problem. Or regional planners may produce a variety of approaches to the economic development of a region. Planning in this sense may be related to particular policy objectives or to a variety of objectives.

Programming denotes a further step in the direction of finality and feasibility, and may involve selection among alternative plans or a combination of elements from a number of plans. When a program is adopted to achieve a particular policy objective or if, for instance, the President announces a comprehensive program, it is implied that the program is considered feasible and can be carried out. The aspect of feasibility that is of most concern to us here is, of course, the willingness of the organization to bear the cost of the program. Both particular and comprehensive programs, however, are frequently promulgated before they have been exposed to the rigorous tests of budgeting. One reason for this situation lies in the operations of a complex organization, which will be examined later.[3] Another arises from the fact that it is frequently desirable to program for a period into the future, longer than the period for which it is feasible to prepare budgets. Budgets to be useful must relate to a future that is reasonably foreseeable. It may nevertheless be desirable to program for a future that can only be foreseen dimly—provided that the program is subject to revision as the future unfolds.

Basic decisions that greatly influence the size of the budget may be taken at the programming stage. As dramatic examples, the distribution of the defense program among the three Services and of the Air Force program among the various commands are budgetary questions, since the national objective is to obtain the most efficient use of resources devoted to defense. While these questions are largely settled before a budget is prepared, the programming decisions should be based on the relative costs of the various defense alternatives.

The formulation of a budget is an extension of the programming stage. Programs become expenditure programs and thus are expressed in terms of a common denominator, money. They can then be compared with each other and with their cost in terms of taxation or of borrowing with greater precision than is feasible in the earlier stages of the process. Furthermore, the question of economy—the attainment of given program results at minimum costs—can be effectively considered only when all the elements of the program are expressed in terms of money.[4]

The comparisons and calculations that comprise the formulation of the budget are likely to call for revision of programs, since more light is thrown on implications of those programs than was previously available. On the other hand, if the budget in a particular year fails to provide for the year what is called for by a longer-term program, the program may nevertheless be adhered to and may exert an upward pull on the budget in the following year. The budgeting stage is the first point at which rational economic calculation—consideration of how scarce resources can best be allocated among various alternative uses—comes fully into play. Although these comparisons enter in the earlier stages to some extent, they cannot be fully carried out until all programs are considered together and are expressed in a common denominator. The major thesis, stated above, that expenditure commitments for any particular program should not in general be made until this stage is reached rests on the view that this process of rational calculation and comparison can further the total objectives of an organization.

Budget or program execution should be regarded as a separate stage in the decision-making process since, even in a budget for as short a period as a year, it is impossible to prescribe what is to be done with complete specificity or to provide for all contingencies. The objectives of the budget can be more nearly achieved if there is some discretion exercised in the execution of the budget than if it is followed slavishly. During the budget period, external factors may require minor revisions in policy objectives, and possibilities of economy may become apparent that could not be foreseen at the time the budget was prepared. Successful execution of the budget therefore requires scrupulous adherence to its intent but departure from its detail where necessary to give effect to its intent. In the course of the execution of the budget new methods for achieving economy and efficiency in the conduct of operations should be tested and explored. This should be the continuing purpose of administrative management based on actual experience. The talents and techniques required for this task are essentially different from those required to secure an efficient allocation of the budget among the various programs.

Budget or program review has three main purposes. In the first place, expenditures should be reviewed from the point of view of their legality and propriety. Such a review is the traditional purpose of an audit of the organization's accounts. In the second place, a review of actual performance provides a link between the past and the future in the determination of policy objectives and the formulation of a budget. In the third place, a review of actual performance is essential for the purposes of administrative management. And the kind of review required for this purpose may be different from that needed for programming purposes. For instance, a classification of expenditures by purposes or functions is needed for the formulation of a budget. But the traditional classification by organization units or objects may be more suitable for administrative management.

The behavior of the organization depends on the way in which it performs each of these operations and the ways in which it relates them to each other. One organization may make virtually all its decisions at the policy-making stage. Its determination of objectives may also involve determination of its program. In other words, it leaves the allocation of resources among alternatives to look after itself. Another may be so preoccupied with costs and economy that it loses sight of its purposes and objectives. Organizations may vary also in the degree to which they permit review of the past to influence their future plans. Some may look only to the future and forget the past. The behavior of others may depend far more on the forces of inheritance and tradition than on the shifting contemporary scene.

Organizations can also differ widely in the way in which they define their policy objectives. In some the objectives may be defined with precision, and the subsequent stages of the process may consist mainly of refinements and elaborations of the initial determination. The "firm" of the economics textbooks, for instance, has a single objective—to maximize profits. When the supply and cost conditions faced by the firm are assumed to be known, its program can be worked out by mere computation. At the opposite extreme, it is difficult if not impossible to define with any precision the policy objectives of a university. Its policies grow out of the activities of members of the faculty who are motivated by a general belief in the university's traditions and purposes. Yet their ideas of policy may vary widely. In fact, the success of the university may be held to depend on the existence of such a variety of viewpoints. Nevertheless the university's resources are limited, and, despite the diversity of its objectives, the university must adopt a definite budget program. Clearly the formulation of the budget has more serious policy implications for the university than for the hypothetical firm. In government, the role of budget formulation usually falls somewhere between these extremes.

How an organization combines the several stages of the decision-making process depends largely on its basic purposes and on temperaments and attitudes of the individuals who comprise it. Such factors may be decisive in the simpler forms of organization, such as the small New England town meeting, where all members of the town deliberate together. The analysis of their behavior then falls within the province of the social psychologist.

The economist, however, can still point to the degree to which rationality enters the decision-making process. He can say to the town, "If you want to act more rationally, you will stress the formulation of a definite budget more heavily than you now do." He may also be prepared to say, "In my judgment you will be better off if you make more conscious selections among alternatives than you now do, and I can suggest to you some habits of thought that will assist you to do so."

The behavior of the more complicated organizations—of which the Federal Government may well be the most complicated—depends not only on the attitudes and habits of thought of their members but also on their formal procedures and structures. The rules under which an organization operates and the relationships established among its parts have an important bearing on the ways in which the various parts of the decision-making process affect its total behavior. Proposals for improvement in the process must therefore consist largely of suggestions for procedural and structural changes.

ORGANIZATIONAL STRUCTURE AND PROCEDURES AND THE DECISION-MAKING PROCESS

Discussion of the government decision-making process and of budgeting in particular has frequently tended to take an unduly simplified view of the structure of an organization and the distribution of functions within it. For instance, the relations of the legislature with the executive have often been embodied in these familiar statements: the legislature determines policy; the executive formulates a budget to carry out that policy; the legislature considers and enacts the budget; the executive executes the budget; the legislature reviews the accounts of the executive.

That formulation conveys the impression of a simple sequence of technical operations. Policy-making is disposed of in the first stage. Budgeting is merely a matter of determining the costs of the "policies determined by the Congress." Appropriation involves a technical review of the executive estimates and the formulation of detailed directives for the executive. Execution means carrying out both the letter and therefore the spirit of those directives. Review means an audit of the accounts of the executive from the point of view of their legality and propriety. This description is by no means a caricature of traditional views. It is faithfully reflected in the procedures of the appropriations committees and in the procedural association of budgeting with accounting to the exclusion of its association with policy formation. Whether or not this approach ever furnished an adequate guide to organization, it is thoroughly inadequate for a government performing its modern functions. The legislature does not distill policy once and for all out of the air. Policy objectives are being continually revised in the light of experience and the changing needs of the situation. The legislature is largely influenced in this respect by the recommendations of the executive.

The formulation of a budget is far more than a translation of predetermined objectives into financial terms. Policy objectives—particularly in the defense area—may, of necessity, be capable of definition only in imprecise terms. Consequently, when the legislature undertakes to review the executive budget, it has more to do than merely check details. It must decide whether it approves or wishes to alter the program content of the executive budget. Or, as occurs in the parliamentary system of government, the legislature surrenders the right to amend the budget but retains the right to dismiss the executive and in that way to get a new budget. Furthermore, the need to relate expenditures to revenues makes it impossible to regard budgeting as a mere translation of policy into financial terms. Only the peculiar conditions of the nineteenth century made it possible to overlook this essential point in connection with the Federal Government.

The budget enacted by the legislature cannot be formulated in complete detail. The executive must be permitted discretion to adapt the program to the needs of a changing situation as it unfolds, subject to the overriding policy objectives established by the legislature. It follows that review should be much more than a matter of accounting or auditing as commonly understood. For the legislature to perform its functions properly, it needs to appraise the total performance of the executive within the areas of executive discretion. Finally, the executive cannot be treated as a whole. The operation of the decision-making process depends heavily on the relations of the chief executive and his subordinate departments and on those of department heads with their subordinates. In the Federal Government the situation is even more complicated since the executive departments have responsibilities to the Congress in addition to their responsibilities to the President. Consequently a more elaborate view of organizational structure and procedures is needed—one that recognizes the continuing nature of the decision-making process, the thoroughgoing interdependence of the various stages, and, therefore, the fact that no single part of the organization is exclusively concerned with any one stage.

As groundwork for such an approach it is necessary to stress both the vertical and the horizontal aspects of the structure of an organization. The nature of its decisions will depend first on the hierarchical structure of the organization, that is, on the vertical division of functions. It will depend also on the horizontal arrangements made at each level in the hierarchy—on how legislatures or executives at any level divide and combine their activities with respect to policy objectives, budgeting execution, and review.

Vertical Division of Functions

An organization is normally divided vertically into a legislative or representative body, a chief executive, and executive departments and their subdivision. The need for a vertical division arises first from the fact that legislative bodies are normally too cumbersome to carry out completely some of the top-level functions in the decision-making process. While in some organizations the legislature is clearly superior to the chief executive, in others it shares top-level authority with him.[5] The latter situation is typified by the power of the President to veto laws passed by the Congress and by the power of the Congress to exert direct control over executive departments through formal or informal restrictions on the use of appropriations. Secondly, the vertical division arises from the need for specialization in the Executive Branch. Specialization necessarily means that discretion within defined limits is exercised by subordinate layers. If an upper layer gives complete instructions to a subordinate layer, no specialization will be achieved. Specialization also implies that a subordinate official sees less of the total picture than his superior. While he should be aware of the objectives of the whole organization, he is not competent to compete with his superiors in the performance of their functions.

The behavior of the organization will depend largely on the relationships and the lines of communication that are established among the successive layers in the vertical hierarchy. These fall within three main categories: (*a*) Directives, which flow down the organization. Directives, whether given to the executive by the legislature or by one executive level to another, have two main functions: first, they prescribe what shall be done; and second, they determine the degree of discretion that may be exercised at the subordinate level. (*b*) Recommendations, which flow up through the organization. The recommendation made by one level to the next above it depends first of all on the functions that are assigned to it; second, on its view of the policies that the organization should follow; and third, on the recommendations it receives from below. It should be emphasized that an executive is not likely to be performing his functions adequately if he merely transmits recommendations received from a subordinate. He presumably has a more complete knowledge of the policies of the organization as a whole than does his subordinate, and he should revise the recommendations he receives in the light of his greater knowledge. (c) Reviews and reports on past performance, which flow up through the organization—both to show how far directives have been carried out and to provide a guide to decisions for the future.

The nature of the vertical relationships differs widely among organizations. An army narrowly limits the areas in which subordinates may exercise direction and make recommendations. On the other hand, the policies and programs of a university are likely, in the main, to originate in the faculty. There is no rule for the optimum form of an organization for all purposes. There is likely, however, to be an optimum structure of vertical relationships for an organization that is designed to serve some given purpose.

Horizontal Division of Functions

The need for a horizontal division of functions is most evident in a legislature. All the members of even the simplest legislative body cannot collectively perform the several decision-making operations. It therefore divides into committees, say, a policy and planning committee, a budget committee, and an execution and review committee. The nature of the legislature's decisions will depend both on the ways in which it divides the process and on the way in which it relates the decisions of the various parts to each other. For instance, one that divides its budgetary function between separate expenditure and revenue committees is likely to reach different decisions from one that has a single budget committee. And the way in which committees are coordinated may result in the policy and planning committee being stronger than the budget committee or vice versa.

The question of horizontal organization arises not only in legislatures but at every level of a vertical organization. An executive is concerned with policy objectives in areas where he can exercise discretion or can make recommendations to his superiors. He must submit a budget for his future activities. He must execute his budget when it is enacted. He must report on his operations. Within his own orbit the head of a division may be as much concerned with policy as the head of a government department. But the division head bases his policy recommendations and decisions on a narrower and more specialized set of criteria than does the head of the department. Horizontal arrangements thus give rise to the same kinds of questions in executive departments as in legislatures.

Notes

[1]This chapter has been greatly influenced by Herbert Simon's *Administrative Behavior* (New York: The Macmillan Company, 1947), and Paul H. Appleby's *Big Democracy* (New York: Alfred A. Knopf, Inc., 1945). But neither of these authors can be held responsible for the conclusions reached.

[2]Needless to say, the word, "planning" as I use it here has no connotation of central control of economic activity. I am using it rather in the sense in which it is used in military circles.

[3]See, "Organizational Structure and Procedures and the Decision-Making Process" section of this article.

[4]Money is used as the common denominator for budgeting because in normal terms it represents in general the cost of scarce resources. In times of extreme scarcity, such as total war, the money measure of scarcity becomes inadequate. Budgeting in terms of critical scarce factors such as manpower or strategic materials then tends to replace monetary budgeting; it is usually called "programming" rather than "budgeting."

[5]I shall speak of the chief executive as a single individual for the sake of simplicity. It is important to realize, however, that this is merely a simplification. The chief executive may be a cabinet, as in the British Government. In some corporations the board of directors constitutes the chief executive. In others the president is the chief executive, while the board of directors acts rather as the representatives of the legislature (the shareholders). In still others chief executive authority may be vested in an executive committee. In the Federal Government the President is constitutionally the chief executive.

II

Some Institutional Contexts

Shared powers, multiple access, and complex dynamics

An old European peasant saying has it that the wise man puts all his eggs in one basket, and he watches that basket. Given due attention and strength or lack of thieves, that man can conveniently protect all his eggs. If his attention wavers or his strength is inadequate, however, all of the eggs may be lost in one fell swoop. The underlying strategy thus minimizes the risk of a small loss. Alas, the strategy also maximizes the risk of a total loss.

The men who helped shape our political institutions followed an opposed strategy. They advised, in sum, that we distribute our political eggs among several baskets. The negative root belief is that the electorate cannot be expected to be either eternally vigilant or broadly informed. The positive root belief is that the interests of the electorate can, will, and should be engaged in enough significant cases to make their impact felt.

The working accommodation in America has been the despair of doctrinaire thinkers, having as it does dual goals: the control of necessary (but dangerous) political elites, and the control of vital (but lethargic) mass electorates. Native cunning, therefore, called for political institutions set against one another so that some degree of mutual surveillance was built into the system without rigidifying it. As a result our political eggs are scattered, with dual expectations, in several institutional baskets. Thus the chances are increased that no faction can steal all our political eggs. Relatedly, any really ambitious egg-snatchers are more likely to receive the multidirectional attention that sooner or later will motivate the electorate to turn the rascals out. The underlying strategy minimizes the chance of maximum loss and is prepared to absorb smaller losses as a major cost.

How American political institutions put their eggs in several baskets may be suggested via the late Morton Grodzins's image of a political layer cake.[1]

Grodzins described the "vertical" sharing of power in our federal system between the central government, the states, and local governments as the several multicolored strata of a layer cake. The differing widths of the various strata of the cake reflect the differing powers of the several levels of government in various issue areas. The analogy permits multiple comparisons with life. The thicknesses of the several layers in a cake vary from point to point, for example, just as the power of various levels of government varies in different areas. Further, the several layers of a cake subtly blend into one another in some places and stand boldly distinct at others. Just so is power usually shared, although at times one level or another may exercise a virtual monopoly. Grodzins's image can be extended to the "horizontal" sharing of powers at the federal level between the legislative, executive, and judicial branches, which is commonly referred to as the "separation of powers," plus "checks and balances." The analogy also applies to state and local governments in much the same ways.

Putting our political eggs in several baskets has profound effects on public finance and budgeting. Indeed, perhaps the central issue of all public administration today concerns the basic redefinition of the scope of the power of various governments. The nature of this power has been a recurring problem, and observers increasingly agree that the issue is as central today as it was (for example) during the 1860s. Disagreement begins beyond this point.

Some observers thank their lucky stars for the welter of countervailing governmental powers which operate vertically between national, state, and local levels, as well as horizontally between the several branches at each level of government. Basically, in this view, the tangle of countervailing and shared powers provides the major bulwark against using public policy as a vehicle for drastic or at least premature social experimentation. In this view, the country tends to get into serious trouble only when too many eggs get transferred into too few baskets, especially the national government's basket.

Oppositely, the dominant opinion seems to be that the pattern of pervasive countervailing and shared powers is at the heart of the crisis of contemporary governance. In short, that pattern impedes, and probably prevents, needed adaptations to new conditions. The orthodox criticisms of national expenditure and taxation decisions, for example, clearly imply that (at best) too much has been made of countervailing and shared powers. The results are massively untidy. Thus Charles E. Lindblom details the characteristics of expenditure and taxation decisions that most economists criticize:

1. The lack of specific policies and procedures for coordinating revenues and expenditures.
2. The conflict between the President and Congress, between the two houses of Congress, and the multiple subcommittees within each house.

3. The committees of Congress that authorize programs typically do so in relative independence of the committees that make appropriations.
4. The appropriations committees tend to review segments of the budget, not the entire package, so many meaningful cost/benefit comparisons are not even attempted.
5. Many budgetary results are outcomes of unrelated decisions, as opposed to decisions deriving from some comprehensive review.[2]

The selections below illustrate the impact of shared powers on public budgeting and finance, with the initial emphasis on horizontal sharing between units of the federal government. Three charts preceding Reading 4 provide a comprehensive overview of the formulation of the budget and congressional action on appropriations and revenue measures. That the sharing of powers is both profound and widespread is indicated graphically in these charts, which are entitled "Major Steps in the Budget Process," "Formulation of Executive Budget," and "Congressional Action on Appropriations."

An Office of Management and Budget publication, "Preparation and Execution of the Federal Budget," provides some flesh for the bare bones of the schema of the budget cycle in the preceding charts. The focus in Reading 4 is on the complex cycle of 28 months for each budget, as well as on the multitude of actors participating directly in the complex decision-making required during that cycle. Given obvious differences in scale, much the same processes generally characterize budget-making in many state and some local jurisdictions.

Frederick J. Lawton's "Legislative-Executive Relationships in Budgeting as Viewed by the Executive" (Reading 5) incisively analyzes the various institutional features that reinforce the growing impact of the presidency on budgeting and financial processes. Because of where he sits and the nature of the interests he represents, the president has seen his office become institutionalized as a presidency of some 4,000 immediate aids, including the vital Office of Management and Budget. Prior to World War II, the president had only a handful of immediate aids. The influence of the presidency on budgeting and finance has burgeoned correspondingly, although limits on that influence are still great. Thus it is a mistake to think of this massive presidency as a unity, for its several members have been known to speak in diverse tongues, both formally and informally. Nor have executive agencies always accepted presidential direction without question. Also, the power of congressional committees and subcommittees is legendary, presidency or no.

Despite these qualifications, however, the trend line for the presidency is up, very sharply.

The ability of the presidency to focus the great and growing resources at its command so as to influence budgeting and financial decisions is perhaps most dramatically reflected in the occasional use of the ultimate presidential weapon, the power to "impound" funds whose expenditure Congress has authorized. The presidency's power of impounding—an "implied power" at best—is a super item veto for which no specific constitutional sanction exists.[3] In any case, several presidents have made their decisions to impound funds stick and have thereby created precedents on which succeeding presidents can rely.

To put it boldly, the president can impound funds and in effect negate either complete legislative bills or individual items in them that have received both legislative authorization and appropriation. And he can do so without the possibility of his action being formally overridden by the legislature, as is the case with his constitutional power of veto. Of course, the use of impounding by the executive runs the risk of stirring up countermeasures by the legislature. Less ultimately, the Office of Management and Budget —a unit within the Executive Office—also exerts influence over spending by federal agencies via quarterly allotments.

The growing disadvantage of Congress vis-à-vis the president—at least up to Watergate!—has received full attention in many places. Nelson W. Polsby's "Policy Analysis and Congress,"[4] for example, points up numerous limitations on congressional ability to accomplish effective policy analysis, against the background of existing institutions, practices, and history. The very existence of two houses of Congress—with different terms, constituencies, personalities, and styles of decision-making—generates powerful centrifugal forces that fragment the legislative overseeing of financial and policy matters, for good or ill. Polsby dramatically characterizes the two legislative houses:

> Where the House of Representatives is a large, impersonal and highly specialized machine for processing bills and overseeing the executive branch, the Senate is, in a way, a theater where dramas—comedies and tragedies, soap operas and horse operas—are staged to enhance the careers of its members and to influence public policy by means of debate and public investigation.[5]

Such differences in thrust can at least complicate comprehensive legislative supervision of the executive branch.

Overall, Polsby's analysis reinforces the validity of Lawton's observation in Reading 5 that legislative-executive relations are not simply a "direct and inevitable outgrowth of the separation of powers." In massive reinforcement, Congress and its electoral system "foster localism" (in Lawton's terms) and provide multiple points of access for diverse organized interests who seek to get their concept of public or private advantage embodied in legal principle or in actual practice. These "organized interests" include

both executive agencies and multifarious associations representing industries, the professions, veterans, and so on.

J. Leiper Freeman provides valuable perspective on this legislative fragmentation in "The Setting and the Participants in Bureau-Committee Relations" (Reading 6). In his view, the special flavor of the legislative product
comes from the semiautonomy of three sets of critical actors:

1. The legislative committees and subcommittees that are often more meaningful and impactful than that collective abstraction, "the Congress."
2. The bureaus of federal agencies, which sometimes go substantially their
   own way because of the vagaries of political control and the concentration of long-tenured specialists in the bureaus.
3. The "interests" or "associations," whose focus is understandably particularistic rather than comprehensive.

Much the same characterization applies to legislative bodies at all levels of
government.

Granted that Congress may be characterized as relatively "diffuse" and
the presidency as relatively "focused" in making budget and financial decisions, one need not make the value judgment that the legislature must be
or can be only a mirror image of the institutionalized presidency. Maintaining a certain substantial difference between the Congress and the presidency, of course, is consistent with the practice of keeping our political eggs
in several baskets. The orthodox expert opinion does not take this point of
view, however, but tends toward the mirror-image role for Congress, toward "executive leadership" over "disciplined political parties." This is the
"put all your eggs in one basket" approach. Both strategies have their patent
costs, and it is perhaps the guiding genius of our institutions that we can
peacefully maintain the two strategies in confusing and ever-changing sets
of balances in various issue areas at different times. That we tolerate complexity while safeguarding personal freedom and at the same time supplying
an unparalleled prosperity to increasingly larger segments of our population
is the despair of dogmatic thinkers. Perhaps our "mixed" institutions do
not, overall, do as well as they might. But perhaps also they are therefore
unlikely to do as poorly as more "pure" institutions might.

The vertical sharing of powers—between federal, state, and local jurisdictions—raises similar issues about interpenetration and the locus of control. In general, the working solutions are similar to those in the case of the
horizontal sharing of powers. We can take here as granted the interpenetration of federal and local spheres of influence and control. Even the humblest
unit of local government may be depicted by a very complex layer cake, as
noted above. Any local government's bundle of services, for example, diversely involves federal and local officials. In some cases, services are provided completely outside the context of local government by state or federal
agencies. In other cases, local jurisdictions are the sole or prime providers

of services and of the resources they require. In between, complex varieties of sharing exist.

Given this complex interpenetration of levels of government, three related questions assume massive proportions: (1) Who will exercise control? (2) What will be controlled? (3) How will controls be exercised? Working solutions cover a wide range. At times firm and relatively unflinching federal attempts to control can be observed. More typically, local governments are given only the variously specific outlines of policy limits. Perhaps the dominant pattern is one of a complex sharing of controls, in keeping with the prevailing shared responsibilities for running an effective program. The root issue, in any case, involves developing some relatively effective and relatively acceptable mix of centralization and decentralization.

Not all observers are satisfied with today's solutions of the "who," "what," and "how" of exercising control. Harold M. Groves addresses himself to the complex issue of the nature and locus of public control, with the purpose of arguing a particular point of view. In "Centralized versus Decentralized Finance" (Reading 7), he argues that existing institutional arrangements do not encourage decentralizing financial authority to local jurisdictions. He makes the usual point for putting our eggs in fewer baskets, if not necessarily in one basket. Thus some jurisdictions are so numerous (e.g., school districts) that in many cases they are too small to support economically a desirable array of services. Many requests for "local control," if honored, will in actuality or by intention result in reducing the level of public expenditures or the quality of services. This illustrates the heart of Groves's argument.

Not that the issue is a black/white one for Groves. He notes the values inherent in numerous local jurisdictions, for example; local school districts provide opportunities for actual experience by many citizens in control over the complexities of their own governance. Again, there is a crucial rub. Achieving the value of local involvement may compromise achieving the value of educational enrichment. And if education is less effective, so also will people be less equipped to take good advantage of the opportunities for local involvement.

Although cries against "power-hungry central officials" are common at all levels of government, Groves continues, numerous harsh realities concerning "factions" or "interests" argue for a considerable centralization of authority. Consider an obvious case, Groves's charge that local governments in many cases are characterized by a "civil service infested with patronage and with the inferior talent that must be expected at highly inadequate salary scales." Realistically, the reason may be that some constellation of local interests, like a "courthouse gang," finds it convenient to preserve such a state of affairs despite the long-run costs. Centralizing a certain amount of authority in such cases may be the *sine qua non* of getting effective action on a program. Any "power-hungry central bureaucrats" would be certain to note such a necessity. And even administrators with strong preferences for decentralizing authority could either give up on their program or attempt to force necessary changes at the local level.

Indeed, less obviously, authority is often centralized because local officials want it that way. Thus local officials may lack the necessary skills or knowledge to act authoritatively with confidence. Local officials also often can use central authorities to insulate themselves from demanding local interests or individuals who have no real claim but to whom the official does not feel he can safely say no. Thus the local official can have his cake and eat it too. "Now you know I would like to help you," the official might explain, "but headquarters really has my hands tied in this case. Sorry." Of course, the official's hands also may be tied in ways he does not appreciate, but many are the cases in which he is thankful that central authorities took some of the heat off him.

There are complex ways in which special interests are a significant factor in helping shape the institutional contexts within which issues of public finance and budgeting must be resolved. A real sense of that dynamic interplay at the federal level is introduced in Freeman's Reading 6, discussed above. The general view—and sometimes the appropriate one—sees the capitol domes of our various seats of government as giant nipples around which "the interests" crowd to wax fat on the milk of public monies. A more sophisticated and subtle view is commonly appropriate, for the interests give to the commonwealth as well as take from it. They can induce creative activism by government agencies on programs that are broadly necessary. They can also tie public agencies to serving a narrow clientele that might better be left to wither away. Maximizing the former and minimizing the latter constitute the dual challenges facing public budgeting and finance.

No simple conclusions can be drawn about the impact of interests on budgetary decisions. One public agency studied by Rufus Browning[6] was submissive and docile, yet a second agency attempted to create interests it could live with, while it strived to manage creatively the interests that confronted it. Why agencies differ in responding to interests cannot be answered simply. Agency traditions will help determine whether interests are toadied to or respected, whether their every whim is served or some creative amalgam is attempted between what clients want or could use and what an agency feels it can and should provide. Whether the agency contains many "professionals" or whether it is staffed by "nonprofessionals" also will be an important factor in helping determine the response to interests.

If the "organized interests" are crucial to an understanding of decisions about public finance and budgeting, there also is ample room for the "unorganized masses" to influence policy. Occasionally, public interest will be deeply stirred by some event or cause; then public officials are well advised

Major Steps in the Budget Process

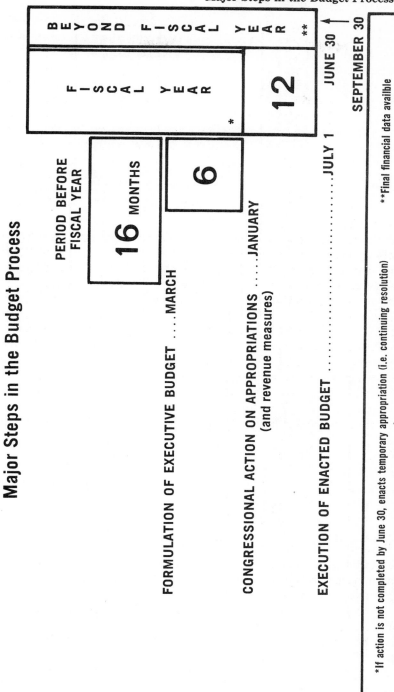

PERIOD BEFORE FISCAL YEAR

16 MONTHS

FORMULATION OF EXECUTIVE BUDGET .....MARCH

6

CONGRESSIONAL ACTION ON APPROPRIATIONS ......JANUARY
(and revenue measures)

FISCAL YEAR *

12

BEYOND FISCAL YEAR**

EXECUTION OF ENACTED BUDGET ....JULY 1 .... JUNE 30 .... SEPTEMBER 30

*If action is not completed by June 30, enacts temporary appropriation (i.e. continuing resolution)

**Final financial data availble

Source: Executive Office of the President/Office of Management and Budget, December 1972.

Formulation of Executive Budget

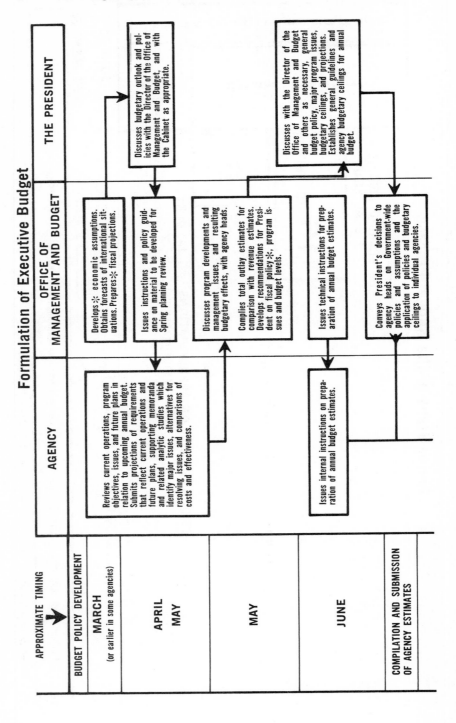

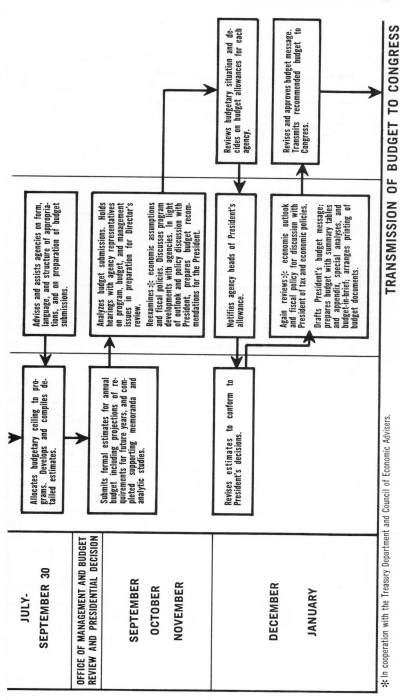

Source: Executive Office of the President/Office of Management and Budget, December 1972.

TRANSMISSION OF BUDGET TO CONGRESS

* In cooperation with the Treasury Department and Council of Economic Advisers.

Reviews budgetary situation and decides on budget allowances for each agency.

Revises and approves budget message. Transmits recommended budget to Congress.

Advises and assists agencies on form, language, and structure of appropriations, and on preparation of budget submissions.

Analyzes budget submissions. Holds hearings with agency representatives on program, budget, and management issues in preparation for Director's review.

Reexamines * economic assumptions and fiscal policies. Discusses program developments with agencies. In light of outlook and policy discussion with President, prepares budget recommendations for the President.

Notifies agency heads of President's allowance.

Again reviews * economic outlook and fiscal policy for discussion with President of tax and economic policies.

Drafts President's budget message; prepares budget with summary tables and appendix, special analyses, and budget-in-brief; arranges printing of budget documents.

JULY-
SEPTEMBER 30

OFFICE OF MANAGEMENT AND BUDGET
REVIEW AND PRESIDENTIAL DECISION

SEPTEMBER

OCTOBER

NOVEMBER

DECEMBER

JANUARY

Allocates budgetary ceiling to programs. Develops and compiles detailed estimates.

Submits formal estimates for annual budget including projections of requirements for future years, and completed supporting memoranda and analytic studies.

Revises estimates to conform to President's decisions.

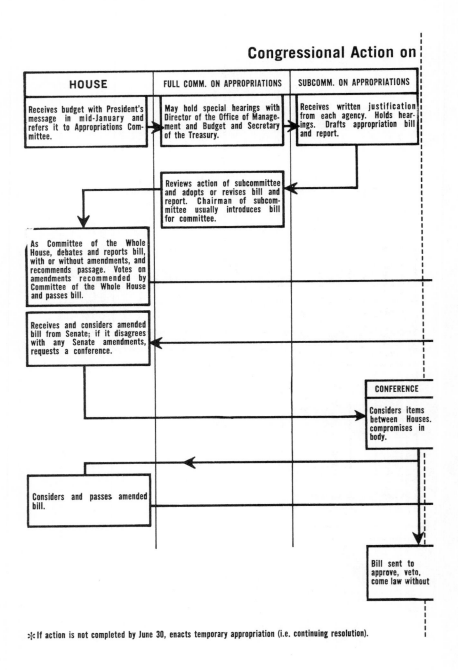

Congressional Action on

HOUSE	FULL COMM. ON APPROPRIATIONS	SUBCOMM. ON APPROPRIATIONS
Receives budget with President's message in mid-January and refers it to Appropriations Committee.	May hold special hearings with Director of the Office of Management and Budget and Secretary of the Treasury.	Receives written justification from each agency. Holds hearings. Drafts appropriation bill and report.

Reviews action of subcommittee and adopts or revises bill and report. Chairman of subcommittee usually introduces bill for committee.

As Committee of the Whole House, debates and reports bill, with or without amendments, and recommends passage. Votes on amendments recommended by Committee of the Whole House and passes bill.

Receives and considers amended bill from Senate; if it disagrees with any Senate amendments, requests a conference.

CONFERENCE

Considers items between Houses. compromises in body.

Considers and passes amended bill.

Bill sent to approve, veto, come law without

∗ If action is not completed by June 30, enacts temporary appropriation (i.e. continuing resolution).

Appropriations, January-July*

SENATE	SUBCOMM. ON APPROPRIATIONS	FULL COMM. ON APPROPRIATIONS

Receives budget with President's message in mid-January and refers ia to Appropriations Committee.

Note: Senate hearings are sometimes held before House completes action.

Receives bill from House and refers it to Appropriations Committee.

Receives agency justifications and appeals from House action. Holds brief hearings. Drafts amendments to House bill.

Adopts or revises subcommittee amendments and reports to Senate.

Debates bill and passes it, usually with amendments. If not amended, bill goes to President in same manner as amended bill.

Action on revenue measures follows the general course indicated here, being channeled through the Ways and Means Committee prior to action by the House and through the Finance Committee prior to action by the Senate.

COMMITTEE(S)

of disagreement Recommends report to each

Considers and passes amended bill.

President who can or permit to be-approval.

Office of Management and Budget prepares Summer Review, a summary of congressional determinations and revised budget outlook for new fiscal year.

DECEMBER

Source: Executive Office of the President/Office of Management and Budget, December 1972.

To take respectful notice. In addition, broad public opinion must support any long-run program. Manipulation and restricted information may suffice to protect administrators and politicians in the short run, but at least in the long run our institutions cannot remain inconsistent with deeply held public attitudes.

Notes

[1]Morton Grodzins, *The American System* (Chicago: Rand McNally & Co., 1966), pp. 156–71.

[2]See Charles E. Lindblom, "Decision-Making in Taxation and Expenditures," esp. pp. 295–98, in National Bureau of Economic Research, *Public Finances* (Princeton, N.J.: Princeton University Press, 1961).

[3]For an introduction to the complex legal and historical background, see Louis Fisher's, "The Politics of Impounded Funds," *Administrative Science Quarterly,* 15 (September 1970), 361–77.

[4]Nelson W. Polsby, "Policy Analysis and Congress," in U.S., Congress, Subcommittee on Economy in Government, Joint Economic Committee, *The Analysis and Evaluation of Public Expenditures: The PPB System* (Washington, D.C.: U.S. Government Printing Office, 1969).

[5]*Ibid.,* n.p.

[6]Rufus Browning, "Innovative and Non-Innovative Decision Processes in Government Budgeting," pp. 128–45, in Robert T. Golembiewski, *Public Budgeting and Finance* (Itasca, Ill.: F. E. Peacock Publishers, 1968).

4

Preparation and Execution of the Federal Budget

Office of Management and Budget

The preparation and execution of the Federal budget for any fiscal year covers at least 28 months. Thus, each spring attention is directed to (1) the control of obligations and outlays (expenditures and net lending) during the final months of the year in progress; (2) the planning of programs for the next fiscal year, which will begin the next July; and (3) the development of preliminary plans and policies for the succeeding fiscal year. Even

---

Reprinted from a publication of the Executive Office of the President, Office of Management and Budget, dated October 1971.

during the period of specific work on a particular budget, attention is given to projecting the effect of program decisions to subsequent budgets and to identifying major issues or problems affecting the budgets in the future.

The preparation and execution procedures change somewhat from year to year. However, the following description outlines the process in its most recent form.

PRELIMINARY STEPS

Staff of the Office of Management and Budget, in cooperation with staff of the Treasury Department and the Council of Economic Advisers, keep under continuous review the relationships between Government finances and the economy generally. This review includes study of recent and current conditions, as well as the outlook for coming years. Each spring the outlook goes into more depth with respect to the fiscal year for which a budget will be submitted in the following January, and projections are developed for future years. Consideration is given to tentative assumptions on the economic environment, projections of revenue expected under these assumptions, and the aggregate range of outlays which would be appropriate in view of current fiscal policies.

Agencies utilizing program planning and evaluation systems provide the Office of Management and Budget, upon request, program and financial plans, selected program memoranda, and special analytical studies on identified issues. The program and financial plans set forth data on outputs and financial requirements for a 7-year period, extending 5 years beyond the current year. The program memoranda and study papers reflect the application of systematic analysis to the programs, plans, and work design for various objectives and subjects with which the agency is concerned. These program memoranda include the agency head's tentative choice among alternative solutions to the problems discussed.

Agency program planning and evaluation are critically examined in the Office of Management and Budget. Proposed program expansions and new programs are viewed in terms of anticipated measurable benefits. Efforts are made to discontinue the application of resources to marginal and obsolete activities. Discussions between the Office of Management and Budget and the agency often help to shed light on specific problem areas.

In the late spring and early summer the Office of Management and Budget conducts the Spring Planning Review. Staff prepares estimates indicating a probable range of outlays for each of the major programs and agencies for the forthcoming budget. In preparing estimates, staff draws upon its knowledge of agency programs, agency estimates for particular programs in program evaluation materials provided in the spring, and informal discussions with responsible agency budget and planning personnel.

The Director reviews the fiscal and economic situation, the spending outlook, and the individual program, budget, and management issues posed in the agency presentations. He discusses the results of the review with agency heads and with the President as appropriate. Guidance is sought and obtained as needed, and "budgetary ceilings" are given to the agencies so that they may reshape their plans and prepare their budgets accordingly.

COMPLICATIONS AND SUBMISSION OF AGENCY BUDGET ESTIMATES

During the next several months agencies revise their program plans in accordance with budgetary ceilings and program guidance received, and decide upon the budget requests they wish to make for the upcoming budget. They compile schedules and supporting information in accordance with the instructions prescribed by the Office of Management and Budget (Circular No. A–11).

The process of compiling the detailed estimates begins with the personnel who are responsible for carrying out the agency's programs. They prepare information on costs or obligations, personnel, workload, and other supporting data, for the year just ended (the past year), the amounts planned for the year just beginning (the current year), and the estimates for the budget year, which still will not begin for almost a year.

In most agencies preparation of the budget begins at the field station level. It then goes through successive stages of review within the agency. At each level of review the viewpoint is different—the regional office must consider the estimates of each field station in relation to other field stations and to the total requirements for the region. Finally, at the departmental level, the estimates for bureaus and major programs must be judged in comparison with other bureaus and programs and with the total for the agency.

Agency budget submissions are due in the Office of Management and Budget in September. The submission covers all accounts in which money is available for obligation or expenditure, whether or not any action by Congress is requested. Schedules are based on amounts already available for the current fiscal year and those specifically requested for the budget year for programs in effect as of the date of the budget submission. These amounts include programs for which additional authorizing legislation is required in order to carry them on during the budget year. The agencies also submit summary information with respect to items to be formally requested later covering (1) anticipated additional requirements for the current year which were not foreseeable at the time the appropriations were enacted, and

(2) amounts which are expected to be required to finance new legislative programs recommended by the President.

REVIEW OF AGENCY ESTIMATES IN THE OFFICE OF MANAGEMENT AND BUDGET

When the estimates are received in the Office of Management and Budget, they are referred to the examiners assigned to the programs involved. All the knowledge the examiners possess about the agency—whether based on long-run analysis, field investigations, special studies, or conferences held with agency officials—is brought to bear on the estimates at this time. The examiners must be thoroughly familiar with the President's budget policy and previous congressional action, as well as with the programs of the agency and their relationship to activities of other agencies. They give considerable attention to the bases for the individual estimates: the volume of work on hand and forecast; the methods by which the agency proposes to accomplish its objectives; the costs of accomplishment; and the estimates of requirements in terms of supplies, equipment, facilities, and numbers of people required. They review past performance, check the accuracy of factual information presented, and consider the future implications of the program. They identify program, budget, and management issues of major importance to be raised for discussion with agency representatives at hearings conducted in the Office. The hearings, held in October and November, usually last only a few hours for a small agency, but may run into weeks for a large department.

After the hearings are completed, the examiners prepare their summary of the issues and their recommendations for the Director's Review. This review concentrates attention principally on the major test check on other aspects of the recommendations.

The Director's Review provides an opportunity for the principal officers of the Office of Management and Budget to obtain from the examiners an understanding of the agency's program aspirations and budget requests, an analysis of the significant issues involved, the relationship of the agency requests to the budgetary ceiling set for the agency in the spring, and recommendations as to budget allowances. The Review process is pointed toward applying the President's policies to the agency budget under consideration, identifying the phases of each agency's budget which require specific Presidential attention, and reaching a judgment by the Director on the recommendations he will make to the President regarding such items.

The process of review occupies the Office of Management and Budget from the latter part of September through most of December. During this period, the economic outlook is again assessed by the Treasury Department, the Council of Economic Advisers, and the Office, and revenue estimates are prepared for presentation to the President.

DECISION BY THE PRESIDENT

Because of the scope and complexity of the budget, the recommendations are placed before the President as portions of the Office of Management and Budget review are completed.

The President is faced with the task of recommending a budget which meets the most urgent needs of the country and still is prudent within the constraints imposed by the availability of resources. This task is complicated by the large segment of the budget which is relatively unaffected by the annual budget process. For the last few years such items as interest on the public debt, social security, veterans benefits, grants for public assistance, and agricultural price supports have accounted for more than three-quarters of the total nondefense budget outlays. The level of these outlays depends upon provisions of the laws which authorized the programs and on other factors not readily subject to annual budgetary control.

As soon as the President makes his decisions, each agency head is notified by the Director of the amounts which will be recommended to Congress for his agency's programs for the ensuing fiscal year.

PREPARATION OF THE BUDGET DOCUMENT

When the agency receives its budget allowance, the initial budget estimates are revised—in conformity with the President's decisions—for inclusion in the printed budget documents. The Budget Appendix sets forth the exact wording of the appropriation language last enacted by the Congress, with the changes proposed by the President, followed by detailed schedules supporting each estimate. In line with the policies set forth in Public Law 84–863, cost-based budget presentations are used for most accounts. This type of presentation, based on accrual accounting systems, provides information on inventories and other resources available to finance the agency's program and on the costs for the resources consumed within each fiscal year.

As soon as revisions of the individual schedules for each agency are completed, the figures from the individual appropriation and authorization schedules are summarized. Figures from the agency summaries are then consolidated to make up the tables which, together with final revenue estimates prepared by the Treasury Department, set forth the budget totals.

SUBMISSION TO CONGRESS

The President's budget is transmitted to the Congress—generally in January—but staff of the House Appropriations Committee may start work on the estimates before that time, based on advance proofs of certain chapters. As an initial step in Congressional budget review, the Director of the Office of Management and Budget and the Secretary of the Treasury are usually invited to appear before one or both of the Appropriations Committees to explain the general basis for the budget proposals.

Agencies prepare and submit justifications providing additional detailed information for consideration by the Appropriations Committee, and agency witnesses appear before its subcommittees to explain the estimates and answer questions. The justification material presented to the Committee generally is the same type of material given to the Office of Management and Budget earlier—revised to reflect the President's decisions on the budget. However, if the Committee wishes additional information or a different format of justification, it is provided.

The Committee reviews performance in the past year and the latest available information on the status of current year programs, as well as the estimates proposed for the budget year. Agencies also present information on balances of prior appropriations. In the case of major procurement programs (as in Defense) which require a long period of time between placing the orders and the delivery of material, the justification usually includes information on delivery schedules.

In many cases, the Committee regularly receives agency financial and work reports, and information from the General Accounting Office on the results of its audits of the agencies. It also has available its own staff and investigative staff on detail to it from executive branch agencies.

About 13 appropriation bills are prepared and adopted each year. After an appropriation bill is passed by the House, the Senate Appropriations Committee receives further statements and justifications from the agencies and its subcommittees hold hearings on the estimates.

After action on an individual appropriation bill is completed by the House and the Senate (including action on the Conference Committee report) the bill as passed is presented to the President, who has the power to veto the bill as a whole but not specific items in it. Congressional action on some appropriation bills has not been completed in recent years until sometime in October or later. When a bill has not been enacted by the beginning of the fiscal year for which the funds are requested, Congress enacts a temporary appropriation act, i.e., a "continuing resolution," which authorizes the agency to continue its operations until the bill is enacted.

BUDGET AMENDMENTS AND SUPPLEMENTAL ESTIMATES

Even while congressional review of the budget is in process, continuing attention in the agencies is being given to the need for revising the original estimates upward or downward, due to developments which have arisen since the estimates were originally submitted to the Congress. Additional funds for the budget year may be required to carry out programs for which new legislation is enacted or to meet emergencies which have arisen since the budget was prepared. Preliminary estimates are included in the budget totals for the new legislation anticipated at the time the budget is prepared. Specific amounts which are subsequently recommended to the Congress are the result of detailed analysis and review, based on the conditions at the time the recommendation is transmitted.

During this same period, additional amounts required for the current year are recommended in the form of supplemental estimates.

APPORTIONMENT BY THE OFFICE OF MANAGEMENT AND BUDGET

The Anti-Deficiency Act—Section 3679 of the Revised Statutes, as amended—requires that the Director of the Office of Management and Budget apportion, with a few exceptions, appropriations and funds made available to the executive branch. This consists of dividing the total available funds into specific amounts available for portions of the fiscal year or for particular projects or activities. It is a violation of law when an agency incurs obligations or makes expenditures in excess of the amounts apportioned.

The apportionment system is intended to achieve the most effective and economical use of the funds available and, for appropriations available for a definite period of time, to prevent the necessity for supplemental or deficiency appropriations. The Anti-Deficiency Act permits apportionments which anticipate the need for a supplemental appropriation, only when the appropriation is needed for outlays required by laws enacted subsequent to the transmission of appropriation estimates (e.g., Government-wide salary increases), or to cover certain specified emergency conditions. In each case where an apportionment is made on the basis of an anticipated supplemental, a report of the facts is required by law to be submitted to the Congress.

Agency requests for apportionments must be submitted to the Office of Management and Budget by May 21 of each year or within 15 days after approval of the appropriation act, whichever is later. The requests are referred to the examiners responsible for the programs involved. They review the request and the supporting material in arriving at their recommendations on amounts to be apportioned. The Office is required to act on the apportionment request by June 10, or 30 days after the approval of the appropriation act, whichever is later.

Reserves may be established "to provide for contingencies, or to effect savings whenever savings are made possible by or through changes in requirements, greater efficiency of operations, or other developments subsequent to the date on which such appropriation was made available."

Amounts reserved may not be obligated by the agency unless they are released by reapportionment action by the Office later in the year.

AGENCY CONTROLS OVER FUNDS

Each agency is required by law to have a system of administrative control to (1) restrict obligations or outlays against each appropriation or fund to the amount of the apportionments of such appropriation or fund, and (2) enable the agency head to fix responsibility for the creation of any obligation or the making of any outlay in excess of an apportionment or reapportionment.

In most agencies, the system of administrative control is based on the allotments made to the responsible personnel in the various organization units who have authority to incur obligations in carrying out the programs of the agency.

By the time the appropriation bill for a fiscal year is enacted, the agency's plans for the fiscal year must be brought up to date. The revisions take account of changes in the amounts expected to become available and of changes in conditions which affect the agency's program. The plans at this stage are usually more specific than they were at the time the original estimates were prepared. The revised plans are usually prepared in the same office which prepared the original budget estimates, and are again reviewed and consolidated at successive levels in the agency to serve as a basis for both the apportionment requests to the Office of Management and Budget and for allotments within the agency.

REVIEW OF PROGRESS DURING THE YEAR

Progress on the budget program is reviewed throughout the fiscal year at successive levels, both in the agency and the Office of Management and Budget. Periodic reports on the status of apportionments are supplemented by more specialized reports which relate accomplishments to cost. Shifts in the agency budget plans are frequently required to meet changing conditions—to finance unforeseen emergencies or to provide savings where the workload is less than was estimated or where increased efficiency permits accomplishment at less cost than was anticipated.

5

Legislative-Executive Relationships in Budgeting as Viewed by the Executive

Frederick J. Lawton

[I]t happens that my vantage point has been on the executive side. You have to bear that fact in mind in considering my line of reasoning. Yet I myself would like to forget any particular angle and keep before me only what I know to be the requirements of effective government. These requirements are of great urgency at a time when the United States has assumed vast responsibilities not only for the welfare and security of the American people but also for the survival of freedom throughout the world.

I shall discuss first some of the controlling factors in legislative-executive relationships. Then I shall outline the budget process in the context of these relationships. Finally, I shall deal briefly with some of the more recent proposals for strengthening Congress in its budgetary operations.

The problem of legislative-executive relationships is frequently seen as the direct and inevitable outgrowth of the separation of powers. It is true that the system of divided powers as written into the Constitution in categorical language has no counterpart in any other political system. Nowhere can one observe as sharp a distinction as is established by the Constitution in giving the legislative power to Congress and the executive power to the President as the embodiment of a coequal branch of government.

Still it is easy to see that the separation of powers would be something quite different if it did not operate on the basis of an electoral system which fosters localism and pressure groups. The separation of powers would be something quite different if it operated under the influence of a party system which developed solidarities around general programs for governmental action—equally meaningful for the membership of Congress and the President. In other words, those who simply lay the complications of legislative-executive relationships to the separation of powers see only part of the

From *The Influences of Social, Scientific, and Economic Trends on Government Administration* (Washington, D.C.: The Graduate School, U.S. Department of Agriculture, 1960), pp. 38–49.

picture. The other part—and the larger part—comes to light in those factors of law and usage that explain the difficulty experienced by Congress in attempting to function as a unified and self-directed institution.

To be sure, we have learned from experience that the most productive type of society is the kind of diversified society which exists in our country. A diversified society must reflect its divisions in the composition of the national legislature. If it were otherwise, it would be hard to see how representation could be attained in a democratic manner. What is important for my purpose here, however, is to suggest that the splintering effects of interest representation in Congress run counter to the practical maxim that the business of governing makes necessary a unified structure.

In this matter, the executive branch, under the Constitution, is more satisfactorily organized. For reasons persuasive in their own day—and increasingly persuasive in our time—the Founding Fathers insisted upon unified direction of the executive business of the nation under a single Chief Executive. This arrangement has provided the executive branch with considerable capacity for compounding different interests into a working formula for the pursuit of the common good. Congress, on the other hand, has for the most part remained without suitable machinery for initiating and enforcing broadly balanced programs for the attainment of national goals.

In the light of these considerations, it becomes very plain that legislative-executive relationships will continue to be molded by the stubborn realities of Congressional-Presidential government. The natural pulls and strains that run through a society of autonomous interest groupings will normally keep Congress and the President on different tracks. The basic reason, as I have tried to indicate, does not lie simply in the division of legislative and executive power. It lies in differences of political perspectives, which in turn are influenced by interest relationships. The political perspective of Congress is affected closely by the perspectives of its individual members, who have their political roots in their district. The President's perspective is necessarily national—not local.

It follows that those who have prescriptions for the improvement of legislative-executive relationships should first give appropriate attention to the controlling facts in the constitutional situation. Only by assessing these facts with calm objectivity can we discover the points where it would be practicable to attempt modifications in the existing arrangements in order to increase the effectiveness of our public management.

Against this background the tested value of the national budget system stands out in a doubly impressive way. Here, in the annual formulation of a comprehensive work plan for the Federal Government, a bridge has been erected between the legislative and the executive branches. A means of cooperation was found thirty years ago by the congressional architects of the Budget and Accounting Act which, as a basic governmental procedure, has been effective in a continuing way. Under this procedure, with the groundwork done in large measure on the executive side, Congress provided itself with a practical basis for instructing the departments annually about the programs to be carried out and the scale of individual activities.

Development of the budget process has introduced significant refinements into congressional control over the executive branch. Legislation, of necessity, confers responsibilities and grants authorizations to departments in quite general language. If an agency is directed to perform defined functions under law, it would still have wide discretion in determining how much or how little should be done in the performance of each individual function. Budgeting is like a mechanism for pumping fuel into the engines of government. It reserves for Congress the full opportunity for saying, on a year-to-year basis, in what scope and at what rates of progress departments should carry out their statutory assignments.

Budgeting is a bridge between the legislative and the executive branches also because it provides a method of reaching decisions of policy and administration in an orderly and informed way. Under the Budget and Accounting Act, the President was charged with the task of placing before Congress each year a complete budget as the plan of work for the whole Government. It was recognized clearly that the President alone has the constitutional standing to give a proposed budget the support of political responsibility. It was also recognized that he alone, as Chief Executive, was in a position to make available to Congress all the detailed technical information at his disposal throughout the executive branch. Congress, in turn, thus gained a stronger foundation for critical examination and final approval of the budget proposed by the President.

The importance of the Budget and Accounting Act as a milestone of responsible management has been pointed out frequently. Perhaps it is useful here to stress what I would like to call the constitutional significance of this legislation. Its constitutional significance lies in the achievement of a durable procedure for cooperation between the legislative and the executive branches. This bond of cooperation is of ever increasing consequence because the budget has emerged as the key document which controls the conduct of the entire business of the Federal Government.

The budget process as a procedure for cooperation between the legislative and the executive branches gains its strength from three basic elements. As I see it, the first of these, though sometimes pushed into the background, is the mutual appreciation by both branches of the need for approaching the budget as a joint effort. Only when there is acceptance of the cooperative implications of budgeting can one expect the greatest benefit from the budget process. A second element is the full utilization of the President's responsibility as constitutional head of the executive branch for the budget he submits to Congress. The largest returns accrue to Congress when it helps to keep the exercise of the President's responsibilty unimpeded. The third necessary element of the procedure is free flow of budgetary information from the executive branch to Congress.

When I emphasize the value to Congress of the President's direct responsibility for the budget I do not mean to suggest that the President would or should ignore the interests of his principal advisers—the heads of the executive agencies. In actual fact, as many of you know, the preparation of the budget in the executive branch is a large-scale and intensive operation which, at various points in the sequence of stages, brings into play the judgments of a large number of responsible operating officials. This is both good and inescapable. One reason for wide participation in budgetary decisions is the obvious fact that budget-making for the entire Government is too big a job to be done by any agency singly, even when the agency is charged with explicit statutory responsibilities in the field, as is the Bureau of the Budget.

No less important is the fact that the President would hardly want to speak for the executive branch without being sure that he has tapped all the counsel available to him in his official family. In order to come forth with a well-considered budget, the President must place much reliance not only on the factual information but also on the evaluative judgments contributed by experienced and politically sensitive administrators. Consultation is essentially a way of give-and-take. In other words, although even the soundest advice is never automatically compelling upon the one charged with making the decision, nevertheless under normal circumstances he will not find it easy to brush aside thoughtful advice once it has been supplied.

Moreover, as a knowing observer once put it, department heads, whether or not possessed of political ambition, may be conscious of standing in a competitive position to the President. They may show little solidarity with him on issues affecting their own agencies. It is clear, therefore, that the budget submitted by the President could fall apart in Congress if strong subordinates undertake to convey their opposition.

When the President presents Congress with his budget, he therefore submits a document that rests on many vital agreements. But he must retain and defend the integrity of decisions that result from his more inclusive field of vision. There is reasonable assurance in the operation of the budget process that the various special points of view within the executive branch find recognition, yet they cannot be allowed to run roughshod over the more general points of view typical of the level of the President.

In brief, the pressure within the executive branch for specialized functional objectives—as in the promotion of business, labor, or agriculture and in a host of similar fields—is met by a strong counterpressure in support of general solutions based on coordination. But reconciliation of positions is accomplished not by command but by a meeting of minds. It is not to be assumed, of course, that the end product is perfect. It is important that the end product come as close as possible to representing a general executive position, by and large accepted by all concerned.

One thing that is not understood widely is the degree to which the budget process, in compounding executive positions, at the same time brings to the fore the attitudes of interest groups and the tendencies likely to emerge in Congress. One reason is that the President is naturally anxious to come forth with a budget that would appeal to public opinion as well as to most of those who exercise influence in the political arena. As Chief Executive interested in carrying out the Government's program, the President is obviously more concerned with a practical work plan than with a propaganda document.

In addition, of course, the individual departments in most instances have quite close relations with particular clienteles and individual committees or leading figures in Congress. As a result, internal consultation within the executive branch about the President's budget has also external aspects. Such consultation casts light not only on departmental preferences but also on the political scene, especially the trends of thought prevailing in Congress.

What this means is that the President, when making his final decisions on the budget, has the advantage of many different strands of information. He acts on the results of examination carried on in the first instance within the different departments, and subsequently on a broader scale by the Bureau of the Budget. All of this serves to relate governmental programs and performance to the needs of the next fiscal year. But the President also has before him a picture of the positions taken by interest groups and congressional committees, and of the currents of public opinion and general congressional sentiment as well. In this respect, the Bureau of the Budget will regard itself responsible for bringing to the notice of the President any congressional expressions of general budgetary policy, especially the views of the Appropriations Committees and other congressional committees having across-the-board responsibilities, like those of the Budget Bureau itself.

True enough, there will always be occasions when the President feels duty-bound to press for the recognition of issues on which members of Congress may have a neutral or even a negative attitude. To draw the attention of Congress to these issues—including issues that do not enjoy universal popularity—is one of the burdens of statesmanship. It is at the same time an essential feature of Congressional-Presidential government. On the other hand, in order to foster the general interest as he sees it, the President needs to give thought to what support is likely to emerge for his proposals within the legislative branch.

As a staff agency of the President, the Bureau of the Budget exerts no direct influence in the legislative handling of the budget. Its indirect influence is confined to what it contributes toward a satisfactory presentation to Congress of information helpful particularly to the Appropriations Committees. One thing, however, should be remembered. The budget as submitted expresses the President's policy recommendations. The Budget Bureau is not meant to have a policy position of its own. Nor could the Bureau be expected, in view of its staff character, to depart from the policy positions of the President. What the Bureau is intended to do—and what it is reasonably well equipped to do—is to serve as a dependable source of interpretive as well as factual information.

Only in a secondary respect does the Budget Bureau move outside its information role, and then only upon congressional demand. For example, the Bureau may be given specific authorizations under appropriation language to take care of certain minor budgetary problems, like approval of transfer of funds. On the basis of general law, the Bureau has the additional duty to report promptly on instances of departmental use of funds that would lead to deficiencies. Sometimes Congress has charged the Bureau with the task of determining reductions all across the executive map to meet a figure set by Congress in acting upon the President's budget. This, however, is a rather rare arrangement.

There are different ways in which the Budget Bureau provides Congress with information. In the first place, in accordance with the Budget and Accounting Act itself, the Bureau must furnish such information as is called for by any of the committees of Congress concerned with finance, whether revenue or appropriations. These requests fluctuate in numbers, and are usually more frequent during the period when the President's budget is in preparation and when things are being gotten ready for the hearings held by the Appropriations Committees.

Another customary form of making available to Congress the budgetary information of the executive branch is through testimony by the Director or other officials of the Budget Bureau. As you will recall, the explanation of detailed budgetary requests before the Appropriations Committees is offered generally by the individual agencies. Testimony by officials of the Budget Bureau usually centers upon matters of general significance for the executive branch as a whole or upon amplification of information previously supplied in the testimony of officials of individual agencies.

As may be expected, there are usually discussions between Appropriations Committee staff and staff of the Budget Bureau. These discussions, however, look to particular problems and respect the separate institutional responsibilities of the two branches under the Budget and Accounting Act. Special reports asked for by congressional committees are another avenue of information transmitted from the Budget Bureau. Occasional details of Bureau staff to congressional committees and a considerable variety of informal staff contacts are further illustrations of the exchange of knowledge.

But in this whole picture I wish to refer especially to the Budget Bureau's role as the President's legislative clearing house. Under the legislative clearance procedure—established by the President at the suggestion of the Chairman of the House Appropriations Committee as early as 1921—both congressional committees and executive agencies use the Budget Bureau to find out whether a specific legislative proposal is in accord with the program of the President. This procedure has the significance of a signal system by letting congressional committees and individual members of Congress know what the position of the executive branch is with respect to particular legislative proposals.

As I indicated earlier, the importance of the budget process as a method of regularized cooperation between the legislative and the executive branches should always be appreciated anew because it might otherwise too readily be taken for granted. I do not mind adding that in the protracted discussion of ways of improving legislative-executive relationships in the field of budgeting there is often too much of an implication of presumably serious deficiencies yet to be overcome. It would be better to begin with a thoughtful appraisal of the structure of relationships that has developed between the two branches since the adoption of the Budget and Accounting Act, and specifically during the past decade or so, in order to figure fruitfully what might be done further.

It is in this light that I should like to touch briefly upon the innocent panacea that has been suggested off and on throughout the years—the idea of an "independent" Budget Bureau. It is not too clear just how such independence could be guaranteed and what results might flow from it. It is obvious to me that this whole concept falls outside the frame of our Congressional-Presidential system of government, because true independence of an agency that made fundamental financial determinations binding on all other agencies would actually amount to political irresponsibility. There is implied in the concept of an independent Budget Bureau a bureaucratic supremacy exercised by a body of experts who would impose their infallible judgment on all concerned. If the experience of the last three decades has made clear anything, it has borne out the wisdom of the congressional builders of the budget system in embedding the budget process in the structure of constitutional responsiblity.

Another suggestion that has been made at times is for a congressional Budget Bureau. This might mean a transfer of the existing Budget Bureau to Congress. If it meant that, the proposal would entail grave weakness by bringing about three highly undesirable consequences. The first would be the divorce of budget preparation and budget administration from the judgment of the Chief Executive about what activities and what funds are needed for the effective conduct of the Government's business. The second would be the destruction of the intimacy of the Budget Bureau's contacts with the wealth of detailed information now available to it within the operating services. The third would be the elimination in the budget process of that focal point for nationwide perspective and coordination which we possess in the Presidency. If, on the other hand, the idea of a congressional Budget Bureau rather meant an agency to serve as the congressional counterpart to the Budget Bureau as we have it now, the matter would reduce itself to a question of congressional staffing, especially of the Appropriations Committees. Such staffing, of course, must not lead to the result of having the same job done twice at different places.

Both of these ideas—that of an "independent" Budget Bureau and that of a congressional budget agency—have proved alluring to those who see a simple remedy to the tremendous increase in the size and scope of the budget during recent years. No one would deny that this development has produced entirely new and challenging problems for Congress. Forty years ago, the Federal Government's expenditures were less than 700 million dollars or about two and one-half percent of our total national income. With such a level of Government, problems presented by spending, borrowing, or debt management were of a lesser order. Today the economic and social implications of fiscal policy are of far-reaching importance to all of us. In a fiscal year, for example, when the Government takes more than 25 percent of our national income, the budget is certainly one of the most significant factors in the economic and social life of the nation.

I always have been impressed by the knowledge and understanding which so many members of Congress, particularly those on the Appropriations Committees, apply to the countless budgetary issues coming before them. Yet I feel that in approaching the budget, there is a tendency to get immersed in the complexity of the detail without first considering the broader determinations which have generally dictated the size and scope of the budget.

As I have suggested on previous occasions, the problem is a twofold one. First, there is the need for identifying and agreeing in Congress on the kind and amount of information that is required to evaluate both the budget as a whole and its thousands of component parts. And second, there is the need for providing within the Congress itself the kind of arrangements to insure the best use of this information.

With respect to the first part of the problem I believe that there is a general misconception about the kind of information necessary to test the validity of the budget. The size and emphasis of the President's budget is not governed by a multitude of unrelated decisions on individual items and activities. The major determinant in any budget is whether a given activity should be conducted at all, and if so at what level. All decisions on individual activities must be made in the light of broader factors—primarily the expenditure and revenue outlook, the international scene, economic conditions, and provisions of existing law.

These are the kinds of questions the President faces again and again in the preparation of the budget. Long before detailed estimates are prepared by the agencies, the basic decisions have been reached which, together with mandatory expenditures under existing law, control the broad outlines of the forthcoming budget. A forecast of changed economic conditions in relation to requirements of existing law, for example, may change the expenditure needs for veterans programs by more than $1 billion. The same assumption applied to other programs, such as public assistance grants, can also add or subtract hundreds of millions in the Federal Government's expenditures.

Certainly Congress, for its scrutiny of the budget, should have all the information that is needed to view independently and with full understanding the budgetary needs of the Government. I am inclined to think, however, that this is not simply a matter of increasing the quantity of information to be placed before Congress. Instead of being a matter of quantity, it is first a matter of the relevance of information. That is to say, instead of knowing more about the lesser detail of individual budgetary proposals, Congress might want to know more about those matters, issues, and problems that govern the budget in its main elements and as a whole.

I think that Congress, particularly in recent years, has made progress in obtaining from the executive branch much of the information that is essential to an appraisal of the Government's fiscal requirements. There has been, however, considerable debate within Congress over the question of the best organization and procedure to permit an adequate review of the information now available to it.

Three major types of congressional action affect the budget—authorizations, appropriations, and taxation measures. The authorizing bills are handled by the substantive committees. The appropriations are considered by the two Appropriations Committees. And taxation bills come before the Committee on Ways and Means in the House and the Committee on Finance in the Senate. Nowhere, however, does Congress pull the whole picture together.

To repair this situation is the motivation behind the idea of a Joint Committee on the Budget. In its more recent form, the proposal—going beyond the Legislative Reorganization Act of 1964—would provide an investigative committee with staff to do for the Appropriations Committees the work which the Joint Committee on Internal Revenue Taxation now does for the House Committee on Ways and Means and the Senate Committee on Finance. This would add to the facilities already at the disposal of the Appropriations Committees. While a joint staff might save overlapping and duplication between the two houses, I believe that the proposal would be successful only if the Appropriations Committees themselves came to the conclusion that they want a joint staff and will use it. Actually, there is sharp division on this point.

My own criticism of the proposal from the standpoint of equipping Congress with a method of evaluating fiscal requirements is that the projected role of the joint committee rests heavily on the expenditure side of the budget. It touches only very lightly on the two equally significant aspects of budgetary consideration—revenue requirements and authorizing legislation. The revenue side of the budget must be considered in relation to the expenditure side. Still more important, however, is the review of the fiscal effects—especially the effects upon subsequent budgets—of authorizing legislation, which is introduced and considered in every session of Congress. Such analysis is at present beyond the purview of the Appropriations Committees or any other single committee in either house.

Another idea is that of a single annual appropriation bill, as a sort of logical counterpart to the fiscal integration achieved in the budget submitted by the President. A more sweeping proposal, discussed at some length in recent years, would make a number of changes in existing budgetary practices and procedures. (1) It would enact into law as a statement of congressional policy the objective to balance the budget and provide for a reduction of the national debt under conditions of high employment, production, and purchasing power. (2) It would require that the annual economic reports of the President or the economic reviews of the Council of Economic Advisers set forth a four-year estimate of desirable levels of governmental expenditures and receipts. (3) It would give the President the item veto, exercised by most governors. (4) It would require that budget estimates transmitted to Congress be based on a consolidated cash statement. (5) It would require a separation in the budget of investment-type expenditures from operating expenditures and, in addition, four-year estimates of investment-type expenditures in appropriate detail. (6) It would provide for appropriations for major nonmilitary investment-type programs to be available for four years.

In the matter of a statutory "freeze" of fiscal policy, it might be questionable whether such policy can or should always be based on only one or two major objectives. In time of war, for example, whether hot or cold, even though production and employment are high, it may be impossible to balance the budget without such drastic tax increases that incentives to needed war production are impaired. Similarly, a statement of major objectives of fiscal policy should probably also take into account the need to meet essential levels of public service and to provide a balanced and equitable tax system.

As for four-year projections of desirable levels of expenditures and receipts related to the gross national product, our experience in the Bureau of the Budget indicates that long-range estimates are an important and necessary step in developing better guides for fiscal policy. Many problems remain to be solved, however, before the present exploratory work reaches a stage which would warrant the establishment of a statutory requirement.

The increasing recognition by both the public and Congress of the usefulness of consolidated cash totals has contributed to a better understanding of the economic significance of fiscal policy. While therefore greater emphasis upon this approach to budget presentation is desirable, some limitations should perhaps be pointed out. Even in measuring the economic impact of the Government's financial operations, presentation on a consolidated cash basis goes only part way. It does not, for example, differentiate between those expenditures or receipts which have immediate or pronounced effects on the economy and those which have not. Moreover, since fiscal policy cannot be based exclusively on economic considerations, more than one type of budgetary presentation is necessary as a guide for policy decisions.

There is no single "all-purpose" classification or presentation of budgetary facts which will meet all the needs of Congress, the President, and the operating agencies.

With respect to a separation of operating expenditures from capital and other investment expenditures, the Budget Bureau has long recognized the need for a budget classification which would identify expenditures of an investment or similar character. A special analysis published for the first time in the budget for 1951 was presented as an experimental effort to provide a tentative new classification of expenditures according to the duration and nature of benefits flowing from them. Improved data have since then become part of the budget document. One of the major problems is, of course, the definition of investment and similar expenditures.

Four-year availability of appropriations for investment programs may both encourage advance planning and allow the executive branch greater flexibility in timing expenditures for these programs in the light of changing economic conditions. Orderly planning of advance commitments for such investment programs is one of the most difficult but most important objectives to achieve.

The most important and most controversial of the proposals for budgetary reform is the item veto. There have been differences of opinion as to whether a constitutional amendment would be required to give the President this power or whether legislative action would be sufficient. The need for the item veto is increased in case Congress makes use of the so-called omnibus appropriation bill, as it did in 1950. A single appropriation bill magnifies the problem of legislative riders on appropriation acts. The experience in 1950 with the consolidated appropriation bill strengthens my belief that a single bill is fertile ground for the inclusion of legislative riders, despite restrictions in the Senate and House rules relating to legislation in appropriation bills. Practically speaking, therefore, it would be better first to provide for the item veto before action is taken to consolidate appropriations into one bill. Unfortunately, the probabilities of successful legal attacks upon the item veto when this is based simply on legislative rules seem somewhat greater with respect to riders than with respect to appropriation amounts.

So much for some indication of the nature of proposals advanced in recent years to strengthen further the legislative-executive relationships which have developed in such remarkable consistency under the Budget and Accounting Act. As I conclude, I seem to end up with these principal points:

First, only a utopian would imagine that the underlying factors of Congressional-Presidential government would yield to mere procedural elaborations of the budget process. A significant improvement in legislative-executive relationships must cut more deeply. Here the critical question is how Congress itself looks upon the way it is organized internally for asserting its institutional identity and unity.

Second, there is nevertheless wide agreement that room exists for procedural perfections in the present state of legislative-executive operations in regard to the budget. In fact, in matters of management nothing should ever be regarded as the last word on how a thing is to be done. Complacency in this matter is a dangerous narcotic. But I am far from sure that each proposal for improvement brought forth during these past years has been examined with sufficient care in all of its implications. Nor do I feel that it would always be to the benefit of good government to enact proposals into inflexible statutory requirements when cautious experimentation appears a more fruitful course. Above all, the mental reservations toward many of these proposals expressed in the Appropriations Committees certainly deserve respectful attention.

Third, it might be well for me to refer in this context to the pioneering activities of the joint accounting project, which was undertaken with strong congressional support by the General Accounting Office, the Treasury Department, and the Bureau of the Budget. What we need perhaps is some such joint project to explore with care the field I have discussed here, with continuing participation of the Appropriations Committees or also other committees of Congress. No one could know what would be the outcome. But it might help to clear the air.

And fourth, in whatever is done we should be a little closer to earth than we have been so often of late and firmly reject the implication that this or that innovation will in itself produce telling economies. The reckless overselling of ideas is one of the less satisfying aspects of the political process. When it comes to significant economies, no device and no mechanism can automatically do the trick. This is a matter of unwavering determination of priorities, and the resistance to such priorities is spread all over the political landscape.

6

The Setting and the Participants in Bureau-Committee Relations

J. Leiper Freeman

[E]xcept in the case of issues which in modern terminology become "escalated" to the level of compelling national concern, the resolution of most policy questions tends more often to be left to secondary levels of the political setting. Policy-making is often left to essentially subordinate units of the Administration and Congress. Similarly, the parties often leave issue politics to interest groups. In this sense, such sub-units of the political setting, encouraged by diffused power and functional specialization of political expertise, tend to enjoy a relatively wide range of autonomy. Policy tends to be "farmed out." Although this is not complete autonomy, it is significantly more than would be found in a centralized and strongly hierarchic model.

This semi-autonomous status of lesser units in the general system deserves a brief overview because such units furnish the most intimate portion of the setting of the subsystem. It is from their positions as leaders of these specialized organizations that subsystem participants derive their status as policy-makers.

SEMI-AUTONOMY OF BUREAUS IN THE ADMINISTRATION

First, in the complex and interdependent structure of the Administration the bureau or its equivalent is frequently the unit of continuity and specialization in a given area of policy. To a considerable extent, departments and agencies are assemblages of bureaus. Although much has been done within the last generation to centralize departmental control through reorganization and departmental staff innovations, many departments and agencies are still to a great degree "holding companies" for bureaus. Of course, during the Eisenhower Administration there occurred an extensive expansion of departmental officers—particularly at the level of assistant secretary. The intent here was to give the political administrators at the departmental level a greater control over the career bureaucracy, and to some extent this development may have brought the focus of legislative-executive relations closer to the departmental heads. Yet in the many more specialized policy decisions which must be reached apart from the main political arena the importance of bureau chiefs is still great.

In this situation departmental leaders are essentially the agents of the Administration's party, that is, of the coalition which controls the Presidency. This tends to be their primary orientation. It is their job, for as long as they are in temporary positions of departmental leadership, to attempt to assert the views of the Administration before the array of bureaus in their charge and to gain compliance with these views. At the same time, of course, they must rely upon the bureaus for expertise and special knowledge, and they must often accede to what may appear to them to be "bureaucratic inertia" or "bureaucratic eccentricity." The bureaus, composed wholly or almost wholly of career personnel and possessed of the technology and the capacity to perform the tasks of the agency, are neither easily moved by the party in power nor overly embarrassed at urging their time-tested viewpoints upon "non-career" leaders in the Administration.

The result is a not-too-delicate seesaw between the politics of the Administration's party and the politics of bureaucratic expertise, specialization, and self-preservation, with bureau leaders frequently fulcrums in the balance.[1]

SEMI-AUTONOMY OF COMMITTEES IN CONGRESS

In its own way the Congress is a complex structure of many interdependent and important subdivisions. Although the total sizes of both the Senate and the House of Representatives have remained stable for several decades, both houses have not particularly abated their tendency to maintain committees on special subjects. The number of standing committees was reduced by the LaFollette-Monroney Reorganization Act of 1946, but this proved only a temporary or partial curtailment of some active sub-units. What was once a standing committee may carry on as a semi-independent standing subcommittee under the new organization. The standing committees are supplemented from time to time with select committees investigating special topics. Senior members of both parties gain status and prerogative with the accumulation of years of service on these committees. They also build up a certain special knowledge about and familiarity with the issues, individuals, and groups concerned in the policy matters handled by their committees.

Furthermore, each house of Congress is in itself a legislative body, since all acts have to pass both houses in identical form in order to become law.

This means that each house tends to some degree to duplicate the work of the other as well as to maintain duplicating committee structures. In order to iron out differences between the houses on particular bills, conference committees are used on an ad hoc basis. All of these facts essentially add to the complex and pluralistic committee matrix within which so many decisions are reached in a decentralized fashion. The usage of joint committees on a sustained basis has been limited and has been only partially successful. The committees of each house are baronial centers of power, as Cater, along with every other student of Congress, has noted.[2] And, indeed, the two houses are jealous of each other, leading to such events as the recent inter-committee warfare between the two appropriations committees.[3]

The general consensus of students of Congress, moreover, is that seniority linked to committee power serves effectively to curtail party government, except under conditions of unusual skill in leadership probably coupled with unusual pressure from public opinion. The majority party in each house gains the power to fill the posts of leadership both on the committees and for the houses as a whole. Yet the norm of seniority, in and out of committee, generally means that long-time legislators can exert influence and achieve status somewhat independent of party regularity. Although both parties have tried to maintain semiformal devices for general policy leadership, the policy committees have seldom tried to bind the party members in the two houses. They explore problems and attempt to arrive at acceptable stands. In addition, majority leaders, minority leaders, and their aides try to enforce some party coherence, especially upon major items at issue. But the management of legislation typically is a task shared by several leaders in each house, and often entails cooperation which crosses party lines and must invariably satisfy the committee leaders concerned. Not since the days of Speaker Joe Cannon has the House of Representatives had truly centralized leadership. That power was dispersed among committee leaders—especially the Rules Committee leaders—and party elders. Yet the House seems highly organized in comparison with the individualistic Senate, where Majority Leaders such as Lyndon Johnson and clotures on filibusters are rarities indeed. There, the prevailing power is customarily shared by "the Establishment" composed largely of senior committeemen.[4]

Eighty years ago Woodrow Wilson pointed out that the real decisions of Congress were made in standing committees.[5] Over twenty years later he found that "each committee is a miniature House," although he detected a greater central control over that body in the powerful Speaker of that period.[6] Today, the centrally organized control of the House is somewhat weaker than it was in the early 1900's, and neither the House nor the Senate has fundamentally altered the importance of committees. The basic validity of Wilson's view on committees still seems to hold. Thus in Congress there is a seesaw between the politics of the congressional majority leadership and the politics of the committees in which the influence of special interests and seniority are concentrated. Here committee leaders are often fulcrums in the balance.

SEMI-AUTONOMY OF INTEREST GROUPS IN RELATION TO THE PARTIES

The parties should be viewed as general organizations striving to achieve majority support and interested in the broadest consensus possible. In the United States, while there is a difference in the broad concerns of the two major parties, they are more distinct from each other on the basis of the geographical distribution of their support, social characteristics, and traditional voting habits than because of hard and clear ideological contrasts and disciplined pursuits of interests.

Not having to pursue the entire range of concerns confronted in the attempt to man the government and win the next election, the specialized interest groups are relatively free to seek narrowly those things nearest and dearest to their hearts, pocketbooks, and clients. They can appropriate a party's viewpoint or ignore it, according to its relevance to their limited cause. These groups are organized as limited-purpose groups, whether their association is based on occupation, profession, geography, ideology, or any of a number of common grounds of cohesion. They do not usually seek to control the whole machinery of policy-making, but rather to prevent policies from being made which would injure their special interests and to secure other policies favorable to their interests. In the aggregate, however, these groups are often a basic counterforce to party politics, and they do an effective job of seesawing with the parties. Here interest-group leaders are often fulcrums in the balance.[7]

CHARACTERISTICS OF SUBSYSTEM LEADERS

Having reviewed briefly some of the factors which emphasize the semi-autonomy of subdivisions of the Congress, the Administration, and the public with relation to the larger entities, and having observed that these subdivisions furnish the immediate setting of subsystems of policy-making somewhat isolated unto themselves, it is now appropriate to examine briefly some characteristics of the major participants in such a subsystem. We will consider bureau leaders, committee leaders, and interest-group leaders in sequence.

Bureau leaders tend to occupy an ambiguous status in the Administration. They may be viewed on a continuum from more partisan to more professional or more technical. Though some are still appointed by the President, others are members of the career service. Almost all of them are expected to be closer to the professional and technical end of the spectrum than are departmental leaders, and the trend over the last few decades has been to view bureau heads increasingly on the "career" side of public officialdom. Consequently, bureau leaders are increasingly apt to "stay" when department leaders "go." Furthermore, bureau leaders are judged on the basis of special knowledge and technical performance and less on party adherence. Conversely, bureau leaders are expected to adjust to the orientation of the party in power insofar as it is possible for them to do so within the general limits of their professional and technical standards. They are not expected to be so deeply embedded in the bureaucracy that they are either inaccessible or handicaps to departmental leaders or, on occasion, to the President.

At present, the bureau leader is the mid-level entrepreneur of policy in the executive branch. Standing between the partisan position of the core of the Administration and the special knowledge, interests, and skills of his bureau, he is a spokesman for the civil servants and the clientele of his organization. Frequently, he is a quasi-monopolist of vital information. Finally, he is a major agent of continuity in a particular area of public policy.

On the congressional side, committee leaders are in positions somewhat analogous to bureau leaders in the Administration. Due to the method of their election committee leaders, like all senators and representatives, reflect geographic and other special interests to a considerable degree. Moreover, since they owe much of their own status in the legislative hierarchy to seniority, they usually respect the seniority of others on their committees, to a certain extent without regard to party allegiance. Serving together over the years on a committee may even breed real loyalty and mutual good will among senior members. Still further, the senior members of a committee may establish a close and mutual relationship with committee staff members so that something of a small, legislative "bureaucracy" may exist, with characteristics of stability, endurance, and cohesion not unlike those in an executive unit. Consequently, it is not unusual to find on a committee an in-group composed of senior members of both parties plus staff members of long standing or great prestige. Even with a majority-party affiliation, a newcomer may be an outsider for quite a while. The members of the in-group will tend to make the decisions and to mediate between the committee and the legislative body as a whole.

The interest-group leaders who play important parts in a subsystem are spokesmen for and symbols of special sets of values held by segments of the public. Like bureau leaders and committee leaders, they are usually middle-level entrepreneurs of policy. Within their special subject-areas they are usually well-informed and are likely to be heard; outside these areas, however, they are less likely to prevail. They make it their business to maximize the satisfaction which will appear to flow from their efforts to the members of their associations. A concomitant of this function is that they furnish continuous, special attention to and take constant parts in the deliberations between the bureaus and committees handling the policies affecting their groups. These leaders keep uppermost in their minds and activities the nature of their constituencies, which are frequently similar to the clientele or part of the clientele of the bureau concerned, and which may be parts of the constituencies of the committee members. Occasionally, they claim to speak authoritatively for larger segments of the public than they actually do. They may be prone to ignore the fact that their constituents often are either members of, or are sympathetic toward, other groups with perhaps conflicting interests. Nevertheless, there is little in our system of policy-making that aids in the determination of the true extent of the representativeness of interest-group leaders, and they tend to be heard insofar as they are vocal, organized, cohesive, clever, knowledgeable, and persistent.

SUMMARY

The general political system which centers upon Congress and the Administration furnishes the political setting for policy-making subsystems formed by the interactions of the leaders of congressional committees, executive bureaus, and interest groups. This political setting is the scene of the activities of the major political parties as they attempt to organize and control the government. In both the Administration and Congress, however, party government tends to be characterized by factionalism, necessitating coalitions which cross strict party lines and which are also assemblages of divergent interests held together by rather volatile political cement. In such a general system, policy issues are rarely found to be clearly partisan, for the chief, enduring partisan concern is to capture the government.

Consequently, policy issues tend to be consigned to lower levels of Congress and the Administration for specialized consideration and extensive resolution by those units most intimately concerned. Similarly, the parties tend to leave doctrinal and technological fine points to interest groups. Thus, the overall setting promotes considerable autonomy for bureaus, committees, and interest groups, which are the organs forming the most immediate setting of the subsystems under discussion here. It is out of their positions as leaders of these semi-autonomous, specialized organizations that the major participants in subsystems derive status as policy-makers. As mid-level entrepreneurs of policy, they stand between tightly organized functional groups on the one hand and loosely mobilized general political power on the other.

Notes

[1]In the period since World War II, some of the "fulcrum" function of bureau chiefs has been passed upward, to assistant secretaries, perhaps. But the basic pattern is still there. In 1954, articles were being written, e.g., concerning the problems of coordinated policy-making in the State Department. Ten years later, the Secretary of State was complaining of problems of "layering," of being far removed from actual confrontation with his agency's work, due to layers of subordinates. See Frederic W. Collins, "New Tests for 'State,' " *The New York Times Magazine,* May 23, 1954, pp. 8–9; and Ellis O. Briggs, "Case against a West Point for Diplomats," *The New York Times Magazine,* May 3, 1964, p. 20 ff.

[2]Douglass Cater, *Power in Washington* (New York: Random House, 1964), Chap. IX.

[3]Joseph S. Clark, *Congress: The Sapless Branch* (New York: Harper & Row, 1964), pp. 137–39.

[4]*Ibid.,* Chap. VI.

[5]Woodrow Wilson, *Congressional Government* (Boston: Houghton Mifflin Co., 1885).

[6]*Ibid.,* p. 92.

[7]David Riesman in *The Lonely Crowd* (New Haven, Conn.: Yale University Press, 1950) speaks of these groups as primarily veto groups. Although much of their effort is defensive, this term is inadequate for the roles which they play within limited arenas of policy-making. There they take the offense, while outside their special domains of effective action they do not always have the complete defensive power which the term veto implies. See also the comments of Earl Latham, *The Group Basis of Politics* (Ithaca, N.Y.: Cornell University Press, 1952), pp. 36–37.

====

7

Centralized versus Decentralized Finance

Harold M. Groves

It is an accepted rule that the Government should not perform functions that can as well be performed privately and that the Federal Government should not perform functions that can as well be performed by State and local governments. Unfortunately this doesn't help very much in making decisions as to whether functions should be assumed by the Federal Government or left to the States.

From H. M. Groves, "Centralized versus Decentralized Finance," in U.S., Congress, Joint Economic Committee, *Federal Expenditure Policies for Economic Growth and Stability* (Washington, D.C.: U.S. Government Printing Office, 1957), pp. 188–94.

PRESUMPTION FAVORING DECENTRALIZED FINANCE

The presumption in favor of State and local government is based on the faith that decentralization is an important constituent of democracy. This faith is particularly plausible insofar as it applies the rule that matters which are solely or perhaps mainly of concern to a particular area should be left to the people of that area for decision. This interest in local autonomy carries the title "Home Rule" and it is guarded as jealously (and as frequently violated) as the similar right of the private individual to mind his own business when it does not conflict with that of somebody else.

Beyond this interest in home rule there are values in local government that are lost when responsibilities are assumed by central governments. One of these is participation—government by the people. The private citizen undoubtedly finds opportunities to participate in government at the local level which cannot be duplicated at the national level. At the city hall or State Capitol any public-spirited citizen can reach his alderman or legislator in person and he can appear to express his views at a public hearing. An ordinary "dirt farmer" can do all of this and get home in time to milk the cows. It may be prohibitively expensive for him to go to Washington and, anyway, he would need an elaborate organization to make much impression there. Rated by degree of participation, most democratic government is that by popular assembly or referendum where representatives can be dispensed with entirely. Next best is representative government in a small enough circle so that the ordinary citizen without undue sacrifice can make himself heard and felt.

Local government also offers to many an opportunity to participate in government in positions of responsibility. There are thousands of people whose career as a representative of the people is and will be confined to membership on the school boards of our some 65,000 school districts. This is not only of some value in itself—it is a training school and a testing ground from which the upper echelons of government recruit talent.

Local governments also serve as experiment stations in which new ideas may be tried out without the risk and expense (to say nothing of the inertia) that would be involved if the experiments were national in scale.

These positive values of local government are reinforced by the negative aspects of far-flung centralized bureaucracy. Distrust of such is deeply rooted among Americans, especially those who lean toward an anti-monopoly philosophy. Central government is not only big; it is also single; it possesses unique coercive powers; and it offers no alternatives to its customers. Like all large monopolistic organizations it suffers the inefficiencies that rise from inadequate knowledge at the center of what is really needed at the periphery.

Of course, it can be argued plausibly that some central sharing in the financial support of local functions is quite different from Federal assumption of sole responsibility and control in these areas. It is argued that in communities with limited resources, grants-in-aid may increase local independence by freeing some of their limited funds for services of their own choosing. But this new freedom is like that of a son who earns part of his support and gets the remainder in a regular (but not guaranteed) allowance from his benevolent parents. He is not really fully free and responsible until he subsists on his own income supplied by himself.

THE CASE FOR CENTRALIZED FINANCE

All of the above is widely appreciated in this country. But there is another side of the picture that offers persuasive support for a degree of centralized responsibility at least greater than that which prevailed in the 1920's.

Slow Progress and Undemocratic Procedures in State Government

The States and municipalities (particularly the former) would be in a stronger position as candidates for more responsibilities if they had (or would) put their own house in order. Following the Commission on Intergovernmental Relations one can list the areas that need attention as follows:

1. There are antiquated representation systems that underrepresent large and recently developed centers of population in one or both legislative bodies. What becomes of the democratic principle when a majority in the legislature can be elected by a quarter of the eligible voters and when A's vote counts for 10 times as much as B's? Some of this might be defended on the dubious ground of area representation; most defense is the obvious rationalization of a special interest. Some progress in reapportionment is being made continuously but it is not enough to offset population changes now going on; thus on balance the problem is a growing one. Some effort has been exerted to devise machinery that can cope with vested interests in this area but it has been successful in only a few States.

2. There are antiquated constitutions providing for weak executives, too many elected officers, too infrequent legislative sessions and budgets, and too limited financial powers.

3. There are still many cases of civil service infested with patronage and with the inferior talent that must be expected at highly inadequate salary scales.

4. There is the record of neglect in dealing with the metropolitan problem regarded by many critics as the No. 1 domestic issue. This is the problem which has resulted from the recent vast movement of population

into some 168 metropolitan areas and out of their centers to their peripheries. If these areas had governments coterminous with their functions they would still be hard pressed with such matters as strangulating traffic, decadent sections, crowded schools, delinquent gangs, and of course excessive tax rates. Usually added to all this is an antiquated political geography with many units of government, some of them poaching on their neighbors. One district may have a factory and another the workers. These problems will not yield except to great courage and imagination at the State level. Not too much of this kind of leadership has developed.

Regressive Taxation

The States and municipalities have on the whole a regressive tax system based at the local level on the general property tax and at the State level on the retail sales tax. The Musgrave studies[1] have indicated that in State and local taxes the poorest bracket of taxpayers ($0 to $2,000 net income) pay almost half again as much per thousand dollars of net income as the well-to-do (over $10,000 net income). Moreover, there is ground for the view that the trend is toward more regressivity. Eleven States have enacted sales taxes since World War II and no States have enacted new net income taxes. This means that a vote for decentralizing the financial responsibility for a function is a vote for regressive as against progressive taxation. This is not a matter of equity alone; it also involves economics. It is the progressiveness of the tax system that gives it much of its built-in flexibility—its propensity to produce automatic surpluses and deficits to meet the needs of compensatory budgeting.

Those who favor decentralization should logically be in the front rank of the crusaders for better and more aggressive State and local government. Actually this is often not the case and it leads to the conclusion that these people are probably more interested in less government, less total taxes, and less taxes for themselves than in decentralization as such.

Interstate Competition

The States and municipalities are in a relatively weak financial position because they are amenable to interterritorial competition to a far greater degree than the Federal Government.

The proposition that Federal aid involves only the collection of revenue that might have been raised locally, the sending of this revenue to a distant capital, from whence it is returned with some part missing, is at most a half-truth. The full truth would add that if the central government (for better or for worse) did not support this function and raise the tax for it, the function probably would not be supported at all and the tax for it would not be raised. The competitive factor, among others, also provides a rationale for distributing aid to strong districts as well as weak ones.

The degree to which taxation influences industrial location and the degree to which competition influences State and local decisions concerning taxation are matters long in dispute. It is evident that State and local governments are not completely captive and that the deductibility of State and local taxes on Federal income-tax returns gives them some protection. State and local government under the pressure of earlier public works postponement and increased population have been expanding their outlays for public services with some aggressiveness. It is true also that no empirical study has ever established the alleged fact that areas with high taxes or relatively progressive tax systems have suffered in industrial development. But anyone who observes legislative bodies cannot doubt that the pressure is real and important. It is nonetheless real because a lot of it is mainly fear psychology.

The degree of interterritorial competition is probably increasing. A perusal of newspapers and magazines indicates that the "booster spirit" is everywhere going strong. It takes the form of advertising, developmental corporations, subsidies, tax exemption, and a "favorable tax climate." Concerning the latter, one former director of a State division of industrial development observed:

> In an era of industrial mobility, no State can stand alone in its adherence to a tax structure strongly oriented to the "ability to pay" theory. Continued adherence to this theory, in the face of defections by contiguous or "competitive States" will have the certain long-range effect of decreasing the rate of personal-income growth and denying improved employment opportunity to the very persons supposedly benefited by the application of this theory.[2]

Interdependence

The trend of the times is toward more interdependence. This thesis can be supported by the impressive evidence concerning migration, travel, and interterritorial exchange of all sorts. This interdependence means that the people of Podunk, N.Y., have some equity in the maintenance of public standards in Podunk, N. Mex., and vice versa. It is characteristic of the satisfaction of human wants through government that the benefits derived from government outlay are largely indirect and frequently extraterritorial.

The growth of interdependence is particularly relevant with regard to education. Educational standards may seem at first to be of concern mainly to pupils and parents or at most the citizens of the community in which the youth are reared. But what becomes of this conclusion when we confront the statistics of migration and observe how many now being educated in one community turn up eventually as workers and citizens of another?

Interdependence means that the interest in many matters formerly of strictly local concern is now a divided one. The degree of interest for parties involved is difficult to discern and to implement. Our Federal aid system is one means by which a partnership of interest is combined with a partnership of financial responsibility and control. The control issue is the most sensitive one; the Kestnbaum Commission surveyed this area with great care and although it recommended some changes in detail, it is fair to say that on the whole it found the controls conservative and salutary. They have encouraged such State improvements as merit-system civil service and State highway departments.

The General Level of Public Expenditures

It is apparent that one's reaction to the question of Federal versus State financial responsibilities is conditioned considerably by his reaction to public expenditures as such. If he thinks they are too high he will probably favor decentralization. The States and municipalities for reasons previously cited will not spend as freely as does the Federal Government with its far superior taxing power. The proper level of overall public expenditures is the subject for other panels. Here it may be said that proponents of liberal government spending have these points on their side:

As the economy advances and per capita income increases, free income (above biological necessities) increases still faster. This free income is subject to a degree of discretion not true of the hard core of necessities. It is everywhere devoted in large measure to services where the Government competes with private disposition most effectively. Some of the ugliest aspects of the American way of life, such as slums, crowded schools, youth delinquency, and mental illness are in the area where government programs are most effective. The wastes of government are regrettable but they probably are minor compared with those of private consumption which in the United States are legendary. The typical American consumer thinks nothing of driving a station wagon across town to mail a letter. Governments are sometimes extravagant but they also frequently are niggardly. The case I know best is the Internal Revenue Service which in the opinion of many critics has always been substantially undermanned. Under present conditions the belief that the acceleration of private expenditures as against government expenditures necessarily results in the healthiest society is not tenable.

CENTRALIZATION AND ECONOMIC CONTROL

One would be insensitive to the wave of the present if he did not attempt to relate our problem to that of controlling inflation. For the maintenance of at least the present Federal role in the overall expenditure picture it can be said, looking at the long run, that Federal expenditures and taxes are more amenable to control than those of the States; that the government's large role in the economy is what makes compensatory controls effective and that this role would diminish if the Federal Government relinquished a large area to the States; that it is the predominantly progressive overall tax system that affords built-in flexibilty and that this is maintained only by the Federal Government's role. On the other hand controllability is no good if it isn't used; this seems to indicate a reduction in Federal expenditures now that inflation is our gravest problem; if the States do not take up the slack, so much the better. Those who cherish Federal expenditures for their nonfiscal or institutional objectives have the obligation to offer some remedy for inflation other than reduced public expenditures.

Of course, what would really now aid the States would be an acceleration of economic growth, an end to inflation, a loosening of tight money (which interferes with their borrowing), and a continuance of Federal spending at least insofar as it supports the States. This program sounds a little like the politician's platform of a soldiers' bonus, reduced taxes, and a balanced budget. But we have not exhausted the field when we have accepted a high level of public expenditures and rejected tighter money as remedies for inflation. Simplest but not the most popular remedy is to plug loopholes in existing taxes and thus add to the Federal budget surplus. Obviously cutting taxes and letting expenditures ride is a perverse answer. Perhaps we should look for something new as an inflation control; for example, decelerated depreciation, a tax on bank loans, and a sales tax on industrial equipment have been suggested. A graduated overall expenditure tax to supplement the income tax would be a promising instrument of control if it could be administered.

On the other hand, if as alleged and as seems probable, our present inflation problem is due in large part to cost-push causes; that is, to monopolistic pressure (business and labor) upon the price level, then we surely have to look for something new in inflation controls. The nearest thing to a fertile suggestion that has so far come to our attention is that of Sumner Slichter to disallow wage increases (for a time) as corporate income-tax deductions. Alternatively we might levy a special payroll excise tax in much the same way and to the same effect. These proposals involve the administrative problem of separating wage increases from payroll additions due to expansion; and they throw all the bonus of monopolistic pricing on labor. It would be more logical to levy a special sales tax on the receipts from price increases; but in only a few cases are commodities sufficiently standardized to separate genuine price increases from changes due to innovation in product. To all of these possibilities the objection will be made that they constitute government tampering with the free market. But here the ready answer is that it is the absence of a free market that creates our problem to begin with.

At any rate it seems inadvisable to reorder our intergovernmental fiscal relations as a remedy for inflation. That some Federal expenditures can and should be cut is conceded, but most of them (from our point of view) are inelastic in the downward direction. And in some areas expenditures should be increased.

This is not to say that nothing should be done about inflation. The author will not attempt here to arbitrate among the several suggestions listed above, but he does wish to leave the thought that the time is ripe for the exercise of some further ingenuity with regard to the inflation problem.

QUANTITATIVE PICTURE OF FEDERAL-STATE FINANCE

We may turn before drawing a conclusion to the quantitative picture and ask what it shows regarding the alleged encroachment of the Federal Government on the States. Over the long view, the relative position of State and local governments in total expenditures has undoubtedly dropped sharply. In 1927 State and local expenditures were nearly three-quarters of the total (73.1 percent); in 1940 they were still more than half (52.8 percent); and in 1956 a little more than one-third (33.6 percent). The 1956 proportion is the same as that of 1948, indicating no postwar trend. Much of the recent alleged aggrandizement of the Federal Government has been for military items; if they are abstracted from the picture, Federal, State, and local outlays are not far from equal. This was true during the late 1930's when the military proportion of the Federal budget was much less. As to Federal aid, since 1940 it has increased more rapidly than State and local expenditure but less rapidly than total expenditure. Over the longer pull, however (comparing the present Federal position with that of the late twenties), the Federal role by any standard has increased quite substantially. The expansion occurred during the thirties and included, of course, the important area of social security.

Comparing the United States with other countries as to centralization one finds such data as the following[3] (the figures indicate the ratio of local taxes to total taxes 1947–53):

United Kingdom	8	Italy	18
France	13	Switzerland	51
Germany	14	Canada	26
Sweden	25		

In conclusion and to indicate a personal position on our problem, the author finds himself in general agreement (as to the matters discussed in this paper) with the Kestnbaum Commission's report which may be summarized as follows: The Federal system on the whole was found to be in healthy condition; the values of local autonomy are real and important and always need stressing; these values may be overbalanced by the great advantages of national or joint action in particular areas changing with time; it behooves the States deploring Federal encroachment to put their own houses in order. The States and municipalities are still finding plenty of scope for such vision, energy and ingenuity as they are able to summon. The Federal system in this country has preserved a degree of local autonomy unsurpassed at least by that of any of the world's great powers.

The pragmatic and sensible solution of Federal problems is not likely to lie in loyalty to any slogan but in the balanced weighing of values in the case of each new issue as it arises.

Notes

[1] Richard A. Musgrave, "Incidence of the Tax Structure and Its Effects on Consumption," *Federal Tax Policy for Economic Growth and Stability,* Joint Committee on the Economic Report, 84th Cong., 1st sess. (Washington, D.C.: U.S. Government Printing Office, 1955), pp. 96–113.

[2] Robert D. Siff, "Some Pertinent Points on Industrial Development Policies," *Tax Policy,* Vol. 24, Nos. 2–3, Tax Institute, Princeton University Press, Princeton, N.J., 1957, p. 11.

[3] Economic Commission for Europe, Research and Planning Division, "Changes in the Structure of Taxation in Europe," *Economic Bulletin for Europe,* Vol. 2, No. 3, Geneva, 1951, p. 59; Canadian Tax Foundation, *The National Finances,* 1954–55, Toronto, p. 10.

III

Some Economic Contexts

A basic framework and specific issues

In essence, public finance and budgeting encompass basic economic questions of who gets which scarce resources. To be sure, the economic sciences and arts are still far from providing precise guidelines for public spending, but, fortunately, some real help is available.[1] Whatever the state of the art or science, the world will not wait until we have firm answers to basic economic concerns. Ready or not, here I come: That is the unavoidable motif.

This chapter turns to consideration of several central economic issues related to budgeting and finance, organized in terms of seven specific questions. These questions will introduce the pieces reprinted below, each of which both summarizes specific problems and details progress in putting economic analysis in the effective service of executive and legislative officials.

1. *What is the "federal budget"?* No simple answer exists at either the descriptive or the prescriptive level.[2] The "federal budget" is not a very specific notion, and conceptual variations of what it is and what it should be also differ significantly. In addition, in a number of important senses, the yearly "budget" presented by the president to Congress has, like Topsy, more or less "just grew." Finally, there are several distinct if overlapping uses of budgeting processes and products. Financial data may be put to these three uses:

1. Program analysis, e.g., for monitoring the current status and for programming future states of a specific program or service.
2. Financial analysis, e.g., for determining whether debt management and cash flow policies are adequate to support some total mix of public goods and services.
3. Economic analysis, e.g., for attempting to manage the various types of "inflation" by fiscal policies and public spending.

2. *What rules should guide budgeting practices?* The classical budgetary rule, perhaps, holds that you certainly cannot spend more than you take in during (for example) a year, and you cannot spend very much more than you take in during the short run. This "balanced budget rule," as Gerhard Colm and Marilyn Young argue in "In Search of a New Budget Rule" (Reading 8), can at once be reasonable and have serious consequences. For example, attempts to balance the public budget when the economy is faltering may only deepen the downswing. In fact, such economies might paradoxically result in larger deficits (income minus spending) than policies less concerned with balanced budgets each year. Whatever the case, our deep national commitment expressed in the "full employment" legislation of 1946 sharply underscores the conclusion of Colm and Young that the balanced budget rule has serious inadequacies. "No budget rule can be accepted," they note "which is not compatible with a policy designed to support balanced economic expansion and stabilization."

The liabilities of the balanced budget rule seem clear enough, but Colm and Young are tentative about a specific replacement. Thus they analyze critically a second rule, a balanced budget over some more or less extended cycle. The authors devote even closer attention to an alternative budget rule which presumes the existence of valid and reliable tools for sophisticated economic analysis. If nothing else, Colm and Young demonstrate that those sanguine days are gone forever when persons in authority could support the simple balanced budget rule without serious reservations. The new age of working through and testing a rule and analytical techniques more congenial to "full employment" has been well begun, but only begun.

3. *Must government spending always be too little and/or too late?* Even given an appropriate budget rule, the timing of government spending as a vehicle for economic stabilization remains a central concern. Given the often-substantial lead time between the decision to spend and actual significant public outlays, arguments against government attempts at stabilization by spending gain force. These antispending arguments apply particularly where relatively full employment exists, where large numbers of employables are in the armed services, or where public spending requires skills that are already in short supply. Timing is crucial under any conditions, however; thus public spending might come too late to keep the economy from "cooling down." More seriously, gearing up for public spending might be completed just as the economy somehow recovers and a flood of growing confidence triggers private spending that had been deferred by economic warning signs. In such a case, increased public spending could "overheat" the economy and contribute to an inflationary spiral.

That timing is often a serious problem can be suggested by an argument drawn from Murray Weidenbaum.[3] Exquisite timing problems inhere in the need to integrate these four stages of the spending process:

1. The sequence of events leading to and including legislative authorization of appropriations.
2. The period during which contracts are placed.
3. The complex processes of gearing up for production in private sectors of the economy.
4. The completion of the processes leading to payments in private sectors of the economy.

The whole process need not grind to a conclusion before any effects are noticeable, of course. Government spending has a variable impact on private consumption and investment at all stages of the spending process. Consequently, public spending need not always be too little or too late. It can have at least some impact almost as soon as the formal announcement is made.

Exacerbating the issue of the timing of governmental expenditures, however, is the elemental fact that a substantial share of the budgets of most governments cannot be transferred from one program to another through budget review and new appropriations. Weidenbaum sketches the condition at the federal level in "Budget 'Uncontrollability' as an Obstacle to Improving the Allocation of Government Resources" (Reading 9). He stresses four categories of federal expenditures which are beyond such annual legislative action: trust funds, permanent and indefinite appropriations, fixed charges, and ongoing projects.

The details would differ widely, of course, but much the same condition prevails at all levels of government. The consequence is also common: what the economists refer to as a less-than-optimum allocation of resources. As Weidenbaum concludes resignedly: "Under present law it is almost futile to perform benefit/cost . . . analyses which may demonstrate that the Government obtains a lower return on its investments in highway transportation than in air transportation or some other alternative and, hence, that some shifting of funds might improve economic welfare."

4. *What are the dimensions of the public sector?*   Even if we are assured about timing and an applicable budget rule, any public spending must be further concerned with crucial issues about the content of the public/private sectors. Many observers—like John Kenneth Galbraith—have noted that we spend too much on automobile tail fins and too little on education. He advises shifting resources in such cases from spending in the private sector to the support of the public sector. Galbraith's emphasis can be juxtaposed with that of Colm and Young in Reading 8, who were concerned with a ceiling for public budgets in their search for a budgeting rule. Galbraith is interested in raising the "floor" of public spending by enlarging our working definition of acceptable uses of public monies.

Henry C. Wallich's "Public versus Private: Could Galbraith Be Wrong?" (Reading 10) looks at the scope of the public sector and opposes the prevailing current of opinion in the literature. Wallich reviews Galbraith's position and urges that bloated working definitions of the public sector can significantly endanger individual freedom. As Wallich recognizes, the issue is a profoundly difficult one, for too-zealous reservation of matters to the private sphere also could threaten individual freedom, and some necessary things might never get done. Wallich's prime concern is that too much may be done, with consequent danger to individual freedom in the haste to right social wrongs and distribute the benefits of prosperity more widely.

5. *What is the history of spending in the public sector?* The issues raised by Wallich are illuminated by a review of the history of spending in the public sector. Patently, some kinds of public spending could reduce individual freedom; expenditures for concentration camps, as an extreme example, clearly would have that effect. Other public spending—as for defense—might be largely necessary to preserve individual freedom.

As usual, the issues are more complex than they appear on the surface. As Francis Bator notes, merely "to add up all the money paid out each year by public agencies . . . is not a very revealing exercise."[4] To do so would be to add apples and oranges. Thus Bator distinguishes two types of expenditures: nonexhaustive and exhaustive. In a direct sense, nonexhaustive spending does not absorb economic output; it redistributes income or assets. Such spending consists of transfer payments like unemployment compensation, old-age and retirement benefits, and so on. Exhaustive expenditures do absorb goods and services. They are a measure of the public claims on output that is thus made unavailable for private consumption or investment. Nonexhaustive expenditures have the sharper growth rate.

There is no watertight distinction between the two kinds of spending but, overall, they do raise different challenges to individual freedom. Nonexhaustive spending essentially requires a redistribution of income, with important implications for the individual freedom (however that is defined) of all parties. Assume that some citizens contribute more and others receive more than the average contribution. The former citizens might complain that their freedom has been restricted by the provision for unequal contributions, which was enacted because of the lobbying of the officials in charge of the program. If the transfer payments have no strings attached to them, however, those individuals receiving more than they contributed may have their lives and freedom enhanced. Individual freedom faces at least two derivative challenges. The difficult decision first concerns the point at which the felt deprivation of the former people is so great as to require ceasing or postponing further need gratification of the latter people. There is no substantive rule for such a decision. Rather, the basic rule is procedural. When "enough" resistance is generated through our existing institutions and procedures, then the redistributing has tended to stop. To go further might endanger the moving consensus among the overpayers on which our relatively peaceful political life in part depends; to stop short of "enough" resistance is to lose an opportunity to increase the commitment of the overreceivers to their society. In any case, the second challenge is that both parties would have to develop controls to help assure the responsibility and responsiveness of the public officials monitoring the program, a challenge that is always with us.

What the resultant impact on individual freedom would be in either case above, however, is problematic. Perhaps that is the wisdom of our traditionally lesser concern with the kinds of decisions made and our greater concern with the processes used to make decisions and with the resulting consensus about these decisions.

Exhaustive governmental expenditures imply other, perhaps more serious, challenges for individual freedom. For example, they reduce the total pool of goods and services available to private consumers and investors during an economic boom, and thus they may contribute to inflation. And once made, the objects of exhaustive expenditures also tend to remain under the direct control of the "public sector." These two examples suggest a broad challenge to individual freedom.

Bator provides valuable data on the distribution of public spending of both kinds in various areas. These data should enlighten discussions of the impact on individual freedom of spending in the public sector. The sharp increase over time in nonexhaustive versus exhaustive expenditures, for example, has a significant place in any discussion about the growing size of our public budgets.

6. *Who gets the benefits of public spending?*   Even if a broad-based consensus does support some program of public spending such as social security, it is not always clear who gets what at whose relative expense. The issues commonly are that complicated.

James T. Bonnen considers this complexity as to who gets how much in "The Lack of Knowledge and Data on Distributional Impacts" (Reading 11). The selection is excerpted from a much longer contribution to the Subcommittee on Economy in Government of the Joint Economic Committee of the Congress. Basically, Bonnen argues that our historical concern with equity is usually far greater than our present knowledge of the distributional consequences of public spending. Bonnen introduces 11 questions relevant to judging the distributional impacts of public programs which are also useful for evaluating the desirability of such programs. The selection also sketches an analysis of the distributional costs and benefits of higher education.

7. *How are choices to be made from among desirable programs on which public monies could be spent?*   A brief review of the six emphases above generates still another basic question for public expenditure theory. If a budget rule is accepted, a ceiling on public expenditures may be defined, and their timing can be made easier. A working definition of the "public sector" involves determining the minimum level of public services that is considered

tolerable, as well as indicating the particular beneficiaries of those services. However, still another class of choices must be made: given that every desirable program cannot be supported at once, which specific ones should be supported?

This seventh question will be postponed for now. A number of selections that are helpful in sharpening criteria for selectivity are presented in Chapters VIII and IX which focus on a number of techniques for economic analysis which will facilitate making choices between alternative policies and programs. They also tend toward a useful generalization: Available techniques or approaches always significantly influence what our policy can be, and they can sometimes predetermine what it will be.

Notes

[1] For a balanced and still-applicable summary of what is available and what is elusive, see Walter W. Heller, "Economics and the Applied Theory of Public Expenditures," in *Federal Expenditure Policy for Economic Growth and Stability* (Washington, D.C.: U.S. Government Printing Office, 1957).

[2] Gerhard Colm and Peter Wagner, "Some Observations on the Budget Concept," *Review of Economics and Statistics* 65 (No. 2, 1963), esp. pp. 122–26.

[3] Murray L. Weidenbaum, "The Timing of the Economic Impact of Government Spending," *National Tax Journal* 12 (March 1959), 79–85.

[4] Francis M. Bator, *The Question of Government Spending* (New York: Harper & Bros., 1960). See especially pp. 9–28.

===

8
In Search of a New Budget Rule

Gerhard Colm and Marilyn Young

THE BALANCED BUDGET RULE

The search for a new budget rule is predicated on the conviction that the balanced budget rule is not suitable for guiding public policy. Simple as this rule appears, it is meaningless unless it is said what budget ought to be balanced—the conventional budget, the consolidated cash budget, or a budget of current expenditures. Furthermore, there is hardly anybody to-

From National Planning Association, *The Federal Budget and the National Economy* (Washington, D.C., March, 1955), pp. 41–54. Used with permission of publisher.

day who would advocate that a budget should be balanced each year, irrespective of economic circumstances. *It is generally recognized that an attempt to balance the budget under adverse economic conditions may not only aggravate the situation, but may even lead to larger budget deficits than would result from a budget policy designed to support an expansion of markets. No budget rule can be accepted which is not compatible with a policy designed to support balanced economic expansion and stabilization.*

The balanced budget rule is not only deficient from an economic point of view but, also, it has little relevance for the attainment of economy and efficiency in government. It makes little sense if the drive for economy in government is pursued intensively only when a deficit exists or threatens to develop. To the extent that there is extravagance in government, reductions in expenditures should be made, irrespective of whether there happens to be a surplus or a deficit in the budget. It should not be assumed that maximum efficiency has necessarily been achieved when the budget is balanced.

Curtailing important programs such as the national security programs for the purpose of balancing the budget makes again, for different reasons, no sense. Such curtailments must be made on grounds of foreign and military policy, and the world situation. The fact that there happens to be an "X" billion dollar deficit in the budget, does not prove that an "X" billion dollar curtailment in national security programs is the best course of action. *Evaluating the necessity and merits of various programs, and searching for real waste and inefficiency in government operations, are more difficult than an appeal to the balanced budget rule, but the latter cannot be substituted for the former.*

With respect to the method of financing needed programs, whether by taxes or borrowing, it makes more sense to refer to the need for a balanced economy than to the need for a balanced budget. Must we then substitute the balanced economy rule for the balanced budget rule? Skeptics may say that, by accepting this formula, we would not be substituting a new rule for an outmoded one, but would be abandoning budget rules altogether. Those who have little confidence in economic analysis fear that the balanced economy argument would often be used to rationalize an expenditure, tax, or borrowing policy which might be politically expedient. They insist that the traditional budget rule, in spite of its defects, has one advantage: Once one has agreed which budget is to be balanced, the rule is definite and does not permit argument about its interpretation. This is true, but it is equally true that the balanced budget rule cannot be reconciled with the economic necessities of fiscal policy. Is there any way out of this dilemma? Is it possible to devise a guide for budget policy which establishes some rule of budget policy, and yet avoids the rigidity of the balanced budget rule?

BALANCING THE BUDGET OVER THE CYCLE

One suggested modification of the balanced budget rule has been the idea that the budget need not be balanced in any one year, but should be balanced over the period of the business cycle, which would include both years of business slack and years of prosperity. The deficit incurred during the bad years would be offset by a surplus during the good years.

This rule presupposes a regularity and foreknowledge of the cycle which actually does not exist. It also presupposes that over the long run a rise in the public debt would not be needed in support of economic growth. While it is possible that during certain periods private expansion and absorption of credit may be adequate for the support of continuing growth, it is equally possible that at times expansion will require that the public debt grow along with the level of total activities. If under such circumstances a budget surplus were enforced in order to repay the debt incurred during a previous recession, the expansion might be brought quickly to a halt.

The rule of balancing the budget over the cycle appears neither feasible nor, as a general rule, desirable. It should be added, however, that recognizing the possibility that the national debt may increase over the cycle does not imply any complacency about a rising national debt *burden*. A rising absolute amount of debt may mean a declining debt burden, if the national income rises more steeply than the interest service on the debt.

BALANCING THE CONSOLIDATED CASH BUDGET

A step toward loosening up the rigid budget rule is taken when the consolidated cash budget is considered as a guide for budget policy rather than the conventional budget.

The government's financing must be done with broad economic considerations in mind, and the budget statement which is used to guide the government's financial policy should be that which comes nearest to taking account of all government transactions, irrespective of the organizational, administrative, or legal form in which they are conducted. The consolidated cash statement comes much closer to meeting this objective than the conventional budget.

Under prevailing conditions, if the Federal budget, measured in the conventional manner, is balanced, about $4 billion more is collected from the public than is disbursed to the public. The consolidated cash budget can therefore be balanced with about $4 billion less revenue than the conventional budget.

Nevertheless, it cannot be said that a balanced consolidated cash budget means that the government contributes as much to the flow of funds through the economy as it absorbs, or that the government is "neutral," causing neither inflation nor deflation. *For instance, a very large balanced budget is probably more inflationary, or less deflationary, than a smaller balanced budget.* The type of expenditures and the type of taxes, in addition to their amounts, also play a role. Besides, neither the consolidated cash budget, nor any other budget statement, really reflects all government operations.

None of the budget statements reflect government guarantees of private credit, though these guarantees may have much the same economic impact as government outlays. For instance, residential construction financed under an FHA or VA guarantee, which would not appear in the budget, might have much the same economic effects as residential construction financed through outright VA loans, which would appear in the budget. And the economic impact of a lease-purchase agreement for the construction of post offices, the cost of which would be spread in the budget over a period of years, might be similar to that of outright Federal construction of post offices, in which case the full cost would appear in the budget at the time of construction.[1] It should be noted that although the economic effects would be similar in these cases, they would not be precisely the same for there might be different effects on the private credit market.[2] Therefore, even a balanced budget does not mean that government operations are neutral with respect to the economy.

But should the government's budget policy be neutral? *Does not budget policy belong to the instruments which the government, in accord with the Employment Act, should use for promoting economic growth and stability?*

The budget policy which should be pursued depends to a large extent on the effectiveness of other government policy measures which are not, or not fully, reflected in the budget (e.g., credit policy, guarantees, wage and price policies, and foreign trade policies). Nevertheless, these nonbudgetary policies of the government are not so effective that the government could rely exclusively on them for accomplishing the purposes of supporting steady economic expansion.

BALANCING THE BUDGET UNDER CONDITIONS OF HIGH EMPLOYMENT

Another approach to the problem of modifying the balanced budget rule was suggested by H. Christian Sonne and Beardsley Ruml in the NPA pamphlet, *Fiscal and Monetary Policy,* published in 1944. They recommended that "tax revenues should balance expenditures at some agreed level of high employment and high production, and should provide for the amortization of the national debt when employment and production exceed those levels; but not before." A footnote qualified the term "balance" by saying that "a budget may be balanced in a financial sense, and still be very much unbalanced in an economic sense."

The idea that taxes should be adequate to meet expenditures under conditions of full employment found many supporters, among them the Committee for Economic Development. This rule requires that for the ensuing year expenditures and revenues should be estimated under the *assumption* that economic activity in the ensuing year will be on a high level. Government expenditure programs and tax measures should be so formulated that the budget thus computed will be at least balanced or, preferably, show a moderate surplus. If booming economic conditions should carry economic activity above what is regarded as a "high" level, tax yields and budget surplus would be higher than estimated. If economic activity should remain below that level, the tax yield would be lower too, and some expenditures (e.g., for unemployment compensation) would rise. Thus, without any change in legislation, a deficit would occur.

Only in case of a truly severe depression should this "built-in" flexibility be supported by a reduction in tax rates and the adoption of *additional* expenditure (e.g., public works) programs. If, under conditions other than a severe depression, additional expenditures should be adopted, additional tax measures would also be needed in order to satisfy the rule. Or if tax rates should be reduced, expenditures should be curtailed correspondingly, so that the budget would remain in balance or yield a moderate surplus under conditions of high employment.

This proposal has several advantages, namely:

1. The rule relates additional expenditures to the need for additional taxes, and tax reductions to curtailments in expenditures. Thereby it serves the requirements of budget discipline.

2. The rule permits deficits when a slack develops in the economy, thereby avoiding the harmful effects of a perverse budget balancing policy which would, in a recession, raise tax rates or curtail expenditure programs, and thereby aggravate the economic difficulties.

3. The rule does not require changes in expenditure programs or revenue legislation based on economic analysis and forecasting (except in case of severe inflation or depression). Once set for a particular year, expenditure programs and tax rates would not be changed for stabilization purposes, since the variation in tax yields and outlays would occur automatically. It should be mentioned, however, that new projections would be needed yearly for the full employment levels of production, incomes, profits, sales, etc., so that expenditure programs and tax rates could be reset. In a growing economy with a growing tax base, the rule implies that either government expenditures should grow proportionately with the growth of the economy or that tax rates should be gradually reduced.

Compared with these advantages the rule has also several limitations:

1. The rule assumes that a balanced budget or a moderate budget surplus under conditions of high employment is always in accord with the economic requirements of maintaining full employment.

This basic economic assumption can be questioned on the following grounds. During some periods it might be desirable that the government run not only a balanced budget or a small surplus but a very substantial surplus. This could be true, for instance, in case of a boom with inflationary tendencies. On the other hand, there can also be envisaged situations in which individuals, under conditions of high employment, might desire to save more than the amount of private capital which business wished to invest over and above the funds derived through internal business saving. The rule of balancing the budget under conditions of high employment assumes that, under full employment, the amount which private individuals and corporations will desire to save will be no greater than the amount of funds needed for financing private investment. While this may be the case sometimes, there is no assurance that it will always be the case. Many economists believe that there is more reason to expect that, with rising income, over the long run the desire to save may exceed the desire to invest. In any case, the rule is based on an unproven economic assumption.

2. The rule assumes that in case of an economic contraction (short of an emergency) the deficits created automatically by the built-in flexibility of revenues and expenditures will be sufficient to support recovery to the full employment level. What the rule really accomplishes is that it avoids a "perverse" fiscal policy. However, to give positive support to recovery, a reduction in tax rates (not only a drop in yield), and an increase in expenditure programs (not only a rise in expenditures under existing programs), may be needed. Even in the relatively mild recession of 1954, the government found it necessary to reinforce the effects of built-in stabilization by a tax reduction.

3. The rule provides for positive measures of tax reduction or additional expenditure programs only in case of a severe depression. It abandons the notion that fiscal policy measures may be more effective when adopted before a severe depression has developed. Its main dependence on the automatic stabilizers makes it necessary to sacrifice the notion of preventive fiscal action. Policies designed to counteract a depression in the early stages would have to depend on other measures, such as credit and monetary policies.

The rule of balancing the budget (or aiming at a moderate budget surplus) under conditions of high employment represents a great improvement over the traditional rule of balancing the budget under all conditions. Its greatest advantage is that it does not necessitate adoption of economically harmful fiscal measures, as would result from adhering strictly to an annually balanced budget in case of economic fluctuations. *The rule fails, however, if fiscal and budget policies are considered as necessary instruments of an active stabilization policy.* Is it possible to further refine the budget rule to make it still more responsive to economic requirements, and yet to maintain some kind of budget discipline?

BALANCING THE BUDGET OF CURRENT EXPENDITURES

A less restrictive budget policy could be obtained if the balanced budget rule—in the traditional or improved form—should be applied only to the budget of current expenditures. This would permit financing outlays for public investments by borrowing without violating the rule of balancing the budget of current expenditures.[3]

This would have the following advantages:

1. The further modification of the balanced budget rule would permit some government borrowing even under conditions of full employment. If the opinion is correct that in a period of rising income the desire to save may tend to exceed business's needs for outside funds, then this modification would move in the direction of supporting a better balanced economy. If, under certain circumstances, government borrowing for financing of capital outlays should have an inflationary effect, it could be counteracted by a restrictive credit policy on the part of the central bank.

2. This modified rule would also give some leeway for a more active stabilization policy in case of an economic contraction. It would permit stepping up of government investment programs without adoption of additional tax measures.

Thus this policy would give a somewhat greater scope to an active stabilization policy, designed either to maintain or to restore full employment. On the other hand, this modified balanced budget rule still has certain limitations and possible disadvantages:

1. The rule permits borrowing under conditions of full employment of a maximum amount equal to certain outlays of the government. *However, there seems to be no reason to assume that the amount of borrowing which is required for supporting balanced economic growth should always or even generally happen to be identical with government outlays for specified capital investments.* Furthermore, the significance of this modification depends in part on the definition of capital outlays which is used. And whatever definition is used, if capital outlays are excluded from the current budget, it would become necessary to include in the current budget allowances either for the amortization of loans issued for the financing of the capital outlays, or depreciation allowances for those assets which are taken out of the current

budget.[4] This would somewhat diminish the difference between balancing the total budget and balancing the budget of current expenditures.

2. The proposal exempts capital outlays of a specified nature from the prescription that additional expenditure programs should be financed by additional tax measures. This exemption might introduce a bias into the budget process. The government might be more willing to adopt additional capital programs than other programs, regardless of the respective merits of the programs under consideration. For instance, there might result a tendency to favor large road construction programs as against aids to education irrespective of the relative urgency of the programs.

3. The fact that the rule would permit stepping up of investment programs in a contraction might lead to the freer use of this device, rather than of tax reduction, for combatting a recession—again irrespective of the relative merits of the two policies.

These merits and shortcomings would be more or less common to any form of a policy of meeting current expenditures by tax revenue and capital outlays by borrowing. Proponents of this rule, however, often make the further proposal that capital outlays, should, so far as possible, be administered by government corporations (or authorities), and that these corporations should place their own bonds on the market. Furthermore, these corporations should be entirely "taken out of the budget."[5] Although the question of independent financing of government corporations is only indirectly related to the matter of choosing an appropriate rule for budget policy, some of the ramifications of such a technique may be mentioned here.

Government corporations (or authorities) have proved to be useful instruments for quasi-commercial operations. The corporate form permits more flexible methods of management and budgeting than the departmental organization. It is another question as to whether government corporations should or should not place their own bonds on the market. Good experiences have been had with the revenue bonds of toll road authorities, which sometimes were more attractive to investors than the bonds of the states under whose jurisdiction those authorities operate. In the case of the Federal government, the situation would, however, be quite different. Bonds issued by government corporations without government guarantee would, in all probability, have to carry a higher rate of interest than bonds issued by the Treasury. It should be carefully considered whether outside financing of these public ventures has such advantages that it is worth paying the additional costs. Furthermore, if very large issues are expected for financing Federal capital outlays, for instance, for a road construction program, their effect on the capital market should be considered.

In general, the government has the responsibility for choosing those methods of financing for public purposes which are most conducive to the maintenance of a high level of employment and production. This may require, under certain circumstances, government financing by short- or middle-term bonds, in order to leave the long-term market for private financing, for instance for housing mortgages. If government corporations should be entirely independent in their financing, they might wish to issue long-term bonds irrespective of general economic considerations.

We have already had the problem of coordinating Treasury and Federal Reserve policies. *If a number of government corporations should independently determine the terms for very large issues, the chance of obtaining a unified Federal economic and financial policy might be further impaired.*

During the 1930's, a number of government corporations had the right to float their own issues. The Treasury was given a sort of veto power. This arrangement did not work satisfactorily, and the Treasury bought most of the bonds issued by the corporations. Subsequently, the issue of such bonds was severely restricted. The government corporations received their advances from the Treasury. The financing of the capital outlays of these government corporations thus became part of the whole financial program of the Treasury. Whatever method of financing government undertakings should be used in the future, it should not reduce but should rather enhance the ability of the government to influence the capital market in the interest of economic stabilization. *Therefore, in case of large-scale financing by government corporations, adequate provision should be made to assure a method of financing which would not work at cross purposes with the objectives of Federal credit policy.*

The separate financing of government corporations has the special appeal that it would demonstrate the independence of capital investments from the budget. It suggests a "business-like" approach. The complete separation of these outlays from the budget, and from Treasury financing, would demonstrate to the public that there is in principle no difference between the floating of a loan for financing a self-supporting road system and the financing of private enterprise. If one believes that it will be in the interest of desirable economic expansion to promote a large amount of investments of this character, it may well be that acceptance by the Congress and the public can be won more easily if they are organized and financed as separate undertakings. This may be a wise policy for obtaining a desirable result with the least resistance.

Before accepting this policy as the only solution available, it should be asked whether there might not be a more direct way in which budget policy could be formulated so as to contribute to economic growth and balance. *However, even if some other formulation of a guide for budget policy should be found and adopted, government outlays for the various projects and functions should be so classified as to show, at least for information purposes, outlays for capital assets of various characters as distinct from current expenditures for the administration of the various government functions.* Such a classification of expenditures can be adopted without taking capital outlays out of the budget and without using the amount of capital outlays as the sole criterion for determining the permissible amount of borrowing.

Notes

[1] In the case of a lease-purchase agreement, the total government outlays would be greater than they would be in the case of outright government construction.

[2] Subsidies granted in the form of tax privileges (e.g., provisions for accelerated depreciation) provide another example of governmental transactions which affect the economy, but are not visible in the budget. Though subsidies in the form of payments are included among budget expenditures, tax subsidies are reflected only indirectly in reduced revenue. If the subsidies shown in the budget are added up, the result will always be incomplete. Tax subsidies are different from loan guarantees, however, in that tax subsidies do affect the budget surplus or deficit—even though the amount of their effects is unknown.

[3] See Beardsley Ruml, *A Budget Reform Program,* 1953, and *Budget Reform—Round Two,* 1953.

[4] Inclusion of an amortization allowance in the current budget may be the most natural procedure, if the capital outlays are financed by issues of government corporations, and if the amortization period is in some reasonable relationship to the expected period of useful life of the assets.

[5] It should be mentioned here that, according to established practice, the budget expenditures total includes gross expenditures of general and special funds and the net expenditures of corporations wholly owned by the government, regardless of source of financing. Therefore, self-financing of government corporations in itself would not change the budget total.

9

Budget "Uncontrollability" as an Obstacle to Improving the Allocation of Government Resources[1]

Murray L. Weidenbaum

INTRODUCTION

The increased efforts that economists and others have been making in recent years to improve the concepts and procedures for allocating public resources make it especially necessary and desirable to focus greater attention on the obstacles to making these improvements operational. One major

Reprinted from U.S., Congress, Subcommittee on Economy in Government, Joint Economic Committee, *The Analysis and Evaluation of Public Expenditures: The PPB System, A Compendium of Papers,* Vol. I (Washington, D.C.: U.S. Government Printing Office, 1969). Some footnote material has been omitted.

set of obstacles to improving public resource allocation is the legal and other institutional constraints that limit the discretion of governmental policy-makers.

For example, under present law it is almost futile to perform benefit/cost or similar analyses which may demonstrate that the Government obtains a lower return on its investments in highway transportation than in air transportation or some other alternative and, hence, that some shifting of funds might improve economic welfare. The futility arises from the simple fact that the major financial authorizations for highway programs are not contained in the appropriation bills requested by the President and enacted by the Congress, but in the relatively long-term legislation which authorizes the Federal-aid highway program. Thus, the Congress cannot, through the budget review and appropriations process, in practice effect a transfer of funds from surface to air transportation by reducing the appropriations for the Bureau of Public Roads and increasing those for the Federal Aviation Agency, two component units of the Department of Transportation.

Similarly, there is no discretion through the budget process to shift funds from an income-maintenance program such as public assistance to aid to education, both functions of the Department of Health, Education, and Welfare—or to any other purpose whether it involves expenditures or tax reduction. This rigidity arises because the expenditures under the public assistance program are in the nature of fixed charges; they are predetermined by statutory formulas governing Federal matching of State disbursements for public assistance. Given the permanent statute on the books, the amount that the Federal Government spends on this income-maintenance activity each year is determined by the pattern of state welfare disbursements. Neither the President nor the Congress can much influence the amount of Federal expenditures in this area within the confines of the budget process. Changes in the basic social security legislation would be necessary.

There are many other examples of these institutional obstacles to improving the allocation of public resources, as will be shown later on a more comprehensive basis. The end result of course is that the process of public resource allocation is hardly that deliberate and systematic choice among alternatives that economists try to envision. Rather, it is a fragmented and compartmentalized affair. Many of the key decisions are not made during the budget process or within the budgetary framework at all.

It is an earlier stage of the process which is the effective point of decision-making on numerous government spending programs—the enactment of substantive and often permanent legislation. This is the birth stage, and rebirth and growth stages, of a substantial proportion of Federal spending. This is the stage where many of the basic policy decisions are made—the nature of farm subsidies, the types of public assistance payments, and the level of highway grants. However, since it is the substantive committees of the Congress which handle enabling or authorizing legislation (e.g. Commerce or Foreign Relations or Public Works), rather than the appropriations committees, cost implications of the new programs often are relegated to secondary consideration or even ignored.

As will be demonstrated below in quantitative terms, the effectiveness of appropriations control over Federal Government expenditures is far less than it superficially appears to be.[2]

This study of the techniques of governmental budgeting may shed some light on the substantive issues involved in the allocation of government resources. It may help to explain, for example, why the military budget goes through cycles of alternate expansions and contractions, while the expenditures of domestic-civilian activities—notably the social welfare programs—continue to rise almost without interruption. The basic explanation presented here is in terms of the differences in the relative controllability, through the appropriations review process, of the different types of government spending programs.

TYPES OF BUDGET CONTROLLABILITY

This study focuses on the effectiveness of congressional power over the public purse, as measured by the degree to which the Presidential budgetary recommendations are subject to substantial modification through the appropriations process. In most cases, the discretion of the Executive Branch in preparing the budget estimates is also limited by similar institutional obstacles.

The rather narrow definition of controllability of government funding used here needs to be emphasized. The analysis is being made from the viewpoint of annual action by the Congress on the appropriation bills that finance the various government agencies. Given a long enough time span and the support of the Congress as a whole, virtually all Federal spending programs are susceptible to modification, if not elimination. If it so wished, the Congress could repeal the substantive, permanent legislation requiring public assistance grants or veterans pensions or farm price supports, or at least modify the statutes to make them more permissive. In time, it could conceivably retire the public debt and thus obviate the need for annual interest payments or at least reduce the size of the debt to be serviced.

Nevertheless, in practice the President and the Congress do not face each year's budget preparation and review cycle with a clean slate; they must take account of large accumulations of legal restraints within which they must operate.

From the viewpoint of appropriations review, there are thus numerous exogenous forces and factors which they must take account of and cannot effectively control: the number of eligible veterans who apply for pensions or compensation, the amount of public assistance payments made by the states and for which they must be partially reimbursed according to prescribed matching formulas, and so forth. The relatively controllable portion of the budget, from this viewpoint, consists of those government spending programs where the determining factors are endogenous to the appropriations process, which may modify them, at least to a considerable extent.

Four categories of exogenous institutional barriers to improving (or at least changing) the allocation of government resources are identified here: trust funds, permanent and indefinite appropriations, fixed charges, and ongoing projects. These categories are not mutually exclusive and thus individual programs have been assigned to them sequentially; that is, all Federal Government activities operated through trust funds have been assigned to that category, even though the great bulk is financed through permanent and indefinite appropriations. Thus the category of permanent or indefinite appropriations is limited to Federal activities not operated through trust funds. Similarly, activities financed under permanent appropriations may be viewed as a fixed charge on the annual budget. Nevertheless, only programs which do not fall within the two categories mentioned previously (trust funds and permanent or indefinite appropriations) are shown as fixed charges. Thus, double counting is avoided.

Trust Funds

The first category of relatively uncontrollable items dealt with here are the so-called trust funds. These vary from the large social insurance type of mechanisms, such as the old-age, survivors', and disability insurance program, to the gift fund for the Library of Congress. The common characteristic of these trust funds which is relevant for the present inquiry is that they are generally financed through permanent appropriations which do not require annual action by the Congress. As stated in one recent Budget Document: "Most trust fund receipts are made available for use by permanent law, without requiring further action by Congress."[3]

Another clear indication of the relative uncontrollability of these trust funds through the budget process is that they generally do not even appear in the annual appropriation bills. In the case of the social insurance funds, the actual level of expenditures is determined by the number of eligible persons who apply for benefits during a given year.

For grants to states for highways, the Federal-aid Highway Act of 1954 and amendments to it not only authorize the program but also provide authority to enter into obligations, in this case to commit the Federal Government to make grants to the States at a later date. This bypassing of the appropriations process is often referred to as "backdoor spending." Technically, however, it is backdoor financing. The actual disbursements of the Federal funds to the states require the Congress to enact so-called "appropriations to liquidate contract authorizations." The latter is a mere formality. There is virtually no Presidential or Congressional discretion over these liquidating appropriations—the Government was financially committed at an earlier point, at the time the obligations were incurred.

In the Federal budget for the fiscal year 1969, trust funds accounted for $55.1 billion or 27 percent of the total budget authorizations requested for the year.

Permanent and Indefinite Appropriations

In addition to the trust funds, there are numerous permanent appropriations which are contained in budget funds. The largest of these is the permanent and indefinite appropriation for the payment of interest on the national debt: "Such amounts are appropriated as may be necessary to pay the interest each year on the public debt" (31 U.S.C. 711 (2) and 732).

Other permanent accounts cover such items as the appropriations to the Department of Agriculture for removal of surplus farm commodities and to the Department of the Interior for range improvements. Thirty percent of gross customs receipts is automatically available to finance the agriculture program each year, regardless of estimated need or relative desirability vis-à-vis the changing mix of public sector activities. One-third of grazing revenues from Federal lands are similarly available for range improvement work.

A related category of funding is the "indefinite" appropriations. Although these are contained in the annual appropriation bills, they are in the nature of a blank check good for one year. Indefinite appropriations authorize a government agency to spend the sums necessary to meet a given specified requirement. For example, the Post Office Department is financed through an annual indefinite appropriation. So is the retired pay of commissioned officers of the Public Health Service.

In the fiscal 1969 budget, permanent or indefinite appropriations (other than to trust funds) accounted for $20.2 billion or 10 percent of the total budget authorizations requested.

Other Fixed Charges

A third type of budget request which is relatively uncontrollable through the appropriations process is often termed a "fixed charge." These are programs where the level of spending is determined effectively by basic statutes rather than through the review of annual appropriation requests. The largest programs in this category are the appropriations for public assistance and for veterans' compensation and pension payments. The Department of Health, Education, and Welfare makes grants to states to reimburse them for a fixed share of the public assistance payments that they make. Similarly, the Veterans' Administration provides statutorily determined benefits to all qualifying veterans or their widows and children who apply.

Although programs such as these are funded through annual definite appropriations, there is little effective control over the actual level of disbursements. Frequently, the initial appropriations turn out to be too low and supplemental appropriations are subsequently requested and routinely approved. There is considerable incentive for the Congress to appropriate less than the initial amount requested in the budget for these items. Thus, it gains some political benefit for supposedly "cutting" the budget. They then can later and much more quietly vote supplemental funds.

In the fiscal 1969 budget, fixed charges (other than those arising from trust funds and other permanent appropriations) amounted to $19.0 billion or 9 percent of budget requests.

Partially-Completed Projects

The final type of relatively uncontrollable budget activity analyzed here is the amount of new funds requested to continue or complete construction and similar long-term projects started with money voted in the budgets of earlier years. The almost unassailable justification for these appropriations is the old question, "What is the value of just half a bridge?" Typically for government agencies with large construction programs, such as the Army Corps of Engineers and the Department of the Interior, each year's budget request is dominated by funds needed for projects begun under prior year budgets.

One indication of this influence of previous commitments is the fact that the Federal Budget for 1969 estimated that $2.4 billion would be spent in that year to carry on construction projects previously begun and for which a total of $28.8 billion already had been spent prior to the budget year. Even though these expenditure figures are not directly comparable to the appropriation or budget authority estimates used in the present study, the contrast between large amounts of what in effect are sunk costs and relatively small increments of additional funding is clear.[4]

The National Aeronautics and Space Administration (NASA) may constitute a special case at the present time [1969]. The great bulk of its current expenditures is devoted to completion of Project Apollo, the effort to land a man on the moon prior to 1970. Theoretically, the program can be reduced or stretched out and thus the President or the Congress could reduce the funds requested for Apollo. In practice, there is a very natural reluctance to interfere with the successful completion of an undertaking in which the Nation already has invested such sizeable funds (over $15 billion for Apollo during the fiscal years 1959–68 alone).

The data for funds requested to continue or complete ongoing projects, as shown in the tables that follow, are incomplete. In many cases it was not possible from publicly available information to identify the specific long-term projects of many agencies. Thus, the funds shown as relatively controllable are overstated, and the uncontrolled funds understated.

The Department of Defense (military functions) constitutes the major example of this gap in our knowledge and thus no military projects are shown in this category of relatively uncontrollable programs. On occasion individual weapon systems have been cancelled after substantial investment of development and production funds. Nevertheless, budget reviewers in both the executive and legislative branches often are reluctant to terminate a large project, even though the changing course of events indicates that the returns may not be as attractive as originally envisioned.

It may be that nonstatutory, implied commitments may be of overriding importance in military budgets from time to time. During the Vietnam War, for example, the Congress has appropriated virtually all of the funds requested in support of that specific and costly military endeavor. Formally, the $30 billion a year request for Vietnam was subject to substantial reduction by the appropriations committee, and is therefore included in the controllable portion of the budget in this analysis; in practice no substantial modifications of the Vietnam estimates were considered by the Congress. However, the Congress did critically review and modify the non-Vietnam portions of the budget of the Department of Defense.[5]

In essence, what is involved here is justifying this military situation, and comparable civil ones, in an implicit incremental benefit-cost analysis: will the returns from the completion of the total project exceed the additional cost to be incurred in completing it? Clearly, many projects midway in the construction state may show incremental benefit-cost ratios substantially in excess of unity, whereas freshly computed total benefit-cost ratios would indicate far less attractive results. There may be substantial political onus attached to abandoning an effort after the investment of substantial public funds. The completion and operation of a public undertaking where the newly determined estimated costs are greater than the estimated benefits is hardly likely to attract great public attention.

ESTIMATES OF RELATIVE BUDGET CONTROLLABILITY

On the basis of the foregoing analysis, Table 9.1 was prepared in an effort to indicate the relative controllability of the budget requests of the various Federal departments and agencies. The data cover all of the recommended budget authority (new obligational authority as well as loan authority) contained in the Federal Budget for the fiscal year 1969. Table 9.1 includes both budget and trust funds and is based on the unified budget concept, the most comprehensive measure of Federal finance available at the present time.

TABLE 9.1

Controllability of Federal Government Budget Requests,
Fiscal Year 1969 (in millions of dollars)

Department or Agency	Trust Funds	Permanents, Indefinites	Fixed Charges	Ongoing Projects	Relatively Controllable	Total
		Relatively Uncontrollable				
Funds appropriated to the President .	1,324	—	—	—	4,819	6,143
Agriculture	68	735	3,831	—	2,896	7,530
Commerce	134	214	—	—	679	1,027
Defense—military.	7	—	2,313	—	76,796	79,116
Defense—civil	9	4	—	950	344	1,307
Health, Education, and Welfare.	37,670	41	7,456	13	6,190	51,370
Housing and Urban Development . . .	159	1,821	358	—	3,004	5,342
Interior	97	268	—	180	312	857
Justice	—	—	—	—	542	542
Labor.	4,095	—	145	—	596	4,836
Post Office	—	920	—	—	—	920
State	12	2	—	—	414	428
Transportation.	4,703	70	51	—	1,701	6,525
Treasury.	39	15,425	—	—	-54	15,410
Civil Service Commission	3,626	—	42	—	131	3,799
General Services Administration	—	1	2	—	327	330
Railroad Retirement Board	1,064	—	18	—	—	1,082
Veterans' Administration.	746	12	4,664	—	2,368	7,790
NASA	1	—	—	2,133	2,235	4,369
Export-Import Bank	—	608	—	—	—	608
Farm Credit Administration	535	—	—	—	—	535
All other	773	97	91	—	896	1,857
Total	55,062	20,218	18,971	3,276	104,196	201,723

Note: Includes requested new obligational authority and loan authority.
Source: Based on data contained in Budget of the United States Government, Fiscal Year 1969, and appendix.

In the aggregate, the trust funds, the ongoing construction projects, and the other permanent and indefinite appropriations and fixed charges account for a major share of the budget—$97.5 billion or 48 percent of the total budget authority requested in the fiscal year 1969. It should be emphasized that where the budget document and available supporting materials did not provide sufficient detail, or where any doubtful cases existed, the items in question were treated as controllable. Hence, there may be some significant underestimation of the relatively uncontrollable portion of the budget shown here. As mentioned earlier, there undoubtedly is an underestimation in the ongoing project category.[6]

Variations by Agency and Program

Were the fixed charges and other relatively uncontrollable items distributed proportionally to the size of the budgets of the various Government agencies, the interference with the allocation of Government resources might be less than is presently the case. However, as shown in Table 9.2, this is hardly the case. Some agency programs virtually escape the scrutiny of effective annual budgetary review—the Post Office, the Export-Import Bank, the Railroad Retirement Board, the Farm Credit Administration, and the great bulk of the Treasury Department.[7]

TABLE 9.2

Relatively Controllable Portions of Agency Budgets—Fiscal Year 1969 Budget Requests

Justice	100
General Service Administration	99
Defense (military)	97
State	97
Funds appropriated to the President	78
Commerce	66
Housing and Urban Development	56
NASA	51
All other	48
Agriculture	38
Interior	36
Veterans' Administration	30
Defense (civil)	26
Transportation	26
Health, Education, and Welfare	12
Labor	12
Civil Service Commission	3
Post Office	0
Treasury	0
Railroad Retirement Board	0
Export-Import Bank	0
Farm Credit Administration	0
Average for Federal Government	52

Source: Table 9.1.

At the other end of the controllability spectrum, all or almost the entire annual budgets of the Department of Defense (excluding civil functions such as the Corps of Engineers' construction work), the Departments of Justice and State, and the General Services Administration are subject to effective control through the annual budget process.

An interesting contrast appears between the two departments with the largest budgets, one military and the other civilian. The Department of Defense—which received most of the funds appropriated for national defense purposes—operates with very few and very small trust funds and other fixed charges. Almost all of its budget is subject to annual scrutiny.[8] In comparison, only one-tenth of the HEW budget can effectively be altered during the annual budget cycle. Most of the funds spent are insulated by permanent and indefinite appropriations and other long-term statutory commitments.

Upon further examination, it can be seen that a relatively small number of large programs account for the bulk of the funds which are relatively immune to effective budgetary control. The following 12 programs of over

$1 billion each account for over $85 billion or 88 percent of the portion of the fiscal year 1969 Budget which is here estimated to be "relatively uncontrollable":

	In millions
Social security trust funds	$37,670
Interest on the public debt	15,200
Public assistance	5,765
Veterans' pensions and compensation	4,654
Highway grants to states	4,650
Unemployment insurance	4,095
Civil service retirement payments	3,626
CCC (Farm price supports)	3,362
Military retired pay	2,275
Project Apollo	2,133
Medicare (Treasury contribution)	1,360
Railroad retirement payments	1,064

The Relatively Controllable Portion of the Federal Budget

Table 9.3 shows the distribution by agency of the relatively controllable portion of the Federal budget authorizations requested for the fiscal year 1969. It is apparent that the Department of Defense accounts for the great bulk of the funds where the President and the Congress possess substantial discretion over the amounts initially requested (74 percent). For purposes of comparison, it can be noted that the DOD represents 38 percent of the total Federal budget.

A handful of other departments and agencies—Agriculture, HEW, Transportation, NASA, and the Veterans' Administration—account for the bulk of the remainder of the relatively controlled portion of the budget.

REDUCING THE INSTITUTIONAL OBSTACLES

The data presented earlier lead to the rather striking conclusion that the great bulk of the expenditures for the domestic civilian agencies of the Federal Government is authorized virtually automatically as a result of the basic, continuing commitments previously enacted by the Congress, rather than through the deliberations of the annual budgetary process. Somewhat less conclusively, it appears that the military programs are susceptible to effective budgetary review to a far greater extent.

For most of the nondefense programs, the effective point of control appears to occur not at the time that the appropriations are voted, but at the earlier period where the Congress enacts the basic legislative commitments, that is, the rates of veterans' pensions or social security benefits.

TABLE 9.3

Distribution of Relatively Controllable Budget Requests, Fiscal Year 1969 Budget Requests

	Percent
Defense (military)	74
Health, Education, and Welfare	6
Funds Appropriated to the President	5
Agriculture	3
Housing and Urban Development	3
Transportation	2
Veterans' Administration	2
NASA	2
Commerce	1
Labor	1
All other	1
Defense (civil)	*
Interior	*
Justice	*
State	*
Civil Service Commission	*
General Services Administration	*
Post Office	0
Treasury	0
Railroad Retirement Board	0
Export-Import Bank	0
Farm Credit Administration	0
Total	100

*Less than one-half of 1 percent
Source: Table 9.1.

For purposes of analysis, it may be helpful to divide the various uncontrollable items into two categories, "natural" and "artificial" (this attempt at labeling by no means exhausts the possibilities).

The "natural" type of uncontrollable item is exemplified by the permanent, indefinite appropriation for the payment of interest on the public debt. These payments arise directly from the amount and types of public debt issues which are currently outstanding. There is no discretion left at the disbursement phase of the process; the Federal Government simply must honor its promise to pay the interest on its obligations as it falls due. The natural uncontrollability of this item expense is acknowledged by the Congress in the form of a permanent appropriation to pay interest with no fixed dollar limit.

Similarly, the making of monthly compensation payments to veterans on account of service-connected disabilities is a program which is naturally uncontrollable within the confines of the budget process. The law requires monthly payments to all those certified by VA doctors as possessing a given percentage impairment of earnings. However, in this case the Congress insists on annually reviewing the appropriation for the payment of veterans' pensions and compensation. It is hard to characterize this congressional review as anything other than wheelspinning or having "fun and games" with the budget. Moreover, this exercise in futility diverts executive branch and congressional time and attention to the budget away from the areas where they can significantly alter the results.

In sharp contrast, there are numerous government programs which are artificially uncontrollable as a result of statutory law, but which lend themselves, through changes in substantive legislation, to effective annual budgetary review. For example, under section 32 of the act of August 24, 1935 (U.S.C. 612 C) an amount equal to 30 percent of annual customs receipts is automatically appropriated into a permanent, indefinite special fund for the "removal of surplus agricultural commodities." These amounts bear little relationship to the requirements for such funds. In fact, recent appropriation acts have authorized transfers of funds to the school lunch program and for related activities. Clearly, the amount of funds automatically appropriated exceeds the needs of the basic activity financed by the appropriation.

The annual grants of $50,000 paid to each state and Puerto Rico for A & M colleges similarly are made under a permanent appropriation act. Neither the Bureau of the Budget nor the President nor the Congress has any opportunity to review the annual appropriation request and thus annually redetermine the continued need for or desirability of these payments.

There are numerous other examples. Many permanent indefinite appropriations to the Department of the Interior are tied to a portion of revenues from sales or rentals of government assets and bear little relationship to the current requirements for Federal expenditures for the activity to which they are earmarked. Thus, visitor fees at Yellowstone National Park are automatically used to provide educational expenses for dependents of park personnel, while visitor fees at Grand Teton National Park are used automatically as payments to the state of Wyoming, in effect in lieu of taxes.

CONCLUSIONS

Although the analysis of individual government programs presented here is incomplete (partly due to the lack of available data), it is clear that the effectiveness of appropriations control over Federal Government expenditures is far less than is generally appreciated. The following changes might be considered toward reducing these institutional obstacles to improve the allocation of public resources.

1. *A review of the necessity for the numerous trust funds that have been established.*   Some of them—such as those for the financing of social security benefits—appear to somewhat approximate the general notion of funds

held in trust. In many other cases—such as the Federal-aid highway program—it is hard to make a case for segregating the activity from ordinary budget operations. In that particular case, the program of Federal grants to the states did operate out of general revenues until 1954. In good measure, the highway-related excises which are now funneled through the highway trust fund may be viewed more properly as a form of earmarked taxes and treated as a special fund within the regular budget procedure.

2. *A reevaluation of the need for the various permanent and indefinite appropriations.* Some of them may have outlived their usefulness. However, there is no automatic or periodic review of their status and a clean slate examination might be most useful.

3. *A reexamination of the "fixed charges" on the budget.* Some of them might usefully be converted into permanent or indefinite appropriations. In other cases, discretion might be restored to the appropriations committee to determine annually the amount to be voted for the stipulated purpose, in the light of then current conditions and completing requirements. This latter action, of course, would require changing the substantive legislation governing the program.

4. *A focusing of greater attention on "new starts" of construction and other long-term projects.* It is a natural tendency to place greater emphasis in the budgetary review process on the items with the largest price tags. However, as has been shown, most of the appropriation requests in this category of long-term projects are to continue or complete projects already underway. The point of most effective control is at the outset, prior to the investment of public resources in the project. However, it is precisely at the starting-up stage where the appropriation requests are most modest and thus perhaps more readily approved. A careful weighing of the expected full or long-term costs and benefits is thus extremely important at the outset.[9]

The reduction of these institutional obstacles to maximizing the taxpayers' return on their investment will not of itself result in eliminating relatively low priority and less efficient government activity, but it should make efforts in that direction less difficult.

Notes

[1]An earlier version of this analysis appears in M. L. Weidenbaum, "On the Effectiveness of Congressional Control of the Public Purse," *National Tax Journal,* December 1965. The author is indebted to Mr. Suk Tai Suh for assistance in developing the statistical materials used here.

[2]This substantive point is developed more fully in M. L. Weidenbaum, *Federal Budgeting: The Choice of Government Programs* (Washington, D.C., American Enterprise Institute for Public Policy Research, 1964).

[3]*The Budget of the United States Government for the Fiscal Year Ending June 30, 1965,* Appendix (Washington, D.C.: U.S. Government Printing Office, 1964), p. 898.

[4]*Special Analyses, Budget of the United States, Fiscal Year 1969* (Washington, D.C.: U.S. Government Printing Office, 1968), p. 82.

[5]See U.S. House of Representatives, Committee on Appropriations, *Department of Defense Appropriations for 1969* (Washington, D.C.: U.S. Government Printing Office, 1968).

[6]For what was perhaps the pioneering attempt to analyze the controllability of Federal spending, but limited to the administrative budget, see "Controllability of 1952 Budget Expenditures," in Joint Economic Committee Report, U.S. Congress, *January 1951 Economic Report of the President* (Washington, D.C.: U.S. Government Printing Office, 1951), pp. 89–103.

[7]Interfund adjustments complicate the Treasury figures. In practice, the budgets of the operating bureaus are generally subject to effective annual review.

[8]As pointed out earlier, the Congress may be reluctant to exercise this potential control over the military budget during wartime and similar emergency periods.

[9]In recent years, the budget requests for military and selected other areas have been prepared on the basis of "full funding" of proposed projects, that is of appropriating the entire estimated cost of a project at the time it is started. This procedure helps to enable the Congress to ascertain the total cost of a project before the work actually begins. However, water resource projects continue to be an important exception to this desirable change. See *Special Analyses, Budget of the United States, Fiscal Year 1970* (Washington, D.C.: U.S. Government Printing Office, 1969), p. 81.

10

Public versus Private: Could Galbraith Be Wrong?

Henry C. Wallich

In addition to free advice about growth, the nation has received helpful suggestions of another sort, in a rather opposite vein. It has been argued that we have all the production we need and to spare, but that too much of our growth has gone into private consumption, too little into public. We are said to be wasting our substance on trivia while allowing urgent public needs to go uncared for. This view does not complain of inadequate growth. But it sees us riding in tail-finned, oversized automobiles through cities that are becoming slums, finds our children sitting glued to the latest TV models but lacking schools where they can learn to read properly, and generally charges us with putting private profligacy ahead of public provision.

The general doctrine that in the United States public needs tend to be underfinanced in relation to private I first heard many years ago from my old teacher Alvin Hansen. It has always seemed to me to possess a measure of appeal. Throughout this book, I have been at pains to argue that with rising wealth and industrialized living, the need for public services advances, and probably faster than living standards. In part this reflects simply the familiar fact that the demand for services tends to expand faster than the demand for goods. In part, the social conditions of modern life are also accountable for the growing need for government services. Private business is learning to meet many of these new needs—for instance in the field of insurance. It is not inconceivable that some day we shall become rich enough to be able to indulge increasingly a preference for privately supplied services. But at present, and as far ahead as one can see, the trend seems the other way. I would footnote this reference by observing that to recognize a rising trend in the need for public services and to claim that at present we have too little of them, are two different things. The more than doubling of federal and also of state and local expenditures since 1950 should drive home that distinction.

The thesis that public services are neglected and private consumption inflated with trivia has found its most eloquent interpretation in *The Affluent Society* by John Kenneth Galbraith, to whom we were previously indebted for important insights into the workings of American capitalism. Galbraith argues that this imbalance is nourished by advertising, which creates artificial wants. He sees it further accentuated by an obsession with production, which keeps us from realizing that our problems are not those of want, but of affluence. The imbalance is epitomized by our supposed tendency to limit public expenditures to what is strictly essential, while we apply no such criterion to private expenditures.

TOO MANY TRIVIA?

One may reasonably argue that Galbraith exaggerates the distorting influence of advertising. That would not alter the basic assumption on which his thesis rests—the assumption that there are better wants and worse wants. Scientific detachment notwithstanding, I find it extraordinarily difficult to disagree with this proposition. To rate an attendance at the opera and a visit to an (inexpensive) nightclub as equivalents, because the market puts a similar price on them, goes against my grain. So does the equation of a dollar's worth of education and a dollar's worth of chromium on an automobile. And a plausible case would probably be made, on the basis of the evolution of the species, that opera and education do represent more advanced forms of consumption.

But what consequences, if any, should be drawn from such judgment? It is one thing to be irritated by certain manifestations of our contemporary civilization—the gadgets, the chrome, the tail fins and the activities that go with them. It is quite another—and something of a *non sequitur*—to conclude from this that the only alternative to foolish private spending is public spending. Better private spending is just as much of a possibility.

And does this judgment yield a basis for trying to discourage the growth of the less "good" expenditures? In a free society, we obviously want to move with the utmost circumspection. It is worth remembering that even Thorstein Veblen, who went to some extreme in deriding the "leisure class" and its "conspicuous consumption," did not take an altogether negative view of all conspicuous waste. In *The Theory of the Leisure Class* he said, "No class of society, not even the most abjectly poor, foregoes all customary conspicuous consumption. . . . There is no class and no country that has yielded so abjectly before the pressure of physical want as to deny themselves all gratification of this higher or spiritual need."

For fair appraisal of the case against trivia, we would also want to know the approximate size of the bill that is being incurred for various frills and frivolities. Gadgets in cars and homes have drawn the special ire of the critics. It is interesting to note, therefore, that expenditures for all kinds of durable consumer goods, including automobiles, run about 14 percent of personal consumption. The greater part of this, presumably, goes for the essential parts of fairly essential equipment. What is left for ornaments and gadgets does not loom impressively large. After all, not all the income in this country is spent by people for whom life begins at $25,000. The median family income is $5,600. Would the critics of the affluent society want to live on much less than that?

Whatever our private feelings about the gadgetry in our life, we probably do well not to stress them too hard. It is only too easy for some members of a community to work themselves into a fit of righteousness and to feel tempted to help the rest regulate their existence. In an extreme form, and not very long ago, this happened in the United States with the introduction of prohibition. Some of us may lean toward special taxation of luxuries, but surely no one wants sumptuary legislation banishing from our show windows and homes the offending contrivances. A new puritanism directed against wasteful consumption, however understandable, would make no great contribution to an economy that requires incentive goods to active competition and free markets. Neither would it be compatible with the freedom that we value.

ENDS AND MEANS

It is the positive side of the case—the asserted need for more public services—that must chiefly concern us. My contention here will be that to talk in terms of "public vs. private" is to confuse the issue. More than that, it is to confuse means and ends. The choice between public and private money is primarily a choice of means. The sensible approach for those who are dissatisfied with some of the ends to which private money is being spent, is to specify first what other ends are important and why. Having determined the ends, the next step is to look to the means. That is the order in which I propose to proceed here.

The critics are right in pointing out that new material needs have been carried to the fore by social and economic evolution—even though they mislabel them as public needs. In the good old days, when this was still a nation of farmers, most people had no serious retirement worries, there was no industrial unemployment problem, good jobs could be had without a college degree, most diseases were still incurable—in short, social security, education, and health care found primitive and natural solutions within the family and among the resources of the neighborhood. Today, these solutions are neither adequate nor usually even possible.

Mounting wealth and advancing technology have brought within reach the means of meeting these needs. We can afford to live better in every way —more creature comforts, more leisure, more attention to matters of the mind and spirit. At the same time we can take better care of retirement, of unemployment, of illness, of education, of the possibilities opened by research, than ever before.

There are indeed new needs. The citizen-taxpayer has his choice of meeting them, as well as all his other needs, in one of two ways. He can buy the goods or services he wants privately, for cash or credit. Or he can buy them from the government, for taxes.

The nation as a whole pays taxes to buy public services as it pays grocery bills to buy groceries. The tax burden may be heavier for some individuals than for others. But the nation as a whole has no more reason to complain about the "burden" of taxes than about the "burden" of grocery bills—and no more reason to hope for relief.

Of the two stores, the private store today still is much the bigger. The public store is smaller, but it is growing faster.

Each store has some exclusive items. The private store sells most of the necessities and all of the luxuries of life, and in most of these has no competition from the government side. The public store has some specialties of its own: defense, public order and justice, and numerous local services that the private organization has not found profitable. But there is a wide range of items featured by both stores: provision for old age, health services, education, housing, development of natural resources.

THE NEW NEEDS

The bulk of the new needs are in this competitive area. The fashionable notion is to claim them all for the public store and to label them public needs. The statistics say otherwise. They say in fact two things: First, the supply of this group of goods and services has expanded very rapidly in recent years; and second, they are being offered, in varying degrees, both by the private and the public suppliers. Let us run down the list.

Provision for old age is predominantly private.   The average American family, realizing that while old age may be a burden, it is the only known way to achieve a long life, takes care of the matter in three ways: (1) by private individual savings—home ownership, savings deposits, securities; (2) by private collective savings—life insurance, corporate pension funds; and (3) by public collective savings through social security. Statisticians report that the two collective forms are advancing faster than the individual. The increases far exceed the rise in the Gross National Product of almost 80 percent (in current prices) over the past ten years; they do not indicate either that these needs are neglected or that they are necessarily public in character.

Education: The bulk of it is public; but a good part, particularly of higher education, is private.   Total expenditures for all education have advanced in the last ten years from $9.3 billion to $24.6 billion ($19.3 billion of it public). Education's share in the national income has advanced from 3.8 percent to 5.8 percent. The silly story that we spend more on advertising than on education is a canard, though with its gross of over $10 billion, advertising does take a lot of money.

Health expenditures are still mainly private.   At considerable expense, it is now possible to live longer and be sick less frequently or at least less dangerously. In the past, most people paid their own doctors' bills, although health care for the indigent has always been provided by public action or private philanthropy. Since the war, the proliferation of health insurance has given some form of collective but private insurance to three-quarters of our 182 million people. This has greatly reduced pressure for a national health service along British lines. For the aging, whose health-care needs stand in inverse proportion to their capacity to pay or insure, public insurance has finally been initiated and needs to be expanded. The total annual expenditure on health is estimated at over $25 billion, a little more than on education. Of this, about $6 billion is public.

So much for the allegation that the "new needs" are all public needs. Now for some further statistics on the public store, which is said to have been neglected. Some of them could make an investor in private growth stocks envious. Research expenditures (mainly for defense and atomic energy) have gone from about $1 billion to over $8 billion in the last ten years. Federal grants to the states have advanced from $2.2 billion to $7 billion during the same period. Social-security benefits rose from $1 billion to over $10 billion. All in all, public cash outlays (federal and state) advanced from $61 billion to $134 billion over ten years, 57 percent faster than the GNP.

For those who feel about public spending the way Mark Twain felt about whiskey, these figures may still look slim. (Mark Twain thought that while too much of anything was bad, too much whiskey was barely enough.) To others, the data may suggest that the advocates of more public spending have already had their way. Could their present discontent be the result of not keeping their statistics up-to-date? In one of his recent pamphlets, Arthur M. Schlesinger, Jr., claims that the sum of the many neglects he observes (including defense) could be mended by raising public expenditures by $10 to $12 billion. That is well below the increase in public cash outlays that actually did take place in one single fiscal year, from $118.2 billion in 1958 to $132.7 billion in 1959. In the three fiscal years 1957–59, these outlays went up more than $31 billion, though the advance slowed down in 1960. More facts and less indignation might help to attain better perspective.

Some parts of federal, state, and local budgets have expanded less rapidly than those cited—in many cases fortunately. The massive buildup in defense expenditures from the late 'forties to the 'fifties has squeezed other programs. Unfortunately, on the other hand, some programs that both political parties have favored—including aid to education, to depressed areas, for urban renewal—have been delayed unduly by the vicissitudes of politics. But the figures as a whole lend little support to the thesis that politicians don't spend enough, and that the government store is not expanding fast enough.

THE CITIZEN IN THE STORES

The two stores—private and public—work very hard these days to capture the business of the citizen-taxpayer. Here is what he hears as he walks into the private store:

"The principal advantage of this store," the private businessman says, "is that you can shop around and buy exactly what you want. If I don't have it I'll order it. You, the consumer, are the boss here. To be sure, I'm not in business for charity but for profit. But my profit comes from giving you what you want. And with competition as fierce as it is, you can be sure the profit won't be excessive."

If the proprietor has been to Harvard Business School, he will perhaps remember to add something about the invisible hand which in a free economy causes the self-seeking of competitors to work for the common good. He will also, even without benefit of business school, remember to drop a word about the danger of letting the public store across the street get too big. It might endanger freedom.

As the citizen turns this sales talk over in his mind, several points occur to him. Without denying the broad validity of the argument, he will note that quite often he has been induced to buy things he did not really need, and possibly to neglect other, more serious needs. Snob appeal and built-in obsolescence promoted by expensive advertising don't seem to him to fit in with the notion that the consumer is king. Looking at the brand names and patents and trademarks, he wonders whether most products are produced and priced competitively instead of under monopoly conditions. The invisible hand at times seems to be invisible mainly because it is so deep in his pocket.

Bothered by these doubts, the citizen walks across the street and enters the public store.

"Let me explain to you," says the politician who runs it—with the aid of a horde of hard-working bureaucrats doing the chores. "The principles on which this store is run are known as the political process, and if you happen to be familiar with private merchandising they may seem unusual, but I assure you they work. First of all, almost everything in this store is free. We simply assess our customers a lump sum in the form of taxes. These, however, are based largely on each customer's ability to pay, rather than on what he gets from the store. We have a show of hands from the customers once a year, and the majority decides what merchandise the store is to have in stock. The majority, incidentally, also decides how much everybody, including particularly the minority, is to be assessed for taxes.

"You will observe," the politician continues, "that this store is not run for profit. It is like a co-operative, run for the welfare of the members. I myself, to be sure, am not in politics for charity, but for re-election. But that means that I must be interested in your needs, or you would not vote for me. Moreover, there are some useful things that only I can do, with the help of the political process, and in which you and every citizen have an interest. For instance, everybody ought to go to school. I can make them go. Everybody ought to have old-age insurance. I can make that compulsory too. And because I don't charge the full cost of the service, I can help even up a little the inequalities of life.

"By the way," the politician concludes, "if there is any special little thing you want, I may be able to get it for you, and of course it won't cost you a nickel."

The citizen has some fault to find with the political process too. He notes that there is not even a theoretical claim to the benefits of an invisible hand. Majority rule may produce benefits for the majority, but how about the other 49 percent? Nor is there the discipline of competition, or the need for profits, to test economy of operation. There is no way, in the public store, of adjusting individual costs and benefits. And the promise to get him some small favor, while tempting, worries him, because he wonders what the politician may have promised to others. The political process, he is led to suspect, may be a little haphazard.

He asks himself how political decisions get to be made. Sometimes, obviously, it is not the majority that really makes a decision, but a small pressure group that is getting away with something. He will remember that

—after payments for major national security and public debt interest—the largest single expenditure in the federal budget is for agriculture, and the next for veterans. He may also recall that one of the first budgetary actions of the new Administration was to increase funds for agriculture by $3 billion.

THE EXPANDING BELT

Next, the citizen might consider the paralyzing "balance-of-forces" effect that often blocks a desirable reshuffling of expenditures. The allocation of public funds reflects the bargaining power of their sponsors, inside or outside the government. A classical example was the division of funds that prevailed in the Defense Department during the late 'forties. Army, Navy, and Air Force were to share in total resources in a way that would maximize military potential. By some strange coincidence, maximum potential was always achieved by giving each service the same amount of money. It took the Korean War to break this stalemate.

What is the consequence of the balance-of-forces effect? If the proponents of one kind of expenditure want to get more money for their projects, they must concede an increase also to the advocates of others. More education means more highways, instead of less; more air power means more ground forces. To increase a budget in one direction only is as difficult as letting out one's belt only on one side. The expansion tends to go all around. What this comes down to is that politicians are not very good at setting priorities. Increases in good expenditures are burdened with a political surcharge of less good ones.

The last-ditch survival power of federal programs is a specially illuminating instance of the balance of forces. If a monument were built in Washington in memory of each major federal program that has been discontinued, the appearance of the city would not be greatly altered. In contrast, when the Edsel doesn't sell, production stops. But the government is still reclaiming land to raise more farm surpluses and training fishermen to enter an occupation that needs subsidies to keep alive. Old federal programs never die, they don't even fade away—they just go on.

The citizen will remember also the ancient and honorable practice of logrolling. The unhappy fate of the Area Development bill illustrates it admirably. As originally proposed, the bill sought to aid a limited number of industrial areas where new jobs were badly needed. It got nowhere in the Congress. Only when it was extended to a large number of areas with less urgent or quite different problems, were enough legislators brought aboard to pass it. Because of the heavy political surcharge with which it had become loaded, President Eisenhower vetoed the bill. A bill was finally enacted early [in 1961], long after aid should have been brought to the areas that needed it.

Finally, the citizen might discover in some dark corner of his mind a nagging thought: Any particular government program may be a blessing, but could their cumulative effect be a threat to freedom? He has heard businessmen say this so often that he has almost ceased to pay attention to it. He rather resents businessmen acting the dog in the manger, trying to stop useful things from being done unless they can do them. He is irritated when he hears a man talk about freedom who obviously is thinking about profit. And yet—is there any conclusive rebuttal?

THE CITIZEN'S FAILURES

The citizen would be quite wrong, however, if he blamed the politician for the defects of the political process. The fault lies with the process, or better with the way in which the process, the politician, and the citizen interact. The citizen therefore would do well to examine some of his own reactions and attitudes.

First, when he thinks about taxes, he tends to think of them as a burden instead of as a price he pays for a service. As a body, the nation's taxpayers are like a group of neighbors who decide to establish a fire department. Because none is quite sure how much good it will do him, and because each hopes to benefit from the contribution of the rest, all are prudent in their contributions. In the end they are likely to wind up with a bucket brigade.

But when it comes to accepting benefits, the citizen-taxpayers act like a group of men who sit down at a restaurant table knowing that they will split the check evenly. In this situation everybody orders generously; it adds little to one's own share of the bill, and for the extravagance of his friends he will have to pay anyhow. What happens at the restaurant table explains—though it does not excuse—what happens at the public trough.

Finally, in his reaction to public or free services, the citizen takes a great deal for granted, and seldom thinks of the cost. Public beaches mistreated, unmetered parking space permanently occupied, veterans' adjustment benefits continued without need—as well as abuses of unemployment compensation and public assistance—are some examples. This applies also, of course, to privately offered benefits, under health insurance, for instance. The kindly nurse in the hospital—"Why don't you stay another day, dearie, it won't cost you anything, it's all paid for by Blue Cross"—makes the point.

By removing the link between costs and benefits, the political process also reduces the citizen's interest in earning money. The citizen works to live. If some of his living comes to him without working, he would be less than rational if he did not respond with a demand for shorter hours. If these public benefits increase his tax burden so that his overall standard of living remains unchanged, the higher taxes will reduce his work incentive. Why work hard, if much of it is for the government?

THE POLITICAL DOLLAR AT A DISCOUNT

These various defects of the political process add up to an obvious conclusion: the dollar spent by even the most honest and scrupulous of politicians is not always a full-bodied dollar. It often is subject to a discount. It buys less than it should because of the attrition it suffers as it goes through the process, and so may be worth only 90 cents or 80 cents and sometimes perhaps less. The private dollar, in too many cases, may also be worth less than 100 percent. But here each man can form his own judgment, can pick and choose or refuse altogether. In the political process, all he can do is say Yes or No once a year in November.

The discount on the public dollar may be compensated by the other advantages of government—its ability to compel, to subsidize, to do things on a big scale and at a low interest cost. Whether that is the case needs to be studied in each instance. Where these advantages do not apply, the private market will give better service than the political process. For many services, there is at least some leeway for choice between the private and public store—health and retirement, housing, research, higher education, natural-resource development. Defense, on the other hand, as well as public administration, public works of all kinds, and the great bulk of education —while perhaps made rather expensive by the political process—leave no realistic alternative to public action.

The argument I have offered is no plea to spend more or less on any particular function. It is a plea for doing whatever we do in the most effective way.

11
The Lack of Knowledge and Data on Distributional Impacts

James T. Bonnen

As one reviews Congressional hearings and agency program materials, one is impressed by the lack of knowledge or even raw data on program impact, including the distribution of program benefits. It is as if these were impolite if not impolitic questions to raise.

A recent experience of the author is instructive. At the invitation of Charles L. Schultze, then on the senior staff of the Brookings Institution, and more recently U.S. Budget Director, I attempted to measure for a Brookings conference the distribution of benefits of certain Federal subsidy programs. It was decided that these should be the Bureau of Reclamation's irrigation water development program, the Maritime Administration's ship construction and operating subsidies, and the Federal Aviation Administration's subsidy programs. Despite eight months of consistent work, it was not possible to put any really useful numbers together. The Maritime Administration and the Federal Aviation Administration provide very little public information. They put minimal effort into systematic data collection or analysis. The apparent reason is that the demands made upon the administration of these programs do not require much data. The number of direct beneficiaries of the Maritime subsidies run only to about twelve or thirteen firms in any one year. One gets the impression that as far as quantitative records are concerned these programs are managed from the lower left-hand drawer of the administrator's desk.

The Bureau of Reclamation is another matter. Here there is a wealth of data, but readily available only in forms that tend to defeat any comprehensive analysis of the programs' distributional impacts. The total reclamation program data that the Bureau reports is aggregated from reclamation project reports but the project level detail is not given. Thus, it is not really possible to connect the statistics that are reported for the projects with the

From U.S., Congress, Subcommittee on Economy in Government, Joint Economic Committee, *The Analysis and Evaluation of Public Expenditures: The PPB System: A Compendium of Papers,* Vol. I (Washington, D.C.: U.S. Government Printing Office, 1969).

Some references have been deleted.

statistics that are reported for the U.S. Both sets of data must be integrated for any comprehensive analysis of the program's distributional impacts. It almost seems as if these data were consciously arranged to avoid the possibility of any distributional analysis.

For the purposes of the Brookings paper I was forced to abandon my original ideas and to use some data that were available from the 1964 agricultural price support program for cotton. The U.S. Department of Agriculture's Agricultural Stabilization and Conservation Service (ASCS) produces for its own administrative purposes strikingly detailed statistics on allotment acreage and number of farmers by allotment size group. From this and certain of the pricing and other value data it was possible to produce an estimate of the distribution of benefits [2].

ASCS deals with about two and one half million beneficiaries for whom detailed records must be kept as to their eligibility for allotments and the size of those allotments and their compliance. Due to the administrative complexity of the program a substantial amount of internal data collection is necessary. Over time much of this has come into the public domain. It is important to note, however, that a lot of the data in the public domain today is there only because Congressmen or Senators initially asked for it and saw that it was published.

After reviewing a number of Federal program areas one must conclude that we are unlikely to improve the situation, with respect to data availability for this type of analysis, until Congress asks some of the more important distributional questions of those administering the programs. Congress is going to have to be willing to put additional resources into more sophisticated data retrieval systems than presently exist. These data are not currently demanded in the administration of the programs. If Congress and the President do not demand them they will never exist.

The facts are that we do not even fully exploit presently existing data. Economists have not done the analysis of distributional issues that is now possible in those policy areas where some data are available. The PPB system has already helped to some extent to bring distributional questions into focus and to establish the relevance of equity issues and the urgency of many distributional questions. However, in a general sense, economists are still shirking the responsibility to move beyond efficiency criterion in their analytic interests.

The Information Necessary to Appraise Distributional Impacts

What do we need to know if we are to estimate the distributional impacts of public programs and judge their desirability? Look first at the ideal situation. We need to be able to answer the following questions in something like the order in which they are stated.

For benefits:

1. What is the purpose or objective of the public program or legislation, part of which is the question, *who should benefit?*
2. *Who actually benefits,* what groups? It is sometimes not easy to identify beneficiary groups clearly.
3. How much are the *total benefits* of the program? Placing a value on the benefits of many programs is also not an easy analytical proposition.
4. What is the *distribution of program benefits* among beneficiaries?
5. What is the *current distribution of incomes and assets* or other relevant dimensions of welfare among (a) actual beneficiaries and (b) intended or potential beneficiaries?

For costs:

6. *Who should pay the program costs?* Sometimes the nature of the program contains strong implications as to who the burdened should be; other times this is almost an unanswerable question.
7. *Who actually does pay* the cost of the program? Identification of the burdened groups should consider not only the tax structure, but direct price and income effects and the indirect effects of major factor and product substitution caused by the program.
8. What are the *total program costs?* Many times this includes, as it does in question 7, economic and social costs not reflected in federal budget expenditures but market and non-market costs generated through the operation of the program itself. Thus, these are not simple questions.
9. *How are program costs distributed* among the burdened groups?
10. What is the *current distribution of incomes and assets* among (a) the actual burdened groups and (b) the intended or potential burdened groups?

Finally:

11. Integrating the above information, what are *the alternatives* in achieving the same program objective and which alternative is most efficient; that is, attains the same desired distributional (or other) impact but at a lower cost?

When one can answer all of these questions with some degree of clarity and when this information can be reasonably well integrated, it should be possible to evaluate the distributional impacts of the public program involved. I know of no case in which such an ideal has been obtained to date. Major theoretical as well as data gaps must be filled first. Until then, decision makers will operate with far less information. It should be pointed out, too, that economists as economists cannot answer all of these questions. The normative matter of who should benefit or who should pay involves value judgments which economists may not make as scientists. Of course, if some general statement of norms or objectives can be provided, the economist like any logician can develop certain conditionally normative deductions upon which to base a decision as to who should benefit and who should pay.

It is often not possible to answer with any clarity questions one and six about who should benefit and who should be burdened. The evidence from the legislation or from the program's history may not be that clear. The economist, however, may make a substantial clarifying contribution if he can answer questions two and seven; that is, who actually does benefit and who actually is burdened by the costs of these programs. By injecting positive information of this nature into the policy process one often helps produce a clarification of the objectives.

The economic theory literature most related to these questions is focused on the classical theory of factor shares and national income distribution.[1] Little of it is of value for our needs and even on its own grounds it is an intellectually underdeveloped area today. That which does serve to some extent is the eclectic benefit-cost and public finance literature. We are in need of theoretical and analytical constructs that will allow us to interrelate in a causal manner changes in macro-economic variables, public program impacts, and changes in the economic and social rules of society with the distribution of income and assets, not only for the Nation but for regions, various sociodemographic subsets, and interest groups. This is a tall order, but the needs are more and more urgent and economists must pursue this task.

Economists have spent most of their conceptual and empirical energy on questions three and eight, that is, in attempting to measure the total benefits and the total cost of particular programs. The empirical part of the benefit-cost measurement literature focuses almost exclusively on these questions.

Answering questions four and nine on the distribution of benefits and costs is rarely a simple problem for it varies profoundly with differences in the nature of the program and the variety of funding techniques used. Both funding and program influences are discussed in some detail in the following two sections.

Questions five and ten, about the prevailing income and asset distributions among actual or intended beneficiaries and burdened groups, are not independent of the first two questions about who the beneficiaries or burdened groups are or should be. Indeed, collecting data on such very specific incidence groups can be a difficult analytical and data collection problem. Not only are asset distributions generally nonexistent but getting income distributions for specific incidence groups can be extremely difficult, if not impossible, in many cases today. However, it is absolutely necessary to proceed through this stage, for even after you have measured the distribution of program benefits and burdens, it is not possible to judge the welfare or equity impact of the programs until you know the welfare and equity situation of those affected. Weisbrod and Hansen have a recent interesting treatment of this problem [11].

In the case of none of the programs that I am aware of, are we in a position today to mesh the information on the distribution of program benefits with really adequate knowledge of the prevailing welfare conditions of the target population. In fact, about the best we are able to do in most of these programs is to identify who the beneficiaries are. In few cases are we able to say how much of the benefits individuals with various characteristics receive. In even fewer cases can this then be matched with a little data on income characteristics of beneficiaries. In almost no case can we match benefits with current asset distributions for the target population. If you do not know what a program is currently doing to a target population you cannot possibly work intelligently and systematically to improve the direction and character of impact. Generally, we do not really know today what we are doing to ourselves in equity. Our state of knowledge is frankly pitiful.

Finally, answers to question 11 on the cost of alternatives to attain a program objective are necessary to provide information on the trade-off between alternative distributional (as well as other) features of a program.

The Effect of Funding Source

The funding of the social insurance programs out of trust fund sources presents a fundamentally different problem from that of a welfare program transferring money income to dependent children out of general funds collected directly from taxpayers. Measuring the distribution of burden presents a different problem if the program is funded from an income tax rather than a sales or property tax. In the situation where the program is funded out of general revenues, one has to assume a cross section of the revenue sources in structuring one's analysis of the distribution of burden.

In many cases where a program involves a product that is eventually sold to consumers (as in the wheat price support program) part of the cost of the transfer of benefits (to farmers) is funded not by taxpayers but by consumers through some device, the cost of which is passed on directly in the price to the consumer. In the case of the wheat program, a certificate payment system produces this consequence. Wheat price supports also result in higher than current free market prices and thus create a direct transfer from consumer to producer. In other cases public laws or programs may affect real wealth transfers directly between groups in the society without use of the market. Other programs are funded in a manner that transfers the incidence of burden over time, classically through the sale of debt. There are other issues that involve substantial spatial differences in the distribution of burden so that one region, in net effect, may be subsidizing another even though both are eligible for the program. Other questions of burden may require measurement of the impact on different income groups and various economic interests. In any case, it is readily seen that the problem of measuring the distribution of burden of program costs can be quite a different analytical problem from one program to another.

The real incidence of burden is not always obvious. Factor and product substitution effects can be very substantial and are rarely included in calculations of program costs. Structural factors intervene. The incidence literature in taxation identifies many situations in which incidence is shifted. Analogous situations arise in measuring the distribution of burden of program costs.

The Effect of Program Differences

The nature of the individual program also has a profound effect on the analytical problem. Expenditure programs are of many different forms. Capital investment programs, particularly of the natural resource development type, have been the primary focus of most of the benefit-cost type of analyses. Some of the most common Federal expenditure programs, however, are those that transfer real income. These programs can be quite varied in nature. Some transfer income directly, others provide social services and even others transfer real income in kind, as in the food distribution programs. While equity considerations are not given very high priority in most capital investment programs, they tend to be a prime objective of most public expenditure programs that transfer real income directly to some group in society. In any case, some equity considerations are eventually imposed on most direct income transfer programs even if they were not an original consideration in the intent of Congress or of the political interest groups that generated the support to create the program.

Government research and development (R. & D.) expenditures constitute a third type of public expenditure program that has distinctive implications for data needs and analysis. While the immediate beneficiaries of a federally subsidized R. & D. investment may be the initial recipients of the funds, the long run consequences of these programs transform the technologies of society and through technology many of society's social rules. These programs are of singular importance for they cast long shadows into all parts of the society.

Closely related are the regulatory programs and legislation that change the social organizational rules of society. Some of these, such as the antitrust laws, attempt direct manipulation of markets by imposing rules on the structure of markets or on market behavior. Much legislation deals directly with the rules by which society lives. Many of these rules, as for example, the patent and copyright laws, specify criteria that attempt to affect who shall get the initial direct benefit of a new idea or technology.

Finally, there are some additional matters. It is worth noting that the distributional impacts of program changes are likely to be different in the situation where the change in the program involves an expansion than where expenditures are cut. In short, there is a need to analyze distributional impacts at the margin when evaluating programs. The experience of tight budgets over the last several fiscal years has underlined this rather dramatically in some cases. Every economist understands that most changes in prices not only have a price effect but an income effect on both household and firm behavior. Similarly, most income changes have a price effect as well as an income effect. It is well to keep in mind in analyzing public programs that most changes in programs will have both a resource use effect as well as an income redistribution impact. Both will have incentive and disincentive consequences. In short, our responsibility in analyzing public programs does not end with the goal of efficiency and its measurement in a benefit-cost ratio. Indeed, efficiency and equity are frequently intertwined analytically as well as in social policy.

Additional Considerations

Besides gaining command over the distributional impacts of individual programs there is another level of knowledge that is necessary for intelligent and comprehensive policy planning. Congress and the executive branch must know something more about the aggregated impact of Federal programs by regions and for the United States as a whole. That is, it is well that we know the regional effects of individual programs and thus their differential regional impacts. It would be most useful to be able to aggregate the natural resource development investments of various resource development programs into regional aggregates with distributional knowledge within each region and between regions. The same would be true for the whole of our educational input or of the full range of our health programs. There is a need to gain an overview of the plethora of individual programs which presumably add up to some comprehensive whole but for which at this point in time we have very little in the way of knowledge about how they actually add together, if they do. Nor do we have any real notion of the spatial implications for these general program areas. There are indications in our development literature and in studies of the social pathologies of this society, such as poverty, that some of our difficulties today arise as a result of the systematic long term differentials in the distribution of investments in education, in natural resource development, etc. Before we can avoid these kinds of problems we need to know they exist.

There is, in addition, a need to develop a measurement of the distributional impacts of total Federal program expenditures. In other words, we need an overview of the national picture of public expenditures and funding with their impact by various distributional characteristics—income, age, sex, family status, degree of urbanization and race, for example. Again some subcategorization such as educational programs, health, manpower, etc., would be useful as well. An interesting, though given the state of the arts a necessarily rather assumption-ridden, approach to this problem has been produced by Gillespie. His general finding is rather striking. His results indicate that for total Government expenditures and funding:

The Federal pattern of fiscal incidence generally favors low incomes, burdens high income, and is mainly neutral over a wide middle income range. The State and local pattern also favors low income but is essentially neutral over both the middle and upper income ranges. A comparison of the two patterns controverts the conventional view that the State and local tax structure is regressive and the Federal tax structure progressive: indeed, just the reverse is true, for in net terms the State-local structure grants larger benefits to the lower income range than does the Federal [3].

Gillespie goes on to conclude:

More basically, the question arises whether equity . . . should be considered only with reference to tax burden distribution, or whether the relevant criterion should be defined in terms of net benefit (or burden) distribution. If the latter view is taken, tax reform and expenditure reform can no longer be considered independent problems [3].

There are several reasons why one might question Gillespie's results but his attempt at empirical measurement of the overall impact of public programs on the distribution of income underlines dramatically the very significant conceptual and data needs we face before genuinely satisfactory measurement will be possible.[2] Indeed, one of the conclusions that should be drawn from Gillespie's effort is that this kind of empirical measurement of public program performance can best be done by the Federal Government itself or in very close cooperation with the Bureau of the Budget and other immediate sources of internal program data.

Perhaps we need again to repeat the model that was followed in the creation of our national income statistics. Much of the intellectual investment in the primary design of concepts and system was executed by the National Bureau of Economic Research in close conjunction with Federal statistics agencies. It was then implemented by the Government as a Federal system. Certainly the conceptual and data problems are on the same order of difficulty and we are in a similar early stage in developing these numbers for program analysis purposes. Such a system, of course, would be designed to collect data for the full range of program analysis needs, including distributional questions.

DISTRIBUTIONAL CONSEQUENCES OF THREE GOVERNMENT PROGRAMS

This Nation has a long history of creating public programs at least in major part for equity reasons. Among older examples are the farm programs, Corps of Engineers and Bureau of Reclamation programs, and many of the public assistance or welfare programs; examples from recent years include the poverty programs, the food distribution programs, many of the manpower and some of the education (title I of ESEA) programs. Much of the current aid to urban areas has a major equity element among its purposes.

Yet the distributional consequences of our equity programs often turn out to be perverse. We seem to manage these programs without much continuing thought to their equity objectives. Equity objectives or standards are rarely spelled out in the legislation. Once enacted equity concerns seem to recede. Measurement of goal attainment is often reduced to gross rules of thumb, smearing and confusing the original legislative intent. The efficiency of administrative organization is substituted for program efficiency as an overriding congressional concern once clientele support develops. In execution this seems eventually to lead to a fuzziness if not outright drift in the purpose of some programs. The PPB system should lead to improvement but until Congress concerns itself with these matters more systematically, programs are likely to develop dynamics of their own, running on in a self-serving contemplation of the use of public wealth for private ends. This should be a source of concern to the Congress.

We know that, in some cases, the distributional characteristics of a program, while perhaps not to begin with, have become over time quite perverse when measured against current equity standards or even the program's original purpose. This would appear to be the case in the instance of the farm programs which were created because farmers as a group were receiving far less for their labor and resources than nonfarm people. Today the program is under criticism because the distribution of program benefits *among* farmers is highly concentrated, with a large number of farmers receiving very little and a small number receiving very large payments and price-support benefits.

More commonly, the distributional consequences of a program may have been perverse but we have not really known this with any certainty because it was not obvious and we never bothered to measure it. Investment in higher education, for example, may not, as we tend to assume, provide general upward mobility on the basis of ability rather than wealth.

There is evidence, too, that some natural resource investments such as those made in the West by the Bureau of Reclamation have very perverse, and, one assumes, unintended distributional consequences on the growth of other regions.

Let us look briefly at [one of] these three cases as [an example] of the kind of analysis that can be done in the context of public program analysis for policy decisionmaking. By some standards at least, all exhibit distributional characteristics that are not now being considered adequately in program decisions and design.

The Distribution of Benefits and Costs of Higher Education

What do we know about the distributional consequences of society's investment in public higher education? The belief is fairly general that most youth have access to this system on the basis of ability, that education provides an avenue for upward mobility in this society based on ability rather than wealth. Certainly this society holds normative beliefs that suggest that the direct benefits of higher education should be distributed in this manner. What are the facts about the distributional impact of this investment in human resources? W. Lee Hansen and Burton A. Weisbrod have analyzed this question for the State of California [4, 5]. Their work is instructive for its ingenuity, for the kind of distributional analysis that it suggests is possible in human investment programs, and for the kind of surprises that distributional analyses can provide.

The California system of higher education has the general reputation of being one of the most open and accessible and as well financed and with as low tuition as any in the Nation. Yet Hansen and Weisbrod's data suggest strongly that the effect of the system is most regressive. It can be seen in Table 11.1 that the subsidy as a percent of income rises from 12 percent at $8,800 of income to 41 percent at the $12,000 level of income. The authors find that while the tax structure is slightly regressive the benefit distribution is quite regressive.

This results from several factors. The total subsidy to a student's education averages $4,870 at the University of California, $3,810 in the State college system, and only $1,050 in the junior college system. Since the average family income rises progressively from $7,900 for those who have no children in California public higher education to $12,000 per family with children at the University of California, the effect is to provide the largest educational subsidy to the wealthiest. This is partly the consequence of academic entry requirements, since 80 percent of the high school graduates are not eligible to enter the University of California. But that is not the end of it. They go on to state:

Even more interesting is the fact that the percentage of all students qualifying for the University of California [Table 11.2, column 1] rises quite dramatically by family income level—from about 10 percent in the lowest bracket (under $4,000) to 40 percent in the highest (over $25,000). Thus, the correlation between high school achievement and family income—and all that it reflects—is startling indeed. This pattern persists as we widen our view to include those eligible for both the university and State colleges [Table 11.2, column 3]. But a close examination of the differences between the two columns shows that the percentage of those eligible only for the State college system is roughly constant at all income levels; thus, university eligibility requirements account largely for the unequal distribution of opportunity [4].

TABLE 11.1
Average Family Incomes and Average Higher Education Subsidies Received by Families by Type of Institution Children Attend, California, 1964

	California Families without Children in California Public Higher Education	California Families with Children in California Public Higher Education, Children in—		
		Junior College	State College	University of California
Average income	$7,900	$8,800	$10,000	$12,000
Average subsidy	0	1,050	3,810	4,870
Subsidy as percent of income . .	0	12	31	41

Source: W. Lee Hansen and Burton A. Weisbrod, "Benefits, Costs and Finance of Public Higher Education" (Chicago: Markham Publishing Co., 1969), Ch. IV, Table 6.

TABLE 11.2
Distribution of High School Graduates by Eligibility for Public Higher Education in California, by Type of Education and Family Income (in percent)

	Percentage Distribution of High School Graduates by Eligibility for—		
Family Income	University of California (1)	State Colleges (2)	University of California and State Colleges (3)
0 to $3,999	10.7	17.3	28.0
$4,000 to $5,999	11.5	14.8	26.3
$6,000 to $7,999	11.9	18.6	30.5
$8,000 to $9,999	16.2	17.0	33.2
$10,000 to $12,499	19.4	17.7	37.1
$12,500 to $14,999	22.5	17.3	39.8
$15,000 to $17,499	27.9	17.5	45.4
$17,500 to $19,999	29.5	15.6	45.1
$20,000 to $24,999	33.3	12.8	46.1
$25,000 and over	40.1	14.2	54.3
Not reported	13.3	14.7	28.0
All	19.6	16.7	36.3

Source: W. Lee Hansen and Burton A. Weisbrod, "Benefits, Costs, and Finance of Public Higher Education" (Chicago: Markham Publishing Co., 1969), Ch. IV, Table 7.

Hansen and Weisbrod also estimated for California that "the combined State and local tax structure is regressive below $8,000 and is essentially proportional above that level." Thus, they conclude that:

The general nature of the redistributive effects of the current method of financing public higher education in California is clear. Some low-income people have benefited handsomely from the availability of publicly subsidized higher education. But on the whole, the effect of these subsidies is to promote greater rather than less inequality among people of various social and economic backgrounds, by making available substantial subsidies that lower income families are either not eligible for or cannot make use of because of other conditions and constraints associated with their income position. To overcome the effects of the present system would require a substantial overhaul of the pricing system in public higher education, a realignment of the tax structure, and/or a broadening of the eligibility base for public expenditure programs. With respect to the latter, alternative eligibility for public subsidies to young people might well be expanded so as to embrace all young people —not only those who go on to college but those who opt for alternative ways of expanding their earning power, such as apprenticeship or on-the-job training, or even investments in businesses. In any case, it is clear that whatever the degree to which our current higher education programs are rooted in the search for equality of opportunity, the results still leave much to be desired [4].

.   .   .   .   .

CONCLUSION

This paper has argued that distributional consequences of public decisions have major and increasingly important impacts in our society. We have a long history of public commitment to equity purposes. Yet we know very little about the social processes by which distributional impacts are institutionalized and are filtered through the society. We know even less about how to redesign distributional systems without incurring excessive political and social cost. In fact, we do not at this point even have good descriptions of the distributional impacts or characteristics of our public programs. What little we do know suggests, as in the three cases just presented, that there are many surprising and apparently perverse distributional impacts.

Both the integrity of our many public commitments in equity and our efficiency in the use of tax monies to attain public ends require far greater effort to collect data for program analysis of the distributional impacts of public decisions.

The three cases—higher education expenditures, Bureau of Reclamation investments, and the farm program—contain several lessons. If we do not systematically attempt to collect data and assess distributional impacts, we shall always be surprised by the many unintended consequences of our public decisions. Even if we accept the original objectives of older programs, we fail to attain our ends because we have failed to keep the equity objectives clearly before us. The use of indirect means, such as price supports, is a tricky and uncertain way of attaining equity objectives.

Finally, past decisions made without adequate distributional knowledge now appear (given our objectives) often to lack in economic and social wisdom. But even more importantly, these past decisions cannot now be easily or cheaply reversed. This is particularly true in light of the irrevocable specialized capital investments in the reclamation program and the past farm program benefits that are now capitalized into the cost structure of agriculture. The cost of our past ignorance of distributional impacts is dearly high. There is no need to persist in such error. But we must now collect the data and do the analysis of the distributional impacts that are needed for today's decisions.

LITERATURE CITED

[1] American Economic Association, *Index of Economic Articles,* vols. 1–7, Homewood, Ill., Irwin, 1961–67.

[2] Bonnen, James T., "The Distribution of Benefits from Cotton Price Supports," in Samuel B. Chase, Jr., ed., *Problems in Public Expenditure Analysis,* Washington, D.C., The Brookings Institution, 1968, pp. 223–48.

[3] Gillespie, W. Irwin, "The Effect of Public Expenditures on the Distribution of Income," in Richard A. Musgrave, ed., *Essays in Fiscal Federalism,* Washington, D.C., The Brookings Institution, 1965, pp. 112–183.

[4] Hansen, W. Lee and Burton A. Weisbrod, *Benefits, Costs and Finance of Public Higher Education,* Chicago, Markham Publishing Company, 1969.

[5] Hansen, W. Lee and Burton A. Weisbrod, "The Distribution of Costs and Direct Benefits of Public Higher Education: The Case of California," *Journal of Human Resources,* Spring 1969, pp. 176–191.

[6] Kravis, I. B., *The Structure of Income: Some Quantitative Essays,* Philadelphia, 1962.

[7] Mishan, E. J., "A Survey of Welfare Economics, 1939–1959," in Mishan, ed., *Welfare Economics,* New York, Random House, 1964.

[8] Morgan, James N., Martin H. David, Wilber J. Cohen, and Harvey E. Brazer, *Income and Welfare in the United States,* New York, McGraw-Hill, 1962, pp. 15–24.

[9] Peacock, Alan T., ed., *Income Redistribution and Social Policy,* London, Jonathan Cape, 1954, pp. 178–267.

[10] Weintraub, Sidney. *An Approach to the Theory of Income Distribution.* Philadelphia, Chilton, 1958.

[11] Weisbrod, Burton A., and W. Lee Hansen, "An Income-Net Worth Approach to Measuring Economic Welfare," *American Economic Review,* vol. 58, No. 5, Part 1, December 1968.

Notes

[1]See the review of literature in [6, 7, 8] and the volume on the theory of income distribution by Weintraub. [10]. Also look through the A.E.A. Index of Economic Journals [1]. Note that the classification scheme of the Index contains no major distribution category except for factor shares.

[2]For an earlier interesting study of total Federal Fiscal distributional impact see Alfred H. Conrad's study in [9].

IV

Some Strategic Contexts

Analytic models and actual patterns of decision-making

Economists once made life simple for themselves; they let assumptions take the place of descriptions. Thus classical economists assumed widespread consumer knowledge, more or less perfect competition between producers, and rational decision-making by both producer and consumer. Under such conditions, even in the relatively short run, people reflected what they valued by the prices they were willing to pay for any array of goods. There was little need for strategy in all this, little need for long-range planning. Economic Man got what he could while he could, basically. This is an elemental strategy.

Similarly, public finance and budgeting would be simple indeed if some cousinly assumptions are made. Classical Budgeting Man could spring from a small handful of assumptions. The assumptions include:

1. Relatively complete and comparable knowledge by both voters and policy-makers about what individuals and groups want and how to get it.
2. Meaningful comparisons between alternative programs or agencies so that scarce budget dollars can be assigned in terms of such criteria as the relative efficiency of attaining social ends of various orders of preference.
3. Rational decision-making by both voters and policy-makers.

We have long since learned that simplicism in economics does not help in either understanding what is or prescribing what should be. Thus a consumer's knowledge about what he does want is far from perfect, and he is perhaps best off in this area. Comparatively, at best, his knowledge about the degrees to which alternative products meet his specific needs is imperfect.

TABLE IV.1
Two Models of Decision-Making

Rational Comprehensive Model	Successive Limited Approximations Model
1a. Values or objectives are determined and clarified separately, and usually before considering alternative policies.	1a. Objectives and action alternatives are considered to be intertwined.
1b. Policy-formation is approached through ends-means analysis, with agreed-upon ends generating a search for appropriate ways of attaining them.	1b. Means-end analysis is often inappropriate because means and ends are not distinct.
1c. A "good" policy is therefore one providing the most appropriate means to some desired end.	1c. A "good" policy is one about which various analysts agree, without their agreeing that it is the most appropriate means for some objective.
1d. Every important relevant factor is taken into account.	1d. Analysis is limited in that important possible outcomes and important values are neglected.
1e. Theory often is heavily relied upon.	1e. Successive comparisons greatly reduce the need for theory.

Based on Charles E. Lindblom, "The Science of Muddling Through," *Public Administration Review*, 19 (Spring 1959):79–88.

A few massive enterprises also have a great advantage in shaping particularly the short-run tastes of the great multitudes, as by advertising that exploits our deepest needs to be loved or admired. The assumptions of the classical economist, in short, must be modified or rejected.

This chapter seeks to encourage a sophistication about public finance and budgeting similar to what has been achieved in economics. The basic focus here is dual, on analytical *models* of decision-making and actual *patterns* of decision-making.

The broad approach can be usefully framed in terms of two models of decision-making that are relevant to all types of administration. Table IV.1 sketches the properties of these two models, which derive from the insightful contribution of Charles E. Lindblom.[1] Basically, the Rational Comprehensive model of decision-making is consistent with the ideal assumptions detailed above for Economic Man and Budgeting Man. Classical Economic Man, for example, has the knowledge of values and reality demanded by the Rational Comprehensive model. In addition, because all consumers and producers are assumed to have small and relatively equal shares of influence in the model's marketplace, everyone's knowledge and desires are afforded full and equal but minor play. There is no special need for alternative strategies under these conditions.

The Successive Limited Approximations (SLA) model of decision-making stands in sharp opposition. Economic Man and Budgeting Man would not find the SLA model congenial. Indeed, they would be immobilized by conditions like those assumed by the SLA model. Thus the SLA model implies incomplete knowledge of what is desired and how it may be obtained. Here alternative strategies take on considerable significance and chance and insight play major roles. Under the SLA model, Lindblom advises, the premium is definitely on "muddling through."

The selections below in various ways reflect and elaborate on these two basic models of decision-making. Some cautions are appropriate. The connections between the selections and the models, of course, are usually in terms of "more or less." That is, the selections tend to reflect more of one model than the other; they reflect differences in degree more than in kind. As a related caution, neither model is more appropriate than the other in all cases. Thus the SLA model is clearly inappropriate where the assumptions of the Rational Comprehensive model can be met in reality, as in the solution of a linear programming problem which yields the lowest transportation costs of moving specified quantities of specific goods between known points having different freight charges. Here also the issue is one of greater or lesser usefulness, rather than of all or none. The relevant art is determining those circumstances under which one model or the other is more appropriate, not trumpeting the one and excoriating the other. The two models have their specific uses, while they vary significantly in their general applicability.

Certain specifics may help establish the value of the two models of decision-making as analytical end points approached but variously modified by various commentators. The Rational Comprehensive model's most prominent acceptance is reflected in the "program budget," and even more particularly in a systemic notion of interrelated planning, programming, and budgeting activities. Chapter IX will present considerable detail about this systemic approach, the basic propositions underlying which are straightforward and well understood. Relying on Arthur Smithies, the major propositions of a systems approach to planning, programming, and budgeting can be stated as:

1. Each public objective should be defined as clearly as possible.
2. A unified and consistent set of public objectives is the goal.
3. Each alternative policy should be viewed as an alternative way of achieving these unified public objectives.
4. Each possible expenditure should be assessed in terms of its comparative contribution to meeting the unified social objectives.
5. Each possible expenditure should be systematically appraised as to its balance of economic costs and benefits.
6. No decisions on expenditures should be made until all claims are in, so as to permit meaningful comparisons of alternative uses of resources.
7. All decisions about taxes and expenditures should be made as part of a unified budget process.[2]

Smithies is aware that these components of a systemic approach can be approached only in degree, but he maintains that the idealized model still is worth working toward. In Reading 3 (Chapter I), for example, Smithies provides evidence of the formidable problems confronting Rational Comprehensive approaches to finance and budgeting. Some of these problems are unique and circumstantial, but some exist almost everywhere and apparently most of the time. For example, Smithies's notions of division of an organization both horizontally by function and vertically by levels reflect a ubiquitous practical difficulty in approaching the Rational Comprehensive model. In essence, organizations tend to fragment in two basic ways: up and down between different hierarchical levels, and across between units at the same level performing different organization activities. Both varieties of fragmentation reduce the degree to which planning, programming, and budgeting can be delicately articulated and integrated into a comprehensive system. Note only that the different needs and problems of the various fragmented subgroups may not be expressed or compared, even if those needs and problems are comparable, compatible, and can be met. Suborganizations will develop within any agency, that is, and their members will tend to "play close to their chests" with financial and budgeting data. The point holds for horizontal relations with peers, as well as for vertical relations with superiors. And the point holds most forcefully when the inherent tendency to form horizontal suborganization is reinforced by the kinds of separations of powers, plus checks and balances, that define the basic relationship between legislatures and the executive and administrative units of American government.

What some observers see as deviations, others see as normal and perhaps as desirable. James D. Barber and Aaron Wildavsky illustrate the point in terms of their approaches to "incrementalism," which has a strong flavor of the Successive Limited Approximations model of Table IV.1. Smithies requires a statement of the nation's goals before he begins budgeting. An incrementalist, in a rough but approximate sense, looks first at what the budget was last year and in the few preceding years. The incrementalist's basic budgeting rule thus becomes: "base level, plus or minus." This basic rule is crude, but it may also be realistic, and the most that can be expected in many cases.

The selections below provide two perspectives on incrementalism. Barber looks long and hard at the criteria policy-makers actually used in making budget decisions in response to a problem situation imposed by the experimenter. Barber's "Complexity, Synopticism, Incrementalism, and the Real Questions" (Reading 12) reports some of the results of an ingenious laboratory experiment with real governmental decision-making groups. Since these groups were local boards of finance, Barber in effect gives us a look at incrementalism from the "top, down." Wildavsky's "Ubiquitous and Contingent Strategies" (Reading 13) provides a "bottom, up" complement. Essentially Wildavsky details the ways in which government agencies seem well advised to act so as to maximize the chances of getting favorable consideration from those who have formal control over appropriations, particularly legislators.

Viewing budgeting as comprehensive or as incremental is no mere play on emphasis. For many purposes, the theoretical and practical differences are substantial. First, the two views differ because their proponents are looking at somewhat different things in somewhat different ways. Incrementalists tend to stress how things actually are; in contrast, comprehensive budgeters are given to emphasizing how they ought to be. Budgeters of the two persuasions, consequently, are liable to find themselves at odds on a wide range of issues. The "is" and the "ought," in short, commonly do not coincide. Indeed, the predisposition to emphasize one or the other may reflect basic unyielding personality differences.

Second, strategy is all-important to the incrementalist view, while it is distinctly secondary in any comprehensive approach to budgeting. The comprehensive approach strongly tends to seek support for a program in terms of its consistency with national objectives. Its bias thus is toward articulating those objectives, and perhaps complaining if movement toward them is sluggish. Although this view admits of some exaggeration, the incrementalist seeks strategies that are acceptable even if agreement about objectives has not been achieved or is in fact unlikely or impossible. Illustratively, even if no agreement exists about "national objectives," life must go on regardless. Of course, agreement about objectives probably always is desirable. Failing that, the question is: Is there some program we can agree is a good one, lack of agreement about objectives notwithstanding?

Thus proponents of the two views about budgeting and financial decisions will find themselves leaning in opposite directions. The contrast is not absolute; strategies are relevant in the comprehensive approach, and objectives cannot be neglected by the incrementalist. Usually, however, the emphases are so opposed that the contrast is all but absolute.

Third, deep philosophical differences may underlie the two approaches to budgeting and financial decisions. The incrementalist position is more at home with a pluralist concept of what the basic form of government is or ought to be. The comprehensive approach inclines more toward some form of elitism as a descriptive or prescriptive guide for governance. Again the point must not be pushed to extremes, for pluralism and elitism may have developmental ties. For example, "too much" pluralism may in practice lead to social and political chaos. In such a case, pluralism may then lead to elitism.

The theoretical differences between the two approaches to budgeting decisions, in any case, may reflect or be strongly reinforced by the philosophies or world views of the individuals espousing them. The differences in approach in such a case may rightly be called ultimate.

A final selection points up other significant theoretical and practical differences between the incremental and comprehensive approaches to budgeting. Charles E. Lindblom, in "Incremental Decision-Making" (Reading 14), essentially compares a number of characteristics of the federal budgeting processes with certain norms supported by orthodox budgeting principles. He provides detail on the major slippages between practice and principle, moreover.

Lindblom does not despair that reality and the norms of orthodox budgeting practice are at significant odds. The closing part of his argument, in fact, sketches several senses in which decision-making about budgets is better off for the differences between what actually happens and what is often accepted as desirable. Lindblom develops his position via an analysis of coordination through "partisan mutual adjustment" in which he often finds a rationality and effectiveness that others have argued can be found only in a comprehensive approach to budgeting. Lindblom also suggests that a commitment to the comprehensive approach can be dangerous as well as misguided in the many cases in which the required means-ends analysis is awkward or impossible. In sum, he sees means-ends analysis as most applicable to "low-level problems." Much that is of budgetary and financial significance in governance does not qualify as a low-level problem, however.

And therein, lies the rub of a general commitment to the comprehensive approach as Lindblom sees it.

Notes

[1]Charles E. Lindblom, "The Science of Muddling Through," *Public Administration Review* 19 (Spring 1959), 79–88.

[2]Arthur Smithies, *Budgetary Process in the United States* (New York: McGraw-Hill Book Co., 1955), esp. pp. 12–45.

=======

12
Complexity, Synopticism, Incrementalism, and the Real Questions

James D. Barber

Potentially at least, budgetary decisions are immensely complex. They can involve calculations covering the entire range of detailed governmental functions and operations. from the chemistry of water purification to the psychology of social work. Aaron Wildavsky's examples from the congressional budgetary process—e.g., should more money be spent on studies of homopoiesis or lymphomatosis[1]—could be matched at the local level. Potential complexities also exist in coping with relations among levels of abstraction, in assessing the implications of past actions for future ones, and in applying ethical standards to uncertain choices. . . . [T]he most determined budgeter can never hope to take into account all the complexities implicit in the decisions he must make.

Consider the "ideal" budget-maker. He begins by surveying the goals of the community, ranking them in order of importance and determining the temporal priority of each in relation to the others. He bases this initial step on a comprehensive knowledge of his town's economic, political, historical, and ecological character, projected into the future by means of appropriate techniques. Then he proceeds to determine the best means to these ends, making a detailed analysis of each department's resources, operations, and

From James David Barber, *Power in Committees: An Experiment in the Governmental Process,* © 1966 by Rand McNally and Company, Chicago, pp. 34–46.

plans. Finally, he allocates funds among these activities in accordance with the priorities previously established and the probabilities of various unforeseen contingencies.

This "synoptic ideal"[2] is obviously impossible to obtain in its pure form, but is often held out as a goal to be approximated as nearly as possible. Budget-makers are advised to move in this direction, to take into account as many facets of the problem as they can. At its worst, such advice is simply exhortation to try hard and do better. Analysts of actual budget-making processes as they are performed from day to day by human beings in official positions have come forth with a radically different picture of the budget-maker. In fact, they report, budgeters operate incrementally by restricting their attention to very small segments of the total problem, comparing a few alternative marginal departures from the existing situation, and considering only what can be done with readily available resources. While this view can be offered as a strictly empirical observation, it can also be used to elaborate a series of recommendations.

However, to concentrate on the stark contrasts between the synoptic ideal and the incremental reality is perhaps to miss some real questions of practical importance. The interesting questions regarding budget-making practices are:

1. *Matters of degree.*   The alternatives are not incrementalism versus synopticism, but more-or-less incrementalism versus more-or-less synopticism. To what extent can (should) the budgeter take into account a somewhat broader range of calculations than he does? To what extent can (should) he devote more of his time to marginal calculations at the expense of large and long-range considerations?

2. *Matters of method.*   There are any number of ways to simplify an excessively complex problem. What are the implications of choice among these various possibilities? What particular intellectual devices can (should) the budgeter adopt?

3. *Matters of rationality.*   Decision-makers may pursue strategies for simplification largely consciously, with an awareness based on rational choice, or largely unconsciously, in accordance with unexamined habits or predilections. Cognitive complexity is a psychological problem, a source of strain, which can be resolved by inadvertence or design, accidentally or purposefully.[3] The data to be presented next bear on these questions, and I shall come back later to some possible answers.

BUDGETARY CRITERIA

. . . [E]ach board of finance spent approximately thirty minutes in the small groups laboratory on a budget-reducing task, looking over its own most recent budget figures to determine where and by how much the total could be cut if this were necessary. These deliberations were tape recorded and, subsequently, complete, typed transcripts were prepared. To find out what criteria were actually employed as the members approved and rejected reductions, a content analysis of this material was performed. First, all comments which could be identified as favoring specific reductions were distinguished from those opposing specific reductions, giving totals of 559 and 420 respectively. Then these comments were assigned to categories meant to catch the main substantive content of each as this emerged inductively from the data. In Table 12.1, the frequencies of these comments are detailed. These figures and a freer perusal of the transcripts cast light on several board of finance techniques for simplifying an extremely complex set of problems.[4]

Criterion 1: Controllability

The distinction between controllable and uncontrollable costs is a preliminary criterion, applied when the members of the board attempt to decide where to focus attention rather than how much to cut. Certain expenditures have been committed by previous long-range decisions, or are tied in closely with basic legal requirements, or are mandatory accompaniments of other fundamental costs such as retirement funds or wage levels. Excluding these from consideration enables the board to devote its efforts to those matters on which it has discretion in the short run. This is the most frequent of the reasons advanced against cutting particular items. Obviously it can be a useful device when it is consciously applied from the beginning.

In a good many cases, however, the reasons for categorizing an item as uncontrollable are not clear. The borderlines between expenses which are irrevocably committed, those which could be affected by changes in other areas of the budget, and those which are thought to be difficult to change without disrupting essential services are not well defined. Often the members seem to be referring not to some fixed commitment but to a general *consensus* among themselves that changing an item would be undesirable. Typically, the item is mentioned, comments that it "can't be touched," all quickly agree, and they pass on to the next item. In these cases ambiguities in the meanings of controllability are not consciously explored, and it is possible for many specific appropriations to drift over into the uncontrollable category.

Criterion 2: Size and Increase

Most boards appear to recognize that cutting budget requests "across the board" by some fixed percentage or amount is, in the long run, destructive of budgetary rationality. The lesson is learned through a series of feedback processes. Over the years, such flat cutting teaches the requesting agencies to anticipate losing a fixed proportion of their requests, regardless of the merits of the case, and thus to adjust the requests accordingly. The

TABLE 12.1
Budgetary Criteria: Percentage of Comments Expressing Reasons for and against Proposed Reductions

Reasons for Cuts		
Magnitude and Change of Expenditures		
Appropriation was increased in last budget...............16.8%		
New item................11.8		
Large item...........9.1		
Account shows surplus; current expenditure rate...........8.9		
Subtotal...........		46.6
Effects on Operations		
Cuts will not hamper services...........13.6		
Expenditure can be postponed...........8.9		
Subtotal...........		22.5
Uncertainty		
Original appropriation based on rough estimate, was not considered carefully by BF...........10.9		
Funds may not be needed; can correct later...............6.3		
Subtotal...........		17.2
Other		
Effect on tax rate.......................4.7		
Comparison with other departments.....................2.3		
Probable public reaction to cut.....................1.6		
Probable reaction of department to cut...................1.3		
Comparison with other towns...........0.9		
Competence or sincerity of requester...................1.3		
Miscellaneous.......................1.6		
Subtotal...........		13.7
Total...........		100 (N = 559)

Reasons against Cuts		
Uncontrollable items		
"Can't be touched"...................27.4%		
State requirements...................8.1		
Subtotal...........		35.5
Appropriation Already Minimal		
BF cut from last request...........10.5		
BF considered last request carefully.....................9.1		
Appropriation has decreased...........5.0		
Request was minimal; tight...........4.3		
Subtotal...........		28.9
Effects on Operations		
Cut will hamper services...........16.0		
Effect uncertain, perhaps harmful.....................7.4		
Urgent; cannot be postponed...........0.5		
Subtotal...........		23.9
Other		
Probable public reaction to cut...........3.8		
Effect on tax rate.......................2.4		
Competence or sincerity of requester...................2.1		
Probable reaction of departments.....................0.2		
Comparison with other departments.....................0		
Comparison with other towns...........0		
Miscellaneous.......................3.3		
Subtotal...........		11.8
Total...........		100.1 (N = 42(

budget reviewers eventually catch on to this ploy and automatically deduct the traditional "fat" or excess before beginning their real cutting. The requester may then be motivated to pad even more, and so on. Eventually both sides begin to lose confidence in one another, and to realize how ridiculous the game is becoming. The spiral may end with mutual confessions of sin, prayers for forgiveness, and oaths of reform. Judging from comments offered in the boards of finance discussions, across-the-board cutting is passé.

Generally, attention is fixed on the large items in the budget and those requests which have increased over the previous request and/or appropriation. Large requests indicate large and, thus, important programs and therefore, members conclude, large opportunities for savings. The focus is on agency *totals* as clues for the allocation of attention. This is the easiest way to distinguish among requests, and chopping down a large appropriation may pay off in money terms much more than many smaller-scale decisions.

There is, however, a hidden assumption in this line of reasoning which may be fallacious: that a large item contains roughly the same proportion of "fat" as the smaller items do—or perhaps more. This would be a valid conclusion if, for example, the requests were padded on a percentage basis, by adding, say, 10 percent. But otherwise the following proposition would probably hold for most departments: the larger the request, the more times it has been carefully reviewed during the request-making process. The board of education budget, almost always the largest single item, has filtered up to the board of finance through a long series of preliminary stages: teachers, principals, superintendent of schools, board of education budget committee, and full board of education. The tree warden, on the other hand, may bring his comparatively small but unreviewed request directly to the board of finance. Insofar as each successive review tends to reduce initial estimates, many large final totals may indicate budgetary muscle rather than fat.

The technique of concentrating on the large items, then, may be undertaken consciously, but it is often practiced without complete awareness of critical assumptions.

But, in fact, the board of finance may make few comparisons from department to department on the basis of size or other principle. The main procedure in practice is to consider the budget *horizontally*—this year versus last year—rather than *vertically*—Department A versus Department B. Increased requests stand out; sometimes the difference between last year's and this year's request is calculated and entered on the budget forms in order to highlight this aspect. The operative assumption seems to be that stable expenditure levels are *prima facie* valid and need not be closely examined, while raises are suspicious and need detailed scrutiny. As a simplifying device, this technique reflects the much more general tendency for a person to notice objects in motion amidst a collection of fixed objects.

However, designating what is moving and what is still depends on a further specification: moving in relation to what? A *stable* or constant money figure may conceal marked instability in the level of services rendered, in real expenditure terms (considering prices), in changes in the revenue side of budgeting, and so forth. A *raise* in the salary schedule of 2 percent a year represents a *decline* in real incomes if the cost of living is going up 3 percent a year. If more state funds are made available for road work, a *stable* figure for the town highway department in fact represents an *increase*. In periods of increased welfare needs, as in a recession, a *stable* welfare expenditure conceals an actual *drop* in spending per case. Thus simplification by means of concentration on departures from previous spending levels risks distortion and substantive error in the budget. If most other conditions are stable, however, it offers one more way to cut down the burden of calculation.

Criterion 3: Concreteness

If asked to describe their procedures in budgeting, most members of the boards of finance would, I believe, refer to the above techniques in one form or another. The budgeter is usually aware that he uses such techniques—these are the reasons which he advances overtly. But frequently there is an aspect of each technique of which he remains unconscious: the bases for the reasons which he advances are seldom explored and, I think, seldom thought about. The remaining criteria to be discussed fall largely in the latter category of simplification techniques employed unconsciously, or at least according to no regular design.

When a person must make a decision in an ambiguous situation, he searches for some familiar element or set of elements with which he has had much experience, and concentrates on that. In a discussion of education, for example, the philosopher is apt to focus on the general goals, the psychologist on the learning process, and the economist on the marginal utility of various resource allocations. Board of finance members often bring to their official tasks considerable experience in practical affairs, gathered over years of business activity. This means that they are familiar with budgets and can quickly grasp the practical implications of budgetary details. But these very strengths may divert attention toward the concrete, down-to-earth details of a problem and away from certain less tangible but relevant matters.

Take the recreation budget, for example. Questions such as what variety of fencing is best for a playground, what it is reasonable to pay for grading a ball field, and the like are quite similar to those encountered in the course of business. But other matters of key import to the recreation program seem strange: Which of several alternative teenage sports programs would contribute most to the health and welfare of the youngsters? What balance should be struck between programs for the various age groups? These kinds of questions are in fact decided by the ways the board allocates funds. But they may be answered indirectly, without discussion or adequate information, because of the board's tendency to wrestle with physical details rather than policy alternatives. Many of the comments scored above as effects on operations are of this nuts-and-bolts variety.

Criterion 4: Immediacy

The pressure to keep the discussion in board meetings focused on the here and now is intense. Exaggerated in the laboratory situation, scarcity of time is a problem also in the normal budget deliberations, as the deadline for completing the budget approaches inexorably. The member who brings up the long-range picture, or who reaches too far back into the past for his illustrations, may be made to feel that he is interrupting an emergency meeting to introduce irrelevancies. This year's problems are bad enough without adding in those of a decade hence. Simplification is thus achieved by restricting attention to the present and near future.

Yet, of course, decisions made in the immediate context do shape long-run community developments. This is especially evident in large capital expenditures. When a bridge is built in a certain location, the town is, in effect, committed for years to come to a certain pattern of traffic flow in that area. Other land uses are excluded for a long time. Long-term effects on real estate values, business fortunes, and the like may be fixed. Attitudes expressed in the board of finance deliberations regarding community planning agencies often discount these implications but they cannot disprove them.

Viewing time in the other direction, if the board focuses only on what is immediate, it tends to eliminate much relevant evidence from the past. This is not to reintroduce all the complications which simplification techniques are meant to handle, but only to point out that there may be particular decisions upon which particular past experiences might bear, and that an unconscious decision to exclude from consideration everything that happened before last year may not be entirely reasonable. The key problem is one of information retrieval or feedback. Some relevant historical information will be stored in the minds of the members and they may be motivated to introduce it, but the imposition of group restraints on such expressions excludes this vital resource. Other information might be kept in systematic written form, readily available for reference when needed.

Here again, then, a device for simplifying complexity bears with it the possibility of introducing unnecessary additional complexities, as the same problems are encountered and muddled through again and again, without benefit of ordered hindsight.

We have negative evidence of another variety of immediacy or insularity as a criterion: the rather surprising lack of reference to experiences in other towns. The members of a board of finance focus on their own community almost exclusively. Fewer than 1 percent of the comments favoring cuts and none of those opposing cuts refer to comparisons with other towns. In part this is a result of lack of information, few boards being aware that comparative statistical data on town budgeting decisions are readily available. In part it reflects community pride—"Ours is a unique town"—and in part reasonable doubts about the transferability of findings from one setting to another. But among the 169 towns in Connecticut there are undoubtedly many which face similar problems in education, law enforcement, municipal financing, and so on. The small town of Bethlehem may gain little enlightenment from the teeming city of Bridgeport, but it might profit from a look toward Canaan or Bozrah or Hebron.

Criterion 5: Uncertainty

All of these criteria could be considered methods for reducing uncertainty. In a more complex way, however, the boards appear to use the certain-uncertain distinction itself as a simplifying device. We notice in Table 12.1 such items as "Original appropriation, based on rough estimate, was not considered carefully by BF," "Funds may not be needed; can correct later," "BF considered last request carefully," "Effect uncertain, perhaps harmful." The thrust of these comments seems to be that any given time the board will (a) not reconsider decisions about which the members have been certain in the past, and (b) make new decisions, without feeling entirely certain about them, only if such decisions can be taken tentatively and any ill effects can be corrected later. The latter gambit is a prediction that in some cases (usually those involving small expenditures) risks can be progressively eliminated on the basis of future feedback. For example, most towns can expect to encounter sudden needs for additional snow removal funds from time to time, and to draw on various contingency funds to meet these needs as they arise. Money for hiring new school teachers, on the other hand, is needed once and for all near the first of the year in order to complete contractual arrangements. This invites gambling a bit with the snow but taking a cautious approach with the teachers.

The retrospective dimension of uncertainty as a criterion is somewhat simpler. The board looks back at its prior deliberations and recalls that in some cases decisions were made with considerable confidence and in others with considerable doubt. The more uncertain they were, the more willing they are to reconsider. On the surface this appears to be an obvious and reasonable way to proceed, but it is open to at least one kind of irrational inference. That is, estimates of past certainty may be based almost entirely on past effort—on the time and energy previously devoted to reviewing a request. Members seem to feel that if a problem was initially considered at great length the solution was very likely right, or at least that new deliberations on the problem are unlikely to improve the solution. In many cases this makes sense, but in others the fact that much effort went into the making of a decision may indicate that members had many doubts, that many contingencies had to be taken into account, and/or that opinions had to be substituted for missing information. In other words, effort expended is sometimes, but not always, an accurate index of results achieved.

Criterion 6: Dollars and Cents

Another way to simplify the complexity of a decision is to focus on its formal details—in this case, the figures on the pieces of paper at hand. The numbers provide the fundamental basis for calculation, the expression of wants and costs in comparable monetary units. And arithmetic furnishes the fundamental techniques for comparing this program with that one, this year with last year, and so on.

The danger inherent here is that of falling into a kind of symbolic reification in which the representation is cognitively detached from the thing represented, the link between symbol and reality forgotten. In budgeting it is possible to become so absorbed in dollars-and-cents calculations that one loses track of what the figures stand for. This problem arises especially when a great deal of time is spent on arithmetic in order to bring together a coherent set of requests. The numbers come to have a life of their own as they are summed and subtracted and divided. This can lead to mistakes in emphasis and interpretation; for example, a decision to cut a request from one department by a certain amount may be treated as a precedent of sorts for cutting another department by the same amount. The forest is lost sight of as the trees fall all around.

These six criteria for simplification in budgeting: (1) Controllability, (2) Size and increase, (3) Concreteness, (4) Immediacy, (5) Uncertainty, and (6) Dollars and cents appear to be the main ones employed by the boards of finance. Of course, any aspect of budgeting not attended to suggests a technique for reducing complexity—for instance, little attention is paid to revenue-raising problems or to public opinion in these deliberations—but these half-dozen criteria seem to shape budgeting most determinatively. They bring us back to the "real questions" raised earlier.

Close study of the discussion transcripts leads to the conclusion that if these boards err, it is not in the direction of the "synoptic ideal." We come away with the impression that far too little attention is devoted to the broader, longer-range implications of the decisions being made, and that evidence which could be highly useful is systematically ignored.[5] The temptation is strong to preach the gospel of the bigger picture, to urge more effort on all fronts. But this is unlikely to increase the effectiveness or rationality of the budgetary process. More to the point are considerations of how simplification can be accomplished without sacrificing so much of the larger dimensions of budgeting.

INCREMENTAL IMPROVEMENTS IN INCREMENTALISM

If the major problem for the budgeter is economizing his attention, then strategic decisions— those which subsume or predetermine some aspect of many lesser decisions—are of prime importance.[6] Strategic decisions pay off in savings in time and energy as the same types of problems come up repeatedly. For example, once a man decides to shave every morning, he need not concern himself further with the matter. The time taken to make this decision represents a saving, not a waste, of effort. The rule need not be applied rigidly; there will be occasions for breaking it. But by concentrating attention for a while on a recurrent problem and resolving it, one conserves mental energies for years to come.

For the boards of finance, and perhaps for other budget-making bodies, three kinds of strategic decisions appear to offer the best possibilities. None is new, but they are unevenly attended to.

1. Basic Policy and Timing Decisions

By consciously devoting time early in the budget process to determining the boundaries between all controllable and all uncontrollable costs, setting general cost-of-living salary adjustments, and the like, these matters are removed from the agenda of many meetings on specific budget items. Similarly, paying attention early to long-range community planning can dispose of conflicts which might otherwise crop up repeatedly. Timing decisions, particularly setting a schedule for the submission and consideration of requests, can save many an hour's *ad hoc* discussion about what to do next. The simple matter of setting a definite time for meetings—especially for *ending* meetings—removes another set of unnecessary uncertainties. Such cross-cutting decisions on specific, clearly defined topics offer much better possibilities for improvement than vague discussions of general goals or theories of administration.

2. Information-Processing Decisions

Part of the problem here is simply that of creating and collecting information: keeping accurate minutes, requiring reports from operating agencies, gathering statistics on various facets of town finance. The more serious problems involve organizing and communicating available information for maximum utility in making individual decisions. For example, one of the boards of finance regularly has before it, at budget time, a breakdown of the appropriations to each department over the last decade, including the percentage of the total town budget spent annually by each. Standardized budget forms facilitate quick access to relevant comparisons. By setting up a system for training new members and for distributing agendas and pertinent documents to all members for study before they come together at the meeting, the board can save much collegial learning time. Again, the significant pay-off results from *deciding,* consciously and definitely, how information is to be created, stored, and retrieved.

3. Delegation Decisions

The possibilities of delegation are largely unexploited by most boards of finance. Yet it is evident that much relevant research could be farmed out to finance officers, department heads, and clerks. If a program budget, in which each requesting agency spells out in simple narrative form the main services rendered in the past year and the program for the next year, is submitted, the members of the board will not have to dig this information out of the requesters at joint meetings. Research and recommendations on long-term community trends can also be delegated. And perhaps the biggest saving in time could be accomplished by assigning simple calculation tasks to a clerk with a desk calculator. The man-hours consumed by problems in simple arithmetic add up impressively in many boards.

These are, of course, matters of detail on which there can be valid disagreement. The point which needs to be stressed is that analysis of such methods offers better possibilities for the incremental improvement of incrementalism than does a focus on grand alternative models of decision-making. If the goal is rational efficiency in exercising the power of the purse, such mundane moves have much to recommend them. If the purpose is to attain a position of power in the framework of town government, other devices . . . may be called for.

Notes

[1] Aaron Wildavsky, *The Politics of the Budgetary Process* (Boston: Little, Brown, & Co., 1964), p. 9.

[2] David Braybrooke and Charles E. Lindblom, *A Strategy of Decision: Policy Evaluation* (New York: Free Press of Glencoe, 1963), chap. 3. On synoptic versus incremental approaches, see also Charles E. Lindblom, "The Science of 'Muddling Through,' " *Public Administration Review,* Vol. 12 (1952), pp. 79–88; Yehezkel Dror, Charles E. Lindblom, Roger W. Jones, Mickey McCleery, and Wolf Heydebrand, "Governmental Decision-Making: A Symposium," *Public Administration Review,* Vol. 24 (1964), pp. 154–65; James W. Fesler, "Administration in the Federal Government," *Yale Papers in Political Science,* No. 6, Yale University Press, New Haven, Conn., 1963; and Rufus P. Browning, "Innovative and Non-Innovative Decision Processes in Government Budgeting," a paper delivered at the 1963 Annual Meeting of the American Political Science Association.

[3] On conscious versus unconscious decision rules, see Karl W. Deutsch, *The Nerves of Government* (New York: Free Press of Glencoe, 1963), chap. vi.

[4] Many of these themes are similar to those Wildavsky found at the federal level. See Wildavsky, *op. cit.,* chaps. ii and iii.

[5] On the conservative tendencies of incrementalism, see John T. Lanzetta and Vera T. Kanareff, "Information Cost, Amount of Payoff, and Level of Aspiration as Determinants of Information Seeking in Decision-Making," *Behavioral Science,* Vol. 7 (1962), pp. 459–73; Randall B. Ripley, "Interagency Committees and Incrementalism: The Case of Aid to India," *Midwest Journal of Political Science,* Vol. 8 (1964), pp. 143–65; and Vernon Van Dyke, *Pride and Power: The Rationale of the Space Program* (Urbana: University of Illinois Press, 1964), chap. xvi.

⁶On strategic simplification, see Deutsch, *op. cit.,* pp. 251–52; and Thomas C. Schelling, "Bargaining, Communication and Limited War," in *The Strategy of Conflict* (New York: Oxford University Press, 1963), pp. 53–80. On similar simplification techniques in Congress, see Ralph K. Huitt, "Congressional Organization and Operations in the Field of Money and Credit," in William Fellner *et al.* (eds.), *Fiscal and Debt Management Policies* (Englewood Cliffs, N.J.: Prentice-Hall, 1963), particularly pp. 436–40.

13

Ubiquitous [and Contingent] Strategies

Aaron Wildavsky

What really counts in helping an agency get the appropriations it desires? Long service in Washington has convinced high agency officials that some things count a great deal and others only a little. Although they are well aware of the desirability of having technical data to support their requests, budget officials commonly derogate the importance of the formal aspects of their work as a means of securing appropriations. Budget estimates that are well prepared may be useful for internal purposes—deciding among competing programs, maintaining control of the agency's operations, giving the participants the feeling they know what they are doing, finding the cost of complex items. The estimates also provide a respectable backstop for the agency's demands. But, as several informants put it in almost identical words, "It's not what's in your estimates but how good a politician you are that matters."

Being a good politician, these officials say, requires essentially three things: cultivation of an active clientele, the development of confidence among other governmental officials, and skill in following strategies that exploit one's opportunities to the maximum. Doing good work is viewed as part of being a good politician.

Strategies designed to gain confidence and clientele are ubiquitous; they are found everywhere and at all times in the budgetary system. The need for obtaining support is so firmly fixed a star in the budgetary firmament that it is perceived by everyone and uniformly taken into account in making the calculations upon which strategies depend.

"Contingent" strategies are particular; they depend upon conditions of time and place and circumstance; they are especially dependent upon an agency's attitude toward the opportunities the budgetary system provides for. Arising out of these attitudes, we may distinguish three basic orientations toward budgeting in increasing order of ambition. First, defending the agency's base by guarding against cuts in old programs. Second, increasing the size of the base by moving ahead with old programs. Third, expanding the base by adding new programs. These types of strategies differ considerably from one another. An agency might cut popular programs to promote a restoration of funds; it would be unlikely to follow this strategy in adding new programs. We shall take up ubiquitous [strategies only here].

CLIENTELE

Find a clientele.   For most agencies locating a clientele is no problem at all; the groups interested in their activities are all too present. But for some agencies the problem is a difficult one and they have to take extraordinary measures to solve it. Men and women incarcerated in federal prisons, for instance, are hardly an ideal clientele. And the rest of society cares only to the extent of keeping these people locked up. So the Bureau of Prisons tries to create special interest in its activities on the part of Congressmen who are invited to see what is going on. "I wish, Mr. Bow, you would come and visit us at one of these prison places when you have the time. . . . I am sure you would enjoy it." The United States Information Agency faces a similar problem—partly explaining its mendicant status—because it serves people abroad rather than directly benefiting them at home. Things got so bad that the USIA sought to organize the country's ambassadors to foreign nations to vouch for the good job it said it was doing.

Serve your clientele.   For an agency that has a large and strategically placed clientele the most effective strategy is service to those who are in a position to help them. "If we deliver this kind of service," an administrator declared, "other things are secondary and automatic." His agency made a point of organizing clientele groups in various localities, priming them to engage in approved projects, serving them well, and encouraging them to inform their Congressmen of their reaction. Informing one's clientele of the full extent of the benefits they receive may increase the intensity with which they support the agency's request.

Expand your clientele.   In order to secure substantial funds from Congress for domestic purposes, it is ordinarily necessary to develop fairly wide interest in the program. This is what Representative Whitten did when he became a member of the Appropriations Committee and discovered that soil conservation in various watersheds had been authorized but little money had been forthcoming: "Living in the watersheds . . . I began to check . . . and I found that all these watersheds were in a particular region, which meant there was no general interest in the Congress in this type of program. . . . It led me to go before the Democratic platform committee in 1952 and urge them to write into the platform a plank on watershed protection. And they did." As a result, Whitten was able to call on more general support from Democrats and increase appropriations for the Soil Conservation Service watersheds.

Concentrate on individual constituencies.   After the Census Bureau had made an unsuccessful bid to establish a national housing survey, Representative Yates gave it a useful hint. The proposed survey "is so general," Yates said, "as to be almost useless to the people of a particular community. . . . This would help someone like Armstrong Cork, who can sell its product anywhere in the country . . . but will it help the construction industry in a particular area to know whether or not it faces a shortage of customers?" Later, the Bureau submitted a new program that called for a detailed enumeration of metropolitan districts with a sample survey of other areas to get a national total. Endorsed by mortgage holding associations, the construction material industry, and Federal and state housing agencies, the new National Housing Inventory received enthusiastic support in Congress, where Representative Preston exclaimed, "This certainly represents a lot of imaginative thinking on your part. . . ." In another case the National Science Foundation made headway with a program of summer mathematics institutes not only because the idea was excellent but also because the institutes were spread around the country, where they became part of a constituency interest Congressmen are supposed to protect.

Secure feedback.   Almost everyone claims that his projects are immensely popular and benefit lots of people. But how do elected officials know? They can only be made aware by hearing from constituents. The agency can do a lot to ensure that its clientele responds by informing them that contacting Congressmen is necessary and by telling them how to go about it if they do not already know. In fact, the agency may organize the clientele in the first place. The agency may then offer to fulfill the demand it has helped to create. Indeed, Congressmen often urge administrators to make a show of their clientele.

SENATOR WHERRY: Do you have letters or evidence from small operators . . . that need your service that you can introduce into the record. . . . Is that not the test on how much demand there is for your services?

RALSTON (Bureau of Mines): Yes. . . . If it is important, as a rule they come to talk.

When feedback is absent or limited, Congressmen tend to assume no one cares and they need not bother with the appropriation. ". . . A dozen or more complaints do not impress me very much. . . . We cut this out last spring and we did not hear any wild howls of distress. . . ." When feedback is present it can work wonders, as happened with the Soil Conservation Service's Small Watershed program. Representative Andersen waxed enthusiastic:

> . . . Will you point again to Chippewa-Shakopee? I know that project well because it is in my district. I wish the members of this subcommittee could see that Shakopee Creek watershed as it is today. The farmers in that neighborhood were very doubtful when we started that project. Now many of them tell us, Mr. Williams, that the additional crops they have obtained . . . have more than repaid their entire assessment. . . .

Guarding the treasury may be all right but it becomes uncomfortable when cuts return to haunt a Congressman. This is made clear in Representative Clevenger's tale of woe.

> CLEVENGER: I do not want to economize on the Weather Bureau. I never did. I do want an economical administration. . . . I have been blamed for hurricane Hazel. My neighbor, who lived across the road from me for 30 years, printed in his paper that I was to blame for $500 millions in damages and 200 lives. . . . His kids grew up on my porch and yet he prints that on the first page and it is not "maybe." I just "am." He goes back to stories that related to cuts that I made when I was chairman of the Committee.

Most agencies maintain publicity offices (under a variety of titles) whose job is to inform interested parties and the general public of the good things the agency is doing, creating a favorable climate of opinion. There may be objections to this practice on the part of Congressmen who do not like an agency and/or its programs, but those who favor the agency consider it desirable. House subcommittee Chairman Kirwan urged this course on the Bureau of Indian Affairs in connection with its Alaskan Native Service, a worthy but not overly popular program. "Why don't you make some arrangement to tell the Americans every year," Kirwan suggested, "instead of telling this committee what is going on? If you write a letter when you go back to Alaska . . . I will guarantee you the press will get it." The Weather Bureau was urged to put out some publicity of its own by Representative Flood, who observed that

> . . . forecasts . . . were obviously, literally and figuratively all wet. Somebody pointed out in this [New York Times] editorial where this . . . forecast has been "a little cold, a little wet, a little snow, but not bad." . . . But something took place which . . . dumped the whole wagonload of snow on Broadway and made them very unhappy. This happened repeatedly over a period of 30 days, which did not make you look very good, if I can understate it. . . . All right. Why do you not prepare a statement for the many newspaper readers in the area and point out to them that you know the problem is there, and that this is what you want to do about it. . . .

A final example comes from a student who wrote away for a summer job and received in reply a letter from an administrator refusing him on account of budgetary limitations. "Because of our inadequate funds at this critical time," the official wrote, "many students, like yourself, who would otherwise receive the professional training that this work provides, will be deprived of that opportunity. ... Only prompt action by Congress in increasing these funds can make the success of our mission possible."

Divided we stand.   The structure of administrative units may be so arranged as to obtain greater support from clientele. It may be advantageous for a department to create more bureaus or subunits so that there are more claimants for funds who can attract support. "We have had the rather disillusioning experience that too often when we create a new agency of Government or divide up an existing agency," a Representative concluded, "that we wind up with more people on the payroll than we ever had before. ...." There can be little doubt the division of the NIH into separate institutes for heart research, cancer research, and so on has helped mobilize more support than lumping them together under a general title with which it would be more difficult for individuals to identify.

United we fall.   The Weather Bureau is an example of an agency that did rather poorly until it took the many suggestions offered by its supporters in Congress and established a separate appropriation for research and development. The new category was the glamorous one and it was easier to attract support alone; being lumped in with the others hurt its appeal. Indeed, putting projects under the same category may be a way of holding down the expenditures for some so that others will not suffer. One of the imposing difficulties faced in building up the Polaris missile program was the fear that it would deprive traditional Navy activities of resources.

Advisory committees always ask for more.   Get a group of people together who are professionally interested in a subject, no matter how conservative or frugal they might otherwise be, and they are certain to find additional ways in which money could be spent. This apparently invariable law was stated by Representative Thomas when he observed that "All architects [doctors, lawyers, scientists, Indian chiefs] are for more and bigger projects, regardless of type. I have not seen one yet that did not come into that classification."

Advisors may be used to gather support for a program or agency in various ways. They may directly lobby with Congress or the President. "I happened to have lunch with Dr. Farber (a member of the quasi-governmental advisory committee of the NIH) the other day," Congressman Fogarty reveals, "and I learned there is considerable sentiment for these (clinical research) centers." Congressman Cederberg did not know of "anyone who would in any way want to hamper these programs, because I had lunch with Dr. Farber. ...." Advisors may provide a focus of respectability and apparent disinterest to take the onus of self-seeking from the proponents of greater spending. They may work with interest groups and, indeed, may actually represent them. They may direct their attempts to the public media of information as anyone can see by reading the many columns written by Howard Rusk, M.D., a writer on medical subjects for the *New York Times,* requesting greater funds for the NIH.

Do not admit giving in to "pressure."

CIVIL AERONAUTICS BOARD OFFICIAL: . . . One of the reasons there has been such substantial expansion in local airline service, believe it or not, is largely due to the members of Congress.

REPRESENTATIVE FLOOD: I hope you are talking about Hazleton, Pa.

CAB OFFICIAL: I am talking about Pennsylvania as well as every other state. I do not want to leave the impression here that there has been undue pressure or that we have been unduly influenced by members of Congress, but we have tried to cooperate with them.

REPRESENTATIVE FLOOD: I do not care what the distinction is.

But if they press make them pay.

CAB OFFICIAL: . . . Senator . . . if there are any members of Congress apprehensive about the increasing level of subsidy, this has not been evident to the Board. . . . I cannot think of any local service case in which we have not had at least 15, 20, or 25 members of Congress each one urging an extension of the local service to the communities in his constituency as being needed in the public interest. . . . We felt that they, if anyone, knew what the public interest required . . . as to local service . . . with full knowledge that this would require additional subsidy.

Avoid being captured.   The danger always exists that the tail will wag the dog and the agency must exercise care to avoid being captured. Rival interests and Congressmen may be played against each other. New clientele may be recruited to replace the old. The President and influential Congressmen may be persuaded to help out. Or the agency may just decide to say "no" and take the consequences. Dependence upon the support of clientele, however, implies some degree of obligation and the agency may have to make some compromises. The interests involved may also have to compromise because they are dependent upon the administrators for access to decisions, and they may have many irons in the fire with the agency so that it is not worth jeopardizing all of them by an uncompromising stand on one.

Spending and cutting moods.   Unfortunately, no studies have been made about how cutting and spending moods are generated. Yet changes in the climate of opinion do have an impact on appropriations. Possibly a great many groups and individuals, working without much direct coordination but with common purpose, seize upon events like reaction to World War II controls and spending to create a climate adverse to additional appropriations, or upon a recession to create an environment favorable for greater expenditures.

Budget balancing and end-runs.   It is clear that the slogan of the balanced budget has become a weapon in the political wars as well as an article of belief. This is not the place to inquire whether the idea has merit; this is the place to observe that as a belief or slogan budget balancing is one determinant of strategies.

When the idea of a balanced budget becomes imbued with political significance, the Administration may seek appropriations policies that minimize the short-run impact on the budget although total expense may be greater over a period of years. In the Dixon-Yates case a proposed TVA power plant was rejected partly because it involved large immediate capital outlays. The private power plant that was accepted involved much larger expenditures over a 25 year period, but they would have had comparatively little impact during the Eisenhower Administration's term of office.[1]

When clientele are absent or weak there are some techniques for making expenditures that either do not appear in the budget or appear much later on. The International Monetary Fund may be given a Treasury note that it can use at some future date when it needs money. Public buildings may be constructed by private organizations so that the rent paid is much lower in the short run than an initial capital expenditure. The Federal Government may guarantee local bond flotations. An agency and its supporters who fear hostile committee action may also seek out ways to avoid direct encounter with the normal budgetary process. This action is bitterly opposed, especially in the House Appropriations Committee, as back-door spending.

I do not mean to suggest that getting constituency support is all that counts. On the contrary, many agencies lay down tough criteria that projects must meet before they are accepted. The point is that there are ordinarily so many programs that can be truly judged worthwhile by the agency's standards that its major task appears to be that of gaining political support. Priorities may then be assigned on the basis of the ability of the program and its sponsors to garner the necessary support.

CONFIDENCE

The sheer complexity of budgetary matters means that some people need to trust others because they can check up on them only a fraction of the time. "It is impossible for any person to understand in detail the purposes for which $70 billion are requested," Senator Thomas declared in regard to the defense budget. "The committee must take some things on faith." If we add to this the idea of budgeting by increments, where large areas of the budget are not subject to serious questions each year, committee members will treat an agency much better if they feel that its officials will not deceive them. Thus the ways in which the participants in budgeting try to solve their staggering burden of calculation constrains and guides them in their choice of means to secure budgetary ends.

Administrative officials are unanimously agreed that they must, as a bare minimum, enjoy the confidence of the appropriations committee members and their staff. "If you have the confidence of your subcommittee your life is much easier and you can do your department good; if you don't have confidence you can't accomplish much and you are always in trouble over this or that." How do agency personnel seek to establish this confidence?

Be what they think they are.   Confidence is achieved by gearing one's behavior to fit in with the expectations of committee people. Essentially, the desired qualities appear to be projections of the committee members' images of themselves. Bureaucrats are expected to be masters of detail, hard-working, concise, frank, self-effacing fellows who are devoted to their work, tight with the taxpayer's money, recognize a political necessity when they see one, and keep the Congressmen informed. Where Representative Clevenger speaks dourly of how "fewer trips to the coffee shop . . . help make money in most of the departments . . . ," Rooney demonstrates the other side of the coin by speaking favorably of calling the Census Bureau late at night and finding its employees "on the job far later than usual closing hours." An administrator is highly praised because "he always knows his detail and his work. He is short, concise, and to the point. He does not waste any words. I hope when it comes to the economy in your laundry soap it is as great as his economy in words."

To be considered aboveboard, a fair and square shooter, a frank man is highly desirable. After an official admitted that an item had been so far down on the priority list that it had not been discussed with him, Senator Cordon remarked, "All right, I can understand that. Your frankness is refreshing." An administrator like Val Peterson, head of the Federal Civil Defense Agency, will take pains to stress that "There is nothing introduced here that is the field of legerdemain at all . . . I want . . . to throw the cards on the table. . . ."

The budget official needs to show that he is also guardian of the treasury: sound, responsible, not a wastrel; he needs to be able to defend his presentations with convincing evidence and to at least appear to be concerned with protecting the taxpayer. Like the lady who gets a "bargain" and tells her husband how much she has saved, so the administrator is expected to speak of economies. Not only is there no fat in his budget, there is almost no lean. Witness Dewey Short, a former Congressman, speaking on behalf of the Army: "We think we are almost down to the bone. It is a modest request . . . a meager request. . . ." Agency people soon catch on to the economy motif: "I have already been under attack . . . for being too tight with this money. . . ." Petersen said. "I went through it [a field hospital] very carefully myself to be sure there were no plush items in it, nothing goldplated or fancy."

If and when a subcommittee drops the most prevalent role and becomes converted into an outright advocate of a program, as with the Polaris missile system, the budget official is expected to shoot for the moon and he will be criticized if he emphasizes petty economies instead of pushing his projects. Democratic Subcommittee Chairman Kirwan and ranking Republican Jensen complained that the Bureau of Land Management did not ask for enough money for soil conservation. "It is only a drop in the bucket," Kirwan said, "they are afraid to come in." "This committee has pounded for the seven years I know of," Jensen responded, "trying to get them to come in with greater amounts for soil conservation and they pay no attention to it." The norm against waste may even be invoked for spending, as when Kirwan proclaimed that "It is a big waste and loss of money for the U.S. Government when only 6 million is requested for the management of fish and wildlife." In 1948 the head of the Cancer Institute was told in no uncertain terms, "The sky is the limit . . . and you come in with a little amount of $5,500,000 . . ." It is not so much what administrators do but how they meet the particular subcommittee's or chairman's expectations that counts.

Play it straight! Everyone agrees that the most important requirement of confidence, at least in a negative sense, is to be aboveboard. As Rooney once said, "There's only two things that get me mad. One is hare-brained schemes; the other is when they don't play it straight." A lie, an attempt to blatantly cover up some misdeed, a tricky move of any kind, can lead to an irreparable loss of confidence. A typical comment by an administrator states, "It doesn't pay to try to put something over on them [committee members] because if you get caught, you might as well pack your bags and leave Washington." And the chances of getting caught (as the examples that follow illustrate) are considerable because interested committeemen and their staffs have much experience and many sources of information.

Administrators invariably mention first things that should not be done. They believe that there are more people who can harm them than can help and that punishments for failure to establish confidence are greater than the rewards for achieving it. But at times they slip up and then the roof falls in. When Congress limited the amounts of funds that could be spent on personnel, a bureau apparently evaded this limitation in 1952 by subcontracting out a plan to private investors. The House Subcommittee was furious:

REPRESENTATIVE JENSEN: It certainly is going to take a housecleaning . . . of . . . all people who are responsible for this kind of business.
OFFICIAL: We are going to do it, Mr. Chairman.
REPRESENTATIVE JENSEN: I do not mean "maybe." That is the most disgraceful showing that I have seen of any department.
OFFICIAL: I am awfully sorry.

If a committee feels that it has been misled, there is no end to the punitory actions it can take. Senator Hayden spoke of the time when a

bureau was given a lump-sum appropriation as an experiment. "Next year
... the committee felt outraged that certain actions had been taken, not
indicated in the hearings before them. Then we proceeded to earmark the
bill from one end to the other. We just tied it up in knots to show that it
was the Congress, after all, that dictated policy."

Four months after a House subcommittee had recommended funds for
a new prison, a supplemental appropriation request appeared for the purchase of an institution on the west coast that the Army was willing to sell.
Rooney went up in smoke. "Never mentioned it at all, did you?" "Well,"
the Director replied, "negotiations were very nebulous at that time, Mr.
Rooney." "Was that," Rooney asked, "because of the fact that this is a
first-rate penal institution . . . and would accommodate almost 1,500 prison-
ers?" It developed that Rooney, catching sight of the proposed supplemental, had sent a man out to investigate the institution. The supplemental did
not go through.

Integrity.   The positive side of the confidence relationship is to develop
the opinion that the agency official is a man of high integrity who can be
trusted. He must not only give but must also appear to give reliable information. He must keep confidences and not get a Congressman into trouble by
what he says or does. He must be willing to take blame but never credit.
Like a brand name, a budget official's reputation comes to be worth a good
deal in negotiation. (This is called "ivory soap value," that is, 99 and
44/100% pure.) The crucial test may come when an official chooses to act
contrary to his presumed immediate interests by accepting a cutback or
taking the blame in order to maintain his integrity with his appropriations
subcommittee. It must not be forgotten that the budget official often has a
long-term perspective and may be correct in trying to maximize his appropriations over the years rather than on every single item.

If you are believed to have integrity, then you can get by more easily.

ROONEY: Mr. Andretta [Justice Department], this is strictly a crystal ball operation; is it?

ANDRETTA: That is right.

ROONEY: Matter of an expert guess?

ANDRETTA: An expert guess. . . .

ROONEY: We have come to depend upon your guesswork and it is better than
some other guesswork I have seen.

A good index of confidence is ability to secure emergency funds on short
notice with skimpy hearings. No doubt Andretta's achievement was related
to his frequent informal contact with Rooney.

ROONEY: I am one who believes we should keep in close contact with one another
so we understand one another's problems.

ANDRETTA: I agree.

ROONEY: You very often get in touch with us during the course of the year when you do not have a budget pending, to keep us acquainted with what is going on.

ANDRETTA: Exactly. . . .

Make friends: The visit.   Parallel in importance to the need for maintaining integrity is developing close personal relationships with members of the agency's appropriations subcommittee, particularly the Chairman. The most obvious way is to seek them out and get to know them. One official reports that he visited every member of his subcommittee asking merely that they call on him if they wanted assistance. Later, as relationships developed, he was able to bring up budgetary matters. Appropriations hearings reveal numerous instances of personal visitation. A few examples should suggest how these matters work: Representative Jensen: "Mr. Clawson [head of the Bureau of Land Management] came in my office the other day to visit with me. I don't know whether he came in purposely or whether he was just going by and dropped in, and he told me that he was asking for considerably more money for . . . administrative expenses and we had quite a visit. . . ." A subordinate employee of that bureau showed that he had caught the proper spirit when he told Representative Stockman, "If you would like some up-to-date information from the firing line, I shall be glad to call at your office and discuss the matter; will you like for me to do that?"

When columnist Peter Edson editorially asked why the Peace Corps did so well in appropriations compared to the difficult times had by the State Department and the Agency for International Development, he concluded that Sargeant Shriver, head of the Corps, "has tried to establish congressional confidence in him and his agency. Of the 537 members of Congress, he has called on at least 450 in their offices."

The pay-off.   Wherever possible, the administrators seek to accommodate the Congressman and impress him with their interest and friendliness. This attitude comes through in an exchange between a man in the Fish and Wildlife Service and Senator Mundt.

OFFICIAL: Last year at the hearings . . . you were quite interested in the aquarium there [the Senator's state], particularly in view of the centennial coming up in 1961.

MUNDT: That is right.

OFFICIAL: Rest assured we will try our best to have everything in order for the opening of that centennial.

The administrator recognizes and tries to avoid certain disagreeable consequences of establishing relationships with Congressmen. The Congressman who talks too much and quotes you is to be avoided. The administrator who receives a favor may get caught unable to return one the following year and may find that he is dealing with an enemy, not just a neutral.

I'd love to help you but . . .   Where the administrator's notion of what is proper conflicts with that of a Congressman with whom it is desirable to maintain friendly relations, there is no perfect way out of the difficulty. Most officials try to turn the Congressman down by suggesting that their hands are tied, that something may be done in the future, or by stressing some other project on which they are agreed. After Representative Natcher spoke for the second time of his desire for a project in his district, Don Williams of the Soil Conservation Service complimented him for his interest in watershed activity in Kentucky but was "sorry that some of the projects that were proposed would not qualify under the . . . law . . . but . . . they are highly desirable."

The "it can't be done" line was also taken by the Weather Bureau in an altercation with Representative Yates.

WEATHER BUREAU OFFICIAL: We cannot serve the public by telephone . . . because we cannot put enough telephone lines or the operators to do the job. . . . We expect them [the public] to get it through the medium of newspapers, radio, television. If you have six telephones you have to have six people to deal with them. You have no idea. . . .

YATES: Yes; I do have an idea, because I have been getting calls from them. What I want to do is have such calls transferred to you. . . . But as long as you have only one phone, I shall get the calls and you will not. . . .

WEATHER BUREAU OFFICIAL: We find we must do it on the basis of mass distribution.

Sometimes, action may be delayed to see if the committee member will protest. The Weather Bureau tried for a while to cut off weather reports from Savannah to the northern communities that constitute its major source of tourists despite the fact that the Bureau's House subcommittee chairman represented that city.

REPRESENTATIVE PRESTON: I wrote you gentlemen . . . a polite letter about it thinking that maybe you would (restore it) . . . and no action was taken on it. Now, Savannah may be unimportant to the Weather Bureau but it is important to me.

WEATHER BUREAU OFFICIAL: I can almost commit ourselves to seeing to it that the Savannah weather report gets distribution in the northeastern United States.

Give and take.   At other times some compromise may be sought. Secretary of Commerce Averell Harriman was faced with the unpalatable task of deciding which field offices to eliminate. He first used internal Department criteria to find the lower one-third of offices in point of usefulness. Then he decided which to drop or curtail by checking with the affected Congressmen, trying to determine the intensity of their reactions, making his own estimate of whom he could and could not afford to hurt. Harriman's solution was a nice mixture of internal and political criteria designed to meet as many goals as possible or at least to hold the Department's losses down.[2]

Truth and consequences.   In the end, the administrator may just have to face the consequences of opposing Congressmen whose support he needs.

Even if he were disposed to accommodate himself to their desires at times, he may find that other influential members are in disagreement. He may play them off against one another or he may find that nothing he can do will help. The best he may be able to do is to ride out the storm without compounding his difficulties by adding suspicions of his integrity to disagreements over his policies. He hopes, particularly if he is a career man, that the Congressmen will rest content to damn the deed without damning the man.

Emphasis.   The administrator's perception of Congressional knowledge and motivation helps determine the kind of relationships he seeks to establish. The administrator who feels that the members of his appropriations subcommittees are not too well informed on specifics and that they evaluate the agency's program on the basis of feedback from constituents, stresses the role of supporting interests in maintaining good relations with Congressmen. He may not feel the need to be too careful with his estimates. The administrator who believes that the Congressmen are well informed and fairly autonomous is likely to stress personal relationships and demonstrations of good work as well as clientele support. Certain objective conditions may be important here. Some subcommittees deal with much smaller areas than others and their members are likely to be better informed than they otherwise would be. Practices of appointment to subcommittees differ between House and Senate and with passing time. Where Congressmen are appointed who have direct and important constituency interest at stake, the information they get from back home becomes more important. If the composition of the committee changes and there are many members without substantial background in the agency's work, and if the staff does not take up the slack, the agency need not be so meticulous about the information it presents. This situation is reflected in the hearings in which much time is spent on presenting general background information and relatively little on specifics.

Subcommittee and other staff.   Relationships of confidence between agency personnel and subcommittee staff are also vital and are eagerly sought after. Contacts between subcommittee staff and budget officers are often frequent, intensive, and close. Frequency of contacts runs to several times a day when hearings are in progress, once a day when the bill is before the committee, and several times a month during other seasons. This is the principal contact the committee staff has with the Executive Branch. Even when the staff seeks information directly from another official in the agency, the budget officer is generally apprised of the contact and it is channeled through him. Relationships between ordinary committee staff members and Budget Bureau personnel are infrequent, although the people involved know one another. The top-ranking staff members and the Budget Bureau liaison man, however, do get together frequently to discuss problems of coordination (such as scheduling of deficiency appropriations) and format of budget presentation. At times, the BOB uses this opportunity to sound out the senior staff on how the committee might react to changes in presentation and policy. The staff members respond without speaking for the committee in any way. There also may be extensive contact between committee staff and the staff attached to individual Congressmen, but there is not a stable pattern of consultations. House and Senate Appropriations Committee staff may check with one another; also, the staff attached to the substantive committees sometimes may go into the financial implications of new bills with appropriations staff.

When an agency has good relations with subcommittee staff it has an easier time in Congress than it might otherwise. The agency finds that more reliance is placed on its figures, more credence is given to its claims, and more opportunities are provided to secure its demands. Thus one budget officer received information that a million-dollar item had been casually dropped from a bill and was able to arrange with his source of information on the staff to have the item put back for reconsideration. On the other hand, a staff man can do great harm to an agency by expressing distrust of its competence or integrity. Asked if they would consider refusing to talk to committee staff, agency officials uniformly declared that this refusal would be tantamount to cutting their own throats.

Notes

[1] See the author's *Dixon-Yates: A Study in Power Politics* (New Haven, Conn.: Yale University Press, 1962).

[2] Kathryn Smul Arnow, *The Department of Commerce Field Offices,* The Inter-University Case Program, ICP Case Series, No. 21, February, 1954.

14
Incremental Decision-Making

Charles E. Lindblom

Among the ways of simplifying decision-making tasks to avoid irrationalities . . . is one I have elsewhere described in some detail under the label

From Charles E. Lindblom, "Decision-Making in Taxation and Expenditures," in *Public Finances: Needs, Sources, and Utilization* (Copyright © 1961 by Princeton University Press), published for National Bureau of Economic Research, pp. 305–323. Reprinted by permission of Princeton University Press. Footnotes have been renumbered.

of the incremental method.[1] I suggest that it is actually the most common method through which public policy decisions, including decisions on taxes and expenditures, are approached. That it is a method commonly practiced has led us to take it for granted rather than formalize it in terms like those that formalize incremental consumer choice, to which it is obviously related.

The incremental method is characterized by its practitioner's preoccupation with: (1) only that limited set of policy alternatives that are politically relevant, these typically being policies only incrementally different from existing policies; (2) analysis of only those aspects of policies with respect to which the alternatives differ; (3) a view of the policy choice as one in a succession of choices; (4) the *marginal* values of various social objectives and constraints; (5) an intermixture of evaluation and empirical analysis rather than an empirical analysis of the consequences of policies for objectives independently determined; and (6) only a small number out of all the important relevant values.

Of these six characteristics, the first three are recognizable characteristics of political decision-making, as practiced by both officials and most policy-minded academic analysts. I shall not linger over them except to point out that anyone whose approach meets the first three conditions has enormously simplified his policy problems compared to what they would be if he literally and strictly followed the conventional prescription to attempt a comprehensive overview. The fourth and fifth strike at the value problem in policy-making; and the sixth strikes at the general complexity of policy analysis, although in what appears to be a shocking way.

Let us first consider problems of handling values. In the incremental method, political decision-makers handle values through marginal comparisons in the same way that consumers do. Although economists describe rational consumer behavior by reference to utility surfaces, indifference curves, demand schedules, and the like, a rational consumer need know nothing about them. He need not first determine his indifference curve for oranges and apples and subsequently decide his purchase policies accordingly. Nor need he first try to comprehend all possible product mixes (or even a few alternative product mixes), then decide which one he prefers, and only then make those purchases necessary to attain the preferred mix. The rational consumer proceeds directly to marginal comparison of alternative specific purchases. The way in which we economists can, for our own professional purposes, conceptualize consumer choice obscures the great difference between what the consumer can be conceived of as having done but does not actually do—ascertain a function, then choose so as to maximize it—and what he actually does—simply compare policies at the margin and choose directly the preferred policy.

Like the consumer, the incremental decision-maker in governmental affairs does not make use of a utility function, in his case a social welfare function. He does not think in terms of "all the variables that might be considered as affecting welfare: the amounts of each and every kind of good consumed by and service performed by each and every household, the amount of each and every kind of capital investment undertaken, and so on."[2] He can hardly be said to know even a point or two on such a function because he does not think in terms of alternative social states; and, if he can be said to value one social state higher than another, this fact is more to be inferred from his choices than said to control them. He makes specific choices, as does the consumer, at the margin.

Similarly, incremental decision-makers closely intermix empirical and value elements in choice as do consumers. We may describe a consumer who buys a car as having decided upon such a purchase policy in order to attain such objectives or values as speed of movement, ready accessibility of transportation, improved status, and conformity, as well as the pleasures of novelty, display, color and form, and acquisition itself. To decide whether to buy a car and, if so, which car, requires then that he both choose among combinations of such values as these and empirically investigate the consequences of alternative purchase policies for the attainment of each of these values. Thus he must make two kinds of choices: (1) the preferred value-mix and (2) the purchase best suited to the attainment of the preferred value-mix. In actual fact, however, he makes these two choices simultaneously when he decides upon his purchase; he does not in one choice determine the preferred value-mix and then make his purchase in its light.

Moreover, he would find it difficult to describe, even to himself, his preferences among the objectives except by pointing to the purchase made and those rejected. Furthermore, he would confess that many of the objectives or values served by his purchase appeared to him as relevant only after alternative purchase policies began to compete in his mind. He did not, for example, first consider buying a car in order to satisfy his esthetic senses, but esthetic values quickly became relevant once he contemplated buying a car.

Although it is customary to analyze values as a first step in policy-making, it is a characteristic of the incremental method that such an analysis is cursory, short-lived, and only a prefatory clarification of a few of the many goal-values that will be affected by policies to be considered. Sometimes such an analysis is omitted entirely. Either at once or very quickly in incremental decision-making, the analysis turns directly to alternative policies. *Predicting* consequences of alternative policies and *evaluating* the consequences then become intertwined to the degree that, as in consumer choice, only in the final choice among policies is the final choice among objectives or values itself made.

For example, many policy analysts find it extremely difficult to decide how much inflation they are willing to tolerate in order to achieve some specified reduction in unemployment except in contemplation of some particular set of policy alternatives offering marginally different prospective amounts of inflation and unemployment. Or, again, none of us do very well in describing to others—or even to ourselves—the relative value of economic security and rapid economic growth. But we make the choice when confronted with alternative policies offering different increments of the two values. Again, we do not determine our welfare function, then choose, but instead choose directly and, in so doing, simultaneously both indirectly define a part of a welfare function and maximize it.

It is also a characteristic of the incremental method that the decision-maker is much more tentative about his objectives or values than he is considered to be in conventional models. He counts on policy choices to lead him to fresh perceptions about values, he expects to learn about his values from his experiences with pursuing and enjoying them, and he is inclined to think that in the long run policy choices have as great an influence on objectives as objectives have on policy choices.[3]

If incrementalism is a method through which a single decision-maker can rationally evaluate alternative policies, it also offers a solution to the problem of disagreement among decision-makers on values. Incrementalism sidesteps problems posed by disagreement on values because decision-makers deal directly with policies, as has just been explained; no virtue attaches, as it does in the conventional method, to prior discussion of and agreement on objectives or values.

This characteristic of incrementalism makes agreement possible in at least three distinguishable ways. First, ideological and other differences in values that loom large when considered abstractly do not necessarily stand in the way of agreed marginal values. Second, the practice of evaluating only in actual choice situations often leads decision-makers to reconsider values in the light of practical constraints, and reconsideration often moves them toward agreement. Third—and much more important—individuals can often agree on policies even if they hold conflicting values. A group of decision-makers can agree, for example, on the desirability of a sales tax without agreeing on objectives; they may have quite different values and reasons in mind. It will be shown in a later section that incrementalism makes still another attack on the problem of disagreement: sometimes incremental policy-makers are coordinated by methods that do not require them to agree with one another on either values or policies.

As for the general problem of complexity in policy-making, the most drastic simplification of complex problems achieved in incremental decision-making is, as already indicated, through outright neglect of important consequences of policies. Neglect of important variables is so widely preached against that it may be worthwhile to make the point that all policy analysts practice such neglect and intend to go on doing so. In academic policy analysis, we economists routinely leave a mound of unfinished business for the political scientist, sociologist, or psychologist to attend to; and we only sometimes remember to qualify our results accordingly. We leave to the psychologist, for example, the appraisal of malingering when we analyze the desirability of liberalizing benefits under unemployment compensation. Less obvious but no less common is every policy analyst's neglect of imponderables, even when they are considered to be important. Beyond these omissions are many others, some of which appear at least superficially to be arbitrary or random, others of which are traceable to our ignorance. Examples are extremely long-run consequences for family solidarity of increasing urbanization achieved as a result of agricultural expenditures (or restrictions of expenditures) that induce farmers to leave the land; short-term consequences for corporate concentration of military procurement decisions; and consequences for the development of socialized medicine of liberal expenditures on veterans' medical care.

If important consequences are neglected, can the method still be described as one suitable for rational decision-making? Or is omission of important consequences a proof of irrationality? Whatever one's concept of rationality, I suggest that the answer in principle is clear. If the consequences are not neglected in the processes by which policies are determined, then that they are neglected by any given decision-maker is not evidence of irrationality in decision-making. Less cryptically, if values neglected by some decision-makers are the concern of other decision-makers, public policies taken together can be rational. We often permit the fallacy of composition to obscure this insight. Or, to put it another way, we often miss this point because we have applied to politics a confusion of partial and general equilibrium analysis.

Consider a hypothetical example. The President and some of his advisers agree on a greatly expanded program of highway expenditures. Their objectives are national defense, reduction of highway congestion for civilians, and economic development. Consequences of the program for the parity of the 50 states as recipients of federal funds are ignored, as are possible consequences for auto fatalities, design of automobiles, profits of existing toll roads, destruction of homes and recreational areas, sales of automobiles, sales of home furnishings, character of home life, participation in organized religion, and so on.

When the program is presented to Congress, if not before, some of the neglected values will be spoken for by representatives of the states or of toll-road authorities. These interests may come to terms immediately with the original proponents of the program, not necessarily by each representative's taking into account each other's values but by agreement directly on modifications of the program. Other interests will wait until congressional consideration of the program is underway, and still other interests will be brought to bear on the administrative officials eventually responsible for implementing the program. And years later, when it becomes apparent to churchmen that too many people are out driving on Sunday rather than attending religious services, they will stir themselves to find ways of combating the tendency. When they do so, they will not necessarily associate the tendency with the earlier highway program, and it is not at all necessary that they do so in order to deal with their problem.

I intend the example to do no more than show the possibility that decisions can be rational even if each decision-maker ignores important values, if only the values neglected at one point are attended to at another. It is not necessary to show that all values are given equal consideration; they are not in the conventional method. Nor is it necessary to show that their inequalities are systematic or are understandable in terms of some formula; they are not in the conventional method. Nor is it necessary to show that all important values are brought somehow to bear on each decision, even if not on each decision-maker. For sometimes a neglected value will move no one to action until a decade later when it becomes clear that it is being endangered.

The example I chose was not after all very hypothetical; the processes illustrated are familiar. Let us, therefore, explore further the possibility that interconnections among decision-makers in actual fact accomplish rational decision-making despite the apparent irrationalities of each decision taken by itself. We turn thus to an aspect of decision-making that can be posed explicitly as the problem of coordination.

COORDINATION THROUGH PARTISAN MUTUAL ADJUSTMENT

Coordination is worth exploring for several reasons. First, we have been led into it by an exploration of ways in which decision-makers simplify their problems and hence achieve a rationality that would be denied them if they tried to comprehend their problems fully. The possibilities that decision-makers are achieving some notable degree of rationality through the practice of what we have called the incremental method depend in large part on how the decisions are related to each other. Second, quite aside from incrementalism, coordination is an aspect of decision-making with its own special difficulties usually not sufficiently distinguished from decision-making in general. Third, in the study of expenditure decisions, budgeting usually emerges as the dominant coordinating process, and we shall want later to reconsider budgeting in the light of alternative coordinating mechanisms actually in use or potentially useful.

One group of possible coordinating devices includes, of course, the very same procedures that have already been described for decision-making generally; the conventional method with its attempt at comprehensiveness of overview; and the alternative methods for simplifying decision-making, i.e., bottleneck planning, satisficing, and incrementalism. These are all similar in that, if they are used for coordinating decisions, the principal coordinating mechanism is a centrally located mind or centrally located, closely cooperating group of minds. Consideration of their prospects for achieving rational coordinating decisions raises the same questions as we have already raised about them, and I shall consequently pass them by with only two comments.

With respect to the conventional method, because limitations on rationality are posed both by value conflicts and by the complexity of problems, these limitations would appear to be even more serious in the case of coordinating decisions than for decisions generally. With respect to the incremental approach to decisions, it is indeed a possible coordinating method; but, because one of our claims for it is that individual decision-making irrationalities are compensated for by characteristics of a coordinating mechanism appropriate to it (and yet to be explored), to defend incrementalism itself as an approach to coordinating decisions is, though not impossible, difficult.

To what extent the coordination of, say, total federal revenues and expenditures—they are coordinated, even if not ideally—is accomplished through this first group of coordinating methods is not clear. As we have seen, the absence of formal machinery for a centrally comprehended coordinating decision does not prove the absence of central coordination. Assuming some degree of central coordination, achieved perhaps through informal consultation, we do not know what mixture of such approaches as the conventional and the incremental is employed. In any case, inspection of such a problem in coordination as this one would quickly lead us to believe that a second type of coordination, not marked by central comprehension, is also exploited.

The second type, so far as I know, has been best elaborated, though with some troublesome ambiguities in presentation, by Michael Polanyi in a little known essay in which he attempts to generalize from market coordination processes.[4] This is a method in which each of a number of decision-making centers desiring a solution to a commonly recognized problem that cannot be centrally solved independently makes an adjustment to the positions taken at each other decision-making center. A long succession of such independent adjustments eventually achieves a solution to the problem when no center needs make a further adjustment. Polanyi draws an explicit analogy with certain forms of mathematic problem-solving.

His assumption, on which he perhaps wavers, that participants in such a process recognize a common problem and deliberately cooperate is an assumption explicitly to be denied in describing still a third kind of coordination: the mutual adjustment of partisan decision-makers. In this kind of coordination, adjustments to each other are made by decision-makers who do not share common criteria, differ in the values they think important, do not necessarily cooperate with each other or recognize any common problem. It is an especially significant kind of coordination for incremental decision-makers because, to the extent that they simplify their problems by concentrating on some values to the exclusion of others, they become the very kind of partisan we have just described. It is in this third kind of coordination that we shall find the mechanisms through which incremental decisions are often made parts of a larger rational policy-making process.

Partisan mutual adjustment is commonplace for coordination of any two or more of such individuals and groups as the President, Director of the Budget Bureau, individual legislators, congressional committees and sub-committees, administrators at various levels, and countless private groups. At least three major types of partisan mutual adjustment can be distinguished, although any one individual or group is often simultaneously engaged in all three.[5]

Atomistic.   This first type is suggested by atomistic mutual adjustment in the hypothetical purely competitive market. Each decision-making group simply ignores the repercussions of its decisions on other groups in deciding upon its own policies. The decision-maker may or may not know that his decisions have repercussions for other groups; in either case he ignores them. It follows that he does not attempt to manipulate other groups. In the example above, protagonists of a highway program can simply ignore the consequences of their policies for church groups, for taxpayer associations, or for wildlife conservationists. Typically, a group acts atomistically with respect to some but not all other groups. The atomistic method is, I think, the equivalent of Polanyi's method except for what I believe to be his assumptions of a common recognition of a problem and of deliberate cooperation.

In the atomistic method, each partisan group will find itself constantly adjusting its policies as it finds that other groups have created the need for an alteration in its course of action. A continuing process of mutual adjustment could conceivably work through successive approximations to an equilibrium in which no further moves are necessary; but, equilibrium tendencies or not, it interlocks the various groups whose policies are consequential for each other.

Deferential.   In this adjustment process, each decision-maker avoids any policy that would constrain or adversely affect another group. In our own private affairs, each of us is accustomed to leaving unchallenged to each of our associates certain areas of personal choice. Similarly, there develops in the political arena a set of mutual concessions of jurisdiction or authority among decision-makers, individual or group. In addition, private citizen and public policy-maker alike defer in order to avoid adverse counter moves. In such a process as this, decision-makers seek a way to attain their objectives in the areas of free movement left open by the activities of other decision-makers. Some congressmen will not pursue their policy objectives if they turn out to challenge the President's program; and similarly in some areas of choice formally open to the President, he will defer, say, to a congressional coalition. Again, decisions are closely interlocked by this process of mutual adjustment.

Strategic.   In this method, decision-makers manipulate each other in a variety of ways. They may do so by partisan discussion, in which they try to win other decision-makers over to their preferred decisions by whatever purely verbal appeals they think might be effective. This kind of discussion differs from discussion that proceeds in the light of agreed objectives or end values, and its possibilities for achieving coordination throw, I suggest, a new light on the loose but stimulating older concept of democracy as government by discussion. It is the kind of discussion in which an advocate of tax reduction in the Senate might appeal to his high-expenditure colleague not through values shared but by calling the colleague's attention to facts favorable to tax reduction or by reference to his colleague's values or objectives.

Second, decision-makers may manipulate each other by the exchange of effective threats and promises. The Pick-Sloan plan for the Missouri River is an example of the product of an exchange of promises, in this case between the Army Engineers and the Reclamation Bureau. An exchange of threats and promises is a common outgrowth of partisan discussion, but I mean to define partisan discussion to exclude it, so that it can be seen as distinct. Such an exchange I shall refer to as bargaining, following, in so doing, one common usage. Partisan discussion and bargaining, as I have defined the latter, are typically intermixed.

Third, they may manipulate each other by a variety of pressures on each other beyond partisan discussion and bargaining, that is, by injuring, forestalling, or crippling each other directly. For this no intercommunication is required, as in partisan discussion and bargaining; and the frustrated group or decision-maker may not even know the source of the frustration. Here, as also in bargaining, one of the principal strategies is to form an alliance or coalition. Among several advantages gained through alliance, one is that, where one group is without a direct method of influence on a third, it may use a second as an instrument, as when the President is induced by one group to dismiss the head of an agency that stands in the way of the first group. The National Wildlife Association and the American Forestry Association are examples of a pair of conflicting decision-making groups both powerless to make legislation and administrative decisions alone, hence both engaged in building alliances with legislators, other interest groups, and individual voters.

How often these methods for partisan mutual adjustment achieve a rational coordination of decisions is not realized. That they interlock decisions made at various points in the body politic is clear enough; that they are methods for interlocking a multiplicity of incrementally approached decisions is also clear. In addition, whatever its defects, partisan mutual adjustment achieves whatever coordination it does achieve without making coordination a staggering intellectual task. To the extent achieved, coordination is a by-product of decision-making, as in market processes. Nor does coordination, so achieved, make staggering demands for information, because the facts needed to achieve an intellectual coordination are required by no one. Finally, coordination so achieved does not depend upon agreed objectives or values. In short, partisan mutual adjustment strikes at both the complexity problem and the values problem.

But what if the interlocking of decisions is without any perceivable desirable pattern? It has to be shown that coordination so achieved is rational in some sense going beyond what we have already said. I suggest the following hypotheses:

1. *Partisan mutual adjustment is a process through which any value held to be important by any group of people can be made influential on policy-making.* The common objection that not all important interests are participant in each decision is, for reasons discussed above, not valid; it is sufficient for the truth of this hypothesis that each interest be somewhere influential.

2. *It often achieves a satisfactory weighting of conflicting values or interests in policy-making.* Because, as argued above, there is no agreed formula for weighting of conflicting values in our society, any one of a large range of possible systems of weights is no less satisfactory by any agreed standard than another. And since any system of weight used in conventional methods of coordination is to a degree arbitrary, it need only be shown that the system of weights used in mutual adjustment is sometimes better.

While accidents of strategic position and other factors will produce a wide variety of weight from one policy area to another, a supporting hypothesis is that policy will respond relatively more to widely shared and/or intensely held values than to less widely shared and/or less intensely held values and that, consequently, values will in effect often be weighted in a satisfactory way. This supporting hypothesis is all the more probable because of the practice of groups to form alliances around common or adjacent interests. It does not imply that all individuals express their values and the intensity of their values by the degree to which they participate in the mutual adjustment of groups in the political arena. On the contrary, a satisfactory system of weights could evolve from the mutual adjustment of groups representing a small minority of citizens if the distribution of values and intensities among the participating minority corresponded roughly to its distribution in a larger population consisting of citizens not indifferent to policies even if not participating. Again, the system of weights does not have to meet any very restrictive conditions in order for it to be satisfactory in the light of alternative methods of coordination.

3. *In particular, the weighting of interests in mutual adjustment meets the requirements of consent.*   Put down roughly, for brevity's sake, the hypothesis takes account of the alleged precondition of democratic government: that citizens must agree on certain fundamental values and procedures, despite their disagreements on others. Societies can be thought of as purchasing this agreement, or consent to continuation of democratic government, by conceding to each interest group whatever it requires as a price for its consent. (If too many groups demand too high a price, their demands cannot be met, and democratic government is impossible.) Mutual adjustment is a process in which, when the intensity of frustration of group interests threatens democratic consent, the fact is plain; and the option is open to other groups to pay the necessary price. This is an aspect of mutual adjustment much to be prized, I suggest, even if it is sometimes converted into blackmail, as perhaps it has been in the fight against desegregation.

These three hypotheses deal directly with the suspicion almost all of us entertain that mutual adjustment is an arbitrary coordinating mechanism. I suggest that they are sufficient both to call into question the widespread view that central coordination is generally superior and to argue the desirability of comparative study of the two methods, with the hope of discovering just when the one is superior to the other.

Three additional hypotheses throw further, though indirect, light on the value of mutual adjustment as a coordinating process.

4. *Partisan mutual adjustment clarifies citizens' perception of their own preferences and leadership's knowledge of citizens' preferences.*   I can only allude briefly to competition among potential group leaders for followers as having the effect of stimulating each leader to outdo his rivals in articulating for the group its preferences and its best avenues toward their gratification.

5. *It also often dissipates conflict stemming from narrow or hastily considered views of group interests by group members.*   The search for allies in multilateral bargaining, for example, puts enormous pressure on group leaders to find a way of defining a group's interest so that it can be harmonized with the interests of potential allies. Mutual adjustment will often achieve not merely a compromise of interests but what Mary Parker Follett has called an integration of interests.[6]

6. *Whether mutual adjustment is or is not more coercive than centrally achieved coordination depends upon the rules of the game by which the mutually adjusting groups play.*   In view of some tendencies to stress the coercive aspects of mutual adjustment, it is relevant to emphasize its contribution to winning consent, to point up the inevitability of coercion in central coordination, and finally to point out that, while mutual adjustment could and does under some rules lead to violence, as between nations, in other circumstances it can be and is played by rules that respect traditional constraints on the use of coercion.

IMPLICATIONS FOR NORMS AND PRINCIPLES

We now turn to the implications of all the foregoing for norms and principles for decision-makers and designers of decision-making machinery in the field of taxation and expenditure decisions. To the extent that incrementalism together with partisan mutual adjustment is a set of processes for rational decision-making, its first implications for norms and principles in decision-making are already obvious from the foregoing discussion. Although these first implications are destructive more than constructive, to go very far beyond them requires research and reflection that has hardly yet been attempted and which has in fact been inhibited by the common preoccupation with conventionally conceived decision-making.

The first and obvious implication is that, to the extent that incrementalism and mutual adjustment are defensible, every single one of the conventional norms explicitly listed in the early pages of this paper is invalidated. Some of them are reduced to norms appropriate to particular circumstances in which central comprehension is possible; others are entirely inappropriate.

It would be tedious to discuss each in turn; inspection of them in the light of the foregoing argument should be sufficient. But it may be helpful to recapitulate some principal points of the foregoing argument as explicit comment on each of the seven listed principles on which the more numerous prescriptions rest. Each of the seven is in some substantial way invalidated.

1. *Comprehensive overview.*   It follows from all the foregoing that deliberate omission of important relevant values from the analysis of a decision is desirable for sufficiently complex decisions, or for decisions in which decision-makers cannot agree on values; and the circumstances in which each omission is satisfactory increase with the adequacy of partisan mutual adjustment for the coordination of the decisions so made.

2. *Defined social objectives.*   For collective decisions, they cannot be defined if they cannot be agreed upon, as is typically the case for large-scale social choice. Often social objectives can be defined only through actual marginal policy choices by individuals or by groups within which values are agreed upon. It is then sufficient that such individuals and groups agree on policy, even if they do not agree on objectives; and atomistic and deferential mutual adjustment achieve policy-making even without agreement on policy. Hence the principle is often inappropriate in that it defines a quite unnecessary requirement for rational collective choice.

3. *Means-end approach.*   Where values cannot be agreed upon, it is not desirable that participant decision-makers look upon their problem as a collective means-end problem; it is sufficient that they simply find a basis for agreement without regard to which variables are means and which are ends. Or it is sufficient in some types of mutual adjustment, such as atomis-

tic and deferential, that they see the policy problem only as a problem of adaptation of means to their own private partisan ends. Moreover, since ends and means are simultaneously finally chosen in incremental policy-making, it is not desirable that policies be chosen as means to previously clarified ends. Finally, it is desirable that ends be considered as quite tentative and that they be reformulated with each policy choice in such close interconnection that it can be said that ends follow choice of means as much as means follow choice of ends.

4. *Deliberate and explicit choice.*   It is desirable that some policies be set as a by-product of partisan mutual adjustment rather than deliberately and explicitly. Just as we do not have in a price system a deliberate and explicit choice among resource allocations but permit allocation to be determined as a by-product of a multiplicity of market decisions, so policy on, say, income distribution in the United States may be an example of a policy best achieved as a by-product of more particular decisions on factors affecting income distribution. Or, for another example, it may be desirable to let the aggregate size of the military budget emerge as a by-product of decisions on specific expenditure programs and not raise the aggregate as an explicit problem at any time. On values and objectives, it follows from comments on the means-end approach that values or objectives should quite commonly not be made the object of explicit and deliberate choice but should be chosen implicitly at the margin through an actual policy choice and should not be articulated as an unnecessary obstruction to agreement on policy.

5. *Unified decision process.*   This normative principle, specifying the general appropriateness of hierarchical forms of organization to knit decision-makers together, simply leaves no room for coordination through partisan mutual adjustment.

6. *Reason and cooperation.*   The whole point of the argument of this paper might be reduced to the proposition that reason runs out, cannot bear the burdens imposed on it, therefore has to be employed in the light of its limitations. A general prescription to employ reason in decision-making, however persuasive, is less wise than a prescription to use reason in establishing such decision-making machinery as reduces the demands made on reason and achieves a coordination of only partly reasoned decisions through processes of adjustment other than those that go on in the human mind.

Because partisanship is an asset (because it simplifies), conflict becomes not a problem but a method of coordination. Conflict is as useful, therefore, as cooperation. Conflict between the President and Congress, for example, or between two administrative agencies is, within limits still to be explored, to be prized as an essential element in partisan mutual adjustment.

7. *Calculation and minimization of cost.*   This principle requires more extended comment than given to the others, although the principal grounds

for qualifying the principal are inferrable from the above comments on the means-end approach.

Let us take the example of expenditures for inspection of income tax returns, an allegedly clear case in which a larger expenditure than at present would easily recoup its cost in increased tax receipts. Assume that those making the decision are divided among those who want the increased receipts and are willing to expand the necessary funds to accomplish their objective, those who welcome an opportunity to weaken income taxation, and those who, while favorably disposed to income taxation, are not happy about the extent to which its enforcement requires detailed investigation of personal affairs by revenue officials. Each can calculate costs as he sees them, both monetary and intangible. Typically, at some stage a policy will in fact emerge; but, given the assumption that their values differ, they will not have aggregated their values into a pay-off or welfare function (assuming, of course, they do not have an overriding agreed value in the form of such a function). Hence the policy finally arrived at by agreement or by other mutual adjustment is just that—a policy, not their response to an agreed compromise or aggregation of their conflicting values.

Given this solution to their problem, it cannot be asked and answered whether the costs of achieving a social objective were minimized or not, except by the arbitrary injection of the personal values of the observer who asks the question. In this case, a prescription that costs be calculated and minimized could be appropriate only for the partisan problem-solving of the participant decision-makers, which is not the way in which such a prescription is ordinarily intended. As a prescription intended for some collectivity like the House of Representatives, it is not operational, for the House as a whole cannot agree on what is value received and what is cost.

To go further, it would not even always be desirable, even if possible, for the House to agree on an aggregating rule for conflicting values so that, in the light of such an aggregation, choices could be made that did maximize values received or minimize costs. For presumably such a rule would itself be a product of partisan mutual adjustment. To minimize costs under such circumstances would therefore be simply to make policies consistent with prior partisan adjustment of conflicting values. It is not at all clear that this is to be preferred to the direct partisan mutual adjustment of policy conflicts without prior resolution of value differences. The arbitrary element is only more apparent in the one method than in the other.

The same line of argument holds for choice among expenditures on, say, heavy bombers, medium bombers, and missiles of various kinds. It is easy to advocate the policy of providing the biggest bang for a buck; but, in the absence of agreement among bargainers for various branches of the military or among congressmen on just what weapon has the biggest bang, the prescription reduces to the advice to the partisan interests to minimize costs or maximize objectives as they narrowly see them, or else the prescription is again nonoperational.

One appropriate alternative prescription in cases such as these is that expenditures should be undertaken that participant decision-makers can voluntarily agree on, assuming only that each participant has, in his own limited view, acted economically. Another appropriate prescription is simply that each decision-maker act economically and that their independently decided courses of action be coordinated (policy achieved as a by-product) through atomistic, deferential, or some type of strategic adjustment not even requiring their agreement, assuming only that the process of adjustment meets certain conditions.

Still further, let us assume no disagreement whatever on values but a problem so complex as to go beyond the successful comprehension of any individual or committee. Under these circumstances, breaking the problem down into its aspects and throwing decisions into the hands of partisan groups linked through mutual adjustment may still be desirable. If so, the appropriate prescription is, again, not that costs be calculated but that the policy be that on which the participants can agree or be that policy achieved as a by-product of mutual adjustment without agreement. Here the impossibility of achieving a value aggregation in the light of which costs can be minimized stems not from conflict but from complexity. . . .

Notes

[1]Charles E. Lindblom, "Policy Analysis," *American Economic Review* (June 1958): 298–312.

[2]Abram Bergson, "Socialist Economics," in H. S. Ellis (ed.), *A Survey of Contemporary Economics* (New York: The Blakiston Company, Inc., 1947), p. 417.

[3]How then distinguish, it might be asked, a rational and irrational decision? The conventional model defines a rationally chosen policy by its relation to a set of objectives. A rational policy, for example, is one that attains its objectives, or maximizes the probability of doing so, or is, by warranted beliefs, best suited to attainment of its objectives. But since for complex public policy decisions, the decision-makers' objectives are defined by the policy choice he makes, the principal characteristic of the rational decision—perhaps the defining characteristic —turns on the accuracy of the decision-maker's predictions about the outcome of his policies. We shall, however, say more about this below.

[4]Michael Polanyi, "Manageability of Social Tasks," *The Logic of Liberty* (Chicago: University of Chicago Press, 1951).

[5]It will be apparent to many that in exploring these processes I am following the tradition of the pluralists in political theory. But my professional interests in the application of the results of these inquiries to problems of collective expenditure and other economic decisions turns my interest toward the calculation aspects of these processes rather than the control aspects. More concretely, where a political scientist asks whether these processes safeguard us against an overconcentration of power, I ask whether they can aid us in rational choice.

[6]H. C. Metcalf and L. Urwick (eds.), *Dynamic Administration: The Collected Papers of Mary Parker Follett* (New York: Harper & Row, Publishers, 1942), pp. 31 ff.

V

Some Administrative Contexts

Perspectives on internal and external control of agency spending

Expenditure processes wend their way—often torturously—from agency request through final audit of the agency's spending. This chapter focuses on a paramount part of those processes—the diverse ways and means of exercising control over public spending. Such scrutiny usually is multiple, for complex internal controls manned by the agency's own employees exist to monitor its spending, and should those internal controls fail, external controls also have been developed. Figure V.1 lists major control elements of both kinds. The particular emphasis here is on nonlegislative controls. The distinction between internal and external controls is not watertight, and complex feedback loops exist. The two types of controls serve, however, as a first approximation of that which exists.

Figure V.1 sketches the overall federal system to which internal and external controls are applied. The process depicted in the chart begins with the formal legislative decision to authorize a public program and ends with the audit of the ways in which the monies actually were spent. The major activities in this complete flow are:

1. Authorization.
2. Appropriation.
3. Apportionment, quarterly allocation of funds monitored by the Office of Management and Budget.
4. Obligation to buy.
5. Expenditure.
6. Renegotiation, which occurs in the case of a relatively small proportion of government contracts, as in defense.
7. Audit, both internal to the agency and externally by the General Accounting Office.

FIGURE V.1
Some Prominent Features of the Flowchart of Control over Agency Spending

External Controls: Budgetary Processes	Internal Controls: Regulating Processes	External Controls: Auditing Processes
External executive control:	Budget Controls	Contract renegotiation: as by the Renegotiation Board
Office of Management and Budget	Agency Budget Office	
Overall budget preparation	Requests	External audit: Government Accounting Office
Oversight of legislative activities	Allotments	
Monitoring formal executive-legislative contacts	Program Controls	External regulation: substantive and appropriations committees and sub-committees of Congress
Negotiating allotments for spending by executive agencies	Planning	
	Evaluation	
External legislative control:	Cost Controls	
Substantive and appropriations committees and sub-committees of Congress	Agency Accounting Office	
	Cost accounting	
Statutory legislation	Production Controls	
Authorizations to spend	Scheduling and production control	
	Work standards	
	Quality control	
	Evaluation of Controls	
	Agency Auditing Office	
	Internal audit	

Similar flows—and similar issues—characterize all levels of government.

Overall, at the federal level executive monitoring of the complex process sketched above is entrusted to the Office of Management and Budget, once called Bureau of the Budget and even now often referred to as "the Bureau." OMB is a vigilant and wide-ranging defender of the interests of the presidency, and often of its own interests as well. Its leverage comes from several sources. Consider an apparently mundane one, to begin: OMB plays a major role in monitoring budgetary allotments, a fact noted in Figure V.1 and is also patent in the chart below titled "Execution of Enacted Budget." That is, usually on a quarterly basis, Bureau officials help determine schedules for expending specific portions of an agency's budget. The apportionment has direct purposes: to facilitate fiscal planning, as by the Treasury in its concern about when payments will be required; and to prevent an agency from launching an unwise "buying spree" toward the end of a fiscal year to spend all available monies. Patently, this allocation process is at once a delicate and significant one, and OMB's role in that process makes the agency important, by definition.

OMB's leverage also increasingly derives from a fundamental shift in emphasis of its mission-and-role, although some have been disappointed with progress in the degree of shift that has been achieved. John Walsh provides insightful perspective on the evolving concept in his "Office of Management and Budget: New Accent on the 'M' in OMB" (Reading 15). He observes that "despite the emphasis on the "M" [for Management] in OMB, the management role of the agency has not blossomed quite as rapidly as was expected." Walsh's survey of why the emphasis on "M" was considered important and of the factors limiting the effectiveness of the new emphasis deals with much that lies at the heart of federal governance and politics.

More detail on the administrative context within which budget issues get worked over is provided by the visual that immediately follows these notes, "Execution of Enacted Budget." The chart depicts a complex scene. It pictures the attempted integration within the presidency at the onset of the spending cycle. Yet it also pictures the complex fragmentation or parceling out of various phases of the spending processes, as to legislative subcommittees. Thus a General Accounting Office is at the terminal end of the spending cycle, and it is also accountable in law and largely in practice to the Congress. The whole reflects a peculiarly American stamp. The relevant summary is not who controls the spending process, but that numerous people and offices share in its control in complex ways under incredibly complicated conditions.

The overall picture of the spending process is further detailed by a number of sources. Carl W. Tiller's "Agency Budget Problems" (Reading 16) examines the external controls exercised by the Office of Management and Budget (OMB) over agency spending. Moreover, he touches on the complex relations that exist within an agency as it seeks to apply internal controls to the spending of its component units. The total picture is one of great potential for Bureau/agency friction, as well as one of potential for friction between (for example) budgeting and accounting staffs within the same agency. Tiller reports that budgeting and accounting personnel even in the same agency do not share close formal and informal relations. The "good guys" and the "bad guys," in sum, cannot be defined solely in terms of who is inside and who is outside an agency.

Note that Tiller writes both as an observer describing what exists and as a professional budgeting official prescribing what ought to exist. Thus he speaks of "the regrettable diffusion of budget responsibility in a number of agencies." Empirically, as an observer, he refers to "the splitting up of the former functions of budget offices." Evaluatively, as a budgeting professional, Tiller regrets that there "are many aspects of the job of helping executives reach decisions which used to be lodged in the budget staff but are now found elsewhere." The cause may lie in the behavioral and organizational dynamics emphasized in the following two chapters. For example, budget staffs in agencies just might identify with their fellow professionals at department headquarters or in the Office of Management and Budget. Indeed, Tiller may provide some evidence of this tendency in his observation that: "Throughout the budgetary process, agency officers and the staff of [OMB] have a great common interest." Operating officials within any agency might not always have a similar shared interest, however. And such operating officials might complain that the agency budgeting staff is more interested in pleasing OMB contacts or in meeting professional standards than in serving the line officials in its own agency.

In this matter, as in most others, apparently, where you sit determines what you see. Consider Thomas J. Anton's "Agency Budget Roles" (Reading 17), a summary of his study of the expenditure process in the state of Illinois. Although there were exceptions, Anton found a "subculture of budgeting" to be characteristic of Illinois agencies. Anton's picture contrasts sharply with that reflected in Tiller's selection, no doubt reflecting two different stages of development of budgeting traditions at the federal level and in Illinois. Relevantly, also, major changes seem to have occurred in Illinois since the period during which Anton completed his research.

Related to the fall from power of budget staffs in some federal agencies observed by Tiller has been the recent emphasis on "internal auditing." What is this activity, and why has it attracted so much attention recently? First, Army regulations define "internal audit" as "the independent appraisal activity within the Army for the review of financial, accounting and related operations as a basis for constructive service to command and management at all levels." Second, the sharply greater concern with "managerial controls" inside the executive agencies of the federal government since World War II generally underlies the growing importance of the internal audit. Earlier perhaps the dominant emphasis was on external control by the presidency through budgetary tools. Still earlier, the emphasis was on legislative control of administration.

This general approach to the growing concern about internal audit can be given more specific roots. The head of each executive agency of the federal government, for example, has responsibility for establishing and maintaining an adequate system of internal control. The lesser contemporary problem is the tight budgeting of monies for spending on intra agency activities. The contemporary task is more to see that very large amounts are spent effectively and legally, often by complex tiers of contractors and sub-contractors working for (but not in) a public agency. Roughly, per dollar spent, less money now goes into the kind of internal activities, many of them mundane, that budgeting offices coped with historically. "Cost consciousness" is the major cry, moreover, and most budgeting agencies are not well staffed for cost-cutting services. Relatedly, government agencies now increasingly face the task of presenting "one face" to contractors. Here again internal audit is more crucial than budgeting. Crudely, the end of the spending pipeline is a strategic spot to police the overall system of internal control of large volumes of "outside spending." Internal audit is at the end of the pipeline, and budgeting is at the front.

Proponents of the crucial role of the internal audit have labored hard to reinforce history. History helped mightily, no doubt of it. One observer isolated three powerful historical trends supporting an enlarged role for internal audit:

1. The General Accounting Office has been active in unearthing deficiencies of management, especially in relation to contracts with outside organizations. Agency managements thus were motivated to discover and remedy the deficiencies before GAO review. Hence the growing importance of internal audit.
2. Congress gives close attention to reports of the GAO, and reports of alleged irregularities also get wide publicity. For obvious reasons, then, executive agencies have been anxious to isolate irregularities by internal audit.
3. Consequently, internal audit commonly has enjoyed access to top management, who are anxious lest irregularities be suppressed within the hierarchy of their own organizations.[1]

Other historical forces were at work. The recent large-scale introduction of automatic data-processing equipment, for example, probably aided internal audit. Such powerful machines encouraged a systemic and overall view of managerial control. The location of internal audit in the agency spending process again permitted unusual opportunities for systemic oversight. At any rate, perhaps most basically, supporters of internal audit have emphasized the broad aspects of managerial control which are such a challenge in today's public organizations. And these advocates also have attempted to tie internal audit closely to top management. Overall, proponents of internal review did not default on their opportunities.

To be sure, there are strong ebbs as well as flows in the overall tide toward an increasing emphasis on internal audit. Three particular resisting factors will be noted here. First, the early history of auditing in the federal government is overall one of punitiveness and restriction. Consider the early strong tendency of the GAO to attempt to control expenditures as well as to audit them. Up until World War II, roughly, Gerald Schulsinger reports that rather than emphasizing reports to Congress, the GAO tended to intervene in executive processes as government officials. These officials could attempt to undo the transaction, or they could personally reimburse the government. This GAO approach was well designed to alienate administrative officials. As Schulsinger concluded:

> By the use of the disallowance power, GAO personnel were able to substitute their conclusions of law and fact for those of agency administrators having responsibility for the conduct of government activities. Their authority to do this was frequently questioned, but their power was only in rare instances effectively limited.[2]

Such early history of auditing has not been completely lived down. Memories (and myths) die slowly in government.

Auditing still carries a certain stigma to many operating officials, although times have changed. Beginning in 1949, for example, the GAO began a "comprehensive audit" program. The number of GAO employees shrank by some 60 percent between 1946 and 1953, largely due to a sharply diminished concern for checking individual transactions at a central office to find evidences of failures to follow procedures or the law or to supply "adequate" evidence that public monies were expended properly. In contrast, as Schulsinger notes, the "comprehensive auditor" worked at the site of operations rather than at a remote Washington GAO desk. His sights also were raised. As Schulsinger explains, "the comprehensive auditor" cut down substantially the amount of voucher examination or other scrutiny of individual transactions and concentrated instead on surveying management procedures and controls generally, with a view to helping management develop its own controls.[3]

Second, and relatedly, auditing's history reflects a concern with errors untempered by a recognition that some are unavoidable, either in actual fact or because of cost. Spending a dollar to prevent a ten-cent error illustrates the point at issue, and the early history of federal auditing (or perhaps its mythology) is full of examples. Understandably, operating officials were concerned about such an auditing approach. One business executive complained about the repeated citation in audits of errors of omission and commission, explaining that he did not advocate error for error's sake. He criticized the "usual implication" that these things should never occur.

"Perhaps they should not," he explained, "and it may be that with superhuman effort on our part they would not, but to prevent their occurrence may well cost five or ten times as much as it would if we were to take the risk of their occurrence on a self-insurance basis." The executive drove his point home. "On the whole," he concluded, "we may sometimes find it more economical not to try to prevent every mistake but to operate on the philosophy that, when we do err, we will uncover the error and guard against its repetition in the future."[4] This "management orientation" stands in sharp historical opposition to the "auditing orientation," although some of the sharper edges of the difference have worn away over time.

Third, the philosophy underlying the early history of auditing was one of centralization. In contrast, decentralization is an increasingly common answer to providing managerial control. And never the twain do meet. To be sure, things are far removed from those days when the GAO demanded to examine all relevant papers relating to all expenditures at GAO headquarters. But the practice of auditing still reflects some bias toward a centralized system.

There are compelling attractions in an effective internal auditing unit, of course. Control over expenditures is always important, especially if the negative and unintended effects of audit can be kept to a minimum. Specifically, internal auditing can most handsomely pay its way other than in the traditional sense of a postaudit of expenditures, or a kind of discovering of open organizational barn doors through which the monetary horses have already fled. Rather, status for internal audit requires the development of methods and systems for control that will alert management with an immediacy beyond that possible in most of today's organizations.[5] To extend the earlier metaphor, the internal auditor must determine where the financial barn doors may be, when they are likely to be left open, and which doors are more expensive to close than are the runaway horses that may escape. Additionally, all this intelligence must be available well before the actual facts.

Whether or not this view correctly assesses the developing role of the internal auditor, there seems no question that the activity need not search for challenges. The challenges to financial reporting abound and, if anything, become evermore important. Ellsworth H. Morse, Jr., describes the full sense of these challenges in "Internal Auditing Principles and Concepts for Federal Agencies" (Reading 18). Morse especially sketches the in-betweenness of the role of internal audit in federal agencies as it applies the policies of the GAO to its home agency.

Some specific sense of the newer problems facing today's internal auditor is reflected in the sharply increased tendency of government agencies to contract out for good and services. Contracting out has some real advantages in many cases, but it always implies problems of controlling costs and encouraging efficiency. With cost-plus-fixed-fee contracts, for example, a government agency motivates little or no contractor concern for efficiency. Sensitive government accounting and auditing controls patently are necessary. If incentive contracts are used, on the other hand, great care must be taken in setting targets lest the contracting party make great profits or lose its organizational shirt.[6] Again, sensitive financial controls are vital.

If an agency's internal controls are not adequate to the job, as Figure V.1 shows, further protection is available. The focus here is on the external postaudit provided by the GAO. Other external controls also exist, of course, and they may be powerful. Thus congressional investigating committees can have a massive impact, for good or ill.

Any realistic approach to the GAO must reflect forces in opposition, for that agency has been and perhaps must be Saturday's child. While monitoring executive agencies, the GAO is an arm of Congress that strives to assure that public monies have been adequately spent. Beyond that statement, little can be written that is simple or incontestable. The GAO does more than provide reports about irregularities, which action characterizes the "independent audit" of business organizations. Although not in the executive branch, that is to say, the GAO has power over executive agencies. The office has not been above using that power, in addition, as in voiding payment of vouchers for services provided or goods delivered. Hence the GAO has been a major storm center, and feelings about it can become intense in both proponent and opponent.

Given the GAO's past and its promise, observers have tended to polarize into defenders and detractors. Basically, Richard E. Brown is a defender,[7] basing his conclusion on an effort to measure GAO's effectiveness in terms of six criteria of how well the agency meets its mandate of aiding Congress to control administrative performance. On definite balance, Brown gives the GAO good grades on these six criteria:

1. GAO must be independent of the executive branch and responsible only to Congress.
2. GAO must provide a true postaudit, rather than an audit which merely delays executive action by predecision reviews.
3. GAO's postaudit must be comprehensive, intensive, and prompt.
4. GAO must have such relationships with Congress that the latter is appropriately organized to receive, consider, and act on audit reports.
5. GAO must be professionally competent and objective in a highly politicized environment.
6. GAO's audit work must deal with timely and important issues rather than with remote history or trivia, as judged from the perspective of both Congress and the public agencies being audited.

The GAO gets much the worse of it from Joseph Harris.[8] Clearly an advocate of presidential leadership, Harris comes down hard on the GAO and its past, while noting the marked recent improvements in its relationships with executive agencies. That the external audit is provided by the GAO, that the GAO's role involves more than a little control over executive agencies, and that the GAO is basically Congress's creature, are hard facts for Harris. He never becomes reconciled to them, especially not to the fact that GAO not only audits but also has the power to settle accounts of executive officers as well as the power to make interpretations as to whether particular transactions are in accord with law and regulations. These are very big clubs, indeed, Harris notes. Despite some countervailing forces, "the fact that the departments must eventually settle with the GAO requires them to give great weight to its views on all questions of policy and procedure, even when they involve matters on which the department's competence and judgment ought to be superior."[9]

These perspectives on the GAO patently apply at the federal level, but they also serve to highlight the tension between legislative and executive branches that commonly exists at all levels of government. The details above will not apply to all state and local jurisdictions, that is to say, but they clearly reflect the basic character of the American political framework of separate and shared powers.

Lennis M. Knighton provides support for this summary conclusion in "An Integrated Framework for Conceptualizing Alternative Approaches to State Audit Programs" (Reading 19). Knighton distinguishes several kinds of postaudit at the state level, and he meaningfully relates them to the developments he has seen in state audit, which he calls an "important but long-neglected function."

The audit function has lately come on so strong for some, indeed, that they have argued that it should take on a "fourth power" status, as a new and separate branch of government, coequal with the legislative, executive, and judicial branches.[10] These observers do not believe the separation of powers is effective today, with the legislative branch being variously overpowered by the executive. The head of the proposed auditing branch would be directly elected by "the people" and report to them, as a way of seeking to control the burgeoning executive branch at state and local levels, as well as at the federal level. The prevailing federal practice, of course, has the audit function reporting to the Congress. In sharp contrast, many observers would prefer that that function, except for postaudit, be given to the executive.

Notes

[1]Daniel Borth, "Accounting in the Federal Government," *The Federal Accountant,* 13 (June 1964), 32–33.

[2]Gerald G. Schulsinger, *The General Accounting Office: Two Glimpses,* Inter-University Case Program Series No. 35 (University, Ala.: University of Alabama Press, July 1956), p. 4.

[3]Ibid., p. 5.

[4]Dudley E. Browne, "Uses and Misuses of Accounting in Reducing Costs," *The Federal Accountant,* 13 (December 1963), 60.

[5]Haver E. Alspach, "Internal Auditing Today and Tomorrow," *The Federal Accountant*, 13 (September 1963), 114–27.

[6]See Victor K. Heyman, "Government by Contract: Boon or Boner?" *Public Administration Review*, 2 (Spring 1961), 59–64.

[7]Richard E. Brown, *The GAO: Untapped Sources of Congressional Power* (Knoxville, Tenn.: University of Tennessee Press, 1970), esp. pp. 72–84.

[8]Joseph Harris, *Congressional Control of Administration* (Washington, D.C.: Brookings Institution, 1964), esp. pp. 128–52.

[9]Ibid., p. 144.

[10]Robert V. Graham, "Is Auditing a Fourth Power? Yes," *State Government*, 43 (Autumn 1970), esp. pp. 259–66.

15

Office of Management and Budget: New Accent on the "M" in OMB

John Walsh

Every recent American president has sought to remold the machinery of the Executive branch to make it more responsive to his policies, and Richard Nixon, more than his predecessors, has put his faith in the efficacy of modern management techniques. In the process, he has used the Office of Management and Budget (OMB), not only as a model of management, but as a source of managers for other federal agencies.

George P. Shultz, now Secretary of the Treasury and Nixon's chief adviser on economic matters, proved himself as the first director of OMB, which was established under a 1970 reorganization plan. Caspar W. Weinberger was Shultz's deputy at OMB and succeeded him as director before going to his present post as Secretary of Health, Education, and Welfare (HEW). James R. Schlesinger, now serving as Secretary of Defense after relatively short stints as chairman of the Atomic Energy Commission and director of the Central Intelligence Agency, got his start in the Nixon Administration as an assistant director of the budget agency. OMB staff members colonized the new energy office, and OMB's associate director for

Reprinted from *Science* 183 (January 1974): 286–90. Copyright 1974 by the American Association for the Advancement of Science.

natural resources, energy, and science, John C. Sawhill, was picked as deputy director of the new agency. Members of the OMB alumni are spotted in many other jobs throughout the federal hierarchy, rather like new branch managers sent out from the home office.

It is true that OMB has become a wellspring of men and ideas comparable to the Department of Defense under Robert S. McNamara during the Kennedy and Johnson administrations. But, despite the emphasis on the "M" in OMB, the management role of the agency has not blossomed quite as rapidly as was expected.

This is attributable in part to resistances within the system, to which presidents Truman, Eisenhower, Kennedy, and Johnson all ruefully testified. Reforms of the federal system, even those firmly backed by presidential power, tend to get lost in the wastes of bureaucratic time. And the Nixon Administration may have had unreasonably high hopes of managerial miracles. One sarcastic semiepigram repeated by a former insider now on the sidelines makes the point. "The Kennedy Administration operated on the fallacy that, if you appoint a good man, the organization doesn't matter. The Nixon Administration operates on the fallacy that, if you get the organization right, you can appoint a third-rate tractor salesman and it doesn't matter."

More concretely, OMB has run into stronger resistance from Congress. There is a consensus on Capitol Hill that OMB has greater power than its predecessor agency, the Bureau of the Budget (BOB), and OMB has been cast in the role of direct antagonist to Congress on the issue of Administration impoundment of appropriated funds. Congressional attitudes were expressed in the action to require Senate confirmation of the director and deputy director of OMB. The Administration view was that this infringed the President's untrammeled right to appoint his own personal advisers, while the feeling in Congress was that the director of OMB and his deputy had acquired new policy powers and should be subject to the same congressional scrutiny as other top political appointees.

It would be wrong, however, to suggest that there is little momentum behind the push for better management, particularly since the arrival a year ago of Roy L. Ash as director of OMB and Frederic V. Malek as his deputy. Ash and Malek are the Administration's two leading apostles of management, and both are updated versions of Horatio Alger heroes. Ash came to the Administration from the presidency of Litton Industries, a pioneering if now somewhat uneasy conglomerate, and Malek, a graduate of West Point and of the Harvard business school, is a self-made millionaire. Before he joined the Nixon Administration, Ash served as head of the President's Advisory Council on Executive Organization, dubbed the "Ash commission," which provided a comprehensive blueprint for federal management. Now, as director of OMB, he is in an excellent position to put into practice what he preached.

The reorganization plan under which OMB replace BOB grew directly out of Ash commission recommendations and was part of a grander design. As the President's message on the reorganization plan said, "Improving the management processes of the President's own office, therefore, is a key element in improving the management of the entire Executive Branch."

The Executive Office of the President includes both the personal staff of the President, comprised mostly of political appointees, and the institutionalized agencies such as OMB and the Council of Economic Advisers, which have a larger proportion of career civil servants on their staffs. The 1970 reorganization plan called for an expanded Domestic Council in the White House, under presidential assistant John Ehrlichman, which would take a stronger hand in policy matters, and for a restructured budget agency (OMB), which would put increased emphasis on management.

A New Symmetry

As the presidential message phrased it, "The Domestic Council will be primarily concerned with *what* we do; the Office of Management and Budget will be primarily concerned with *how we* do it, and *how well* we do it."

The expanded Domestic Council, with an increase in staff to perhaps 100 professionals, was envisioned as a counterpart in domestic matters of the National Security Council, which deals with military and foreign affairs. The intention was to largely eliminate the need for the task forces that were increasingly relied on to formulate policy and develop legislative proposals during the Kennedy and Johnson administrations (*Science,* 18 January).

To many observers at the time, the proposed changes seemed to further undercut the authority of Cabinet Officials in setting policy and proposing legislation. The opposition to increasing the concentration of power in the White House also affected other proposals for change on a grander scale. A 1972 plan to consolidate the 11 existing Cabinet-level departments into 8, for example, was simply ignored by Congress. After the 1972 election, a supercabinet composed of three powerful counselors to the President was created by presidential directive, but it never really worked out, in part perhaps because Watergate went critical.

In any case, the 1970 plan to upgrade the Domestic Council never went through, despite the fact that this was a period when the star of Nixon domestic affairs adviser John Ehrlichman was rising, and the idea of a phalanx of councils reporting to the President through top White House aides was congenial to Nixon.

There are differing stories about what prevented implementation of the plan, but the episode was widely interpreted as a showdown between Ehrlichman and Shultz that the latter won.

Shultz had been named as first director of the newly constituted OMB, and one close observer who was in OMB at the time says Schultz sized up the move to give the Domestic Council power over policy and to let OMB simply handle the financial end of things and stopped it. According to another source, "Ehrlichman was riding high at the time, but he learned a few things about government and backed off."

At any rate the Domestic Council never metamorphosed, and OMB survived its identity crisis. Within OMB, the development was interpreted as Administration recognition that OMB possessed a unique capability. A handy symbolism was found in a sequence of actions which occurred after OMB was established. Pictures of former BOB directors were taken down but some time later were replaced, a nod to continuity which agency regulars noted with quiet satisfaction.

This is not to say that the budget agency has not changed. In fact there has been a steady increase in concern for the management aspects of the agency's task. This has been an evolutionary process which antedates the Nixon Administration and which has been aided by progressive changes in the training and interests of OMB staff.

In the 1950's, BOB directors had banking or accounting backgrounds while the career staff had a heavy representation of public administration graduates, the dominant strain in the previous decade. The next phase, the advent of the economists, was clearly defined in the early 1960's. As William D. Carey, a longtime BOB offical and now an Arthur D. Little, Inc., vice president, put it, these economists "wanted to measure, quantify, look at output. They changed the old habits and style of budgeting." The process became more sophisticated, says Carey, and BOB "never gave up the hope that the budget would become a financial and policy program related to some more or less coherent set of objectives, instead of a sort of vacuuming process which sucked up the junk with the jewels."

With the coming of the Nixon Administration, the recruiters turned to the business schools and management consulting firms for their quarry. One BOB-OMB veteran says, "Under Shultz the mother church was the University of Chicago. Under Ash and Malek it's the Harvard business school."

Not an "Open" Agency

OMB is not an "open" agency in discussions of its actions with Congress, the press, or the public, and it is particularly secretive during the months preceding release of the budget. Junior members of the OMB staff approached for interviews by *Science* during the preparation of these articles, for example, made the stock response that it would be better to talk to "policy-level" officials. The budget agency staff has always been a discreet and elusive group. But, in this reporter's experience, it should be noted that those policy-level officials in OMB today are, if anything, more accessible to the press than their counterparts were in previous administrations.

When Malek is asked to discuss the Administration's stress on management he does talk a little like a management casebook, but hardly like a zealot. The main thrust of the Ash commission, he says, going back to first principles, was "to give the President stronger executive assistance in managing the government." BOB played a key role in developing the federal budget and in giving analytical support to the President. BOB had also done some work in promoting effective management. Malek says that both the Ash commission and the President felt the budget agency "should play a more effective role in assisting the President to manage government—to set goals, to chart directions, to do the kind of things that the chief executive of any enterprise is concerned with."

When Ash and he took over last year, Malek says they felt there had been "considerable transition" but that a lot more could be done to improve management. The immediate target was "to change the focus from mechanical things, like data processing, purchasing, and so forth, to an orientation to broader management aspects to assist the President."

This meant meshing the management and budget functions of the agency. Under the 1970 reorganization, OMB had started out with a bifurcated structure with separate management and budget branches. "Our feeling is that management and budget are one and the same tool of management and that it was important to integrate them." OMB's organizational structure was changed by eliminating a dual chain of command and consolidating activities under four associate directors with direct "line" authority. "The change was not traumatic or even dramatic," Malek asserts. Each associate director presided over budget and management divisions in his field. Some routine management responsibilities were transferred to the General Services Administration, the government's housekeeping agency. And a number of new upper-level staff positions for "management associates" were created. Efforts were reportedly made to recruit "hotshot management types" from outside government to fill these new posts.

The management associates do a variety of things, but they are expected to spend about a third of their time working with other agencies on so-called "MBO's." The Ash-Malek formula for achieving better management features the concept of "Management by Objectives (MBO)." Malek calls MBO "a tool for the President [to use in managing government], a way to delegate responsibility to the Cabinet without abdicating responsibility." Each agency submits objectives each year. These are carefully reviewed in OMB, discussed with the agency, and submitted to the President. If he decides they are acceptable, the agency is held accountable for achieving the objectives. Progress is to be monitored at monthly meetings at which Ash and Malek are expected to be present. Most issues that arise, however, are supposed to be settled at the staff level rather than at the meetings.

How is MBO going so far? "Objectives link up with the budget, but not to the degree they should," says Malek. "We're not satisfied yet." Pressure on the agencies in behalf of MBO continues to be applied. Each agency was asked to submit its objectives for fiscal 1975 along with its budget requests. A task force has been commissioned to determine how the linkup between objectives and the budget process can be made more effective. "If [MBO] is going to endure, we think it is necessary to link it to something as old and established as the budget process."

In the case of research and development Malek concedes that it is difficult to set objectives. He thinks that the National Science Foundation (NSF) "has done a very good job in this area" in trying "to get something quantifiable or at least measurable."

It is true, says Malek, that with basic research you can't measure too well, but that, "given [good] information, you can set priorities. The cancer program is a good example," he says. "HEW has an objective related to the effectiveness of implementation of the cancer program and subobjectives related to the direction research on cancer is to take. Cancer has a little higher priority than other types of research.

"NSF is in the process of identifying all areas of research it could enter into—for example, how to contribute to the assessment of ocean resources. Objectives should have real influence—provide a solid foundation on which to base budget decisions." When will this happen? "Remember, this has only been going on since spring," is Malek's reply. Reception of MBO in the agencies is now a "a mixed picture," according to Malek, "But across the board at the top of the agencies there is enthusiasm and good cooperation. The real test is when you look down the line in an agency. Then it varies."

MBO is inevitably compared to the late, unlamented PPBS (Planning-Programming-Budgeting System) in the Johnson Administration. PPBS was based on the use of cost-benefit analyses to compare alternative ways to achieve policy goals. It was evolved in the Department of Defense, and its application in other agencies was made mandatory by presidential order. PPBS is remembered for being awkward to adapt to civilian programs and for inflicting masses of paperwork of dubious value.

"What we're trying to avoid that was present in PPBS are the rigid requirements and a lot of paperwork," says Malek. "We're not trying to establish a system. We're trying to get across that this is a way of life, a way of thinking, how you do business. In an agency like NASA, this is extremely well established. It's nothing new to them. In other agencies it's slower in developing."

Budget Examiners

Inside OMB, the reorganization has effected a not so subtle change in the way the budget agency functions. The archetypal figure in the agency is the budget examiner, who has been responsible for a group of programs or a small agency. A budget examiner might be a relatively junior civil servant, but still wield decisive influence in the budgetary process. One budget agency veteran says, "Here, a Grade 12 (there are 18 grades in the

civil service scale) deals with assistant secretaries, elsewhere they're nobo-
dies."

This is still true, but the examiners have a diminished role. In the old
days, the budget examiner, his division chief, and perhaps the director of
BOB or his deputy might negotiate with an agency head and his budget
officers on final budget items. According to those who have watched the
process, the examiners now have less contact with the agencies during the
year and less direct impact in the review. The division chiefs have apparently also lost clout; the associate directors are said to have absorbed power
formerly exercised by those above and below them in the chain of command.

In terms of relations with the White House, the reorganization has also
had a decided effect on OMB. Shultz, the first OMB director, was soon
drawn into the White House, where he functioned as an adviser to Nixon
on broad matters of economic policy. He spent the balance of his time in
an office in the West Wing rather than in the old Executive Office Building
where OMB was located. OMB deputy Caspar Weinberger became de facto
budget director. The same pattern has been repeated with Ash and Malek.
Malek presides over the director's review sessions and Ash functions as a
White House adviser and is somewhat removed from the day-to-day process
of fashioning the budget.

OMB regulars see a "fragmentation" of the agency occurring. Before the
present review began, Malek was regarded as more interested in management problems and executive development than in the budget process, and
the verdict on him will have to await completion of the budget cycle. Under
the circumstances, however, it is suggested that now, with four highly
independent associate directors dealing directly with the White House on
their separate fields of responsibility, there are "four little OMB's" operating.

This fragmentation in turn is traced to the 1970 attempt to reorganize
OMB in parallel with an augmented Domestic Council that never came off.
Another of the "oddball things that have happened," according to one
observer, affects the route of decision-making on R & D issues. Shultz and
his assistant, Kenneth W. Dam, were tapped to fill the vacuum left by the
abolition of the post of President's science adviser early last year. But, as
the observer said, "The Shultz science operation is the vestigial remains of
the supercabinet which didn't work." The arrangement may have its conso-
lations for scientists, however, since Shultz is thought to be better informed
and more open-minded on science than anyone close to the President,
including Ash, who is reputed to take an "industry view" of R & D. Dam,
by no great coincidence, is a former assistant director of the budget agency.

Does OMB have any other problems? A too rapid turnover in staff, says
one staff member. "If you're responsible for an education program, you

can't just look at the education budget; you've got to know what's going on in the country, and you have to have some feeling of where the agency is moving." (Although there has been a steady expansion of the White House staff during recent administrations, especially during Nixon's first term, the growth of OMB itself has been relatively restrained. The regular staff now numbers about 630, roughly two-thirds of them professionals, compared with a total of about 450 during the early days of the Kennedy Administration.)

Some critics charge that OMB has been "politicized" and point to the interposition of the associate directors as proof. It is true that a number of top budget officials are Administration appointees who presumably were picked for their sympathy with the President and his policies. But what these critics see as a break with the past is that these appointees are from outside OMB and outside government. Three of the four associate directors came to OMB by way of successful careers in management consulting firms or industry. One of these is Sawhill, whose post as associate director for natural resources, energy, and science has been vacant since he moved to the energy office. The fourth associate director has a government background. He is Paul H. O'Neill, whose domain, human and community affairs, includes biomedical research. In his service in both the Veterans Administration and the budget agency, however, O'Neill distinguished himself as a new model manager.

Longevity No Bar

Long service in the budget agency is not a disqualification for key assignments. Hugh F. Loweth, for example, who was recently named to head the energy and science division under Sawhill, joined BOB in 1950 and has been dealing with science programs since the middle 1950's. His division handles most of the civilian R &D programs outside the health field.

Other critics insist that politicization is less of a problem for OMB than is a lack of policy guidance. William A. Niskanen, a recent OMB insider as assistant director for evaluation and now a professor of economics at Berkeley, argued in a recent monograph* that the White House lacks an adequate formal process for communicating policy on major issues to OMB, and he makes suggestions for remedying the deficiency.

Old hands at OMB demur on the existence of a policy gap. "It's an iterative process," says one veteran staff member. [Policy] is not handed down on tablets. It's very fuzzy. We're told, for instance, that the President wants to hold down civilian employment. You rarely get signals clearly."

What is implied in these divergent views are differing general conceptions of how OMB should operate. Those imbued with the old "bureau" tradition seem to feel there is nothing wrong with OMB that a return to closer

---

*W. A. Niskanen, *Structural Reform of the Federal Budget Process* (American Enterprise Institute, Washington, D.C., 1973).

communications downward with client agencies and upward with the President and his chief aides would not remedy. On the other hand, the new breed of managers clearly believes that OMB should continue to move in the direction of improving formal policy structures and increasing the active management of programs.

There is a third view based on the belief that OMB has acquired too much power by default. From this perspective, reform of the whole budget process is needed to restore authority to Congress. OMB is not a popular agency with Congress, and the budget which is about to appear is unlikely to make it more popular. What is different this year, however, is that Congress has taken the first faltering steps toward disciplining its appropriations process to keep spending within budgeted limits. Congress, however, has shown an almost feudal inflexibility toward the kinds of internal transfers of authority that such a major reform would require. So unless and until such radical reform occurs, OMB, under whatever name and organization chart, is likely to persevere, because the budget remains the most effective combination of carrot and stick available to a president.

═══════════

16
Agency Budget Problems

Carl W. Tiller

Budgeting in the Federal Government serves as a means, both at the national level and at the individual agency level, of weighing choices and determining priorities. Since governmental programs cannot be carried on without money, the necessity for making decisions about money forces decisions about program and efficiency. Implicit in nearly every decision on obligating or spending money is a decision on what will be done with the money. And what will be done with the money involves decisions as to program and the degree of managerial efficiency which is contemplated.

The inevitability of the budget cycle is another aspect of budgeting which contributes to decision making within Government. Whether an executive is ready to make decisions or not, budget time comes around at least annually and forces administrators into decisions they might otherwise prefer to postpone.

From *The Federal Accountant* 13 (September 1963): 58–67. Used with permission of publisher and author.

Execution of Enacted Budget

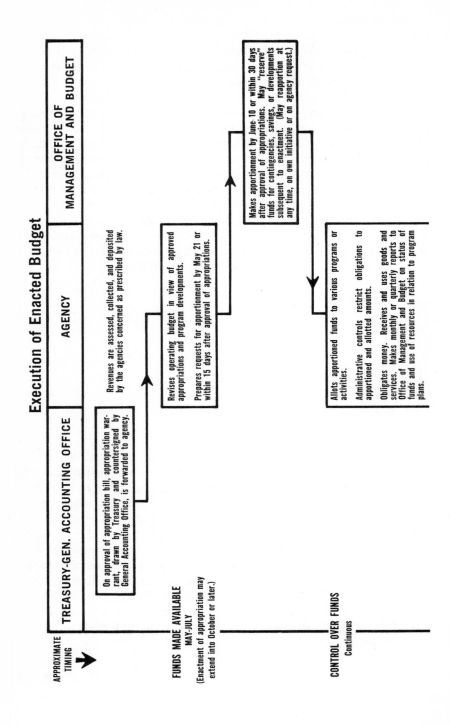

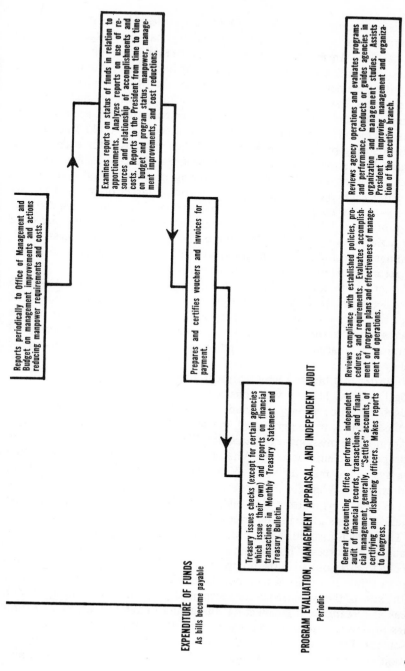

Reports periodically to Office of Management and Budget on management improvements and actions reducing manpower requirements and costs.

Examines reports on status of funds in relation to apportionments. Analyzes reports on use of resources and relationship of accomplishments and costs. Reports to the President from time to time on budget and program status, manpower, management improvement, and cost reductions.

Prepares and certifies vouchers and invoices for payment.

Treasury issues checks (except for certain agencies which issue their own) and reports on financial transactions in Monthly Treasury Statement and Treasury Bulletin.

EXPENDITURE OF FUNDS
As bills become payable

PROGRAM EVALUATION, MANAGEMENT APPRAISAL, AND INDEPENDENT AUDIT
Periodic

General Accounting Office performs independent audit of financial records, transactions, and financial management, generally. "Settles" accounts, of certifying and disbursing officers. Makes reports to Congress.

Reviews compliance with established policies, procedures, and requirements. Evaluates accomplishment of program plans and effectiveness of management and operations.

Reviews agency operations and evaluates programs and performance. Conducts or guides agencies in organization and management studies. Assists President in improving management and organization of the executive branch.

Source: Executive Office of the President/Office of Management and Budget, December 1972.

BASIC BUDGET CONSIDERATIONS

The Government's approach to budgeting reflects its keen awareness of the importance of careful planning and of the vital role budgeting plays in national decision making. National decision making involves plans, not merely forecasts. The budget is not primarily a forecast, although there are forecasting elements within it—for example, what the tax yield will be at present rates. Essentially that which the President budgets, that which an agency head budgets, and that which subordinates budget, are a series of plans and proposals, not merely a set of forecasts of what is likely to happen.

Each spring programs under way and those proposed for adoption are evaluated in terms of feasibility, need, progress and cost. A five-year forward projection is made during this spring preview period and shortly thereafter each agency head is given a planning target or series of targets to be used as a guide in the development of detailed agency financial and program plans. These combined agency financial and program plans are thoroughly reviewed during the fall months of the year in a process which culminates the following January with the President's submission of the Budget of the United States to the Congress.

Congress of course also uses the budget process, as a way not only to make decisions about the budget itself but also to make decisions about the scope and nature of an agency's program. For many agencies, the budget process provides the one regularly recurring opportunity for congressional appraisal of what has been taking place and is proposed to take place in the agency.

In order that budgets may represent good plans, it is necessary that the budget process lead to well-considered decisions on program needs. A budget should be so prepared and presented that it focuses consideration on the missions to be performed and on the steps which are necessary to perform those missions. For example: What is needed in order to have an appropriate defense posture? What are the needs for successful operation of a system of mail delivery? What should be the national program of reforestation? What are the Government's needs with respect to immigration and customs matters? The budget process must bring to attention and obtain decisions annually on over 5,000 programs of the Government.

These decisions are influenced, and necessarily so, by consideration of available resources. There is never as much money in sight as would be needed to carry out all of the programs which the various program administrators think desirable. Sometimes there are not enough persons available with skills of the type needed for specialized programs, particularly in such areas as research and engineering. Budgeting therefore must assist executives in setting priorities and determining the best allocation of available resources. Decisions on the budget as a whole are also influenced by the nation's economy and considerations of the role that the budget should play in the nation's economy. Budget presentations of the agencies might well give attention to the relationship between program proposals and the state of the nation's economy.

One of the hardest phases of budgeting occurs when two or more objectives seem to come into conflict. Such a clash takes place many times in the preparation of the President's budget. For example, the objective of a bigger program to meet national goals with respect to education may conflict with the objective of reducing the budget deficit. Again, the objective of reducing the gold outflow may conflict with the objective of economizing. Which objective should yield and which should triumph—to hold down payments abroad or to hold down total payments? The answers do not come easily, for there is no exactly right answer; decisions must be reached in the light of weighing the circumstances and alternatives in each individual case.

AGENCY BUDGET OFFICERS

Agency budget-making necessarily involves the participation of all senior officials in the agency but the agency's budget officer is its general focal point for budgetary endeavors. By the very nature of the budgetary process, the budget officer in most agencies has the major responsibility for reviewing and integrating the agency's budget and thus exerts a rather considerable influence on agency decisions. Among the various facets of a budget officer's responsibilities, these five may be distinguished as having special importance:

1. To aid the process of executive decision making, including decisions on programs, administrative requirements and finances.
2. To present the proposed program and financial plan of the agency, or of his segment of the agency, to subsequent reviewing authorities.
3. To communicate decisions made and guidance adopted at higher levels, with reference to program and finances, to and through his organization.
4. To influence decisions through his own store of information, analysis and advice.
5. To provide a focal point within his organization for efforts to obtain efficiency, eliminate waste and to see that the Government gets the highest possible return on every dollar spent.

In his budget-making responsibilities, the agency budget officer typically functions in a staff capacity and his contribution to decision making constitutes what probably is his most important role. Decision making requires facts, alternatives, evaluation of possible consequences and recommendations from subordinates. A competent budget officer accordingly draws on accountants, statisticians, line operators and many others within his agency for the factual data needed for budget presentations. Effective budget presentation involves a statement of and consideration of alternatives, both with respect to ways to accomplish the agency mission and with respect to the probable consequences of spending more or less than proposed for the purpose within the fiscal year.

Agency budget officers could make greater contributions to decision making if they gave more attention to the possible consequences of alternatives and submitted data thereon along with their recommendations. A consideration of alternatives is a basic part of the budget evaluation that occurs in the Bureau of the Budget, as policy issues are readied for the President's consideration. Above all, budget officers should remember that no budget is really made by the budget staff; it is made by the principal executive in charge of the Government agency concerned and should be made in the light of relative needs, alternatives and possible consequences.

SOME AGENCY PROBLEMS IN BUDGETING

Budgeting, involving as it does estimates of an uncertain future, is inherently a difficult process but not all of the problems encountered by agency budget staffs as they seek to carry out their responsibilities can be attributed to the uncertainty of the future. Many of the problems can be characterized as organizational in nature and some of the most troublesome problems are of an individual agency's own making. For discussion purposes, however, agency problems in budgeting will be considered under three general headings: Problems of Environment; Problems Inherent in the Budget Process; and Problems Relating to Budget Presentation.

An overall comment pertinent to all three of these headings concerns the regrettable diffusion of budget responsibility in a number of agencies. Too often in the last ten years or so, budget staffs have been stripped of significant portions of their responsibility. There are many aspects of the job of helping executives reach decisions which used to be lodged in the budget staff but are now found elsewhere. While "empire building" should be avoided, the splitting up of the former functions of budget offices may result in less coordinated staff work and perhaps less adequate budget plans. It is most important that there be the greatest possible coordination between the budget staff and other agency staffs concerned with planning, management, accounting, statistics, reporting and related activities.

Problems of Environment

A basic group of agency budget problems can be associated with the environment in which budgeting occurs. Probably the most common problem in this category relates to horizons and time span. Modern society has become so complex the Government simply cannot do a good job of budgeting by considering only one year at a time. It is difficult, however, to get some agency executives to look very far into the future. In the national interest, there must be more appraisal of long-range objectives and more long-range programming (even though firm decisions and commitments of money may not come for long periods of time) as a basis for sound annual budgets.

Some of the multi-year plans that have been presented to the Bureau of the Budget the past three budget seasons have been very good, but on the whole the quality of these plans has been disappointing. There has not been adequate multi-year planning on the part of the doers, the line officials in the agency who are going to carry out the plans and who really should initiate much of the planning. An over-concern with day-to-day operations—and lack of concern with long-run objectives—is a significant roadblock in the path towards better budgeting.

Probably a majority of the Government's agency budget officers consider as one of their problems the fact that they are always working in a "tight budget" environment. This criticism is the reverse of what the public generally thinks about the budget as a whole. Actually, the budget is always tight, but consideration is always given to worthwhile programs and financial needs. No agency is kept from voicing its aspirations in its budget submission for the President's consideration, although there may be disagreement as to how worthwhile are particular proposals.

Perhaps no catalog of agency budget problems would be complete without noting that an almost universal problem is lack of success in getting all the program authority and financial resources that an agency wants. Because any one agency's needs must be weighed against other needs and against overall factors relating to the fiscal policy and the nation's economy, it is not possible to budget as much for some programs as might seem warranted. But, after taking account of such elements of decision making, an agency officer may still improve his performance by establishing with successive reviewing levels the highest degree of confidence in his integrity. There is no substitute for confidence in the integrity of the budget presentation and in the integrity of the budget officer personally—confidence that his facts and figures are accurate, honest, reliable and completely frank. Of course, integrity alone is not enough; an agency must also have worthwhile programs, and worthwhile and genuine financial needs, in order to get its budget proposals accepted at successive levels of review.

Problems Inherent in the Budget Process

A very common complaint is that the budget process is too long—that it is too spread out, beginning too soon and ending too late. For no apparent reason, some agencies begin their annual budget process as early as February—17 months before the fiscal year starts. In every agency the overall process is undoubtedly too long and too spread out, and too many man-hours are devoted to it. There is a widespread need for critical self-evaluation of the budget process at various levels within Government.

A related problem is the difficulty of obtaining firm decisions at the time they are needed. Even when the process starts early, it becomes difficult to get decisions nailed down at the various levels of review. This is probably more characteristic of legislative program items in the budget than of continuing programs, but it applies to both. Are decisions being sought at an earlier stage than is absolutely necessary? How can decisions be obtained promptly when they are really needed? The answers to these questions may seem elusive, and they probably are, but part of the difficulty undoubtedly lies in too little attention to these areas within the agencies themselves.

Another problem, and a very serious one for many reasons, is the delay in congressional action on legislation and appropriations, which slows down preparation of the next budget. Even though most budget officials agree that budgeting should be done from a zero base, it is desirable to know what the congressional attitude has been toward the last budget before the next one is prepared, or at least before decisions on it become final. Congressional delays on the budget in recent years have been aggravated by the practice of requiring annual authorizations—the double budget system—for more and more programs. Almost 35 percent of the dollars in the latest budget are for programs on which Congress requires annual authorizations before the appropriations may formally be acted upon under the rules of Congress. That is, the agency must first present a request for legislation to extend the expiration date of a law or to authorize a larger amount to be appropriated, and obtain needed legislation, before the appropriation process can move very far. Late appropriations have become a common and unfortunate handicap for agency operations as well as for both budget execution and preparation of the following budget.

One final problem with respect to the budget process is that budget personnel are tied up the year around in too many routines. Not only is the annual budget preparation process itself long, but there are so many supplementals and budget amendments, special forecasts, special analyses, reports and other duties, that budget personnel have too little opportunity to think, to plan and to evaluate carefully. There is a need for more fortitude to keep the budget process in the normal cycle, and to eliminate consideration of supplemental estimates and budget amendments which should have been planned earlier or might wait until the next fiscal year. Perhaps, too, some of the routines of reports and some of the special analyses might be shifted from budget staffs to other portions of an agency organization.

Problems Relating to Budget Presentation

By far the most frequent criticism made of budget presentations is that too much detail is required. Part III of the Budget Appendix (details of personal services) might well be an early candidate for omission. But, as in the case of many other details, the law requires it, and members of Congress may well need such detail even if others find little need for it as a part of the printed budget documents. Often detail presently required stems from a real interest in Congress—for example, in budgets for automobiles—that in part has arisen because of past abuses of discretion by particular agencies or officials.

Some agencies express concern that budget submissions must include classifications of data that are of no particular interest to them. But they may overlook the fact that some classifications of data which are not of direct managerial interest in the agency may be of importance in managing the Government as a whole. Decision making with regard to the relation of Federal finances to the economy involves the analysis of information on the economic impact of Government transactions, even though an individual agency may not find such information vital in its own day-to-day operations.

Incidentally, agency personnel might be surprised if they knew how often the Bureau of the Budget resists requests and suggestions that additional details, classifications and other data be obtained from the agencies. The budget submissions are handy vehicles for carrying annual reports and statements of plans on a variety of subjects that are important but may make the total budget submission burdensome instead of helpful.

Another budget problem is the fact that the data obtained by budget offices are not always in the best form. A few budget submissions still need "activity" classifications that reflect the programs carried out, and they need data on the cost of carrying out those programs and on the changes in the resources available for future program needs. Many agencies still need to develop or improve their measures of program accomplishment. This is true also at various levels within many agencies.

Lack of appropriate accounting and budget liaison is still a problem in some agencies. Accounting offices sometimes give their budget offices data in a form that has to be reworked for presentation to a higher level, and budget assistants who rework the material may know what the required form is but often do not really know how to put the data into that form. The result is the compilation of queer and inaccurate budget schedules and statements, which must be revised subsequently. With respect to "actual year" data, there can be little reason for an accounting office not to provide the data in the form required for review and submission to other levels, and those in the budget office ought to use their time to better advantage than reworking data that comes from the accounting offices.

Inadequate budget justifications are a more general problem, applying to estimate material which department and bureau budget officers receive as well as to some they create. Many words saying that this is needed and that is needed do not demonstrate need, but this problem goes beyond the financial management community. Line officials may have legitimate program needs and legitimate financial needs, but some of them have not learned how to communicate their needs in a way that enables someone else to appraise and evaluate those needs wisely. More should be done to help officials outside the financial management community to learn how to explain and justify their needs.

COMMON OBJECTIVES

Throughout the budgetary process, agency budget officers and the staff of the Bureau of the Budget have a great common interest. Budgeteers at various "levels" are working in staff capacities for "line" officials who have the ultimate responsibility. All participants in the budget process thus have a common interest in seeing that the data and the considerations for decision making are presented in such a way that wise conclusions can be reached by those in decision-making roles.

By working together, agency budget officers and staff examiners in the Bureau of the Budget can do much to improve budget procedures. Their interests are mutual in making the budget process more effective as a means toward reaching decisions and providing for their execution. Many improvements have been made in the past 15 years and a few changes may have been made which have not represented progress. Additional improvements can be made if everybody concerned will undertake to cooperate in solving basic problems, working together towards the objective of making the budget process a better servant of those with responsibility for making Government decisions—both in the Executive Branch and in Congress.

17
Agency Budget Roles

Thomas J. Anton

Strictly speaking, no two agencies are or can be exactly alike. Differences in personnel, program, and purpose—no matter how slight—must exist between each of the separate agencies which make up the state organization.

Reprinted from Thomas J. Anton's, *The Politics of State Expenditure in Illinois* (Urbana: University of Illinois Press, 1966), pp. 44–52.

Does it therefore follow that each separate agency must pursue a different course in determining its finances? Not at all, for regardless of differences, every agency must prepare a "budget" every two years, and must do so within a framework established by the central fiscal agency, the Department of Finance. While the operations required by this framework do not produce the same consequences in each agency, they do encourage the development of decision-making rules which appear to differ very little from one agency to the next. These rules, in turn, are based upon certain assumptions made by budget officials concerning the nature of their political-administrative environment. The striking similarity of these assumptions and rules, as revealed in discussions with budget officers from a variety of departments, suggests the existence of what might be called an organizational subculture. We begin here, accordingly, by sketching out the assumptions and rules which constitute this subculture. In order to show the impact of the subculture on budget practices, a rather detailed examination of budget preparation in one agency is then offered.

THE SUBCULTURE OF BUDGETING

Doubtless one of the chief contributing factors to the uniformity of outlook among agency budget officials is the amount of schooling they have had in the operations of the state organization. Interviews in eleven major state agencies revealed that the average length of state service for the budget officers of these agencies was twenty-two years, with individual periods of service ranging up to thirty-four years (Table 17.1). Not all of these officials, of course, have spent all their years in the state service as budget officers, but each of them has prepared at least two budgets, and most have been involved specifically in budget preparation for a decade or more. Given this level of experience, and considering the stability of format and control exercised by the Department of Finance, similarity of views among this cadre of officials is to be expected.

Four assumptions are particularly important in shaping the point of view of state budgeters:

1. *The term "budget" refers to the forms distributed by the Finance Department which, when filled out, will appear in the budget document submitted to the legislature by the Governor.* By and large, budget-makers do not see themselves as makers of policy. When asked to describe his approach to the job of budgeting, the typical agency official will simply recite the procedures he follows in filling out the budget forms and submitting them to Finance. These procedures and forms need not have any necessary relationship to the agency appropriations finally approved by the legislature or, indeed, to any changes in agency policy which may develop after the "budget" has been submitted. As a result there is no need to

Table 17.1
Length of State Employment, Budget Officers in Selected State Agencies (as of
   January, 1963)*

Agency	Budget Officer's Title	Years of State Employment
Agriculture	General Auditor	22
Aeronautics	Controller	16
Conservation	Accounting Supervisor	9
Financial Institutions	Executive Assistant	17
Highways (Div. of)	Chief, Bureau of Administrative Service	34
Insurance	Clerk	28
Mental Health	Deputy Director, Administrative Service	29
Mines and Minerals	Secretary	20
Public Aid	Chief, Division of Research and Statistics	20
Public Health	Assistant to Director	20
Public Safety	Chief Clerk	27
	Average:	22

*Agencies in this table include all code departments (except Finance) in which I was able to interview the budget officer.

develop any rationalization of budget development from either a philo-
sophic or strategic point of view. "Budgeting" means nothing more than
filling out budget forms and . . . the skills necessary to accomplish this task
are frequently available in the form of a secretary or clerk who can add and
subtract and copy figures from Finance Department reports with reasonable
accuracy. Budget officials who think of budgeting in terms any larger or
different from these are exceedingly rare.[1]

   2. *The budget is prepared for someone external to the agency itself.*   The
very fact that the budget is seen as a financial statement that is not necessarily related to agency policies encourages agency officials to view the
budget as something essentially artificial, designed for external consumption only. Few of the small agencies make any attempt to utilize budget
categories to control expenditures, while attempts to fit the budget into
some over-all management plan are unheard of at this level. Indeed, many
smaller agencies rely more heavily on the reports issued by Finance than
on their own accounts. Moreover, even those officials who do emphasize
their own accounts for use in budget preparation tend to treat budgetary
accounts as obstacles to be overcome rather than as constraints to be
obeyed. As one such official put it, "Any budget officer with half a brain
knows perfectly well that he can cover up any expense he wants to cover
up simply by juggling his accounts; I've done it many times myself."

Though perhaps exaggerated, this statement does illustrate the widespread disregard for budget categories as mechanisms relevant to internal agency operations.

A similar lack of relevance is characteristic of many of the large agencies, such as Highways, which control their internal operations through highly sophisticated accounting systems. The difficulty at this level is that the relatively simple budget forms cannot easily accommodate more sophisticated systems of information, with the result that budgets prepared by these agencies become little more than watered-down translations of the accounts used to record agency activities. Conscious preparation of such "translations" not only emphasizes the artificial nature of the budget but also underlines its external, rather than internal, relevance. At least one of the largest agencies, for example, prepares two "budgets," one for itself (which is not available for inspection) and one for submission to the external reviewing authorities.

3. *The budget is not taken seriously.*   This is a somewhat loose way of stating the twin expectations of budget officials (a) that little time will be devoted to their budgets once they leave the agency itself and (b) that decisions on their budgets will *not* be made according to criteria which are either consistent or relevant to agency operations. Obviously such expectations must be oriented toward a "who" as well as a "how," and as far as agency officials are concerned the "who" is quite clear. All such officials who were interviewed agreed that the Finance Department seldom, if ever, made any changes in the forms submitted, though the examiners were reported to be occasionally helpful in solving technical problems or revealing errors in calculation. Similarly, and perhaps surprisingly, many agency officials did not view the Governor as an especially important decision-maker on budgetary matters. Some, in fact, appeared to have no very clear-cut notion of just what the Governor was supposed to do with regard to the budget. The important reviewing body, from the agency point of view, is the legislature, particularly its surrogate on budgetary affairs, the Budgetary Commission.

According to agency budget officers this commission seldom tampers with requests that do not exceed current appropriation levels. Instead, the commission tends to concentrate on supplemental proposals, almost all of which—again according to agency budgeters—are eliminated. Agency personnel are particularly anxious to point out that the elimination process is normally a quick one (the most common agency estimate of time spent before the commission was five minutes) which appears to have no obvious rationale. Thus one administrator reported that he had experienced hearings at which the only question asked by the commission membership was "Is this budget okay?" Another, from an agency with a long history of reductions imposed by the commission, argued that commission members appear to know very little about the operations of his agency and to have very little desire to learn. As far as he was concerned, hearings before this body are "mostly a joke." Still a third allowed that lengthy consideration and detailed questioning are not altogether unusual in commission proceedings, but when such events take place, policy differences are not the cause. Instead, "Some senator may not like the way a guy combs his hair, or maybe he just wants to get his name in the papers."

The inability of agency officials to see any obvious rationale for commission decisions leads to frequent criticism of the commission as "disinterested," "irrational," or even "ignorant." Inevitably, too, it creates a cynical reaction among agency people, who conclude that "something else" (i.e., politics) motivates commission decisions that they are unable to understand. However critical of the commission agency officials may be, they also assume that the commission is the principal—indeed the only—body likely to pay much attention to their budget requests and this is the principal hazard to the achievement of agency budgetary objectives. The difficulty of this hazard is enormously magnified, of course, by the lack of any publicly recognized rationale for its actions. Lacking such a rationale, decisions made by the commission appear to be completely arbitrary—an appearance which frequently generates considerable apprehension among agency personnel as they look forward to their biennial confrontation with the commission.

4. *The budget will be cut.* To say that agency officials are unable to see any rationale behind Budgetary Commission decisions is not to say that they are unable to predict the actions likely to be taken by the commission. On the contrary, their predictions are freely made, uniform, and generally accurate. Both the uniformity and the accuracy of these predictions stem from their familiarity with the informational categories developed by Finance and their expectation that the decisional rules implicit in those categories will be followed by the commission. With considerable confidence, the typical agency official predicts that his budget will encounter little or no questioning if the new request does not exceed the current appropriation, that any "lapse" that shows up will be closely scrutinized, and that any request for a supplemental increase will be cut, regardless of the adequacy (from the agency's point of view) of the justification provided.

Underlying such assumptions is a sense of the peculiar significance of the budget in Illinois finance. For any given agency the budget is seen as primarily a financial summary of current operations, designed to provide a financial cover for those operations and, when the occasion presents itself, to make room for some slight expansion. This view does not reduce the importance of the budget, but it does remove budget officers from any necessary connection to major policy decisions and it does permit them to act within the framework of a well-defined subculture of their own. To the extent that maintenance of the organizational status quo is problematic, as is sometimes the case, the rules of this subculture assume an importance that can hardly be exaggerated. For the most part, however, budgeting presupposes that the future is, and of right ought to be, a simple extension of the present and is therefore characterized by rules designed to ensure that result. Fashioned in anticipation of the "review" expected at the hands of the Budgetary Commission, these rules may be thought of as falling into two classes: rules for spending money and rules for preparing budgets.

Rules for Spending Money

Wise budget officers very quickly learn two things. First, they learn that questions concerning their budget requests almost always arise from the record of expenditures made by the agency. Second, they learn that the accounting system is sufficiently ambiguous to offer them considerable leeway in determining charges to be made against particular accounts. Certain rules governing expenditures follow as a matter of course:

1. *Spend all of your appropriation and, if possible, a little bit more.*   This rule, which has been commented on above, flows directly out of the instructions distributed by Finance. Those who have appeared before the Budgetary Commission and who expect to do so again, however, are in a position to understand its deeper significance. Failure to use up an appropriation indicates that the full amount was unnecessary in the first place, which in turn implies that the Budgetary Commission did not do its job. Such an implicit slap in the commission's face is extremely dangerous and can lead to a reduction in the next appropriation. Spending slightly more than was appropriated to selected accounts (by a judicious use of accounts in which a surplus is expected), on the other hand, can lay the groundwork for an appropriation increase. At the very least, it can provide justification for maintaining the total over-all appropriation.

2. *Avoid any sudden increase or decrease in expenditures.*   Changes in expenditure levels are recorded by the Department of Finance. If brought to the attention of reviewing officials, such records tend to raise questions and create situations in which cuts are likely to be made. To avoid such questioning it is best to maintain a constant expenditure level, even if this requires a certain amount of juggling between accounts. It is particularly important to keep expenditures up during the first year of the biennium, because those figures tend to be given greatest weight by the Budgetary Commission.

3. *In case of conflict between these two rules, the former is to be preferred.* Not infrequently, maintenance of a constant level of expenditure turns out to be impossible with the result that some agencies approach the end of a biennium with large sums of money remaining unspent. Where this situation occurs it is normally better to spend as much of these remaining sums as possible, for several reasons. Chances are that the agency's budget re-

quest has already been reviewed, since meetings of the Budgetary Commission usually conclude by February of the legislative year. Thus expenditures which pick up during the final months of the biennium are likely to go unnoticed until sometime after the legislature adjourns. Review of such expenditures will come, if at all, some fifteen to twenty months later, when the commission will be far more interested in new projections than in past excesses, especially if the excesses help to prevent lapses.

Officials who follow these simple rules for spending their money will seldom do worse than to maintain what funds they have, for their careful husbandry of sums available will have created financial records which raise few questions and offer fewer opportunities for criticism. In the event that these rules are not, or cannot, be followed, it is still possible to achieve a similar result through application of an alternative set of rules governing budget preparation.

Rules for Preparing and Submitting Budgets

1. *Avoid requests for sums smaller than the current appropriation.*   This rule has been mentioned above and follows from the expected tendency of the Budgetary Commission to give little or no attention to requests that do not exceed the present level of support. In the context of the discussion provided in this chapter, however, it is possible to amplify this basic rule by adding others, as follows:

2. *Put as much as possible of the new request (particularly items with top priority) into the basic budget.*   For a variety of reasons it is frequently impossible to avoid "lapses." The imposition of a "freeze" on new employees during the 72nd biennium, for example, made it impossible for many agencies to avoid lapsing considerable sums, since they were unable to replace employees who retired or otherwise left state service. In such circumstances, the new basic budget should include the sums lapsed, even though this is a formal violation of Finance Department regulations for preparing "basic" and "supplemental" budgets. The Budgetary Commission can be expected to be sympathetic to agency desires to maintain what is considered to be "their" money. Or, if a "lapse" in one account provides the basis for a reduced basic request for that account, it is desirable to make up that reduction by asking for an increase in some other account, again on grounds that the increase really does not increase the current level of financial support. The basic principle here is that the current appropriation must be preserved.

3. *Increases that are desired should be made to appear small and should appear to grow out of existing operations (the appearance of fundamental change should be avoided).*   If a new program or change in program is desired, a large portion of its cost should be included in the basic budget. The remaining supplemental portion will then appear to be nothing more

than a part of ongoing operations and will have an accordingly greater chance of approval.

4. *Give the Budgetary Commission something to cut.*   Normally it is desirable to submit requests for substantial supplemental increases. This helps to divert attention away from the basic budget and, more significantly, provides the Budgetary Commission with an opportunity to justify (by eliminating such requests) its continued existence. The commission and other knowledgeable officials will understand perfectly if you do not press your demand for supplemental amounts with an extraordinary degree of enthusiasm.

The assumptions and rules delineated here represent a synthesis of ideas and attitudes toward budgeting expressed by numerous agency budget officers. If there is one theme which stands out, it is that agency budgeting cannot transcend the limits imposed by the conceptual categories used to shape the budgetary informational system. In addition to defining the kinds of statements that will be treated as "information," those categories shape the purposes that can be achieved through budgeting, the strategies likely to be effective in achieving them, and the rules for selecting strategies. The informational categories, in short, determine the way officials *think* about finances, and thus structure agency budget roles.

Note

[1]One such rare official is employed by the Department of Mental Health. Both the official and the Department are discussed below.

18
Internal Auditing Principles and Concepts for Federal Agencies

Ellsworth H. Morse, Jr.

On October 1, 1968, the Comptroller General of the United States released a revised statement of basic principles and concepts for the guidance of Federal agencies in the design and operation of their internal audit systems.[1]

Reprinted from *The Federal Accountant* 19 (March 1970): 34–50.

This statement replaces an earlier one issued by the General Accounting Office in 1957 to assist Federal agencies in carrying out an important objective stated in the Budget and Accounting Procedures Act of 1950, namely, that the management control systems of Federal agencies should include internal auditing.[2]

Section 113 of the act, for example, which is concerned with executive agency responsibilities, requires the head of each such agency to establish and maintain systems of

... internal control designed to provide ... effective control over and accountability for all funds, property, and other assets for which the agency is responsible, including appropriate internal audit.

In addition, section 117 of the act, which is concerned with the audit responsibilities of the Comptroller General, specified that he give

... due regard to generally accepted principles of auditing, including consideration of the effectiveness of ... internal audit and control, and related administrative practices of the respective agencies.

The purpose of the revision is to reflect the benefit of over 10 years experience in the development and practice of internal auditing in Federal agencies and programs. As the foreword by the Comptroller General, Elmer B. Staats, to the revised statement notes, it also reflects:

... the benefit of extensive discussions with representatives of agencies, staff members of congressional committees and individuals outside of Government with experience in private industry and other public and private organizations.

The revised statement also gives recognition to the specific interest of the Government Activities Subcommittee of the House Government Operations Committee on this subject. In 1962, this committee incorporated into its studies of the efficiency and economy of operations in a number of Federal departments and agencies a review of their internal audit function. In a report[3] released the next year, the committee expressed strong endorsement of the need for strong internal audit systems in the Federal agencies and set forth several criteria which in its opinion should be applied by Federal agencies in their systems. Since the committee's report represented an important and constructive statement on the subject, pertinent excerpts from the report were appended to the revised GAO statement.

GAO AUDIT POLICY

GAO's concern with good internal audit systems is a direct outgrowth of its responsibilities for making audits of the affairs of Federal departments and agencies and promoting the development of good financial management systems throughout the Federal Government.

In the evolution of auditing concepts away from detailed examination of all transactions to a pattern of testing the effectiveness of internal control systems of the organization being audited, the role of internal auditing gradually assumed greater importance insofar as the external or independent auditor was concerned. This change has been just as applicable in government auditing as in independent audits of private enterprises.

In enacting legislation in 1945 providing for GAO auditing of Federal corporations,[4] the Congress directed the Comptroller General to audit the financial transactions of Government corporations "in accordance with the principles and procedures applicable to commercial corporate transactions." This important principle laid the foundation then for applying in Federal auditing the same basic approach that had been successfully developed by independent public accountants for private industry. In essence, this approach called for a review and evaluation of the effectiveness of the audited organization's system of management control first as a basis for decision on the extent to which the independent auditor would perform detailed audit work in order to support his conclusions or opinions.

This concept was applied in the GAO audits of Government corporations under the 1945 legislation from the start. One of the first major reports on a corporation audit under this legislation pertained to the Reconstruction Finance Corporation for the fiscal year 1945. Volume 1 of this report (it was a 10-volume report) expressed the conclusion that the "internal audit activity in RFC . . . has been less effective than we would consider acceptable."[5] After reviewing at some length how the internal audit organization was operating, as brought out during the GAO audit, the report went on to state:

We find, in summary, that the internal audit activity during the period ended June 30, 1945, except insofar as the lending activities were concerned, was administered unaggressively, without adequate imagination, and with considerably less useful over-all result than the Corporation would have been justified in expecting. Whether this condition may be attributed primarily to circumstances existing within the chief auditor's office, or whether it should be attributed to the general approach to management adopted by the Board of Directors is not known to us.[6]

The comprehensive audit policies of GAO have always provided that the nature and scope of its audit operations be determined with due regard to the effectiveness of the management control system of the agency being audited. Internal auditing has been regarded as a key part of each control system. Accordingly, direct GAO concern with internal audit systems continued with the extension of comprehensive auditing into all departments and agencies of the Federal Government. An early example may be found in the audit report on the United States Maritime Commission for the fiscal years 1948 and 1949. That report stated:

Internal auditing has not been utilized by the Maritime Commission in the management and conduct of its affairs . . .

Assurance of adequate control and protection of the Government's interests cannot be obtained without effective internal auditing . . . Internal audit activities must be Commission-wide, unbiased, and free from influence which may alter the scope of the auditing program or color the reporting thereon.[7]

Joint Financial Management Improvement Program

Effective internal auditing in Federal agencies has been one of the important objectives of the Joint Financial Management Improvement Program since its beginning over 20 years ago. In a joint policy statement dated January 6, 1949, the Comptroller General, the Secretary of the Treasury, and the Director of the Bureau of the Budget, cited as one of the underlying concepts of the joint program the need for "an audit independent of the executive branch which will give appropriate recognition to necessary features of internal audit and control."[8]

The current statement of the objectives of this program specifies as one objective: "Establishment of suitable internal control practices, including internal audit, in the agencies."[9]

Annual published reports of progress under this program have regularly included information on improvements achieved in internal auditing systems in various Federal agencies.

RELATION TO ACCOUNTING PRINCIPLES AND STANDARDS

As a principal partner in the Joint Program and in furtherance of its statutory mandate to promote good financial management systems in the Federal agencies, GAO is also continuously concerned with encouraging strong internal auditing systems. In August 1952, for example, the then Comptroller General, Lindsay C. Warren, addressed the heads of Federal departments and agencies with a statement on the contribution of accounting to better management which included the following brief but vigorous exposition of the importance of internal auditing to a good management system:

Internal controls essential to good management—to which accounting can so effectively contribute—require a carefully planned organizational structure, well-defined operating policies and procedures, clear delegations of duties to subordinates, competent personnel, and a strong internal audit program. A broadly constituted internal audit program provides the administrator and his subordinates not only with the auditor's findings on financial transactions but also with objective views of the manner in which policies and procedures, whatever their nature, have been carried out along with recommendations for improvements. Prompt action on such reports is, of course, a necessary step in the functioning of the system of internal control.

This concept was similarly stated in the first comprehensive statement of accounting principles and standards for guidance of Federal agencies issued as Accounting Principles Memorandum No. 1 by the Comptroller General later in 1952 pursuant to the Budget and Accounting Procedures Act of 1950.

In the restatement of accounting principles and standards for Federal agencies, published in 1965 by the then Comptroller General, Joseph Campbell, the essential importance of internal auditing in an effective internal management control system was expressed as follows:

> The performance of all duties and functions should be under proper supervision. All performance should be subject to adequate review under an effective internal audit program so as to provide information as to whether performance is effective, efficient, and economical; management policies are adhered to; applicable laws and prescribed regulations are complied with; and unauthorized, fraudulent, or otherwise irregular transactions or activities are prevented or discovered (2 GAO 7).

SECOND HOOVER COMMISSION ENDORSEMENT

The First Hoover Commission (1947–49) did not deal with the internal audit function. However, in its study of budget and accounting functions in Federal agencies, the Second Hoover Commission endorsed the need for internal auditing. Its report, issued in 1955, called attention to the need for such systems in the Federal agencies and recommended that the Bureau of the Budget and GAO "make an intensive study to determine the adequacy of internal auditing in Government agencies and what steps should be taken to improve it."[10]

The Commission's Task Force on Budget and Accounting observed that internal auditing organizations that had been inaugurated in many agencies were still in the pioneer stage of development and that really effective and useful internal auditing was rare.[11]

In commenting to the House Committee on Government Operations on the Commission's recommendation for an intensive study, the Comptroller General stated that as a regular part of its comprehensive audit program and in the discharge of its accounting systems responsibilities, the GAO continuously studied the adequacy of internal auditing in Government agencies and made recommendations designed to improve the quality and effectiveness of their internal audit programs, where appropriate.[12]

The Bureau of the Budget informed the same committee that the subject of internal audit was given continuous attention under the joint accounting program and that it would consider with other agencies having leadership responsibilities for this program "the question whether the current emphasis on internal audit improvement will achieve the objective sought by the Commission or whether there should be established a special project or projects in this area."[13]

No special joint study of the internal audit function in the Federal agencies was ever made in response to the Commission's recommendation, however.

REVISION OF GAO STATEMENT

The 1957 GAO statement on internal auditing was widely used in the Federal agencies for general guidance in the development of their internal audit systems and in training programs of the Civil Service Commission and individual Federal agencies. With the passage of time and more experience with the function, not only in the Federal agencies but in industry, a major revision of the original statement was undertaken to provide a clearer and more comprehensive presentation of the basic principles for application in the Federal Government in the light of experience and in the face of vastly increased Federal expenditures and new and expanding programs.

What kinds of changes have been introduced into the revised statement? A detailed comparison of the revised statement with the 1957 statement is not feasible here but an identification of the major changes with some explanatory comments should be useful.

CENTRALIZATION OF FUNCTION

One very important change was the much stronger emphasis placed on the value of a single centralized internal audit organization within a Federal department or agency. The 1957 statement reflected the general viewpoint that the pattern of organization was a matter for top agency management to decide and that the method of organization was not important as long as the needs of top management were effectively served, appropriate internal reviews were made, all internal review work was properly coordinated, and duplication avoided. The 1957 statement also recognized the possible desirability of combining internal and contract auditing in one organization.

The revised statement delineates clearly the advantages of a single internal audit organization reporting to the agency head or to a principal official reporting directly to the agency head. The advantages[14] cited include:

Greater independence.
Broader viewpoint fostered on the interrelationship of organizations and
    functions within an agency.
Improved position for making systematic and independent evaluations
    of and reports on agency programs, activities, and operations.

Increased ability to attract and retain good managerial and staff capability.

Better staff utilization.

Better coordination of audit effort.

ORGANIZATIONAL LEVEL OF INTERNAL AUDIT FUNCTION

The advantages of a centralized organization are closely tied in with the level in the department or agency at which the internal audit organization is located. The revised statement specifies that the internal auditor must be independent of the officials who are directly responsible for the operations he reviews. In order to be appropriately independent, he must therefore be located at the highest practical organizational level. Preferably, the statement points out, he should report directly to the agency head or to a principal official who does report directly to the agency head.

This requirement is much more specific than that reflected in the 1957 statement. There the general concept was stated that the internal auditor should be responsible to an official at a sufficiently high level to assure adequate consideration and action on his findings and recommendations. The stronger requirement in the revised statement reflects the increased importance of the internal audit function in the Federal agency management control systems, at least in the eyes of the General Accounting Office. It also reflects the experience of those agencies where the internal auditor has been organizationally located at the highest levels—increased stature, better management of function, more efficient operation, better staffing, etc.

Arriving at the position stated in the revised statement required a very thorough consideration of a number of interrelated factors. Among these were:

- The variety in size, nature, and complexity of the different organizations comprising the Federal establishment.
- The known variations among Federal departments and agencies in top management concepts and philosophies of management control and operation.
- Differing attitudes toward the usefulness of the internal audit function as a part of a management control system when related to other mechanisms in existence.
- Turnover in department and agency head positions.

From the standpoint of expressing a guiding principle, it would have been easy to simply state that the internal auditor should report directly to the head of his department or agency in all cases. While this is considered to be a desirable pattern where the agency head has a strong interest in this function and is willing to devote time to it, not all agency heads take this view. It was concluded that it would be unrealistic to ignore this fact and therefore the alternative was included of having the auditor report to a principal official who did report directly to the agency head. At this stage of evolution of the internal audit function—and it is still a relatively new function in management control systems—this requirement places the function at a suitably high level and we will look to further experience with it as a guide in refining these principles and concepts in the future.

One factor that was considered very important was to have the internal auditor report to an official who is a strong supporter of the function. Without such support, an internal auditor's place in an organization can be precarious. There is little to be gained and much to lose from the standpoint of improved management control systems by having the organization chart show that the internal auditor reports to an agency head who has no real interest in or time to devote to its operations. It is much preferable to have the internal auditor accountable to a principal official who understands the function and knows how to make use of it to improve management in the agency.

Even where the internal auditor reports to a principal official other than the agency head, the revised statement points out that some involvement by the agency head is needed. For example:

- The official to whom the internal auditor does report should have direct access to the agency head.
- All significant audit findings should be made available to the agency head.
- The agency head should satisfy himself that the official to whom the internal auditor reports encourages the auditor to exercise latitude in determining the scope of his work and reporting on it, including coverage of activities under the official to whom the internal auditor reports.
- The agency head should concern himself with the scope and effectiveness of the internal audit function, its staffing, and the adequacy of attention paid to audit findings and recommendations.
- When the internal auditor deems it necessary to the fulfillment of his responsibilities, he himself should have direct access to the agency head.

In a statement of internal audit principles and concepts addressed to the diverse organizations that make up the Federal Government, the possibility of internal audit staffs being located in subordinate organizations could not be ignored. While a strong case for centralization of all such staffs is made, the revised statement notes that when internal audit staffs are located in subordinate organizations, the following conditions should apply:

- Such an arrangement should not be made or continued unless the staff is of sufficient size to attract and retain qualified personnel and to make possible the productive and flexible use of staff resources.

- Decisions on establishing such staffs should be made or approved by the agency head.
- The central internal audit activity in the agency should furnish general policy direction and coordinate the efforts of such staffs.
- The audit work of the staffs in subordinate organizations should be used in carrying out the work of the central internal audit organization and the effectiveness of the work at the lower level should be evaluated.
- The internal audit group in a subordinate organization should be accountable to an official at a sufficiently high position to assure access to any activity in the organization and adequate consideration and action on its findings and recommendations.

SCOPE OF OPERATIONS

The 1957 statement suggested a broad scope of operation of agency internal auditors. The revised statement retains this breadth with some changes in emphasis and wording and enunciates clearly that the scope of work should not be restricted. The suggested scope of operation is described under the following broad categories:

Appraising performance
Evaluating efficiency and economy
Testing the reliability and usefulness of records and reports
Examining financial transactions

The statement also cautions against diluting the auditor's capacity to function by assigning him responsibility for developing and installing methods, systems, or procedures. His best contribution to improved management comes through his independent evaluations of performance of all kinds and such evaluations should include identification of methods or procedures that need improvement. Actual design and development of such improvements should be performed by experts in the field, rather than divert auditors away from their primary purpose.

The role of the agency head in defining the auditor's scope of operations is important. The statement brings out that the duties of the internal auditor should be clearly stated by the agency head. This information should be disseminated throughout the agency so as to promote proper recognition of his place in the management system.

The statement of this requirement follows, and needs to be considered in the light of the expressed caution against restricting the scope of the internal auditor's activity. As a practical matter, while a very broad scope of operation is favored, the top management has to fit the internal audit function into a management system that is seldom started from scratch and one which often includes other arrangements for checking on performance. In addition, top management will tend to have preferences as to the areas where they will look for the assistance from the internal auditors. Finally, independence in internal auditing, important though it is, is still a relative matter and can never be complete.

As a part of a management system, internal auditors are bound by the management concepts and attitudes within the organization they serve. Even though their charter may be unlimited, there are practical constraints on their competence and freedom to examine into everything. These constraints are particularly applicable in the scientific and technical phases of management and operations. They may also be applicable to the level of management performance within an organization since the internal auditor's scope of operation is one to be set by the top management itself and not one of functional right. Top management may prefer to have the internal auditor concern himself with other phases of operation than top management performance.

RELATION TO EXTERNAL AUDITING

The term external auditing has come to be applied to auditing of the performance of third parties who render service to an organization.

This subject was included in the 1957 statement under the heading of contract auditing. There its importance as an aid to good contract administration was brought out and the principle was clearly stated that such auditing should be reviewed from an internal auditing standpoint to ascertain on behalf of the management whether it was being carried out properly and effectively. As far as organizational arrangement was concerned, the 1957 statement left the matter for management decision in particular circumstances—the contract auditing could be performed by a separate group or if practical considerations so dictated, the internal and contract audit functions could be assigned to the same group.

The revised statement retains the concept of flexibility as to the best organizational arrangement for the internal and external auditing functions.

The concept is based on the fundamental proposition that quality and effectiveness of performance of the audit function are the primary tests of usefulness in a management control system rather than a uniform organizational arrangement. In this case, if all of the audit work is properly performed and management's needs—at all levels—are served, the organizational alignment is not important. If these objectives are not accomplished, however, the method of organization should be considered as one of the possible contributors to ineffective performance.

The revised statement also reasserts the principle that, regardless of the form of organization adopted, provision should be made for independent internal review of the external audit work in the same manner as other operations are reviewed to ascertain whether it is being properly performed.

In addition to Federal agency contractors, the revised statement also refers to grant and loan programs as an important area of third party auditing. Federal programs involving grants of funds to State and local governments have expanded greatly since the earlier statement was issued. For example, from a level of about $5 billion in 1958, such outlays have risen to about $21 billion during the current year and the estimate for fiscal year 1970 is about $25 billion. The problems of auditing these large, numerous, and growing programs are requiring increasing attention and there are no pat answers to determining the best way to provide appropriate and effective auditing and at the same time avoid over-auditing.

Approaches followed in the past do not necessarily point the way to the most efficient and effective way to provide audit coverage for these massive programs in the future. The concepts being tested in the Department of Health, Education, and Welfare which administers the greatest number and some of the largest Federal grant programs are to be followed with great interest. There, from both organizational and functional standpoints, a distinction between internal and external auditing has been subordinated and efforts are being made to examine the operations of both agency personnel and of grantees as an integrated review of performance under a program. Under this approach, the audit resources to be applied will include not only the agency's audit organization but also the work of auditors in grantee organizations (such as State auditors) and independent public accountants.

PERSONNEL

The 1957 statement noted the need for competence and experience as a prerequisite for carrying out internal auditing of the scope contemplated. It also recited some of the subject matter areas in which the internal auditor in a Federal agency needed to be well informed.

The revised statement restates the essential requirements as to the nature of auditor training and qualifications. Then, recognizing both the expanding scope of operation of internal auditing and the utilization by managers of additional techniques, the revised statement adds several additional fields in which a working knowledge is needed. These include statistical sampling, electronic computers, management information systems, economics, and operations research. While accounting with auditing training and experience is still noted as the most common background for internal auditors, staff specialists in such fields as mathematics, engineering, and computer operations are mentioned as desirable when warranted by the nature of an agency's programs and activities.

OTHER CHANGES

The section on reporting by the internal auditor has been expanded to spell out more specifically to whom (in general terms) audit reports should be submitted.

A new feature of the revised statement is the inclusion of a resume of reporting standards requiring observance if internal audit reports are to be effective.

The section of responsibilities for following up on audit findings and recommendations has been clarified by pointing out that primary responsibility for action and follow up on these rests with the management itself. The internal auditor should, however, keep informed on the nature of management's consideration of his recommendations and whether satisfactory corrective action has been taken. The statement further suggests that agency internal auditors also concern themselves with GAO audit findings and recommendations.

GAO REVIEWS AND EVALUATIONS

In addition to inquiring into the nature, extent, and quality of internal audit work with respect to agency operations being examined by GAO, the GAO audit program includes the making of reviews from time to time of the overall functioning of agency internal audit systems. Reports on such work are sent to the Congress when deemed warranted by the significance of the findings or the importance of any recommendations being made. Otherwise the reports are addressed to the agency heads concerned.

In a special summary report on this work submitted to the House and Senate Government Operations and Appropriation Committees early in 1969, the Comptroller General expressed the belief that significant progress had been made toward achieving effective internal audit systems in the Federal agencies. He noted that GAO had found that in a number of cases the internal audit organizations were doing a satisfactory job of providing management with independent, objective, and constructive appraisals of the financial and operating activities of the agency. In other cases, a need for improvement in the organization or functioning of the internal auditors was found and recommendations were made as to such matters as:

- Consolidating separate internal audit activities into a central organization in the department or agency responsible to the highest practicable level.
- Relocating the existing internal audit organization at a higher level in the agency to obtain greater independence and objectivity.
- Expanding the internal audit function commensurate with the needs of the agency.

- Making more comprehensive reviews with increased emphasis on evaluations of operating efficiency and economy.
- Assuring that important matters disclosed through audits are brought to the attention of top-level management.
- Following up on recommendations contained in internal audit reports to assure that proper action is taken on them.
- Improving the documentation of internal reviews so that adequate evaluations could be made of the quality and scope of audit work performed.

CONCLUSION

As the magnitude, variety, and complexity of Federal Government operations continue to grow, the need for good internal audit systems in all departments and agencies will increase. And the opportunities for internal auditors to be of assistance to agency managers in managing and administering public programs, activities, and resources will also grow.

The Congress looks to the executive branch agencies to carry out Government operations and programs not only effectively, efficiently, and economically but, in doing so, to prevent irregularities, abuses, and illegal actions with respect to public resources. The executive agencies must utilize all available mechanisms to achieve these easily stated but difficult objectives. Internal auditing is recognized by the Congress as one of the needed management functions in Government operations to help achieve the kind of control and results sought in the conduct of Federal programs and the related employment of public funds and resources.

The principles and concepts for good Federal internal auditing systems as spelled out in the Comptroller General's statement were published to assist Federal agencies in the further strengthening of their management systems. The revised statement distills the best of experience gained so far with the internal audit function and further refinements in the statement can be expected in the future as more experience is gained.

Notes

[1]This statement was issued in pamphlet form and also is included as a chapter of Title 3 of the *GAO Manual of Policies and Procedures for the Guidance of Federal Agencies.*

[2]The 1957 statement was printed in full in *The Federal Accountant,* December 1967, pp. 36–49, and in *The Internal Auditor,* March 1958, pp. 13–25.

[3]Report by the House Committee on Government Operations, *Survey of Selected Activities,* Part 1 ("Efficiency and Economy in the Department of Commerce"), House Report No. 456, 88th Congress, 1st Session, June 25, 1963.

[4]First by section 5 of the act of February 24, 1945 (59 Stat. 6) and later the Government Corporation Control Act, approved December 6, 1945 (59 Stat. 597).

[5]Report on Audit of Reconstruction Finance Corporation and Affiliated Corporations for the fiscal year ended June 30, 1945, Volume 1, printed as House Document No. 316, 80th Congress, 1st Session (1947), p. 18.

⁶*Ibid.*, p. 100.

⁷Report on Audit of United States Maritime Commission for the fiscal years ended June 30, 1948 and 1949, printed as House Document No. 465, 81st Congress, 2d Session (1950), pp. 94–95.

⁸This document was signed by Lindsay C. Warren, Comptroller General of the United States; John W. Snyder, Secretary of the Treasury; and James E. Webb, Director of the Bureau of the Budget.

⁹"The Joint Financial Management Improvement Program in the Federal Government of the United States, Its Scope, Objectives, Methods—1967," p. 6.

¹⁰*Budget and Accounting,* a report to the Congress by the Commission on Organization of the Executive Branch of the Government, June 1955, p. 60.

¹¹Task Force Report on Budget and Accounting in the United States Government, Commission on Organization of the Executive Branch of the Government, June 1955, pp. 77–78.

¹²Letter dated October 26, 1955, to Chairman, Committee on Government Operations, House of Representatives, included in Committee Print on Budget and Accounting: Executive and Legislative Reorganization Subcommittee of the House Committee on Government Operations, 84th Congress, 2d Session (May 12, 1956), p. 14.

¹³Letter dated February 20, 1956, included in same Committee Print, p. 19.

¹⁴Some of these advantages were referred to in the research study of this function in the Federal Government made by a Federal Government Accountants Association committee in 1962. *Internal Auditing, Review and Appraisal in the Federal Government,* Research Bulletin No. 2, Federal Government Accountants Association, p. 12.

19

An Integrated Framework for Conceptualizing Alternative Approaches to State Audit Programs

Lennis M. Knighton

INTRODUCTION

Over the past few years, there has been considerable discussion of alternative approaches to conducting state post-audit programs; and terms or expressions such as Performance Auditing, Operational Auditing, Financial Auditing, Compliance Auditing, and Program Auditing have become popular themes for discussions at professional meetings, audit seminars, and legislative hearings. Yet, in spite of the vast interest in these topics and the many attempts to explain them, both in seminars and in writing, there still exists today a tremendous confusion over the terms that are used and the concepts that are embodied in them.

Reprinted from *The Federal Accountant* 20 (March 1971): 6–23.

As one who has contributed extensively to these discussions, both as a speaker and as an author, I have become increasingly aware of the need to develop a framework that permits the integration and correlation of these concepts one with another. The purpose of this paper is to attempt the development of such a framework.

This effort is necessitated, as well as compounded, by several important factors that should be recognized at the outset. First, proliferation of terminology seems to have become the favorite sport of authors and speakers everywhere, and the subject of auditing has certainly not escaped this trend. Moreover, with numerous individuals at every level of government struggling to come to grips with this important but long-neglected function, each trying to build a more appropriate structure for audit policy and programs in the public sector, it is only natural that many labels or expressions will be used to describe the various approaches or concepts formulated, often with conflicting or contradictory meanings. No one can doubt the sincerity of those who have thus contributed to the many new terms that are used today. Neither can one fault their lack of familiarity with expressions or labels used by others in the field; for there has not been an effective exchange of ideas and information on this subject in specific, concrete terms. And while discussions abound and questions multiply, conclusive answers and clear definitions have not been forthcoming.

Certainly this short paper cannot hope to lay to rest the issue of terminology or to reconcile once-and-for-all the many conflicting and over-lapping concepts of audit in use today. What this paper can do, hopefully, is to set forth a proposed framework for bringing together and reconciling some of the more common concepts and to do so in such a way that others may build upon it, challenge it, or modify it until a meaningful generalized model emerges that can satisfy the needs of communication and understanding. What is proposed here, then, is merely a modest beginning of an effort that may well take years to finish; but the time has come to at least begin.

WHAT IS AN AUDIT?

Before one can meaningfully engage in discussion of alternative approaches to auditing, he must first agree on the definition of an audit. Yet, definitions themselves are seldom blessed with universal acceptance, partly because of the many ways in which definitions may be expressed, and partly because of the lack of agreement on the meaning or connotation of words used in definitional expression. For purposes of this discussion, however, an audit will be operationally defined as an examination of records or other search for evidence, conducted by an independent authority, for the purpose of supporting a professional evaluation, recommendation, or opinion concerning (1) the adequacy and reliability of information and control systems, (2) the efficiency and effectiveness of programs and operations, (3) the faithfulness of administrative adherence to prescribed rules and policies, and/or (4) the fairness of financial statements and performance reports that purport to disclose the present condition and the results of past operations of an organization or program.

This definition is admittedly comprehensive, flexible, and nontraditional; yet, it is sufficiently specific and descriptive that it conveys a common understanding of the nature, scope, and intent of audit effort. It is comprehensive so as to embrace each of the audit concepts to be discussed hereafter; it is flexible in recognition of the fact that not all audit effort is undertaken for the same purpose, in the same degree of depth, with the same breadth of scope, or by the same type of auditor. And it is of course non-traditional, as traditional definitions tend to be far too narrow and restrictive for our purposes or are sufficiently vague and imprecise as to be operationally meaningless. Finally, this definition encompasses essentially what is popularly called the "post-audit," although it may apply to "interim" or "concurrent" audit work as well. The "pre-audit"—the checking of vouchers or other claims before payment or settlement—is specifically excluded in this definition.

RECENT TRENDS IN STATE AUDITS

Not many years ago, only one or two audit concepts were even discussed in connection with state audit work. Most states adopted a policy of conducting "financial audits" of the various agencies and other state organizations, particularly of those agencies and activities which handled the collection and disbursements of large sums of money. Under the concept of financial auditing, procedures were developed to check the legality of expenditures and to insure honesty in fiscal affairs. The key tests made by the auditor were to determine that expenditures were properly documented and authorized, that they were for valid claims against the state, and that funds were properly receipted, accounted for, and safeguarded. Most states conducted such audits infrequently and on a very limited scale except in the central financial agencies, and some states only checked those areas where there was suspicion of fraud or other mishandling of public funds.

As state programs grew in size and complexity, however, the demands made of the auditor for additional information also grew. Consequently, the traditional financial audit became inadequate, and the audit scope began to expand into other areas. As this extension of the audit scope began, various names were given to the new phase of audit effort, including compliance audits, operational audits, performance audits, and many more. Some authorities viewed these new extensions of audit inquiry as simply an enlargement of the traditional financial audit, while others saw them as wholly new and different audit concepts, to be undertaken separately and apart from the financial audit. Neither extreme, however, has been victorious in the debate, as the overlapping nature of all of these concepts is apparent to anyone familiar with them. Indeed, it is precisely in understanding the similarities and the differences among them—the areas of overlap and duplication as well as the areas of unique contribution and the complementary purposes of each—that we can come to see and appreciate each element of the overall comprehensive, integrated, audit package or program in its true perspective.

THE COMPREHENSIVE AUDIT AND ITS VARIOUS PARTS

It has been common to speak of state audits as being either financial audits or performance audits and to include in the latter category all aspects of auditing not traditionally found in financial audits. Experience has shown, however, that such a simple dual classification scheme is inadequate for communicating and discussing the many activities that thereby fall into the performance-audit area. Yet, such a distinction is not without merit, for it at least recognizes the many extensions of audit scope to be something other than financial auditing.

One way of classifying the various audit concepts that retains this dual distinction yet recognizes the need for further division is to begin by first dividing the overall comprehensive audit into *financial auditing* and *performance auditing* and then to break the performance audit down into *compliance auditing, operational auditing,* and *program auditing.* Each of these terms must be more specifically defined so as to remove much of the ambiguity that presently surrounds them and also to insure that the manner in which they are used here is clearly distinguished from the manner in which other persons or organizations may define or use them. Briefly these distinctions are as follows:

> *Comprehensive Audit:*
> an all-inclusive, umbrella-like concept, encompassing all audit policies and programs, and including both financial audits as well as performance audits, as outlined below.
> *Financial Audit:*
> an examination restricted essentially to financial records and controls, for the purpose of determining that funds are legally and honestly spent, that receipts are properly recorded and controlled, and that financial reports and statements are complete and reliable.
> *Performance Audit:*
> an examination of records and other evidence to support an appraisal or evaluation of the efficiency of government operations, the effective-

ness of government programs, and the faithfulness of responsible administrators to adhere to juridical requirements and administrative policies pertaining to their programs and organizations.

Compliance Audit:

that portion of the performance audit which pertains to the faithfulness of administrative adherence to juridical requirements and administrative policies.

Operational Audit:

that portion of the performance audit which pertains to the efficiency of operations—focusing primarily on operating policies, procedures, practices, and controls; including the utilization and control of nonfinancial resources, such as property, equipment, personnel, supplies, etc.

Program Audit:

that portion of the performance audit which pertains to the effectiveness of government programs—focusing essentially on the management control system and the reliability of data contained in performance reports that purport to disclose the results of operations in terms of program accomplishment.

In the discussion that follows, these concepts will be more fully explained, and the opportunities as well as the limitations of each will be briefly explored. Also, a few examples of alternative testing or examination procedures that are useful in conducting the search for evidence under these concepts will be noted for purposes of illustration, although the constraints of this discussion prohibit extensive discussion of these testing procedures.

Finally, whereas the above classification scheme seems to set each concept apart from the others in a mutually exclusive fashion, they are all integral parts or components of a comprehensive audit program. Each fills a special role so that the whole is complete and perfect. Moreover, it is unlikely that many (if any) fully integrated, complete, comprehensive audit examinations of government programs have ever been conducted or will be conducted in the near future. Most audits focus on selected aspects of the overall approach, and seldom does an auditor even pretend to be conducting an overall, comprehensive audit. Moreover, in many cases the overall approach may not be desirable or practical. Yet, the conceptual model must be built completely, with every essential element identified and described, and with the relationships among them clearly disclosed.

COMPLIANCE AUDITING AND THE FAITHFULNESS OF PERFORMANCE

In every organization, public or private, there develops a body of rules and policies to which each responsible manager at every level of the organization is expected faithfully to adhere. These rules and policies are designed to set the boundaries within which managerial performance is desired and to provide direction and continuity in the decisions of responsible administrators. In government, these rules and policies have their origin primarily in the juridical and administrative requirements that are prescribed for each program or operation. In addition, commitments of various types are made between different levels of management as well as between executive officials and the legislature, and faithfulness in keeping these commitments is expected of all parties.

It is a basic management responsibility to see that adequate control procedures are established to insure compliance with these requirements. It is also a basic management responsibility to account for its own conduct as well as to review and evaluate the faithfulness of the performance of lower level executives and other public employees under its direction. The purpose of the compliance audit is simply (1) to test the adequacy and reliability of controls that are designed to insure faithful performance and (2) to ascertain that management has met its responsibility by complying with these requirements, policies, and commitments.

To conduct such an audit, the auditor must first become familiar with the rules and policies in question. To ascertain the juridical requirements, the auditor must gather together all of the statutory, judicial, constitutional, and other legal provisions and requirements relating to the organization or program to be audited. Once these items have been collected, they may be conveniently stored in a permanent data file where they will be available for each subsequent audit. New laws, judicial decisions, constitutional amendments, or other legal changes will need to be noted in the permanent file in order to keep it current and relevant, but the major work is the collection of the original information.

Likewise, administrative policies and requirements that are imposed on management by higher level executives or other regulatory agencies and authorities should similarly be gathered and stored in the permanent file. These policies should be examined to determine their conformity or consistency with the juridical requirements. Where conflicts are found, recommendations should be made to harmonize the differences; but juridical requirements, having the force of law, will always take precedence over other policies and requirements.

With this information assembled, the auditor is prepared to formulate an audit program, which is his plan of work covering the testing, examination, and evaluation of evidence to support a judgment concerning the faithfulness of performance. As in the case of the financial audit, the auditor is not normally concerned with determining that no violation of rules and requirements occurred, however insignificant, isolated, or exceptional that violation might be. Rather, the auditor is primarily concerned with determining that management controls are appropriate and adequate to insure that faithful performance will generally be achieved and that exceptions will be brought to the attention of responsible officials for follow-up action and review.

To accomplish this objective, the auditor must first test the control system. This testing may be accomplished through statistical sampling or other appropriate procedures as determined by the auditor. Part of the professional competence the auditor is expected to possess and bring to his job is an understanding of the essential elements of a good control system and the recognition of appropriate methods or techniques by which such controls may be tested and evaluated. This point is an extremely important one, and it has important implications for those who would prescribe long and detailed compliance questionnaires for auditors to fill out and sign. In the absence of professionalism in the audit examination, there is justification for the fear that adequate and appropriate tests may not be made; but where professionalism exists, and where professional audit standards are met, it is sufficient to provide the auditor with complete information as to the requirements to be met by management and leave it to the auditor to determine the nature, scope, and extent of tests to be made. This fact is as applicable to federal assistance programs and grants as it is to state requirements covering their own programs.

A corollary of this fact, however, is equally true. If auditors are to be worthy of this trust and confidence in their professional judgment and in their ability to satisfy the requirements of compliance audits without the long and detailed compliance questionnaires, they must meet unequivocally the demands of true professionalism by strictly adhering to the standards that are applicable to such audits. Failure to do so will bring upon them the harsh judgment of administrators and legislators alike, whereas true professionalism will win the confidence and trust that must accompany this function if auditing is to truly achieve its potential as an effective element of positive control in promoting faithful performance at all levels of public administration.

OPERATIONAL AUDITING AND EFFICIENCY IN GOVERNMENT OPERATIONS

Operational auditing is not a new concept or practice, for operational audits have been conducted for many years by internal auditors in industry as well as in some agencies of government. One of the oldest operational audit programs in government, and also one of the best examples of operational auditing today, is that found in the Atomic Energy Commission of the Federal Government. Several states have also extended their audit programs to include examinations of operational controls and practices, including most of the states that have in recent years formally embarked on performance post-audit programs. Because of the extensive literature available elsewhere on operational auditing, and due to the limitations of this paper, only a very brief sketch of operational auditing will be given here. However, the importance of understanding this concept and its promise for improved efficiency in government operations cannot be underscored too strongly.

Simply stated, an operational audit is nothing more or less than an examination of operating policies, practices, and controls, for the purpose of ascertaining those areas in which improved efficiency may be achieved in the use of public resources and in the conduct of government programs. Operational auditing extends beyond financial audits, for the latter are concerned solely with the receipt, control, and disbursement of funds, and with the acquisition of goods and services through public expenditures. For example, a person conducting strictly a financial audit would examine payroll records to determine that amounts were properly computed, that payments were made to legitimate employees, and that the employee was actually on the job during the period for which he was paid. A person conducting an operational audit would extend his examination to include a review of employment policies and practices, training and assignment of personnel, productivity records relating to work accomplished, incentive and reward systems, personnel turnover, and other such items. In other words, the operational auditor is concerned with whether or not policies exist and controls are adequate to insure that a maximum of public service is obtained through the use of personnel resources.

Similarly, the financial auditor tests to insure that equipment purchased is properly authorized, that it meets the required specifications, and that the proper amount was expended for its purchase. The operational auditor will test to determine whether the machine is properly maintained, whether it is operated by one qualified to do so, whether it is presently in use or sitting idle, and whether it is adequately meeting the needs for which it was acquired.

Many other examples might be given pointing out similar extensions of audit effort as required under the concept of operational auditing, but the point that is important here is that as an expert in control systems, the auditor can make a valuable contribution to improved efficiency through this type of examination and evaluation. Moreover, and perhaps more importantly, the auditor can best determine whether adequate, timely and relevant information is available to management to permit administrators themselves to monitor the efficiency of their own operations; for improvements in efficiency will always be the product of management action, not audit findings. And the important objective of operational auditing is to insure that management is aware of conditions as they exist and has the necessary information to make an informed judgment as to preferable alternative courses of action where they exist.

An important point to remember here is that managers are seldom able to be physically and personally close to the many operations of their organizations, and the auditor needs to approach his review of operations as if he were the manager himself. He must ask the question: If I were the manager of this program, what would I like to know about my operations in order to bring about improvements in efficiency? Where are the areas of overlap and duplication? Where are the weaknesses in inspection, control, and enforcement of quality standards? What assets could be more efficiently or effectively utilized? What are the causes of idle time, breakdown in communications, loss of employee morale, or lack of pride in workmanship? And the corollary questions must also be asked. What accounts for the exceptionally high performance of some personnel, for the improvements in productivity in certain areas, for the degree of coordination in the performance of some tasks, or for the absence of idle equipment (or equipment breakdowns) where these conditions are found? And how can the experiences of these strong areas assist in understanding how to improve the weak areas?

If the auditor conducts his audit in a positive, constructive manner, and if he has as his objective the rendering of a meaningful service to management, it is difficult to see how any manager would not welcome an operational auditor on the job and give him his full cooperation and assistance in the conduct of the audit. No manager is able to conduct such an in-depth review of his own operation unless his operation is extremely simple and very small. Every manager needs this type of analysis for his own knowledge and understanding, for improving his own operating results, and for accomplishing his own objectives. And that is the purpose of an operational audit —to assist management in improving the efficiency of operations.

Many organizations employ their own staff of internal auditors to undertake these operational reviews, and that is as it should be. Fundamental to every management control system is the element of internal review and evaluation of operating performance. Indeed, without such an internal audit staff or something comparable to it, an agency or department is missing one of the most important means of management information and most valuable tools of management control. Where such a program exists, the independent auditor will first be interested in testing the effectiveness and determining the scope of internal audit work, including managerial response and follow-up action. In addition, the independent auditor will want to look at overall organizational efficiency, including those aspects associated with top management responsibility which may be proscribed from internal audit review because of the location of the internal auditor within the organization itself. Wherever it occurs, however, and regardless of who the auditor may be, operational auditing holds great promise for improving the efficiency of public programs.

Finally, there are many examination, testing, and review techniques that have been found useful in operational auditing, and one who embarks on an audit of this type would be foolish and irresponsible not to familiarize himself with the extensive literature on the subject, especially that published by the Institute of Internal Auditors. A few brief examples will suffice for our purposes here.

One approach that has been found to be very effective in some instances is the "walk through" audit. This approach is especially useful where large amounts of equipment are required for an operation, where tangible products are produced or handled, and where construction activity is underway. As the auditor walks through the operation, he observes conditions as they are and raises questions about all sorts of items. What is this machine used for? What is this employee's responsibility? What kind of training or skill is required for this job? Who determines the specifications for this material? What happens to products that are spoiled? Why are these dusty stacks of supplies not being used? Who authorizes overtime? Who approves the printing of these items? Is there any possible use for this idle space? Who has access to these vehicles? These and similar questions will lead the auditor to examine and explore many items that he would never think of or discover merely sitting behind a desk in the office.

Another approach is to flow-chart the patterns of responsibility, the document flow, or the processing of various items. Using this approach an auditor may discover inconsistencies, overlap, and duplication that curtail efficiency. By extending this procedure to include estimates of time required for performing given tasks, the order in which tasks must be performed, and the control objective of each procedure or policy required, the auditor can often spot problems that increase costs and cause unnecessary delay in the rendering of service. Similar studies conducted recently by the Bureau of the Budget in Washington, for example, revealed that Federal processing time for some grant applications from state and local governments could be cut by as much as 60 to 80 percent, with corresponding savings in processing costs.

Still another approach that is extremely useful might be called the systems approach. Here the auditor attempts to analyze an activity or segment of an operation by (1) determining each task to be performed, (2) identifying the individual responsible for performing each task, (3) ascertaining the information needed by the responsible individual to insure appropriate action, and (4) identifying and evaluating each policy, procedure, or other element of operational control designed to promote improved performance of the tasks required. Such an approach would be useful in reviewing the acquisition, control, and use of drugs and pharmaceutical supplies in a hospital, for example. The auditor in this instance would not undertake to question the medical decisions of doctors in prescribing drugs for hospital patients, for these decisions are clearly out of the realm of the auditor's competence. But it is important to determine what steps or tasks are involved in the whole process of securing and dispensing drugs to hospital patients, to understand where responsibility for each step lies, and to ascertain what information is needed as well as what is presently available to support appropriate decisions by responsible persons. Further, it is important to identify each policy, procedure, or other element of control designed to insure that adequate quantities of the right drugs and supplies are acquired to meet hospital needs; to determine that inventories are stored and controlled in such a way as to minimize spoilage, loss, stock outs, and carrying costs; and to ascertain that all items are dispensed to the right parties, in the right quantities, according to the request of the doctor.

These are but a few of the approaches that are used by auditors in the conduct of operational audits. In most instances the auditor will probably find that operational auditing is most easily and naturally accomplished as simply an extension of financial auditing. While reviewing the financial aspects of drug acquisition, for example, why not also look at the operational aspects relating to drug storage and use? And what of the other acquisition policies and practices? These are the elements of control which most contribute to operational efficiency in government.

PROGRAM AUDITING AND THE EFFECTIVENESS OF GOVERNMENT PROGRAMS

The third and final classification of performance auditing is what we shall call program auditing. This term or designation is not nearly as well known as those already discussed, but the concept is equally important. The objective of a program audit is to test additional elements of the management control system and to collect other evidence to support an evaluation of the effectiveness of programs to achieve their intended or desired objectives.

There are really two parts or aspects to this type of an audit. First, the auditor must identify and evaluate the various elements of management control to judge their effectiveness in enabling management to chart or measure its own progress towards the achievement of the objectives sought. Second, the examination is conducted to determine the reliability of data included in management reports that purport to disclose program accomplishment.

The purpose or objective of a management control system is to insure that planned accomplishment becomes actual accomplishment, and the degree to which planned objectives are actually achieved is the measure of effectiveness in any operation. In order for management to successfully administer programs and accomplish the objectives, however, there must be a constant flow of relevant information to responsible officials so that timely and appropriate action can be taken as necessary to keep the program on target. Indeed, managing a program of any kind is not unlike sending a manned spacecraft to the moon and back. Prior to launch there must be extensive planning relative to all phases of effort to be undertaken, including the design of an information system to provide a steady stream of data on the progress of the mission. For each planned operation or activity, responsibility must be assigned in advance; and policies must be set not only to guide decisions in the normal course of events but also to handle possible contingencies in the event something unexpectedly goes wrong. Moreover, it is not sufficient just to provide for feedback of information; there must also be relevant performance standards against which actual data can be compared in order to evaluate the progress of the mission at every major decision point.

Finally, the control system is only complete when there is also a mechanism or means by which appropriate corrective action can be taken when necessary. Without any one of these control elements, successful completion of the mission would be difficult if not impossible to accomplish. The same is true with an organization and its programs. Each of these elements of control is essential, and each must be provided for in the planning process. It is the responsibility of management to see that each element of control is included in the overall management control system, and it is the responsibility of the program auditor to test for the existence and effectiveness of each element and to point out areas in which improvements can be made to strengthen the overall system.

It is the responsibility of management to account for the results of operations under its direction. This responsibility includes accountability not only for revenues and expenditures but also for program accomplishment. This fact is often overlooked by those who would send the auditor out to "find out what happened" under a given program, evaluate its effectiveness, and render a report of accomplishment together with recommendations for improvements. Management should be required to report what happened and to explain any deviations between planned and actual results. The function of the auditor, as it relates to performance reporting, should be only that of testing the reliability of data included in management's reports. The auditor is not one whose expertise renders him qualified to judge subjectively the effectiveness of program accomplishment. Legislators and executive officials who desire such information must agree in advance on the objectives, establish performance standards, and identify performance data or criteria that they are willing to accept as indicating effective performance. The same is true for executive officials when they give their approval to program and budget requests.

It is not enough, however, to simply agree on the kind of information to be included in performance reports. Effectiveness is defined as achieving one's objectives. Consequently—and this point cannot be overemphasized —legislators and executive officals must also agree on a statement of conditions that will exist when intended objectives are achieved. This statement of conditions, expressed in the same terms and based upon the same criteria that are to be reported in the performance report, will then constitute a set of performance standards by which management and others can evaluate program effectiveness. Only then will the program objectives become useful standards to guide management actions.

Finally, when there is agreement on criteria and standards, it is possible to design an information and reporting system that will systematically or scientifically collect the information desired in performance reports. Then, and only then, can the auditor meaningfully undertake to professionally evaluate the reliability of reported performance data.

True program auditing, as defined here, is seldom undertaken today, primarily due to the lack of performance reports and standards. The audit skills required for this type of examination are essentially no different from those required for operational or compliance audits, except that the auditor must understand additional elements of management control. The auditor is still testing and evaluating information and control systems. To require the auditor to go beyond the parameters of program auditing as set forth here is to require that he violate one of the most fundamental standards of professional auditing, which is that he never extend his examination into nor render a professional judgment on matters that are beyond his areas of professional competence. An auditor is an information and control specialist. And any auditor who yields to the temptation or demands that he go beyond his professional competence is both foolish and irresponsible. There are numerous opportunities for meaningful audit work that are well within his professional competence, and they can be found in each of the three areas of performance auditing as well as in financial auditing. When auditors have achieved their potential in these areas, new horizons will undoubtedly open up for public service in other ways.

SUMMARY AND CONCLUSION

We have seen that a meaningful classification scheme for state audits is possible, one that differentiates the various significant audit concepts and, at the same time, integrates those concepts into a meaningful framework of comprehensive audit theory and policy. The key to our analysis was the division of the performance audit into three parts, which we called Compliance Auditing, Operational Auditing, and Program Auditing. While these divisions appear natural, they are in fact simply conceptualizations of different areas of emphasis that actually overlap and coalesce; and it is naive to assume that one auditor can be assigned to perform compliance audits, another to perform operational audits, and still a third to perform program audits without each one treading frequently and significantly into the other man's land. Equally naive is the notion that financial audits and performance audits should be separated and undertaken by different auditors, for once again there are so many common features that would require analysis by both auditors that it would be far better to have one unified comprehensive audit program that correlates all of the tests and evaluations and reports on each aspect of performance in its proper perspective.

The model system outlined in this discussion cannot presently be found in full bloom in any of the states. That condition, however, does not detract from the usefulness of the model, for it is not intended as a description of practice. Rather, it is offered for the purpose of stimulating discussion, for increasing conceptual understanding, and for use as a standard against which each state may compare its own programs. Hopefully it represents an ideal toward which all states will continue to move. And while this model has been developed and discussed primarily with state programs in mind, the concepts should prove equally relevant to Federal agencies as well as to local units of government.

With Federal agencies now more willing than ever to rely on state and local audits to satisfy the requirements of Federal assistance programs, with studies now underway to define more precisely the audit standards applicable to government programs, and with most states facing serious fiscal crises where both efficiency and effectiveness in state operations are coming under increased scrutiny, there probably has never been a climate more conducive to the development and implementation of a comprehensive state audit program than there is now.

Happily, trends in recent years indicate that many states are moving in this direction; and it is not unlikely that history will record that the decade of the Seventies was for auditing what the decade of the Sixties has been for budgeting—a time of unparalleled progress in the development of bold new systems for making government programs more responsive to the needs of our modern society.

VI

Some Behavioral Contexts

Differences and similarities between people

The study of human behavior must wrestle with two apparently contradictory strains. For genetic reasons, as well as philosophical ones in the Western civilizations, the uniqueness of the individual must be stressed. However, it is clear that if people do differ in many significant ways, they are also similar in equally significant senses. Perhaps more precisely, many people in fact behave similarly under enough conditions that one would be foolish to insist in principle on the unmodified uniqueness of the individual. Such behavioral similarities in no way deny that people are also unique in significant senses.

There is no settling the tension between uniqueness and similarity. Behavioral science must continually seek generalizations that respect individual uniqueness. At the same time, however, behavioral scientists must frame their concept of human uniqueness in ways that acknowledge what is similar enough in nature that it cannot be ignored.

Public finance and budgeting similarly are in the differences/similarities business. The pieces reprinted in this chapter establish the point in diverse ways. By way of introductory support, note only that budgets set goals. Immediately, then, the budget-maker is involved in balancing the differences and similarities of those people subject to the budget. Will any thousand individuals best respond to a "tight" budget and work frantically even though the budget is realistically unattainable? Or does Sam work best when he experiences the success of "bringing a project in under budget," and the more so the better, as far as he is concerned? Setting a "loose" budget is appropriate in such a case, even though it is unrealistically high. The practical difficulty, of course, is that the budget-maker can seldom have it both ways. He must be acutely conscious of that point where enough people will respond similarly and positively enough to the standards he offers.

Chris Argyris's "What Budgeting Means to People" (Reading 20) goes right to the heart of important differences that characterize relations with budgeting and finance personnel in organizations. He finds that those specially charged with responsibility for budgeting or finance are likely to see their activity in different ways than those performing other activities of which budgeting and financial considerations constitute only a part.

The differences between the perceptions of those in budgeting and line foremen often are sharp, as Argyris develops them. For example, he compares the perceptions of the two types of organization members concerning this theme: What are the uses of budgets? As might be expected, budgeting personnel see their activity as crucial and strategic. Budgeting is "the watchdog" of the firm. Consequently, it closely identifies with top management because it supplies the data required for overhead control. Foremen have a different view. Budgets tend to complicate the foreman's job of dealing freely with individual cases, and budgeting personnel are seen as uninformed and pretentious, and sometimes as malicious.

These differences in perceptions suggest the delicacy of relations of budgeting and finance personnel with other organization members, especially because perceptual differences are reinforced by a wider family of issues that could reduce effectiveness. Argyris develops a list of major bones of contention between budgeting and line supervisors. Some of these complaints are pretty clearly what may be called "objective dilemmas." That is, they exist as an inherent part of budgeting and finance activities. The problems of handling objective dilemmas, whether more or less acute, will exist. Other difficulties may derive from "standard practices," that is, from established ways of doing things. Standard practices may be changed, of course. Thus this second class of difficulties may be sharply reduced if organization members are willing.

The variety of difficulties deriving from objective dilemmas and from standard practices can be illustrated briefly. Patently, for example, budgeting and finance personnel monitor money. Since money is the lifeblood of all organizations, both business and government, budgeting and finance often will be where the heated action is. Examples cover a far broader range as well. Reports about meeting budgets must treat "ancient history"; the interval during which the report is prepared may be shortened with "on-line" automatic data-processing equipment, but such history must be included. Other complaints are more or less clearly the results of usual practices. That budget reports are full of "results" but few "reasons," for example, is often true, but it also can be changed.

There are no easy ways to solve the many issues faced by budgeting and finance personnel. Inherent issues will remain, of course. Their severity can be reduced, but only by getting mutual cooperation, and the sharp differences in perceptions identified by Argyris suggest that getting cooperation will be difficult. Usual practices can be changed, but again only if free and open communication is possible. Sharp differences in perceptions close channels of communication, however, and perceptions are difficult to change. The magnitude of the challenge is plain.

In summary, given the sometimes-extreme differences in perceptions of budgeting people and those of foremen, the most reasonable prediction calls for considerable stress and inefficiency in coping with complaints, whether they derive from objective dilemmas or from usual practices. The summary might have to be softened as the organization, the level, and the job are varied. What Argyris saw in four factories does not necessarily apply universally to organizations. Even with such qualifications however, striking commonalities exist between Argyris's description and the relationships that exist in many actual organizations.

Notice we are firmly back in the differences/similarities business, based upon the preceding summary paragraph. The point can be made explicit as follows: Students and practitioners can neglect only at their own peril the differences in perceptions that Argyris isolates, nor can they neglect the marked similarities between other organizations and those described by Argyris.

Andrew C. Stedry provides useful elaboration on the differences/ similarities theme. Excerpts drawn from his *Budgetary Control and Cost Behavior* variously approach the crucial role of "levels of aspiration" in budgeting. Stedry surveyed the applicable literature and found it wanting for his purposes. Consequently, he designed a laboratory experiment to test the validity of a variety of hypotheses about levels of aspiration, performance, and kinds of budgets.

The issues confronted by Stedry in "Budgets and Forming Levels of Aspiration" (Reading 21) can be put in skeletal form. Basically, all people tend to develop "levels of aspiration," internalized standards of performance toward which they are committed to strive. "Estimates of performance" must be distinguished from levels of aspiration, in addition. For example, consider a Major Leaguer who could realistically be a .400 hitter in baseball. If he is motivated to extend himself only when he is below .350, however, his aspiration level in this case would be below a realistic estimate of performance. Of course, estimates of performance may coincide with levels of aspiration, and they can even surpass them.

Raising the issue of levels of aspiration immediately calls forth a host of important questions which beg for attention. What happens to his performance if any individual settles on a level that is easy to achieve? Or simply impossible? And do some people habitually overestimate or underestimate their actual performance? With what consequences in each case? Such questions imply great challenges to the behavioral sciences and far outstrip the available answers in theory or practice, but such are the questions which daily confront budgeters and financial officers.

Fortunately, some useful behavioral benchmarks exist. For example, an individual will tend to decrease his level of aspiration in response to failure. The practical implications seem direct. Budgets ought not be so demanding that they preclude success. If budgets are impossibly high, individuals will tend to reject them. Levels of aspiration may be lowered, as a consequence, by an approach that seeks to raise them.

Despite our existing knowledge, much remains to be learned about the interaction of internal estimates of performance, internal levels of aspiration, and externally imposed budgets. Consider only that in budgeting an external demand is more or less imposed on the individual to accept a specific level of aspiration. The situation is complex, for the individual may estimate that the required performance is unattainable under any conditions. In addition, even if the subject (S) estimates he could attain the budget goal, S's own levels of aspiration may be such that he is unwilling to do all that might be necessary to attain the external goal. Of course, S could accept the external goal as his own internal level of aspiration. The likelihood of his doing so will be a direct function of the specific management practices used in formulating and administering the budget.

Matters could be further complicated, but it should be clear that it is a glorious can of worms that Stedry must sort out. The excerpt below suggests the real progress he made, and it also should suggest the value of a full reading of the original source.

If nothing else, one of Stedry's findings has triggered a useful airing of differing points of view. Stedry notes that the experimental subjects (Ss) who performed best in his experiment were individuals who first received their high performance budget imposed by the experimenter (E) and then set their own aspiration levels. The worst performers were those Ss who first set their own aspirations and then were given E's high performance budget. Stedry explains:

An hypothesis which might satisfactorily explain this phenomenon is as follows: The high performing group formed its aspirations with the high budget levels in mind, while the low performing group rejected the high budget after forming aspirations with relation to their last performance . . . [Alternatively,] the stress, at least for some subjects, was so high that they may have been "discouraged" and may have ceased to try to improve performance.

Other possibilities also exist, but Selwyn Becker and David Green, Jr., in "Budgeting and Employee Behavior" (Reading 22) pick up the theme that "participation" in the making of budgets "can lead to better morale and increased initiative." Their analysis usefully covers much ground, starting with the basic belief that participation is no panacea but that it can produce beneficial results under specified circumstances. Roughly, participation is one way of increasing the chances that an employee's level of aspiration will be more or less consistent with the demands and standards in an organization's budget. Without participation, a wide divergence of individual aspirations and formal goals is more likely.

Care must govern any conclusions about the efficacy of participation, because the associated phenomena are complex. Becker and Green argue that sufficient employees respond similarly enough to participation that under specified conditions the student or organization for many practical purposes can devote less attention to the differences that patently do exist between individuals. Directly, management use of participation often can increase the likelihood that Ss will accept a budget as their own internal level of aspiration. The generalization does not hold for all individuals or all cultures, but it apparently applies quite broadly. Of course, participative techniques also could generate resistance to management's budget, as by permitting group forces to mobilize when employees come to feel that management is employing pseudoparticipation, the results of which are only accepted when they coincide with management's desires. Participative techniques generally have more sanguine effects, however.

The work of Stedry and Becker and Green constitutes a major effort to deal with critical phenomena, and hence the authors raise many more issues than they can settle.[1] That progress is being made, however, is clearly reflected in Roger L. M. Dunbar's "Budgeting for Control" (Reading 23). Dunbar begins with a model of the budgetary system, or "machine." He then surveys the research literature, much of it completed since the debate matching Stedry with Becker and Green, in search of answers to four questions relevant to the kind of inputs that will maximize the efficiency of the budgetary system, or machine:

1. Should the goals built in a budget be easy to reach, difficult, or even impossible to achieve?
2. Should the individual subject to a budget participate in the setting of its goals?
3. What system of financial rewards will increase the probability of goal attainment?
4. What is the relationship to goal achievement of rewards that are extrinsic and those that are internal?

Dunbar concludes with a list of specific unknowns that will help generate more detailed answers to these four questions than he can presently provide. Dunbar's account does suggest, however, that real progress is being made down some torturous roads.

This chapter must end as it began, coping with the apposition of differences and similarities of the various behavioral contexts within which public finance and budgeting are performed. Epigrammatically, the level of aspiration of this chapter has been to introduce the reader to some of the behavioral complexities that probably will be essentially unraveled within our lifetimes. Today, however, these behavioral complexities remain as massive experiential Everests that still defy the scientific mountain climber. No student of administration, to justify the attention given here, can be unaware that the complexities are there and must be conquered.

John W. Cooley provides broad perspective on the significance of these complexities in "The Federal Accountant's Role in Providing Organizational Incentives" (Reading 24). The basic incentives implied by most financial and budgeting controls can be characterized as an elemental reward-and-punishment model. Such controls have generally relied on *external motivation,* as when executives use financial data to discipline or reward subordinates, more or less on the pattern sketched by Argyris in Reading 20. Such a usage will always exist, of course, but Cooley essentially calls for more attention to financial data that induce *internal motivation* in the subordinate. What Cooley cites as a need at the federal level, it is important to note, is at least as critical at state and local levels of government.

The swing away from external motivation sketched by Cooley is reflected in many ways, and perhaps especially in the recent emphasis on Management by Objectives (MBO) programs.[2] There is no way here to adequately define the MBO approach, but it can be briefly described as "a process whereby the superior and subordinate managers of an organization jointly identify its common goals, define each individual's areas of responsibility in terms of the results expected of him, and use these measures as guides for operating the unit and assessing the contribution of each of its members."[3] Given wide variation in its details, MBO has three common thrusts:

1. It seeks to clarify objectives and responsibilities.
2. It seeks to assign these specific objectives and responsibilities.
3. It seeks to build shared commitments to specific objectives so as to reinforce the sense of individual generalized responsibility for doing a good job.

The reader might consult Chapter IX, which provides additional information about MBO as a technique, especially at the federal level. See Rodney H. Brady's "MBO Goes to Work in the Public Sector" (Reading 37).

An important behavioral perspective on MBO is provided by Harry Levinson in "Management by Whose Objectives?" (Reading 38). Levinson argues in sum, that "the typical MBO effort perpetuates and intensifies hostility, resentment, and distrust between a manager and subordinates." Those are grim behavioral consequences, to be ardently avoided.

In general, then, MBO seeks to increase the degree of internal motivation and to decrease the reliance on external motivation. The hoped-for consequence is dual: to induce a new sense of individual control and freedom as the individual polices his own behavior so as to achieve agreed-upon objectives, and to decrease the close oversight component of supervision, thereby reducing the load on superiors and decreasing the punitiveness associated with supervision.

Notes

[1] For the resulting debate, see Andrew C. Stedry, "Budgeting and Employee Behavior: A Reply," *Journal of Business* 37 (January 1964), 195–202; and Selwyn W. Becker and David Green, Jr., "Budgeting and Employee Behavior: A Rejoinder to a 'Reply,'" *Journal of Business* 37 (April 1964), 203–5.

[2] See George S. Odiorne, *Management by Objectives* (New York: Pitman Publishing Corp., 1965), and also his *Management Decision by Objectives* (Englewood Cliffs, N.J.: Prentice-Hall, 1969).

[3] Odiorne, *Management by Objectives,* pp. 55–56.

20
What Budgeting Means to People

Chris Argyris

The purpose of the study is to examine problems and to raise questions concerning the possible human relations effects budgets have upon supervisors. Because of the nature of the problem this study cannot present final solutions to problems, nor answer questions in any definitive way. It can merely define a wider aspect of the budget problem and suggest possible solutions. Each controller must light up these approaches with his own experience. In short, this study, the first of its kind attempted by the Foundation, is primarily exploratory.

Because of the indefinable limits of the human problems in this area, the research team decided to focus its attention on how the supervisors feel about budgets and how the finance people feel about the same budgets. The group sought answers to questions such as these.

1. How do the finance people see their job?
2. What problems do the finance people see in relation to factory people? What problems don't they perceive?
3. Similarly, how do the factory supervisors see their job?

From Chris Argyris, *The Impact of Budgets on People* (New York: Controllership Foundation, 1954), pp. 2–14. Reprinted with permission of author and publisher.

4. What problems do factory supervisors perceive in relation to the finance people and/or budgets? What problems don't they perceive?
5. What similarities and differences exist between factory people and finance people with regard to values, attitudes, and feelings toward budgets?

WHAT BUDGET PEOPLE THINK ARE:

The Use of Budgets

To the budget people, budgets have an extremely important function in the organization as the "eyes and the ears of the plant." They provide the answers to most questions and the budget people see themselves as the "answer men" of the organization. Consider the following examples:

First let me say that budgets are the watchdog of this company. What do I mean by that? Two things: First, if we have profit, there's no problem; Second, if we are losing money, what can we do about improvement—any kind of improvement?

We guard the fields. The budget department has to constantly strive to improve the goods and make the plant better. There is always room to make things better.

There is, therefore, an important emphasis made on budget people constantly finding things that are "sour," looking for weaknesses and, in general, looking for things that are wrong, not right.

Another emphasis is equally important. All the budget people interviewed insisted that the errors found and the weaknesses uncovered should immediately be sent to top management.

If I see an inconsistency, I'll go to top management and report it. No, I never go to the supervisor in charge. It is our job to report any inconsistencies to the top management.

Once the information is in top management's hands, it is up to it to take action. In other words, budget results are primarily top management control instruments.

Coupled with the task of finding weaknesses and reporting them to top management is a third emphasis on doing the reporting soon. Budget results can be effective only when they are "hot off the griddle." Whatever pressure budgets may generate to "motivate" a factory man to better his record would be lost if action was not taken immediately.

It's our philosophy that we've got to get these figures to top management when they're hot. They're no good when the job is cold. As it is now, with our records, top management can get the factory supervisors together and do something right away.

A fourth emphasis is on using the budget as a means for putting pressure on operating supervisors.

As soon as we examine the budget results and see a fellow is slipping, we immediately call the factory manager and point out, "Look Joe, you're behind on the budget. What do you expect to do about it?"

True, he may be batting his brains out already on the problem but our phone call adds a little more pressure—er—well, you know, we let them know we're interested.

Finally, budget people believe that budgets present a goal, a challenge to factory people. They think that without budgets factory people would have nothing "to shoot for"—would lack the help of a great motivating instrument. For example:

Production budgets set the goals. The budgets, yes, the budgets, set a challenge for those fellows (factory). It's something for them to shoot for. They need something to shoot for. All of us need a goal.

In summary, budget personnel see budgets as performing at least the following important functions:

1. They are a means to make things better. There is always room for improvement. Inconsistencies, errors, weaknesses are constantly being discovered, examined, and reported to top management.
2. Properly used, they are a means of instituting improvements quickly. Budgets are of most value when their results are in the hands of top management as soon as possible.
3. They are a means of putting pressure on factory supervisors.
4. They provide a goal, a motivating force for the factory people.

The Differences between Their Outlook and That of Factory Supervisors

If the budget people see any important differences between the outlook of operating people and themselves, such information should be of value in ascertaining how "basic" are the causes of misunderstanding between the budget and production parts of the organization.

The results indicate that budget people see some very basic differences. For example:

I would say that factory people have a different outlook on life. They tend to be more liberal toward others.

The financial people, on the other hand, look at life more coldly. To them, it's all figures. The only thing they look at is what amount of money is involved. It's the total figure that counts.

The factory supervisors' outlook on things is different. They emphasize today. Yes, they're looking at only the short run. We have to look at things in the long run. We have to see the whole unit. They worry about their individual departments.

I think you'd almost say there are personality differences between factory and finance. We (finance) tend to approach everything with figures. We have to. We've been trained that way. Factory people approach it without worrying about costs.

Yes, there are differences. We (finance) have been trained to see things as they are—to study them logically and systematically. We've been trained to look at a problem and say, 'Well, this is it, one, two, three, bang, that's it.'

The differences described above may be clues for understanding the human problems that arise. For example, if the factory supervisors are, in fact, only interested in the short run and if the budget staff does not see the short run as being crucial, then trouble will arise. Similarly, if the budget staff has a basically different outlook on problems from the factory supervisors, this difference will tend to increase disagreements.

Their Problems with Factory Supervisors

The budget people were asked to describe what they felt was the most difficult problem they faced in their relationships with factory supervisors. The majority of the replies fell into a very consistent pattern. The most pressing problem was "selling" budgets to factory supervisors. The budget people believed that the task was almost insurmountable. It was interesting to see that the three most often stated reasons for this problem with factory supervisors were (a) lack of education on the part of factory supervisors, (b) lack of interest, and (c) misunderstanding and/or mistrust of budgets.

Some of the Solutions to These Problems

Most of the solutions suggested by budget people seem to revolve around educating, or training, factory people in the appreciation and use of budgets. These are some of the suggestions:

1. Supervisors should be taught the use and need for budgets in the company and specifically in their departments.
2. If possible, budgets should be explained so the supervisor would know exactly how and why budgets are constructed the way they are. Most finance people were quick to caution against overwhelming the factory man with minute details of financial "buzz words." (They all pointed out that the explanations should be kept as simple as possible.)
3. Closely connected with the above is the budget staff's desire that factory people have more acquaintance with, and therefore respect for, the everyday problems of the finance staff in administering budgets.
4. Interestingly enough, most of the top controllers believed that the problems of administering the budget would not be alleviated until finance people, as well as factory people, changed. They felt that the budget people should be given a thorough course in self-understanding and in understanding and getting along with others—in other words, a course in human relations.

These, then, are the human problems involved in the administration of budgets and what can be done about them, as seen by the budget people.

WHAT FACTORY SUPERVISORS THINK ARE:

The Use of Budgets

Just how important are budgets and budget departments to factory supervisors? Each factory supervisor was asked to name the department which affected him the most and then the second most important. Fifty-seven percent considered production control as number one and forty-five percent chose the budget department as number one. Of the fifty-seven percent who picked the production control department as number one, all but one supervisor chose the budget department as the second most important department.

It seems relatively safe, therefore, to say that budgets wield an important influence in some typical comments:

Well, if you want to study a department that has its clutches everywhere, go into the budget department. That's all over this plant.

In general, the supervisors close to the employees hardly ever used budgets. In fact, they suggested that the best way to cause trouble was to mention a budget directly or indirectly to the employees. The supervisors higher up in the line of authority did use them. Of course, their usage varied, but in general the budgets were used. We shall see subsequently that the amount of use by upper-level supervisors was closely related to the way they handled their subordinates.

Use by Top-Factory Supervisors

We have seen that front-line supervisors are not able to use budgets freely with their employees. Top-factory supervisors, on the other hand, seem to use budgets quite frequently and strongly on the supervisors below them.

Clearly, the closer one is to the employees, the less one can use budgets to increase production or arouse interest in production. If such is the case, one begins to wonder about the supervisor who is in the position of receiving all the pressure from above, but cannot pass on the pressure to the people below him. Does all this pressure stay with the supervisor?

Budget Problems

Although there may be some differences among levels of supervision in the use of budgets, all the supervisors, regardless of their rank, were pretty much agreed concerning the limitations of budgets. Some of the limitations mentioned were:

Budget reports only include results, not reasons.   Perhaps one of the greatest criticisms of budgets was the fact that they never included the reasons why they were not achieved by a certain supervisor. There was considerable feeling about this problem. Supervisors disliked intensely the fact that their departments would look "sick" on the budget while the reasons for the "sickness" were never published along with the results.

Budgets never show the reasons why they have not been met. They never take into account all variables that affect production.

The budget might contain the finance man's explanation: e.g., "The reason 'why' this budget has not been met is excess labor costs, or too much waste of time getting the job ready to be produced, etc.," but such reasons were not the real explanations as seen by the supervisors. They wanted the budget to state why they had excess labor costs, or why it took too long to get the job ready.

In other words, the supervisor's why was never included. Only the why of the budget man was included.

The following supervisor sheds additional light on the subject. It is interesting to note that he realizes why the budgets are not broken down further. But it is perhaps more interesting to note that even though he understands why budgets give only the total picture, he still feels quite strongly about them. Such data cannot help but lead one to wonder if a knowledge about budgets will really alleviate the feelings about them.

As I see it, budgets are for top management. Top management is only interested in the total picture. They just want to see the results. They're just interested in knowing if the goal has been met.

The deviations, the headaches are all ironed out for them at the end of the budget. But, you can bet your boots, they are not ironed out for me. They remain, to remind me of the many things that can go wrong in my department. It's like this: I'm in the forest. I see hundreds of different trees (problems) that go to make it up. Top management is up in the air looking down on the forest. They see a mass of green. Now the budget measures that mass of green, but they don't tell the top management anything about the different trees that make up the green. You might put it this way —my job is to worry about the feelings that go to make up these figures. Finance peoples' job is to worry about the figures without the emotions.

Emphasis on history.   Another closely allied problem is that budgets emphasize past performance. Budgets are historical documents. As such, they are used primarily to project some predictions about the future based on the past.

Factory supervisors, on the other hand, place little emphasis on the past and hardly ever have time to think of the future. Their emphasis is on the present day-to-day situation.

Rigidity of budgets.   In addition to the emphasis on the past, supervisors felt there was an equally negative emphasis on rigidity of standards.

Once established, budget people seemed to dislike changing standards. Most budget people, the factory supervisors stated, were inflexible.

This rigidity of the finance people, as seen by the factory supervisors, leads to some important feelings on the part of the latter. For example:

I'd say one of the biggest problems is that budgets are set up on past performance. Once they come up with a figure, they hate to leave it. Two years ago, my budget on errors was 100, now it's 150, but our production has increased a lot more.

Somehow the budget people freeze the figures in their minds and they just don't want to change.

Budgets apply pressure for an ever-changing goal.   One of the more important criticisms the factory people had was the feeling that the people who set the budgets were never satisfied. For example:

If I meet this budget, those guys up there will only raise it. Or, You can't let them know that you made the budget without too much trouble. If you do they'll up it as sure as hell.

These were typical remarks made by most of the factory supervisors. (In no case did the top-factory supervisor consider this to be a criticism.) It was quite obvious that the factory supervisors wondered when, if ever, the optimum level would be reached. For example:

They make a budget and then constantly increase it. There's too much of that constant raising and raising that thing. Pretty soon the boys catch on and figure out it's the same old stuff. So they don't respond.

The implication that budgets motivate supervisors to do a better job.   As we have seen earlier, the finance people perceive budgets as goal-setters for factory supervisors. They feel that the supervisors are "kept on the ball" because of budgets. Some finance people suggest that factory supervisors would be "lost" without budgets. On the other hand, factory supervisors resent quite strongly being thought of as people who would lose their motivation if it were not for budgets.

Some of them agreed that budgets had a function of helping them accomplish their work, but few if any saw budgets as the creator of their motivation. To accept budgets as motivators is to imply that supervisors do not have adequate interest in their jobs. This is seen as an insult to a man's integrity and the factory supervisors resent it strongly. For example:

I don't care much for budgets. I can use them, but I don't need them. My job is to get out the production, and I do the best I know how. What do I need budgets for? Now budgets can't help me in that.

Budget! Well, I know this is the way the other fellows feel about it. They don't want to be bothered with them. We do our job, and we do the best job we can. That's it. No matter what comes out, we know we've done our best.

Budgets are not realistic.   Another important criticism made by factory supervisors was that some budgets were purposely kept high so that they were almost impossible to meet. The supervisors definitely and sincerely resent this practice. They resent it primarily for two reasons:

Such a practice places a supervisor in a situation where he can never succeed. One supervisor expressed this when he said:

There's not much sense in setting a budget that's too high. What good is it? If a man doesn't meet it, he's going to say, "to hell with it." It's going to get him to think they're never satisfied. If you ever want to discourage a guy, just give him a budget you know he can't meet.

Such a practice implies that the company does not believe the supervisor's own desire to do a good job is sufficient to meet reasonable budgets. The unrealistic budget is used to spur supervisors on, but it does not work and is resented.

The Differences between Their Outlook and That of the Budget People

In the first part of this article some differences in outlook between financial people and factory people as seen by the financial people were described. What are the differences in outlook as seen by the factory supervisors?

The first four basic differences as seen by the factory supervisors have already been discussed. They were:

1. Finance people are primarily interested in the past and the future. They don't think of the present.
2. Finance people tend to be too rigid once they have set up their figures.
3. Finance people see only the total picture. They never see the many problems that go to make up the total picture. They worry only about end results.
4. Finance people tend to see life only as a set of figures. They take the emotions out of life and deal only with the cold figures.

Some other differences have not been previously mentioned:

5. Finance people cannot see the other person's point of view. They know almost nothing about the problems a supervisor is faced with daily.
6. Finance people have a language of their own. It is completely different from the language of the shop.
7. The final difference is more in the area of attitudes. It was best expressed by one supervisor who said:

A big problem with budget people, and all finance people for that matter, is that basically they are—well, let's see, yes—sarcastic.

I think that they think they're the whole show. If you're asking for our opinions we think they have an overexalted opinion of their position.

Solutions to Some of These Problems

1. By far the most frequent and most stressed recommendation made by factory supervisors was that the finance people should learn to see the other person's point of view. The supervisors recommended that the finance people be given a "taste" of factory problems. Some typical comments were:

They are not fully acquainted with our everyday production problems. They don't realize our troubles and our difficulties. The best thing to do is to bring them down and see our problems.

I'd tell you what I'd teach them: to know my job. See the problems I have. Bring them down here and see what really goes on.

2. The financial people should undergo some training to learn that budgets are not final. They are merely opinions. One supervisor stated:

Yes, I could recommend a good thing. I wish they could have their thinking about budgets changed. They are too rigid. Budgets are statements of opinions not facts. That's their big trouble. They think budgets are facts.

3. The financial people should change their belief that the employee is lazy and wants to do as little work as possible. For example:

I'd like to see them change their attitude that employees are not out to get them (budget people) and do as little work as they can get away with.

4. Closely related to recommendation (3) above is one that recurred often: Finance people should change their belief that the best way to raise production is through pressure.

5. Financial people should be taught that they are not superior to factory supervisors. Some typical comments:

I'd deflate their ego—I'd give them something to take them down a peg.

21

Budgets and Forming Levels of Aspiration

Andrew C. Stedry

Having established the need for a particular kind of budget whose aim is control, as opposed to planning or forecasting, it is now desirable to investigate the relationship between the control budget figure and actual performance.

. . . A "good" *control* budget is one which produces "good" results. If it is desired to minimize cost in a given department, and if a budget of $1000 produces a cost of $1001, and a budget of $300 produces a cost of $1000, the latter is a better budget. The magnitude of the budget figure is unimportant other than in terms of its impact on cost.

The budget is a goal imposed on an individual, who shall be called a "department head," by his supervisor or supervisors (management). To its attainment are occasionally attached positive rewards, but more frequently, negative rewards are attached to its nonattainment. If it could be assumed that the department head took the budget as his personal goal and worked toward this goal with maximum effort, the criterion of budget control for a single individual would be trivial—i.e., choose a cost goal at the technological minimum for the operation and let him work toward it. It is not difficult to visualize the effects of such a goal in practice. If there is negative reward attached to its nonattainment, some change must be made in the system or the department head will resign, be discouraged, or possibly simply sabotage and oppose the system, perhaps soliciting the help of others to form a group for this purpose.[1] Regardless of the amount of positive reward attached to its attainment, the expected value of reward, statistically speaking, is zero; and the net expected value of rewards and penalties is negative.

In practice the budget may exist on paper at the technological minimum, and doubtless some budget or engineering departments may make just such

From Andrew C. Stedry, *Budget Control and Cost Behavior* (Englewood Cliffs, N.J.: Prentice-Hall, Inc., 1960), pp. 17–19, 24–26, 40–43, 59–61, 89–91. Reprinted by permission of the author.

forecasts for their own guidance. But in actual execution it is usual to secure assent of persons who are to be controlled so that some deviation or adjustment may be applied to this figure. This means that there is some "acceptable" level of cost which, in general, will be above the theoretical optimum. If cost descends below this level the performance is rated as meritorious, but if cost is above this level then there is an implied criticism which may receive explicit form when this fact is called to the department head's attention, and an investigation of causes supplemented by a report (perhaps by outsiders) may ensue. Reprimands, promotion passover, and dismissal are possibilities.

It is a postulate of this thesis that unwritten "acceptable levels" are the common bases of control budgets. Alternatively, there may be an acceptable rate of approach to the technological optimum, which in practice becomes the control element, and the cost level is then determined from the acceptable rate of improvement of the control budget.

Another hypothesis whose logic and empirical content will be investigated is that *a stationary budget*[2] *is not an effective control budget.* If the budget level is never attained, then some other criterion is in fact replacing it as a control element. If the level is consistently attained, the question of the possibility of consistently obtaining operation at a lower cost will never be answered, because there is no incentive to improve performance. If a level is obtained part of the time, either it must drift toward consistent attainment or nonattainment, or the percentage of the time it will be attained will become stable at some value which produces an acceptable balance of positive and negative reward for the department head. Another and related issue is whether anyone whose performance displays such characteristics would strive for the same reward balance at a lower budgeted cost level. It is part of the task of this thesis to provide a formal basis against which such questions may at least be asked (as they are not in the present literature) and thereby provide a start towards a formal theory of budgetary control. In particular, it is proposed to deal minimally with the question of budgetary level setting in order to focus on the dynamics which center about the question of when (and how) a budget should be changed.

THE BUDGET AS A DETERMINING FACTOR IN FORMATION OF ASPIRATION LEVELS[3]

When management presents the department head with a budget, it can only present its goal. It is a hypothesis of this thesis that management can increase the tendency of the department head to aim at or below this goal by increasing the positive reward associated with its attainment and/or increasing the negative reward associated with its nonattainment.

Management can enforce absolute compliance with the budget by dismissal for noncompliance. After this policy has been in effect for a short time, management would retain only the department heads who aimed at or below the budget and were successful at achieving their aims. It would seem, however, that for this procedure to be in operation without a decimation of supervisory personnel, the budget levels would need to be set for above expected cost in order to allow for random fluctuations. Such a procedure seems unlikely to cause the department head to drive his costs far below the budget, since safety will take priority over innovation. The fear of a lowering of the budget if he performs too well will undoubtedly dominate a desire to impress management with superior performance.[4] Barring this undesirable procedure, the budget may be considered at best a candidate for the department head's goal but more generally as one factor which operates in its determination. This level of cost toward which the department head strives will be termed his *aspiration level.*

EXISTING MODELS OF ASPIRATION LEVEL DETERMINATION

The definition of aspiration level which will be used here is consistent with the definition of J. D. Frank: "The level of future performance in a familiar task which an individual, knowing his level of past performance in that task, explicitly undertakes to reach . . ."[5]

. . . . .

The assumptions of the model can best be comprehended in the following set of postulates for the behavior of a hypothesized department head.

1. If there is a *discrepancy* between the *expected actual level of expenditure* and the *aspired level of expenditure,* he will attempt to reduce this discrepancy by moving his aspiration level toward the actual level at a rate which depends on the size of the discrepancy.

2. In addition to the effect caused by the discrepancy, the *aspired level of expenditure* will be lowered in response to a lowering of the *budgeted level of expenditure.*

3a. The department head will be *encouraged* if the discrepancy (actual expected cost minus aspired cost) does not exceed some positive value known as the *discouragement point.*

3b. The department head will be *discouraged* if the discrepancy exceeds the *discouragement point* but does not exceed a larger value known as the *failure point.*

3c. If the value of the discrepancy exceeds the *failure point,* the system will cease to exist, or a new one will come into being; "the department head will resign."

4a. If the department head is *encouraged,* he will attempt to reduce a positive discrepancy by reducing the *expected actual level of expenditure;* he will react to a negative discrepancy by allowing expected cost to rise.[6]

The rate of reduction or increase depends upon the size of the discrepancy.

4b. If the department head is *slightly discouraged,* he will reduce the discrepancy by reducing expected cost at a lower rate relative to a given discrepancy than he would if encouraged. If he is *moderately discouraged,* he will allow expected cost to increase, but at a sufficiently small rate that the discrepancy will not be increased. If he is *extremely discouraged,* he will allow expected cost to increase at a rate which increases the discrepancy.

Postulate 2 describes a situation in which the budget is a figure about which there are several auxiliary points, each of which defines a particular set of rewards. Using the Simon model of aspiration level determination, the department head will find a point at which the rewards are "satisfactory." He will then study the relationship of this point to the budget, find out about how much it changes for a given change in the budget, and then change his aspiration level accordingly, responding to changes in the budget. Postulate 1 is essentially Lewinian in nature, in that the department head may be interpreted as responding to a positive discrepancy as a reduction of the perceived probability of success of the original aspiration, adjusting his aspiration level in the direction of increased probability of success. The discrepancy between the expected actual level of expenditure and the aspired level of expenditure is appropriately termed a measure of *stress,* since clearly the department head's "emotional tension, produced by frustration,"[7] varies with the size of the discrepancy. A compromising of goals is a well-known reaction to stress,[8] and hence postulate 1 may be interpreted directly as a stress-reducing mechanism without considering the existence of subjective probabilities.

Postulate 4a describes the department head as exhibiting another "normal" form of reaction to stress—striving to improve performance. A primary assumption of this model is that man is an improvable animal and that, given sufficient motivation, cost reduction is a possibility. J. C. March and H. A. Simon (*Organizations,* New York: John Wiley & Sons, Inc.) have confined their discussion of improvement to an increase in search behavior.[9] It is assumed here that improvement is possible through increased experience with the task, diverting of effort from nonorganizational goals, development of increased "cost-consciousness" (diverting of effort from other organization goals in which there is less stress), or mere harder work—all of which may be considered part of or in addition to search behavior. Postulate 3a notes a limitation on the amount of stress which the department head can tolerate and still devote his efforts to cost reduction at maximum effectiveness.

Postulate 4b describes the various stages of withdrawal within the range of stress denoted by postulate 3b. Caused by sublimation or ineffective effort due to stereotype of response, the department head will be less successful in reducing costs. The neurotic response of extreme discouragement will eventually lead to ultimate withdrawal (postulate 3c), provided some change does not occur within the system. The assumption that exceeding the discouragement point will evoke one of only three types of behavior depending on the individual department head is made for the sake of simplicity rather than necessity.

. . . . .

To comprehend the more complex situations which are likely to be encountered in practice it would undoubtedly be necessary to complicate the model, and this would, in turn, vitiate the objective of simplicity and clarity which is a *sine qua non* of a theoretical formulation at this stage of scientific work in budget control and cost behavior. But simple as it is, the analysis here presented does present some highly plausible clarification. For instance, once the department head's goal-setting pattern has been established, a static budget will tend to produce stationary expected cost, subject only to random variation about an expected value, in a viable ongoing situation. It is evident, furthermore (and psychological considerations appear to be strong enough to warrant this conclusion), that management cannot choose a rate of budget reduction for a particular department independent of considerations of the motivation structure of the department's head. Although this would appear to be obvious, the emphasis in today's literature is on budgeted costs and their relation to technology and not on their relationship to the individual being budgeted.[10] Technological constraints are an additional factor which must be considered, but technology,[11] important though it may be, does not obviate the necessity of also considering in any measure motives in a budgetary system which ultimately depend on some real consensus for their implementation. It is paradoxical that those who criticize mechanistic approaches to accounting (e.g., the research which treats human beings as servomechanisms[12]) fall into the trap of mechanistic approach themselves when applying (or explaining) rules of thumb to the problems of budgetary control.

The mathematics used in this chapter (and the logic with which it is associated) [have been deleted in this reprinting. But it is important to generally observe that the use of mathematics] has been directed primarily to laying bare (and clarifying) certain issues which, though sometimes recognized in practice, are often concealed—or go completely unattended —in the existing literature on budgeting.[13] Certain by-products have also been achieved which will be explored in various ways in the chapters that follow. Thus certain issues involved in the strategy of setting budgets have been uncovered and related to each other in a way which related certain major factors to one another. Thus the budgeted amounts of the person to be controlled have been related to his actual cost performance with the aspiration levels acting as an intervening variable. Moreover, possible interactions between aspiration levels and cost performance have been examined. Finally, the objectives of those who seek to influence cost performance have been brought into the analysis, via the budgetary variables, in a way which raises most issues of strategy relative to the objectives of central management and thereby brings to the fore certain questions which are germane to adequate performance of the controller's office, as that office is now conceived.[14]

It is obvious, for example, that blanket budget reductions which are common in government bureaus and similar cost-saving "drives" in large corporations on a plant-wide scale are of dubious merit. Furthermore, the treatment of all subordinates "impartially" when it comes to budget demands, which essentially means treating them equally, regardless of their motivation structure, appears not only irrational from the cost standpoint but from the standpoint of welfare of the subordinates as well. For example, if a man at middle management level is directed to cut his budget, he may be able to "push" one man whose discouragement point is high to the limit and by so doing avoid discouraging a few others whose discouragement points are lower, thus preserving morale and reducing costs further than he could by behaving "impartially." More specifically, if management desires to behave consistently over time, it must choose a more modest rate of budget reduction for the man who is easily discouraged than for the man who appears perpetually enthusiastic. Given two men with the same discouragement point, management must avoid discouraging the man who "when he is bad, is horrid," whereas the man who "when he is bad, is still slightly good" and doesn't give up easily can be kept on the verge of resignation for best cost results.

The [mathematical] models explored in this chapter indicate that an increase in stress, up to a point, is desirable in the reduction of costs. The assumption that standard costs must be "attainable," which pervades the current budget literature, is based on the assumption that the people who operate under them must be satisfied if they are to turn out a reasonable but unexceptional performance. But under even the very simple assumptions of the models in this chapter, it is evident that this need not be the case. Under certain circumstances the cost expected to be obtained by a department head must be above his aspirations in order to ensure that he will work diligently toward reducing costs. Insofar as budgets affect his aspirations this kind of behavior must be taken into account; references to "loose" and "tight" budgets, with blanket approvals of the latter and condemnation of the former, as is common in the literature,[15] are not an adequate basis for dealing with this problem. Pending an explicit quantitative characterization in particular circumstances, the equations used in the models of this chapter have at least established a provisional qualitative characterization which suggests, instead, that budgets should be set rather in a way which allows an affected department manager to achieve his aspirations part of the time. In conclusion we note that this opens a rather broad range of questions concerned with the value of accuracy and timeliness of accounting (as distinct from budgeting) reports in terms of both their immediate and ultimate consequences for cost behavior.

If, as is sometimes said, "Control exists in the minds of men rather than the books of account," then the theoretical model of this chapter helps to highlight and formalize the kinds of psychological concepts that need to be considered. Of course such formalisms, however logical or elegant, are not enough in and of themselves to justify a theory. An empirical foundation is greatly to be desired or, failing this, some kind of testing and validation is required. Apart from the study of Argyris,[16] which does not really deal with the central problem of cost responses to budgetary control procedures, there is (unfortunately) no systematic accumulation of evidence where the desired empirical foundation can be readily secured.

Failing access to a broadly based and systematic series of studies of managerial behavior under different budgeting arrangements, the following seem to be the best immediate alternative sources of empirical information: (1) studies that have been made of worker reactions to various incentive pay schemes, and (2) psychological (laboratory) studies (e.g., in aspiration level theory) which are more or less germane to the topic of interest. After these topics have been discussed in the sections immediately following, attention may be turned to one other source of information and possible validation. This information will be reported in the form of a laboratory experiment designed explicitly for the purpose of testing salient aspects of the theory which has now been advanced.

.   .   .   .   .

The studies presented in this chapter provide a cross section of the evidence available about human behavior which might be applicable to an individual in a budget-controlled activity. More, of course, could be presented, but it is hoped that this brief survey will at least provide some background for the analyses and experiments which will be dealt with in the following chapters.

To summarize, there is evidence that individuals form either individual goals or estimates of their performance (or perhaps both). On the other hand, it is not precisely clear which of these is being formed at any given instant. These aspirations (or expectations) tend to be decreased following a failure in a previous trial in the same task, or increased by a success in that task. The aspirations are affected by external reference points other than performance, but this effect tends to decrease as experience with the task increases. (However, the effects of rewards have not been clearly determined.) The aspiration level is subject to change with success or failure on related tasks, but it is not clear whether the effects can be explained by stimulus generalization or by similarities of need.

Animal studies of motivation are a potential source of information, but the problems of inference relating them to human behavior are not solved even in general, so that use of information gleaned from these studies is of dubious value for the subject with which this thesis deals.

Experiments in utility maximization have used, as a basic premise, the "rationality" of man. On the one hand, these studies are by and large oriented only to an individual's tastes and performance. On the other hand, there is no universal agreement on the basic postulates. Furthermore, these experiments have been conducted with amounts of money whose expected values are, as Dreze notes, in danger of being regarded as trivial by the subjects. This further attenuates the results secured (since they become even more difficult of extrapolation to an actual situation) and, hence, tends to reduce the reliability of conclusions that might otherwise be drawn.

Field studies have shown conflicting results, and only isolated examples of studies which indicate the possibility of introducing an adequate control scheme appear. A further weakness (from the standpoint of this study) is that almost all of the more substantial studies in this area have been directed primarily towards the behavior (motives, etc.) of production workers, as distinct from budgeting or budgeted management.

Business experience, though voluminous, tends to be so loosely phrased (or reported) and to contain such a mixture of complex and unresolved factors, that little can be gained, at this time, by a recitation or analysis of this experience. It therefore has seemed best to confine the presentation here to a single instance where the management has at least been more articulate than most. It is interesting—although, of course, not decisive—that this company (the Lincoln Electric Company) has issued its series of pronouncements in a form which is not wholly incompatible with the theory covered in the preceding chapter.

The brief survey of received evidence, analyses, and hypothesis (i.e., the survey just concluded) does not reveal any body of material which is sufficiently pointed either to validate or even to give satisfactory guidance for a theory of budgetary control of the kind which is of interest here. With this in view, an experiment was designed to see what could be uncovered by the laboratory techniques of experimental psychology when these are combined with the principles and tools of modern statistical inference, as exhibited by the theory of experimental design, and the tools provided by the analysis of variance, etc.

In the experiment which will now be reported, a major objective was to investigate relations that might exist between individual performance and aspiration levels and the relations that might also exist between these variables and the kind of "external"[17] goals which are represented by a budget of the kind commonly employed in management practice.

.   .   .   .   .

The results of the experiment have shown that performance in a situation where the attainment of a goal is rewarded and its nonattainment penalized is significantly affected by the type of budget chosen, the conditions of administration and the way in which aspiration levels for the task are determined.

The experimental results indicate that an "implicit" budget (where the subject is not told what goal he must attain) produces the best performance, closely followed by a "medium" budget and a "high" budget. The "low" budget, which was the only one which satisfied the criterion of "attainable but not too loose," resulted in performance significantly lower than the other budget groups.

However, there is a strong interaction effect between budgets and the aspiration level determination grouping. The group of "high" budget subjects who received their budgets prior to setting their aspiration levels performed better than any other group, whereas the "high" budget group who set their aspirations before receiving the budget were the lowest performers of any group.

An hypothesis which might satisfactorily explain this phenomenon is as follows: The high performing group formed its aspirations with the high budget levels in mind, while the low performing group rejected the high budget after forming aspirations with relation to their performance. However, aspiration level data indicate that the low performing group had a much higher goal discrepancy so that, if anything, their goals were closer, on the average, to the budget than were the high performers.

The low performing group also had a very high achievement discrepancy score. If achievement discrepancy is interpreted as a measure of stress, this would give rise to an alternative hypothesis—viz. that the stress, at least for some subjects, was so high that they may have been "discouraged" and may have ceased to try to improve performance.

A major difficulty is involved in the use of achievement discrepancy scores. This results from the functional dependency of such scores upon performance. For example, a constant aspiration level would produce a negative correlation between achievement discrepancy and performance (ignoring the trivial case where performance equals aspiration level throughout). This conceptual deficiency of the current state of psychological theorizing makes it difficult to establish a causal relationship between this discrepancy and performance—as hypothesized in this model. It is, however, significant that the ordering of the stress (achievement discrepancy) corresponded fairly closely to the ordering of performance in spite of the opposing effect of the functional dependency.

It is also observed from the analysis that the size of the achievement discrepancy can be affected significantly by the size of the budget, a result which is consistent with the requirements for the validity of postulate 2 in the model of this chapter.

The investigation of the goal discrepancy also indicated a significant budget effect, and this again tends to corroborate postulate 2, since in the continuous model the two discrepancies are indistinguishable. A somewhat surprising (even though not statistically significant) effect is also present. This is the tendency of the groups who formed their aspiration levels without knowledge of the budget to come closer to their budget than is true for the group which had the advantage of the budget information supplied to them. A possible explanation is that a moderate departure from the budget can come about gradually in the groups that form aspirations first, while a departure in the other groups (since the budget is associated with reward) is likely to be a large shift downward.

The types of aspiration levels, under the procedures used, did play a part in performance differences. This was to be expected. But the fact that it did not play a part in the discrepancies which occurred requires some explanation. One possibility is that the greater variability of the aspirations noted in the aspirations of the β subjects (who did not have the budget when forming their aspirations), in spite of roughly the same average aspirations, may have produced a greater number of discouraged subjects (who had aspired to extremely high levels). In the group whose aspiration levels tended to remain close to the budget, there was relatively few extremely high or low discrepancies. Hence this group would tend to exhibit high but not intolerable levels which according to postulates stated earlier, would lead to high performance as well.

Although not conclusive on the point, the study does shed some light on participative schemes of budgetary management insofar as these are connected to aspiration levels. The group which determines its aspiration level first, in the experimental situation, is closest to the solution proposed by McGregor. He suggests that the department head should plan his budget and then take it to his supervisor who will give him his budget based on his estimate. The experimental data raise some questions as to the universal validity of this recommendation, for under the experimental situation if "management" decides on a "high" (performance) budget, its use of McGregor's participation plan coincides with the worst possible result. On the other hand, it would probably help performance in a "low" budget situation.

This summary of the findings may now be concluded by a few observations on the causal connection between stress and performance. As already noted, the experiment did help to separate and distinguish between goal discrepancy and achievement discrepancy. The best that the data and subsequent analyses will bear on the subject of "stress" suggests only the possible use of achievement discrepancy as either a surrogate or a direct measure of stress. The value of the achievement discrepancy as a measure of stress is dubious and the effect of stress and/or achievement discrepancy on performance requires further documentation before such usage is fully warranted.

Notes

[1]Cf. Chris Argyris, *The Impact of Budgets on People* (New York: Controllership Foundation, 1954).

[2]That is, a budgeted cost for a given operation which does not change over time.

[3]My initial contact with aspiration levels was aided immensely by William H. Starbuck and his excellent survey of the field (W. H. Starbuck, "Level of Aspiration Theory and Market Behavior," Pittsburgh: Carnegie Institute of Technology, Graduate School of Industrial Administration, Behavioral Theory of Firm Project, Working Paper No. 7, November, 1957).

[4]Cf. C. I. Barnard, *The Function of the Executive* (Cambridge: Harvard University Press, 1954).

[5]J. D. Frank, "Individual Differences in Certain Aspects of the Level of Aspiration," *American Journal of Psychology,* Vol. 47 (1935), p. 119.

[6]If a multiple commodity or multiple cost structure was hypothesized, it would be assumed that negative stress in one area would direct attention to another. Cf. W. Edwards, "Probability-Preference in Gambling," *American Journal of Psychology,* Vol. 66 (1954), pp. 349–364.

[7]Ruch, *Psychology and Life,* Chicago: Scott, Foresman and Company, 4th ed., 1953, p. 154.

[8]*Ibid.,* p. 162.

[9]But cf. *Handbook of Experimental Psychology,* chap. xiii, Neal E. Miller, "Learnable Drives and Rewards," where this same kind of search for improved situations is ascribed to fear and anxiety ["Learnable Drives and Rewards," in *Handbook of Experimental Psychology,* S. S. Stevens (ed.) (New York: John Wiley & Sons, Inc., 1951), pp. 435–72].

[10]E.g., I. W. Keller, *Management Accounting for Profit Control* (New York: McGraw-Hill Book Company, Inc., 1957), p. 98, states that, "The setting of standards is the responsibility of the technical staffs of a plant such as industrial engineers, design engineers, and chemists," although he later concedes that the foreman must agree that the standard is "fair." The problem of what to do if agreement is lacking, or what proportion of standards should be made to come into the area of questionable "fairness," is not related to the motivations of the individual concerned.

[11]In the literature of theoretical economics such technological factors (in the form of a production function) are accorded preponderant importance. But it must be remembered that the economic theory of the firm is based on a highly simplified model of the firm's "human" structure which, in turn, is justified by the fact that this model is designed primarily for analyzing "market" or general economic behavior and not the behavior of agents within a single firm.

[12]See, for example, R. N. Anthony ["Cost Concepts for Control," *The Accounting Review,* Vol. 32, No. 2 (April, 1957)], who (rightfully) states that, "Human control systems cannot be so easily or so precisely designed as mechanical or electrical ones." Although he rejects the servomechanical analogy, he can only offer in substitution such comments as, "The method of constructing costs for control purposes is governed by management policy."

[13]Cf. e.g., J. B. Heckert, *Business Budgeting and Control* (New York: The Ronald Press Company, 1946); J. H. MacDonald, *Practical Budget Procedures* (Englewood Cliffs, N.J.: Prentice-Hall, Inc., 1939). This literature is almost completely occupied with mechanics of budgeting to the point where it has assumed an almost standard form of presentation and development.

[14]Particular reference is made to the "control," as distinct from the "service," function in the sense in which these two terms are used in the controllership literature.

[15]Some authors entirely dodge this issue by favoring only "accurate" budgets failing to make clear whether they are speaking of the budget as a planning instrument or a control instrument.

[16]Argyris, *op. cit.*

[17]See remarks in Existing Models of Aspiration Level Determination section regarding stress.

22

Budgeting and Employee Behavior

Selwyn W. Becker and David Green, Jr.

Writing in *Number: The Language of Science,* Tobias Dantzig observed: "The concrete has ever preceded the abstract. . . . And the concrete has ever been the greatest stumbling block to the development of a science. The peculiar fascination which *numbers as individuals* have exerted on the mind of man from time immemorial was the main obstacle in the way of developing *a collective* theory of numbers, i.e., an arithmetic; just as the concrete interest in individual stars long delayed the creating of a scientific astronomy."[1]

And so it has been with budgeting, where for some there is still question on whether or not a theory has developed. Business budgeting is a twentieth-century innovation; its development has been characterized by a fragmentary literature and an emphasis on technique. A review of its history indicates that progress has largely been through learning from mistakes—a "cut-and-try" approach. In this paper we will review this history as a background toward an understanding of the relation of the budget to the motivations of those who effect and are affected by it. In a sense this will be an excursion—an attempt to determine "what the behavioral scientists can tell us or find out for us about . . . the impact of (budgets) on people and on their aspirations."[2] In the process, we will point out that the attempt to make use of motivational factors in the budgeting construct raises many difficult and imperfectly understood problems. Further, we will attempt to explain why the style of managerial leadership is of critical importance in the choice of budget procedures—an issue largely overlooked. Also, we will consider the role played by the communication of performance results and the timing of budget revisions.

In the United States, budgeting by state and local government started with the municipal reform movements around the turn of the century. At the outset, the budget was viewed as an instrument of control—"control over the officers . . . of administration by placing limitations on their author-

Reprinted from "Budgeting and Employee Behavior" by Becker and Green from *Journal of Business,* Vol. 35, October 1962, pp. 392–402, by permission of the University of Chicago Press. © University of Chicago Press, 1962.

ity to spend."[3] These early budgets were, and for the most part still are, authorizations to spend—appropriations—for particular "objects of expenditure" such as personal services, commodities, travel, and the like. The appropriation was the "upper limit" much like a thermal control on a furnace—when the limit is reached the fuel, or, in the fiscal sense, the money is stopped. The upper limit was imposed through the approving of the budget by the governing body—the board, the council, the legislature, etc.

These governmental budgeting procedures provided for a second type of control—a restraint control. Each claim presented had to be approved for payment by the chief financial officer. The question of "what is a legal or bona fide obligation?" was resolved by considering (1) whether the budget document provided for such an expenditure, (2) whether sufficient funds were left in the appropriation to pay the claim, and (3) whether the necessary documents were on hand. To know if the remaining appropriation was sufficient, fairly elaborate records were maintained. To these were posted the dollar amounts of issued purchase orders as well as the specific expenditures.

Both types of transactions reduced the "available" balance. This was a practice of *clerical* control—a technique employed to insure the completeness of record and one that is still unique to governmental accounting (with the possible exception of retail "open-to-buy" records). To the extent that interim reports were prepared and distributed to department heads, rudimentary *communicative* control was practiced.

Governmental purposes were served well enough by these budget procedures. Revenue and expense forecasts were relatively simple. Because changes were not contemplated, the budgets were for fixed amounts for the designated time period. Where actual revenues fell short of the estimates, unilateral demands to cut expenditures by a designated percentage were issued—sometimes by resort to payless paydays.

Early business budgeting largely imitated governmental practice and technique. It began with "imposed" budgets[4] and the obvious controls—limit, restraint, clerical and communicative. During the early and middle 1930's, it became fashionable to speak of "budgetary control" and to view the budget as both (1) a financial plan and (2) "a control over future operations."[5] Also in the thirties, the inadequacies of the static budget became obvious when business activity took a sharp downturn and profits disappeared.[6]

A budget form that provided for intraperiod changes in the level of sales or manufacturing was introduced and was called a flexible or variable budget. It attempted to provide "bench mark" numbers for a range of contemplated activity.

Primarily, budgetary control has been the attempt to keep performance at or within the acceptable limits of the predetermined flexible plan. In a sense the plan controls—but for how long? And how is the plan to be modified?

BUDGET PERIODICITY

The recurring cycle of early governmental and business budgets was simple. The budgets were imposed, there was performance, and the comparison of the performance against the budget influenced the next budget. The cycle could be depicted as [shown in Figure 22.1]*

FIGURE 22.1

Ordinarily, the budget period was one year or two. The comparison of performance and budget often had curious results on the subsequent budget. Where expenditure was less than budget, there was a tendency to revise the subsequent budget downward. As a result, managers would engage in a spending spree the last few weeks of an appropriation year to avoid being cut down next year.

The budget period in business has also been calendar oriented—the quarter or twelve-week period extended twelve or fifteen months. Ordinarily, budget revisions are restricted to future periods. Later in the paper we will discuss reasons for cycling budget revisions on a basis other than the calendar.

BUDGET MODIFICATION

By 1930 it was recognized in business circles that imposed budgets "resulted in some dissatisfaction and advice was given to prepare them in the departments and have them revised or edited in the central offices."[7] Thus *participation* was introduced into the budgeting construct. It has been said that the "real values of participation at all management levels . . . , aside from better planning are the psychological values that accrue as the result of participation. A high degree of participation is conducive to better morale and greater initiative".[8]

There is some evidence of the extent (and degree) to which participation is currently employed in business. Sord and Welsch interrogated managements of thirty-five companies to determine the level at which principal

---

*Figure numbers have been added to facilitate page makeup and improve clarity.

budget objectives were developed. No companies said they used totally imposed budgets. Six firms (17 percent) prepared objectives at higher levels and allowed subordinate managers to consider and comment on them before final adoption. Twenty-nine firms (83 percent) said they requested subordinate managers to prepare their own goals and objectives for review and approval at higher levels.[9]

Theirs obviously was a very small sample. Furthermore, it is questionable that the interrogatories used did, in fact, investigate participation. As Chris Argyris discovered, there is such a thing as "pseudo-participation." "That is, participation which looks like, but is not, real participation."[10]

Participation may have great value in improving budgets by drawing together the knowledge diffused among the participants, although we do not treat this objective here. Our interest is in participation as a useful technique for dealing with the psychological problems of employee satisfaction, morale, and motivation to produce; that is, the belief that increased participation can lead to better morale and increased initiative. The evidence supporting this belief will be evaluated, as well as other psychological effects associated with participation that may be of even greater importance. But first the question: What is participation? We will use the following definition: Participation is "defined as a process of joint decision-making by two or more parties in which the decisions have future effects on those making them."[11]

FIGURE 22.2

A collateral question: How does the introduction of participation affect the budget cycle? At first glance, it seems that the chart would appear as [in Figure 22.2].

However, we believe this is too simple. Participation adds a separate "psychological path." Participation is *not* a single-value variable but rather is a concept encompassing several explicit variables. Instead of a simple cycle we have a sequence that might be depicted as [in Figure 22.3].

In paragraphs that follow we will attempt to identify these unspecified psychological variables by examining what we consider to be the relevant available research results. Before proceeding it is imperative to make one

FIGURE 22.3

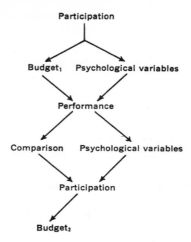

fundamental point: *Participation is not a panacea.*[12] Indeed, there is evidence to suggest that it is inappropriate in certain "environments." When participation is employed, the concept of control, as outlined above requires modification. Instead of the budget being the plan to which performance is conformed, compared, and evaluated irrespective of changes in environment (other than those provided for in the flexible budget), the plan is influenced, at least in part, by the environment. That is, control limits and informs those operating under the budget; in turn, they determine and limit the succeeding budget.

PARTICIPATION, MORALE, AND PRODUCTIVITY

In an industrial setting Coch and French investigated the effects of prior participation on production after work changes were introduced.[13] Difficulty of work and percentage of work changes were equated for a no-participation group (NP); for participation by representation (PR); and for a total participation (TP) group. With a prechange standard of sixty units per hour, after relearning, the NP group reached a level of fifty units per hour; the PR group sixty units per hour; and the TP group sixty-eight units per hour, or an improvement of about 14 percent over the standard rate. Another important finding was that 17 percent of the NP group quit their jobs in the first forty days after the change, and the remaining members of the group filed grievances about the piece rate, which "subsequently was found to be a little 'loose.'" There was one act of aggression against the supervisor from the PR group, none from the TP group, and no quits in either the PR or TP groups.

If employee turnover and stated grievances can be taken as a measure of morale, then it seems clear that the two groups that participated in the initiation of change were better disposed toward their job situations than was the no participation group.

Based only on this study one cannot decide if participation directly increased incentive to produce, as measured by subsequent productivity, or only improved morale, which in turn led to increased motivation. This is a point worth considering since morale is not perfectly correlated with productivity.

An inference about this relationship can be drawn after examination of a study by Schachter *et al.* on group cohesiveness and productivity.[14] (Group cohesiveness is usually defined as attraction to the group—desire to become or remain a member—and reluctance to leave the group. Another way of looking at cohesiveness might be the amount of "we" feeling generated in an individual as a result of his association with others.) Schachter and his associates experimentally created high and low cohesiveness in two groups. A task was chosen in which output could be easily measured. In half of each group subjects were individually given instructions designed to induce production at a high rate; the other half instructions designed to induce production at a low rate. It was found that group cohesion and acceptance of induction were significantly related. The high-cohesive groups more frequently accepted induction than did the low-cohesive groups. This was especially true of the negative induction, or "slow-down" situation.

The Coch and French study suggests that morale and/or productivity are enhanced as a result of employee participation in the initiation of change. The Schachter *et al.* study suggests that with participation held constant (all groups worked under constant conditions) change in productivity is related to group cohesiveness. Cohesiveness, it can be seen from the definition is related to morale. Morale is most frequently defined as satisfaction with one's job, supervisors, and working associates. It has also been defined as the *degree* to which an employee identified himself as part of the organization. In either case morale and cohesiveness with a group imply some similar reactions and attitudes toward an organization or group.

Since participation affects morale (cohesiveness) and productivity, but cohesiveness without participation affects production, the most likely conclusion is that cohesiveness is dependent on participation but that changes in productivity are more directly related to cohesiveness.

ELEMENTS OF PARTICIPATION:
PROCESS AND CONTENT

Let us consider participation as conceptually divisible into process and content. Process means the *act* of participating with the possible consequences stemming from the act; content is the *discussion topic* toward which are generated the positive or negative attitudes. The *act* of participating enables the participants to know one another, communicate and interact with one another—conditions that easily can lead to increased cohesiveness. As we have seen, however, increased cohesiveness also can result in lower production if that is the sentiment of the cohesive group. Thus it becomes clear that the content of participation is an important determinant of final production levels. What should the content consist of and what should it accomplish? These questions can be answered on the basis of some data on group decision-making collected by Kurt Lewin and his students.[15] One experiment was designed to induce housewives to use previously unused foods (sweetbreads, etc.). Positive communications describing the foods were presented to two groups; one by the lecture method, the other by a group-discussion method. A subsequent check revealed that 3 percent of the women who heard the lectures served one of the meats never served before, whereas after group discussion, 32 percent served one of the meats. This experiment was repeated with a different leader, different groups, and a different food—milk—and yielded essentially similar results.

As compared to individual instruction and the lecture method, group discussion was superior in inducing change—a result attributed to the hesitancy of individuals to accept goals that depart from the group standard. (Psychological nonacceptance of a goal by an individual virtually precludes its attainment by him.) The group-discussion method allows the group member to assess the standards of all other members so that, if the group apparently accepts a change, he too can accept it and retain his group membership.

It is clear that the content of participation should be directed toward setting a new goal with discussion of a sort sufficient to enable each participant to realize that the goal is accepted by the others in the group. The fulfillment of these conditions could serve as a definition of successful participation by (1) providing the opportunity for enough interaction so that a cohesive group can emerge and (2) directing the interaction so that each participant's analysis of the content will enable him to accept as his own those goals adopted by the group. Thus, we can see that the process and content of a participation program interact, and that such interaction can lead to one of several outcomes:

1. High cohesiveness with positive attitudes (goal acceptance), a condition of maximally efficient motivation;
2. Low cohesiveness with positive attitudes, an unlikely but possible condition that probably would result in efficient performance;
3. Low cohesiveness and negative attitudes, a condition resulting from unsuccessful participation that would tend to depress production within the limits of the integrity or conscience of each individual; and

4. High cohesiveness and negative attitudes, the occurrence most conducive to a production slow-down.

Level of Aspiration and Performance

Ideally, in the budgeting process, participation results in a plan of action including a proposed amount of accomplishment and an estimate of the costs to achieve it. If participation has been successful, then these proposed levels of cost and accomplishment are accepted as goals by the participants. In effect, these projected levels of achievement become the levels of aspiration of the managers of the organization. (In a smoothly running organization the managers induce acceptance of the same levels of aspiration in the members of their departments.)

Level of aspiration has been defined in the psychological literature as a goal that, when just barely achieved, has associated with it subjective feelings of success; when not achieved, subjective feelings of failure.[16] From an extensive review of the literature Child and Whiting summarize many findings into five conclusions:

1. Success generally leads to a raising of the level of aspiration, failure to a lowering.
2. The stronger the success the greater is the probability of a rise in level of aspiration; the stronger the failure the greater is the probability of a lowering.
3. Shifts in level of aspiration are in part a function of changes in the subject's confidence in his ability to attain goals.
4. Failure is more likely than success to lead to withdrawal in the form of avoiding setting a level of aspiration.
5. Effects of failure on level of aspiration are more varied than those of success.[17]

Recently Stedry has utilized this psychological variable in an attempt to establish some relations between level of aspiration, imposed budgets, and subsequent performance.[18] Stedry, not a psychologist, may have overlooked some of the relevant psychological literature. Seemingly he selected an inaccurate method of measuring aspiration level which weakens his several conclusions and recommendations. For his measure of level of aspiration, Stedry asked his subjects to express what they "hoped to achieve" on the next set of problems. Festinger found that the D score (the difference between performance and aspiration) was greater between performance and expressions of "like to get" than between performance and expressions of "expect to get."[19] Diggory found the correlation between "hope" statements before and after failure significantly higher than statements of expectations before and after failure.[20] In other words, "hope" and "expect" represent different attitudes. Since level of aspiration is defined as the goal one explicitly undertakes to reach rather than the goal one hopes to achieve, it seems clear that Stedry's conclusions are based on an inaccurate measure of his major variable. Subsequently, Stedry has indicated his belief, based on questionnaire information, that his "subjects appeared . . . to have given the right answer to the wrong question."[21] In any event, his attempt is valuable heuristically because it highlights a possible relation between budgets, budgeting, and human motivational performance.

We have already hypothesized a relationship between participation and the formation of levels of aspiration. There remains a specification of the effects of level of aspiration on the remaining segments of the budget cycle.

After the budget has been adopted, the attempt to translate it into behavior constitutes the performance part of the cycle. The degree of effort expended by members of the firm as they attempt to achieve budgeted goals is partially dependent upon their levels of aspiration. Maximum effort will be exerted to just reach an aspired-to goal. In fact, according to level of aspiration theory if, for example, five units of effort are required to reach goal $x-3$, ten units to reach goal $x-2$, fifteen units to reach goal $x-1$, and twenty-five units to reach goal x, the level of aspiration goal, an individual will expend the disproportionate amount of energy to achieve at level x to derive that subjective feeling of success. Thus we can see how a budget that is partially derived through a successful program of participation can result in greater expenditure of effort on the part of employees to reach goals specified in the budget.

Such expectations are not without foundation, of course. Bayton measured the levels of aspiration of three hundred subjects of roughly equivalent ability prior to their performance on seven arithmetic problems. He found that subjects with higher levels of aspiration followed with higher performance.[22] From a finding of this sort one cannot conclude that greater motivation to achieve is associated with the level of aspiration goal, but it is well known that increased motivation leads to increased effort, a condition usually followed by an increase in performance. We can thus find indirect support for our contention. Another bit of evidence may illustrate the point further. Siegel and Fouraker set subjects to bargaining under bilateral monopoly conditions.[23] With no control of levels of aspirations, the subjects maximized their joint profits and split the profits nearly equally. However when high and low levels of aspiration were induced into the bargaining pairs (despite the fact that a better bargain meant more money for the subject), those with a low level of aspiration gained only about one-third of the joint profits. Thus, it seems clear that level of aspiration not only describes a goal for future attainment, but also it partially insures that an individual will expend a more-than-minimum amount of energy, if necessary, to perform at or above that level.

Depending, then, on the conditions under which a budget is drawn the budget can act as a motivating force and can induce better performance from the members of the organization. On the other hand, the budget can specify aims and goals so easy of attainment that the organization's members will be induced to produce at less than their usual capacity.

After the performance phase of the cycle a comparison is made between the costs and income previously predicted in the budget and the actually attained income and costs. We are not here concerned with how the comparison is made but rather with its utilization, since that may have considerable effect on employee behavior and morale.

Much has been written on the effect of communication within an organization. With reference to the comparison, or control, function of the budget, the use or misuse of communication can be critical especially when viewed in the context of participation and level of aspiration.

First and foremost, it is imperative for each participant to know whether he should feel subjective success or failure. If he is not informed of the results of the comparison he cannot know whether his striving for a particular level was worthwhile or not. Nor can he, in turn, pass on the word to his subordinates in whom he induced specific levels of aspiration. They, too, will not know whether to feel success or failure. We can see that communicating knowledge of results acts, in this case, as reward or punishment. It can serve either to reinforce or extinguish previous employee behaviors. Where subjects were given a learning task and provided knowledge of results, learning increased; but when knowledge of results was withheld performance fell, that is learning not only stopped but performance was decreased.[24] In discussing these results, Munn argued that "the rapid drop in performance which followed this point may be attributed to the loss of motivation which came with withdrawal of knowledge of results, not from forgetting what had been learned up to this point."[25]

Failure to communicate knowledge of results adversely affects not only performance but also morale. Leavitt and Mueller, in an investigation of effects of varying amounts of feedback, found that task accuracy increased as feedback increased. They also found that zero feedback is accompanied by low confidence and hostility while free feedback is accompanied by high confidence and amity.[26]

The question may now be asked: "So what if the employees don't know how they did? They already performed and the profit is recorded." The answer obviously concerns the effects this lack will produce on subsequent behavior and, more specifically, on the goals to be set in the succeeding budget.

The next budget will be affected because omitting feedback not only precludes certainty regarding a previous level of aspiration but also affects the subsequent level of aspiration. Most generally an individual will raise his level of aspiration after success and lower it after failure.

In the budgeting cycle, after the comparison phase, the new budget is started. The participating supervisors bring to the new participation situation all their new aspirations resulting from past feelings of success or failure. If they have been deprived of a rightfully achieved feeling of success, their subsequent aspirations are likely to be lowered. This could result either in a less efficient budget, that is, lower goals than could easily be achieved or, after disagreeable argument, an imposed budget from an adamant management. In the first case succeeding performance will be unnecessarily low; in the second, participation will be ineffectual with the possible result of poor performance and, almost certainly, lower morale. The *proper* budget cycle then is really a dual, interacting sequence of budgeting and psychological events. It can be depicted as [in Figure 22.4].

FIGURE 22.4

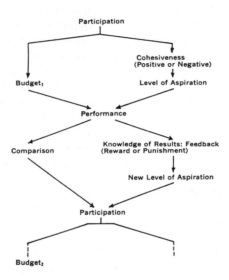

A successful participation budget does two things: (1) It induces proper motivation and acceptance of specific goals, and (2) It provides information to associate reward or punishment with performance. These lead to new aspirations and motivations that set the stage for the next participation budget.

CONCLUSIONS

An understanding of the psychological variables stemming from participation is valuable, perhaps, for its own sake, but it is hardly likely to provide concrete assistance in a decision to institute such a program. We have seen that participation can lead to either increased or decreased output. It is not unlikely that the setting in which participation occurs is one determinant of the production outcome. Some organizations can be characterized as operating under relatively authoritarian leadership. By definition, participation is essential to democratic process and very probably is antithetical to an authoritarian organization. To illustrate the latter, assume that the various department heads participate in the decision-making process, prepare a budget, only to have it rejected by upper management without explanation other than that a more satisfactory budget is necessary. The best prediction here is that the participating group will be highly cohesive and hold negative attitudes toward management, a precondition to lowered output.

It is also likely that under authoritarian management status differences will be rigidly adhered to. If the participants in the budgeting process occupy different status levels influence on decisions will be directly related to status—the more status the more influence. Status differences would probably mitigate against high cohesiveness. Presumably status differences that did not affect the decision-making process would not preclude either a cohesive group or positive goal acceptance, especially if the occupants were secure in their positions or perceived the possibility of upward mobility.[27]

We do not wish to enter the controversy over the relative merits of various styles of leadership but merely wish to point to some possible limitations on the use of participation. In order to be successful, the participants must participate, that is, must have influence on the adopted decisions. If participation can be achieved under more or less authoritarian conditions, it is likely to be effective, just as it can be undermined (by disregard) with democratic leadership. Only management itself can determine whether it is worthwhile to initiate or continue the participation segment of the budgeted cycle.

At any rate, presuming an organization has determined that it can benefit from participation, are the psychological effects such that participation simply can be "grafted" onto existing procedures or are other changes necessary? Or indeed, if no changes are necessary, are there any that can be made so that efficiency, motivation, and productivity will be enhanced?

Suggested changes in budgeting are not difficult to find. Stedry, recognizing the possible motivating forces produced by budgets, seems to suggest that "phony" budgets be prepared while the real budget is kept secret.[28] The "phony" ones would be designed to induce maximum motivation through a manipulation of level of aspiration. This plan would require different phony budgets for each department and, indeed, for each individual. If different budgets are viewed as discriminatory and unfair devices, company morale might suffer. Further, if already disgruntled employees learn that they were striving to attain phony goals the effectiveness of future budgets, real or phony, might be seriously impaired.

A knowledge of the effects of level of aspiration may lead to changes designed to increase employee motivation and output. The budget cycle characteristically is tied to an arbitrary time schedule. Even with no other information, this is defensible logically and perhaps economically as well. If, however, the budget is to be used as a control device (in the sense of prohibiting excessive expenditures) as well as a motivating device, then it clearly should be tied to the level of aspiration cycle rather than to a time schedule. We know that success leads to a rising level of aspiration and, generally, failure to a lowering. Failure can also result in "leaving the field," that is, psychological or physical withdrawal from the goal-oriented environment.

It is suggested here that much more frequent comparisons of performance and budget be made, including feedback to the employees of the results of the comparison. This recommendation is made for the following reasons: (a) If the performances meet or slightly exceed expectation, then level of aspirations will rise and budgets can and should be revised; otherwise employees will perform at the budget level when they could be performing at a higher budget level. Maximum efficiency can only be achieved by revising the budget upward. (b) If performances are just slightly below the budget expectations, budget changes are not necessary, but feedback is so that employees will continue to strive for the budget goals. (c) If performances are well below the budget, it may be well to revise the budget downward. If such revision is not made, employees' level of aspiration will fall, the budget will be viewed as unattainable, and output will fall. The danger here is that levels of aspiration and output may fall much more than is necessary. If the budget is revised downward just enough so that it is perceived as being attainable, then maximum output will be achieved again.

Notes

[1]4th ed. (New York: The Macmillan Company, 1956), chap. iii.

[2]David Solomons, "Standard Costing Needs Better Variances," *National Association of Accountants Bulletin,* Vol. 43, No. 4 (December, 1961), p. 30.

[3]Frederick A. Cleveland, *Chapters on Municipal Administration and Accounting* (New York: Longmans, Green & Co. 1909), p. 72.

[4]Imposed budgets have been characterized as ones "dictated by top management without the full participation of the operating personnel" (R. N. Anthony, "Distinguishing Good from Not-So-Good Accounting Research," in *Proceedings of the 22nd Annual Institute on Accounting,* Columbus: Ohio State University, 1960, p. 68).

[5]Eric Kohler, A *Dictionary for Accountants* (Englewood Cliffs, N.J.: Prentice-Hall, Inc., 1957), p. 75.

[6]F. V. Gardner, "How About That 1935 Operating Budget?" *Factory Management and Maintenance* (November, 1934); C. E. Knoeppel and E. G. Seybold, *Managing for Profit* (New York: McGraw-Hill Book Co., 1937), p. 206.

[7]*Budgetary Control in Manufacturing Industries* (New York: National Industrial Conference Board, 1931), p. 52.

[8]B. H. Sord and G. A. Welsch, *Business Budgeting* (New York: Controllership Foundation, Inc., 1958), p. 97.

[9]*Ibid.,* p. 95.

[10]*The Impact of Budgets on People* (New York: Controllership Foundation, Inc., 1952), p. 28.

[11]J. R. P. French, Jr., J. Israel, and D. As, "An Experiment on Participation in a Norwegian Factory," *Human Relations,* Vol. 13 (1960), p. 3.

[12]A useful discussion—"Participation in Perspective"—appears as chap. ix in *The Human Side of Enterprise* by Douglas McGregor (New York: McGraw-Hill Book Co., 1960).

[13]L. Coch and J. R. P. French, Jr., "Overcoming Resistance to Change," *Human Relations,* Vol. 1 (1948), pp. 512–32.

[14]S. Schachter, N. Ellerston, D. McBride, and D. Gregory, "An Experimental Study of Cohesiveness and Productivity," *Human Relations,* Vol. 4 (1951), pp. 229–38.

[15]"Studies in Group Decision," in D. Cartwright and A. Zander (eds.), *Group Dynamics* (Evanston, Ill.: Row Peterson & Co., 1956), pp. 287–88.

[16]K. Levin, T. Dembo, L. Festinger, and Pauline Sears, "Level of Aspiration," in J. McV. Hunt (ed.), *Personality and the Behavior Disorders,* Vol. I (New York: Ronald Press Co., 1944), pp. 333–78.

[17]J. L. Child and J. W. M. Whiting, "Determinants of Level of Aspiration: Evidence from Everyday Life," in H. Brand (ed.), *The Study of Personality* (New York: John Wiley & Sons, 1954), pp. 145–58.

[18]Andrew C. Stedry, *Budget Control and Cost Behavior* (Englewood Cliffs, N.J.: Prentice-Hall, Inc.), 1960.

[19]L. Festinger, "A Theoretical Interpretation of Shifts in Level of Aspiration," *Psychological Review,* Vol. 49 (1942), pp. 235–50.

[20]J. C. Diggory, "Responses to Experimentally Induced Failure," *American Journal of Psychology,* Vol. 62 (1949), pp. 48–61.

[21]Stedry, "Aspiration Levels, Attitudes, and Performance in a Goal-Oriented Situation," *Industrial Management Review,* Vol. 3, No. 2 (Spring, 1962), p. 62.

[22]J. A. Bayton, "Interrelations between Levels of Aspiration, Performance and Estimates of Past Performance," *Journal of Experimental Psychology,* Vol. 33 (1943), pp. 1–21.

[23]S. Siegel, L. Fouraker, *Bargaining and Group Decision Making* (New York: McGraw-Hill Book Co., 1960).

[24]J. L. Elwell and G. C. Grindley, "The Effect of Knowledge of Results on Learning and Performance," *British Journal of Psychology,* Vol. 29 (1938).

[25]N. L. Munn, *Psychology* (Boston: Houghton Mifflin Co., 1946).

[26]H. J. Leavitt and R. A. H. Mueller, "Some Effects of Feedback on Communication," *Human Relations,* Vol. 4 (1951), pp. 401–10.

[27]Harold H. Kelley, "Communication in Experimentally Created Hierarchies," *Human Relations,* Vol. 4 (1951), pp. 39–56.

[28]*Budget Control and Cost Behavior,* pp. 5, 17, 41–42, and 71. Stedry does not use the term "phony."

23
Budgeting for Control

Roger L. M. Dunbar

Many writers have defined the principal purpose of a business as making profits (for example, Dill, 1965); however, other objectives may also be important such as the coordinating of separate parts of the organization and the development of new products. To achieve these various objectives, the behavior of organization members must be directed and, if necessary, restricted (Tannenbaum, 1968); in many large-scale businesses this control is effected by the budgetary system (Sord and Welsch, 1958).

The term, budget, has been used rather loosely and may refer to at least two methods of control: (1) a budget may be used as a part of the allocation process authorizing expenditures, the budgeted manager being required to restrict spending to this authorized level; or (2) it may be used to set specific organizational goals such as the increase of sales or the reduction of costs. It is the latter focus which is of interest here, and an attempt will be made to integrate both laboratory and field research findings to describe how such a system may influence behavior.

THE BUDGETARY SYSTEM

With some notable exceptions such as Hofstede (1967) and Stedry (1960), attempts to understand how budgets control behavior have been rare. In this paper ideas derived from general systems theory are used to formulate the characteristics of a budgetary control system; then the implications of some empirical findings for this model are considered.

A system is a collection of interconnected elements; and if it has a purpose, general systems theorists refer to it as a machine. Each machine can have only one goal; therefore, to obtain a multipurpose system, machines must be combined. In order to achieve its particular purpose, a machine must have a feedback mechanism to sense changes away from its goal and then make appropriate adjustments. The adjustive reaction may be positive in that progress is reinforced by a continual increase of the goal

Reprinted from *Administrative Science Quarterly* (March 1971): 88–96.

in the desired direction, or negative, in that deviations are inhibited and the machine is brought back to a present goal.

Stedry (1960: 2) said the primary objective of budgeting "is to increase long-run profit at the fastest possible rate"; however, a second goal of the budget is to facilitate organizational coordination by providing an accurate forecast of future results. Therefore, an ideal budgetary system would consist of a machine to increase profit and another to facilitate coordination by accurately forecasting results.

In the present model, the elements of the machine to increase profit are assumed to appear primarily in the process of setting the budget goal, implying a positive feedback mechanism. On the other hand, the elements of the machine to facilitate coordination are assumed to appear primarily in the process of achieving the budget, implying a negative feedback mechanism. Since the goal-setting machine sets the goal for the goal-achieving machine, there is clearly a hierarchical link between the two machines.

Members of the goal-setting machine, who may include the budget department, top management, and possibly the budgeted individuals themselves, must provide the positive feedback which will ensure the continual advancement of budget goals. The process whereby budget goals are set is here viewed as a black box. However, inputs to this goal-setting box can be isolated and then associated with performance outputs. Four inputs are considered: (1) whether goals set are difficult or easy to achieve; (2) whether the organization allows the budgeted individual to participate in the setting of the budget goal; (3) whether the organization provides monetary incentives for favorable performance relative to the budget; (4) whether the organization provides what the budgeted individual perceives as inadequate extrinsic rewards for favorable performance relative to the budget.

Goals must not only be set but also achieved. The critical step between the setting of a goal and its achievement is the acceptance of the goal by the goal-achieving machine, that is the budgeted individual. There is fairly convincing evidence that cognitively, human beings are negative feedback or homeostatic machines (Festinger, 1957; Brehm and Cohen, 1962). Therefore, it is assumed here that if the budgeted individual can be persuaded to accept the budget goal, his homeostatic nature can be relied upon to achieve it, or to bring performance as close to it as the environment will allow.

GOAL DIFFICULTY AND PERFORMANCE

Stedry (1960) found that when subjects were given a budget goal of a specific number of correct solutions to a series of algebraic water-jar problems to be obtained within a fixed time period, those given a relatively low budget had significantly fewer solutions than those given a higher budget. Locke (1968) found that without exception, and in 12 separate studies, higher goals led to higher performance. Siegel and Fouraker (1960) found that in a bargaining situation, those subjects who had evidently been induced by the experimenter to adopt a high aspiration level negotiated contracts which were significantly more profitable ($6.25) than those with a lower level of aspiration ($3.35). Finally Likert (1967) noted that high-performing sales offices set higher goals than low-performing offices.

Hofstede (1967) hypothesized that while up to a certain level of difficulty, higher goals would be accepted with resulting improved performance, beyond that, the goal would be rejected and performance would decline. It is this possibility of goal rejection that makes a positive feedback mechanism necessary to ensure a controlled increase of the budget which can be accepted as feasible by the goal-achieving budgeted individual. Unfortunately, little is known about the critical level at which budget goals are likely to be rejected rather than accepted. Stedry and Kay (1966) set foremen normal (that is, achieved 50 percent of the time in the past) and difficult (that is, achieved 25 percent of the time in the past) goals on two different job measures. The difficult goals were associated with either very good or very bad performance. Interviews indicated that good performance resulted when the foreman thought the goals challenging, but bad performance resulted when they thought them impossible.

Stedry (1962), in the water-jar experiment mentioned, distinguished three levels of goal difficulty and found that acceptance was not linearly dependent on difficulty, as Table 23.1 shows. However, when harder goals were set, Table 23.1 also shows that the probability that subjects set still higher goals declines. These studies by Stedry and Kay (1966) and Stedry (1962) might indicate that to increase profit and obtain predictable results, the positive feedback mechanism could be designed to set goals that can be achieved, based on past performance, not more than 40 percent of the time but more than 25 percent of the time.

TABLE 23.1
Probabilities of Achieving and Accepting Different Levels of Goal Difficulty (Stedry, 1962)

	Level of Goal Difficulty		
	Low	*Medium*	*High*
Probability of achieving goal	.69	.59	.39
Probability of accepting goal	.64	.53	.62
Probability of setting a higher goal	.25	.14	.00

If goals are too difficult, the performance of the goal-achieving machine will not always reach the planned level, and it will be necessary to trade off the costs and benefits of more profit for more coordination difficulties, as shown in Figure 23.1. The goal is shown as increasingly difficult, but actual performance in terms of profit increases at a slower rate up until the point where the goal is rejected, then it falls off rapidly. Also, as the goal is increased, the discrepancy between planned and achieved performance increases, leading to an increase in coordination costs and a consequent reduction in profits.

PARTICIPATION IN GOAL SETTING

The organization may allow the budgeted individual to be incorporated into the goal-setting machine. Such participation has consequences for goal setting, goal acceptance, and performance. Vroom (1964), after citing a number of empirical studies, concluded that as subordinates were given a larger influence in decisions, their performance improved, partly because of the ego involvement which participation generated. In a budgetary context this may be interpreted to mean a greater willingness by budgeted individuals to accept the budget goal; with a difficult goal, this acceptance would be likely to result in improved performance.

Participation may also bring responsibilities the budgeted individual was not previously aware of to his attention. Hofstede (1967) found that participation was associated with the relevance of financial standards, but not technical standards. First-line managers had considered technical standards their responsibility but not financial performance, until participation in the setting of financial budgets made financial standards relevant.

However unless participation involves the setting of specific goals after discussion, there is little effect on performance. Lawrence and Smith (1955) introduced group discussion into four industrial work groups. Although there was a slight improvement in the performance of the two groups which did not set goals, production increased very significantly in the other two groups which had set objectives after the discussion.

The timing of goal determination in the participation process may be important. Stedry (1960) found that subjects given a very difficult goal and then asked to specify their personal level of aspiration performed significantly better than subjects asked to specify their levels of aspiration and afterwards given a very difficult goal. He estimated the difference in performance to be equivalent to six standard deviations. He suggested that the first group formulated their level of aspiration with the high budget in mind, but the second group rejected the difficult goal because they could not reconcile it with their already specified aspiration level.

Hofstede (1967) also expected participation to help ensure a perception among budgeted individuals that goals were fair, and therefore the budget would be more relevant to them. However, the association between responses to a question on whether the goal setting took account of special problems and the relevance of the budget was not significant. Stedry (1962)

FIGURE 23.1
Trade-off between Harder Goals, Performance, and Coordination Costs

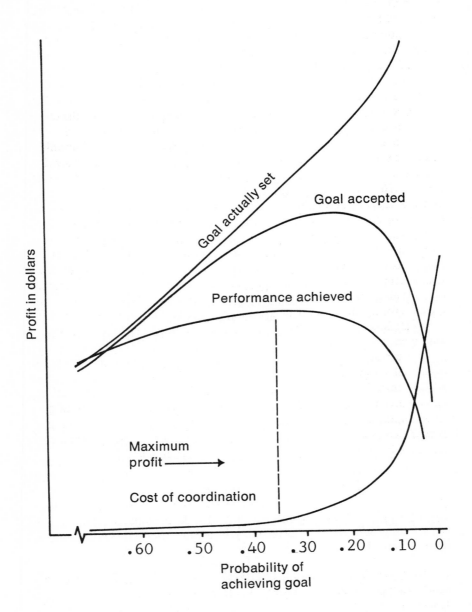

found no association between perceptions of how accurate budget setting had been and performance.

Vroom (1960) hypothesized that participation and personality characteristics will interact to affect performance. He found that for persons with a high need for independence, the extent of their psychological participation in decision making was significantly associated ($r = .31$) with their performance, but not significant for those with medium or low independence needs. He found similar high associations for persons with moderate ($r = .38$) and low ($r = .33$) authoritarian scores, but no significant correlation for those with a high authoritarian need. When he partialled out the effects of age, education, and occupational level, the differences between the correlations attributable to the personality variables generally increased.

Hofstede (1967), using a slightly different measure of authoritarianism, obtained even more significant results in a budgetary context. After dividing managers into low, medium, and high authoritarians, he obtained correlations of .76, .64, and .47, respectively, between participation in goal setting and the budget's perceived relevance to performance. Probably Hofstede's (1967) correlations were much higher than Vroom's (1960) because Vroom associated participation with actual performance as assessed by the superior, whereas Hofstede associated participation with the relevance of the budget as perceived by the budgeted individual. In Vroom's (1960) analysis, goal acceptance intervened between the setting of the goal and performance. Nevertheless both studies indicate that personality factors have consequences for the influence of participation on performance, and may, according to Hofstede's (1967) results, determine whether the budgeted individual will accept the budget.

In summary, discussions have little effect on performance unless coupled with goal setting. Participation may ensure that goals are not advanced so rapidly that they cannot be accepted by the budgeted individual, and the ego involvement produced by discussion, together with the timing of goal determination, may lead to greater goal acceptance. The extent of goal acceptance as a result of participation is probably affected by personality characteristics such as authoritarianism and dependence.

MONETARY INCENTIVES AND GOAL SETTING

Stedry (1960: 19), referring to cost goals and cost performance, hypothesized "that management can increase the tendency of the department head to aim at or below this goal by increasing the positive reward associated with its attainment and/or increasing the negative reward associated with its non-attainment." Similarly, Rath (1960: 172), a management consultant, concluded from "personal observation in hundreds of plants" that there is no motivational force as powerful as a wage system which related indivdual earnings directly to output "by means of a formula linking performance to a predertermined standard."

Toppen (1965a, 1965b) provided fairly convincing evidence in an experiment that subjects performed a very routine task faster, at least in the short run, if offered monetary incentives. In one experiment, the number of pulls on a manipulandum by subjects paid at the rate of 25 cents was significantly greater than the number by those paid at the rate of 1 cent. In another experiment, subjects paid by piece rate had a significantly greater output than subjects paid a fixed amount, irrespective of output.

Locke *et al.* (1968) argued that monetary incentives would only affect performance to the extent that the rewards persuaded the subject to set higher goals for himself. In an experimental task requiring subjects to list as many uses as possible for a common object—for example, a cardboard box—subjects were either assigned difficult goals, allowed to set their own goals, or else not required to set any goals. No significant difference in performance was found between subjects who were rewarded and those who were not; but subjects assigned higher goals showed a significantly greater improvement than those assigned lower goals. Locke *et al.* (1968) concluded that differences in goal difficulty dominated any direct effects of monetary incentives.

In another experiment Locke *et al.* (1968) showed that monetary incentives resulted in the setting of less difficult goals, if this was perceived as a way of increasing income. In a word-unscrambling task, subjects could choose the word length, but were paid according to whether they successfully un-scrambled a word, irrespective of length. As the level of incentive pay increased, subjects set goals, that is, recorded intentions of decreasing word length, and also chose shorter words to unscramble. A significant association was found between incentive and intentions, but when the effect of intentions was partialled out, no relation was found between incentive and choice. This finding suggests that monetary incentives directly affect goal setting, and then the subject behaves in such a way as to achieve the goal he has set.

The Locke *et al.* (1968) experiment also emphasized that monetary incentives may encourage subjects to set less difficult goals, and since goal levels affect performance, higher monetary incentives may be associated with lower performance. This is not the association usually assumed in the literature. Like Georgopoulos *et al.* (1957: 346), most writers have assumed that "It is doubtful whether many people see low productivity as helping the achievement of many of their goals." Yet if rewards are strictly contingent on goal achievement, then lowering goals allows the rewards to be obtained more easily, and therefore may result in lower performance.

Top management may be aware of this potential link between incentives and lower performance, for it is almost universally accepted that information about pay and salary assessment should be kept secret (Lawler, 1967). Such secrecy allows the link between lower performance and either higher income or the same income for less effort to be hidden, but it also fosters the opposite belief, that higher performance is associated with higher income. Georgopoulos *el al.* (1957) collected questionnaire information from a population of incentive workers, nearly half of whom had had less than a year's experience on the job, and found that 62 percent felt that high productivity reduced their earnings in the long run, and 64 percent felt that low productivity did also. Evidently, most workers saw the link between income and performance quite clearly. As long as income depended on performance relative to standards, and standards could be adjusted so that take-home pay was within an appropriate range, higher performance could result in increased goals; to avoid such punishment for higher performance, less ambitious goals could be set, thus lowering performance.

Monetary incentives, therefore, do affect goal setting which in turn affects performance. If budgeted individuals set their own goals, they will set them so that their personal income is increased. When payment depends strictly on goal achievement, budgeted individuals will reduce their goals and therefore performance. Only if incentive payments depend on some direct measure of performance, rather than on a relative performance standard, are difficult goals likely to be set and performance improve.

INADEQUATE EXTRINSIC REWARD AND GOAL SETTING

Hypotheses derived from Festinger's (1957) theory of cognitive dissonance suggest that when an individual chooses to carry out an activity for which he will receive inadequate reward from his environment, he will increase the effort he invests in the activity. As a result, the person's performance may improve, allowing the attainment of personal rewards from significant achievements. This sense of personal achievement substitutes for the original inadequate environmental reward and reassures the person that his original decision to engage in the activity was justified. Specifically, Weick (1966) held that inadequate environmental reward for performance will lead a subject to focus on his own inputs and shift the responsibility for his behavior from an external to an internal source. If a suitable dissonant cognition could be created with respect to budgeting, goal setting and hence performance might improve.

Hofstede (1967) recognized this possibility, though not the link with dissonance theory. His thesis was that budgeted individuals, not top management, should regard budgeting as a game. Such a perception is certainly in contrast to arguments that budgeting is an important element of organizational control and that extrinsic rewards, specific and implicit, should depend on budget achievement. To create cognitive dissonance, extrinsic rewards would not be dependent on goal achievement, and for maximum dissonance, the organization would allow managers to work without budgets if they wished. Then the reason for having a budget, that it was needed to be facilitate organizational control, would be removed. To resolve the dissonance of choosing to commit himself to a budget in such a situation, a manager would have to wish to obtain the sense of individual achievement which comes from meeting a goal, rather than because of any extrinsic rewards provided by top management.

Two laboratory experiments provide some insight into how cognitive dissonance might effect budget performance. Stedry (1962) found a significant negative association between performance and subjects' beliefs that high monetary rewards would make them work harder. He also found a significant positive association between performance and the enjoyment obtained from the inherent challenge in the task, in contrast to the satisfaction of earning money. Stedry (1962) explained these results as due to subjects' differential financial needs and differential abilities to do the experimental problems. However, since the experimental task was presented to subjects (Stedry, 1962: 61), "as a game in order to avoid possible antimathematical blocks associated with problems in algebra," an alternative explanation might be that subjects who accepted the experimental task as a game then sought to overcome challenging goals, whereas those who saw achievement of the goal as a means to earn money did not perform as well.

Weick (1964: 534) asked students to take part in a "study of problem-solving to receive credit toward fulfilling a course requirement." The experimental task required subjects to identify, by means of cues, a concept chosen by the experimenter. Subjects were asked to set time goals and to identify the concept as quickly as possible with as few cues as possible. They were also told that other people had performed the task, that fairly complete norms had been developed, and that afterwards, they would be able to compare their performance with that of others. Low-dissonance subjects carried out the experiment as they had been led to expect, but high-dissonance subjects were told that they would not receive the credit that had been promised them and that, therefore, they were free to leave even though the experimenter preferred that they stayed. Four out of 54 students left so that 50 students took part in the experiment. Weick's (1964) main hypothesis was that the performance of high-dissonance subjects would be superior to that of low-dissonance subjects.

As Table 23.2 shows, the high-dissonance group performed only slightly below their goal, but, the low-dissonance group was much below. All the differences between the two conditions were statistically significant and in the expected direction. Performance improved in both groups, but while the attainment time on the fourth trial for the low-dissonance group was 117.4 seconds, it was only 43.71 seconds for the high-dissonance group.

TABLE 23.2
Performance of Groups Getting Credit and Getting No Credit (Weick, 1964)

Performance of groups	Condition	
	No credit	Credit
Average goal time (seconds)	62.44	125.40
Average performance time (seconds)	70.64	191.38
Attainment discrepancy (seconds)	-8.20	-65.98
Average cost of cues (points)	72.57	118.77

Weick's (1964) results are impressive, and a provocative analogy can be made with business budgeting. Top management could carry out its long-range planning independent of managers at the operating level. Then, like Weick's (1964) students, managers could be allowed a choice as to whether they would participate in the budgeting game. If they chose to use a budget, both top management and the budgeted individual would want challenging goals, because then achieving the goal would give a sense of accomplishment to the budgeted individual and it would also increase profit for top management.

SUMMARY

A budgeting system was described as a hierarchical combination of a goal-setting machine and a goal-achieving machine. The goal-achieving machine sets goals which should increase corporate profit; the goal-achieving machine endeavors to achieve exactly the budgeted goal in order to facilitate organizational coordination and planning. Evidence presented showed that goals significantly affect performance, that participation in goal setting of itself, had little discernible direct effect on the goal levels set, that monetary incentives encouraged the setting of less difficult goals when the reward depended strictly on goal achievement, and it was suggested that inadequate extrinsic rewards may result in the setting of difficult goals and higher performance.

As a result of the survey, a number of problems for further research have become apparent.

1. Evidence is needed as to whether personality characteristics such as needs for dependence or authoritarianism are associated with a budgeted individual's acceptance of a goal set by higher management.

2. Evidence is needed about the relation between managers' perceptions of how their budgetary performance affects their salaries and how this perception affects their goal-setting behavior. The effect of other variables on goal-setting behavior should also be considered.

3. In particular, evidence is needed from industrial settings of the effects on goal setting and performance when cognitive dissonance has been created by allowing managers to choose whether they will work with a budget when it is known that there are extrinsic rewards for goal achievement.

4. Evidence is also needed about how variables such as those discussed in this paper may interact with each other to affect goal setting, budget acceptance and budget achievement.

REFERENCES

Brehm, Jack W., and Arthur R. Cohen. *Explorations in Cognitive Dissonance.* New York: Wiley, 1962.

Dill, William R. "Business organizations." In James G. March (ed.), *Handbook of Organizations,* 1071–1114. Chicago: Rand-McNally, 1965.

Festinger, Leon. *A Theory of Cognitive Dissonance.* Evanston: Row, Peterson, 1957.

Georgopoulos, Basil S., Gerald M. Mahoney, and Nyle W. Jones. "A path-goal approach to productivity." *Journal of Applied Psychology,* 41 (1957): 345–353.

Hofstede, Geert II. *The Game of Budget Control.* Assen: Van Gorcum, 1967.

Lawler, Edward E. "Secrecy about management compensation: are there hidden costs?" *Organizational Behavior and Human Performance,* 2 (1967): 182–189.

Lawrence, Lois C., and Patricia C. Smith. "Group decision and employee participation." *Journal of Applied Psychology,* 39 (1955): 334–337.

Likert, Rensis. *The Human Organization.* New York: McGraw-Hill, 1967.

Locke, Edwin A. "Toward a theory of task motivation and incentives." *Organizational Behavior and Human Performance,* 3 (1968): 157–189.

Locke, Edwin A., Judith A. Bryan, and Lorne M. Kendall. "Goals and intentions as mediators of the effects of monetary incentives on behavior." *Journal of Applied Psychology,* 52 (1968): 104–121.

Rath, Arthur A. "The case for individual incentives." *Personnel Journal,* 39 (1960): 172–175.

Siegel, Sidney, and Lawrence E. Fouraker. *Bargaining and Group Decision Making.* New York: McGraw-Hill, 1960.

Sord, Bernard H., and Glen A. Welsch. *Business Budgeting, A Survey of Management Planning and Control Practices.* New York: Controllership Foundation, 1958.

Stedry, Andrew C. *Budget Control and Cost Behavior.* Englewood Cliffs, N.J.: Prentice-Hall, 1960. "Aspiration levels, attitudes, and performance in a goal oriented situation." 1960.

Stedry, Andrew C. "Aspiration levels, attitudes, and performance in a goal-oriented situation." *Industrial Management Review,* 2 (1962): 60–76.

Stedry, Andrew C., and Emanuel Kay. "The effect of goal difficulty on performance: A field experiment." *Behavioral Science,* 11 (1966): 459–470.

Tannenbaum, Arnold S. *Control in Organizations.* New York: McGraw-Hill, 1968.

Toppen, J. T. "Effect of size and frequency of money reinforcement on human operant (work) behavior." *Perceptual and Motor Skills,* 20 (1965): 259–269. (a)

Topper, J. T. "Money reinforcement and human operant (work) behavior: 111 piecework-payment and time-payment comparisons." *Perceptual and Motor Skills,* 21 (1965): 907–913. (b)

Vroom, Victor H. *Some Personality Determinants of the Effects of Participation.* Englewood Cliffs, N.J.: Prentice-Hall, 1960.

Vroom, Victor H. *Work and Motivation.* New York: Wiley, 1964.

Weick, Karl E. "Reduction of cognitive dissonance through task enhancement and effort expenditure." *Journal of Abnormal and Social Psychology,* 68 (1964): 533–539.

Weick, Karl E. "Task acceptance dilemmas: A site for research on cognition." In Shel Feldman (ed.), *Cognitive Consistency,* 225–255. New York: Academic Press, 1966.

24

The Federal Accountant's Role in Providing Organizational Incentives

John W. Cooley

In the evolution of Federal financial systems, one objective has been to promote economy by motivating people to work efficiently. The techniques introduced for this purpose were based on assumptions about the nature of people and their interaction in organizations. Due to rapid changes in environment, the motivating role of financial systems needs to be reappraised. In making this reappraisal, the key questions are: (1) What motivates people to accomplish organizational objectives? (2) What assumptions about motivation underlie Federal management control systems? (3) What are the weaknesses in present organizational incentives? (4) Why have twenty years of efforts by Federal accountants failed to correct these shortcomings; and finally, (5) What are prospects of achieving the long sought

Reprinted from *The Federal Accountant* 20 (December 1971): 3–19.

objective of installing systems that will motivate Federal managers to be productive?

THEORY OF MOTIVATION

Psychology of Motivation

The limited but growing body of knowledge about human motivation cannot be synthesized into a solitary set of explanatory principles. But, as one authority said: "In designing a management control system, principles of psychology, imperfect though they are, are much more important than generally accepted accounting principles."[1]

Abraham Maslow concluded that motivation results from an unsatisfied need. He identified five basic needs and placed them in a hierarchy from the physical need for survival through needs for safety, social acceptance, and status to the desire for self-fulfillment. Motivated behavior, Maslow says, is goal seeking and directed toward reducing discomforts. A satisfied need ceases to motivate and the higher needs are not activated until the lower needs are satisfied. For example, when a human lacks oxygen, no other need has meaning. The need for oxygen, when satisfied, ceases to be a motivator.

Recently, the methods traditionally used to motivate employees, such as higher pay and better working conditions, have been questioned by behavioral scientists. For example, Frederick Herzberg found that salaries, when fairly administered, would promote a reasonable level of performance from people, but increases did not cause much improvement beyond a "get by" level. Factors such as recognition, opportunity for professional growth, and independence on the job, were found to be strong motivators.

Modern Organizations

Human motivation is affected by institutional arrangements. Years ago, Mary Parker Follett observed that organized activity requires an integration of personal and organizational goals and that conflict should be resolved in a way whereby neither party has to sacrifice anything. In practice, perfect goal congruency is most difficult to achieve.

Some authorities maintain that behavior in modern, bureaucratic organizations is largely institutional in nature and not explainable by theories of individual psychology. Technical specialization has advanced rapidly, but cultural definitions of authority roles have not kept pace. The result is dysfunctional role playing, due to a large gap between those at the top who have the right to make decisions and those specialists who have the ability. The degree of real centralization is influenced strongly by the degree of specialization which, in turn, is a function of the degree of technology. An attempt to organize and control in a way that does not recognize the "facts of the situation" can lead to gross inefficiency. In commenting on the widely observed harmful impact of centralization on motivation and performance, Dr. Victor Thompson stated that: "Strict control from above encourages employees to 'go by the book,' to avoid innovations and changes of errors which put black marks on the record. It encourages the accumulation of records to prove compliance. . . ."[2] Centralization tends to cultivate officials prone to "pass the buck."

Management Style

Management is the art of getting jobs done through people. Douglas McGregor classified managers into two categories: Theory X and Theory Y. These represent two different sets of assumptions about people reflected in a manager's style and strategy and in the way he uses accounting as a tool of his trade.

Under Theory X, managers motivate people through control of their productive behavior by reward and punishment and thereby cause them to seek organizational objectives. Behind this theory is the implied assumption that people are lazy and must be motivated to work by reward and threat of punishment.

In contrast, Theory Y says that people are motivated by factors already within themselves, such as the will to achieve. Management's job is to create conditions whereby these inherent drives are used to the best advantage of the organization. Behind this theory is the assumption that people generally enjoy work under proper conditions; that people like to achieve things; and that they will try to direct their own behavior in a way that meshes with the objectives of the organization.

There is growing recognition that decentralization and a participative management style bring into play the higher motivators, and that Theory Y represents the best strategy for getting people to achieve organizational objectives. Current usage of accounting is predominantly oriented toward Theory X. In his best selling book, Robert Townsend said: "Your people aren't lazy and incompetent. They just look that way. They're beaten by all the overlapping and interlocking policies, rules, and systems encrusting your company."[3]

Needs are based partly on the perception of the individuals involved. Young folks seem more humanistic oriented than their parents. In selecting a career, today's college graduates are less interested in security and more interested in an opportunity to develop their abilities and make a maximum contribution to society. Some people believe that the younger generation will resist becoming slaves to technology and bureaucracy. These changing attitudes may spur the trend toward decentralization and the participative style of management.

ASSUMPTIONS ABOUT MOTIVATION UNDERLYING FEDERAL SYSTEMS

Philosophy of Management

The U.S. Constitution infers a management philosophy of minimum Government. The founding fathers relied on the private market place as a motivator and regulator of economic activity. For the few essential Governmental activities, the policy was maximum decentralization. Each state and community was expected to finance local public services. Thus, people could see what they were buying without sophisticated financial systems.

As the Federal Government grew it became inefficient. Under the spoils system, Federal employees appeared to consider the ". . . faithful discharge of their duties and prompt transaction of the public business mere incidents to their main pursuit—an easy, pleasant, social good time in Washington."[4] The Civil Service was established in 1883 to promote recruitment of career personnel who could be relied upon to do a professional job of managing public affairs. Later, Woodrow Wilson said that the best way to achieve efficiency in Government is through hierarchial ordering of professionally trained public servants. This arrangement, dehumanized with relationships between institutional roles rather than between people, became, and remains, the pattern for large organizations and the framework around which financial systems are tailored.

Evolution of Management Systems

Many improvements in financial administration were instituted in the late 1800's based on the scientific approach to management then in an embryonic stage. In 1910, President Taft's Commission on Economy and Efficiency was organized to consider "employment of accountants and experts from official and private life," to attain more effectiveness and greater efficiency in public activities. The Commission concluded that: "In every case where technical processes have been studied it has been demonstrated beyond question that large economies may be effected. . . ."[5] In the late 1930's, the President's "Brownlow" Committee concluded that, ". . . to make democracy work today in our National Government . . . the Government needs thoroughly modern tools of management."[6]

With the "New Deal" and World War II, the Federal Government exploded in size and complexity. In the late 1940's and early 1950's, the Hoover Commissions found extensive waste and mis-management. These Commissions demonstrated that professionalism and previous efforts to improve economy in the Federal Government were inadequate. This resulted in legislation providing that budgets for obligations by object of expenditure would be replaced by performance (or program) budgets based on accrual accounting. The objective of the change was to establish responsibility accounting by relating costs and program performance in a way that would promote better management.

Adaptation of Commercial Accounting

In compliance with the laws, programs were initiated to improve financial systems. Recognizing the absence of a profit motive, Government accountants (educated and experienced in commercial accounting) tried to take advantage of every practicable administrative device to create management incentives for maximizing benefits from available resources. Financial arrangements were sought that would cause human nature to work for organizational objectives, rather than against them. Numerous innovations, borrowed from industry based on commercial practices, were introduced into the Federal Government. These transplanted commercial systems were expected to cause Government managers to act more like the presumably more efficient managers in private industry. These commercial techniques, introduced to promote efficiency, have paid dividends, but they have not always produced a full measure of potential benefits.

One technique, introduced to aid in performance budgeting, was working capital funds for interim financing inventories and work-in-process at some production and service organizations. By use of these funds, an internal consumer/supplier relationship was established that served as a partial substitute for the profit motive. Under this arrangement, managers of "supplier" activities were expected to be motivated to operate more efficiently because of indicators of efficiency. Consumers buying the items were expected to search for cheaper substitutes and ways of using less of the no longer free products or services. Also the outputs were expected to be allocated more efficiently because they would be rationed by "market prices." In a 1956 discussion of working capital funds, the Defense Comptroller, W. J. McNeil, concluded that: ". . . every place where we have established a revolving fund, we have made real profit for Uncle Sam."[7]

The systems promoted with varying success in the 1950's generally provided for straight responsibility accounting for funds and property. The explicit motivational foundation was that if you give a manager with a clear mission and matching resources needed information, he will make the right decisions. As Karney Brasfield said in 1956: "We believe that managers generally want to do a good job. We think the mistakes they make are primarily because they do not have the facts to operate on. . . ."[8] But, there was also an implicit underlying assumption that good accounting would expose mismanagement—that fear of such exposure would motivate managers. Internal auditing was established on a large scale to highlight waste and mismanagement so that corrective action could be taken. Where output could be measured easily, unit cost standards were established and comparative analyses were made to expose uneconomic units.

Of course, the accounting and internal auditing improvements made during the 1950's were sold as a tool of management, not as a motivator of managers. But in practice, a tool of one manager is often a motivator of other managers.

Redirection of Financial Systems

The improvements in the 1950's were directed primarily toward increasing cost consciousness at operating level. But, in the late 1950's, certain economists demonstrated that the systems then used led to suboptimization —that better methods were needed for choosing among major alternatives. Thus, the planning, programming and budgeting (PPB) system was introduced in the early 1960's to improve top management decisions in allocation of resources. In establishing the PPB system, a top-down approach was used entailing a high degree of centralization. The planning, programming and budgeting functions were tied together; resource requirements were related to objectives; programs were priced five years into the future; and a systems analysis capability was established to identify and analyze alternatives, using computers and quantitative techniques where applicable.

The motivation theory underlying the PPB system is that all programs are in competition for limited resources and that the sponsor of each program will want to minimize his cost and thereby fare better in cost/benefit comparisons. Also, additional information about alternatives was expected to produce decisions more likely to promote organizational goals. The system is based on the presumption that the decision-maker is an "economic man" devoted to maximizing public utility.

WEAKNESSES IN PRESENT ORGANIZATIONAL INCENTIVES

What the Boss Really Wants

The fact that Parkinson's Law relative to empire building is an international joke shows that motivational problems in large organizations remain unsolved. But, in both industry and Government, most people respond to what they think the boss wants, perceived by the way rewards are distributed more than by what the boss says. Notions about incentives underlying most Federal financial systems have relied upon supervisory officials who themselves may benefit from high costs.

The main problem is that the message has not been forcefully conveyed to Federal employees that their bosses are aggressively interested in overall economy. Yes, there has been lip service in abundance on the subject. How could pleas for efficiency be taken seriously when disciplined accounting systems have not been installed to properly measure either cost or productivity?

Rewards for a Good Manager

Incentives for more efficient management in the Federal Government can occur only when the good manager can be distinguished from the poor. Objective criteria of efficiency are not readily available in the Federal Government and even where they are, incentives to seek more efficient methods are not strong. Where efficient organizations can be identified with reasonable objectivity, means of reward are not available under existing financial systems. When by diligent effort, a manager increases productively and accomplishes objectives at less than expected cost, he is likely to be rewarded by having the savings given to another organization (possibly a rival) less interested in pressing for efficiency. After years of accumulated work by capable and dedicated Federal accounts, some operating level managers are still padding budgets. Budget reviewers are still making annual percentage cuts in some cases based on last year's funding level.

An important missing ingredient in Federal systems has been inability to allow managers to benefit from efficiencies. There remains a strong tendency to judge and reward a Government manager by the size of his budget. The number and pay of subordinate employees even influence a Federal supervisor's salary. As Charles L. Schultze said:

To the extent that public employees are themselves judged and 'rewarded' by criteria which relate to the effectiveness and efficiency rather than to the mere size of the programs under their control, individual and institutional incentives can be made consistent.[9]

As no ready measure of success and no easy way to reward successful Federal managers have been found, the selfish advantage of a Federal manager often is served by keeping the budget high—by building empires.

The Accountant's Dream vs. Real World

Suppose a manager plays by the accountant's rules and trims all of the fat from his staff and his budget. When the cut comes, he likely will be asked to absorb a percentage along with other activities. Also, the lower budget is likely to result in a reduced allowance for him next year. This kind of motivation, Paul R. McClenon observed:

. . . is clearly wrong: the situation is like that of unneeded appropriation balances which "must" be sent to avoid reduction in the base for next year. In both instances one might wish that the undesirable pressures did not exist, and one finds sanctimonious expressions of faith that they have been abolished, but one also can find evidence of their continued existence.[10]

Cost, even when given active and sympathetic recognition, tends to assume a role secondary to the desire for nice-to-have items and slack in the system. Slack permits the manager to earn a "can do" reputation and allows the organization to survive crises that inevitably arise. Financial systems deteriorate and valid cost information is concealed when managers don't play by the rules. Under the rules, resources should be given to cover the added costs of any new assignments. But frequently managers are asked to take new assignments (or arbitrary fund reduction) "out of their hide." The knowledge that new, unfunded assignments (or budget cuts) will come provides a strong incentive to pad the budget.

GAPS BETWEEN TODAY'S SYSTEMS AND THE ACCOUNTANT'S MODEL

Where Have Accountants Gone Wrong?

Since the Hoover Commissions, Federal accountants have tried steadfastly to center attention on objectives by placing both accomplishment and costs in a clear light. Systems that related cost and performance information were expected to motivate cost consciousness in decision-making. However, negative organizational incentives have not been overcome. Something has gone wrong!

The model system recommended by the Hoover Commissions and prescribed by public law requires disciplined, systematic measurement of cost and performance of programs. The sad fact is that Federal accountants still have not succeeded fully in properly measuring either cost or performance. Many of the easier changes directed toward the model system have been made. As a result of the succession of new initiatives toward the model system, the economical way of attaining objectives has become less likely to be overlooked. But, some of the easier financial innovations, made in anticipation of more difficult changes, may have produced interim systems with at least partially negative incentives.

A manager's ability to perform his mission within the authorized budget became one measure of his efficiency in using resources. This produced a tendency for managers to place greater emphasis on remaining within fund pockets than on maximizing efficiency of performance. The financial systems, in their evolutionary stage of development, have tended to undervalue certain resources while drawing heavy attention to other resources highlighted by the budget review process. Efforts to increase the budget may have become more rewarding to managers than effort to get greater utility from resources already available. Resources not highlighted in the budget, such as the rental value of real estate, and the differential from market value of the salary of military draftees, tend to be undervalued.

Problems in Measuring Cost

To relate cost and performance, an essential ingredient is valid cost information. Cost approximations used in budget formulation have improved, but the goal of establishing a management control system over budget execution founded on disciplined cost accounting has been elusive. For valid comparison of actual cost and performance during a given period, accrual accounting at a low level of detail is required. In spite of extensive efforts (especially in the last three years) to install accrual accounting systems, attention is still focused on obligations. Year-end windfalls and pressure to get funds obligated before they are lost are still facts of life.

Generally, Congress provides funds through an input oriented appropriation structure to cover acquisition of resources. This structure is unsuitable for cost benefit comparisons and objective oriented management decisions. But, changes in funding structure are resisted because funding channels are tied closely to the power structure. Managers recognize that if they don't fund an activity, they don't control it.

The primary purpose of Federal accounting systems is for fiscal controls in terms of funding provided by Congress. Simultaneous accounting by a Government Agency, in terms of both the source of funds, and the use of resources introduces complex conversion problems, complicates the program/budget cycle and is very expensive. In such cases, the fiscal records are properly given first consideration and the duplicate accounting for program status is usually undisciplined, untimely and unuseful. Back in 1956, when W. J. McNeil was the Defense Comptroller, he recognized that: "The development of an accounting system . . . which disregards the source of the funds is not a system which will ever give . . . meaningful information."[11]

The Missing Link in the PPB System

Before the PPB system was installed, some agencies had not even identified all outputs. Earlier performance measurement efforts were directed toward intermediate outputs of functional organizations at operating level. The PPB system could have been a big step toward achieving the model accounting system.

However, in designing the PPB system, instead of changing the appropriation and organizational structures to correspond with major objectives, a separate program management structure was superimposed in many cases from the top down over traditional organization and appropriation patterns. Since Federal accounting systems must satisfy fiscal requirements in terms of appropriations, a gap was left in the management control system. Generally, the accounting systems failed to provide variances from planned cost and performance in terms of the program structure used when decisions were made.

The PPB system was designed to aid in justifying resources for the right purpose, not for managing resources efficiently after they are obtained. The program decisions are based on estimate cost and performance that are never related to actual accomplishment as part of a disciplined, integrated system. This strained the cost estimating process, since the incentive of a program sponsor is to keep the estimate low until favorable decisions are made. In some cases, the PPB system became merely an auxiliary exercise while hard resource rationing decisions remained in terms of the established appropriation structure and funding process.

Problems in Measuring Performance

Even where cost accounting systems are in use, progress in developing suitable productivity measures has been slow. As Charles L. Schultze said:

> There is usually no . . . single measure which commensurates all of the various aspects of the output of a public program—indeed that is why it is a public rather than a private output. The measurement of the output of public programs, therefore, is usually extremely complex.[12]

To avoid unwanted side effects, care is required in using productivity statistics. For example, pressure on the Strategic Air Command to decrease the cost per flying hour could cause an increase in the number of flying hours to spread the fixed costs over a bigger base. Thus, facilities would be wasted in a way detrimental to the goals for which they were obtained.

Output measures represent an essential variable in the model Federal accounting system. If satisfactory productivity measures cannot be established, then the accountant's model needs major adjustments. Some accountants seem to have given up on the task of developing productivity measures. True, the job is difficult and requires common sense in selective application of quantifiable factors. However, improvements are possible in this area. Better performance measures are essential if the negative management incentives in the Federal Government are to be replaced with more positive ones. In devising incentive programs, the set of outcomes desired must be known.

Using the Profit Motive

"So what if we have good cost and performance information," some accountants ask, "We still would not have organizational incentives without a profit motive." But actually profit is a flexible idea useful under a variety of conditions.

While the U.S. Federal Government has been introducing commercial accounting practices, with the hope of improving incentives, large organizations in private industry have found that bureaucratic institutional patterns are weakening the profit motive. Industry has established profit centers with somewhat arbitrary measures of the contribution of each organizational segment to company profit and other objectives. Thus, led by changing technology and standards of living, the problem of motivating efficient management has become, to some degree, similar in all big organizations. Professor Victor Thompson found from his study that ". . . the motivations and behavior of public and private bureaucrats appear to be more and more the same."[13]

In 1965, the Soviet Communist Party started using profits as a yardstick of efficiency and source of incentive to producers. This produced dramatically increased production. Profits in the socialistic system (surplus production) serve both to stimulate and directly measure improvements in the production process. Profits of U.S. industry are not a direct and easy yardstick for production improvements since they are distorted by factors such as the tax laws. Indeed, Leonard Spacek said recently that the question "What is profit?" epitomizes the accounting professions's greatest problem —communication. He said that "profit as now reported is the result of a conglomeration of practices which defy definitions."[14] In the Soviet context which embodies the economic idea of maximizing utility (the same concepts underlying the PPB system), profits can be measured in any case where cost and production can be measured.

Incentives for success remain universally strong, though the role of profits in measuring success has changed. One study indicated that a manager for the Navy Ships Command spends as much time thinking about achievement as a manager in Ford or Sears. But since Federal organizations are not rewarded for efficiencies, productivity measures have been perceived by Federal managers as foundations for punishing noneconomic units. This is the main source of difficulty in measuring productivity. People do not want to be measured. The big problem is to apply each manager's driving, entrepreneurial spirit toward the right goals, recognizing that managers can sometimes succeed by just the appearance of achievement.

Crosswinds of Changing Trends

Proprietary accounting made possible the industrial revolution by allowing the growth of large organizations with absentee ownership when oversight by the investor was extremely limited by technology. Managerial accounting can allow flexibility in managing decentralized operations without loss of essential top management controls. Progressively summarized cost and performance (along with exception reporting) could serve as the primary basis for management control. Toward this objective, Federal accountants promoted flexibility for operating level managers, but higher echelons choose to rely increasingly on numerous auxiliary controls such as manpower ceilings. Thus, the flexibility promoted by accountants was seldom delivered to the degree promised.

While Federal accountants were promoting systems to support decentralization, advances in computer and communication technology permitted rapid transmission of data in massive detail. One item after another was singled out for special attention. Overreactions to individual problems led to a complex patchwork of overlapping controls thus greatly reducing the decision space available to operating managers. Detailed rules were prescribed covering not only what would be done, but how. Few rewards were offered for use of ingenuity and initiative that involved change in comfortable routines.

According to Dr. Carl Hammer, we are now in an era of "data pollution" and the purpose of nearly all of today's data processing is "to keep us honest." Many managers feel that lower echelon employees, if given freedom, would loaf and act irresponsible. This attitude is reinforced by individual mistakes. Dr. Victor Thompson observed that: "Where the need to control exists, . . . it often manifests itself in procedures, reports and clearances governing trivia . . ."[15] Preoccupation with such details detracts attention from important matters.

On the surface, the contention that better accounting with cost control and productivity measures is a step toward better organizational incentives may seem at variance with findings showing that the more freedom people have in their work the greater their accomplishment. But some controls are essential. Dollar values provide the best common denominator for a horizontal view of such diverse resources as personnel, supplies and services. An adequate financial system permits management by aggregates instead of details. Accounting can serve as a substitute for detailed controls over specific items such as manpower and equipment—restrictive additions to essential fund controls required by law. Proper controls can help a manager build his self-esteem in lieu of forcing him to play games to put up a good front. But many Federal managers have never seen such a system in operation.

PROSPECTS

Favorable Signs

There is evidence in abundance that progressive Federal managers recognize that top bureaucrats in Washington should not try to make every operating decision. For example, Federal funds are being given to states and cities with fewer strings attached. Manpower ceilings placed on Federal Agencies and other vertical controls are being relaxed. The PPB system is being reoriented to a bottom-up (building block) approach. But, to date, these changes have not penetrated deeply into the hierarchy. Real progress in reducing controls has been frustrated.

Even public accountants are beginning to realize that current accounting practices are based on the scientific theory of management which is becoming obsolete. For example, Arthur Tone said that the normal accounting model

> ... assumes that: (1) efficiency is the principal objective, (2) managers and employees are motivated primarily by economic forces, (3) work is essentially an unpleasant task which people will avoid whenever possible, (4) human beings are ordinarily disinterested, inefficient, and wasteful, (5) the accounting system is a control device which permits management to identify and correct undesirable performance, etc.[16]

Participative management and decentralization are hard to achieve through a hierarchy of subordinate officials in the Federal Government. Thousands of jobs depend on perpetuation of detailed controls. Government rules and regulations make it difficult to delegate authority to fix wages, hire and fire people, choose vendors arbitrarily or shift funds. However, many existing restrictions can and should be eliminated. The difficult jump from recognition of the need for change to corrective action is ahead. But with luck, we should soon be able to answer emphatically "NO" to Larry Jobe's question "Are We Doing Less with More?"[17]

Many managers do not seem to realize what a valuable tool accounting can be in moving toward decentralization. Accounting has been viewed as a negative control device and a foundation for punishment instead of a tool for providing flexibility by avoiding more rigid controls. The time is right for much progress in Federal accounting. To make progress, a mammoth selling job is required to change the image of Federal accounting. Federal managers need to be shown what good accounting systems can do. The selling job cannot be done by timid, reactionary characters, cringing in the shadows away from the mainstream of management.

Notes

[1]Robert N. Anthony, *Management Accounting—Text and Cases* (Homewood, Ill.: Richard D. Irwin, Inc., 1960), page 333.

[2]Victor A. Thompson, *Modern Organization* (New York: Alfred A. Knopf, 1963), page 159.

[3]Robert Townsend, *Up the Organization: How to Stop the Corporation from Stifling People and Strangling Profits,* paperback edition, Fawcett Crest, February 1971, page 96.

[4]Oscar Kraines, *Congress and the Challenge of Big Government,* Bookman Associates, New York, 1958, page 20.

[5]W. Brooke Graves, *Basic Information on the Reorganization of the Executive Branch,* 1912–1948, Library of Congress Legislative Reference Service, Public Affairs Bulletin No. 66, Washington, D.C., February 1949, page 51.

[6]The President's Committee on Administrative Management, *Administrative Management in the Government of the United States,* U.S. Government Printing Office, Washington, D.C., 1937, page 4.

[7]Honorable W. J. McNeil, Assistant Secretary of Defense (Comptroller), Testimony before the Subcommittee on Reorganization of the Committee on Government Operations, United States Senate, 84th C., 2d Sess., on S. 3362, et al, relating to Budgeting and Accounting, p. 196. Hearings were held March 20, 21, 26, 27, and 28, 1956.

[8]Karney A. Brasfield, Assistant to the Comptroller General, testimony before a Subcommittee of the Committee on Government Operations, House of Representatives on H. R. 11526, 84th C., 2d Sess., on May 21, 1956, page 50.

[9]Charles L. Schultze, "Using Incentives to Improve the Effectiveness of Government," *Monthly Labor Review,* September 1969, page 36.

[10]Paul R. McClenon, "Should Government be Made More Businesslike," *The Federal Accountant,* Vol. XIII, Number 3, March 1964, page 100.

[11]Honorable W. J. McNeil, Assistant Secretary of Defense (Comptroller), Testimony before a Subcommittee of the Committee on Government Operations, House of Representatives, on H. R. 11526, 84th C., 2d Sess., on May 21, 1965, page 160.

[12]Charles L. Schultze, "Using Incentives to Improve the Effectiveness of Government," *Monthly Labor Review,* September 1969, page 35.

[13]Victor A. Thompson, *Modern Organization* (New York: Alfred A. Knopf, 1963), page 22.

[14]Leonard Spacek, *What Is Profit?* A pamphlet based on Summer Course of Institute of Chartered Accountants in England and Wales, Churchill College, Cambridge, England, September 19, 1970, page 5.

[15]Victor A. Thompson, *Modern Organization* (New York: Alfred A. Knopf, 1963), page 161.

[16]Unpublished speech given to the Washington Chapter, Federal Government Accountants Association on February 11, 1971. Mr. Tone is a partner in a large CPA firm.

[17]See *The Federal Accountant,* December 1970, page 26. (Part of Title).

VII

Some Organizational Contexts

Perspectives on inducing and avoiding stress

Finance and budgeting are part of the vitals of any collective enterprise, and the influence is reciprocal. Patently, the style and efficiency with which finance and budgeting tasks are performed will leave their clear marks on the tone and effectiveness of the host organization. The organization, however, is no passive receptor. The diverse properties of various organizations will influence, and sometimes determine, how budgeting and finance activities are performed. The latter point will be emphasized here, for its significance is seldom noted.

The posture of this chapter can be stated broadly. Because of the jobs that budgeting and finance people must do, their contributions inherently are major stress points in any organization. Because of the way the contributions of finance and budgeting typically are organized in collective enterprises, moreover, the worst is often made of relations that are inherently difficult. In part, the stress associated with budgeting and finance activities is unavoidable, for money and the ways it is to be spent are the obvious stakes, and feelings can be expected to run high even under the best of circumstances. This will always be so. In at least some major part, however, the stress commonly associated with budgeting and accounting is induced by the very organizational relations that men impose upon themselves. This need not always be so.

In its most elemental sense, then, the thrust of this chapter is toward more effective coping with the stress often generated in the performance of budgeting and finance activities. Specifically, that thrust has two component vectors. First, the selections will seek to better describe what stress often does exist. Hopefully, greater understanding of what exists may help reduce the sting of the inevitable. In addition, specific ways of moderating stress in budgeting and finance activities also will be considered. These include, in general, two approaches: the restructuring of work, and inducing appropriate patterns of interaction. The two approaches can reinforce one another, of course, but individual applications in organizations typically emphasize one or the other.

As in the total volume, therefore, the focus here is on more effective action through increased understanding. Knowledge of what exists and of why it exists, in sum, sometimes can permit changing what exists. And that knowledge is valuable even if it only highlights how much is still unknown. Only a wise man knows what he does not know.

"The Staff Role and Budgeting/Finance" (Reading 25), by Robert T. Golembiewski, illuminates how typical organizational arrangements carry a high potential for stress in budgeting and finance activities. Briefly, the piece distinguishes between line and staff functions as primary and secondary to the accomplishment of an organization's objectives. This is the usual concept. It also distinguishes three kinds of staff activities: general staff, specialist staff, and control staff.

These seemingly innocuous distinctions imply manifold problems for line-staff relationships. Consider that finance personnel and units generally are specialist staff, although they may also function as a high-level general staff as well. Like all staff activities, then, budgeting and finance begin the organizational race with the serious handicap of being considered secondary. Some budgeting and finance officials resign themselves to this fate and become mere functionaries. Others try harder. In either case, the potential for stress may be great.

How can staff justify its existence? Well, staff could be very careful to discover irregularities at lower levels of organization and to report them upward to their superiors. The tactic is a two-edged sword, however, for focusing on Score-Card Questions places staff in a disciplining role with respect to those at lower levels of organization. In turn, this role may reduce staff's effectiveness in coping with Attention-Directing Questions and Problem-Solving Questions, which are more appropriate for demonstrating staff's usefulness to those at lower organizational levels. Circularly, then, staff may be further driven to seek top-level support via Score-Card activities. The circularity has patent self-heightening tendencies.

Other perspectives on the potential for conflict implicit in the staff role of budgeting and finance permit further insight. Consider that finance and budgeting do—and should—exercise considerable control over the activities of both line and staff units. As Golembiewski indicates, significant stress often derives from the actual exercise of control by those who are formally "secondary." Hence the typical and heated complaint by line officers that staff personnel should only help but that in fact they also regulate and constrain line activities. Service and control being two sides of the same coin, the organizational separation of the two in the line-staff concept is awkward.

Golembiewski also details nine sources of conflict that further demonstrate the senses in which the traditional staff concept is adequate neither for prescribing what line-staff relationships should be nor for describing what they are. In sum, the guiding principle of line-staff relations is in serious senses ill-suited to the realities of the regulation and constraint that are and should be exercised by financial and budgeting personnel. Nature abhors such imbalance, however. As usual, the incongruence of principle and practice is paid for in terms of a heightened potential for stress and perhaps for guilt.

People in organizations are eminently if often unconsciously realistic, and consequently they will tend to prepare for the worst in their interactions with budgeting and finance officials. Such preparations are often highly creative, but they are usually defensive in nature, and whether these preparations contribute to increased organizational effectiveness is problematic. Characteristically, also, these preparations generally focus upon somehow avoiding public evidence of ineffectiveness. Failing that, the focus is upon developing sources of support for the inevitable dark days when it will be necessary to fight to either establish that the figures are inaccurate or to soft-peddle them. Commonly, either of these approaches requires firm and substantial political support.

Chris Argyris's "Budget Pressure: Some Causes and Consequences" (Reading 26) suggests the richness of the ways in which security is sought. Argyris focuses on stress deriving from the use of budgeting to "keep the heat on" in an organization. His analysis clearly implies that such security often is paid for in terms of limitations on output and rigid organizational relations that defy change. Thus the creation of groups is a common way to seek security against the pressure of budgets, Argyris reports. However, such groups often provide security for members in organizationally awkward ways, such as keeping secret a labor-saving innovation. Similarly, the first-line supervisor must cope with the pressure supplied by budgeting personnel. He does so diversely: by channeling hostility into interdepartmental conflict; by punishing others, as via conflict in relations between line and staff; and by punishing himself, or "killing himself" at work. These patterns of coping, at best, imply mixed blessings and punishments for individuals and for their organizations.

Reading 26 reflects the grim legacy of punitiveness in organizations. Basically, Argyris documents the problems induced by the common definition of the success of budgeting and finance in terms of discovering, or attempting to prevent, the failure of others in the organization. The implied role for budgeting and finance is that of exerting pressure, and that role is likely to be an unattractive one for all immediately concerned. That is, few individuals like to pressure or to be pressured over even the short run.

Whether or not individuals tend to shun pressure relations, in any case, no clear evidence supports their general usefulness. Much contrary evidence exists, indeed. Consider the common self-defeating circularity of punishment. Broadly, the search for security becomes more futile as it becomes more frantic. Line personnel try to protect themselves, as by forming groups. And budgeting personnel respond by seeking their security via more energetic efforts to isolate errors. But the latter tactic, in turn, merely heightens the defensiveness of the line. Of course, massive efforts by the hierarchy can break such circularities. Sometimes, indeed, just such massive efforts are necessary and justified in desperate cases. The most probable legacies of organizational hatchetings are a long-standing bitterness or an abject dependence on formal authorities. Each of these legacies has great costs.

A summary conclusion for budgeting and finance seems indisputable. Clearly, shaping organizations more to human needs will require minimizing the tension implicit in so structuring work that some can succeed only as others fail. Fortunately, the self-fulfilling tendencies sketched above do not seem to be a law of nature. A good part of the potential for stress in budgeting and finance activities derives directly from the orthodox structuring of work. Robert T. Golembiewski's "Accounting as a Function of Organization Theory" (Reading 27) attempts to illustrate the fullness of the proof of this important summary proposition. In addition, Golembiewski attempts to depict the broad outline of an alternative model for structuring work that permits the more human use of human beings. The alternative model eases the tension implicit in budgeting and finance activities in several important senses, as the article notes.

Two major considerations particularly recommend this unorthodox model. Basically, the alternative model increases the probability that budgeting and finance personnel can succeed as the line succeeds. Moreover, the model is consistent with a wide range of research that permits substantial confidence in the usefulness of the alternative structure.

Detailed support for the major thrust of the selection by Golembiewski is provided by Herbert A. Simon and his collaborators in "Centralization versus Decentralization in Organizing the Controller's Department" (Reading 28). The excerpts below come from the study of the controller's departments of several business firms with geographically dispersed operations. The goal was to determine the effectiveness of different forms of departmental organization. A controller's department was considered effective to the extent it: (1) provides information services of high quality, (2) provides these services at minimum cost, and (3) facilitates the development of competent executives over the long run, in both accounting and operating areas.

Wisely, Simon and his colleagues refrained from applying such criteria of efficiency as "adherence to orthodox principles of organization," for the article makes plain such a criterion would have been awkward. Consider here only, for example, that many of the controller's departments consid-

TABLE VII.1
Four Value-Loaded Dimensions of the Laboratory Approach to Organization Development

A Meta-Values of Lab-Training*	B Proximate Goals of Lab Training	C Desirable Means for Lab Training	D Organization Values Consistent with Lab Training†

1. An attitude of inquiry reflecting (among others):
  a. A "hypothetical spirit"; and
  b. Experimentalism
2. "Expanded consciousness and sense of choice"
3. The value system of democracy, having as two-core elements:
  a. A spirit of collaboration; and
  b. Open resolution of conflict via a problem-solving orientation
4. An emphasis on mutual "helping relationships" as the best way to express man's interdependency with man
	1. Increased insight, self-knowledge
	2. Sharpened diagnostic skills at (ideally) all levels, that is, on the levels of the
	  a. Individual;
	  b. Group;
	  c. Organization; and
	  d. Society
	3. Awareness of, and skill-practice in creating, conditions of effective functioning at (ideally) all levels
	4. Testing self-concepts and skills in interpersonal situations
	5. Increased capacity to be open, to accept feelings of self and others. To risk interpersonally in rewarding ways
		1. Emphasis on "here and now" occurrences
		2. Emphasis on the individual act rather than on the "total person" acting
		3. Emphasis on feedback that is nonevaluative in that it reports the impact on the self of other's behavior, rather than feedback that is judgmental or interpretive
		4. Emphasis on "unfreezing" behaviors the trainee feels are undesirable, on practice of replacement behaviors, and on "refreezing" new behaviors
		5. Emphasis on "trust in leveling," on psychological safety of the trainee
		6. Emphasis on creating and maintaining an "organic community"
			1. Full and free communication
			2. Reliance on open consensus in managing conflict, as opposed to using coercion or compromise
			3. Influence based on competence rather than on personal whim or formal power
			4. Expression of emotional as well as task-oriented behavior
			5. Acceptance of conflict between the individual and his organization, to be coped with willingly, openly, and rationally

* Adapted from Edgar H. Schein and Warren G. Bennis, *Personal and Organizational Change through Group Methods* (New York: Wiley, 1965), pp. 30–35; and Leland P. Bradford, Jack R. Gibb, and Kenneth D. Benne, *T-Group Theory and Laboratory Method* (New York: Wiley, 1964), pp. 10, 12.
† Philip E. Slater and Warren G. Bennis, "Democracy Is Inevitable," *Harvard Business Review*, Vol. 42 (1964), pp. 51 ff.

ered effective variously violated the traditional model for organizing work. That is, the effective departments tended to have variously decentralized patterns of organization, such as those called for by the unorthodox model developed in Golembiewski's Reading 27.

The last two selections raise a momentous question: Is it possible to reorganize in ways that make more livable the large public organizations within which finance and budgeting activities are often carried on? It is certainly too early to answer such a question definitively, but early experience with the "laboratory approach" permits real optimism about the evolution of an increasingly more powerful technology for organization development and change. Basically, the "laboratory approach" reflects a specific set of organization values, such as those in Table VII.1, which are to be increasingly built into large organizations as guides for behavior. Generally speaking, these values are consistent with Golembiewski's "unorthodox" organization model and with Simon's decentralized pattern of authority, as these are developed in their readings in this chapter.

Golembiewski briefly describes this new technology in Reading 29. "Organization Development in Public Agencies" does two major jobs: It sketches the objectives of a typical program in the laboratory approach to organization renewal or change, and it illustrates some special difficulties for public agencies, especially those at the federal level, in approaching each of these major objectives. The final piece in this chapter thus outlines a hope and isolates a real challenge. The alternative to accepting that challenge is grim: acceptance of the dynamics sketched by Argyris in the first selection below as not only an accurate description, but also as a static picture of the way the organizational world must always be.

25
The Staff Role and Budgeting/Finance: Nine Perspectives on Conflict

Robert T. Golembiewski

Budgeting and finance officers are often at the center of organizational maelstroms. This is the case in part because they deal with the life blood of administration, and in part because of the double binds inherent in the staff role which budgeting/finance officers commonly fill.

The focus here is on that staff role, on its several forms as well as on the varying potential for conflict implied in those forms.[1] In sum, prevailing staff concepts tend to exacerbate the tension implicit in the delicate monitoring of resources in which budgeting/finance personnel are inherently involved.

SEVERAL KINDS OF STAFF

In most organizations, the basic staff role may be described as the Neutral and Inferior Instrument (NII) model. In this common concept, the staff man or agency is said to be:

- outside the chain of command
- advisory and subordinate to the line man or agency
- having the authority of knowledge or expertise or specialization to convince or encourage but not to order the line man or agency
- secondary to the line man or agency in accomplishing organizational goals

In actual practice, however, a variety of staff activities can be distinguished which diversely fit the NII model. Reliance here is on the comprehensive treatment of Keith Davis.[2] Davis defines "staff" broadly "as those activities which are supplementary to the primary functions of an organization" and isolates two basic varieties of staff and several subtypes of one variety.

I. *General staff.* Davis explains that the general staff is an extension of the manager's capabilities and therefore must operate within an area as broad as that of the manager himself. The assistant to a manager is a general staff man, for example, aiding the chief and serving as his agent. Davis concludes: "His function carries no authority over others. Since he cannot delegate to others, no one owes responsibility to him; however, he may acquire considerable power in various ways."

II. *Specialist staff.* Whereas the general staff serves one manager, the specialist staff relates to a number of managers and departments, including other staff units. Thus a purchasing department not only procures supplies and equipment for all (most) line units, but for other staff units as well.

As Davis notes: "Specialist staffs contribute advanced expertness in a narrow area of activity. Other persons look to them for leadership because of their expertise. Specialist staffs, therefore, represent an authority of ideas, instead of line authority to issue orders."

Davis explains that specialist staffs may have three types of relations with other organization units:

A. *Advisory staff.* A specialist staff which is advisory, Davis explains, acts as counsel to management by its own request in order to help "prepare plans, study problems, and reach decisions." The manager is not compelled to seek the services of advisory staff, nor is he required by formal structure to respect their services.

Davis concludes that the advisory staff is "the least obnoxious of all" for the manager. However, he notes that the relation may be wearing on the staff unit. "It feels insecure," he notes, "because it knows it can be 'put out of business' unless it can convince people to use it. Since it cannot force others to seek its advice, it tries hard to 'sell' its services, sometimes to such an extent that it becomes a nuisance. It feels, properly so, that it must justify its existence."

B. *Service staff.* The service staff does what the name implies, performing for the manager activities which are necessary to run his program. The purchasing department illustrates a service staff.

Davis observes that this service role implies significant difficulties: "It is apparent that service staff relationships are likely to cause more human relations problems than advisory relationships, because the service staff restricts the scope of a manager's actions."

C. *Control staff.* The control staff exercises control over activities of other organization units. Of course, every staff chief has line command over his own subordinates.

Davis considers the control staff to be particularly important because of its potential for line-staff conflict. It gives rise to the complaint about staff units which have all of the authority but no responsibility.

Davis isolates four types of staff control:

1. Functional control, which gives the staff the right to issue orders concerning some aspect of a manager's job and to take action if compliance does not result.

2. Agency control, which gives the staff the right to issue orders in the name of the line manager but not otherwise.
3. Policy control, which gives the staff the right to observe adherence to managerial policy, and to take appropriate action.
4. Procedural control, which gives the staff the right to monitor procedures and to review and approve line decisions.

This taxonomy serves several purposes. Notice that Davis uses the taxonomy to illustrate the kinds of tensions which develop between the line and the various types of staff. The influence of the NII concept also is reflected in the taxonomy, since at least part of the critical line reactions derive from the conceptual assignment of inferior status to staff. The NII concept encourages certain extreme behaviors, for example, expecially by the advisory staff. Most important, outlining the several kinds of staff is significant because each demands a different pattern of relations: "One of the reasons that specialist staffs have so much difficulty in business is that they do not understand these different relationships and consequently do not vary their action to fit the situation," Davis concludes.

In summary, the contradictions between concept and practice imply some subtle problems for the interfacing of line and staff units or officers, who will henceforth be called "program" and "sustaining," respectively. The binds are particularly serious for NII sustaining officials who are control staff or who exercise some control although they are general staff or specialist staff. This is to say that difficulties are common; any large staff unit is likely to reflect aspects of advice, service, and control. Moreover, control is typically a significant feature of the activities of almost any staff unit.

The focus below is on nine sources of tension for staff officials, and especially those who are service or control staff. However, for activities with a very strong advisory and voluntary flavor—as employee counseling on personal problems—this analysis might be quite inappropriate. Indeed, such services often are best provided by an outsider—a consultant, physician, professor, or the like—in whom the employee can confide with reasonable assurance the matters revealed in confidence will not be used against him when promotions or pay increases are at issue.[3]

NINE SOURCES OF TENSION

The problems of interfacing program and sustaining activities derive from role definitions that are commonly violated in practice. Nine sources of tension provide important perspectives on why these violations of concept are so common and so intense. These sources of tension may be considered objective dilemmas which the NII model cannot avoid or resolve and which it may even heighten.

1. *"Control" is the other side of the coin of "service."* That is, tension will exist inherently between program and sustaining activities as both strive to do their jobs effectively. Service often will have control overtones that can affect the performance of program activities. There simply is no getting around it.

The ineluctable blend of service and control is an organizational universal. Consider personnel as a sustaining activity. It may be noted that a personnel department merely does the preliminary screening of potential employees and ministerially forwards to line supervisors a list of candidates for a particular job, from which list the line man makes his choice. Nevertheless, determining who gets on the list patently constitutes control over the head of the program unit as well as service. Final choice does not change this fact.

The impact of sustaining activities in personnel selection can be both profound and subtle. For example, William H. Whyte, Jr., asked the presidents and personnel directors of major enterprises to choose between two types of applicants for a job: the man "with strong personal convictions who is not shy about making unorthodox decisions that will unsettle tested procedures," and "the adaptable administrator schooled in managerial skills and concerned primarily with human relations and the techniques of making the corporation a smooth-working team." The presidents split their choices, but 70 percent of the personnel directors chose the "adaptable administrator."[4] Service becomes control in the long run in such a case, when the trainees chosen by the personnel director (and, more often than not, reflecting the director's preferences) rise to positions of influence.

The control aspects of service can be more obvious, of course. Thus sustaining units can utilize a wide variety of tactics to make their control a matter of fact as well as their service a matter of help, the NII model notwithstanding. Illustratively, Ernest Dale argues that sustaining officials have at least these five major sources of leverage for exerting influence or for "participating in command":

1. Command through superior articulation, since communicative skills and opportunities probably are more common in staff jobs.
2. Command through technical competence.
3. Command through status, since line officials commonly deal with higher level staff officers.
4. Command through sanctions, which range from (apparently) occasional formal power to various nonformal sources of influence, as "having the ear" of some high-level line official.
5. Command by default of line officials.[5]

All of this, indeed, may make too much of a point that has a firm place in common shoptalk about organized effort. Service and control often are not separable, whatever the model of relations between program and sustaining officials. The only relevant consideration is whether the model recognizes this commingling or neglects it.

2. *Sustaining activities allocate scarce resources.* The point holds whether one is considering office space, the delivery of mail, information, or professional advice and services. Often a question of priority is involved, not because anyone wants it that way, but because that is the way things are. Not everyone can get everything they want when they want it. Scarce resources are valuable to the heads of program units, and so the problem of priorities must imply tension between sustaining and program units.

An elemental acquaintance with life in organizations provides ample supporting evidence. The records of a maintenance department often reflect the effects of such bargaining, for example, since both maintenance and its costs are important to program heads. The informal determination of priorities may be reflected in many back orders for some program units and few for others, or maintenance costs may differ for similar jobs in different units.[6] Prompt service and low charges (or their absence) imply control over the program chief's ability to get the job done.

NII model or no, the sustaining official may be moved to just such attempts at control by some power-oriented facts of life in organizations. Favored program units might feel obliged to provide support for the generous sustaining unit in the inevitable contests for other scarce resources, such as the scuffles for budget. Certainly, there are delicate and crude ways by which sustaining officials might encourage respect for their interests from program officials. Illustratively, George Strauss and Leonard R. Sayles describe this strategy of a ship's stores sustaining unit on a large vessel as stemming from the fact that certain groups were always demanding rapid service on complicated requisitions. Ship's stores responded aggressively: "The Ship's Stores workers, moving with speed and efficiency, merely announced that these offending groups would have to fill out in perfect detail the multi-copy, excessively complicated formal requisition sheets that were required by an official, but rarely observed, rule."[7] These pressuring units, in addition, were denied their share of other goods and services (such as ice cream) that were distributed by ship's stores.

The allocation of scarce resources, then, is a source of power to be husbanded carefully. Overplaying one's resources may be catastrophic; underplaying them may invite scorn or the impositions of colleagues. Again, one cannot wish away the problem of scarcity in organizations. It underlies the informal resolutions by power of the many issues that have no strictly technical answer, if any issues permit value-free solutions.

Organizational gamesmanship has broad structural implications. Any line-staff structure can only be more or less useful in providing an arena for the inevitable byplay out of which organizational success or failure evolves. A structure which neglects such dynamics is not likely to provide a congenial ballpark for the organizational game that will be played. If sustaining officials must resort to stratagems to force recognition of their importance, however, performance is not likely to be facilitated over the generality of cases.

3. *Program and sustaining activities have different time orientations.* To simplify only a little, job pressures encourage program officials to be today oriented, while personnel in sustaining units experience pressures that are by-and-by oriented. Patently, being more or less out of phase encourages tension between program and sustaining units and officials. Moreover, personality differences apparently reinforce and complicate these differing time orientations,[8] and matters are gravely aggravated by complementary differences in the difficulty of measuring results. Many program activities have a relatively short lead time in evaluating results, while the positive or negative payoffs of a training program, in contrast, may not show up for a decade or more. Thus for there to be any training at all, program heads must be convinced that it is sensible to take men out of work which has short-run returns and put them on work with a very long-run return, if any at all.

Such differing temporal orientations imply some interesting dynamics that structural arrangements must contain. Consider but a single point. The longer-run payoffs characteristic of sustaining activities often leave staff agencies and individuals disadvantaged in such matters as the allocation of the budget, although management opinion may offset this disadvantage to varying degrees.[9] Sustaining units or officials can be expected to compensate for any bargaining weakness by taking advantage of the complementarity of service and control. A staff model must recognize this datum of power and provide for its effective resolution in organizations.

4. *Performers of sustaining activities, for a variety of reasons, are encouraged to play the role of informant.* There is no dearth of notices that sustaining units and officials perform the "fink function," and compelling factors support such behavior. Sustaining activities were designed to augment the senses of the manager or owner in an organization grown too large for his own faculties. The picturesque analogies expressing this point of view were unhappy caricatures, but they were still influential.[10] They encourage casting sustaining units in the roles of informants or glorified prosthetic devices for management.

This may make too much of a crude organismic mataphor. At the very least, the sustaining official often is privy to much information—often of an interunit nature—which could help overhead program heads. This information is a source of power for sustaining units or officials, as well as a source of tension between them and program units or officials. The advantage of sustaining personnel in being "all over" an administrative unit can be striking. For example, one enterprising staff unit in the Pentagon made extraordinary use of its access to all administrative units. While delivering office supplies via carrier bicycle in the mammoth Pentagon Building, members of the sustaining unit also took "numbers." Their weekly handle was $100,000. Similar access of persons, places, and information can be put to less blatant uses.

Such advantages of access often held by sustaining officials can lead to tension with program personnel, whether the information is merely a casual but choice tidbit or the product of a regular audit. The range of feelings triggered is nicely illustrated by the case of F. Haupt, from industrial engineering at Melville Dalton's "Milo" factory. One of Haupt's roving subordinates learned that one shop was using substitute materials. Haupt informed Tirpitz, a program head from another division, although the matter was none of Haupt's official concern. Dalton suggests that the "leak" was inspired by Haupt's difficulties with T. Kuester—the general foreman of the shop using the substitute materials—over one of Haupt's pet projects. Thus sustaining officials can make their advice difficult to disregard. But such dynamics have broader and subtler motivations as well. Dalton explains the consequences of Haupt's tip in terms of this significant chain of events:

> Tirpitz had ordered that the makeshift material never again be used because of processing difficulties in his own department. According to Haupt, Tirpitz immediately called both Kuester and Kuester's chief . . . "and bawled hell out of them. Tirpitz was so damn glad to learn what was going on that he invited me to have lunch with him." In Milo's executive dining room Tirpitz and Haupt sat at different tables, but this day they lunched together in Tirpitz' home, the better to cement the developing commitment to mutual aid. One of Haupt's intimates reported that he spent an hour in his office that afternoon "crowing about how Kuester had caught hell without knowing who had peeped." Later at parties, Haupt's wife boasted of the "new contact" her husband had made and what a "swell guy" Tirpitz was.[11]

Thus may higher level program and sustaining officials be drawn together, by accident or by design.

Any staff model must contain such dynamics. Given their delicateness, the usefulness of any model will be determined in significant measure by its success in restricting these too-human tendencies within some reasonable bounds.

5. *Can performers of sustaining activities "look the paymaster in the eye"?* This source of tension derives from several features of sustaining activities, among them being the size and growth of staff services and the relatively high rate of failure that characterizes many sustaining activities. Both sources of tension are particularly significant because of the difficulty of evaluating the performance of staff activities.

As for the size and growth of staff services, what may be called the staff "bulge" is common in organizations. Many organizations experience rapid growth of their sustaining activities after passing some minimal organization size. In a general way, one can appreciate why this is so. Given a small organization, single individuals may handle both program and sustaining activities. Witness the small entrepreneur who hires, fires, sets his own budgets, and so on. Given even moderate organization growth, it soon becomes possible and often necessary to spin off some of these activities. And, for a while, sustaining activities seem to grow very rapidly. Mason Haire's study of a small number of firms supports this intuitive explanation. He reported that in the early years of an organization's history, staff grows exponentially as the line grows linearly. Later, the rates tend to equalize. To give some approximate orders of magnitude to this growth, the first doubling of the line saw a sixfold increase in staff. With the next two doublings of the size of the line, staff increased about five times and then threefold. Beyond this point, both line and staff grew at similar rates.[12]

Many organizations have such a history. It can be a source of substantial tension between program and sustaining units. For the heart of administration is scarcity, and what the sustaining units take must come out of the kitty from which the program activities also draw. Given the differing time orientations of the two types of activities, plus the differences in the measurability of results, the taunt of "can you look the paymaster in the eye?" can be a sharp one when directed at sustaining officials.

To a similar end, program officials often have much evidence of "money spent on blunders" or, at the very least, of money spent for purposes whose contribution to performance is difficult or impossible to assess. Program officials will have ample opportunity to make bold use of such charges, given the emphasis upon change in sustaining activities (which is a source of tension in its own right). Change and development can be costly and uncertain, and even slightly sour program-sustaining relations can make the worst of these data. Sustaining officials might react very emotionally to criticism for "just doing their job," a job which includes a great margin for error and also poses uncommon difficulties for measuring performance.

The argument here must not be extended in extremis, but little qualification is necessary. There are cases in which the value of sustaining services may be calculated closely.[13] These opportunities for measuring performance, however, seem relatively rare.[14] Thus if labor turnover is high, inept selection by the personnel department and/or inadequate supervision may be at fault. How are such charges to be allocated? In general, both program and sustaining officials are anxious to take full credit for the successes and no responsibility for the failures. Compelling factors discourage a comely modesty in scuffling over such matters. As one staff officer explained the facts of life with respect to promotion in his company:

The higher you get, the more your advancement depends on impressions that your supervisors have of you. And these impressions are based on almost no real evidence [of technical accomplishment]. If a high staff officer . . . were asked what he'd done for the company during the last year he'd have a hell of a time pulling up anything concrete. When you're in a position like that you know all the time that other people want your job and are trying to get it—and you know that impressions are constantly being formed of you ... the higher you went the more you got involved in politics.[15]

This point of view gets very strong support from a variety of observers and practitioners placed both high and low in organizations.

The two features particularly encouraging tension from source 5—the growth and size of sustaining services and the difficulty of measuring their performance—set a dual task for any satisfactory model of staff relations. The model must tend to reduce requirements for sustaining personnel as compared to alternative models. In practice, this means that a satisfactory model must reduce the number of lower- and middle-level paper-manipulating jobs. A satisfactory model also must permit relatively facile measurement of performance which, in turn, will reduce the need for staff aid.

There is a considerable practical urgency for resolving such problems endemic to sustaining activities. Straightforwardly, if we must admit to some exaggeration, staff commonly is the last to be hired and the first to be fired. No incontrovertible evidence on the point exists. However, personal observation and some research supports the conclusion as a useful rule of thumb for many staff activities. Consequently, an awkward staff model might well encourage sustaining officials to develop power, NII model or no, the better to withstand economic ups and downs. This mode of adaptation is likely to increase line-staff tension while it strives to reduce it. Or an awkward model might heighten the level of frustration among staff officials, a circumstance likely to goad performance over the long haul only under limited conditions. Worse still, staff personnel may turn to the perpetual pursuit of gimmicks, or to overly strident demands for line adherence to procedures, as the means of proclaiming their value to the enterprise.

6. *Sustaining units specialize in change and reorganization; program units specialize in a stable technology.*   Argyris's study of the budget process reflects these sources of tension sharply. Thus a sustaining officer articulated a fundamental bias toward change when he noted that: "We guard the fields. The budget department has to constantly strive to improve the goods and make the plant better. There is always room to make things better." In contrast, a program official saw this persistent orientation toward change as a threat to the stability of operations. "They are not fully acquainted with ... production problems," one program supervisor complained of the budget people. "They don't realize our troubles and our difficulties. The best thing to do is to bring them down and see our problems."[16]

The tension between change and stability can be sharp. The forces supporting stability are great, including as they do the inertia of habit, the fear of the strange, and the suspicion of the untried. Thus in the General Motors of the 1920s, developmental work on a radically new engine was abandoned after millions of dollars had been spent. The engine was lighter and more powerful, used less fuel, and was not subject to overheating or freezing. Whether or not it was feasible or practical no one really knew at that time. Perhaps the question can be settled in retrospect today, perhaps not. In any case, GM program officials did not appreciate the potential of the new engine as much as they feared the production problems its adoption would certainly bring. Being human, they succumbed to the temptation to settle for the problems of the known rather than face the new and unsettling. It was relatively easy to do, for we are told that the innovating staff men were considered "interfering outsiders and theorists."[17]

The bases of tension often are consciously recognized, fortunately.[18] But if it helps to know why you are going to hell in a wheelbarrow, it does not hurt much less if matters end there. That is, consciousness is only the first step toward a structural design that acknowledges such differences and permits some consistently reasonable adjustment of the long run to the short.

7. *There often are substantial differences between the "cultures" of program and sustaining units.* The concept "culture" refers to the sum total of the ways of living that are developed by a group of humans. Considerable forces tend to encourage the development of two such "total ways of living" in program and sustaining units that do not always blend easily, particularly at lower and middle levels of organization.

These cultural differences are not contrived; they develop from a number of potent factors that are associated with the performance of program and sustaining activities. The two activities are not monolithic opposites, to be sure. However, such factors as the greater possibility in program activities of measuring results directly and easily contribute to the sense of "being on the firing line." Sustaining activities commonly permit somewhat more detachment.

Moreover, the careers of program and sustaining officials often differ significantly.[19] Program officials are far more likely to have worked their way up through their present organization and to have done so on the basis of experience and knowledge of particular jobs or operations, rather than on the basis of formal training. In contrast, sustaining officials often are appointed directly to their present job from outside, they often have had considerable formal training, and they commonly have outside professional interests. These differing orientations provide reason aplenty for tension, as when sustaining officials argue for a policy as the only one acceptable to them professionally, and when program officials insist that such frills may be acceptable in theory but one can hardly expect them to work in their company.[20]

These comments may draw a more definite picture than existing research permits, but the slim available data do support the gross contrasts already mentioned. Thus sustaining activities normally draw people with substantially more education than do program activities.[21] Whyte, indeed, complains that the "bright young men" coming out of business schools commonly do not consider any alternative as being acceptable.[22] Moreover, sustaining activities tend to draw younger men. Length of service also tends to be significantly longer in the program activities.[23] Such factors imply and reinforce the differences previously sketched. For example, their shorter length of average service suggests that sustaining officials identify more strongly with their training or profession than with their organization.

The cumulative impact of such factors encourages profound and lasting cultural differences in the performance of the two types of activities. Dress and language often obviously reflect these differences.[24] Such differences are more likely to be characteristic of middle- and lower-level program officials, in addition, for lower-level staff are most likely to "put on the dog" to distinguish themselves sharply from the line by stressing the advantages of their work (such as being able to wear a white shirt and tie). This makes matters seriously worse. For it is at these levels, if anywhere, that healthy program-sustaining relations must exist.

A provisional conclusion, therefore, seems in order. Any staff model that does not promise to reduce cultural differences has little to support it. Certainly, any staff model that aggravates such differences must have extraordinary compensating features. For cultural differences provide an organizational humus in which the several sources of tension can flower splendidly. More plainly, communication is encumbered by cultural differentiae. And this lifeline of cooperative effort is difficult enough to sustain, given such features as the different temporal orientations of program and sustaining activities.

8. *Sustaining activities seem to induce a high degree of frustration in the personnel performing them.* This datum seems of profound significance, although it is difficult to predict the consequences of frustration. For mild degrees of frustration may improve performance, or they may inhibit it. It is an educated guess, made for considerations which cannot be detailed here, that frustration can seldom be managed so as to have mostly favorable consequences for performance.[25] On balance, the frustration implied in sustaining activities will charge the work situation emotionally and often will prove an unproductive source of tension between agencies or individuals performing sustaining activities and those in program activities.

The frustration associated with sustaining activities derives from a number of sources. Sources of tension 3, 4, and 7, particularly, encourage high degrees of frustration. The short promotion ladders common in sustaining units have the same effect. Thus an organization in which there are ten levels in the program units may have three or so levels on the sustaining side. Hence one avenue for alleviating frustration—upward mobility in organizations—is not so available to sustaining personnel as it is to those in program units. Moreover, turnover rates, such as those given in Table

25.1, are consistent with the hypothesis of greater frustration of staff officials. The differences, however, also reflect other factors characteristic of staff, such as the greater commitment to profession than to an organization.

The high frustration potential sets a stern task for any structure. No structural arrangements can eliminate this potential, and it is probably undesirable to attempt to do so. However, a structure which encourages frustration should have very substantial advantages in other respects. If nothing else, the high costs of labor turnover demand such extreme compensating features.

TABLE 25.1
Turnover of Program and Sustaining Personnel in One Factory

	Percentage Turnover*	
Year	Program Units	Sustaining Units
19--	24.2%	78.9%
19--	28.3	88.0
19--	31.7	88.0
19--	31.5	81.5

From Melville Dalton, *Men Who Manage* (New York: John Wiley & Sons, 1959), p. 96.
*Calculated by dividing the average number of employees into accessions or separations, whichever was smaller. Only nonsupervisory employees are considered.

9. *The integration of sustaining activities is a problem of great magnitude.* The problem of integration bedevils any organization, and it has a particular urgency for sustaining activities in today's organizations. "Integration" here refers to the smooth bringing together of all activities—whether line or staff—required for performing some task. In some organizations with parallel activities, therefore, little or no integration in our sense is required. But complex interdependence of activities is increasingly the order of the day, and here integration is vital. Such integration may be accomplished in two ways: either by departmentalizing so as to include all or most necessary activities in the same organization units at the lowest levels; and/or by establishing effective relations between several monofunctional organization units. The NII model rejects the first approach and complicates the second.

More specifically, integrative problems in organizations derive from three major sources in today's organizations. First, the contemporary proliferation of sustaining specialties has been wondrous. Most sizeable organizations house a formidable array of such specialties, ranging from operations research to cost control to human relations. This very proliferation, of course, implies significant integrative problems.

Second, integrative problems are heightened by the tortuous (and sometimes manufactured) complexity of the several sustaining activities. At times, as in operations research, a good deal of the complexity is inherent in the activity. Not infrequently, however, one suspects complexity for its own sake or for the edification of fellow professionals. In either case, the problems of communication between (let alone the integration of) sustaining specialties become pressing.

Third, the problems of integrating sustaining activities seem to increase in direct proportion to the size of the sustaining units involved. Given the history of the substantial growth of sustaining units common in organizations of even moderate size,[26] this is a matter of great significance. George Muller-Thym describes the tendency toward increased fragmentation with growth in size in these terms:

> In companies where groups of staff or specialized personnel have been consistently organized into management pyramids of their own, there has been a tendency to separate the "thinking" or "planning" parts of the organization from the "pushing" or "doing" parts. The effective working contacts of staff and specialized groups have been made primarily with people at the top of the organization. The "thinking, planning, controlling, problem-solving" people transmit their skills to the point of action through a long supervisory chain.[27]

These considerations challenge any staff model. The separation of thinking from doing, the working contacts of staff with top management, the transmission of skills through long supervisory chains—these imply serious roadblocks to integrative effort that must be met in larger organizations. A useful staff model must struggle toward integration against this tide of separatism. A model offering little hope of counterbalancing the pervasive pressures toward fragmentation has little to recommend it.

Indeed, this puts matters too mildly. Integrative problems can only increase. The adequacy of any staff model in meeting the problems of integration has both a great and a growing significance.

Notes

[1]The treatment below derives basically from Robert T. Golembiewski, *Organizing Men and Power* (Chicago: Rand McNally & Co., 1967), pp. 20–21 and 61–75.

[2]Keith Davis, *Human Relations at Work* (New York: McGraw-Hill Book Co., 1962), pp. 208–12.

[3]When such services are provided by an "insider," relevantly, the temptation to use the information sometimes becomes irresistible. The struggles of the line to gain access to relevant files and of the counselor to protect their inviolability may disrupt working relations, encourage the staff to "improve" its position with its information, or compromise the service program. See Nigel Walker, *Morale in the Civil Service: A Study of the Desk Worker* (Edinburgh: Edinburgh University Press, 1961), pp. 15–26.

[4]William H. Whyte, Jr., *The Organization Man* (Garden City, N.Y.: Doubleday Anchor Books, 1956), pp. 148–49.

[5]Ernest Dale, *Planning and Developing the Company Organization Structure* (New York: American Management Association, 1952), pp. 100–104.

[6]Melville Dalton, *Men Who Manage* (New York: John Wiley & Sons, 1959), pp. 32, 24.

[7]George Strauss and Leonard R. Sayles, *Personnel: The Human Problems of Management* (Englewood Cliffs, N.J.: Prentice-Hall, 1960), p. 365. See also Ralph H. Turner, "The Navy Disbursing Officer as Bureaucrat," *American Sociological Review,* 12 (June 1947): 342–48.

[8]See Behavioral Research Service, General Electric Company, *Motive Patterns of Managers and Specialists* (New York, 1960); Lyman W. Porter and Mildred M. Henry, "Job Attitudes in Management: VI. Perceptions of the Importance of Certain Personality Traits as a Function of Line versus Staff Type of Job," *Journal of Applied Psychology,* 48 (October 1964): 305–9.

[9]James N. Mosel, "Why Training Programs Fail to Carry Over," in *Modifications in Manpower Management* (Urbana: University of Illinois Press, 1958), pp. 17–25.

[10]See F. W. Lawe, "Staff Organization," *The Human Factor,* 7 (January 1933): 1–10. Reflections of a gross "organic" concept of "organization" are not rare. As a matter of fact, the concept has captivated students in this country since the late 1800s. For a discussion of the broad dimensions of the organic approach, see Dwight Waldo, *The Administrative State* (New York: Ronald Press Co., 1948), pp. 100–104.

[11]Melville Dalton, *Men Who Manage* (New York: John Wiley & Sons, 1959), p. 75.

[12]Mason Haire, "Biological Model and Empirical Histories of the Growth of Organizations," in Haire (ed.), *Modern Organization Theory,* (New York: John Wiley & Sons, 1959), p. 292.

[13]H. J. Helmer, "You Can Measure the Results of Production Training," *Factory Management and Maintenance,* 110 (March 1952): 128–30.

[14]American Management Association, *Measuring Results of Personnel Functions* (New York, 1947).

[15]Dalton, *Men Who Manage,* pp. 156–57.

[16]Chris Argyris, *The Impact of Budgets on People* (New York: Controllership Foundation, 1952), p. 14.

[17]Thomas A. Boyd, *Professional Amateur: The Biography of Charles Franklin Kettering* (New York: E. P. Dutton & Co., 1957), pp. 119–23.

[18]Alfred D. Chandler, Jr., *Strategy and Structure: Chapters in the History of the Industrial Enterprise* (Cambridge, Mass.: M.I.T. Press, 1962), p. 154.

[19]Melville Dalton, "Conflicts between Staff and Line Officers," *American Sociological Review,* 15 (June 1950): 342–51.

[20]See Peter M. Blau and W. Richard Scott, *Formal Organizations* (San Francisco: Chandler Publishing Co., 1962); and *Administrative Science Quarterly,* 10 (June 1965), entire issue.

[21]Dalton, *Men Who Manage,* pp. 87–88.

[22]Whyte, *The Organization Man,* pp. 81–84.

[23]Dalton, *Men Who Manage,* pp. 89–91, 95–97.

[24]Ibid., p. 94.

[25]Robert T. Golembiewski, *Behavior and Organization* (Chicago: Rand McNally, 1962), pp. 127–48.

[26]Haire, "Biological Model and Empirical Histories," p. 290.

[27]Robert C. Sampson, *The Staff Role in Management* (New York: Harper, 1955), p. 193.

26
Budget Pressure: Some Causes and Consequences

Chris Argyris

One of the most common of the factory supervisors' attitudes about budgets* was that budgets were used as a pressure device to increase production efficiency. Many cases were cited to support this point. Finance people also admitted that budgets helped "keep people on the ball" by raising their goals and increasing their motivation. The problem of the effects of pressure applied through budgets seems to be the core of the budget problem.

THE CAUSES OF PRESSURE

Employers and front-line supervisors believe that the cause for pressure from the top is due to top management's belief that most employees are basically or inherently lazy. Employees and front-line supervisors also feel that top management believes that employees do not have enough motivation of their own to do the best possible job.

The interviews with top management officials revealed that the employees' beliefs were not totally unfounded, as a few quotations from some of the top management (both line and finance) make clear:

I'll tell you my honest opinion. Five percent of the people work, ten percent of the people think they work. And the other eighty-five percent would rather die than work.

I think there is a need for more pressure. People need to be needled a bit. I think man is inherently lazy and if we could only increase the pressure, I think the budget system would be more effective.

Such feelings, even if they are never overtly expressed toward employees, filter through to the employees in very subtle ways. Budgets represent one

From Chris Argyris, *The Impact of Budgets on People* (New York: Controllership Foundation, 1954) pp. 14–22. Reprinted with permission of author and publisher.

*Editors' note: See Reading 20 for an earlier selection from this work which gives some details of the study.

of the more subtle ways. Once the employees sense these feelings exist in top management, they may become very resentful.

THE EFFECTS OF PRESSURE

How do people react to pressure? In three of the plants studied factory supervisors felt they were working under pressure and that the budget was the principal instrument of pressure. Management exerts pressure on the workforce in many ways, of which budgets is but one. Budgets, being concrete, seem to serve as a medium through which the total effects of management pressure are best expressed. As such they become an excellent point of focus for studying the effect of pressure on people in a working organization.

THE CREATION OF GROUPS

An increase in tension, resentment, suspicion, fear and mistrust may not be the only result of ever stronger management pressures transmitted to supervisors, and in turn, to employees. We know, from psychological research, that people can stand a certain amount of pressure. After this point is passed, it becomes intolerable to an individual. We also know that one method people have to reduce the effect of the pressure (assuming that the employees cannot reduce the pressure itself) is to join groups. These groups then help absorb much of the pressure and the individual is personally relieved.

The process of individuals joining groups to relieve themselves of pressure is not an easy one. It does not occur overnight. The development of a group on such a basis seems to have the following general stages of growth.

First, the individuals "feel" the pressure. They are not certain, but they sense an increase in pressure.

Second, they begin to see definite evidences of the pressure. They not only feel it, they can point to it.

Since they feel this pressure is on them personally, they begin to experience tension and general uneasiness.

Next, the people usually "feel out" their fellow workers to see if they sense the pressure.

Finding out that others have noted the pressure, the people begin to feel more at ease. It helps to be able to say, "I'm not the only one."

Finally, they realize that they can acquire emotional support from each other by becoming a group. Furthermore, they can "blow their top" about this pressure in front of their group. Gradually, therefore, the individuals become a group because in becoming a group they are able to satisfy these needs:

1. A need to reduce the pressure on each individual.
2. A need to get rid of tension.
3. A need to feel more secure by belonging to a group which can counteract the pressure.

In short, a new, cohesive group has developed to combat management pressure. In a sense, the people have learned that they can be happier if they combine against this management pressure.

Suppose now that top management, aware of the tensions which have been generated and the groups which have been formed, seeks to reduce the pressure. The emphasis on budgets is relaxed. Perhaps even the standards are "loosened." Does this then destroy the group? After all, its primary reason for existence was to combat the pressure. Now, the pressure is gone. The group should eventually disintegrate.

The answer seems to be that the groups continue to exist!

The evidence for this is not as conclusive as it should be. Therefore, the following explanation should be considered primarily in the realm of inference and conjecture rather than scientific fact.

These factors seem to operate to keep the group in existence:

1. There is a "time lag" between the moment management announced the new policy and the time the workers put it into effect.

2. The individuals have made a new and satisfactory adjustment with each other. They have helped to satisfy each other's needs. They are, as the social scientist would say, "in equilibrium" with each other. Any attempt to destroy this balance will tend to be resisted even if the attempt represents an elimination of a "bad" or unhealthy set of conditions. People have created a stable pattern of life and they will resist a change in this pattern.

3. The individuals fear pressure will come again in the future. Because of this feeling, they will tend to create unreal conditions or to exaggerate existing conditions so that they can rationalize to themselves that pressure still exists and, therefore, the need for the group also exists.

PRESSURE ON FRONT-LINE SUPERVISORS

But what about the foreman? Strong pressures converge upon him. How does he protect himself from these pressures?

He cannot join a group against management, as his work force does. For one reason, he probably has at least partially identified himself with management. For another reason, he may be trying to advance in the hierarchy. Naturally, he would not help his chances for advancement if he joined a group against management.

The evidence of the previous chapters seems to indicate that the line supervisor cannot pass all the pressure he receives to his employees. Time and time again the factory supervisors stated that passing the pressure down would only create conflict and trouble which would lead to a decrease in production.

The question arises, where does the pressure go? How do the supervisors relieve themselves of at least some of the pressure? There is evidence to suggest at least three ways in which pressure is handled by the supervisors:

1. *Interdepartmental strife.*   The foremen release some of the pressure by continuously trying to blame fellow foremen for the troubles that exist. "They are," as one foreman expressed it, "trying to throw the dead cat in each other's backyard."

In three plants observed, much time was spent by certain factory supervisors in trying to lay the blame for errors and problems on some other department.

2. *Staff versus factory strife.*   The foremen released much of the pressure by blaming the budget people, production control people and salesmen for their problems. The data already presented concerning factory supervisors' attitudes towards budget people substantiate this point.

3. *"Internalizing" pressure.*   Many supervisors who do not express their feelings about the pressure have in reality "internalized" it and, in a sense, made it a part of themselves. Such damming up of pressure seemed to be expressed in the following ways:

(a) Supervisor A is quiet, relatively nonemotional, seldom expresses his negative feelings to anyone, but at the same time he works excessively. Supervisor A can be found working at his desk long after the others have gone home. As one supervisor expressed it, "That guy works himself to death."

(b) Supervisor B is nervous, always running around "checking up" on all his employees. He usually talks fast, gives one the impression that he is "selling" himself and his job when interviewed. He is forever picking up the phone, barking commands and requesting prompt action.

Both of these types (or a combination of these types) are expressions of much tension and pent up emotions that have been internalized. People working under such conditions finally are forced to "take it easy," or they find themselves with ulcers or a nervous breakdown.

But that is not the end of the problem. Constant tension leads to frustration. A frustrated person no longer operates as effectively as he was accustomed. He finds that he tends to forget things he used to remember. Work that he used to do with pleasure, he now delegates to someone else. He is no longer able to make decisions as fast as he did months ago. Now he finds he has to take a walk or get a cup of coffee—anything to get "away from it all."

SUCCESS FOR BUDGET SUPERVISORS MEANS FAILURE FOR FACTORY SUPERVISORS

Students of human relations agree that most people want to feel successful. We observe people constantly defining social and psychological goals, struggling to meet them, and as they are met, feeling successful.

Finance and factory supervisors are no exception. The typical finance supervisor does his work as best he can. He hopes and expects just praise of this work from his superior. Most of his success comes, therefore, from his superior's evaluation. It is the "boss" who will eventually say "well done," or commend a promotion. In other words, a finance supervisor measures his success on his job, to a substantial degree, by the reactions of his superior.

The situation is the same for the factory supervisor. He also desires success. Like the finance supervisor, much of his success also derives from the comments and behavior the "boss" exhibits. In short, the factory supervisor is also oriented toward the top for an evaluation of how well he is doing his job.

What is the task of a good and successful finance supervisor? The reader will recall that the finance people perceive their task as being the watchdog of the company. They are always trying to improve the situation in the plant. As one finance supervisor said, "Always, there is room to make it better." And finally, the reader will recall the statement that, "The budget man has made an excellent contribution to this plant. He's found a lot of things that were sour. You might say a good budget man ... lets top management know if anything is wrong."

In other words, their success derives from finding errors, weaknesses, and faults that exist in the plant. But, when they discover these errors, weaknesses, and faults, they also single out a "guilty party" and implicitly, at least, accuse him of failure. This is true because in finding weaknesses, errors or faults in a certain department, one is at the same time telling the factory supervisors that "things aren't going along as well as they could be." This, naturally, gives many factory supervisors a feeling of failure.

To be sure, such an occurrence will not make every supervisor feel he has failed. Some supervisors do not worry much about their jobs. Therefore, we find that the supervisor who really feels the failure is the one who is highly interested in doing a good job.

REPORTING SHORTCOMINGS OF THE FOREMAN

The way in which these shortcomings are reported is also important:

Assume that finance man A discovers an error in foreman B's department. How is this error reported? Does the finance man go directly to the factory foreman? In the plants studied the answer, usually, is "no."

The finance man cannot take the "shortest" route between the foreman and himself. For one reason, it may be a violation of policy for a staff man to go directly to a line man. But, more important (from a human point of view), the staff man derives his success when his boss knows he is finding errors. Therefore, his boss would never know how good a job finance man A is doing unless it came to his attention. In short, perhaps because of organizational regulations but basically because much success in industry is derived from above, the finance person usually takes his findings to his own boss, who in turn gives it to his, and so on up the line and across and down into the factory line structure.

Taking the long way around has at least one more positive value for finance people. The middle and top management finance people also derive some success in being able to go to the plant manager and point to some newly discovered weaknesses in the factory. Therefore, not only one man obtains feelings of success, but all interested people up the entire finance structure obtain some feeling of satisfaction.

But, how about the factory people? The answer seems evident. They experience a certain sense of "being caught with their pants down."

Finally, to add insult to injury, the entire incident is made permanent and exhibited to the plant officials by being placed in some budget report which is to be, or has been, circulated through many top channels.

EFFECTS OF FAILURE ON PEOPLE

One might ask: What effects does this kind of failure have upon an individual? If they were insignificant, obviously we would not be concerned. Such is not the case. Feelings of failure can have devastating effects upon an individual, his work and his relationships with others.

Ronald Lippitt and Leland Bradford, reporting on some ingenious scientific experiments conducted on the subject of success and failure, state that people who fail tend to:

Lose interest in their work.
Lower their standards of achievement.
Lose confidence in themselves.
Give up quickly.
Fear any new task and refuse to try new methods or accept new jobs.
Expect failure.
Escape from failure by daydreaming.
Increase their difficulty in working with others.
Develop a tendency to blame others, to be overcritical of others' work
    and to develop troubles with other employees.

On the other hand, people who succeed tend to:

Raise their goals.

Gain greater interest in the activity in which they are engaged.

Gain greater confidence in their ability in the activity.

Increase their persistence to future goals.

Increase their ability to cooperate and work.

Increase their ability to adapt readily to new situations.

Increase their emotional control.

In summary, we should point out that finance people aren't inherently "out to get them" as factory people in the plants described them. Rather, they are placed in a social organization where the only way in which they can receive success is to place someone else in failure.

27

Accountancy as a Function of Organization Theory

Robert T. Golembiewski

Modern accountancy is ineluctably the product of a wide variety of environmental factors that shaped its tools and approach. This truism can prove very useful. For example, common opinion has it that significant changes in the scope and methods of accountancy must be made. The truism heading this paragraph, then, requires this important qualification: Any lasting changes in accountancy will depend in significant respects upon understanding these environmental factors and upon changing or eliminating them, where possible.

A recent article—"Organization Theory and the New Accountancy: One Avenue of Revolution"[1]—developed this point of view by considering one major environmental determinant that has left a deep impress upon accountancy. The present article attempts to satisfy numerous requests to present the argument in a journal in which both theorists and practitioners in accountancy will have a more convenient opportunity for study and com-

From *The Accounting Review* 39 (April 1964): 333–41. Reprinted with permission of author and publisher.

ment. Mere repetition, of course, seldom has much to recommend it. Therefore, this article takes a different approach to demonstrating the importance of organization theory to accountancy, and to outlining how structural innovation can contribute fruitfully to the present reevaluation of the scope and methods of accountancy. The reader reasonably may move from this piece to the more detailed argument of the original article, and thence to the massive literature on behavior in organizations that underlays both analyses.[2]

PURPOSES, PROCEDURES, AND PROBLEMS OF ACCOUNTANCY: SOME HERITAGES OF THE TRADITIONAL THEORY OF ORGANIZATION

The purposes, procedures, and problems of contemporary accountancy can be approached in useful ways as a function of the traditional theory of organization. Figure 27.1 facilitates making this point in detail. This figure [which will be referred to hereafter as Figure 1, as a type of organization] depicts the conventional organization of three "line" processes A, B, and C, and of one "staff" service D. Symbolically, the contributions of $A + B + C + D$ combine to yield product P_1. Note also that M designates the manager, and that each S refers to a first-line supervisor.

FIGURE 27.1
Organizing a Simple Set of Operations in Terms of the Traditional Theory of Organization

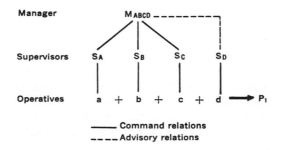

Figure 1 may be drawn with assurance and confidently taken to be a simplified analog of the kind of structure usually encountered in practice. For Figure 1 is based upon the well-known "principles" of the traditional theory of organization that guide most attempts at organizing. These "principles" include such propositions:

1. That work must be specialized in terms of functions at upper levels of organization and in terms of processes at lower levels.

2. That authority must be delegated by a single head to a sharply limited number of subordinates.
3. That supervision must be detailed and continuous.

The effects of these "principles" of organizing are clearly reflected in the purposes, procedures, and problems of accountancy. Some of the senses in which this is the case will be sketched below. For convenience, the emphasis will be upon internal reporting, as opposed to public accounting or the preparation of materials for annual reports and the like.

Purposes of Internal Reporting

Raising the question of the purposes of internal reporting easily could get out of hand. For the enumeration of such purposes is limited only by the ingenuity of the commentator. Let us keep tight rein on ingenuity here by restricting our attention to the several kinds of questions which a full-fledged system of internal reporting should be able to handle successfully. These questions, then, serve conveniently to outline the purposes of internal reporting. Following Simon and his collaborators,[3] three types of questions may be taken to outline the full range of challenges facing internal reporting:

1. Score-Card Questions: "Am I doing well or badly?"
2. Attention-Directing Questions: "What problems should I look into?"
3. Problem-Solving Questions: "Of the several ways of doing the job, which is the best?"

The quoted illustrative questions, of course, are those that a "line" manager might ask himself and those that an internal accountant could help answer.

Procedures for Internal Reporting

These purposes of internal reporting, as it were, provide destinations rather than routes. There are numerous procedures that might be employed to achieve these purposes, that is. In general, however, the procedures actually employed have tended toward a stereotypic pattern. This fact does not reflect the rigid requirements of optimum efficiency in organizations. In fact, the stereotypic approach often significantly curbs efficiency, as will be demonstrated. The stereotypy of the procedures developed in pursuit of the major purposes of internal reporting, rather, reflects the domineering guidance of the "principles" of the traditional theory of organization and of the structure sketched in Figure 1.

The argument of this introductory paragraph is an important one, of course, and requires careful support. To this end, let the focus be upon one major procedural element that pervades so much of the practice of internal reporting in today's business and government agencies, the "line-staff" concept. I have elsewhere analyzed in some detail the classical "staff" model.[4] This classical model was dubbed the "neutral and inferior instrument" (NII) concept, for it prescribes that the "staff" man is outside the line of command, that he merely provides neutral advice or expertise, and so on. This terse characterization suffices for present purposes.

The NII concept of "staff" all but monopolizes the field in prescribing relations in contemporary organizations.[5] Evidence of the impact of this procedural device upon internal accounting is common, for example. Illustratively, and consistent with the NII model, the internal accountant commonly does not report "across" to a lower-level "line" official at his own level. In contrast, he reports *up* his own "staff" hierarchy of one or more superiors, the "staff" superior then reports *over* to the appropriate higher-level "line" official, and the latter in turn communicates *downward* to the "line" official directly concerned, the communication going through one or more levels of intermediate "line" supervision. More generally, much of the content of the role of the accountant engaged in internal reporting is defined in terms of the NII model.[6]

The NII "staff" model did not just happen, of course. In all relevant particulars, it evidences the influence of the traditional theory of organization. Consider but a few factors that establish the point. At the very least, the NII model fits exactly such "principles" of the traditional theory of organization as specialization by function. In its crudest form, that model requires that the "line" specialize in "doing." "Thinking," or "planning," or some such, is reserved to the "staff."

Relatedly, only the NII model avoids a challenge to the unity of command underlying the traditional theory of organization. For the classical "staff" model claims both neutrality and inferiority, and both are necessary if the "principles" are to be respected.

This suggests the weakness of the NII model. Not that logical consistency with the "principles" was the only support of the NII model. That model was aided and abetted by the vigorous complaints of "line" officials around the turn of the century about sharing their authority with the new "staff" specialists. As Dale and Urwick described these complaints and their consequences:

> So the fur flew, and harassed chief executives in business after business were driven into a hysteria of assurances that staff specialists were not meant to do what they had manifestly been hired to do. The line managers were solemnly told that the staff men were "purely advisory" and that no one need take their advice if they did not want to. . . .[7]

Convenience, that is, proved a powerful reinforcement for logical consistency. Both together, however, hardly constitute scientifically desirable criteria for a "staff" model.

Problems of Internal Reporting

Internal reporting has suffered from this molding of procedures to the traditional theory of organization. In sum, the derived procedures proved inadequate to meet the three broad purposes of internal reporting as well as to surmount the mensural and motivational difficulties created by the traditional theory of organization. That is, the three purposes impose requirements different enough—*when the traditional theory of organization is respected*—that they tend to frustrate efforts designed to achieve all of them. Thus Simon and his co-workers noted the tendency of controller's departments to fulfill admirably one or another of the three purposes of internal reporting, while others receive less effective attention.[8]

The point here may be supported by outlining the demands of fulfilling each of the three purposes of internal reporting. Score-Card Questions, to begin, have attracted the lion's share of attention in organizations, and with substantial reason. For the traditional theory of organization requires that an undue importance be placed on score-card data. Referral to Figure 1 helps explain this bias of the traditional theory. Simply, three "line" processes A, B, and C are involved in the production of item P_1. A "staff" service D—internal reporting, let us say—provides valuable service toward the same end. Therefore, crudely, $A + B + C + D = P_1$.

There are motivational and mensural problems aplenty in this simple formulation. Let us forsake comprehensiveness, and attempt to make the most of a single datum. That is, only M_{ABCD} oversees enough of the operations to make reasonable decisions on non-trivial matters related to production of P_1. Understandably, then, M_{ABCD} will place great emphasis on score-card data. Many difficulties are implied and encouraged thereby. Three particular difficulties deserve spotlighting.

First, the traditional theory of organization encourages a separatism of the several units of organization while it requires that the efforts of each must be delicately integrated into a common flow of work. This works at cross-purposes, patently. Thus the units headed by S_A, S_B, S_C, and S_D have only tenuous responsibilities for P_1, the volume and the quantity of which is of obvious significance. The enduring interests of each of these units is more or less rooted in their own particular process or function. It could hardly be otherwise. For the traditional theory of organization stresses them, and individuals are paid to be interested in them. The difficulty, of course, is that total performance commonly comes off the loser in the effort to mesh such particularistic interests.

This phenomenon of separatism in organizations has been observed often, and it has been analyzed in telling detail.[9] We may, therefore, assume the incidence and significance of such organizational separatism and concentrate on its effects. When things go awry, as they often will, this situation obtains: M_{ABCD} will place increasingly great emphasis on score-card data; the individual supervisors will strive all the more mightily to have their own particular function or process appear in a good light, whatever this means for the total flow of work; and accountants will be forced to apply increasingly great pressure to unearth crucial data or to gain some measure of agreement about the allocation of costs. All this is natural enough, given the traditional theory of organization. But the dynamics tend to be self-defeating.

Second, these unfortunate dynamics do not reflect man's consistent and pervasive perversity. Rather, the traditional theory of organization tends to create an environment within which little better can be expected. Thus the traditional theory of organization forces the accountant to handle Score-Card Questions that are at least very difficult, if that theory does not create an ersatz complexity that makes impossible any non-arbitrary assignments of costs to individual organization units. These Score-Card Questions, in the bargain, have great relevance for the lower "line," and great reliance often is placed in them by the upper "line." This outlines an unfortunate condition, and certainly one not likely to exhibit man at this cooperative best. The assignment of the cost of an error to A or B or C, for example, illustrates the kind of issues on which the mischief of the traditional theory is most patent.[10] Matters are delicate enough under the best of circumstances. Consider only one awkward feature of the traditional theory. Each "line" supervisor has a relatively large organization unit, all of whose members are bound by the tie of performing the same function or process. This datum implies the possibility of an organization unit waging substantial political warfare if it feels disadvantaged in the assignment of costs. Relevantly, a single unit in a structure like that in Figure 1 can disrupt the total flow of work. Ample evidence demonstrates that this leverage does not always go unutilized.[11]

The role of "staff" in such jostling for power must be conflicted. Let it not be said that the accountant always shrinks from the effort of developing the power necessary to play the game with some success.[12] An accounting unit hardly could meet the rigorous demands of the traditional theory of organization otherwise. Short of settling for a program of nagging obstructionism or of desperate devotion to minutiae, the effort to develop power —to be taken seriously by others in an organization—must be a constant one. The common reliance of the upper "line" upon internal reporting, in addition, simplifies matters for the accountant via "having the boss' ear." But note that this effort must remain a source of conflict for the "staff" man, even if it is successful. For the NII model does not legitimate such an active role, necessary though it may be. The "line," therefore, can seriously question the legitimacy of "staff's" exercise of power. And "staff" might feel guilty enough about its own efforts to resort to more or less elaborate subterfuges to assuage its discomfort. These conditions are not well designed to induce favorable working relations between "line" and "staff."

Third, score-card data often must be used in attempts to force the integration of operations complicated by the traditional theory of organization. Particularly because of the separatism by functions and processes prescribed by that theory, great demands are placed upon internal reporting as a means of goading cooperative effort or of assigning responsibility in its absence. This punitive motivational use of such data makes mensuration very difficult. For example, it can easily force organization units into a greater resort to devices of self-protection, thereby worsening the separatism already endemic to the traditional theory of organization and thereby increasing the difficulties of meaningful internal reporting. As Worthy perceptively put the matter, respecting the "principles" eliminates

"natural" standards of performance and management is forced to exercise considerable ingenuity in inventing controls which it can use for administrative purposes. Unfortunately, contrived controls such as these, so far from facilitating interdivisional cooperation (which is one of their purposes) often become themselves a source of conflict. The individual supervisor or executive is under strong compulsion to operate in such a manner as to make a good showing in terms of the particular set of controls to which he is subject, and often he does so only at the expense of effective collaboration across divisional lines.[13]

This brief analysis is capable of terse summary. Score-Card Questions in an organization patterned after the classical theory have a punitive bias. Or to say almost the same thing, they tend to induce mechanisms of defense and self-protection. The point is crucial, for these products of generating score-card data outline just the conditions that make it very difficult to meet the other purposes of internal accounting. The point may be put in another way. Given the general acceptance of the traditional theory of organization, the collection of score-card data must preoccupy internal reporting. And to the degree that this is in fact true of any accounting unit, the less likely is that unit to prove effective in handling Attention-Directing Questions or Problem-Solving Questions.

These are not merely logical surmises, be it noted. Relevant research leaves much to be desired. But this conclusion seems generally appropriate to the question of whether internal reporting should develop in the direction of more elaborate periodic score-card reports or toward strengthening special studies: ". . . further development of staff and facilities for special studies is a more promising direction of progress than elaboration of periodic accounting reports."[14] This conclusion reflects both a potential usefulness and a relatively unfilled need.

If this analysis is near the mark, then, merely calling for emphasis on Attention-Directing Questions and Problem-Solving Questions must prove abortive. For the traditional theory of organization remains undisturbed, with all that implies. Tersely, the procedures appropriate for Score-Card Questions under the traditional theory ill suit the requirements of the two former types of questions. The same is true of the tone of relations commonly induced in seeking score-card data, and perhaps of the personality characteristics appropriate for the effort under the traditional theory of organization. It might seem reasonable, as an alternative, to assign responsibility for each of the three purposes of internal reporting to separate units. This possibility is not considered here. Thus, among other consequences, it aggravates organizational separatism, raises jurisdictional questions, and invites overlap and duplication of effort. Moreover, for our purposes, this alternate approach is not very instructive although it might be the best accommodation possible under specific practical conditions.

This position may be supported parsimoniously. Consider Attention-Directing Questions. Thus Simon and his collaborators note that they require "direct and active channels of communication with the operating executives at those points in the organization where operations are being measured." The implied argument needs to be developed only briefly to suggest how the search for score-card data under the traditional theory of organization often fouls the delicate relations Simon sketches. The NII model of "staff," needless to say, greatly complicates just the kind of communication required, if the burdens of "up, over, and down" reporting do not in fact result in a hardening of the communicative arteries. Relatedly, the punitiveness and defensiveness that characterize so much of internal reporting do not provide much encouragement for the kind of interaction required by Attention-Directing questions. Finally, the separatism fostered by the traditional theory of organization and the NII model does not predispose the component units of an organization to the continuing and sensitive co-operation required by the use of internal reporting to indicate the specific problems that "line" personnel might keep in mind.[15]

Much the same, if perhaps more pointedly, might be written of Problem-Solving Questions. They draw on a wide variety of information, including accounting data. They also require a high degree of mutual confidence, intimate knowledge of the needs of the affected units of an organization, and cooperative and continuing relations that permit timely studies. The traditional theory of organization, in general, would not be likely to do tender service to this catalog of prerequisites.

TOWARD A NEW ORGANIZATION THEORY

These few paragraphs sketch some dismal probabilities for cooperative effort, to be sure. Despair, however, is not necessarily in order. Indeed, it has proved possible for men of persistence and inventiveness to avoid the difficulties posed by the traditional theory of organization while meeting the full range of purposes of internal reporting. Guest, for example, provides an interesting record of just such a case of the fruitful cooperation of a new plant manager, his comptroller, and other "line" and "staff" officials in an organization that had suffered grievously from the full list of maladies sketched above.[16] Even in this case, however, some participants were pessimistic. They felt a new era of good feeling would pass quickly with the transfer of the plant manager, who induced and sustained the changes by his skillful handling of men.

FIGURE 27.2
Organizing a Simple Set of Operations in Terms of an Unorthodox Theory of Organizations

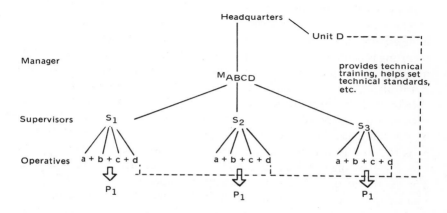

It would be foolish, of course, to place our hopes in managerial supermen. The good intentions of the vast majority of us are combined with lesser talents. Structural innovation can provide the continuing reinforcement of good intentions and average talents, however. Figure 27.2 [referred to hereafter as Figure 2] sketches such a structure for the simplified set of processes considered in Figure 1. Notice that the focus in Figure 2 is upon what may be called "administrative entities," each of which contains all of the elements necessary for producing P_1. Figure 1, in contrast, stresses individual processes and functions. In this sense, a Figure 2 structure may be characterized as holistic, or integrational; a Figure 1 structure may be considered as particularistic, or fragmentary. To illustrate, each supervisor in Figure 2 controls all of the organizational elements necessary for P_1. The individual supervisors in Figure 1, however, each oversee only individuals performing a single activity required for P_1.

The unorthodox structure in Figure 2 is not merely an alternative to the traditional structure. It has been approached in numerous practical situations. Indeed, some aspects of the figure have been stressed by accountants as of great importance in the more effective use of accounting data for managerial control,[17] although such stress is not commonplace. Any organization with strong tendencies toward decentralization, moreover, will have important points of similarity with Figure 2. More or less typically, to illustrate, an accounting service (like D in Figure 2) will report directly to the "line" official at its level (S_1, for example) rather than upwards to Unit D at headquarters. There are many variations in practice on the basic pattern, but their purpose is the same: to reduce time lags between observation and remedial action and to reduce the punitiveness both associated with the "up, over, and down" pattern of "line-staff" relations consistent with the traditional theory of organization.[18]

The several advantages of the structure in Figure 2 have been outlined in detail elsewhere. Here consider only one crucial sense in which internal reporting is facilitated. Thus the managerially significant measure of performance (e.g., variance from standard cost of the units headed by S_1, S_2, and S_3) is also a relatively simple accounting task. The more difficult task of determining the costs to be assigned A, B, C, or D within any unit of organization, moreover, is less significant. For a supervisor's status no longer will depend directly upon whether the charges go to A or B or C, as is the case in a Figure 1 structure. In addition, no supervisor will be threatened by the internal accountant's handling of this more difficult task. For the results of such inquiry can help the supervisor in more effectively managing the total administrative entity for which he is responsible. In a Figure 1 structure, in stark contrast, the results of such an inquiry inherently imply punishment of supervisors for imperfections in a total flow of work, of which any supervisor controls but a part, and for which he often has no clear and unambiguous responsibility. There is a world of difference between the two structures in this particular, needless to note.

There are other convenient features of the structure in Figure 2. Thus much of the pressure is taken off internal reporting—and off accountants! —because it is not used as a goad to superior (or more likely acceptable) performance. For now the units headed by the three supervisors can be compared in terms of simple and meaningful measures of performance.

Thus the relative value of the efforts of units headed by S_A, S_B, S_C, and S_D in Figure 1 can be approached only via arbitrary and often troublesome conventions that are all too vulnerable to sharp dealing. Moreover, these conventions often act as ceilings on performance, a happenstance that motivated one student to argue for the use of bogus budgets so as to avoid limiting effort.[19] In addition, developing or changing these conventions often will prove difficult and seem arbitrary, in that these conventions are not tied to the demands of work in any clear and direct way. The meaningful competition of the several comparable units in a Figure 2 structure, in pleasing oppositeness, should operate so as to induce an upward-orientation in what is considered an acceptable level of performance. The "pressure," in a real sense, is sustained and yet seems natural in that it derives directly from work.

Consider also that a Figure 2 structure reduces the intensity of the forcefield within which internal reporting must take place. Any single unit in a Figure 1 structure, to approach the point, can exercise considerable power. Thus the unit headed by S_4, for example, could seriously disrupt the total flow of work. Indeed, output could fall to zero. In a Figure 2 structure, however, restrictions of output by one unit would disadvantage only members of that unit. Output would fall at most by $1/N$, where N is the total number of similar autonomous units. Realistically, units in a Figure 2 structure would hesitate to punish only themselves, a fact that reduces the probability of resistance by an obstreperous unit of organization.

Simple structure variations, that is to say, can have profoundly different consequences for behavior.

Such description might be extended, but it would come to the same point. The structure in Figure 2 is very congenial to filling the three purposes of internal reporting. Score-Card Questions, that is, are neither so crucial, nor so subject to arbitrary allocations, nor so likely to adversely color the relations of accountants and others, as Figure 1 structures. This of itself makes more probable a telling emphasis on Attention-Directing Questions and Problem-Solving Questions.

But the argument need not be made by default. More positively, the accountant d in the unit headed by S_1 patently has a continuing relationship with the several processes necessary to produce P_1; moreover, he has a direct stake in the successful performance of his unit. He is no longer an organizational "outsider" with interests quite different from those of the unit served, as in Figure 1 structures. He can communicate directly with the official at just the point at which operations are being measured. And it is definitely in the interest of accountant d to draw quick attention to opportunities to improve operations, to know and to anticipate needs, and to help study alternate ways of meeting them. For shoddy work will be subject to facile comparison with the performance of other units. The implied enlargement of the job of accountant d, in addition, also is attractive.[20]

This merely sketches the positive argument, of course. But it suffices to demonstrate that, following Figure 2, it is possible to challenge the full range of purposes of internal accounting with more optimism than one can muster when considering the traditional theory of organization.

SUMMARY

Internal reporting serves as a case in point of the intimate senses in which accountancy is a function of organization theory. The traditional theory of organization has the effect of directing attention to but one of the purposes of internal reporting, the asking of Score-Card Questions, and this at great cost to cooperative effort. An unorthodox theory of organization does not suffer from the same liabilities to the same degree. Of particular significance, this unorthodox theory of organization facilitates asking Attention-Directing Questions and Problem-Solving Questions that must receive a growing proportion of the attention of the accountant engaged in internal reporting, and this if only because electronic data processing will increasingly eliminate much of the accounting time heretofore devoted to Score-Card Questions.

Therefore, it seems appropriate that organization theory receive considerable attention by members of the accounting profession, which is presently in the throes of rethinking its scope and methods. For an inappropriate organization structure can frustrate the most worthy of intentions and, in any case, any fundamental changes in accountancy will require changes in the traditional theory of organization.

Notes

[1] Robert T. Golembiewski, "Organization Theory and the New Accountancy: One Avenue of Revolution," *Quarterly Review of Economics and Business*, Vol. 3 (Summer, 1963), pp. 29–40.

[2] Much of this literature is reviewed and synthesized in the author's *Organizing Men and Power: Patterns of Behavior and "Line-Staff" Models* (Chicago: Rand McNally & Co., 1967).

[3] Herbert A. Simon, Harold Guetzkow, George Kozmetsky, and Gordon Tyndall, *Centralization vs. Decentralization in Organizing the Controller's Department* (New York: Controllership Foundation, 1954), pp. 3–4.

[4] Robert T. Golembiewski, "Toward the New Organization Theories: Some Notes on 'Staff,'" *Midwest Journal of Political Science*, Vol. 5 (August, 1961), pp. 237–59.

[5] Dalton E. McFarland, *Cooperation and Conflict in Personnel Administration* (New York: American Foundation for Management Research, 1962), p. 18 and Table 19, p. 73.

[6] See, for example, David S. Brown, "The Staff Man Looks in the Mirror," *Public Administration Review*, Vol. 23 (June, 1963), pp. 67–73; and Chris Argyris, *The Impact of Budgets on People* (New York: Controllership Foundation, 1952).

[7] Ernest Dale and Lyndall Urwick, *Staff in Organization* (New York: McGraw-Hill Book Co., 1960), p. 165.

[8] Simon *et al.*, *op. cit.*, pp. 3–4.

[9] James G. March and Herbert A. Simon, *Organizations* (New York: John Wiley & Sons, Inc., 1958), especially pp. 36–47; and Eliot D. Chapple and Leonard R. Sayles, *The Measure of Management* (New York: The Macmillan Company, 1961), especially pp. 18–45.

[10] For a case in point, see Argyris, *op. cit.*, pp. 17–19.

[11] Chapple and Sayles, *op. cit.*, pp. 89–97.

[12] Melville Dalton, *Men Who Manage* (New York: John Wiley & Sons, Inc., 1959), particularly chap. iii.

[13]James C. Worthy, "Some Aspects of Organization Structure in Relation to Pressure on Company Decision-Making," in L. Reed Tripp (ed.), *Proceedings of the Fifth Annual Meeting of the Industrial Relations Research Association,* IRRA Publication No. 10, 1953, p. 77.

[14]Simon, *et al., op. cit.,* p. 4.

[15]On this point, see Argyris' analysis of interviews with budget officers in his *The Impact of Budgets on People, op. cit.,* chap. i.

[16]Robert H. Guest, *Organizational Change,* Irwin-Dorsey Series in Behavioral Science in Business (Homewood, Ill.: Richard D. Irwin, Inc., 1962).

[17]Consult, for example, Robert N. Anthony, *Management Accounting: Text and Cases,* 2d ed. (Homewood, Ill.: Richard D. Irwin, Inc., 1960), especially pp. 320–33.

[18]Harry D. Kolb, "The Headquarters Staff Man in the Role of a Consultant," in Mason Haire (ed.), *Organization Theory in Industrial Practice* (New York: John Wiley & Sons, Inc., 1962), pp. 143–46.

[19]Andrew C. Stedry, *Budget Control and Cost Behavior* (Englewood Cliffs, N.J.: Prentice-Hall, Inc., 1960), especially pp. 17, 41–42, and 71.

[20]For numerous examples of the efficacy of job enlargement, see Georges Friedmann, *The Anatomy of Work* (Glencoe, Ill.: Free Press, 1961), pp. 40–67.

======

28
Centralization versus Decentralization in Organizing the Controller's Department

Herbert A. Simon, George Kozmetsky, Harold Guetzkow, and Gordon Tyndall

The study seeks to determine the *effectiveness* of different forms of departmental organization. Ideally, in a business concern the test of effectiveness is profit. But for testing the effectiveness of organizing the controller's department, the question cannot be approached in this direct fashion. Intra- and interdepartmental relations are too indirect and complex to be traced directly to profits. Hence, three indirect measures of effectiveness were used. A controller's department is effective to the extent that it—

Provides informational services of high quality.

Performs these services at a minimum cost.

From *Centralization vs. Decentralization in Organizing the Controller's Department* (New York: Controllership Foundation, Inc., August, 1954), pp. 1–2, 4–9, 13–17, and 18–19. Reproduced with permission.

Facilitates the long-range development of competent accounting and operating executives.

INTRODUCTION

The words "centralization" and "decentralization" are used with a wide variety of meanings. One of these meanings, however, is fundamental to the others, and it becomes the strategically important one for this study:

An administrative organization is centralized to the extent that decisions are made at relatively high levels in the organization; decentralized to the extent that discretion and authority to make important decisions are delegated by top management to lower levels of executive authority.

For example, a measure of the degree of centralization or decentralization in the whole production department would be obtained by observing the relative roles of the vice president for manufacturing, the factory manager, and the factory department head, respectively, in important production decisions. The greater the part of company top level executives in decision-making, the greater the centralization of organization; the greater the role of factory executives, or factory department executives, the greater the decentralization in organization to the factory or factory department levels.

Survey observations indicate that these controllers' departments enter the decision-making process primarily as suppliers and analyzers of information, and as consultants. Therefore, "centralization" and "decentralization" in the controllers' departments must be related to the levels in other departments to which such information and analytical and consulting services are supplied.

The relative degree of centralization or decentralization of the controller's department depends on at least five factors:

1. *The structure of the accounts and reports.* A decentralized account structure is one that provides a maximum of information about individual subordinate organization units (for example, individual factory departments, or sales districts), by means of separate cost statements or profit and loss statements for individual units.[1]

2. *The geographical location of accounting functions.* Geographical decentralization means locating the personnel of the controller's department in the company's factories and district officers rather than largely at the home office.

3. *Formal authority relations.* Decentralization of formal authority means attaching accounting units directly to the operating units whose activities they are recording—for example, placing the factory controller under the authority of the factory manager.

4. *Loyalties.* Decentralization of loyalties means encouraging accounting personnel to regard themselves as members of the operating "team" to which they are providing service.

5. *Channels of communication.* Decentralization of communication means building up direct contact and communication between accounting personnel and the executives and supervisors of decentralized operating units—for example, direct communication between the factory accounting department and factory department heads or personnel.

This study showed rather conclusively that the same degree of centralization and decentralization is not desirable with respect to all five of these factors.

CENTRALIZATION AND DECENTRALIZATION OF THE ACCOUNT STRUCTURE

Two rather different kinds of decentralization are possible. One, which is sometimes called "responsibility accounting," consists in classifying actual and standard (or budgeted) costs according to the organizational unit primarily responsible for incurring the cost, and presenting periodic cost statements for each such unit. The other, sometimes described as "profit and loss accounting," consists essentially in treating interdepartmental and interdivisional transfers of manufactured and partially manufactured goods as "sales," thereby arriving at a profit and loss statement for individual organizational units like divisions, factories, sales districts, and sales branches.

Survey findings leave little doubt that *a decentralized account structure of one or the other of these two forms is desirable—at least down to the level of factory departments, sales districts, and individual sales branches.* A more difficult question is whether the decentralization should be in the direction of responsibility statements or profit and loss statements.

Where a company is divided into a number of relatively self-contained parts, each responsible for manufacturing and selling a group of products, profit and loss statements for these individual parts appear to be meaningful and effective. Decentralized profit and loss accounting runs into real difficulties when the parts of the company to which it is applied are not really self-contained—for example, when separate decentralized statements are prepared for manufacturing and for sales of the same products.

There are four main reasons for avoiding overelaboration of decentralized accounting reports: (a) reporting items not controllable at the respective decentralized units is an unnecessary expense; (b) it decreases understanding of the reports and discourages operating men from using them; (c) it may lead to resentment; and (d) it often causes tardiness in issuance of the accounting reports.

No evidence was found that decentralized profit and loss statements are more effective than decentralized responsibility statements in promoting profit consciousness. It is suggested that profit consciousness is best promoted along two rather different lines:

Informing executives and supervisors from time to time about the company profit picture, and the spread that is needed between costs and sales to maintain profits. But this does not require incorporating profit information in the periodic accounting reports, or arbitrarily allocating overhead items to individual statements.

Developing further the problem-solving uses of accounting information which will help to educate executives and supervisors as to the profit consequences of specific decisions.

ORGANIZATION WITHIN THE CONTROLLER'S DEPARTMENT

There is generally much to be gained from separating, to a considerable degree within the controller's department, the personnel and units responsible for each of three major kinds of functions:

Bookkeeping, and preparation and distribution of periodic accounting reports.

Assistance to the operating departments in current analyses of accounting information for score-card and attention-directing purposes.

Participation in the use of accounting information for problem solving on a special-studies basis.

Perhaps the principal need for separating these functions is to maintain adequate administrative direction and control over the amount of time and effort that is devoted to the different kinds of tasks by accounting personnel. It was repeatedly observed that, when accountants had heavy supervisory responsibilities for report preparation in addition to analytical responsibilities, the pressures of supervision and deadlines led to a relative neglect of analytic work. As a result, when the functions are combined, the controller's department retains little control over the amount of effort that is given to each.

Combining the functions leads to a potential conflict between the accountant's function of providing service to operating departments, and his function of analyzing operations to provide valid and objective data for higher levels of management. Separating the record-keeping functions from analytical work is also an important supplement to an effective internal audit in reducing the dangers of collusion. It may also give the analytical personnel greater freedom to develop close working relationships with operating executives without a feeling of conflicting responsibilities.

Another reason for separating the functions is to allow greater flexibility for organizing each of them in the most economical and effective manner. If there is some organizational separation, each function can be located at the level or levels most appropriate for its particular task. Each can be centralized or decentralized to the extent that appears desirable, independently of the others.

CENTRALIZATION AND DECENTRALIZATION: CURRENT ANALYSIS

An essential condition for the attention-directing use of data is that the accounting reports be reviewed regularly and periodically in order to determine when performance is "off standard" and to initiate inquiries as to the reasons. A principal means for accomplishing this lies in the development of communication channels between the controller's department and the operating departments at the appropriate levels.

There are at least two directions in which the controller's department can take the initiative to strengthen the use of accounting services:

By doing an effective job of funneling reports upward from factories and sales units, and bringing them to the attention of top level executives, so that these executives, in turn, will use the reports in dealing with their subordinates.

By getting top management support for a regular, systematic interpretation of monthly cost variances to be prepared by operating men with the assistance of analysts from the accounting department. This will encourage a regular and growing contact between the controller's department and operating men at middle management levels.

Among the most essential direct communications channels between controller's and operating departments are those between the controller and the factory department head, the factory manager, the district and regional sales managers, and the top company executives responsible for production and sales.

Such channels can be developed by:

Giving accounting personnel duties that can only be discharged by working with operating men.

Giving these assignments high priority by separating them from record-keeping and supervisory functions.

Physically locating the accounting man close to his operating counterpart.

Using for these contacts accounting personnel who have adequate status and character to maintain the relationships on a basis of mutual respect, and who possess a thorough understanding of operations.

CENTRALIZATION AND DECENTRALIZATION: SPECIAL STUDIES

In the companies studied, a very great part of the "spade work" in investigating major operating problems is done by persons outside the controller's department; hence, to a large extent, these problems cut across departmental lines and have to be dealt with from a company-wide or factory-wide viewpoint. For this reason, the special studies work calls for more centralized communications than the current analysis work. An effective organizational arrangement appears to be to establish a unit for special studies in the company offices of the controller's department, and a smaller unit of the same sort in each of the larger factories or other major operating units.

Under most circumstances *the controller's department can most effectively bring its special skills to bear upon problems as a part of a team— formal or informal—that includes staff assistants to operating executives and members of other staff departments as well as accounting personnel.*

Formal procedures that required the preparation of "savings statements" as a basis for capital appropriations were very effective in bringing the controller's department into the decision-making process. Institution of a formal cost reduction program had this same general effect. This suggests that the use of accounting information for problem-solving purposes could be further extended by developing similar procedures in areas like production scheduling, market research, or quality control, which would give the controller's department a broader opportunity to participate formally in the investigatory process. It would also increase effective managerial use of the wealth of data available from the controller's department.

CENTRALIZATION AND DECENTRALIZATION: RECORD KEEPING

For the record-keeping units, the main questions of centralization and decentralization relate to the geographical location of the personnel. How far should the record-keeping and reporting functions be centrally located? How far should they be decentralized to factories and sales districts?

The most important consequences of centralization or decentralization of the records functions have to do with the accessibility of documents and the reliability of the source records. Both of these criteria point in the direction of relatively great geographical decentralization. To give access to detailed records, it is generally advantageous to decentralize record keeping to the locations where the major uses are made of the data. To get reliability, the accounting personnel who are responsible for recording and classifying data need to be as close as possible to the operating situations where the data originate.

There may be definite cost advantages in centralizing to the extent that is necessary for mechanization or clerical specialization. In the surveyed operations, most of these economies can be attained with units centralized to the factory or regional sales level. Further centralization apparently offers little additional gain from a cost standpoint. For this reason it should be possible to retain most of the advantages of decentralization mentioned in the previous paragraph without decentralizing so far as to incur serious clerical "diseconomies."

Questions of promptness, uniformity in classification of data, and auditing control are in most instances of small importance in determining the optimal degree of centralization and decentralization of record keeping.

Manufacturing Records

For manufacturing operations of any size, the volume of clerical work in a single factory is generally sufficient to permit the bulk of the accounting for manufacturing operations to be done at the factory. There remains the question of whether factory record-keeping activities should be further subdivided and decentralized into accounting units paralleling the several operating departments in the factory, or whether they should be assigned to centralized units corresponding to the major accounting activities. The conclusion reached from survey observations is that the net advantage lies on the side of the centralized structure within the factory, although the balance of advantages is less decisive in a very large factory with several separate products and production lines, than it is in a smaller factory.

When the purchasing function is centralized for the company as a whole, the question arises as to whether the accounts-payable work should be handled in the company offices or the individual factories. The project staff were unable to determine that there were important advantages, one way or another.

Sales Records

In sales accounting, the operations involving the greatest volume of clerical work are billing and the maintenance of accounts receivable. There are indications that, primarily for reasons of access to records, evident advantages exist in locating the accounts receivable in the same city or cities as the credit units. But to achieve clerical economy in posting to the accounts, the credit work should not be further decentralized than is absolutely necessary.

In none of these companies was the location of billing a particularly critical matter. When sales are made through company sales branches, locating the billing function with accounts receivable and collections seems generally satisfactory. In other cases, the advantages seem fairly balanced between billing at the factory or sending a copy of the shipping memorandum to a central billing unit located with accounts receivable.

FORMAL AUTHORITY OVER DECENTRALIZED ACCOUNTING OPERATIONS

There are two general types of arrangements of the lines of formal authority in the companies studied. In some, the factory controller or chief accounting executive[2] is completely under the formal authority of the company controller. In other companies he is "functionally" responsible to the company controller, "administratively" to the factory manager.

It was observed that when the accounting department lacks acceptance and active support from the top levels of the manufacturing department, it may be unsatisfactory to divide authority over the factory accountant between the company controller and the factory manager. But in organizations *where top executives of the operating departments regard the controller's services as important management tools, a system of divided authority appears to work as well as a plan in which the factory controller or district office manager reports solely to the company controller.*

Of greater importance than the lines of formal authority is the question of how much leeway should be given the accounting man, at a decentralized location, to run his own shop. Whether authority was centralized or decentralized, *it was found that the greatest service was provided to factory management when the factory accountant felt that he had authority to provide reports to the factory management as requested, within the minimum standards of accounting policy and procedure* laid down by the company controller's department.

Whatever the formal arrangements, it seemed that appointments and removals of factory accountants are almost always a matter of negotiation and agreement between the controller's department and the factory manager. Admitting this joint responsibility, there is probably some advantage in placing the formal power of appointment in the controller's department.

Because of the nature of their duties, office managers in sales groups are more likely than factory accountants to regard themselves, and to be regarded, as members of the operating executive's staff. On the whole, the case for decentralized authority appears stronger in the sales than in the manufacturing area. But, where the normal lines of personnel movement lie within the accounting department, the office managers themselves tend to prefer having personnel and salary administration in the hands of the controller's department.

THE DEVELOPMENT OF ACCOUNTING PERSONNEL

In most organizations, promotion tends to be more or less "vertical." When a position is vacant, the tendency is to fill it by promotion from one of the positions immediately subordinate to it, or in a related part of the organization. If an organization is designed along the lines recommended above, a vertical promotion policy is likely to lead to difficulties. With the separation between analytical work and record-keeping functions, one group of accounting executives would, with vertical promotion, develop their analytical skills but acquire little experience in supervision; another group would acquire supervisory skills with little chance to develop competence in analytical work.

Hence, *in an organization developed along the suggested lines, it is important that there be an intelligent and carefully administered plan for the horizontal transfer of potential supervisors and executives at several stages of their careers.* By horizontal transfer is meant promotion from analytic positions to supervisory positions in record-keeping units, and vice versa.

Personnel development for controllership functions is an organizational problem only to a limited degree. To a far greater extent it is a problem of providing men with training and experience, both prior to and during their employment, that will deepen and broaden their understanding of general business problems. One specific direction for progress is the broadening of pre-employment training for industrial accountants. A second direction is to develop further the opportunities for interdepartmental promotion of promising men. A third direction is to encourage the use of teams and "task forces" drawn from several departments to undertake major planning studies.

·   ·   ·   ·   ·

THE MEANING OF CENTRALIZATION AND DECENTRALIZATION

"Centralization" is a word of many meanings. With reference to management problems, an administrative organization is *centralized* to the extent that decisions are made at relatively high levels in the organization, and persons at lower levels have relatively little discretion. Conversely, an administrative organization is *decentralized* to the extent that important delegations of discretionary and decision-making authority are made from higher to lower levels of the organization.

This study is particularly concerned with:

The degree of centralization or decentralization within the controller's department.

The relationship of this to the degree of centralization or decentralization within operating departments, particularly manufacturing and sales.

Centralization and Decentralization in Controllers' Departments

In some companies a factory accountant is given broad discretion to determine the accounting procedures to be used in the factory, or the kinds of reports to be prepared for the factory manager; in other companies, he is not. In the former case, therefore, there is relatively great decentralization *to the factory level* within the controller's department; in the latter situation there is relatively great centralization *to the company level* within the controller's department.

Centralization and Decentralization in Operating Departments

In some companies a factory manager is given broad discretion to determine manufacturing methods, to handle industrial relations, even, in some cases, to determine what the factory is to produce. The broader the scope of the functions over which the factory manager exercised discretion, the greater the decentralization *to the factory level* in the manufacturing department. In several of the companies studied (Westinghouse Electric is an example) there is an important intermediate stage of delegation between the company level and the factory level—the division. Certain matters are decentralized all the way to the factory, others only to the division. Similarly, on the sales side, in many companies the regional office constitutes an important level between the central company office on the one hand, and the district sales office, on the other.

Relationship between Controller and Operating Department Decentralization

Effectiveness of centralization or decentralization of the controller's department is likely to depend on the relative centralization of operating departments of the company, particularly manufacturing and sales. For example, there would be little apparent point in supplying department foremen with information that would help them schedule production if scheduling decisions are made at the factory or company level with little departmental participation.

What constitutes an effective relationship between the controller's department and operating departments? Is the most effective procedure to feed accounting, statistical and analytical information into the operating organization at the levels where the relevant operating decisions are being made? Or is it better to feed all accounting information in at the top levels of the operating organization, relying on the manufacturing and sales executives to transmit downward information needed for decisions at lower levels. How far should the analysis of data be an accounting responsibility; how far an operating responsibility? It is clear, then, that the study involves examination of centralization and decentralization of the broad accounting functions of controllership *in relation to* operating centralization and decentralization.

Degree and Elements of Centralization or Decentralization Are the Core of the Problem

Centralization may also vary within an administrative unit, some of its functions being centralized while others are decentralized. None of the seven companies studied had completely centralized organizations and functions. Particular activities within the seven companies were found to be centralized or decentralized *to a degree,* varying widely from unit to unit, and from function to function. Thus, posing the problem of centralization became a question of examining the *degree* of centralization and decentralization of the different decision-making functions. It also involved analyzing the *impact* of centralization on five important elements of accounting functions of the controller's department:

1. The *structure of the accounts and reports.* For example, whether the chart of accounts is broken down in such a way that a cost statement or a profit and loss statement can be drawn up for an individual factory or department within a factory.
2. The actual *geographical locations* where accounting functions are performed. For example, whether the records of factory costs are posted at the factory or in the company offices.
3. The *formal authority relations* between accounting personnel and operating personnel. For instance, whether the factory accountant reports to the company controller or to the factory manager.
4. The structure of *group loyalties.* Whether the factory accounting personnel regard themselves as part of the factory "team" or as part of the controller's department, for example.
5. The *channels used* by accounting and operating personnel *in communicating* with each other. For instance, whether the company controller and his home office subordinates communicate directly with the factory controller, or whether their communications with the factory are channeled through the factory manager.

The following paragraphs will attempt to clarify further what is meant by each of these five elements.

Decentralization of accounts and reports.   The first element relates to the structure of the accounts and reports themselves. For example, in a company with a number of factories, the account structure is decentralized to the factory level if most costs for a factory are separately accumulated and a more or less complete income and expense statement prepared periodically for the factory. Similarly, if within each factory costs are accumulated for each department, the structure is decentralized down to the departmental level.

Decentralization of the accounting structure is aimed at the greatest possible decentralization of operating decisions but retaining the operating executive's responsibility for results—results that may be measured in terms of sales, profits, return on investment, or cost reduction.[3]

The idea that the account structure should be decentralized at least to the factory has gained wide acceptance in American industry. In selecting companies for study, the project staff was unable to discover one that did not go at least this far in decentralizing its accounts. Almost all accounting and operating executives of these companies were agreed that the factory manager's job is to make as large a profit as possible, within the limits of company policy, with the manufacturing facilities and investment available to him.

The device most generally used in these companies for securing accountability with a decentralized account structure is the budget, usually of the flexible type, and a monthly comparison of actual with budgeted expenditures. In most, but not all the companies, the determinants of the monthly production cost allowances are tied in directly to the system of standard production costs, adjusted for volume variance. Thus, when the actual manufacturing cost equals the standard, the actual expenditure equals the budget. In about half the companies, a profit and loss statement is prepared for each factory or group of factories in a division. Practice varies as to whether sales are entered in the factory profit and loss statement at actual sales price or at a standard price. One company calculates for each factory the ratio of profits to investment; another is planning to introduce a balance sheet prorating its total capital investment to its various manufacturing facilities, and treating each, on paper, as a separate "corporation."

Generally, decentralization of accounts is not carried as far in sales as in manufacturing. In one case, the manufacturing department "sells" its product to the sales department, and profit and loss statements are prepared for geographically decentralized sales units, but this is not general practice.

There is a wide range in the degree of completeness of the factory accounts. At one end of the range is a company in which purchasing of principal raw materials is centralized. The factory accounts show only the labor actually employed at the factory and operating supplies purchased locally. Material costs and allocations of the company sales and administrative expenses do not appear on the factory statements.

At the other end of the range is a company in which the factory statements include all manufacturing expenses, including materials priced at standard, together with a recirculated allocation of company sales and administrative expenses. The companies which have carried furthest the philosophy of fixing profit responsibility at the factory tend toward this structure of factory accounts.

Geographical centralization and decentralization.   A second, and quite distinct element in decentralization is the *geographical dispersion* of book-keeping and accounting functions to the actual locations where manufacturing and sales activities are carried on. It was this characteristic that a controller had in mind when he stated in an interview: "We have decentralized our factory cost figures. They keep their own records."

There is, of course, no necessary connection between the degree of decentralization of the account structure, as previously defined, and the geographical decentralization of accounting activities. It would be entirely possible to have the account structure decentralized to the departments, for example, and still have all of the original accounting documents forwarded to the central company offices for recording and preparation of reports. On the other hand, it would also be entirely possible to have virtually all the recording activities, including tabulating, carried on at the plants and district sales offices, but no separate cost reports prepared for these individual organizational units.

As a matter of fact, in the companies studied, those that have gone furthest in decentralization of their accounts and reports have generally gone furthest in geographical decentralization of accounting functions. This raises the question, to be discussed in later chapters, of whether there are compelling administrative reasons why these two aspects of decentralization should go hand in hand. Will the efficiency or effectiveness of accounting suffer if there is more or less geographical decentralization than decentralization of accounts? Or has this close connection come about simply through a lack of recognition that two separate sets of organizational decisions are involved here?

In the companies studied, a number of situations existed where these two kinds of decentralization have not been carried to the same organizational levels. . . . Although the *accounts* are decentralized so that reports can be compiled for individual sales branches, the accounts receivable ledgers are maintained and posted in the company central offices. Comparison of National Works with Donora Works yields an example of varying practice in factory departments. The account structure is very similar in the two works, but at Donora many of the recording functions are handled by accounting units located out in the several works departments, while at National most of these functions are performed at the central works accounting offices.

Centralization and decentralization of authority.   A third element in centralization and decentralization relates to the lines of formal authority in the organization. Viewing a multi-plant (or multi-division) company as a whole, it is decentralized if each factory operates as a more or less self-contained unit, with the factory manager responsible for all of the functions carried on within the factory, and having formal authority over all factory personnel.

If the industrial relations director in the factory or the head of the industrial engineering department reports to his counterpart in the company offices, instead of to the factory manager, the organization is centralized to that extent. Similarly, if the top accounting executive in the factory reports formally to the factory manager, accounting control is decentralized; if he reports to the company controller, it is centralized.

Again, this third element in centralization and decentralization may be quite independent of the two previously examined. Indeed, in the companies studied, decentralization of the account structure and geographical decentralization of accounting functions had always been carried further than the decentralization of authority.

In answering questions about formal authority, persons interviewed usually made a distinction between "administrative" authority and "functional" authority. By "administrative" authority they meant the day-to-day relation of a "boss" to his subordinates. This included work assignments, handling personnel and operating questions referred by subordinates, and settling questions involving relations among subordinates. By "functional" authority they meant the right to determine the technical aspects of the accounting function: the chart of accounts, report content and deadlines, bookkeeping procedures, and so on. Obviously, there is some possibility of overlap and of disagreement as to precisely which decisions fall in one category and which in the other. However, little confusion or disagreement was found in the operating departments as to the proper classification of matters which arose in daily operation.

.   .   .   .   .

Group loyalties.   The formal authority relationships do not tell the whole story of a centralized accounting department or a member of a decentralized factory staff. His personal feelings of loyalty must be taken into account. On the organization chart, he might appear as a member of the accounting department, but in fact he might regard himself as a part of the factory management team; the reverse might be true.

It is not easy, in an interview with strangers, for a member of an organization to give a frank and objective appraisal of where his loyalties lie. Hence, the survey team attempted to assess a number of related pieces of evidence to learn whether factory accountants regarded themselves primarily as members of the factory manager's "team" or the company controller's "team." For example, they were asked which of two reporting assignments with close deadlines would receive priority. The interviewer noted whether they spoke of the operating management of the factory as "we" or "they," and similarly, for the home-office accounting department. Whether or not informal lunch-time and other social groups tended to cut across the line between accounting and operations was observed and noted.

Appraisal of this evidence indicates that loyalty tends to be closely associated with the centralization or decentralization of formal authority. In general, the primary loyalty of the factory accountant is with the controller's department in those companies where formal authority in accounting is centralized. In those companies where formal authority is decentralized, the loyalties appear, on balance, to be with factory management. There were two factories, among those in companies with decentralized authority, where the factory accountants felt themselves more or less cut off from *both* the factory management and the controller's department. In these two situations, the factory accountants tended to regard themselves as subject to "cross pressure" from these two sources, rather than as having a strong allegiance to either.

The sample of seven companies and nine factories is far too small to permit a generalized assessment of the factors associated with centralized or decentralized loyalties and their relative importance. A few observations may be mentioned as explanatory factors.

Geographical separation from the home office appears to foster decentralized loyalties. In companies having distant branches, in California, for example, comments were frequently volunteered about the problems of maintaining home-office control over accounting operations in those branches.

Further, the feeling that "we are accountants, but they are operating people," appears to be a powerful force restraining the decentralization of accounting loyalties. Even in the situations with most decentralized loyalties, the accounting personnel felt strongly their responsibility for accurate reporting in accordance with *company* accounting procedures—including procedures they thought incorrect or inadequate.

A number of specific instances were observed where competing claims were made upon accounting personnel to adhere to the professional standards of accountancy on the one hand and, on the other, to get along with factory management by not reporting unpleasant facts. With one possible exception, all observed conflicts of this sort were resolved in favor of the standards of the profession.

Centralized loyalties were also fostered by the tendency of accounting personnel to look to the controller's department for chances of promotion. Except for Eastman Kodak, there was little transfer of accounting employees into manufacturing departments; there was more movement into sales department positions. Where interdepartmental promotions were relatively common, loyalties were more decentralized than elsewhere. Whether the opportunities for promotion are the cause, and the decentralized loyalties the effect, or vice versa, is hard to assess.

Centralization and decentralization of communication.   Closely related to the question of centralization or decentralization of formal authority and of feelings of loyalty is the question of communications. Communications aspects of accounting organization will be considered decentralized to the factory if communications of the factory accounting personnel are more frequent with factory operating executives than with the headquarters controller's department. In the opposite case, the organization is considered centralized. Further, communication is not considered to be the routine flow of accounting documents and reports, but contacts by letter, telephone, or face-to-face for the purpose of assigning work, requesting information, settling problems of accounting procedure, and so forth. Both the amount and importance of such communication will be taken into account in assessing relative strength of communication channels.

As with other elements in decentralization, the pattern of communications within a plant or division may differ significantly from the organization of accounting communication for the company as a whole. At least one situation was found where communication for the *company as a whole* was relatively centralized—that is, communications between headquarters and factory control and accounting. However, *within the factory,* communication was relatively decentralized—in the sense that there was more communication between the factory accounting department and other factory departments than between the accounting department and the factory manager.

Notes

[1]Decentralization, in this sense, is a function of the amount of detailed information supplied about individual organization units. The form in which this information is to be provided (e.g., the chart of accounts) will, of course, be determined primarily at top levels of the controller's department.

[2]To avoid confusion of terms and to reduce necessity for lengthy, qualifying phrases, the term "factory accountant" is used in this report to designate the chief accounting and control executive in the factory. This is not intended to suggest that a division or factory controller's responsibilities are confined to accounting.

[3]For a nontechnical discussion of the philosophy underlying decentralization of the account structure, see Perrin Stryker, "P & C for Profit," *Fortune,* April 1952, pp. 128 ff.

29

Organization Development in Public Agencies: Perspectives on Theory and Practice

Robert T. Golembiewski

The special genius of each age is reflected in distinctive ways of organizing work. If the preceding age stressed stability and consistency, roughly, the emphasis today is on organizing for change and variability. The specific implications are diverse and still obscure, but the general point is overwhelming. John W. Gardner reflects both the certainty and the caution. "What may be most in need of innovation is the corporation itself," he notes. "Perhaps what every corporation (and every other organization) needs is a department of continuous renewal that could view the whole organization as a system in need of continuing innovation."[1]

The major recent response to the need for planned organizational change is the burgeoning emphasis on organization development, or OD. Three themes constitute the core of typical OD concepts. As Winn explains:

> The term "organization development" ... implies a normative, re-education strategy intended to affect systems of beliefs, values and attitudes within the organization so that it can adapt better to the accelerated rate of change in technology, in our industrial environment and society in general. It also includes formal organizational restructuring which is frequently initiated, facilitated and reinforced by the normative and behavioral changes.[2]

Changing attitudes or values, modifying behavior, and inducing change in structure and policies, then, are the three core-objectives of OD programs. In contrast, the reorganization literature in political science is concept-oriented and gives little attention to changes in attitudes and behavior necessary to implement its guiding concept.

This article provides a variety of perspectives on the characteristics of OD programs, and also summarizes experience from a number of OD

Reprinted from *Public Administration Review* 29 (No. 4, July–August 1969): 367–77, bimonthly publication of the American Society for Public Administration, 1225 Connecticut Avenue, N.W., Washington, D.C.

efforts in public agencies at federal and local levels. Not all these agencies can be identified here, unfortunately, but the data-base consists of seven cases. No attempt will be made to evaluate the effectiveness of any particular OD application; and even less is the purpose here to assess the specific technology of OD programs such as the use of sensitivity training.[3]

The motivation of this piece derives from the following propositions. First, government agencies have begun experimenting with various OD approaches, if less bullishly so than business and service organizations. Second, the public sector has a variety of distinctive features that provide special challenges to achieving typical OD objectives. Third, these distinctive features have received inadequate attention in the literature and in the design of OD programs in public agencies. Fourth, applications of OD programs in public agencies probably will become more common. The need to tailor OD programs in public agencies more closely to the distinctive constraints of their environment should consequently increase sharply. Finally, students of public administration can play useful and distinct roles in such OD programs, providing they develop appropriate competencies.

A TYPICAL OD PROGRAM:
AND THE UNDERLYING NETWORK OF FINDINGS AND
HYPOTHESES

Despite their variety, OD programs rest on similar conceptual foundations. These foundations are a mixed bag, including relatively "hard" empirical findings and plausible hypotheses. These foundations of OD programs also prescribe how organizations ought to be so as to be effective, "healthy," or morally acceptable.

Figure 29.1 simplifies the web of findings/hypotheses/values that underlies the typical OD program. The figure focuses strictly on the "front-load" of OD programs; that is, on how sensitivity training or related techniques can induce greater openness, trust, and shared responsibility. Based on such social and psychological preparation, OD programs can flower diversely. For example, early exposure to sensitivity training might encourage greater openness in an organization, which in turn might highlight critical needs for changes in policies, procedures, structure, or technology. An OD program then would be appropriately expanded to meet such needs, as by additions of training programs, etc.[4]

A TYPICAL OD PROGRAM:
MAJOR OBJECTIVES

The findings/hypotheses/values underlying OD programs imply several common objectives. Overall, the goal is to release the human potential within an organization. Specifically, a typical OD program emphasizes major objectives such as these:

1. To create an open, problem-solving climate throughout the organization.
2. To supplement the authority associated with role or status with the authority of knowledge and competence.
3. To locate decision-making and problem-solving responsibilities as close to the information sources as possible.
4. To build trust among individuals and groups throughout the organization.
5. To make competition more relevant to work goals and to maximize collaborative efforts.
6. To develop a reward system which recognizes both the achievement of the organization's mission (profits or service) and organization development (growth of people).
7. To increase the sense of "ownership" of organization objectives throughout the work force.
8. To help managers to manage according to relevant objectives rather than according to "past practices" or according to objectives which do not make sense for one's area of responsibility.
9. To increase self-control and self-direction for people within the organization.[5]

Basically, the organization is seen "as a system in need of continuing innovation," and an OD program begins by stressing the development of attitudes, behaviors, and skills that will support such continuing innovation.

The list of OD objectives does double duty here. In addition to providing additional content for the concept "organization development," the list of objectives helps highlight some of the special difficulties facing OD programs in public (and especially federal) agencies. The discussion below focuses on one major question: What specific properties of public agencies make it especially difficult to approach specific objectives such as those above? Evidence comes primarily from seven OD programs at the federal and local levels in which this author has participated.

CHARACTER OF THE INSTITUTIONAL ENVIRONMENT: CONSTRAINTS ON APPROACHING OD OBJECTIVES

Public agencies present some distinctive challenges to OD programs, as compared with business organizations where most experience with OD programs has been accumulated. Four properties of the public institutional environment particularly complicate achieving the common goals of OD programs.

FIGURE 29.1 A Simplified Model of Findings/Hypotheses Underlying the Typical OD Program

Basic Premise: To the degree that individuals can meet their own needs while meeting organizational needs, two simultaneous conditions become increasingly probable:

- satisfaction of organization members will heighten
- output will increase, both in terms of quality and quantity

Individual

An individual's basic needs center around *self-realization* and *self-actualization*. The former involves a person seeking himself as he is in interaction with others, with the goal of increasing the congruence between his intentions and his impact on others. Self-actualization refers to the processes of growth by which an individual realizes his potential.

An individual whose basic needs are being met experiences corresponding *psychological growth*, the prime conditions for which, and consequences of which, are:

- a growing awareness of the needs and motivations of self and others
- a lessening of the degree to which his relationships and actions are distorted, especially via more actively inducing feedback from others and by more effectively interpreting it
- an increasing ability to modify behavior in response to feedback about its impact on others, to respond appropriately rather than stereotypically
- a growing tendency to seek or develop conditions that promote psychological growth for self and others
- an expanding capacity to determine goals and internal motivations for self

An individual who experiences psychological growth will be correspondingly motivated to search for work, challenge, and responsibility.

Organization

An efficient organization will develop an appropriately shifting balance between *institutionalization* and *risk-taking*. The former refers to *infusing with value* the activities of the organization, so as to elicit member support, identification, and collaboration. Risk-taking is necessary in *innovating* more effective ways to deal with existing activities and in *adapting* to environmental changes in society, markets, technologies, and so on.

An organization's successful balancing of institutionalization and risk-taking will depend upon:

- the increasingly complete use of people as well as nonhuman resources
- the development and maintenance of a viable balance between *central control and local initiative*
- fluid lines of communication—vertically, horizontally, and diagonally
- decision-making processes that solve problems that stay solved without creating other problems
- *infusing the organization with values* that support its existence as a stable institution and that also motivate its developmental change as an adaptive structure

An organization with such a working balance of institutionalization and risk-taking will develop appropriate norms that support efforts of organization members to search for work, challenge, and responsibility.

Satisfaction of both individual and organization needs will be facilitated by, if such satisfaction does not in fact crucially depend upon, skill and competence in interpersonal and intergroup situations.

An individual's growth and self-realization are facilitated by interpersonal and intergroup relations that are honest, caring, and non-manipulative. Individuals can gain convenient experiences with these personal needs and with ways of satisfying them in such learning designs derived from the laboratory approach as sensitivity training. This is a managed process of gaining experience with attitudes and skills for inducing greater openness about positive and negative feelings, attitudes, or beliefs. Such openness leads to greater trust and reduced risk in communicating and is intended to suggest possible transfers into other environments.

Organizational family teams can be exposed to such learning designs derived from the laboratory approach as sensitivity training, with the intention of increasing confidence, trust, and responsibility that can be applied directly to solving organizational issues. Skill and competence in interpersonal and in intergroup situations can be increased in sensitivity training groups composed of strangers, that is, but the real test is the application of such learning in life-relevant situations. Such application will require that substantial numbers of organization members learn appropriate interpersonal skills, as well as that they internalize a set of values which support and reinforce such learning.

Persons in groups which develop greater openness tend to identify strongly with other members and with the goals of the group.

Groups characterized by strong identification with members and goals become increasingly capable of dealing with issues facing their members, and hence increasingly capable of influencing their environment in desired ways.

Groups whose members identify strongly and who can influence their environment are likely to be effective reinforcers of decisions about change. Such groups also can provide emotional support necessary to sustain required changes in the values, attitudes, or behaviors of their members.

Source: Adapted from Robert T. Golembiewski and Stokes B. Carrigan, "Planned Change in Organization Style Based on Laboratory Approach," Administrative Science Quarterly 15 (March 1970): 81.

1. Multiple Access

As compared to even the largest of international businesses, the public environment in this country is characterized by what might be called, following David Truman, unusual opportunities for *multiple access to multiple authoritative decision makers*. Multiple access is, in intention if not always in effect, a major way of helping to assure that public business gets looked at from a variety of perspectives. Hence the purpose here is to look at the effects of multiple access rather than to deprecate it. Figure 29.2 details some major points of multiple access relevant to OD programs in four interacting "systems": the executive, legislative, "special interests," and mass media systems.

Multiple access has its attractive features in beginning OD programs in public agencies. For example, one large OD program was inaugurated in an economical way: a top departmental career official sponsoring an OD program had developed a relation of deep trust with the chairman and the professional staff of a congressional appropriations subcommittee, and that relation quickly, even mercurially, triumphed over lukewarm support or even opposition from the department head, the Bureau of the Budget, and the U.S. Civil Service Commission.

But multiple access can cut two ways. Funds for that very OD program "became unavailable" after its inception, despite strong support from both career and political officers at the top levels. In short, the successful counterattack was launched by agency personnel in the protected/competitive service, an interest group representing these employees, members of a concerned substantive committee of Congress, and the media. The two themes of the counterattack were common to several reactions against OD programs of which I know. First, ordinary decency required allowing the dedicated civil servants affected to complete their careers in peace and in the traditional ways, rather than being subjected to an unwanted program that was seen as having problematic value.[6] Second, the use of sensitivity training in the OD program was disparaged as violating the privacy of organization members, or worse.[7]

Viewed from the perspective of top-level political and career officials intent on inaugurating a public OD program, the "iron quadrangle" in Figure 29.2 inspires substantial pessimism about a fair trial, in the general case. Specific conditions may raise or lower the odds, since the several links in the counterattacking forces above can be variously strong or weak. For example, a public agency may have a very positive constitutional image, which gives its top officials an important edge in presenting their case to congressional committees, the mass media, or the general public. Similarly, top political and career officials can induce—or capitalize on—organized clientele opposition to policies and procedures and use it to force changes at the protected levels. Or political resources and professional skills may

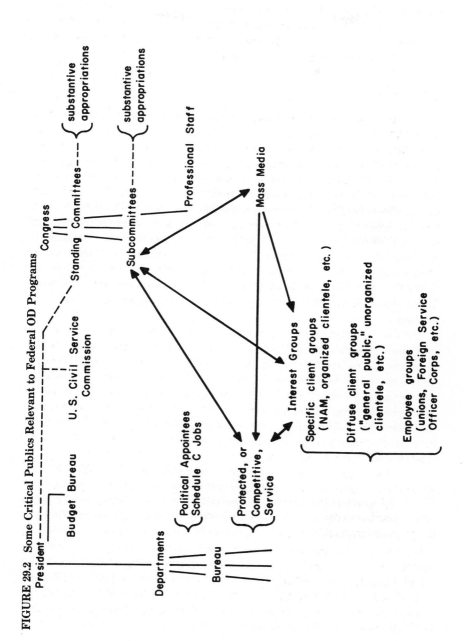

FIGURE 29.2   Some Critical Publics Relevant to Federal OD Programs

provide agency executives with substantial power to control their environment.[8]

Whether the iron quadrangle is more or less integral, the design and implementation of OD programs in public agencies has given that constellation short shift. Perhaps this is because most experience with OD programs has been gained in business organizations, where nothing even remotely like the iron quadrangle exists at managerial levels.

2. Greater Variety

Again as compared to business organizations, the public arena involves in all OD programs a greater variety of individuals and groups with *different and often mutually exclusive sets of interests, reward structures, and values.* In the case outlined above, for example, the appropriations subcommittee was interested in improved operations and reduced costs. But the substantive subcommittee was concerned more with safeguarding program and personnel with which they had developed a strong identification. And never the twain did meet. Role conflicts between legislators and administrators also seem to have been significant. For example, one congressman explained his opposition to an OD program in these terms: "Improvement of efficiency is O.K., but messing with people's attitudes sounds subversive to my constituents." The agency's top administrators felt no such constituency pressure, and their view was that attitudes toward work had to be changed.

Such incongruencies of expectations, rewards, and values also occur in business organizations, of course, as in labor-management issues. In my experience, however, they occur there in less intense and exotic forms.

A conclusion need not be forced. All OD programs have to stress the development of viable "interfaces," that is, relations between individuals or groups with different values and interests. This problem is enormously complicated in public agencies undertaking OD programs, and has received little explicit attention in concept or in practice. For example, in no case that I know of has the development of an explicit interface between legislative and administrative interests been attempted as part of an OD program, apparently in part because of the constitutional separation of powers.

The failure to build such interfaces was a major contributor to the death of a major recent urban OD program. Departmental officers rejected the idea of attempting to build an explicit interface between a substantive subcommittee, an appropriations subcommittee, and the agency as part of an OD program. Tradition, jealousy over prerogatives, and separation of powers were blamed, and with good reason. But it also seemed that departmental officials preferred things as they were. The lack of integration between subcommittees, perhaps, provided alternative routes of access and gave departmental officials some room to operate.

3. Command Linkages

The "line of command" within public agencies, as compared to business and service organizations, is more likely to be characterized by *competing identifications and affiliations.* Again the difference is one of degree, but it approaches one of a kind. Consider only one aspect of the integrity of command linkages common in business organizations. In them, typically, "management" is separated from "labor" only very far down the hierarchy, at or near the level of the first-line supervisor. Moreover, the common identification of all levels of management often is stressed. "Management," moreover, commonly does not enjoy the kind of job security that can come from union contracts. One of the effects of such carrots and sticks, without question, is the more facile implementation of policy changes at all levels of organization.

Hierarchy has its effects in public agencies as well as businesses, but the line of command seems less integral in the former. Thus a unique family of identifications alternative to the hierarchy exists at levels both low and high in public agencies, the apparent underlying motivation being to maximize the probability that evil will not occur, or at least will be found out. That is, the chain of command at the federal level is subject to strong fragmenting forces even up to the highest levels, where political and career strata blend into one another. For example, the ideal of a wall-to-wall civil service is approached closely in practice, and it provides a strong countervailing identification to the executive chain of command. Career officials are "out of politics," but their commitments to programs may be so strong as to inhibit or even thwart executive direction.[9]

That the public institutional evnironment permits (indeed, encourages) a fragmenting of the management hierarchy at points well up in the higher levels may be illustrated in three ways. First, the "neutrality" of civil servants has been a major defensive issue in at least two federal OD programs in which I have participated, the OD efforts having been painted by many career people as sophisticated but lustful raids on a chaste protected service. Second, Congress is an old hand at creating similar countervailing identifications so as to enhance its control over administration,[10] for which the Constitution and tradition provide a solid rationale. Third, the executive has also played the game, sometimes unwittingly. Consider the presidential-inspired Federal Executive Boards. Basically, these Boards were intended to be a horizontal link between field units of federal agencies and vertically between the presidency and top career field officialdom. The FEB's provide career field managers with a potential way to supplement or even bypass departmental reporting relations, both career employees and political appointees. Indeed, President Kennedy may have intended them as just such a bypass around "the feudal barons of the permanent government" whom he saw as obstacles to change.[11]

A conclusion flows easily. Congress often encourages slack in the executive chain of command to facilitate its oversight of the President and his major appointees; and the executive as well as the protected service itself often uses the same strategy. The integrity of the executive chain of command suffers. Although the consequences are mixed, public executives are limited in initiating[12] (for example) OD programs. Witness the furor over the mere handful of Schedule C jobs removed from the protected service during Eisenhower's first term to permit greater executive leverage. Any corporation president would have an immensely broader field to act upon. The motivation to avoid "spoils politics" is recognized, but managerial rigidity is the other side of the coin. Herbert Kaufman concludes that although extensions of the civil service were intended to provide upper-level political administrators with capable help, the latter have often been driven to "pray for deliverance from their guardians."[13]

4. Weak Linkages

Exacerbating the point above, the *linkages between political and career levels* are weak as a consequence of a variety of features of the public institutional environment.[14] This slippage between managerial levels significantly complicates beginning and implementing OD programs, and severely challenges the linkage of executive management with operating management.

The generalization concerning weak linkages in the managerial chain of command is meant to apply in four distinct senses. First, political and career levels often are weakly linked due to the brief tenure of the former. Second, the job of linking the political leadership and the permanent bureaucracy must be handled by a tiny group of executives—political appointees and occupants of Schedule C jobs—who owe diverse allegiance to the chief executive. Third, there is reason to suspect significant slippage between the top career officialdom and lower levels. For example, what lower-level careerists see as necessary protections of tenure, top career officials perceive as cumbersome limitations on managerial flexibility. Fourth, the executive often weakens its own managerial linkages, as it seeks sometimes-unreconcilable political and administrative goals. Thus the unionization of public employees which has been encouraged by presidential executive order hardly discourages labor unions looking for new fields to conquer. But one of the groups of federal employees to organize were inspectors in the U.S. Civil Service Commission who, if anybody, would be seen as "management" in most business organizations.

OD programs consequently must face the issue of somehow interfacing political and career linkages which powerful forces—constitutional, political, and historic—tend to pull apart. Consider only one dilemma facing OD programs. The general rule of thumb is that OD programs should begin "at the top" of organizational hierarchies, or as close to the top as possible. The rationale is obvious: that is where the power usually is in business organizations. Respecting this rule of thumb in public agencies raises a multidimensional dilemma. Basically, "the top" in public agencies is more complex than in most businesses. Initiating an OD program at the level of the political leadership maximizes formal executive support, but it may also raise complex problems. Support of the OD program is problematic because of frequent personnel changes at that level,[15] because of possible well-entrenched resistance from the permanent service, because legislators may fear that any strengthening of the executive chain of command would only mean fewer points of access and sources of information, and because employee associations may resist executive direction. Relying more on support from those in the competitive/protected service maximizes the chances of permanent support, and it may raise congressional and CSC trust in the program. But this approach may encourage executive resistance from such vantage points as the Bureau of the Budget.

The OD specialist faces real dilemmas, then, in choosing the "top" of the hierarchy at which to direct his interventions. I have participated in change programs that have taken both approaches to seeking a power base, and they show only that avoiding Scylla seems to imply meeting Charybdis. The ideal is to appeal to both the political officialdom and to the permanent service, of course, but that is a demanding ideal indeed.

In summary, four properties of the institutional environment of public agencies complicate attaining the objectives of typical OD programs. Consider the objective of building trust among individuals and groups throughout the organization. Technically, viable interfaces should be created between political officials, the permanent bureaucracy, congressional committees and their staffs, and so on and on. Practically, this is a very tall order, especially because the critical publics tend to have mutually exclusive interests, values, and reward systems. Indeed, although it is easy to caricature the point, Congress has a definite interest in cultivating a certain level of distrust within and between government agencies so as to encourage a flow of information. This may seem a primitive approach but, in the absence of valid and reliable measures of performance, it may be a necessary approach. No OD program in a business organization will face such an array of hurdles, that much is certain.

CHARACTER OF THE HABIT BACKGROUND: CONSTRAINTS ON APPROACHING OD OBJECTIVES

The "habit background" of public agencies also implies serious obstacles to approaching OD objectives. Five aspects of this habit background are considered below by way of illustrating their impact on OD objectives.

These five aspects do not comprise an exclusive list, and they are conceived of only as general patterns and behaviors which give a definite flavor to the broad institutional environment sketched above.

Patterns of Delegation

"Habit background" is perhaps better illustrated than defined. First, in my experience, public officials tend to favor patterns of delegation that maximize their sources of information and minimize the control exercised by subordinates. Specifically, the goal is to have decisions brought to their level for action or review. The most common concrete concomitants of the tendency are functional specialization and a narrow span of control, one of whose major consequences is a large number of replicative levels of review.[16]

"Layering" of multiple levels of review is not unique to public administration, indeed it inheres in generally accepted organization theory; but it is supported by forces more or less unique to public agencies that have been powerful enough to substantially curtail innovation of ways to centralize policy and to decentralize operations.[17] The protection of the "public interest" is one such unique factor, for example. The rationale is familiar. Political officials of short tenure often cannot rely on established relations of confidence with personnel at lower levels, nor do they exercise as much control over career rewards and punishments as is common in business organizations or in the military. However, the legislature will hold the political officials responsible. Consequently, political officials seek to maximize information sources and minimize the control exercisable by subordinates. This tendency is reinforced by law and tradition so that it permeates down the hierarchy throughout the permanent bureaucracy. The tendency is often referred to as "keeping short lines of command."

Keeping chains of command short implies constraints on approaching OD objectives in public organizations, based on my experience as well as the logic of the situation. Consider only two of the OD objectives above—three and nine:

> to locate decision-making and problem-solving responsibilities as close to the information sources as possible; and
> to increase self-control and self-direction for people within the organization.

To the degree that the rough distinction above is accurate, public agencies will experience difficulties in approaching both objectives. The prevailing habit pattern in public agencies patently constitutes a tide to swim against in these two particulars, although there are outstanding exceptions to this generalization.

Legal Habit

Second, and again only as a description of what exists, legal patterns make approaching OD objectives severely more difficult in public agencies than in business organizations.[18] The point applies in two major senses. Thus patterns of administrative delegation are often specified in minute detail in legislation, basically so as to facilitate oversight by the legislature. To be sure, we are a considerable distance beyond the first Morgan case, which seemed to argue that only administrative actions personally taken by, or under the direct supervision of, a department head were constitutionally defensible. But flexibility in delegation is still a major problem. Perhaps more important, a corpus of law and standard practice exists which also makes it difficult to achieve OD objectives. For example, considering only those employees on the General Schedule, salary and duties are tied to a position classification system whose underlying model emphasizes trans-departmental uniformity and compensation for individual work.[19]

This legal habit background complicates approaching OD values. Thus efforts to achieve OD objective three above may run afoul of the possibility that relocating responsibilities in one agency is considered to have system-wide implications, with consequences that complicate the making of local adjustments. As one official noted of an OD effort in such straits: "I feel like I have to raise the whole civil service by my bootstraps." Relatedly, OD objective two above seeks:

> to supplement the authority associated with role or status with the authority of knowledge and competence.

This is hard to do to the degree that a pattern of delegation is specified in law. The same point applies to any rigidities due to the duties classification common in public agencies in the United States, and especially to the concepts for assigning authority and for organizing work underlying the duties classification. Job enlargement begun as part of OD programs has run afoul of such concepts, for example.

At the bread-and-butter level, existing legal patterns also inhibit approaching OD objectives. Consider objective six, which proposes:

> to develop a reward system which recognizes both the achievement of the organization's mission and organization development.

Existing law and practice severely limit the search for such a reward system. Thus rewards for exceptional performance—in money payments or in high-er-than-normal GS levels for personnel in the civil service—are now possible, but they still are exceptional in practice. Equal pay for equal work, in sum, still practically means that exceptional work is not rewarded exceptionally. Management in business organizations typically has far greater control over reward systems, and especially at managerial levels. More of a problem, neither existing law nor practice promise much in the way of support for various group compensation plans. Experiments in industry with some such plans have yielded attractive results.

Need for Security

Third, the need for security or even secrecy in public agencies as against business organizations is more likely to be strong enough to present obstacles to approaching OD objectives. Military and defense agencies come to mind first, but they hardly exhaust the list. The "need for security" as used here can concern national security, it can be induced by a general anxiety born of a need to make significant decisions whose results will not be manifest for a very long time, or it can derive from felt needs for protection from such outside forces as a congressman with fire in his eye.[20] The need can also be real, exaggerated, or even imagined in various combinations.

Consider one case which seemed to reflect some of all of these components. Agency personnel were exposed to sensitivity training, one of whose major purposes is to increase skills in being open about both positive and negative emotions or reactions. The training staff provided several settings in which these intentions might be approached, one of which was a "park bench." During one week of sensitivity training some time was set aside each evening for a meeting of all participants in a large room which was the locus of the "park bench." But agency personnel seldom used the arena, although there was a good deal of nervous laughter from the periphery of the "park." After some three abortive tries of an hour each, one participant approached me. "I see the point of the thing," he said, "but a park bench is all wrong." Suddenly, the dawn came. "Park benches," were seen as stereotypic sites for sexual assignations and/or for exchanging secrets with enemy agents. Without doubt, some participants thought the "park bench" a silly notion, and hence did not participate. For most participants, however, the symbolism was so compelling that they could not use the "park bench." Moreover, many agency personnel were so closed, distrustful, and fearful of taking a risk that they could not talk about their guiding symbolism, even if they were aware of it.

This greater need for security cannot be established completely, to be sure, and all that may be said definitely is that to the degree this need exists so are OD objectives more difficult to reach. Consider only OD objective one above:

to create an open, problem-solving climate throughout the organization.

An open climate and a great need for security or for secrecy do not mix well.

Procedural Regularity and Caution

Fourth, for a variety of reasons, government personnel are rather more likely to stress procedural regularity and caution. Perhaps better said, even if agency personnel are convinced that certain heuristics provide solutions that are "good enough," this conviction may conflict with other (and especially congressional) needs for external control. For example, sample checking of vouchers was widely accepted as an efficient enough administrative approach long before relevant publics in Congress and the General Accounting Office recognized it as appropriate for their control purposes.

Good reasons support this bias toward procedural regularity and caution in public agencies, of course, and so much the worse for OD objectives. For example, the bias patently runs against the grain of OD objective eight above, which seeks:

> to help managers to manage according to relevant objectives rather than according to "past practices" or according to objectives that do not make sense for one's area of responsibility.

The underlying rub, of course, is that a "past practice" making little or no sense administratively may seem an utter necessity from the legislative point of view. To be sure, the dictum "where you sit determines what you see" applies to all organizations. But the needs and identifications of administrators and legislators are likely to differ more than is the case for (let us say) the executives and middle managers of a business organization.

"Professional Manager"

Fifth, the concept "professional manager" is less developed in the public versus the business arena, in rough but useful contrast. The relative incidence of business schools and schools of public administration suggests the conclusion,[21] as do the Jacksonian notions deep at the roots of our basic public personnel policies. For example, the "career system" notion has been a difficult one to develop in this country at the federal level. No small part of the difficulty derives from the value we place on an "open service" with lateral entry. Hence the tendency of our public personnel policies to emphasize hiring for a specific position rather than for long-run potential.

Derivations from these taproots have had profound impact. For example, to simplify a little, massive federal attention to training was long delayed by the wrigglesworthian legislative notion that, since the federal service was hiring people who already had the abilities to do the specific job for which they were hired, there was little need to spend money on training.[22] The relative attractiveness of public employment at the federal level at least through World War II provided the proverbial finger in the dike, but conditions changed much faster than did public policy. Instructively, also, the system of regional executive development centers manned by the U.S. Civil Service Commission began as late as 1964, and then only with a miniscule budget and against substantial congressional opposition. Roughly, business has a 10—20 year lead over government in acting on the need for training. Not very long ago, in contrast, the federal government was considered *the* model employer.

The relatively lesser stress on the "public professional manager" implies significant problems for approaching OD objectives. Thus OD objective seven proposes:

> to increase the sense of "ownership" of organization objectives throughout the work force.

No sharp contrast is appropriate. But a definite bias of public personnel policy limits such a sense of identification with, and commitment to, public agencies. If there is one thing most civil services reformers did not want, it was a public work force who "owned" the objectives of their agency. The only "owner" was the public; the model employee was a politically neutral technician who repressed his own values in return for guaranteed tenure. Only thus could an elite and unresponsive bureaucracy be avoided, goes a major theme shot through our public personnel policies and institutions.

CONCLUSION

The body of this paper can be summarized tersely. Organization Development programs are appearing with increasing frequency in both business and public agencies. Moreover, applications of OD programs in government agencies face some unique problems. However, these unique problems tend to go unrecognized or underrecognized by OD teams in part because students of public administration have tended to be underrepresented on such teams. Hence this paper.

Some derivative implications seem appropriate, in addition. First, "poaching" in the public sector by OD teams composed basically of psychologists and sociologists will continue to grow, if only because (as William F. Whyte noted in another connection) such poaching is necessary. Second, students of public administration can play a useful and partially distinct role in such OD programs. But, third, students of public administration are likely to play such a role only as substantial numbers of them develop competencies that complement their special interests in public administration. Such competency enlargement for "change-agents" or organization consultants is provided by the NTL Institute of Applied Behavioral Science and by such university-based programs as those at UCLA and Boston University.

Notes

[1]John W. Gardner, *Self-Renewal* (New York: Harper & Row, 1965).

[2]Alexander Winn, "The Laboratory Approach to Organization Development: A Tentative Model of Planned Change," paper read at the Annual Conference, British Psychological Society, Oxford, September 1968, p. 1. More broadly, see Edgar H. Schein and Warren G. Bennis, *Personal and Organization Change through Group Methods: The Laboratory Method* (New York: Wiley, 1965); and Warren G. Bennis, *Changing Organizations* (New York: McGraw-Hill, 1966).

[3]For an overview of the technique, see Robert T. Golembiewski, "The Laboratory Approach to Organization Development: The Schema of A Method," *Public Administration Review,* Vol. 27 (September 1967), pp. 211–220.

[4]Sheldon Davis, "An Organic Problem-Solving Method of Organizational Change," *Journal of Applied Behavioral Science,* Vol. 3 (January 1967), pp. 3–21.

[5]NTL Institute, "What Is OD?" *News and Reports,* Vol. 2 (June 1968), p. 1.

[6]The theme also appeared in mass-circulation news stories and editorials which argued against Project ACORD in the U.S. Department of State, for example. Stewart Alsop, "Let the Poor Old Foreign Service Alone," *Saturday Evening Post,* (June 1966), p. 14.

[7]For example, sensitivity training has been criticized as "amateur group therapy." For an incisive distinction between training and therapy, see Chris Argyris, "Conditions for Competence Acquisition and Therapy," *Journal of Applied Behavioral Science,* Vol. 4 (June 1968), pp. 147–178.

[8]See, generally, Francis E. Rourke, *Bureaucracy, Politics, and Public Policy* (Boston: Little, Brown, 1969).

[9]For a sensitive summary of the programmatic commitments of career personnel, see John J. Corson and R. Shale Paul, *Men Near the Top* (Baltimore, Md.: Johns Hopkins Press, 1966), pp. 23–51.

[10]Joseph P. Harris, *Congressional Control of Administration* (Washington, D.C.: The Brookings Institution, 1964).

[11]Arthur Schlesinger, *A Thousand Days* (Boston: Houghton Mifflin, 1965), p. 681.

[12]President Truman expressed the point directly in contemplating the problems that General Eisenhower would experience as President Eisenhower, without the discipline and definite career patterns and established ways of doing things he knew in the military. "He'll sit here," Truman predicted, "and he'll say, 'Do this!' 'Do that!' *And nothing will happen.* Poor Ike— it won't be a bit like the Army. He'll find it very frustrating." Richard E. Neustadt, *Presidential Power* (New York: Wiley, 1960), p. 9. His emphases.

[13]Herbert Kaufman. "The Rise of a New Politics," p. 58, in Wallace S. Sayre (ed.), *The Federal Government Service* (Englewood Cliffs, N.J.: Prentice-Hall, 1965).

[14]Dean E. Mann, "The Selection of Federal Political Executives," *American Political Science Review,* Vol. 58 (March 1964), pp. 81–99.

[15]One ambitious OD program, for example, was unable to overcome the rumor that several political appointees were negotiating terms of private employment. Agency personnel were encouraged to inaction, since these officials would "soon be riding their OD hobbyhorse" someplace else. These officials did leave. But all claim that the stories were seeded by career personnel who opposed the OD program, and that it was only the intensity of such "dirty fighting" that encouraged the political appointees to seek private employ after the rumors began.

[16]Before a reorganization inspired by an OD program in the Department of State, some review layers were so numerous that "it could take as long as six months for an important problem to reach the Deputy Under Secretary. Now it takes an average of two days." Alfred J. Marrow, "Managerial Revolution in the State Department," *Personnel,* Vol. 43 (December 1966), p. 13.

[17]Such innovation has been the major trend in large businesses over the last three or four decades. See Robert T. Golembiewski, *Men, Management, and Morality* (New York: McGraw-Hill, 1965); and *Organizing Men and Power* (Chicago: Rand McNally, 1967). Strong pressures for just such innovation are now being widely felt in public administration. Aaron Wildavsky provides a case in point in his "Black Rebellion and White Reaction," *The Public Interest,* No. 11 (Spring 1968), especially pp. 9–12.

[18]A very useful discussion of the antimanagerial thrust of much legislation is provided by Harris, *Congressional Oversight of Administration.*

[19]Robert T. Golembiewski, "Civil Service and Managing Work," *American Political Science Review,* Vol. 56 (December 1962), pp. 961–974.

[20]Great needs for "security" as here broadly defined can rigidify an organization and curb the effectiveness of its members. To the point, see Chris Argyris, "Some Causes of Organizational Ineffectiveness within the Department of State," Center for International System Research, *Occasional Papers,* No. 2 (1967).

[21]Revealingly, it was not until 1946 that Cornell developed the first two-year master of public administration program comparable to the MBA long given by schools of commerce or business administration.

[22]Paul P. Van Riper, *History of the United States Civil Service* (Evanston, Ill.: Row, Peterson, 1958), pp. 429–434.

VIII

Some Technical Contexts
Toward more effective control

Any system of public financial controls rests on an underlying technology of tools and approaches. This chapter presents a diverse collection of these tools and approaches which encompasses the commonplace and the esoteric, stresses definition of financial concepts as well as statistical tools, and considers both individual techniques and their complicated combinations in subsystems or systems of financial controls.

The first selection, "The Local Administrator as Budgeter," by Frank P. Sherwood and Wallace H. Best (Reading 30), casts a wide net. It defines several types of budgets, illustrates typical budget documents, and establishes the intimate connection between estimating costs and developing a budget document. The emphasis in budgets may be on the various kinds of activities or services or equipment for which public funds are to be expended, as in the line-item budget. The emphasis also may be upon the major objects or programs of public spending, as in performance or program budgets. Wherever the emphasis, Reading 30 illustrates (if only in simple cases) the rudiments of budgeting.

As the objects of budgeting become more complicated, approaches and tools of analysis of corresponding power must be developed, for complexity requires that the total budget process be factored into manageable pieces. Factoring, however, complicates the problems of somehow exerting overhead control and of attempting to bring spending in individual areas into some coherent balance in terms of systemic criteria. The more individual factorings and subfactorings there are, the greater the problems of control and coherence. For example, at Factoring I the executive may be convinced that he prefers more spending on A than B. But if a_1, a_2, and a_3 all contribute to A, the budgeter in Factoring II again must develop criteria to assign dollar priorities. So it may go for many additional factorings. In the process, the criteria for choice are likely to become more explicit, and judgments about desirable priorities may shift in complex ways. Consequently, a goal may be considered desirable in Factoring I, but subprograms necessary to achieve that goal may not gain corresponding support in later factorings because alternative uses of monies are somehow more justifiable at that level.

Intentionally, we have projected a mental picture of a duality, of a kind of tug-of-war between irreconcilables. The notion of "suboptimization" conveys much of the essence of the complexity of the factoring problem. Suboptimization refers to the factoring of spending decisions into subparts because no one or no system can meaningfully compare all relevant alternatives. This is not simply a decomposition of big decisions into smaller decisions. The critical issue is that, before suboptimization proceeds very far, the analyst is often in the business of comparing apples and oranges. In the absence of some general criteria that permit meaningful comparisons of the costs/benefits of subdecisions, that is, factoring attempts will be plagued by major problems. Consider two cases:

> Case I: If the costs/benefits of decisions can be estimated in terms of the same unit of measure—for example, dollars—tests of even many decisions for comparative maximum value are possible.
>
> Case II: If output and costs cannot be measured in terms of the same units—that is, if generally accepted and meaningful prices cannot be assigned to alternative decisions—suboptimization routines can quickly become overwhelming.[1]

Factoring will always pose problems but, to some degree at least, we can determine which problems we must face. For example, all budgetary decisions require factoring of some sort, so factoring problems there must be. However, different approaches to budgeting raise different factoring problems. Attention will be devoted to these two perspectives on factoring:

- Coping with whatever factoring problems arise.
- Determining what kinds of factoring problems will arise.

1. *Coping with factoring problems.* Considerable progress has been made in how well we can cope with whatever factoring problems we face. For example, Barry G. King's "Cost-Effectiveness Analysis" (Reading 31) introduces and illustrates one of the major tools that can facilitate comparison of major policy alternatives at top levels, after which decision officials at lower organization levels can be set to work developing specific budget estimates and financial details. This is a "trickle-down," or centralized, approach to budgeting. Among the major advantages of cost-effectiveness efforts (where they are applicable) is that they can be quickly applied to facilitate making a policy decision before detailed budget estimates are requested from executive agencies. In the classic case of a comparison of several critical alternative approaches to strategic bombing, for example,

only six weeks were required to compare the costs/benefits, at least at the level of ballpark figures.[2] Without question, some large multiple of six weeks would have been required if the agencies in question had been asked to submit detailed budget estimates. Moreover, personnel in various agencies might have developed commitments to different alternatives, some or all of which the president or high-level defense officials might later have to violate because of broader considerations. Competition between the several military services might have been generated, and alternative approaches could have received support because of their effects on a service's destiny in addition to (or even in disregard of) their cost-effectiveness merits and demerits. This is a wicked feature of the "percolate-up" budget, at least as far as executives are concerned

Relatedly, quite an arsenal of powerful analytic tools has become available, largely since World War II, the better to cope with whatever factoring problems arise. An old but still useful article—John W. Pocock's "Operations Research" (Reading 32)—provides a gentle introduction to several prominent techniques from this growing analytic arsenal. Among their many uses, such techniques provide the analysis and control required by today's complex budgeting and financial decisions.

Perhaps most prominent among these analytic tools is Program Evaluation and Review Technique (PERT), whose prime applications have been in scheduling and controlling complex interdependent events such as the development of the Polaris missile. Dan A. Bawly and Joseph M. Dotan introduce the technique in "Using PERT in Accounting Reports" (Reading 33), which also deals with the notion of a "critical path." Bawly and Dotan stress a simple application with a small number of events. However, PERT has been applied to very large and complex problems, making particular use of the computer. PERT networks commonly include many hundreds of individual events, each with its own estimated completion time and complex interdependencies with other events. Should the completion of a particular event be delayed, for example, computer runs can reveal the impact of that delay on the total set of events, help reschedule by permitting choice between alternative adaptations to unanticipated delays, and the like.

PERT has a mixed track record.[3] As Ivars Avots concluded a decade ago: "No management technique has ever caused so much enthusiasm, controversy, and disappointment as PERT."[4] Consequently, the reader is well advised to consider these limitations of the technique, as noted by Avots:

1. PERT cannot be used when the occurrence of events cannot be estimated with some accuracy.
2. PERT is not particularly useful for activities that recur regularly, as in most production or processing activities. PERT networks are most useful for one-time programs.

3. The logic of any PERT network cannot be independently verified, so specific applications of the technique critically depend on the skills of analysis, as well as on continuing reevaluation of the network that will generate appropriate revisions plus updating.
4. There are real limits on the number of events that a manual PERT system can conveniently accommodate, and such limits even hold for computerized systems which, of course, can handle many more events than manual systems.
5. Large PERT networks place a premium on skilled interpretation and analysis in the conversion of computer outputs into information that is managerially useful.

On the other side of the picture, the PERT technique and philosophy have a number of major attractions, including four points that deserve especial emphasis. First, PERT requires an integration of planning activities, which is a very useful discipline to cultivate. Second, PERT can permit a rapid evaluation of the status of a program and spotlight specific trouble spots for corrective action by management. Third, PERT networks cut across the boundaries of organization units and provide perspective on total programs. This is a major advantage, particularly in larger organizations. Fourth, PERT attempts to accept uncertainty or probability and to work with it. This encourages a managerial habit of mind that is more realistic and sensitive to complex contingencies, as opposed to a come-hell-or-high-water approach to scheduling with definite but arbitrary deadlines.

"Simulation" is also likely to be used increasingly in public agencies in the near future, and its care and feeding often will be entrusted to officials in finance or accounting. Since there is no such thing as a simple example of a simulation, the temptation will be resisted to provide an extended illustration here. Essentially, however, simulation involves the attempt to specify a set of relationships relevant to some problem area, most usefully in equation form. Once such a "model" of relationships is developed, policy-makers can then play useful "what if?" games. The generic question is: What would happen to the system of relationships in the model if selected variables are manipulated, as required by different policies or programs? The interested reader can consult a variety of examples of simulations, like one which compares three alternative policies for providing health services.[5] Such simulations are not substitutes for executive thought or courage, of course, but they can provide support for both. Such uses are the most that can be expected of any tool. After all, you can cut your neighbor's throat with a knife as well as you can cut your steak. The intention is the critical factor in both cases.

Simulations do have seductive qualities, however, and these must be guarded against. Ida R. Hoos has done an excellent job in this regard. She warns against four dangers of simulation which basically derive from such a fascination with simulation models that real-world concerns get slighted. These dangers are:

1. Overconcentration on the mechanics and details of simulation models.
2. Incorrect or incautious use of any model of relationships, as in considering it a mirror of reality rather than a variously useful simplification of reality.
3. Disregard of limitations that are specifically built into simulations.
4. Neglect of subjective elements or values when taking action based on the results of simulation runs.[6]

More broadly, budget and finance officials will become increasingly involved in the development and operation of Management Information Systems (MIS). MIS seems as much as anything a state of mind, a conviction that systemic managerial problems can be coped with if only comprehensive informational systems can be developed. Typically, definitions of MIS include at least three elements:

1. A standard, integrated data base for an entire organization or growing portions thereof.
2. A system design that provides for the use of these data in the efficient and timely development of required information.
3. The facility or plan to utilize these data for projecting future activity and for planning management action.[7]

Here again, Hoos raises significant questions that provide a tether for MIS overexuberance. Basically, Hoos is concerned that the " . . . management *of* information has receded from view and management *by* information has become the mode." Her concerns derive from the common tendency of early enthusiasm about the ultimate vision to blur certain critical issues, as well as from the mixed track record of MIS applications.[8] Specifically, Hoos urges that MIS applications be clear on five levels of differences about information. That is, there should be information that:

1. Various data-processing equipment can accept.
2. Would be convenient to have.
3. Is economically justifiable in organizations of various sizes and missions.
4. Is managerially useful.
5. Can be reliably gathered.
6. Can be routinely used in making valid inferences or interpretations.[9]

Realistically, Hoos urges, not all (or even most) information meets all six of these criteria. MIS applications must be acutely sensitive as to which information does not meet which criteria; otherwise, much mischief can result, at great cost and despite ponderous effort.

   2. *Determining factoring problems.* Recently, also, major efforts have been made to determine which factoring problems will arise, as distinct

from seeking to cope better with whatever factoring problems do arise because of tradition and past practices.

Various approaches to budgeting imply vastly different factoring problems as can be seen by contrasting a "percolate up" with a "trickle down" process. The traditional line-item process of budgeting has percolate-up characteristics. That is, the chief executive issues a call for estimates, which are generated from below. Thus a strict line-item budget might list "10 stenographers at $4,500 each." This line-item is the product of many factorings, beginning at low levels of organization whose requests were aggregated and perhaps trimmed as they rose through a hierarchy. An overhead authority seeking control probably would attempt to control the number of stenographers. Even if the executive controlled this factoring, his victory would be a slim one indeed, for that executive must be more concerned with what the stenographers do than with how many there are. What the stenographers would do under a strict line-item budget, however, was decided in earlier factorings. Checking the validity and specifics of decisions made in these early factorings poses a difficult problem for the executive. Moreover, in these early factorings agencies develop internal consensus about, and commitment to, specific programs. This consensus and commitment often are difficult for any executive to change.

Roughly, each factoring before the line-item budget reaches the top executive's desk substantially restricts his meaningful control. And traditional budgeting procedures of the percolate-up variety restrict the executive to very late factorings. Allen Schick observes:

> In budgeting, which is committed to the established base, the flow of budgetary decisions is upward and aggregative. Traditionally, the first step in budgeting, in anticipation of the call for estimates, is for each department to issue its own call to prepare and to submit a set of estimates. This call reaches to the lowest level capable of assembling its own estimates. Lowest level estimates form the building blocks for the next level where they are aggregated and reviewed and transmitted upward until the highest level is reached and the totality constitutes a department-wide budget. Since budgeting is tied to a base, the building-up-from-below approach is sensible; each building block estimates the cost of what it is already doing plus the cost of the increments it wants. (The building blocks, then, are decisional elements, not simply informational elements as is often assumed.)[10]

In sum, the line-item budget makes it difficult for the top executive to influence those factorings which he must particularly control. This is an awkward combination.

Under a program budget, in contrast, the executive can and must influence early factorings, which then "trickle down" to subordinates to fill in the details of how the broad programs are to be implemented. In such a way can the executive enhance his control, for this kind of budget in the first factoring deals with crucial decisions by the executive about the priorities assigned to various programs, with what will be done. Thus planning comes first and is the prime executive responsibility. Detailed programming and budgeting decisions come later, at lower administrative levels in later factorings. Hence the common designation PPBS, (Planning, Programming, and Budgeting Systems).

The executive's influence and control over early factorings in a program budget constitute a critical departure from traditional trickle-down approaches. Later factorings must refine how program objectives will be achieved and which specific mix of resources will be used, of course. These later factorings are difficult for the top executive to control, but he also has less interest in them. As Schick observes:

> PPB reverses the informational and decisional flow. Before the call for estimates is issued, top policy has to be made, and this policy constrains the estimates prepared below. For each lower level, the relevant policy instructions are issued by the superior level prior to the preparation of estimates. Accordingly, the critical decisional process—that of deciding on purposes and plans—has a downward and disaggregative flow.[11]

This brief comparison of two approaches to budgeting can be summarized simply. PPBS, basically, it a programmed effort to increase the top executive's control over early factorings in the budgetary process. Thus the technique requires that specific and comprehensive policy choices be made before budget estimates are solicited. The premium is on doing, in broad yet specific form (from the top, down), the planning on which programs and budgets will be based. A line-item budget, in crude but useful opposition, lessens the top executive's control over planning and programming. Such a budget process tends to percolate up the hierarchy from lower levels, where substantial consensus and political support can develop about early factorings which will present the chief executive with *faits accomplis,* or at least will tend to limit his ability to direct and influence budget decisions.

But such simple comparisons need major illustration and analysis. Three summary conclusions can convey the essence of this more detailed view. First, budget reform in the United States is in the midphases of a third and new stage, and two related systems of managerial thought may be said to epitomize this most recent stage. Second, Planning, Programming, Budgeting System (PPBS) is the major and most complex expression of this third stage, even if its star has declined significantly after hopes were so extravagantly raised some years ago, especially at the federal level during the administration of President Lyndon B. Johnson.[12] Third, a related system of thought—Management by Objectives (MBO)—has gained substantial recent support among students and practitioners of public management as a major vehicle for the ongoing third stage of budget reform. In sketching the meaning of these three summary conclusions, both description and critical analysis will be emphasized.

There are many ways of specifying stages in public budget reform, but Allen Schick has developed a particularly revealing approach.[13] He identifies three stages, beginning with the 1920s. First, during the years 1920 to 1935, the focus was on *control of expenditures*, and the major product of this first stage was the Budgeting and Accounting Act of 1921. There is some exaggeration in making the point, but this first stage was definitely biased toward focusing on the individual items for which expenditures were made, with the goal of assuring that all items were legally contracted for and supplied. That is a good place to start, of course, especially if the overriding concern is to limit public expenditures as strictly as possible, consistent with the more-or-less dominant view that the least government is the best government. That concern was overriding in the twenties, and limited government was the dominant view.

In the second stage, major but hardly exclusive attention in budgetary reform began to shift toward what Schick called a *management orientation*, with an emphasis on improving processes and procedures. The characteristic development of this second stage was the evolution of the Bureau of the Budget, later to become the even more revealingly named Office of Management and Budget. The Bureau's evolution as a major presidential aid was accelerated by the New Deal and its associated ferment, a major expression of which was the 1937 Report of the President's Committee on Administrative Management. The goal of the second phase was to induce processes and procedures to permit the more effective spending of public monies. In contrast, as we have noted, the dominant goal of the first stage was a more limited one: to curb the expenditure of public funds.

A *planning orientation* characterizes the third stage of budget reform, and PPBS is its major expression. While necessary attention must be given to the control and management orientations, the focus shifts toward central levels and long-run public goals and policies. Whereas the management orientation of Stage 2 encourages attention to such matters as the best way to accomplish a specific goal, a planning orientation emphasizes profoundly different questions, such as: What should our goals be? How should alternative goals be comparatively evaluated?

PPBS constitutes the most prominent managerial approach to coping with just such questions, and it was accordingly very attractive to many political executives, paramountly President Johnson. Overall, PPBS focuses on simultaneous comparisons and coordination between alternative programs for meeting specified public goals. As Arthur Smithies has observed, PPBS involves:

1. Appraisal and comparison of the full range of public activities in terms of contributions to national objectives.
2. Determination of how objectives can be attained with minimum expenditure of resources.

3. Projection of government activities over an adequate period of time.
4. Comparison of the relative contribution of private and public activities in accomplishing national objectives.
5. Revisions of objectives, programs, and budgets as experience and changing circumstances warrant.[14]

Detail necessary to flesh out the basic description above must stress the evolutionary character of this comprehensive approach. "There is . . . little new in the individual concepts of PPBS," as Harry P. Hatry and John F. Cotton observe. "What is new is the combination of a number of these concepts into a package and the systematic application of the package in toto to government planning."[15] Prominent among these concepts is the program or performance budget, which differs profoundly from the traditional line-item budget. Like many major notions, the distinction here is a subtle one, but its implications are many and profound. Thus the line-item budget is organized around the specific items or objects of expenditures. The program budget focuses on the broad purposes for which expenditures are made. Emphasis on the program budget, in an evolutionary sense, is consistent with the movement toward the third phase of budget reform sketched above. A line-item budget is consistent with the elemental motive of controlling expenditures.

The evolution of PPBS has not been smooth and uneventful, as Jack Rabin specifies in "State and Local PPBS" (Reading 34), which describes the approach and evaluates some of its track record. Overall, Rabin is sensitive to the blatant overselling that accompanied the earlier attempt to extend PPBS throughout the federal agencies, and he seeks to counsel state and local officials that there is a critical need to separate wheat from chaff in considering the installation of PPBS in their jurisdictions. Rabin's selection begins with a description of the theory underlying PPBS, proceeds to a survey of the approach in action, and concludes with a treatment of the pros and cons of attempts to install PPBS.

Of particular significance in Rabin's treatment is the difficulty in PPBS of defining "programs," especially in the continuing presence of multiple agencies whose component activities variously contribute to any set of comprehensive and broad-gauge programs. In principle, one can draw lovely pictures of "crosswalks" between agency structures and program structures, but practical realities are another matter. When the chips are really down, for example, a PPBS "program" does not somehow magically resolve the issues of jurisdictional conflicts between agencies, nor does it eliminate the patent fact that different agencies contributing to the same "purpose" might assign widely differing priorities to their several contributions to that purpose. Usefully, PPBS might dramatize such issues, or perhaps even identify them *de novo*. But PPBS could not resolve such issues, and political executives were seldom very free to use the crosswalks to monitor the agencies. At the federal level, for example, a program budget was developed. But congressional committees tended to demand a line-item budget, or at least individual agency budgets, for their deliberations and decision-making. That was a clear test of what was really important, and who controlled or dominantly influenced what was considered important.

This is no attempt to demean PPBS. Indeed, it can be reasonably argued that PPBS is like Christianity, in the sense that neither has been really tried. For example, there is some evidence that many PPBS applications tended to have a kind of reverse flow. That is, the PPBS principle is that the "purpose" or "program" will determine the needed resources or activities. In practice, however, the existing resources of agencies often have been justified by finding a place for them in some purpose or program. This is a way of having programs without biting the bullet in the way PPBS prescribes. PPBS crosswalks become complex displays in such a case, but they are more useful for reinforcing the status quo than for analysis or managerial control. No agency need be very fearful of such an approach to PPBS, at least in the first few go-rounds.

Some have argued, however, that program structures can be evolved into more potent vehicles for executive control, once some initial acclimatization of legislators and middle-level administrators has been accomplished. Perhaps this will prove to be the case. Rabin's article sketches some evidence indicating an opposite conclusion.

Reading 34 also points to a truism that is often neglected: The specific manner of implementing the PPBS model is the critical factor in the success or failure of individual applications. However attractive the concept, that is, its implementation requires changes in behavior, attitudes, and values. The common tendency is to give inadequate attention to the change process. In this sense, Rabin's capsule histories of local PPBS applications reinforce the relevance to budgeting and finance of the behavioral orientation introduced in Chapters VI and VII, and especially of the introduction to planned change in Golembiewski's "Organization Development in Public Agencies" (Reading 29, in Chapter VII). PPBS is a conceptual and technical thing, but it is put into motion by people operating in the context of agency traditions. If those people do not behave appropriately, and if those agency traditions do not reinforce the appropriate behaviors, the PPBS concept and techniques are lifeless.

The realistic cautions sketched by Rabin are reinforced by James R. Schlesinger's "Uses and Abuses of Analysis" (Reading 35). He urges a comely modesty in the face of the enormous challenges implied in trying to determine the kind of factoring or suboptimization that will be faced. Overall, Schlesinger gives two and one-half cheers for applications of "systems analysis" to public decisions. He devotes much of his space detailing the reservations which explain the one-half cheer he withholds. Witness his concern that systems analysis can be so practiced as to deprive political decision-makers of the opportunity to make decisions, in contrast to helping decision-makers isolate and compare alternatives.

Schlesinger's caution receives a useful emphasis in arguments that systems analysis can be mistakenly interpreted as making technical what must be profoundly political. Aaron Wildavsky provides one such argument in "The Political Economy of Efficiency,"[16] which is not reprinted here. Essentially, he argues that too much can be made of even good things. Thus he sees cost-benefit analysis, systems analysis, and program budgeting as viable enough at "modest" levels of application. As the problems increase in scope, Wildavsky argues, the situation changes in profound ways. It becomes increasingly dangerous to pretend that a political issue is a technical one. The thrust of his argument is direct: " . . . at the highest levels [the techniques above leave] pure efficiency far behind its over-reaching grasp into the structure of the political system. Program budgeting, it turns out, is a form of systems analysis, that is, political systems analysis."[17]

Detailed counterpoint to Wildavsky's broad concerns is provided by a number of sources. The conclusion of one such source will have to suffice here to illustrate that critical literature. Ida R. Hoos criticizes "systems analysis" in a number of particulars, but she is uncertain as to the major target of censure. She sees three possible targets: the technique itself, those specialists who apply the technique, and specific applications. She concludes: "Perhaps it is in the nature of systems analysis . . . that the trio is inseparable, with all three parts of a semantic web permeated with salesmanship, sometimes for the technique, sometimes for the doer, sometimes for the done for."[18]

Yehezkel Dror devotes himself to working on one of Hoos's inseparable trio and, in effect, taking Wildavsky at his word by seeking to develop a preliminary framework for "political systems analysis." Dror's "Policy Analysis: A Theoretic Framework and Some Basic Concepts" (Reading 36) outlines the central concerns of the new form of systems analysis which Wildavsky implied was necessary and which is not provided by PPBS as he describes it. We can only present a selection from Dror's seminal effort, but his argument stands out prominently. Dror begins with a catalog of eight main and interdependent senses in which traditional systems analysis is "inadequate for treating complex social issues." His version of the "policy sciences" seeks to remedy·these inadequacies at the conceptual level by stressing the need for such features as "value sensitivity" that are lacking in traditional systems analysis, at least explicitly. Of course, Dror recognizes that, in practice, stress on such features will be difficult to apply in consistent ways. But it is useful to know what you ought to be doing even if it is not clear how you can or will do it.

Criticisms like those introduced above have been compelling for both theoretical and practical reasons, and even the most ardent advocates of

PPBS have pulled in their horns substantially. Indeed, some observers are writing obituaries for the approach.[19]

Whether PPBS is dead or dying or merely temporarily indisposed, however, two points seem clear enough. First, much of the spirit and especially the techniques associated with the approach will continue to be important to the student and practitioner of public budgeting and finance.

Second, the questions which PPBS addressed are growing more serious as time passes. Consequently, it is not surprising that kindred managerial systems are receiving substantial attention. Perhaps Management by Objectives (MBO) is the most prominent of these alternatives.

MBO, introduced briefly in Chapter VI, has an essential focus that is direct but significant. As Rodney H. Brady explains in "MBO Goes to Work in the Public Sector" (Reading 37), the basic strength of this managerial approach rests in the simplicity of its major premises:

- That the clearer the objective toward which one is working, the greater are the chances of accomplishing it.
- That real progress can only be measured in terms of an objective which is stated with sufficient precision to be useful.

The overall sense is that of a slenderized and modest PPBS, with the same useful thrust toward purposes or objectives, and often making use of the same analytical techniques. But MBO implies a less urgent appeal for centralized control than typically characterizes PPBS formulations.

Experience with MBO has been mixed,[20] in two major senses, at least. First, some observers have noted that the philosophy underlying many MBO efforts could create major problems. Harry Levinson, for example, argues that a "jackass fallacy" mentality has motivated many, even most, MBO efforts.[21] The jackass fallacy implies a view of the employee as one who responds to a narrow range of motivators, the proverbial carrot and the stick. The consequences of such a view underlying MBO programs are pernicious, as Levinson explains in "Management By Whose Objectives?" (Reading 38). He observes that "the typical MBO effort perpetuates and intensifies hostility, resentment, and distrust between a manager and subordinates. As currently practiced, it is really just industrial engineering with a new name, applied to higher managerial levels and with the same resistances." Right or wrong, in whatever degree, Levinson's article deserves careful attention, for the consequences he emphasizes are both unintended and serious if not calamitous. That is a very bad combination.

Second, experience with MBO has been mixed because it is difficult to apply in organizations as they are often structured. Specifically, MBO applications seem particularly chancy in functionally departmentalized structures like the Figure 1 organizations described in Golembiewski's "Accountancy as a Function of Organization Theory," which is discussed and reprinted as Reading 27 in Chapter VII. That is to say, clear and meaningful objectives are difficult to define and monitor where agencies are basically departmentalized by major *purposes,* such as defense, labor, or commerce, or by *functions,* such as personnel, budgeting, or engineering. Such departmentation emphasizes separatism and encourages fragmentation of organization units contributing to a common flow of work.[22] It is a critical fact that most public *and* business organizations are departmentalized by major purposes or functions. In contrast, the thrust of MBO is wholistic and integrative.

Organizations that have Figure 2 structures—which departmentalize around total flows of work, e.g., products or territories with substantial decentralized authority—seem more suited to MBO. Again, Reading 27 may be consulted for a sketch of the properties of Figure 2 structures.

This generalization implies trouble for MBO applications in two senses. First, most public organizations are patterned after Figure 1 structures. Few MBO applications have been preceded by basic structural reorganization from Figure 1 to Figure 2 structures, moreover.

Second, the changeover from a Figure 1 to a Figure 2 structure is often a complicated and touchy matter. For an overview of one philosophical and technological system for inducing organizational change, see Golembiewski's "Organization Development in Public Agencies," reprinted as Reading 29 in Chapter VII.

Notes

[1] Roland N. McKean, "Criteria of Efficiency in Government Expenditures," pp. 252–57 in *Federal Expenditure Policies for Economic Growth and Stability* (Washington, D.C.: U.S. Government Printing Office, 1957).

[2] Gene H. Fisher, "The Role of Cost Utility Analysis in Program Budgeting," esp. pp. 74–88, in David Novick (ed.), *Program Budgeting* (Cambridge, Mass.: Harvard University Press, 1965).

[3] Harvey M. Sapolsky attempts to demythologize the value of PERT in the Polaris missile program, for example. The program's innovativeness in managerial methods like PERT, he concludes, was "as effective technically as rain dancing." Such methods were "quite effective politically," however, in that they contributed to a reputation for managerial efficiency that "allowed the program's technical staffs to continue their frantic work relatively unhindered by concerned but disruptive outside officials." *The Polaris System Development: Bureaucratic and Programmatic Success in Government* (Cambridge, Mass.: Harvard University Press, 1972), p. 246; see also pp. 94–130 for the evidence on which Sapolsky bases his conclusions.

[4] Ivar Avots, "The Management Side of PERT," *California Management Review* 4 (Winter 1962), p. 5.

[5] J. Kane, W. Thompson, and I. Vertinsky, "Health Care Delivery: A Policy Simulator," *Socio-Economic Planning Processes* 6 (June 1972): 283–93.

[6] Ida R. Hoos, *Systems Analysis in Public Policy* (Berkeley, Calif.: University of California Press, 1972), pp. 125–27.

[7] C. R. Jauchem, "Developing the Common Data Base for Management Information Systems," *The Federal Accountant,* Vol. 19 (June, 1970), pp. 22–25.

[8] See Arlene Hirshman, "A Mess in M.I.S.?" *Dun's Review* 91 (January 1968): 26–27, and Tom Alexander, "Computers Can't Solve Everything," *Fortune,* October 1969, pp. 126–29, 168, and 171.

[9] Hoos, *Systems Analysis in Public Policy,* p. 194 ff.

[10]Allen Schick, "The Road to PPB: The Stages of Budget Reform," *Public Administration Review* 26 (December 1966): 257–58.

[11]Ibid., p. 258.

[12]For a documentary supporting this conclusion, see Frederick C. Mosher and John E. Harr, *Programming Systems and Foreign Affairs Leadership: An Attempted Innovation* (New York: Oxford University Press, 1970).

[13]Allen Schick, "The Road to PPB: The Stages of Budget Reform," *Public Administration Review* 26 (December 1966): 243–58.

[14]Arthur Smithies, "Conceptual Framework for the Program Budget," esp. pp. 2–5, in David Novick (ed.), *Program Budgeting* (Cambridge, Mass.: Harvard University Press, 1965).

[15]Harry P. Hatry and John F. Cotton, *Program Planning for State, County, City* (Washington, D.C.: George Washington University, 1967), esp. pp. 14–28.

[16]*Public Administration Review,* 26 (December 1966): 292–310.

[17]Ibid., p. 292.

[18]Ida R. Hoos, *Systems Analysis in Public Policy* (Berkeley: University of California Press, 1972), p. 9.

[19]Allen Schick, "A Death in the Bureaucracy: The Demise of Federal PPB," *Public Administration Review* 33 (March 1973): 146–56.

[20]Herbert H. Meyer, Emanuel Kay, and John French, "Split Roles in Performance Appraisal," *Harvard Business Review* 42 (1965): 123–29; Anthony P. Raia, "Goal Setting and Self Control," *Journal of Management Studies* 2 (1965): 34–53; and John M. Ivancevich, "A Longitudinal Assessment of Management by Objectives," *Administrative Science Quarterly* 17 (March 1972): 126–38.

[21]Harry Levinson, *The Great Jackass Fallacy* (Boston, Mass.: Division of Research, Graduate School of Business Administration, Harvard University, 1973).

[22]Robert T. Golembiewski, *Organizing Men and Power* (Chicago: Rand McNally & Co., 1968), esp. pp. 90–117.

30
The Local Administrator as Budgeter

Frank P. Sherwood and Wallace H. Best

To fully understand the budget process in your city it is necessary to have an understanding of the various types of budgets. In your career as supervisor you will hear reference made to such terms as current or operating budgets, capital budgets, long-range capital improvement programs, line-item budgets, performance budgets, and program budgets.

CURRENT AND CAPITAL BUDGETS

In most cases the current budget (or operating budget as it is often called) covers municipal operations for a year period. It may be contrasted to the

From *Supervisory Methods in Municipal Administration* (Washington, D.C.: International City Managers' Association, 1958), pp. 255–64. Used with permission of publisher and authors.

long-term or capital budget, which is concerned with the acquisition of land and rights-of way and the construction of major public works such as public buildings, streets and bridges, sewer systems, off-street parking, and public utilities. The current or operating budget pays for such things as salaries; materials and services, such as street repair materials, mimeographing services, stationery; and other items essential to the continuing maintenance of the city plant.

The capital budget is distinguished from the current budget in various ways:

1. It represents a long-range plan of capital investment only.
2. It does not have the annuality of the current budget. Projects may be programmed for six years ahead and the effects of the capital program are much longer than that.
3. It is not adopted and executed in the same way as the current budget. The general goals are approved for a six-year period but are subject to yearly revision. The capital projects program for the coming year is made a part of, and executed through, the current operations budget.

All too often a city provides for capital improvements only when the need in a particular case has become sufficiently acute to dramatize the extraordinary expenditure which is usually required. Thus, the city's financial resources may be exhausted by provision for a few capital items, while other needs are neglected.

In contrast to this haphazard method a comprehensive plan (usually drawn up by the planning department or planning commission after consultation with the various departments of the city government and submitted to the citizens of the community for their suggestions and advice) will indicate what things are needed; the relative importance of the various items; and the location, character, and scale of what is to be done to satisfy these needs. The long-range capital improvement program will schedule these items over a period of years so that they can be provided as needed, within the limits of the financial resources of the community.

LINE-ITEM BUDGET

In most cities the budget is regarded primarily as a financial and accounting device with expenditure estimates for various departments being submitted and reviewed as money estimates. Requests are supported mostly by the detailing of objects to be purchased such as materials, supplies, equipment, and salaries to be paid. The validity of the request is judged largely on the basis of comparison with previous expenditure experience. This is the line-item type of budget, based on appropriations to each "object" classification (materials, supplies, equipment, and salaries, for example). Figure 30.1 illustrates one example of a line-item type of budget.

FIGURE 30.1
Example of Line-Item Budget

PUBLIC SAFETY FUND
EXPENDITURES

Account ·Number	Account Title	1956 Actual	1957 Actual	1958 App'ns
2-1	Police Department			
A	Salaries	$387361	$417407	$451460
B-11	Heat and Light	11741	11215	11800
B-21	Telephone and Telegraph	4387	4523	4500
B-23	Postage	18	38	40
B-24	Travel and Training	339	462	950
B-26	Freight	40	75	100
B-29	Ambulance Service	9600	11370	14880
B-37	Doctor and Hospital	2221	819	2500
B-41	Legal Notices	33	30	100
B-45	Printing	498	471	500
B-62	Investigations	4	. . .	100
B-65	Court Costs and Fees	. . .	42	100
B-71	Office Equipment Repairs	593	347	600
B-72	Bldg. and Bldg. Equipment Repairs	1619	1405	2000
B-92	Towels and Laundry	149	67	150
B-93	Dues	15	21	25
B-95	Disinfectants	332	300	350
C-11	Office Supplies	2187	2094	2550
C-21	Gasoline and Oil	10117	10072	10500
C-22	Motor Vehicle Supplies and Repair	6497	5738	6500
C-41	Jail Food	2972	2797	3000
C-42	Janitor Supplies	108	190	250
C-8	Medical Supplies	4	6	25
C-112	Wearing Apparel	4560	4602	6400
C-113	Photo Supplies	845	688	1100
C-114	Radio Repair and Supplies	. . .	. . .	1500
C-12	Other Supplies	1315	1680	1300
D-11	Motor Vehicle Insurance	1568	1732	1780
C-12	Building and·Content Insurance	149	149	200
Z-1	Office Equipment	528	155	1100
Z-2	Motor Vehicle Equipment	2853	16818	12400
Z-12	Other Equipment	1300	2944	1800
	Total	$453953	$498257	$540560

PERFORMANCE BUDGET

In recent years the term "performance budget" has been widely adopted to identify a concept of the budget as a device for planning city programs of service. This terminology was first used by the Hoover Commission in recommending the adoption of improved budgetary techniques by the Federal Government:

We recommend that the whole budgetary concept of the Federal Government should be refashioned by the adoption of a budget based upon functions, activities, and projects; this we designate a "performance budget."

Such an approach would focus attention upon the general character and relative importance of the work to be done, or upon the service to be rendered, rather than upon things to be acquired such as personal services, supplies, equipment, and so on. These latter objects are, after all, only the means to an end. The all-important thing in budgeting is the work or the service to be accomplished, and what that work or service will cost.[1]

Thus the goal of the performance budget is to reach beyond the dollars alone and the mere objects of purchase, to the end result of governmental operation—the services to be performed.

Performance Budgets and Program Budgets

In essence there is little distinction between performance budgeting and program budgeting. As a matter of fact, the budgeting identified as performance budgeting in the Hoover Commission report was first known as program budgeting (see Figure 30.2).

Building expenditure estimates.   Not so long ago the department head in a city with a large annexation program was bemoaning the fact that he could not operate his department on the funds "they gave him." The council's reaction was "we gave you everything you asked for." When the department head pointed out that the council had not provided for the services required for the annexed areas the council's reply was "tell us how much it will cost to service that area and we'll see that you get the money." This placed the department head in a dilemma: all he knew was that he was short on manpower and equipment. He wanted more dollars but when he had to say how many dollars he threw up his hands in confusion.

The line-item approach shows how many clerks are to be hired, how much travel money will be spent, how much will go for printing, mimeographing, paper, typewriters, and stationery. This is a clear and explicit type of budget, but with no precedent for his guidance the department head is not helped out of his dilemma by the line-item practice. A new and different approach is needed.

THE PERFORMANCE APPROACH

The performance approach calls for a budget in which the appropriation figures bear a clear relation to service standards, volumes of work to be performed, methods of performing such work, and the cost element required by such standards and volume.

Performance data has sometimes been called "what we're going to do" data. The supervisor who has been crucified by the newspapers because he

FIGURE 30.2

Example of Program-Type Budget

─────CITY OF HARTFORD─────
ANNUAL BUDGET
PUBLIC WORKS
CURBS AND WALKS   31–11

PERSONNEL DATA	Actual 1955–56	Esti-mated 1956–57	Budget 1957–58
REGULAR POSITIONS			
Clerk Typist 2.........	1	1	1
Clerk Stenographer 2...	1	1	1
Semi-Skilled Laborer....	1	1	1
Sidewalk Const. & Rep. Frmn...............	1	1	1
Cement Finisher.......	1	1	1
Street Inspector........	6	6	6
Street Inspector-Supervisor...............	1	1	1
TOTAL REGULAR POSITIONS......	12	12	12
MAN YEARS PAID.	11.8	11.8	11.9
OVERTIME HOURS PAID................	564	528	528

EXPENDITURE RECAP	Actual 1955–56	Esti-mated 1956–57	Budget 1957–58
PERSONAL SERVICES			
Regular Payroll........	44,988	47,475	48,098
Overtime Payments....	1,078	1,075	1,075
TOTAL PERSONAL SERVICES.......	46,066	48,550	49,173
NON-PERSONAL EX-PENSE			
Inspectors Bus Tickets..	750	750	750
Materials Used by Repair Crew..........	287	845	800
Maintenance City Property...............	35,623	43,425	46,350
Sidewalk Assessment Work...............	14,030	23,000	20,000
TOTAL NON-PERSONAL EXPENSE........	50,690	68,020	67,900
OUTLAY			
Major Installation.	5,958	....	5,700
TOTAL DIVISION..	102,714	116,570	122,773

All activity of the Sidewalk Division has been combined in code 31–11 including the office staff previously reflected in 31–01, the repair crew formerly in 31–12, and sidewalk assessment work once charged to 31–17. However, curb and walk-work included in paving projects is absorbed in the street maintenance account.

This division inspects the condition of all sidewalks, curbs, driveways, ramps, house numbers, street signs, parking meters, and water and gas gates along 215 miles of city streets. Orders are sent to property owners to repair walks and drives. In the event of non-compliance, the city may order the work done and the bill charged against the owner. Revenue code 7316 reflects the amount of reimbursement.

Installation of sidewalk and drive on the north side of Allen Place along the cemetery, $2,700, and replacement of walk at South Green, $3,000, are included in outlay. The maintenance program is outlined below:

CITY RESPON-SIBILITY	Actual 1955–56	Esti-mated 1956–57	Budget 1957–58
WORK MEASURE-MENT			
Curbs-lin. ft........	13,351	21,363	22,000
City-owned walk-sq. ft................	4,394	5,500	5,500
City-accepted walks-sq. ft.............	3,995	5,000	5,000
COST			
Curbs..............	$30,913	$37,395	$39,600
City-owned walks...	2,460	3,445	3,500
City-accepted walks.	2,250	2,585	3,250
TOTAL..........	$35,623	$43,425	$46,350
PRIVATE RE-SPONSIBILITY			
Walks and drives-sq. ft................	20,844	33,424	30,770
Cost..............	$14,030	$23,000	$20,000

didn't remove snow during last winter's snow storm or because the streets flooded due to inadequate cleaning of sewer mains or catch basins will have a happier life if he develops a budget with the "what we're going to do" approach.

The supervisor needs both accounting data and performance data. The accounting division can furnish the dollar amounts required in developing expenditure estimates. Performance data consists of organization charts, work programs, and units for measuring these programs. Accounting information may help the supervisor correlate and interpret the performance data but most of the performance information must be developed by the individual supervisors.

The supervisor first must identify his current program size. He may know, for example, that the city has a policy of removing snow only after a four-inch fall or cleaning catch basins every five years, but perhaps the policies were laid out when there were not as many parking meters and cars or before so much road construction was underway as to create an added burden of dirt on the streets. When the program size has been clearly identified the next step is to compute the costs for the current program and programs of alternate sizes. In this way he can provide an expenditure estimate based on adequate study. The final appropriation can then be proposed by his department head and the chief administrator and determined by the council on the basis of helpful and understandable information.

Measuring Activities

At the heart of any program or performance budget is an adequate system of measurement. In preparing a performance-type budget request the supervisor, if he wishes to clean all residential streets once every two weeks, must have information available which will enable him to compute "how much" gasoline, oil, materials, and supplies will be needed for that schedule; "how many" man-hours will be needed to achieve the program; and "how much" new equipment must be purchased if the program is to be accomplished. The "how much" and "how many" call for measurements. Figure 30.3 shows the units of measurement commonly used in public works and public utility departments. These units provide the public works supervisor with information needed to make a start on measuring the activities of his work group.

All supervisors have rules or standards of operation which they consciously or subconsciously apply to their operations. These standards usually have been developed through years of experience. However, there is a tendency to judge entirely on the basis of past experience and neglect the important factor of changing conditions. In refuse collection, changes in the packaging of foods, method of heating homes, family size, and disposal methods have a bearing on standards.

A recent example of extenuating circumstances affecting the standard is shown in a case concerning water meter reading. The supervisor checked the daily progress of the meter readers by applying his rule-of-thumb: an average of 150 meters to be read each day. The average readings dropped off from this figure until the supervisor began transferring his readers. He discovered that the problem still persisted. Finally in desperation the meter readers asked the supervisor to come with them on their rounds. The supervisor found that the readers were having difficulty getting into the homes. More and more housewives were working, and the callbacks had nearly doubled since the 150-per-day standard was set. The supervisor

FIGURE 30.3 Units of Measurement

PUBLIC WORKS AND UTILITIES DEPARTMENT UNITS
OF MEASUREMENT APPLICABLE TO COST ACCOUNTING

Title		Title	
Function Activity Operation	Unit of Measurement	Function Activity Operation	Unit of Measurement
Inspection Services		Placing Road Materials	
Building Inspection	each	(Solids)	sq. yd. or ton
Smoke Abatement Inspection	each	Low-type Bituminous Streets	
		Scarifying, Grading, Shaping	sq. yd.
Sewer Operation and Maintenance		Rolling	sq. yd.
		Placing Road Materials	
Sewer Operation		(Solids)	sq. yd. or ton
Sewer Operation		Placing Road Materials	
Pumping	000 gal.	(Liquids)	gal.
Purification and Treatment	000 gal.	Patching	each
Sludge Disposal	tons	Paved Streets	
Laboratory		Removing Old Pavement	sq. yd.
Laboratory Testing and		Rolling	sq. yd.
Inspection	each	Placing Road Materials	
		(Solids)	sq. yd. or ton
Sewer Maintenance		Placing Road Materials	
Storm Sewer Lines		(Liquids)	gal.
Excavating	cu. yd.	Placing, Finishing Concrete	
Filling	cu. yd.	(Pave.)	sq. yd.
Removing Pipe	l. ft.	Placing, Removing Forms	
Laying Pipe	l. ft.	(Pave.)	l. ft.
Sheeting and Bracing	sq. ft.	Patching	each
Cleaning	l. ft.	Curbs and Gutters	
Sanitary Sewer Lines		Patching	each
Excavating	cu. yd.	Resetting and Removing	l. ft.
Filling	cu. yd.	Roadsides	
Removing Pipe	l. ft.	Cutting Grass, Weeds, and	
Laying Pipe	l. ft.	Brush	sq. yd.
Sheeting and Bracing	sq. ft.	Culverts	
Cleaning	l. ft.	Major Fixture Replacement	each
Combined Sewer Lines		General Repair and	
Excavating	cu. yd.	Maintenance	each
Filling	cu. yd.	Sidewalks	
Removing Pipe	l. ft.	Placing, Finishing Concrete	
Laying Pipe	l. ft.	(Pave.)	sq. yd.
Sheeting and Bracing	sq. ft.	Placing, Removing Forms	
Cleaning	l. ft.	(Pave.)	l. ft.
Catch Basins		Patching	each
Laying Brick	000 brk.	Laying Brick	000 brk.
Laying Stone	00 blk.	Laying Stone	00 blk.
Sewer Manholes		Resetting and Removing	l. ft.
Laying Brick	000 brk.	Street Cleaning	
Laying Stone	00 blk.	Machine Sweeping	mi.
Open Drains and Brooks		Hand Sweeping	mi.
Laying Brick	000 brk.	Flushing and Dust Laying	mi.
Laying Stone	00 blk.	Sweepings Disposal	ton
House Connections Mainte-		Winter Maintenance	
nance		Sanding	mi.
General Repairs	each	**Sanitation**	
Thawing	each	Garbage Collection and Disposal	
Cleaning and Inspecting	each	Collection	ton
House Connection, Con-		Set Out and Set Back	each
struction		Incinerator Operation	ton
Excavating	cu. yd.	Incinerator Bldg. Operation,	
Filling	cu. yd.	Maintenance	
Laying Pipe	l. ft.	Dry Refuse Collection and	
Tapping	each	Disposal	
Gates and Valves		Collection	ton
Major Fixture Replacement	each	Set out and Set Back	each
General Repairs	each	**Parks, Parkways and Cemeteries**	
		Parkways, Maintenance	
Maintenance of Thoroughfares,		Parkway Tree Maintenance	
Appurtenances		Planting	each
Alleys		Trimming and Removal	each
Removing Old Pavement	sq. yd.	Inspection and Spraying	each
Scarifying, Grading, Shaping	sq. yd.	Other Maintenance	
Rolling	sq. yd.	Cutting Grass, Weeds, and	
Placing Road Materials		Brush	sq. yd.
(Solids)	sq. yd. or ton	Planting Grass	sq. yd.
Placing Road Materials		Spreading Fertilizer	sq. yd. or ton
(Liquids)	gal.	Parks and Playgrounds,	
Placing, Finishing Concrete		Maintenance	
(Pave.)	sq. yd.	Paths and Drives	
Placing, Removing Forms		Scarifying, Grading, Shaping	sq. yd.
(Pave.)	l. ft.	Rolling	sq. yd.
Patching	each	Placing Road Materials	
Unpaved Streets		(Solids)	sq. yd. or ton
Excavating	cu. yd.	Placing Road Materials	
Filling	cu. yd.	(Liquids)	gal.
Scarifying, Grading, Shaping	sq. yd.	Patching	each
Rolling	sq. yd.		

adjusted his schedule so the readers would read at times when people were at home.

Production standards supply supervisors with a definite means of determining when the work load fluctuates upward to a point where more manpower should be added, or downward to a point where surplus manpower should be removed. Two earlier chapters have described the techniques developed for the improvement of methods of doing work. These techniques are available to the supervisor on developing production standards. In using them, if he discovers the job is not being done in the most efficient manner, or that the most efficient method is not being used, then the faulty operations must be corrected before production standards can be determined.

There are three approaches to standard setting: the man-hour approach (Figure 30.4 shows this approach); the cost accounting approach (see Figure 30.5, especially the line headed "Washing Luminaires,"—the total unit cost shown at the end of the line provides a relatively scientific foundation for projecting future costs); and the ratio of personnel approach (under this system the number of personnel required is related to a definite organization index—thus, in the federal government recent standards call for one personnel employee to every 110 civilian workers, and one person performing payroll, leave, and retirement activities for each 235 civilian employees). Whichever these three approaches is decided upon, it becomes the basis for building the expediture estimates.

Nonmeasurable Activities

While it is true that the supervisor has many tools to measure his activities, there are inevitably some activities which defy measurement. Only a portion of governmental activity is amenable to production measurement. An administrator, for example, cannot be expected to produce a prescribed number of "decisions" per day. However, the supervisor should make every effort to "measure" in order to increase the efficiency and effectiveness of his operation.

CONTROLLING THE BUDGET

If the supervisor spends too much his excess will reduce the city's surplus; that is, unless his excess costs are offset by some other supervisor's better cost control. A good supervisor never relies on this because he doesn't want to gain the reputation of always having to be bailed out.

For the supervisor to carry his share of the load he needs to know two things: what expenses are in his budget, and where he stands in money spent at each mile post along the way. Proper charging helps in the effort to control expenses. When right account numbers are applied the supervisor

FIGURE 30.4
Man-Hour Approach to Standard Setting (forms and instructions used by Los Angeles for performance analysis by man-hours)

Form CAO-9 — PERSONNEL REQUIREMENTS - CITY OF LOS ANGELES

Function: Protection to Persons & Property — Code No. 20 — Department: Building and Safety — Code No. 21.1

Subfunctions: Structural Regulations — 21 — Activity: Bldg. Permits & Inspections — 21.11

(1) Code No.	(2) Description	(3) Work Unit	(4) Work Units	(5) Personnel	(6) Total Man-Hours	(7) Man-Hours Per Unit	(8) Work Units	(9) Personnel	(10) Total Man-Hours	(11) Man-Hours Per Unit	(12) Work Units	(13) Man-Hours Per Unit	(14) Total Man-Hours	(15) Overtime Man-Hours	(16) Regular Man-Hours	(17) Personnel
	Subactivities		Last Completed Year				Current Year (Est.)				Next Year (Est.)					
.110	Administration......	B	....	3.9	8083	....	....	4.0	8352	....	....	....	8352	....	....	4.0
.111	Plan Checking....	Bld. Pl. Ck'd	16809	41.8	87334	5.20	15456	39.9	83358	5.40	15500	5.50	85250	1200	82750	40.2
.112	Public Counter.....	" " Issued	60297	18.0	39463	0.65	47790	19.0	39672	0.83	50000	0.89	42750	....	....	20.5
.113	Zoning Enforcement....	" "	60297	10.0	20984	0.35	47790	11.0	22968	0.48	48000	0.50	24000	....	....	11.5
.114	Board Reports.....	Reports	10665	3.8	7934	0.74	10810	4.0	8382	0.77	11000	0.75	8250	....	....	4.0
.115	Inspections........															
.1150	Administration.....	B	....	3.5	7308	....	....	3.8	8004	....	....	....	10440	....	....	5.0
.1151	Inspections.......	Inspections	370691	60.4	126020	0.34	348416	59.7	124584	0.36	350000	0.36	126000	....	....	60.3
.1152	Masonry Inspections.....	Inspection	17076	6.3	13050	0.76	19284	7.0	14616	0.76	20000	0.75	15000	....	....	7.2
.1153	Relocation.......	Applications	1462	5.0	10440	7.14	1444	5.0	10440	7.23	1500	7.25	10875	....	....	5.2
.1154	Maintenance and Occupancy.....	Surveys	44659	27.6	57612	1.29	44716	31.7	66160	1.48	51000	1.40	71400	....	....	34.2
.1155	Parapet Walls.....	Surveys	1096	3.0	6264	5.71	850	3.0	6264	7.40	900	7.22	0500	....	....	3.0
.1156	Slum Clearance & Rehabilitation....	H	....										10440	....	....	5.0
.116	Clerical.........	Documents	107831	41.6	86798	0.80	94936	39.4	82290	0.87	100000	0.88	88000	....	....	42.1
.117	Investigation & Prosecutions....	Cases	317	4.0	8352	26.35	334	4.0	8352	25.00	8750	1.00	8750	....	....	4.2
	TOTALS		....	228.9	479642	....	....	231.5	483442	....	....	....	516007	1200	....	246.4

FIGURE 30.5

Cost Accounting as Applied to Street Light Maintenance Costs in San Diego

FUNCTION: STREETS
DEPARTMENT: PUBLIC WORKS
ACTIVITY: STREET LIGHT MAINTENANCE
MAINTENANCE STANDARDS:

WASHING LUMINAIRES—2 TIMES PER YEAR
LAMPING   —2 TIMES PER YEAR
PAINTING STANDARDS —BIENNIALLY

UNIT COSTS

OPERATION	UNIT Man-hours	RATE PER Man-hour	UNIT LAB. COST	UNIT MAT'L	UNIT EQUIP.	TOTAL UNIT COST
Washing Luminaires .	0.23	$1.29	$0.30	$0.01	$0.02	$0.33
Lamping	0.39	2.11	0.82	0.96	0.12	1.90
Painting Standards . .	0.77	2.23	1.71	1.04	0.08	2.83

NUMBER OF STREET LIGHTS IN SERVICE. 5010

Washing luminaires	5010	×	2	×	$0.33	=	$ 3,307.00
Lamping	5010	×	2	×	1.90	=	19,038.00
Painting standards	5010	÷	2	×	2.83	=	7,089.00

ROUTINE MAINTENANCE BUDGET. $29,434.00

knows what has gone into each set of figures reported back to him. Thus, he can read the score better when he is sure he knows what is in each account.

Oftentimes the supervisor would like to have every kind of expense shown separately but this usually costs too much for the accounting division to supply, and would also be too burdensome. That is why some small amounts are grouped. It adds some difficulty to the supervisor's task of keeping fully informed about the necessary details because there is trouble in remembering what is in each total. For this reason, the supervisor should ask the accounting division to tell him exactly what kinds of expenses are to be charged into each group total.

Many expenses the supervisor controls directly, some only indirectly. There may be expenses he can do nothing about: rent and depreciation are among those. Light, heat, and power are others he cannot do much about unless he has meters in his department. Yet the great majority of expenses he can do something about.

Many supervisors develop expense charts on which they plot the trend in expenses in order to carefully observe their year-to-date costs. Some are constantly analyzing their operating methods in order to determine the weak spots.

Each departmental budget, in addition to being a plan for provision of services, is a part of the whole cost-control plan of the city. Budgets are created to hold expenses within limits and to avoid a deficit. In order to hold the line the best procedure is to plan out expenditures before the money is spent. Costs must be foreseen and controlled. Each supervisor will regulate the flow of expenditures by standards of his own that control his rates of spending. "Beating" the budget, or meeting service standards with less money than is available in the budget, is an excellent way to show your ability as a supervisor.

Note

[1] United States Commission on Organization of the Executive Branch of the Government, *Report Number 7: Budgeting and Accounting* (Washington, D.C.: U.S. Government Printing Office, 1949), p. 8.

31

Cost-Effectiveness Analysis: Implications for Accountants

Barry G. King

Selection from among alternative uses of sizable, but limited, financial resources in order to meet stipulated, but often vague, objectives is a challenge to modern management of both private and public enterprise. Particularly challenging are those situations in which the immediate objectives of management cannot be conveniently reduced to the profit motive, so that alternative means of meeting these objectives cannot be compared on the basis of relative profitability. Recent years have seen the development and refinement of a number of analytical approaches for meeting this challenge. A family of these approaches has become known under such names as (1) systems analysis, (2) cost-effectiveness analysis, (3) operations analysis, (4) cost-benefit analysis, (5) cost-utility analysis, and (6) planning, programing and budgeting system (PPBS). No attempt is made in this article to distinguish the shades of meaning in these terms as they are used in the field and in the literature. All refer to the attempt to apply a systematic, analytical approach to problems of choice. *Cost-effectiveness* analysis has been selected for this discussion, but much of what follows could be said about others of the group.

Cost-effectiveness is a term which has been used in a formal sense only

Reprinted by special permission from the March 1970 issue of *The Journal of Accountancy*. Copyright 1970 by the American Institute of Certified Public Accountants, Inc.

in recent years. Wide publicity was given to the use of the technique in managing the activities of the Department of Defense under Robert McNamara. Many of the top people brought into the Defense Department by McNamara came from the Rand Corporation, where they had been working on problems concerning "the economics of defense,"[1] and where the formal approach had been developed.

In its narrowest sense, cost-effectiveness analysis may be defined as a technique for choosing among *given* alternative courses of action in terms of their cost and their effectiveness in the attainment of *specified* objectives. Treated as given by the analyst are: (1) A specific statement of objectives, (2) a complete listing of the alternative solutions to be considered and (3) acceptable measures of effectiveness in meeting objectives. The decision-maker is viewed as a "higher-order" system who sets these constraints, and for whom the analysis will provide informational inputs for making his choice.

In a broader sense, cost-effectiveness has been defined as simply a "technique for evaluating broad management and economic implications of alternative choices of action with the objective of assisting in the identification of the preferred choice."[2] Here the analyst takes a somewhat more general view of the decisionmaker's problem and is concerned with (1) less explicitly stated objectives, (2) undefined alternative solutions and (3) more subjective measures of effectiveness.

For example, cost-effectiveness analysis may be applied in its narrower sense to the problem of deciding among three proposed aircraft systems. The objective may be one of providing capability of transporting personnel, with effectiveness to be measured in terms of the aircrafts' technical characteristics, such as payload, speed and reliability.

On the other hand, the approach may be utilized in its broader sense, in the case where the objective above becomes one of providing personnel at key locations when needed. The alternatives for meeting this objective go far beyond three competing airplanes, and involve strategies of personnel assignment as well as logistical considerations. Most of the more interesting problems arise in this latter, broader context, and it is this view of cost-effectiveness which is pursued in this article.

Two characteristics of the analysis deserve special emphasis. First, cost-effectiveness analysis is output-oriented. As such, decision situations are analyzed from a program, or mission, viewpoint rather than from a functional one. Problems are treated not as production, marketing or financing problems, but as problems in carrying out a specified program. The impact of this thinking is seen in the increasing tendency on the part of industrial firms to organize their activities, especially those of a planning nature, along project lines as opposed to the more traditional functional organization.

Second, the approach emphasizes effectiveness as opposed to technical economic efficiency in the allocation of resources. In a technical sense, resources are allocated efficiently when an increase in one output can be obtained only at a sacrifice of another output or with an increase in input, whereas effectiveness measures, in terms of an objective, the comparative desirability of alternative efficient allocations. For example, a company's computer and data processing system may operate efficiently, in that it operates 24 hours a day. Furthermore, it may be programed to perform the tasks assigned to it efficiently. Any additional work required of the system will be at the sacrifice of some task it is currently performing. Still this efficient system may well be made more effective in meeting the objectives of the firm for the system by making changes in the make-up of its workload.

Most of the applications of cost-effectiveness analysis reported in the literature have dealt with governmental programs. This was to be expected because these programs require decisions for carrying out policies, the effectiveness of which cannot be measured in terms of profit. Cost-effectiveness analysis has provided a framework for aiding in these decisions. Now we are finding that more and more such decisions are being required of those in profit-oriented organizations. For example, business is being called upon to embark on programs of antipollution and training of the unemployed. Programs such as these cannot be evaluated on the basis of profitability to the individual firm but must be measured in terms of meeting social objectives. Thus cost-effectiveness will, I feel, be found to be increasingly valuable to the profit-seeking enterprise.

It is the purpose of this article to describe and illustrate the methodology of cost-effectiveness analysis in a nontechnical manner, and to specify some implications that the approach seems to have for accountants.

METHODOLOGY

Although it may include the use of models developed as operations research techniques, cost-effectiveness analysis should not be considered as simply another OR tool or technique. Unlike such tools as mathematical programing and queueing theory, which are useful only in solving particular classes of problems which can be structured according to prescribed formats, cost-effectiveness analysis is designed to yield solutions that are uniquely responsive to particular problems. It deals with problems which are ill-structured and which have objectives that are less precisely defined. Thus, the methodology of cost-effectiveness analysis cannot be set forth as a set of standard procedures but must be outlined as a sequence of general steps which constitute an approach. These include:

1. Definition of objectives
2. Identification of alternatives
3. Selection of effectiveness measures
4. Development of cost estimates

5. Selection of a decision criterion
6. Creation of models relating cost and effectiveness.

Objectives

The beginning point for any analysis must be a consideration of objectives. Objectives, the desired goal (or goals) to be attained by the use of resources, must be defined as explicitly as possible. Careless selection and specification of objectives can lead to solution of the wrong problem. Much of the misunderstanding of U.S. defense policy, for example, seems to be related to misunderstanding of objectives. For instance, providing capability to *deter* attack reflects a different objective from providing capability to *repel* attack. In one case the attack is assumed to occur, while in the other the objective is precisely to prevent its occurrence. Thus given strategies may be effective in one case and not in the other.

For another example, reduction of traffic *fatalities* represents a different objective from a reduction of traffic *accidents.* Wearing seat belts has some effectiveness toward meeting the first objective, but none toward meeting the latter. Also, in industrial employee relations the objective of maintaining a stable size for the labor force is quite different from an objective of reducing employee turnover. In many cases the analyst can make a significant contribution by pointing out confusing or conflicting objectives.

Alternatives

The alternatives represent the competing "systems" for accomplishing objectives. They represent opposing strategies, policies or specific actions as well as the necessary elements, such as materials, men, machines, etc. Even though certain elements or tactics may overlap, each alternative is viewed as a complete system. These alternatives need not be obvious substitutes for each other or perform the same specific function. Thus education, antipoverty measures, police protection, slum clearance, and various combinations of these, may all be alternatives in combating juvenile delinquency.[3] Creativity is needed to insure that as many legitimate alternatives as possible are considered. Often new ones are conceived as the analysis of the original alternatives is being performed.

Effectiveness Measures

Overall performance must be combined into appropriate measures that gauge the effectiveness of each alternative. Choosing appropriate measures of effectiveness is probably the most difficult, unique problem in cost-effectiveness analysis. The challenge is to provide measures that are relevant to the objective sought and measurable in terms that allow comparisons of effectiveness among alternatives.

The well-known story of the Soviet nail factory exemplifies the faulty results of optimizing irrelevant measures of effectiveness.[4] An objective of providing nails for a segment of Soviet industry was to be measured on the basis of weight of the output. Soon the factory optimized by producing only huge railroad spikes very efficiently. When the surplus of railroad spikes became quite large, the effectiveness measure was changed to quantity of items produced. The manager was able to quickly switch over to production of huge quantities of tiny tacks, brads and staples, also very efficiently.

In order to compare alternatives, a single quantitative indicator of effectiveness would be ideal. For example to measure the effectiveness of a program having the objective of improving employee morale, one would like to have a means of quantitatively measuring "morale score." As is the case in most situations, such a single measure is not available. However, there are several factors which relate to employee morale which can be quantified to some degree—e.g., absenteeism, turnover and grievances. These measures tempered with judgment concerning nonquantifiable aspects should lead to satisfactory comparisons of effectiveness of given alternatives.

Cost Estimates

To implement a given alternative, it is anticipated that certain resources must be used. Foregoing the use of these resources elsewhere represents a cost in the economic sense. Estimation of the cost of the alternatives constitutes a very important and difficult step in cost-effectiveness analysis.

Basically, two issues are involved: (1) what costs to include and (2) how to measure them. What is desired, of course, is an estimate of all *relevant* costs of each alternative. The concepts of sunk costs, incremental costs and joint costs, all familiar to accountants, are applicable in the same manner as in traditional accounting analyses.

Many costs are general and can be adequately measured in terms of money. Long-range planning problems anticipate largely this type of cost. Often the money constrained resources being foregone are in the future, and, since money can be used to purchase these resources, it provides an adequate measuring tool. However, consideration should be also be given to those costs for which money is not an entirely adequate measure. For instance, the cost in terms of human lives of specific defense alternatives can never be adequately measured in terms of money.

Sometimes a nonmonetary cost may be more rationally expressed as a negative factor in effectiveness, thus leaving the cost portion of the analysis in a "pure" money form. Thus instead of considering the loss of life by friendly forces as a cost, it may be more reasonable to consider it as a negative factor in measuring the effectiveness of a given defense alternative.

Selection of a Decision Criterion

The decision criterion is the standard by which all alternatives are evaluated in terms of cost and effectiveness. Three types of valid criterion from which the analyst must choose are: (1) maximize effectiveness at given cost; (2) minimize cost while attaining a given effectiveness; or (3) some combination of these two which recognizes a tradeoff of cost for effectiveness to maximize a selected utility function of the two factors (e.g., maximize effectiveness minus cost, where the two can be expressed in common terms). Many governmental objectives which are limited to fixed budgets are guided by the first criterion. Industrial firms may be guided by the second.

Adoption of an invalid criterion can be deceptively easy. For example, the statement "maximize effectiveness at a minimum cost" reflects a criterion that can seldom be met. It is not reasonable to believe that the best alternative from a number of feasible ones in terms of effectiveness will also be the one that costs the least. Also, the criterion—maximize the *ratio* of effectiveness to cost, or "effectiveness per dollar"—can also be seen to be invalid unless the ratio remains constant for all levels of activity. For example, an alternative which provides up to 10,000 square feet of warehouse space at a cost of $10 per square foot is not preferable over another alternative which provides up to 20,000 square feet at a cost of $15 per square foot if the objective is to produce a warehouse with 15,000 square feet of space. Obviously if the ratio, $ per square foot, remains constant at all levels of activity the ratio criterion is adequate. However, it provides no better criterion than the valid criterion mentioned above—minimize cost of providing 15,000 square feet of warehouse space.

Creation of Models

Having determined adequate measures of cost and effectiveness, and a criterion by which to compare alternatives, there remains the problem of formulating analytical relationships among costs, effectiveness and environmental factors. Needed are cost models, effectiveness models and a synthesizing model based on outputs from them.

Cost models attempt to describe relationships between the characteristics of a given alternative (system) and its costs. Thus the result of operating a cost model should be an estimate of the cost of each alternative. Effectiveness models attempt to describe relationships between an alternative's characteristics and its effectiveness. The result of operating an effectiveness model should be an estimate of each alternative. Additionally, and very significantly, these models should provide tradeoff relationships between system costs and characteristics as well as tradeoffs between system effectiveness and characteristics. For example besides outputting the fact that alternative A has characteristics X, Y and Z with a cost of C, the cost model should provide relationships such as estimated marginal costs of changes in system characteristics. The synthesizing model should provide relationships between cost and effectiveness among alternatives. It should provide aid in answering such questions as: (1) How much effectiveness can be brought with an additional $X spent on alternative A? (2) What is the cost of a given increase in the effectiveness of alternative B?

Model structure depends on how well the analyst knows the relationships which are to be expressed in the model, along with the complexity of the alternatives involved. If relationships are fairly well known, they may be expressed in algebraic terms and solved by use of the calculus. Other well-developed and understood techniques of operations research, such as mathematical programming, and simulation, are available when applicable. Operational gaming may be used to determine less well-known relationships when the human element is crucial. Finally some relationships may be so uncertain that the only acceptable model is verbal.

Figure 31.1 is an attempt to depict in pictorial form the structure of the analysis.[5] In this figure, the curves relating cost and effectiveness permit illustration of both the criterion of maximizing effectiveness with given cost and minimizing cost of given effectiveness. For example, effectiveness is maximized with a given cost of C by using alternative A or with a given cost of C_2 by alternative A_4. Cost is minimized with a given effectiveness of E_3 by choosing alternative A_2. The ordered alternatives shown in the figure are the result of applying either criterion at the level of C and E.

LIMITATIONS

Several limitations of cost-effectiveness analysis should be considered. First, it must be realized that all results are merely inputs to be judged along with other less systematic factors by a higher-level decision-maker. While the approach should emphasize consideration of as many factors as possible, there will always remain the necessity for the decision-maker to exercise judgment of his own. The breadth of scope of the analysis allows a wide range of problems to be attacked; however, this leaves a good deal of the specifics to the analyst. Judgment is necessary to design the analysis, to determine alternatives, to delineate relevant factors and interrelationships, and to interpret the results. Quade summarizes this limitation by saying,

No matter how we strive to maintain standards of scientific inquiry or how closely we attempt to follow scientific methods, we cannot turn cost-effectiveness analysis into science. Its objective, in contrast to that of science, is primarily to recommend—or at least to suggest—policy, rather than merely to understand and predict.[6]

A second limitation of the analysis is the difficulty in selecting measures of effectiveness. The best that can be done is to reasonably approximate objectives with measures which can aid in guiding decision-making. For example, employee welfare is an objective which everyone understands but which is extremely difficult to measure.

FIGURE 31.1

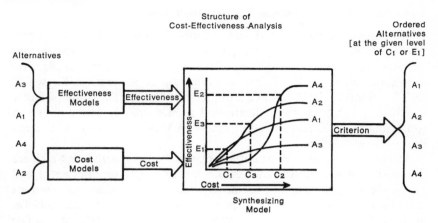

A third limitation results from imperfect information. Insufficient input information in terms of costs and benefits of various alternatives may result in an analysis that is misleading or downright erroneous. Neglect of benefits which are difficult to quantify or which occur in an indirect manner may lead to dismissal of some very advantageous alternatives. On the other hand, exclusion of costs which are difficult to quantify or which result indirectly may make undesirable alternatives seem desirable.

A final limitation which should be mentioned is the lack of a probability orientation in most cost-effectiveness analysis. Whereas several techniques for including probability factors in quantitative models have been developed in an attempt to measure uncertainty, almost no use has been made of these in cost-effectiveness analysis.

IMPLICATIONS FOR ACCOUNTING

The foregoing has been very general and non-technical in an attempt simply to introduce some basic concept of cost-effectiveness analysis. Avoided were the very relevant, but somewhat technical, aspects of the mathematics of maximization,[7] which is the basis for most of the quantitative models in the analysis. There appear to be some germane implications for accounting. These fall conveniently into . . . categories:

1. Implications for an expanded concept of organizational objectives.

2. Implications for an increased knowledge of quantitative management science.
3. Implications for design and operation of management information (data) systems.

Expanded Concept of Organization Objectives

Accountants have been performing a form of cost-effectiveness analysis for some time. Capital budgeting analysis, incremental cost analysis and financial source selection are all decisions to which the basic cost-effectiveness approach is used. All involve evaluation of alternatives for which return is compared with cost as a criterion for selection. The common factor which they exhibit is that effectiveness is measured in terms of return (profitability). Thus cost and effectiveness are stated in terms of a common denominator—dollars.

Modern management must initiate, plan and control activities which are designed to meet objectives which are not primarily profit-oriented and whose effectiveness cannot be adequately measured in dollars. Accountants must be willing and prepared to provide information about and perform analysis of such activities. This includes understanding and helping to define objectives explicitly as well as searching for adequate measures of effectiveness.

Perhaps even more significant for accountants than this responsibility to management for aid in their decision-making is an implied responsibility for external reporting of the results of such activities. Viewed as an institution in our society with goals other than financial ones, business enterprise is being asked to assume a more active part in programs of social action such as manpower training and development of urban areas. We see a trend toward increased protection for the consumer in demands for assurance of quality. Business has a responsibility to the general public in such areas as antipollution and conservation. Along with the responsibility for initiating and carrying out such programs is that of evaluating and reporting the results. Perhaps accountants will adopt a broader view and go beyond reporting on merely the financial objectives of the firm.

Quantitative Management Science

Several concepts of management science are exemplified in cost-effectiveness analysis. These serve to point out areas in which accountants should become knowledgeable. First, the accountant must understand the concept of a model and the modeling process, its uses and limitations. He needs to view models as descriptions or representations of the real world, quantitative or nonquantitative, which are valuable only to the extent that they accurately depict the situation. Also there needs to be the ability to conceptualize problems in an "input-output" format. That is, the accountant must take the approach which takes controllable variables as inputs and manipulates them to learn more about the uncontrollable variables, eventually resulting in an output which optimizes, or at least satisfied, the objectives.

Another valuable aspect of the mathematics in management science is the capacity to express and manipulate relationships in functional form. Cost-estimating relationships (CERs) are nothing more than functions which treat cost as a dependent variable and other factors as independent variables.

Information and Data Systems

Perhaps the weakest link in cost-effectiveness analysis is the "data gap." Models of cost and effectiveness are no better than the data used in developing them and as input to them. Too often, accurate timely data of the type needed are not available. Brussell has the following comment:

> Today the modeling aspects of cost-effectiveness analysis are firmly entrenched. However, there has been a misallocation of research resources as between model building and data inputting or estimating. The conceptual problem of formulating models is relatively easy but probably more interesting and prestigious than the actual bird-dogging, collection, understanding, and estimation of grubby old numbers. There are undoubtedly increasing returns to analysis by improving the input numbers, both cost and performance data, whereas there are diminishing returns when the aim is at better models, cost models included.[8]

The same data gap exists in the use of most management science models and techniques. Information gathering, retrieval, processing, and dissemination are only now getting some of the attention which they deserve. Accountants, because of their interest in information and data processing, should be vitally concerned with development of systems which improve the quality of input data for decision models.

Cost Estimation

Cost-effectiveness analysis offers the challenge of estimating costs of activities which are unique and for which past data are unavailable. Here unavailability is not caused by the cost system, but the fact that the activity has not been tried before. More sophisticated estimating and forecasting techniques must be used. Effects on cost of many factors must be predicted. Accountants have for a long time realized the value of analytical techniques which employ the concept of variable costs. Thus the effect of volume on cost is well recognized. What has not been developed on the part of many accountants is the capability of analyzing costs in terms of other potential independent variables. Techniques of regression and correlation analysis should be mastered.

A related point involves the approach taken with regard to cost estimation. Accountants have traditionally taken a "micro" or "building block" view of cost estimating, based on the breakdown of cost present in the accounting system. Costs of the smallest elements into which costs can be divided are estimated and total cost is derived by aggregating these elementary costs. Such detailed procedures are rather expensive to employ and may not be very responsive to changes in parameters. Trade-off relationships between cost and effectiveness and between costs of two or more competing alternatives are difficult and time-consuming to determine. The alternative is to take a "macro" or "broad brush" approach to estimating costs. This approach involves costing the total system in terms of its parameters, i.e., system characteristics and capabilities. For example, estimating costs of a new airplane may be done in terms of its speed, range, reliability, payload, etc., based on historical data for similar planes, as opposed to a detailed costing of all elements of labor materials, indirect costs, etc., involved in designing and producing it. [However, costing procedures can still] provide some valuable inputs to the cost model. The point is that accountants should be capable of taking the overall total systems view and becoming familiar with estimating techniques based thereon.

In summary, the framework for cost-effectiveness analysis has been outlined in a nontechnical manner. This form of analysis is being used extensively, although sometimes under other names, in government and will be used more extensively in the future in private enterprise. Therefore, accountants should be aware of it, its uses and limitations. These implications are certainly not brought about solely by cost-effectiveness analysis, but reflect some very significant directions for accounting to take as a result of current developments in management science.

Notes

[1]See Hitch, Charles J., and McKean, Roland N., *Economics of Defense in the Nuclear Age* (Cambridge: Harvard Press, 1960).

[2]Heuston, M. C., and Ogawa, G., "Observations on the Theoretical Basis of Cost Effectiveness," *Operations Research,* March–April 1966, pp. 242–266.

[3]Quade, E. S., "Systems Analysis Techniques for Planning-Programming-Budgeting" in *Systems, Organizations, Analysis, Management: A Book of Readings,* edited by David I. Cleland and William R. King (New York: McGraw-Hill, 1969), p. 195.

[4]Niskanen, William A., "Measures of Effectiveness," in *Cost-Effectiveness Analysis,* edited by Thomas A. Goldman (New York: Frederick A. Praeger, 1967), p. 20.

[5]This illustration is adapted from one used by Quade, E. S., "Introduction and Overview," in Goldman, *Cost-Effectiveness Analysis,* op. cit., p. 6.

[6]Quade, E. S., "Systems Analysis Techniques for Planning-Programming-Budgetting," op. cit., p. 201.

[7]For a discussion of the "Mathematics of Maximization," see Hitch, Charles J., and McKean, Roland N., op. cit., Appendix A.

[8]Brussell, Eugene R., "Defense Contractor Use of Cost-Effectiveness Analysis," in Goldman, *Cost-Effectiveness Analysis,* op. cit., p. 114.

32
Operations Research: A Challenge to Management

John W. Pocock

Operations research as an approach to the solution of business and industrial problems is in the headlines today. The power of its unique approach is repeatedly emphasized, yet few can agree on exactly what this approach is. The great variety of its analysis techniques is emphasized, yet few are familiar with more than two or three. The tangible worth of such analysis to the profit-seeking manager is touted, yet specific case material is still relatively scarce.

A synopsized and panoramic picture of operations research may provide some immediate appreciation of the total effort in business applications today and serve as background for the specific discussions that follow.

SEARCH FOR BASIC LAWS

.   .   .   .   .

Every one of us, looking around at some apparently confused activity in the world about us, has probably felt that "there ought to be a law"—some underlying relationship which explains that particular activity and allows us to bring chaos under control. Such a thought may occur to us while we are involved in a traffic jam on the way to a football game or while we are standing in line at a cafeteria. We have the feeling that there must be some basic principle that could help solve the knotty problems we are wrestling with.

This feeling is an essential and basic motivation of all thinking people and has been in the mind of man from time immemorial. The ancient Persians felt it when they looked up at the stars and attempted to determine some rule for describing their erratic courses. The astronomer Brahe was simi-

Reprinted by permission of the publisher from AMA Special Report No. 13, *Operations Research: A Basic Approach,* pp. 7–10 and 12–19, © 1956 by the American Management Association, Inc.

larly motivated when he brought together all the massive data concerning the movement of the stars and planets. So was Kepler as he carried on and worked these data into his studies. But Newton came along with his development of the laws of gravity and the laws of motion before the underlying "law of the heavens" was understood—and he had to invent differential and integral calculus to do it.

.   .   .   .   .

TRANSFER OF EXPERIENCE

This illustrates a fundamental point in operations research that should be brought out early: The experience of a scientist in one field is quite often directly translatable to the totally alien work of a scientist in another field. This transfer, which has quite often led to the use of mixed terms, suggests that the fruits of scientific labor are also translatable into the problems of business operations.

One problem of long standing in scientific research has been this matter of communication between fields of knowledge and the derivation of fundamental laws across all fields. For example, the original work of Darwin has been found to contain data that would have permitted the discovery of the Mendelian principles. However, it remained for the historians to discover this fact, since the scope and experience of Darwin himself did not include the mathematical-statistical insights that Mendel was able to bring to the problem.

Similarly, much of the work that engineers and scientists have done in extensive research activities over the past decade has provided us with new tools and new methodologies that, given proper translation, can be applicable to analysis of business problems.

BODY OF ANALYSIS TECHNIQUES

It has been truly stated that "no war, no strike, no depression can so completely destroy an established business or its profits as new and better methods, equipment, and materials in the hands of an enlightened competitor." Operations research is essentially such a new and better method in the analysis of business operations. However, this new and powerful body of analysis techniques which has been developed over the past 15 years is often cloaked in the formidable language of mathematics; thus the basic approach is often obscured.

As an organized endeavor, operations research originated in England about 1939 as a basis for involving the location of English interception radar. By 1942, the techniques had achieved wide acceptance by top British military planners. The United States soon found, after its entry into the war in 1941, that a similar scientific approach was necessary in the planning of

Army, Air Force, and Navy operations. Such projects as improving patterns of search activities for submarines, evaluating equipment performance, and establishing bombing patterns for most effective and efficient attack were undertaken.

In the late 1940's, industry became interested in operations research, and experimentation was undertaken in some of our larger companies. Its extension has been on the increase during the past several years.

AN OVERALL DEFINITION

Definitions of new areas of activity are generally not fruitful avenues of discussion. This is particularly true of operations research, where scientists are prone to argue at great length concerning a precise meaning. The problem is further compounded by the relative immaturity and newness of operations research, which makes any particular definition exact for only an instant of time. At this point in the history of its development, operations research is an attitude, an approach, a concept. It takes new shape each day.

For our purposes, an overall, rather than a specific, definition will be most appropriate. Thus:

Operations research is a scientific methodology—analytical, experimental, quantitative—which by assessing the overall implications of various alternative courses of action in a management system, provides an improved basis for management decisions.

This definition is given more meaning if we consider basic characteristics of the operations research approach. These characteristics may be listed as follows:

1. Operations research is concerned with the problems of business operations as a system.
2. Operations research utilizes the scientific method in that it is analytical, experimental, and quantitative.
3. Operations research borrows successful methodologies from all the various branches of science.
4. The operations research approach almost invariably involves model building, which is fundamental to the scientific approach. There are many types of models—simulation, mathematical, physical.
5. An operations research study almost invariably involves predicting the effects of alternate courses of action.

Operations research utilizes successful techniques wherever they are found. The professional approaches employed in engineering, mathematics, statistics, physics, economics, and biology have all been found useful in operations research projects. In fact, the use of these various professional disciplines is so widespread that there is a strong inclination for a person to see in operations research those elements with which he is familiar. This often leads him to define operations research in the terms of his own profession. "We have been doing these things for years" is a characteristic remark.

IMPACT OF OPERATIONS RESEARCH

There are four major areas that have been penetrated to some extent by operations research: military, industrial, academic, and consulting.

Operations research has to date found its greatest use and development in the *military services.* It is well-developed activity in each of the service branches and is being expanded continuously into various operating units. Military operations research applications with business situation parallels have been concerned with such typical problems as:

What kinds of weapons and how many of each should the military have in order to accomplish its objective at lowest cost?

How can the Army best allocate each budgetary dollar allowance among its various activities?

How can the Army best deploy troops and weapons in a given situation to place it in the position of greatest line gain?

.   .   .   .   .

METHODOLOGY: PRINCIPAL TECHNIQUES

Operations research seeks to discover regularities in apparently unrelated or random activities. In this research, existing techniques of analysis in many fields of science are drawn upon; and new techniques, peculiar to operations research, are being developed and refined by basic researchers.

The pattern of regularity is generally represented as a "model," which is often mathematical in nature. Certain typical situations, repeatedly met, have inspired development of typical models, or techniques, for solution. Some of the more well-known techniques may be listed as follows:

1. Linear programming.
2. Queueing theory.
3. Game theory.
4. Search theory.
5. Symbolic logic.
6. Information theory.
7. Value theory.

Perhaps a simple example (which can scarcely be viewed as high-level opsearch) will illustrate the main points of the operations research approach.

An abrasive manufacturing company owned seven warehouses, of varying capacities, at widely spread locations. In May, 1953, its single plant was totally destroyed by fire. The problem arose as to whether to rebuild at the present location or seek a location that would make the most effective use of the existing warehouses. The solution of this problem was aided by borrowing the center-of-gravity technique from physics.

In Figure 32.1, we have a physical representative of our problem. In the center is the old plant, which has burned to the ground. The seven warehouses are labeled with the letters A through G, inclusive; these will remain as located. In the lower left-hand corner, we have noted the plant output required, on a monthly basis, for each warehouse. Our problem is to balance

FIGURE 32.1
Example of Center-of-Gravity Analysis

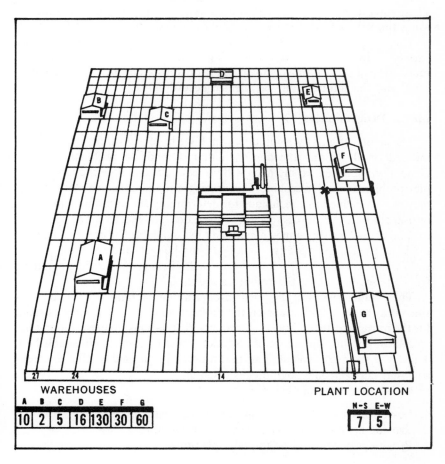

WAREHOUSES								PLANT LOCATION	
A	B	C	D	E	F	G		N-S	E-W
10	2	5	16	130	30	60		7	5

out the distribution pattern so that our new plant will be located in such a way as to provide minimum distribution costs.

The objective, therefore, is to minimize the freight charges. It has been found that, under certain conditions, a satisfactory approximation in determining our ideal plant location is given by the following equations, in which we assume that the *rates are equal in all directions* and that *all routes have approximately the same divergence from the straight line:*

$$x = \frac{x_a A + x_b B + x_c C + x_d D + x_e E + x_f F + x_g G}{A + B + C + D + E + F + G}$$

$$y = \frac{y_a A + y_b B + y_c C + y_d D + y_e E + y_f F + y_g G}{A + B + C + D + E + F + G}$$

These equations may be referred to as a model of our problem. The solution, using the values from Figure 32.1, puts our new plant at $x = 5$, $y = 7$.

This example, of course, is greatly simplified by reduction to a single variable—distance. If we desire to bring in other variables, such as freight rates, time of service rates, and so on, it obviously becomes more complicated and the solution may be affected accordingly.

Linear Programming

The center-of-gravity technique, which we have just discussed, is only a method of illustrating the approach that is made to problem solution. Generally, more refined methods will be required to handle the more complex problems found in real life. Linear programming is such a method, and may be best defined as a technique for determining the optimum allocation, or use, of limited resources to achieve some desired objective. The resources may be defined as the money a company has available for use, the plant or individual machine capacity, the advertising budget, and so forth; the desired objective may be the lowest cost or highest profit possible resulting from the way in which the resources are used.

The characteristics of the linear programming techniques must be considered as to their limitations on the problem solution. First, they assume, for the most part, that a linear or straight-line relationship exists among the variables. Second, the limits of variation must be fairly well established. Third, the volume of calculations that must be performed is often so extensive that an electronic computer is essential.

Linear programming has been applied to:

1. Lower distribution costs from factories to warehouses.
2. Provide better utilization of production facilities.
3. Provide a better method for sales planning.

4. Provide improved price-volume relationships.
5. Determine a better product mix.

Perhaps a simple example will illustrate the nature of a linear programming problem, though not the nature of the detailed solution.

A sugar-refining company had three factories and four warehouses, all geographically separated. A problem existed as to the proper utilization of production and storage facilities in order to achieve minimum freight costs in shipping the finished product from the three factories to the four warehouses. The opsearch unit of the consultants employed to solve this problem used linear programming to obtain an answer.

Figure 32.2 is a graphic representation of the problem. The factories are shown in Roman numerals I to III, and the warehouses are lettered A through D. If we assume that we can "allocate" the production of any of the factories to any of the warehouses, we may draw the arrowed lines shown. The block in the lower left-hand corner indicates the rates or cost of shipping one unit of output from a given factory to a given warehouse. The bottom row, with the numbers 5, 60, 40, and 105, represents the capacity in terms of production units for each of the three plants. This totals 105. The fourth [vertical] row with the numbers 35, 10, 35, 25, and 105, represents the requirements for shipments of each of the warehouses on the

FIGURE 32.2

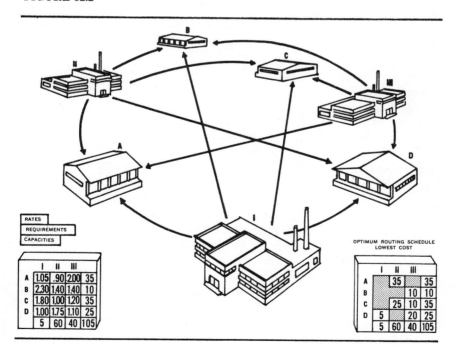

RATES
REQUIREMENTS
CAPACITIES

	I	II	III	
A	1.05	.90	2.00	35
B	2.30	1.40	1.40	10
C	1.80	1.00	1.20	35
D	1.00	1.75	1.10	25
	5	60	40	105

OPTIMUM ROUTING SCHEDULE
LOWEST COST

	I	II	III	
A		35		35
B			10	10
C		25	10	35
D	5		20	25
	5	60	40	105

same unit-of-time basis. Our problem is to allocate the plant, capacities (that is, the production) to the warehouses so that we satisfy their requirements and minimize shipping costs.

The block in the lower right-hand corner of Figure 32.2 represents the solution to this problem. The numbers shown indicate the optimum allocation of production to the warehouses. If this plan were followed, the minimum cost of shipping would be realized.

Linear programming is one of the most powerful and broadly used techniques in the opsearch kit, but some difficulties arise in its use. It is important always to recognize the limitations of the model. The work involved in establishing the necessary equations is usually a task for a well-trained opsearcher, and the technique and solutions sometimes require inspired improvisation. A further limitation of the method occurs when the variables cannot be considered linear. There is, however, considerable work under way to expand the basic technique to more generalized problems and to simplify the mechanics. Linear programming promises to be a standard tool for a long time to come.

Queueing Theory

Queueing theory develops the relationships that are involved in waiting in line. Customers awaiting service, planes waiting to land, machines awaiting the repair crew, items of a production line awaiting inspection—all are typical of the problems that may be approached by the methods of queueing theory.

For an example—an electric company decided to build a factory for the manufacture of television sets. Management could and did define the required plant capacity. However, a problem existed as to the best balance, in terms of cost, between the assembly lines and the servicing operation where the sets were tested and aligned. In other words, it was necessary to minimize the formation of costly stack-ups of unserviced sets or the improper utilization of service capacities. The consulting firm called on to assist in the solution of this problem used the queueing-theory approach to come up with the estimate of cost balance involved (Figure 32.3).

The television sets—all requiring alignment checks and, often, more lengthy service—are shown progressing down the final assembly line. They are moved to the service area for checking. When there are several unusually troublesome sets in a row, the servicing capacity is temporarily exceeded, and a pile-up of sets awaiting service occurs. The problem is that of figuring out the cost of total waiting—that is, the cost of tolerating the "queue" or the stack of goods shown in Figure 32.3 and balancing this cost against the cost of building enough service capacity to lessen the likelihood of the "queue."

FIGURE 32.3

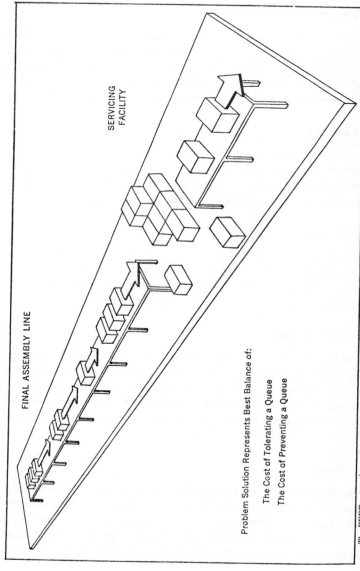

FINAL ASSEMBLY LINE

SERVICING FACILITY

Problem Solution Represents Best Balance of:

The Cost of Tolerating a Queue

The Cost of Preventing a Queue

The PERT network consists of a series of interrelated symbols representing principal events and activities in a program. An event is shown by a box and an activity is indicated by a line or arrow connecting events. When time estimates are assigned to activities, it is possible to compute the critical path of the program, as well as identify activities which have slack time. These may be extended without affecting program schedules.

Applications of queueing theory have shown great power in explaining the rational behavior of many important "waiting" situations. However, applications have been technically restricted by the relatively limited development of basic theory. The ability to handle more complex and generalized situations promises to be of ever-increasing importance but is growing very slowly. For the moment, the use of queueing theory is best left to the professional analyst.

Game Theory

The study of competition between two main factions establishes a mathematical model that can be manipulated for the purpose of determining one player's best strategy and most likely gain. So far, this technique and its application have been developed chiefly by the military, although some work has been done in applying game theory to the timing of advertising.

Search Theory

The study of minimizing the effort required to locate an object—or search theory—arose chiefly from the military problem of locating enemy submarines with limited detection resources. To date, it has had a very limited application to specialized marketing situations.

Symbolic Logic

The algebra of logic substitutes symbols for words, propositions, classes of things, or functional systems. There have been only faltering attempts to apply this technique to business problems; however, it has had extensive implications in the logical design of computing machinery.

Information Theory

An analytical process transferred from the electrical communications field to operations research presumes to evaluate the effectiveness of information flow within a given system. Despite its application mainly to communications networks, it has had an indirect influence in stimulating the examination of business organizational structures with a view of improving information or communication flow.

Value Theory

Value theory is a process of assigning numerical significance to the worth of alternative choices. To date, this has been only a theoretical concept, and is in the status of elementary model formulation and experimentation. When and if developed, this technique should be most helpful in assessing the worth of the various conclusions in the decision-making process.

33
Using PERT in Accounting Reports

Dan A. Bawly and Joseph M. Dotan

With the development of the usage of PERT (Program Evaluation and Review Technique) and CPM (Critical Path Method) in the past decade, the CPA has often been asked to advise his clients on a variety of problems in which PERT could be used. There have been many cases where the CPA, especially in the framework of management services, initiated and developed PERT functions (networks) for his client. Where these plans were fully adhered to and followed up, results were often positive and quite successful.

Many of the large CPA firms have mechanized part of their working procedures; they have all updated their methods of operation; they devote considerable thought to time-saving mechanics of operations; but only in rare cases do they plan their operations by using the relatively recent Critical Path Method.

There are several areas where the use of PERT/CPM may arise. These are usually where heavy pressure of work is expected; where teamwork may be anticipated; where there are great amounts of data to be collected, sorted, and put together again; and, last, where the time element is of great importance.

The use of PERT/CPM by accountants has evolved with the experience gained through the planning of operations around and through the computer. With the increase in computerized operations in the past decade, much attention has been given to the efficiency of programming techniques. This brought about the development of "flow charts," which permit clear presentation of a flow of activities. Designed primarily as an aid in systems analysis and programing, they have also proven useful to picture operations that are not related to computers, ranging from an audit review technique to that for describing the system in, say, a purchasing department. Then there occurred the development of the "decision table," which permits a clear presentation of the analysis of a problem—any problem—even on mundane subjects, ranging in variety from fiscal laws to audit programs.

With the increasing burdens of complicated and costly tasks, tight controls—more sophisticated than those existing heretofore—are required. Basically, the use of mechanics like the "decision table" or PERT/CPM means that the user follows a logical method to solve the problem he tackles. Even in the accounting profession, PERT can be used for multiple purposes. A case of its use in the planning of preparation of consolidated financial statements under pressure and in the carrying out of the work efficiently, effectively, and according to the time schedule is presented in the following description.

The PERT technique was developed for the Polaris submarine project of the United States Navy. In it, the expected sequence of operations is described, with an estimate of the time required to carry out each of them and the spelling out of which requirements should be fulfilled before beginning each new stage. The most important factors in the implementation of any project are the time and often the cost element.

This article deals with a relatively simple case. As the time allowed for completion of the task was minimal and relatively small compared to the complete audit assignment, the cost element was not material and will therefore be disregarded. As the subject dealt with was a known quantity, unlike other PERT projects, it could be planned quite precisely in advance.

AVERAGING TIME

Most PERT networks deal with complicated types of tasks to be performed over a period of time that can range from a number of months to a number of years, often in a field where there has been no prior experience and where estimates may, therefore, be quite unreliable. To solve this problem, an average is often computed of optimistic, realistic, and pessimistic time estimates. Such an average cancels out extremes in time estimates. This problem diminishes if there is past experience to draw on, as was the case in the consolidation procedure described in this article. As the time of the total project was short, any discrepancies between estimated and actual time obviously had to be dealt with on the spot.

One major advantage of planning with PERT/CPM is the clear method of presentation of the critical path, that series of tasks to be performed which necessitates investment of resources and time during the entire period until completion of the project. Tasks not appearing on the critical path can be completed without prolonging the total time required.

The two basic qualities of PERT and CPM are: (1) a sophisticated programing and supervision system and (2) concurrent operation of several subdivisions in coordination with the targets of the project.

Consolidated statements are usually prepared by the accounting division of the client or by its CPA firm. In both cases, the CPA expresses his opinion on the fairness of the presentation of the statements.

BASIS OF STATEMENTS

Usually, the terms of reference for the consolidated financial statements are simple. They should be based on the financial statements of the parent company and its domestic and foreign subsidiaries, completed soon after the year end, and published as early as possible. It is, therefore, important to guarantee the flow of information as early as possible through the design of a method as complete as necessary to ensure that there are no last-minute hitches. The cost element, in such a case, is of minor importance.

The larger the number of subsidiaries in the group and the greater the number of intercompany transactions and minority shareholders, the more cumbersome (and at times lengthy) is the work concerned with the preparation of the consolidated statements. It is impossible in such a case to prepare the consolidation on one sheet of paper. In fact, to prepare the consolidation, a substantial number of schedules is required.

The schedules include: (1) a schedule which handles the statement of income and earned surplus; (2) an analysis of the investments in shares of the subsidiaries; (3) a schedule of investments in debentures of subsidiaries; (4) a schedule collating the other assets of the subsidiaries and the parent; (5) a schedule consolidating all the liabilities of the group; (6) a schedule of the dividends receivable and the proposed dividends at the end of the year; (7) a working paper relating to the rights of the minority shareholders; (8) a calculation of the net asset value at date of acquisition of each subsidiary; (9) an analysis of the development of the capital surplus and the earned surplus.

The expertise required of the person responsible for preparation of such a consolidation includes not only a very profound knowledge and understanding of accounting; it also includes an administrative and organizational capacity for distributing the work among the staff and supervising the assembly of the required data.

Thanks to the planning of the work based on the network, it is at this stage the advantages of PERT first began to be felt. This becomes evident from the following section, which describes the actual work performed in the case dealt with in this article.

WORK ANALYSIS

The first stage of the planning required an analysis of the work done on previous assignments, based on the working papers and other relevant data. A list was drawn up of all the steps to be performed, and it became clear that, in fact, the work consisted of the following stages:

Obtaining the basic data, i.e., the financial statements of all companies to be consolidated and additional information such as questionnaires.
Analysis of the basic data and their compilation in the working papers.
Preparation of consolidation entries.
Preparation of the final product, i.e., the consolidated financial statements.

It is advisable to prepare in advance the layout of the working sheets for the analysis of the financial statements of the parent and all subsidiaries and the anticipated consolidation schedules. In the company working sheets, separate sheets for each of the companies consolidated and the comparative figures for the preceding years, indicating the sources from which these figures were taken, should be shown. A questionnaire should be sent some time before the year end to the various members of the group requesting them to report on all intercompany activities such as sales, sale of property and payments of interest. The questionnaire should be filled out and returned at the time of the preparation of the consolidated financial statements. This step is shown in the network (see Figure 33.1) as Activity 1—2. (Further references herein to the network are shown in parentheses.)

Work can be expedited by obtaining certain of the basic data at an early stage, but most of the consolidation entries are dependent on the receipt of all relevant data, not just most of them. Therefore, the consolidation entries can generally be prepared only after obtaining and analyzing all basic data and copying them into the working papers.

The time schedule of the total work is, therefore, composed of a preparatory period in which data are analyzed as they come in, the pressure period of preparation of consolidation entries, and the final period in which the consolidated financials are drafted. The preparatory period ends at the cut-off date, upon receipt of the last basic data required. Unless such a cut-off date is established and rigidly adhered to, the total period until completion of the task is in danger of being delayed. In the network, this is Event 2.

The real work can start only after completing Event 3. This event represents the stage at which all basic data have been compiled and the working

FIGURE 33.1 Network for Preparation of Consolidated Financial Statements

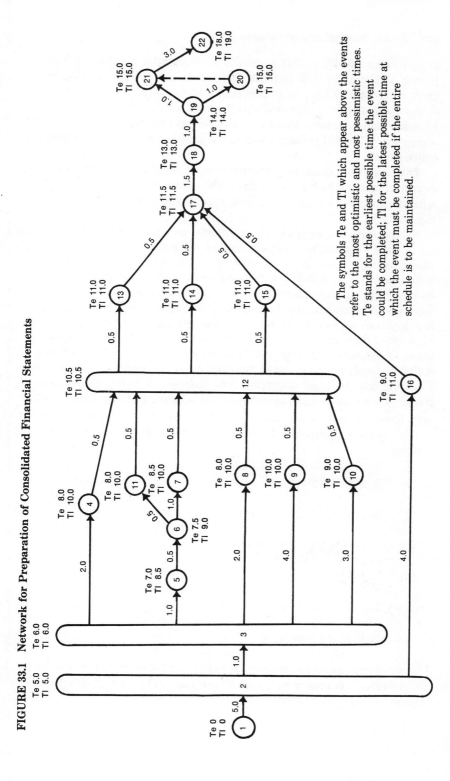

The symbols Te and Tl which appear above the events refer to the most optimistic and most pessimistic times. Te stands for the earliest possible time the event could be completed; Tl for the latest possible time at which the event must be completed if the entire schedule is to be maintained.

papers balanced. From this stage the work may be planned so that, by proper allocation of staff to those activities which are part of the critical path, maximum utilization of time and staff is achieved.

An estimate of the time required for each activity should be made, and no delay should arise in those activities where the slack time is zero, i.e., where any delay will endanger the time schedule for the completion of the entire project.

This analysis is made by preparing a schedule of events which form the interim stages at which certain parts of the work have been completed. This schedule appears in Figure 33.2. The activities between events are listed in Figure 33.3.

Subsequently, a schedule of activities is prepared, indicating the estimated time required to complete each of the activities. On completion of this schedule of activities, it should be possible to ascertain how much time would be required before commencing work on each activity. (E.g., work on new activities depends on completion of Event 3 and can begin after six days have elapsed from the beginning of the project, during which the first five days are devoted to Activity 1–2 and the sixth day to Activity 2–3.)

If more than one activity leads up to a certain event, efforts should be made to minimize the length of time for the preparation of the chain of activities requiring the greatest numbers of days to complete. The activities requiring less than this maximum time span are of lesser importance, although supervision should be given so that they are tied in correctly. In our case, there are six different chains of activities, paths (see Figure 33.1) which require input of resources until completion of Event 12. They are as follows:

(a) 1–2–3–4–12 (8½ days).

(b) 1–2–3–5–6–11–12 (8½ days).

(c) 1–2–3–4–5–6–7–12 (9 days).

(d) 1–2–3–8–12 (8½ days).

(e) 1–2–3–9–12 (10½ days).

(f) 1–2–3–10–12 (9½ days).

The maximum estimated time is on path "e" (1–2–3–9–12), and work on the activities subsequent to Event 12 can start only after the elapse of 10 ½ days.

FIGURE 33.2
Schedule of Events

Event No.   *Description of Events*

1. Start.
2. Completion of analyses of financial statements of consolidated companies.
3. Complete balancing of working schedules.
4. Completion of reviewing and elimination of all intercompany profit and loss transactions.
5. Complete establishing the amounts of shares held by minority shareholders.
6. Completion of calculation of percentages of minority interests.
7. Complete computation of minority interest in capital, and in earned and capital surplus.
8. Complete establishing of earned and capital surplus at dates of acquisition, and amounts paid in excess of net equity value at such dates ("goodwill").
9. Completion of dealing with revaluation of debentures of consolidated companies held by group.
10. Complete analyzing of intercompany balances at balance sheet date.
11. Completion of analyses of dividends paid or payable by subsidiaries.
12. Complete recording of consolidation entries and balancing of various working schedules.
13. End of drafting of balance sheet.
14. End of drafting of statement of capital surplus.
15. End of drafting of statement of income and earned surplus.
16. End of preparation of notes to the financial statements.
17. Complete comparison of the various statements with those of preceding year.
18. Completion of review by senior and by partner in charge.
19. Completion of typing.
20. Completion of review by the reviewing committee.
21. Completion of proofreading and correcting draft financial statements.
22. Approved by board of directors and financial statements signed.

Two additional columns of data could be added to Figure 33.3, and these columns would form the basis of determining the critical plan. The first shows the number of days elapsed at the start of work on each activity plus the time required for its completion. This, in fact, represents the earliest day at which the activity can be completed, assuming that work will continue immediately after completion of all activities leading to the event preceding it.

The last column is based on a calculation prepared by moving from the opposite direction: If it takes 18 days to complete the entire job and the last event takes 3 days, the event before the last one should begin not later than 15 days after beginning the work. Similarly, if activities 17–18–19–21–22 require 6½ days to complete, all activities ending with Event 17 have a latest completion time of 11½ days (18 days less 6½ days).

FIGURE 33.3
Schedule of Activities

Beginning Event

Ending Event   *Description of Activity*

1 – 2   Analysis of financial statements of consolidated companies.
2 – 3   Balancing of working schedules.
2 – 16 Preparation of notes to financial statements.
3 – 4   Dealing with intercompany profit and loss transactions.
3 – 5   Establishing amounts of shares held by minority shareholders.
3 – 8   Establishing earned and capital surplus at dates of acquisition, and amount paid in excess of net equity value at such dates ("goodwill").
3 – 9   Revaluation of debentures of consolidated companies held by group, including computation of deferred taxes on profit arising from revaluation, and minority interest therein.
3 – 10 Dealing with intercompany balances at balance sheet date.
4 – 12 Recording in the working schedules of entries regarding intercompany transactions.
5 – 6   Calculation of percentages of minority interest.
6 – 7   Computation of minority interest in capital and in earned and capital surplus.
6 – 11 Analyzing of dividends paid or payable by subsidiaries.
7 – 12 Recording in the working schedules of entries in respect of minority interest.
8 – 12 Recording in the working schedules of entries in respect of goodwill, etc.
9 – 12 Recording in the working schedules of entries in respect of revaluation of debentures.
10 – 12 Recording in the working schedules of entries in respect of intercompany balances.
11 – 12 Recording in the working schedules of entries in respect of dividends.
12 – 13 Drafting of balance sheet.
12 – 14 Drafting of statement of capital surplus.
12 – 15 Drafting of statement of income and earned surplus.
13 – 17 Comparison of balance sheet to that of preceding year.
14 – 17 Comparison of statement of capital surplus to that of preceding year.
15 – 17 Comparison of statement of income and earned surplus to that of preceding year.
16 – 17 Comparison of notes to financial statements to those of preceding year.
17 – 18 Reviewing of financial statements by senior in charge and by partner.
18 – 19 Typing of financial statements.
19 – 20 Reviewing by reviewing committee.
19 – 21 Proofreading and correcting financial statements.
21 – 22 Approval by board of directors and signing of financial statements.

CRITICAL PATH

After preparation of the schedule as described, the slack time available for each activity is also shown. If there is no difference between the time indicated in the last two columns, i.e., if the earliest date at which the activity will be completed equals the latest allowable date, there is no slack period whatsoever, and the activity is located on the critical path. Full attention should be devoted to it so as to avoid any delay in its completion. On the other hand, if there is a difference between the two dates, the difference indicates that the work on the activity may start later than the earliest date possible, the allowable number of days in delaying the start of work on the activity being the difference in number of days between the two columns. This analysis makes it possible to divert staff from activities with slack time to those without slack time, while being certain that this allocation of staff will not cause delay in the completion of the entire job.

Accordingly, work on the activities along the critical path was carried out throughout the consolidation period, while the other activities were carried on concurrently and when each activity along the critical path was completed, the other data up to that point were ready and did not hold back the work on the next activity. E.g., along the various stages of the work according to the network shown on Figure 33.1 the first task to be completed after the preparation stage was ended was the determination of all amounts relating to elimination of intercompany holdings of debentures issued by group companies. In our case, these amounts were material and involved computations of interest accrued, amounts resulting from clauses providing for increase of return in case of pegging to the cost-of-living index, or, in case of changes in the rate of exchange of foreign currency, deferred taxes on profits recognized only for consolidation purposes and minority interest in such profits. Event 9 represents completion of this activity. Parallel to this, the other activities leading to Event 12 were performed.

Obviously, the results of all computations should be closely examined. It happens repeatedly that in the preparation of the computations new problems arise, partly professional, possibly theoretical, which are not anticipated in advance. These take up additional time. Client operations develop continuously, and adaptation of accounting practices to new circumstances may necessitate research and discussions within the firm and between officials of the company and its CPAs. It may be stated that in every healthy corporation there exists a certainty that new problems will crop up; the only thing which cannot be foreseen is what the nature will be of the specific problem to be encountered in a given year. On the other hand, however, time estimates should be realistic so as to permit a proper follow-up on the progress of the work. It is, therefore, recommended that the required time reserve be expressed by planning the work in advance for completion at an earlier date than that absolutely required so that this built-in slack time can be utilized for the said unforeseen matters.

It may be assumed that the technical working procedures of accountants putting together the consolidated financial statements are different, even though they operate within the same accounting principles and methods. This article does not describe all details specifically performed in the present case. A brief description appears in the schedule of activities, Figure 33.3. This schedule, read together with the network itself, shows the details and the flow of the various activities. It is seen, for instance, that work on activities 6–11 and 6–7 can begin only after Event 6, which means that before work can start on both the analysis of dividends paid or payable by subsidiaries and the amounts of minority interests in capital stock and earned and capital surplus, first the percentages of minority interests should be computed.

MAJOR ELEMENTS LINKED

With the analysis, the completing of data, and the preparation of the consolidation entries carried out, Events 13, 14, 15, and 16 have been reached. Here the major portions in the preparation of the annual consolidated financial statements are linked, viz, the balance sheet, the statement of income and earned surplus, the statement of capital surplus, and the notes thereto.

STATEMENTS COMPLETED

At this stage the work moves along relatively standard practice and is mentioned here only for the completion of the subject. First, the financial statements have to be reviewed, the balances connecting them checked, amounts compared with the financial statements for the preceding year, and the presentation of data and formulation of notes and explanations compared with those appearing in the unconsolidated financial statements of the parent (Event 17). Then the work carried out has to be reviewed by the senior in charge and by the responsible partner (Event 18). The consolidated statements should then be typewritten (Event 19) and passed upon and edited by the reviewing committee of the firm (Event 20). The sequence of these later activities depends on the practice of the firm. The last activity relates to the approval of the financial statements by the board and the signing of the accountants' opinion, and here the work of the consolidated financial statements with the aid of CPM is completed (Event 22).

The network will not be substantially different if the controller of the parent prepares the financial statements and the consolidation is reviewed by the firm of CPAs, or if the firm of CPAs also undertakes the preparation of the consolidated statements.

Although the preparation of the consolidation is not in itself audit work, it requires special expertise, as the statements should present fairly the financial position and the results of operations of the group on a consolidated basis. This is not a question of technical computations only, but especially one of a fair presentation, giving due diligence to the elimination of any material transaction within the group. Care should be taken that no inner reserves be created through the preparation of the consolidated statements. It should be verified that the results only include profits realized through transactions with third parties. (The presentation of facts should be made with the view of the activity of the group as a whole and not of each and every separate individual member of the group; e.g., if one subsidiary rents out buildings to another member of the group which is a manufacturer of goods in the rented building, this building should be shown not as part of buildings for rent but as factory buildings, if such separate headings appear in the consolidated balance sheet.)

AUDITORS HELP THEMSELVES

The PERT/CPM techniques developed in a period when problems of administration and controls multiplied, diversified, and became far more complicated, in a period when costs increased and competition became an even more important factor. PERT and CPM evolved to create a common denominator, a new means of measurement, simplifying procedures through proper planning and detailed description. As with the advent of budgeting, several decades earlier, the method may be misused. Auditors in the past two decades have been conscious of technical developments in methods of administration. They have been aware of the great interest management has had in PERT and CPM. They can do well to study ways by which they can themselves benefit directly from using and applying these modern techniques. They will find that their cost factor will be reduced, their service to clients improved, and possibly that they will even have more free time.

34
State and Local PPBS

Jack Rabin

Planning, Programming and Budgeting System (PPBS) is an analytic tool which is being adopted by many states and localities. It was originally developed by the Rand Corporation in Santa Monica, California, for use by the U.S. Air Force. The technique was adopted by the Department of Defense when Robert McNamara became Secretary of Defense in 1961. In

1965, President Lyndon Johnson, by Executive Order, instructed the executive departments to adopt PPBS, thus making this system the decision-making and financial tool for the federal government.

A number of states (e.g., Arkansas, California) have adopted or are in the process of implementing PPBS as their budget technique; moreover, a growing number of cities (e.g., Dayton, Ohio; Philadelphia) are using a form of the technique. Therefore, an examination of what PPBS is and is not, a review of the major assumptions and techniques employed, and a look at the potential benefits and costs of adopting such a system are in order.

This paper has three global objectives. We shall review (1) PPBS in theory and (2) PPBS in practice. Then (3) we shall confront the question: *Should* PPBS be used by states and localities? Thus, our objectives will be accomplished if the reader can (1) gain an understanding of what PPBS can do for his state or community, (2) realize that PPBS has a number of limitations which may hinder implementation and reduce its potential value, and (3) make a tentative decision as to the adoption of a PPBS for his governmental unit.

PPBS IN THEORY

Considering the theoretical underpinnings behind a Planning, Programming and Budgeting System is a complicated and elusive task. The approach here seeks to answer three questions:

1. What is a useful working definition of PPBS?
2. What is the model of decision-making which underlies PPBS?
3. What is the specific structure of PPBS?

A Useful Working Definition

The scholarly literature is muddled about defining PPBS, although the technique has been in existence for more than two decades. Consider only one reflection on the point in the journal *Public Administration Review,* which has devoted two full issues to PPBS. In responding to the first PAR review, Frederick C. Mosher commented in a letter to the editor:

Over the last few years and particularly the last few months, I have been searching for "satisficing" answers to two questions about PPBS. First, what is really new and distinctive about it? Second, in what directions is it really influencing governmental decision-making and the conduct of governmental operations?

I was therefore particularly gratified to learn that PAR would devote a complete issue to PPBS, and I read all of it with unusual (for me) care and thoroughness. It was a very good and rewarding issue. Yet I cannot honestly say that these articles resolved my questions; indeed, I am somewhat more confused now than before. Most of your authors, like others before them, differ among each other as to what

PPBS really is; few of them say or predict what its real effects are or will be—beyond the confident assurance that decisions will be more rational, governmental operations more efficient (excepting, of course, Mr. Wildavsky's alarums from the wilderness of political science). I am in sympathy with most of PPBS and its constituent elements insofar as I understand what they are. In fact, I have been a supporter for about thirty years—ever since I took a course in budgeting taught by Bob Steadman in 1936. But apparently I have been missing some things. These are what I am searching to identify.[1]

With appropriate caution, then, a working definition is hazarded here. The intent is not to force a standard usage, but to provide a base for elaboration and analysis.

Planning, Programming and Budgeting System is a rational decision-making technique which may be used to make more systematic decisions, given a set of objectives and the information at hand. PPBS emphasizes the long-term benefits and costs of programs, rather than the short-term. PPBS is composed of program budgeting and systems analysis, which typically involves cost/benefit studies.

Program budgeting basically places into common categories all activities necessary to accomplish some broad end or "program."

Program budgeting thus contrasts with the line-item budget, which aggregates similar activities into common categories, without regard to the programs or goals to which they contribute.

There are three documents used in program budgeting: the Multiyear Program and Financial Plan; Special Analytic Studies; and, Program Memoranda. These documents are augmented by systematic analysis, forecasting long-term costs and benefits.

The P.P.B. system should be considered as cyclical. That is, the results of the decisions of previous years provide data for decisions in any current year. The past, as it were, thus provides "feedback" for present and future decisions.

PPBS is only a tool for budgetary forecasting and programming. The tool never makes decisions; decision-makers, choosing to use data derived from the tool, make decisions.

This working definition of PPBS—like all others—implies two levels of purpose. One level is explicit, and the other level of purpose is typically implied but is nonetheless real. Clarity about both levels of purpose is desirable.

Stated purposes of PPBS.   With basic unanimity, observers agree as to the stated purposes of PPBS. As Arthur Smithies explains:

Planning, programming, and budgeting constitute the process by which objectives and resources, and the interrelations among them, are taken into account to achieve a coherent and comprehensive program of action for the government as a whole. Program budgeting involves the use of budgetary techniques that facilitate explicit consideration of the pursuit of policy objectives in terms of their economic costs, both at the present time and in the future.[2]

Consequently it can be said that PPBS exists to serve such stated purposes as:

1. ". . . to improve the basis for major program decisions."[3]
2. ". . . to subject decisions about resource allocation to systematic analysis, comparing alternative courses of action in a framework of national objectives clearly and specifically stated."[4]
3. To use "the rule of efficiency (in choosing) that alternative that optimizes the allocation of public resources."[5]
4. To help ". . . responsible officials make decisions. It is *not* a mechanical substitute for the good judgments, political wisdom and leadership of those officials."[6]

The overall purpose of PPBS, then, is to serve as an aid to human judgment, not to supplant it. PPBS never "decides" an issue; the goal is to have the decision-maker use the data generated to make better decisions.

Derivatively, PPBS implies the existence of three crucial elements in pursuit of this concept of systematic and comprehensive approach to planning, action, and evaluation. In Charles Schultze's terms, PPBS implies:

1. The existence in each agency of an *analytic* capability which carries out continuing in-depth analyses by permanent specialized staffs of the agency's objectives and its various programs to meet these objectives.
2. The existence of a multiyear *planning and programming* process which incorporates and uses an information system to present data in meaningful categories essential to the making of major decisions by agency heads and by the President.
3. The existence of a *budgeting* process which can take broad program decisions, translate them into more refined decisions in a budget context, and present the appropriate program and financial data for Presidential and Congressional action.[7]

Overriding if often implicit purpose of PPBS.   Overall, PPBS reflects the basic if often implicit goal of reserving major and growing decision-making authority in the hands of the executive. In sum, PPBS has a strong "centralizing bias." As Thomas Schelling states:

Any discussion of PPBS is unrealistic unless it is acknowledged that budgetary processes are a means of control, as well as a means of evaluation . . . Almost anyone concerned with administration sooner or later discovers that control of budgetary requests and disbursements is a powerful source of more general control. . . . Anything that makes budgeting more effective will add to the authority of those involved in the budgeting. Budgetary procedures provide invaluable opportunities for holding hearings, demanding justifications, spot-checking the quality of planning, identifying objectives, and even enhancing competition among lethargic subgroups. Furthermore, the budgetary process being geared to an annual cycle, it provides a regular and systematic way of repeatedly examining these subjects.[8]

This control orientation in PPBS may produce a lukewarm to hostile reaction on the part of legislators and lower-level administrators, even when executive decision-makers are committed to PPBS. That is, adoption of PPBS may help to bring about "power redistribution"[9] effects which may not seem desirable to some decision-makers. For example, while top political decision-makers may embrace it, their career subordinates may treat the process as a threat. Thus, anyone embarking upon a program of implementing or "selling" PPBS must take into account its centralizing and power-redistribution effects, and often be prepared for questions relating to both.

Some Underlying Models of Decision-Making

The theory of PPBS implies a specific model of decision-making and thereby generates substantial opposition. The point can be demonstrated by contrasting two broad models of human decision-making: the Rational and the Incremental models. PPBS rests on a Rational decision-making model; opponents of PPBS usually favor the Incremental model as their explanation as to how the process of human decision-making does work, and indeed how it should work.[10]

Rational decision-making model. In this model, objectives (ends, goals, etc.) are known and are accepted by the participants in the decision-making. The sole decision-making task becomes a search for (1) the alternative means to attain the end and (2) the specific approach which costs the least and gives the most benefit (or, in military terminology in use in the 1960s, the "most bang for a buck"). Some major properties of the Rational model are sketched in Figure 34.1.

Early Rational decision-making theorists gave the impression that man could know and predict all alternatives, all costs, and all benefits. Today, the *limits* of man's rationality typically are taken into account. Illustratively, compare the contrasting but developmental views of Gene Fisher and Charles Schultze in Figure 34.2. These men were a Rand analyst and the Director of the Bureau of the Budget, respectively, and both were intimately associated with the development and implementation of PPBS.

Incremental decision-making model. In contrast to Rational models, the several Incremental varieties emphasize five factors: (1) man is assumed to have great and often overwhelming difficulties in foreseeing the consequences (costs and benefits) of his decisions, (2) people do not agree about the goals of government, (3) many ends are means to other ends, (4) many problems are too complex and are related to so many other variables that man cannot fully understand them, and (5) a majority of decisions can be explained in terms of a kind of "domino theory," with one decision stimu-

FIGURE 34.1
The Rational Model of Decision-making

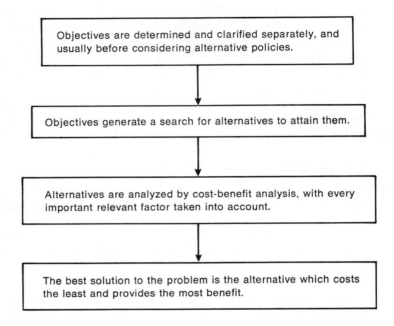

Source: Based upon Charles E. Lindblom, "The Science of Muddling Through," *Public Administration Review* 19 (Spring 1959): 79–88.

lating the need for another decision, *ad infinitum,* as opposed to the simultaneous consideration of all alternatives implied by Rational models. Figure 34.3 sketches the major features of Incremental models of decision-making.

A modified Rational model. The incrementalists made some telling points, to judge from the adjustments increasingly reflected in contemporary versions of the Rational model. Figure 34.4 reflects our conception of these major adjustments.

Basically, Figure 34.4 reflects a substantial dash of humility about what is inevitable, and perhaps even desirable, about public spending decisions. In sum: As long as ʹ ıe keeps in mind that he will not be able to know all alternatives to solving a problem, that his analysis of costs and benefits will not be perfect, and that he will be dealing only with the information that he can get, then the Rational approach to budgeting/decision-making can be a helpful if limited analytic tool.

FIGURE 34.2

Major Characteristics of Cost-Utility Analysis

Gene H. Fisher:
Cost-Utility Analysis (1964)

1. Systematic examination and comparison of alternatives to achieve specified objectives.
2. Assessment of cost and utility of each alternative.
3. The time context is in the future.
4. Quantitative methods should be used "as much as possible," with "uncertain" elements faced up to and treated explicitly in the analysis.

Charles Schultze:
Cost-Effectiveness Analysis
(1967)

1. Systematic examination and comparison of alternatives to achieve specified objectives.
2. Assessment of cost and utility of each alternative under the following provisos: (a) one will never have "all the relevant information" so that (b) analysis is performed only with the information one "can get."
3. The time context is in the future.
4. "... you can put into a cost-effectiveness PPB framework all of the information you can get (although not all of it can be expressed quantitatively)."

Based on Gene H. Fisher, "The Role of Cost-Utility Analysis in Program Budgeting," in David Novick (ed.), *Program Budgeting,* 2nd ed. (New York: Holt, Rinehart & Winston, 1969), pp. 66–67; Charles Schultze, in U.S., Congress, Senate, hearings before the Subcommittee on National Security and International Operations, Committee on Government Operations, 90th Cong., 1st Sess., August 23, 1967, p. 186.

Specific Structure of PPBS

In essence, PPBS builds toward program budgets, and the immediate purpose is to provide a flowchart of the major activities involved in the development of program budgets. The sections below will consider four major elements:

1. Goal definition.
2. The development of a program structure.
3. The major PPBS documents.
4. Cost-benefit analysis.

Goal definition. Ideally, a Planning, Programming and Budgeting System begins with a definition of objectives and subobjectives and extends that emphasis as far as possible. This definition is usually accomplished by elected decision-makers and department heads in policy statements, legislation, and so on. For example, in 1961 President Kennedy stated that a

FIGURE 34.3
The Incremental Model of Decision-Making

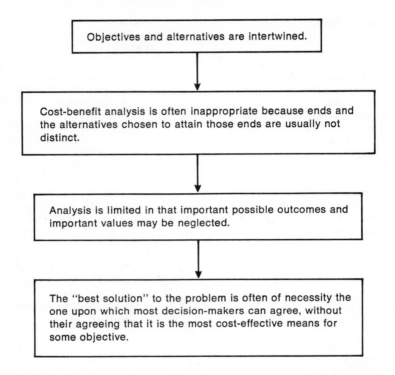

Source: Based upon Charles E. Lindblom, "The Science of Muddling Through," *Public Administration Review* 19 (Spring 1959): pp. 79–88.

national goal for the United States was to place a man on the moon before the end of the decade. In 1965, President Johnson launched a "war" on poverty, seeking to eradicate its causes and consequences in the United States. These are goals. Both were accepted by Congress. Once goals are defined, then program budgets can be developed.

However, the basic question in American government remains *who* should define goals. Are goals to be defined by the people at the "top" or by those at intermediate levels who must find ways of implementing the goals? Paul L. Brown grapples with this dilemma:

What disturbs me about this broad approach (of goal definition) from the top down is that many of these definitions become almost truisms. They have to be refined through several levels before they become meaningful for immediate budgetary or operational purposes. These immediate purposes are areas in which we must make decisions today. ... I see more of a payoff in concentrating initial attention at a lower level of activity than the goals and objectives of government.

FIGURE 34.4
The Modified Rational Model of Decision-making

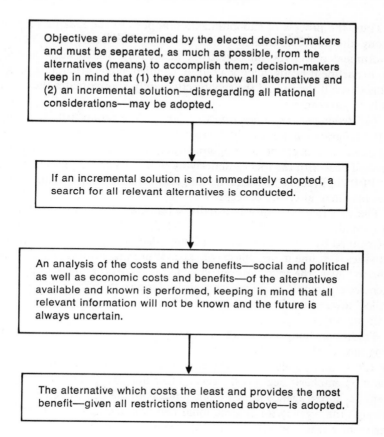

Objectives are determined by the elected decision-makers and must be separated, as much as possible, from the alternatives (means) to accomplish them; decision-makers keep in mind that (1) they cannot know all alternatives and (2) an incremental solution—disregarding all Rational considerations—may be adopted.

If an incremental solution is not immediately adopted, a search for all relevant alternatives is conducted.

An analysis of the costs and the benefits—social and political as well as economic costs and benefits—of the alternatives available and known is performed, keeping in mind that all relevant information will not be known and the future is always uncertain.

The alternative which costs the least and provides the most benefit—given all restrictions mentioned above—is adopted.

I am not convinced that a proper description of the objective cannot be started at an intermediate level, be properly evaluated, measured and combined with statements for higher levels to reach a unified goal which can then be evaluated and worked back down. In this way objectives and subobjectives could be formulated, and perhaps better measurements could be developed more rapidly.[11]

Brown essentially argues for the factoring process involved in "suboptimization." Suboptimization is the process of breaking "problems of choice into manageable pieces or subproblems"[12] and then developing courses of action. As Roland McKean states:

In a government or department, one man or one committee cannot possibly examine all problems of choice simultaneously and select each course of action in light of all the other decisions. The task is divided among various persons along hierarchical lines, some of the broader policy choices being made by high-level officials or groups, and others being delegated to lower levels.[13]

Thus, the process of suboptimization applies to the making of choices among alternative courses of action, and it also concerns the definition of government objectives. Subobjectives, defined by elected decision-makers and department heads, may be usefully handled in constructing a program budget even if the sum of the subobjectives only approximates the ultimate goals of government.

The development of a program structure. A program structure consists of the program categories which are determined on the basis of objectives, but often the concept of the program structure is changed in practice. Here, we shall deal with the theory underlying programs and program structure; in "PPBS in Practice" we shall investigate how environmental and political variables may alter the concept.

The program structure is usually subdivided, based on subobjectives, into smaller components. Last (and definitely last), program categories, determined by top elected and appointed decision-makers, bring together activities (i.e., line items, objects of expenditure), regardless of agency location, so long as the activities contribute to the same program objective. Since agencies commonly share responsibilities for any specific program, "crosswalks" are required to link agency structures and program structures, as is illustrated in Figure 34.5.

Traditional budgeting procedures emphasize agency location rather than program, and line-item budgets thus emphasize agency, division, and activity (or similar labels), as in the right-hand portion of Figure 34.5. This common emphasis neglects the crucial fact that many activities of government cut across agency lines. For example, both the U.S. State Department, through the Agency for International Development, and the Defense Department engage in military-related foreign aid projects. However, these projects are rarely coordinated, due in part to their placement in the organization structure. Similarly, the Defense Department, the Department of Health, Education and Welfare, the Department of Justice, and the Special Action Office for Drug Abuse Prevention in the Executive Office of the President all deal with the drug problem. Whatever the example, the conclusion is the same. A coordinated approach to social problems is often hampered or precluded by agency barriers.

A rough contrast may be helpful. A line-item budget stresses the individual bits of public spending: positions, typewriters, etc. A program budget, on the other hand, stresses the broad product, or objective.

Reconciling the two approaches is easier said than done, but, in essence, program budgets seek to cluster activities necessary to achieve major objectives and consequently must seek coordination between government agencies. Figure 34.5 illustrates such a program structure clustering of diverse

FIGURE 34.5 The "Crosswalk" between Organization Structure and Program Structure

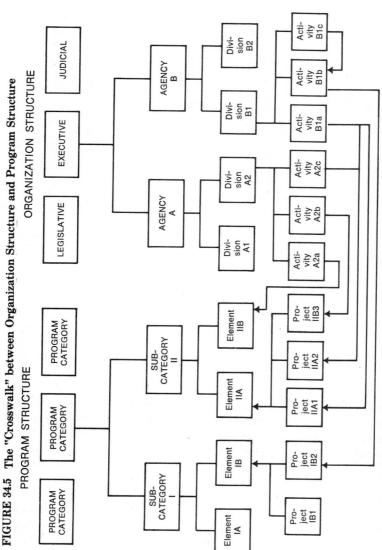

Source: "Planning and Budgeting, A Seminar on Planning and Budgeting Concepts for Florida," presented to the state legislature and all operating departments and agencies by the Planning and Budget Commission and Legislative Auditor, State of Florida, p. 64.

agency activities necessary to meet major objectives. Program structures are typically multileveled and can relate to:

1. The attainment of a major government objective, usually identified as a *program category.*
2. The accomplishment of narrower objectives, usually expressed in terms of *program subcategories.*
3. Specific products, which are grouped under the heading of *program elements.* [14]

In essence, then, program budgets create a new organization or structure of activities, based on broad government objectives, and two factorings of these objectives. Life would be simpler if the individual agencies themselves were organized around programs. Typically, however, a tension exists between the agency and program structures, with the crosswalks identifying which agencies contribute to which programs, in what specific senses, and in what degree.

The major PPBS documents.   Several major documents derive from and add detail to the program structure. Three kinds of such documents will be considered here: (1) Multiyear Program and Financial Plans, (2) Special Analytic Studies, and (3) Program Memoranda.

1. One of the important products of program budgeting is a compact document termed the *Multiyear Program and Financial Plan* (PFP). The PFP:

a. Is based on the program structure.
b. Usually covers a period of years (often five years).
c. Includes activities contemplated as well as authorized.
d. Indicates what the department head thinks will be appropriate over the period covered by the plan.
e. Translates projected costs and receipts into financial, quantitative terms.

A brief excerpt from one PFP is shown in Figure 34.6. In reality, the plan may contain hundreds of categories.

2. *Special Analytic Studies* (SASs) are analytic efforts to examine in depth a specific topic at the request of a decision-maker. SASs typically have one of two time-frames. One type is initiated and completed during one budget year. This one-year study usually is conducted in support of a budget request submitted in a Program Memorandum. Other SASs go beyond one budget year. To illustrate, one such continuing study was designed to develop "on a longer-run basis the conceptual understanding necessary to improve the data available, to evaluate the implications of agency objectives, and to provide an analytic basis for deciding future Major Program Issues."[15] A Major Program Issue is one requiring decision in a current budget cycle, with major implications in terms of either present or future

FIGURE 34.6
Multiyear Program and Financial Plan, Fiscal Years 1972–78 (dollars in millions)

Program Categories	FY 1972 Actual	FY 1973 Current Estimate	FY 1974 Budget Year Estimate	FY 1975 Program Estimate	FY 1976 Program Estimate	FY 1977 Program Estimate	FY 1978 Program Estimate	Total Costs '72–'78
I. Personal Safety								
Civilian law enforcement								
Traffic safety								
Fire prevention & control								
Safety from animals								
Protection and control of natural and manmade disasters								
Total Program Area I								
II. Health								
Physical health								
Mental health								
Drug and alcohol addiction-prevention and control								
Total Program Area II								

Source: State-Local Finances Project, PPB Note 1, George Washington University, p. 5.

costs, the direction of a program or group of programs, or a policy choice. Most centrally, a Major Program Issue identifies specific alternative courses of action, and the costs and benefits of each. Pertinent legislative as well as budgetary considerations can also be emphasized.[16]

3. The *Program Memorandum* (PM) presents

a statement of the program issues, a comparison of the cost and effectiveness of alternatives for resolving those issues in relation to objectives, the agency head's recommendations on programs to be carried out, and the reasons for those decisions. PMs, therefore, provide the documentation for the strategic decisions recommended for the budget year.[17]

In other words, the Program Memorandum:

a. Spells out specific programs recommended by the department for the multiyear period.
b. Demonstrates how the programs meet the objectives specified by the decision-making process.
c. Shows the total cost of programs recommended.
d. Indicates how recommended programs differ from current and past programs.
e. Describes recommended program objectives, expected benefits, and costs for several years into the future.
f. Describes recommended program objectives "insofar as possible in quantitative physical terms.
g. Compares the effectiveness and cost of (1) alternative objectives, (2) alternative types of programs which may meet the same objectives and (3) different levels within program categories.
h. Makes "explicit the assumptions and criteria which support recommended programs."
i. Identifies and analyzes the main uncertainties in assumptions, in costs and benefits.[18]

Cost-benefit analysis.   Cost-benefit analysis—which may also be called cost-effectiveness or cost-utility analysis—is a rational decision-making tool and a variety of systems analysis. The major goal in cost-benefit analysis is to determine the projected costs and benefits of different alternatives to the achievement of an objective or subobjective.

The inability to *meaningfully quantify* all relevant variables is a major limitation of cost-benefit analysis. According to Klaus Knorr, for example, cost-benefit analysis is most useful when ". . . the objective or output is definitely fixed—that is, when there is only one dependent variable, and the sole task is to minimize the costs which are readily and accurately measured."[19] However, ". . . the usefulness of the technique is the more limited, the less the problem is capable of uniform quantification."[20]

Two other important limitations on cost-benefit analysis relate to the definition of "cost" and the availability of information. First, consider the depth of measurement involved in cost-benefit analyses. Many cost-benefit studies disregard all nonmonetary costs; that is, situations or alternatives may involve such costs as morale, "loss of face," and so forth. Since these costs cannot be easily quantified, the tendency is to ignore what may be important considerations. This can be a serious limitation which can seriously mislead incautious interpreters of specific cost-benefit analyses.

Second, applications of cost-benefit analysis are limited by "imperfect information." Many situations may be so uncertain or volatile that accurate information concerning alternative courses of action is either too expensive to obtain or too unreliable to use. Directly, the quality of the input information is critical in interpreting the results of any cost-benefit analysis.

However, given such limitations, the cost-benefit tool should not be hastily discarded. At its best, the technique can help to improve decision-making. Moreover, cost-benefit analysis can heighten the usefulness of a program budget. Pointedly, program budgets are meaningful more or less in direct proportion to the adequacy of their underlying cost-benefit analyses, whether they are implicit or explicit analyses.

PPBS IN PRACTICE: EXPERIENCES IN NEW YORK STATE AND PHILADELPHIA

This section begins with a paradox. PPBS has major attractions, in principle. In practice, however, it has often degenerated into an exercise taking all the items in the line-item budget and finding a place for them in the PPBS budget, and "crosswalks" are considered more as colorful demonstrations than as reflections of cooperation and coordination between agencies providing activities to the same program or programs. This, of course, represents a perversion of the original concept of PPBS and helps to reinforce the status quo. Thus the ideal program seeks to reallocate or eliminate activities inconsistent with program needs. However, most actual programs are political compromises that, because of agency resistance, tend to aggregate all the existing activities of agencies into new "boxes."

The mixed record of success of PPBS applications supports the paradox above. First, it has been all but abandoned by the national government. In addition, its success in states and cities has been mixed. Few governments have rejected PPBS, but few have implemented it in any meaningful way. Most states and cities have conducted either a holding action or rear-guard defense against the implementation of PPBS.

PPBS has not had the success for which its proponents hoped. We shall consider two examples of this mixed success. New York state exemplifies a failure to implement a "true" PPBS budget due to agency resistance, rivalries, and so on. The second example, Philadelphia, is included as an illustration of a successful implementation of PPBS, due primarily to acceptance and implementation of the method by agency officials.

PPBS in New York State

New York was the first state to adopt PPBS (in 1964) and the first to discard it, although the basic program analysis and review portions have been retained.[21] The technique was hindered in implementation by a series of organizational and management problems. First, a jurisdictional fight occurred between the agencies which had been given operational control over PPBS implementation. Second, little effort was made in the beginning to overcome the agency tendency to use PPBS as a planning tool, with budgeting occupying a subordinate role. Third, the various "mini-wars" which affected PPBS implementation soon led to a general disillusionment with it. Finally, these problems contributed to the abandonment of PPBS and the adoption of Program Analysis and Review (PAR), which was an attempt to gain firm executive control over the situation.

The jurisdictional fight.   Three agencies were involved in PPBS implementation in New York: the Office of the Secretary to the Governor, the State Budget Division (which was the "traditional" budgeting agency), and the Office of Planning Coordination.

The development of PPBS programs was given to the Office of the Secretary to the Governor, which soon contained a staff of 100 analysts, many of whom served as staff people assigned to particular program functions. Placing program development in this agency led to the Secretary's Office becoming the center of policy formulation in the state and induced an unpublicized rivalry between that office and the State Budget Division.

A third agency soon entered the picture. The need for statewide comprehensive planning stimulated the creation of the Office of Planning Coordination. This agency was responsible for devising long-range resource plans. The State Budget Division, however, saw the creation of yet another agency as a further threat to its leadership in financial affairs.[22]

This jurisdictional dispute between the State Budget Division and the two planning agencies affected PPBS implementation. When PPBS was adopted by the state, both the State Budget Division and the Office of Planning Coordination established separate PPBS staffs, but neither agency treated PPBS as an important part of its work.

The PPBS staff in the State Budget Division—the program analysis unit—gradually became estranged from the budget director. Moreover, this staff was treated by members of the Budget Division—specifically the examination and the management units—as an outsider:

This ... (estrangement) ... was due as much to the eagerness of the PPBers to be free from the constraints of the old-timers as to the desire of the old-timers to operate without PPB interference. By and large, the examiners were enemies of PPB. They were not really consulted. The PPBers had come to government out of nowhere or out of physical planning. Thriving on their separateness, the PPBers did not recognize that there are other decisional processes outside PPB.[23]

The stress on planning.   Another constraint which limited PPBS almost from its inception was that the system was begun primarily as a statewide planning system, with budgeting in a *subordinate* role. It did not take agency officials very long, according to one student of New York budgeting, to realize that the annual budget cycle was operating virtually independent of PPBS. Documents were consequently viewed as burdens and eventually were consigned for preparation to agency clerks.

After New York enlisted as one of the five states in the State-Local Finances Project in 1967, the State Budget Division was able to expand its PPBS apparatus and began to redirect the system toward budgeting. This move was accompanied by a waning interest in PPBS by the planners in the Office of Planning Coordination.

By 1968, new legislative budget guidelines had legitimized this move on the part of the State Budget Division and had firmly redirected the course of PPBS in New York into the financial management area. Furthermore, in the same year, the State Division was able to supplant the Office of Planning Coordination as the major PPBS agency in the state.

Disillusionment with PPBS.   Although the attempt had been made in 1968 to overhaul the system, it was not enough to rescue PPBS from the *ennui* which had set in during its previous four years' practice. Interagency rivalry prevented the issuance of adequate guidelines for submitting PPBS documents. Furthermore, no attempt was made to inform the agencies why the information they were preparing was important or what would be done with it when submitted.

By 1969, the operation of PPBS in New York had come "to a virtual halt."[24] Key PPBS personnel were looking for other positions. In the summer of 1969, the program analysis and coordination unit in the State Budget Division was abolished. However, PPBS was not abandoned by the state.

Program analysis and review.   In 1970, PPBS was replaced by Program Analysis and Review (PAR). PAR was created to deal with interdepartmental issues, multiyear planning, analysis of alternatives, identification of critical problems, and effective utilization of tools of analysis. Designed to be more agency oriented than PPBS, it attempted to bring the Governor's Office more effectively into the planning and budgeting process.

Conclusions.   Implementation of PPBS in New York was similar to the federal experience in that no attempt was made to gain agency acceptance of a new form of budgetary decision-making which was overlaid on the existing decision structure.

PAR, designed as a low-keyed form of PPBS, has more modest objectives. In New York, it was an accommodation to the existing budget traditions in the state. Its future, according to one student of the New York budget, is uncertain and will depend upon further attempts to reform budgeting in the state.[25]

PPBS in Philadelphia

In contrast with other attempts at implementing PPBS at the state and local level, the technique was introduced into Philadelphia government in December 1966 by local budgeters. Furthermore, a constant effort was made to gain and retain agency acceptance of the new system of budgeting. In fact, only after an agency had accepted the idea of budgeting by program structure were efforts made to introduce further PPBS procedures, such as cost-benefit analysis.

Introduction in Philadelphia.   Although PPBS had the support of the mayor, day-to-day operation was left to the agencies. Moreover, the system was developed through a gradual buildup of staff capabilities, in contrast to New York's establishment of the large staff in the Office of the Secretary of the Governor. In addition, staff capabilities were sharpened by periodic training and orientation sessions, as noted by Selma Mushkin:

> Orientation programs were designed as a "kick-off" to gain a common understanding of PPB among central and staff agency personnel, and to inform heads of departments. The Philadelphia orientation program, the first organized for local officials, achieved a common basis for cooperative agency action and paved the way for a tentative first cut at classification of programs and subsequent revision. To assure that the structures developed by the agencies would have an overall rational relationship to each other, general agreement on a broad basic program framework in the entire city government was reached initially between the Department of Finance, which housed the central staff for the PPB effort, and operating agency personnel.[26]

Thus, from its inception, PPBS in Philadelphia concentrated on agency cooperation. Once an agency accepted a program structure to replace its line-item budget, the next step was taken in introducing cost-benefit analysis.

The use of cost-benefit analysis was first confined to the Health Department, which adopted the procedure on an experimental basis. The success which accompanied the experiment led to the broadening of the analysis effort in other departments.

Conclusions.   In contrast to New York, PPBS in Philadelphia:

1. Was accomplished through the use of "back-door" tactics; i.e., agency personnel were responsible for introducing the procedure instead of the top executive decision-maker.

2. Concentrated on agency acceptance of each part of the new procedure.
3. Did not immediately stimulate the creation of a large staff capability and thus avoided one probable source of interagency rivalry.

As one portion of the Philadelphia PPB system proved itself, the city implemented a second part, and so on. The concentration on agency acceptance of each portion of PPBS led to its gaining firm roots in the City of Brotherly Love.

SUMMARY: SHOULD PPBS BE USED BY STATES AND LOCALITIES?

Any meaningful response to the question posed above must be complex. First, the most important point to remember is that this is a *political* decision involving the major budgetary decision-makers in the instrumentality. As was the case in New York, many planners become disillusioned because the political process is not systematic and decisions on important issues are not made rationally.

The decision to adopt PPBS has implications for vested interests, appropriations committeemen in the legislature, the Governor, and the bureaucracy. With its centralizing and power-redistribution effects, it can have substantial implications for any one of these groups. These implications must be kept in mind by anyone proposing PPBS.

Furthermore, when PPBS is being considered, one should question whether the major budgetary decision-makers have a desire to plan and use the data provided by the system once the project is in operation. Statistical data can be used as a justification or a "smoke-screen" for virtually any alternative course of action. In fact, the likelihood and potential exists for (1) the utilization of machine data to "snow" decision-makers or (2) the production of meaningless data in the agencies if the assent of the bureaucracy is not obtained in implementing PPBS. Thus one must be vigilant even after PPBS has been installed.

Although PPBS has a number of limitations, the system offers numerous potential advantages in that government is forced to take a hard look at the allocation of scarce resources. The technique is one way to force decision-makers to spell out objectives as much as possible. Second, program budgeting groups similar items according to program objectives, thus acting as a hedge against duplication of services, procurement, and so on.

Third, cost-benefit analysis helps government determine, within the limits of man's capabilities, the costs and benefits of alternative courses of action so that another system of making choices is available. Finally, government must plan, and the stress upon multiyear planning in PPBS permits government to operate beyond the traditional one-year time perspective.

Faced with a decreasing tax base on the one hand and increasing demands for services on the other, government can no longer resist some type of systematic approach of problems of budgetary choice. Since this situation does not seem to be improving, the need is immediate.

Notes

[1] *Public Administration Review* 27 (March 1967): 67.

[2] Arthur Smithies, "Conceptual Framework for the Program Budget," in David Novick (ed.), *Program Budgeting*, 2d ed. (New York: Holt, Rinehart & Winston, 1969), p. 24.

[3] "Planning-Programming-Budgeting," Bulletin 68-2, Executive Office of the President, Bureau of the Budget, July 18, 1967, p. 1.

[4] Charles J. Zwick, "Commentary on Recent Developments in the Planning, Programming, and Budgeting System," in "Planning-Programming-Budgeting: *Budget Bureau Guidelines of 1968,*" Hearings before the Subcommittee on National Security and International Operations, Committee on Government Operations, Senate, 90th Cong., 2d sess. 1968. *Planning, Programming, and Budgeting* (Washington, D.C.: U.S. Government Printing Office, 1970), p. 557.

[5] Allen Schick, "The Road to PPB: The Stages of Budget Reform," *Public Administration Review*, 26 (December 1966): 243–58; reprinted in Robert T. Golembiewski (ed.), *Public Budgeting and Finance* 1st ed. (Itasca, Ill.: F. E. Peacock Publishers, 1968), p. 542.

[6] Hearings before the Subcommittee on National Security and International Operation, Committee on Government Operations, U.S. Senate, 90th Cong. 1st sess. August 23, 1967, *Planning, Programming, and Budgeting*, p. 172.

[7] "Planning-Programming-Budgeting," Bulletin 66-3, Executive Office of the President, Bureau of the Budget, October 12, 1965, p. 1.

[8] Thomas C. Schelling, "PPBS and Foreign Affairs," memorandum prepared at the request of the Subcommittee on National Security and International Operations, Committee on Government Operations, U.S. Senate, 90th Cong., 2d sess. *Planning, Programming and Budgeting*, p. 113.

[9] See Aaron Wildavsky, "The Political Economy of Efficiency: Cost-Benefit Analysis, Systems Analysis, and Program Budgeting," paper presented at conference on public policy, Social Science Research Council.

[10] For further information regarding the Incremental model of decision-making, see Charles E. Lindblom, "The Science of Muddling Through," *Public Administration Review*, 19 (Spring 1959): 79–88.

[11] Paul L. Brown, "Establishing a Program Structure," in Fremont J. Lyden and Ernest G. Miller (eds.), *Planning, Programming, Budgeting*, 2d ed. (Chicago: Markham Publishing Co., 1972), pp. 184–85.

[12] Roland N. McKean, "Criteria of Efficiency in Government Expenditures," in Robert T. Golembiewski (ed.), *Public Budgeting and Finance* 1st ed. (Itasca, Ill.: F. E. Peacock Publishers, 1968), p. 517.

[13] Ibid.

[14] "Planning-Programming-Budgeting," B O B Bulletin 66-3 p. 5.

[15] "Planning-Programming-Budgeting," Bulletin 68-9, Executive Office of the President, Bureau of the Budget, April 12, 1968, p. 542.

[16] Ibid.

[17] Ibid.

[18] "Planning-Programming-Budgeting," B O B Bulletin 66-3.

[19] Klaus Knorr, "On the Cost-Effectiveness Approach to Military Research and Development," *Bulletin of the Atomic Scientist* 22 (November 1966). Reprinted in *Planning, Programming and Budgeting* (Washington, D.C.: U.S. Government Printing Office, 1970), p. 581.

[20] Ibid.

[21] Allen Schick, *Budget Innovation in the States* (Washington, D.C.: The Brookings Institution, 1971), p. 117.

[22] Ibid., pp. 119–20.

²³Ibid., p. 120.
²⁴Ibid., p. 126.
²⁵Ibid., p. 128.
²⁶Selma J. Mushkin, "PPB in Cities," *Public Administration Review* 29 (March–April 1969); 171.

35

Uses and Abuses of Analysis

James R. Schlesinger

The Subcommittee's invitation to assess the role that analysis may play in governmental decisionmaking is gratifying for a number of reasons. In its current stocktaking, the Subcommittee is accomplishing something of a turnabout: the analysis of systems analysis. This evaluation takes place at a critical time. Like other offspring in American life, analysis has been absorbed into an environment which has been at once both too permissive and too resentful. There is ample evidence that such a pattern is beneficial to neither the offspring nor the environment. Currently there is a risk that reactions against what may be termed the exuberance of certain claims and activities of analysis could result in the discarding of the substantial benefits that analysis does offer. I shall be attempting to bring out the instances of undue gullibility as well as undue skepticism, but in so doing I should perhaps make my own position clear. My attitude has long been one of two-and-a-half cheers for systems analysis. I recognize—and have emphasized—its limitations. I will make no excuses for offenses committed in its name. But despite the limitations and distortions, I remain an unabashed, if qualified, defender of the value of analysis in policy formation.

In the pages that follow I shall deal with some salient issues regarding the role of analysis: its relation to decisions and decisionmakers, its functioning in a political environment where conflicting objectives exist, and its utility for improving the resource allocation process.

Reprinted from U.S., Congress, Senate, Committee on Government Operations, *Planning-Programming-Budgeting,* 80th Cong., 2nd sess. (Washington, D.C.: U.S. Government Printing Office, 1968), pp. 125–36.

THE AUTHORITY OF ANALYSIS

Systems analysis has been variously defined. In the most ambitious formulation it has been described as "the application of scientific method, using that term in its broadest sense." Certain attributes of science—objectivity, openness, self-correctability, verifiability, etc.—are alleged to apply to systems analysis. Would that it were so, but realistically speaking such assertions must be rejected. Even for science—as those who are familiar with the history of scientific investigations will recognize—this represents a rather romanticized view. In science, however, competition takes the form of establishing hypotheses regarding the workings of the natural order. Evidence and experiments are reproducible, and institutions and personalities consequently play a smaller long-run role. In scientific investigations the search for truth is by and large unfettered. By contrast, in the search for preferred policies such encumbrances as social values and goals, constraints, institutional requirements (both broad and narrow) pertain. Truth becomes only one of a number of conflicting objectives and, sad to relate, oftentimes a secondary one.

An alternative definition described systems analysis as "quantified common sense." By some expositors this definition has been treated as the equivalent of the earlier one, but is really quite distinct. However high the regard in which common sense, quantitative or otherwise, is held in the American community, it never has been regarded as synonymous with scientific method. Nonetheless, the definition is far more apt. Common sense, for example, will accept that within a complicated bureaucratic structure distortions inevitably creep into the process of acquiring and organizing evidence. What one sees depends upon where one sits—an earthy way of describing what is more elegantly referred to as cognitive limits. It may be inferred that a systems analysis shop attached to the Office of the Secretary of Defense will be quite responsive to the perceptions and prejudices of the Secretary and the institutional requirements of his Office. This should be no more surprising than that the Operations Analysis shop at Omaha will be influenced by the doctrine, present activities, and aspirations of the Strategic Air Command.

In the early years of the introduction of the PPB into the Department of Defense, faith in the ease with which scientific objectivity could be attained tended to be high in OSD. For Service staffs, this was a rather painful period, for rather invidious distinctions were drawn regarding *their* objectivity. In recent years an enormous change has taken place regarding the nature of the analytical dialogue. Undoubtedly this new attitude reflects experience and the growing awareness that past decisions and past commitments limit the openness and the freshness with which the OSD staff can address issues in controversy.

This new realism has been reflected in a number of ways. Especially in private appraisals, analysis has been justified with increasing frequency and frankness as part of an adversary proceeding. But such an interpretation is symptomatic of a substantial change. Whatever the merits of an adversary procedure—and these are substantial where there exist clashes of interests and goals and where evidence is difficult to unearth—no one has ever suggested that adversaries seek to be wholly objective. One may hope that the result will be the elucidation of the best possible case for and the best possible case against. But, unfortunately, the emphasis tends to shift to a search for the winning argument as opposed to the correct conclusion. In view of the uneven distribution of debating skills, one cannot fail to have qualms about the probable outcomes. One senior official has observed, only half facetiously, that experience in debate is the most valuable training for analytical work.

Acceptance of the tug-of-war concept, as opposed to the objective-scholar concept, of analysis has coincided with recognition of an even greater limitation on analysis as a guide to policymaking. In recent years it has been recognized in public statements (as well as the textbooks) that analysis is not a scientific procedure for reaching decisions which avoid intuitive elements, but rather a mechanism for sharpening the intuitions of the decisionmaker. Once again this is right. No matter how large a contribution that analysis makes, the role of the subjective preferences of the decision-maker remains imposing. Analysis is, in the end, a method of investigating rather than solving problems. The highest strategic objectives, the statement of preferences or utility, must in large part be imposed from outside. Poor or haphazard analysis may contribute to poor decisions, but good analysis by itself cannot insure correct decisions. This implies two things. First, whatever the complex of decisions, legitimate differences of opinion will persist. Second, disagreement with the decisions should not automatically cast doubt on either the role of analysis in general or on the quality of specific analyses. These must be examined in and of themselves.

To be sure, the judgment of the decisionmakers regarding major objectives and what is or is not important is likely to feed back and influence the analysis. This is not always true, but there are strong pressures to make it come true. Studies are driven by the underlying assumptions, and these may be imposed directly or indirectly from above. Specific terms of reference may indicate which scenarios are acceptable, which unacceptable, and which contingencies should or should not be considered. It is perfectly appropriate, if not obligatory, for the analyst to point out deficiencies in study assumptions or terms of reference. Yet, many will lack the perception or the inclination, while others would regard such action as personally imprudent. In these cases the analysis will only play back to the decision-maker a more sharply defined version of what was already implicit in his assumptions. The role of analysis then becomes not so much to *sharpen* the intuitions of the decisionmaker as to *confirm* them.

Under these circumstances analysis is not being used in its most fruitful form, that of raising questions. But analysis is a tool that can be used in a variety of ways. Much depends upon how the decisionmaker decides to employ it. Considerable fear has been expressed that analysis will usurp the decisionmaking role, that the decisionmaker will become passive, and let analysis (implicitly) make the decisions. This is possible; it is also improper. But whether the decisionmaker will control the tool rather than letting it run away with him strikes me as a less important question than whether he will employ it properly in another sense. Will the decisionmaker tolerate analysis—even when it is his own hobby horses which are under scrutiny?

How many hobby horses are there?

Are they off limits to the analysts?

Dr. Enthoven has quite properly objected to the canard that analysis is somehow responsible for what are regarded as the mishaps of the TFX decisions, pointing out that the new procedures were only tangentially involved. A more penetrating question, it seems to me, is: why did the analysts steer away from the issue?

A slightly different issue arises in the case of Vietnam. Numerous blunders are alleged to be chargeable to analytic errors. But analysis has been employed in the Vietnamese context in only the most cursory fashion. In this context neither the high-level civilian or the military authorities have been eager to exploit the full potentials of analysis. Once again, rather than blaming analytic efforts for the failures, the appropriate question should be: why has analysis been so little employed?

An acquaintance, who has been deeply involved in analytic activities in one of the Departments, recently commented to me on his experiences. Analysis he felt had been relevant in only a small proportion of the decisions. Half the time a decision had been foreclosed by high-level political involvement: a call from the White House, interest expressed by key Congressmen or Committees. In an additional 30 percent of the cases, the careers of immediate supervisors were involved. Analysis could not influence the recommendations; it could serve only as an irritant. But, he argued, in something like 20 percent of the issues, analysis was unfettered and contributed to much improved overall results. This was only the experience of one individual. In other cases the proportions might be quite different. The point is that analysis should be judged on the basis of the only minority of cases in which its influence is in some sense instrumental. Analysis is a useful tool, but it is only a tool. It would be a mistake to turn over a new proverbial leaf—and generally find fault with tools rather than craftsmen.

PRACTITIONERS VERSUS INSTRUMENTS

Accepting that analysis only sharpens the intuitions of decisionmakers, that its powers may be curtailed by unquestioned (or question-begging) assumptions or by imposed terms of reference, and that it is increasingly viewed as a contest between adversaries permits us to be more realistic about analysis in a number of ways. The inflated claims, periodically made in its behalf, may be rejected—along with the misplaced criticisms made in response. Questioning of decisions is turned into questioning of decision-makers' judgments rather than the role of analysis. And analysis itself can be employed more effectively in clarifying the underpinnings of policies, thereby creating the potential for designing more effective ones. We should understand that analysis provides no formula for solving problems, no prescription for sensible policies. It cannot and should not be employed to "demonstrate" that one's own policies are so right and those of others, so wrong.

What analysis provides is an exercise in logical coherence, hopefully with knowledge of and respect for the underlying technical, economic, and organizational data. Coherence does not insure the "correctness" of policy. In fact, an incoherent policy will sometimes be closer to correct than a coherent one. But the incoherence itself scarcely makes a contribution. It is almost invariably a source of waste, and typically of policy muddles.

Analysis may make a contribution, but we should be very clear what it cannot do. It does not provide an instant cure for pigheadedness. In fact, it does not provide an instant cure for anything—not because of its theoretical deficiencies, but because it has to be employed by people and by organizations with divergent goals and views and with stringently limited information about actual conditions.

It is a mistake to identify analysis with the particular judgments, prejudices or arguable decisions of some of its major proponents. Especially is this so when analysis has been employed as a weapon of political conflict. The political process being what it is, it is hardly advisable to admit error in public; that would prove too costly. Human emotions being what they are, it is also unlikely that error will be admitted in private. This does not gainsay the value of analysis before policy commitments are made—or when they are being seriously reconsidered. What it does say is that we should avoid tying analysis to the personal proclivities of the particular individuals who were instrumental in introducing it into government. To do so may be flattering to the individuals. Some may even be inclined to treat their own attitudes and commitments as synonymous with analysis. It would be a serious error for others to accept this view. Disciplined, orderly thought is the characterization given to analysis, but disciplined, orderly thought suggests certain traits: reflectiveness, self-criticism, and the willingness to reconsider past commitments without self-justification. However rarely or frequently encountered in the general human population, these are not traits characteristic of the action-oriented, incisive individuals who reach policymaking positions. Questioning and self-doubt lead to Hamletlike decisionmakers.

Analysts themselves may be self-doubting, bemused by uncertainties, frighteningly candid, but different tactics have been required of the missionaries who have proselytized in behalf of analysis. I do not need to develop this point at any length. It should be plain, for example, that the actual decision to introduce analysis on a government-wide basis (as previously within the DOD) required an act of judgment and courage passing beyond the confines of analysis. Some analysts found the manner in which analytical procedures were instituted disquieting. This no doubt reflects a certain naivete on their part regarding political processes. But analysis was introduced rather suddenly. There was little advance preparation, little attempt to assess resource availability or calculate short-run costs. There was no "program definition phase." What occurred was that the political conditions were ripe,* and the opportunity was seized—for analysis.

I have perhaps belabored the distinction between analysis and judgment and the fact that the act of deciding occurs in the nonanalytical phase. These matters need to be emphasized right now. It is important that analytical procedures in the DOD or elsewhere *not* be identified with particular sets of policies, decisions, or individuals. If analysis comes to be confused with the idiosyncracies of a few dominant personalities, there is some risk that it will disappear along with its original proponents. Its potential benefits for U.S. policy would then be lost for some time to come.

Admittedly there have been overstated claims, planted stories, and an impression generated among the *cognoscenti* of a new, scientific means for grinding out decisions. Admittedly the limitations appeared in the footnotes and not in the fanfare. But these are just the accoutrements of attention-getting. Analysis itself should scarcely be discarded on these grounds. Even if some decisionmakers or analysts have failed to display the mental elasticity that analysis in principle demands, this is only a reflection of the human condition. Why throw the baby out with the bathwater?

PAYOFFS

What is the baby? I seem to have devoted most of my attention to the reasons for refraining from that last half cheer for analysis, and virtually no attention to the reasons for the two and one-half cheers. In part this is

---

*This episode suggests why the politician in his role may find analysis both incomplete and frustrating. Analysis deals in a rather abstract way with resource usage and efficient allocations. It does not deal with the attitudinal issues of support-generation, coalition-gathering or with timing which are so important in the political context.

due to the excellent set of papers and comments that the Subcommittee has published. Therein the potential benefits of program budgeting and analysis are fully presented. Lengthy reiterations of either the potential advantages or the accomplishments seem unnecessary. However, there are some points on which I should like to add a few words.

First, analysis has great value in turning debates over resource allocation toward the realities and away from simple statements of noble purpose. Analysis is not scientific method. Neither will it necessarily be objective in an organizational context. Yet, within the adversary relationship, analysis at least focuses the debate on what particular systems can accomplish and what numbers are required. The emphasis is on the real rather than the symbolic function of weapon systems. Disappointed as many in the Services have been with major policy decisions of the OSD, I believe most knowledgeable officers would agree that the new methods have been beneficial in this respect.

Second and closely related, analysis is oriented toward outputs rather than toward inputs. In this way expenditures can be tied to specific goals, and those expenditures which satisfy primarily the traditions or well-being of individual agencies are brought into question. There are difficulties with goal or output orientation, particularly since we so frequently lack complete understanding of the mechanism that ties inputs to outputs. But the orientation is correct. The government structure is subdivided into agencies that typically concentrate on inputs. Dams, warships, trees, post offices, bombers, nuclear power, supersonic transportation, and, I may add, research expenditures are often treated as ends in themselves—with little examination as to how these instruments serve public purposes. Conscious output orientation, with as much quantitative backup as possible, points in the right direction. It forces agencies to shift attention from their beloved instruments and to explain the goals they serve rather than the functions they perform—and this at a level more practical than the usual rhetoric of noble purpose.

Third, the attempt is made to design systems or policies with practical budgetary limits in mind. The time-honored gap between the planners and the budgeteers has been widely discussed, along with the difficulties it causes. There is little point in plans too costly to be implemented or systems too expensive to be bought in the requisite quantity—if some reduction in quality will provide a feasible and serviceable, if less ideal, posture. (Here we are discussing capabilities and postures which would be effective, if bought—keeping in mind that so many expensive proposals serve little purpose at all.)

Fourth, an attempt is made to take spillovers into account and to achieve better integration between the several Services and Commands. Once again, this is more easily said than done. For example, we are belatedly becoming aware of the spillovers and the integration problems between the strategic offensive force under Air Force management and the new Sentinel system under Army control. This indicates that the attempt to take spillovers into account has not been overwhelmingly successful, but the goal is a correct one. The nation would not wish to duplicate SAC's capabilities for SACEUR or the Polaris force for CINCSAC.

Fifth, the attempt is made to take into account the long-run cost implications of decisions. Perhaps, it is more appropriate to say ... the attempt *should* be made. There has been a certain inconsistency on this account. The costs of some systems have been carefully investigated, before a choice is made. For other (preferred) systems this has not been the case. The Program Definition Phase was originally introduced to insure that technology was in hand and the long-run costs considered before force structure decisions were made. Yet, curiously, in the programmed forces for the '70s our strategic forces are scheduled to become increasingly dependent on MIRVed vehicles, even though the technology is not yet in hand and we have only an inkling of the ultimate costs. The appropriate review of alternatives and hedges did not take place. But this represents, not a criticism of the objective, but a plea for more consistency in its pursuit. It hardly negates the desirability of the careful weighing of alternatives with the long-run cost implications taken into account.

These attributes and precepts of analysis seem unexceptionable.

They are.

An appropriate inference is that many of the complaints couched in terms of "too much analysis" or "the errors of analysis" should be altered into "better and more consistent analysis." In this connection, an editor and friend recently suggested a paper on the impact of systems analysis: "not the general appraisals, we've had enough of that; tell us whether systems analysis has every really been employed in the Department of Defense." An exaggeration perhaps, but as the MIRVing case suggests, analytic techniques have not been consistently applied.

Bernard Shaw observed somewhere that the only trouble with Christianity was that it had never really been tried. An epigram is at best a half truth, designed as someone has commented to irritate anyone who believes the other half. In DOD systems analysis has at least been tried. But there is an element in Shaw's remark that needs to be taken into account. In assessing the success of analysis, both the incomplete implementation and the resistance should be kept in mind.

BUDGETS

Military posture is determined in large measure by the total volume of resources the society is willing to divert from non-defense to defense uses. Yet, understanding the determinants of this resource flow presents a most perplexing problem. No good mechanism or rationale exists for deciding what diversion is proper. Some analysts have shied away from the problem arguing that the main objective should be the efficient employment of whatever resources are provided. A limited feel for appropriate diversion may be obtained by asking such questions as how much more is needed for defense than is needed for other purposes. In principle, senior policymakers may find it no harder to decide on allocation between damage limiting and urban renewal than between damage limiting and assured destruction. They will certainly find it no easier. For a number of practical reasons, they may find it far harder actually to bring about such a resource shift.

The amorphousness of this decision area combined with the repudiation of what were regarded as the rigidities of the Eisenhower years led to some bold words in 1961: there would be no *arbitrary* budget limits; in addition, every proposal would be examined on its own merits. These guidelines have since been regularly reasserted—with perhaps somewhat falling conviction. Originally they might be attributed to sheer enthusiasm; now they can only be taken as either propaganda or self-deception.

However, no matter the source, they will not stand up to *analysis.*

At any time there exists a rough political limit on defense expenditures. For members of this Subcommittee—in fact for any practicing politician—such an assertion will seem like a truism. Something like a consensus develops regarding proper levels of defense expenditures—and in the absence of external shocks this sum will not be substantially augmented. Of course, the *arbitrary* limit is always the *other fellow's.* One's own limit is only proximate and is wholly reasonable. Yet, defense expenditures do tend to become stabilized for years within rather narrow limits. Inevitably, new pressure for funds leads to the sacrifice of programs previously desirable on their own merits. That is as simple as arithmetic.

The only time that budget limits are not pressing (and more or less arbitrary) is when, as during the early Kennedy years, a political decision has been made that much more can be spent on defense. After a brief period of exuberance, the old constraints reappear. The decision does not have to be announced by the President or the Budget Bureau. The Secretary of Defense may get a feel for what is feasible, or he may be trusted to bring in a reasonable figure. But within a rather narrow range he will face a limit, which he may not transcend without either creating a minor fiscal crisis or straining his own credit with the President of the United States.

Save in the rare periods of budgetary relaxation, this, rightly or wrongly, is the way the system works. There is no point in kidding oneself. One may erect a facade intended to demonstrate that there are no arbitrary budget limits and each proposal is examined on its own merits. The pretense can be partially successful, but only because the criteria for choice are so imprecise. Standards can be made increasingly stringent, yet no one can prove how large was the role of budgetary pressures.

Nonetheless, no one should be deceived. What happens is that various alternatives and hedges are discarded; programs become less pressing and are stretched out. The practices are well-known from the bad, old meat-axe days. Under budgetary pressure (arbitrary or not) it is truly remarkable how many options one discovers one can do without. Multiple options just become less multiple. Before uncertainties are resolved, commitments are made and hedge programs are terminated. In the well-advertised adversary relationship, the negotiator-analysts become much harder to persuade. If they are not directly instructed, *they know.*

These are not hypothetical possibilities. With the intensification of budgetary pressures stemming from the Vietnamese war, there has, for example, been a wholesale slaughter of programs in the strategic area. It is important not to be misled regarding the critical role of budgetary pressures —and thus come to believe that so many programs, previously regarded as meritworthy, have suddenly lost their merit. Otherwise, we might gradually come to believe that we are doing far better than is actually the case. One should remain aware that the decimation of a program has long-run postural implications. That is, after all, the message that PPB attempts to convey.

These are elementary propositions. I do not dwell on certain theoretical problems and inconsistencies bearing on the relationship of overall defense spending to the optimality of programs. Suffice it to say that the *quality* of what one buys depends upon how much one wants to spend. This connection between level of demand and cost/effectiveness creates a dilemma in that *neither* the character of the programs nor the size of the budget can be determined initially. But that is a theoretical nicety, the direct consequences of which may not be of major importance.

The vital point is the way in which budgetary limits may control force posture and therefore strategy. Shifting sands seems the best way to characterize the strategic rationales of recent years. In 1961 the suicidal implications of massive retaliation were underscored: the United States would be faced with a choice between humiliation or holocaust. Interest then developed in damage-limiting and coercion. But there has been little willingness to invest money in either. Since 1965 the merits of Assured Destruction have been emphasized—with little attention paid to the suicidal implications found so distressing in prior years. The principal rationale for the current emphasis on Assured Destruction reflects certain recently-developed notions of arms control. It clearly falls within the province of the decisionmakers to adopt a strategy of measured response to any Soviet buildup with the long-term objective of preserving U.S. Assured Destruction capabilities. One should note, however, that to accept this particular guide to action implies that the buildup of the Minuteman force in 1961–62 was a mistake. These newer arms control criteria may be the preferred ones, but they rest on the judgments and intuitions of the decision-makers. They certainly do not emerge by themselves from analysis.

May one infer that the oscillations in strategy have something to do with budget limits, or in this case something more specific: a preconception regarding how much this nation should spend on the strategic forces? I find the conclusion irresistible. The evidence antedates the current phase-down in the face of the Soviet buildup. Once again, these lie within the decision-maker's prerogatives, but particular beliefs regarding budget limits or the "adequacy" of specific strategies should not be attributed to, much less blamed on, analysis.

A USEFUL IF OVERSOLD TOOL

Whatever resources are made available to defense (or any other mission), choices will have to be made.

Allocative decisions inevitably are painful; many claimants will be sorely disappointed.

Few will find fault with their own proposals, almost all with the machinery for selection.

Any procedures for allocation will be criticized—even in a hypothetical case in which the conceptual basis is unarguable and no errors are made. Analysis provides the backup for a selective process. What does it contribute? How does it compare with real-world alternatives—not with mythical alternatives in which all claimants get their requests and no one is disappointed?

It has been emphasized that analysis cannot determine the appropriate strategy. It can shed light on costs and tradeoffs. But the choice to press arms control or arms competition or to rely on tactical nuclears or nuclear firebreaks must be determined by the decisionmaker sustained primarily by hope, conviction, and prayer. Even if a decision could be demonstrated as correct at a given moment in time, there is the certainty that objectives will change over time. For these higher level problems analysis is an aid, but a limited aid. The toughest problems, dominated as they are by uncertainties and by differences in goals, do not yield to analysis.

Happily many problems are more mundane and more tractable. Where analysis has proved its highest value is in uncovering cases of gross waste: points at which substantial expenditures may contribute little to any stated objective. It might be thought that a problem of diminishing returns exists for analysis in that the cases of gross misuse of resources are likely to be uncovered at an early stage. Thus, as the opportunity for major savings through elimination of irrational forms of waste theoretically recedes, analysis would be forced into the more ambiguous areas in which strategic choices become intimately involved. In some cases, where information is readily available and objectives and conditions relatively unchanging, this could prove to be true. The very success of analysis would then undermine near-term expectations of additional returns. However, in defense this turns out to be irrelevant, since the problems are so volatile and information so difficult to unearth.

To say that analysis works best in cases of gross waste should not be taken to imply that analysis accomplishes little. The simple cases involving so-called dominant solutions may involve billions of dollars. The volume of government resources that may be lavished on the care and feeding of white elephants is simply staggering.

Here we have "quantified common sense" in its most direct form. In bureaucracies, units at all levels are concerned with organizational health. Rather than making the hard choices, the tendency is strong to maintain morale by paying off all parties. Analysis provides a means for coping with this problem. The big issues may not be directly involved, though they are likely to be dragged in by the proponents of particular programs.

Should the assessment of analysis be much influenced by the annoyance felt by those whose proposals have failed the tests? Certainly not in the general case. No more than should the decisionmakers be permitted to hide their judgments behind the camouflage of analysis, should the patrons of doubtful proposals be encouraged to argue that acceptance would and should have come—if *only* analysis had not been employed. Budgets are limited and hard choices must be made. If nobody were annoyed analysis would not be doing its job—of questioning both routinized practices and blue-sky propositions. Disappointment is unavoidable. The question is not the existence of annoyance, but to strive to annoy in the right way and for the right reasons.

In this light it may be desirable to examine the issue of the generalist versus the specialist which has been touched upon in the Hearings. In the nature of things specialists become committed to particulars: a piece of hardware, a technological criterion, a disciplinary blind spot. It is a case of suboptimization run wild. Proponents of specific capabilities or gadgets tend to become monomaniacs. In a sense that is the way they should be: totally dedicated to their tasks. But one does not turn to them for detached judgments. There is no substitute for the *informed* generalist. There is a recognizable risk that the superficiality of the generalist may match the monomania of the specialist. However, that need not be the case. Although the generalist's knowledge cannot match that of the specialist in detail, analysis can once again play a useful role, by permitting the organization for the generalist of more specialized information than he alone could master.

How does this relate to the limits of the analyst's role? Two distinctions should be kept in mind: that between the technical specialist and the analytical generalist and that between the analyst and the decisionmaker. The analyst's tools are not circumscribed by discipline or even by subject matter. But general tools are not immediately convertible into broad policies. Many analysts are, in some sense, specialists in the use of general tools. Being a good analytical generalist does not necessarily imply possession of such additional qualities as breadth, judgment, and political attunement. These latter qualities are what many have in mind when they speak of the generalist as policymaker.

CONCLUSION

In closing I should like to underscore three points.

First, the position of the decisionmaker employing analysis is somewhat ambiguous. For tactical purposes this ambiguity may be deliberately augmented. Intermittently he may choose to stress *analysis* or *judgment,* and to shift hats according to the tactical requirements of the moment. His policy judgments may be obscured or defended by cryptic references to detailed analyses which allegedly force the policy conclusions. On the other hand, if any limitations or inadequacies in the analyses should come to light, these can be waved away with the reminder that all issues are ultimately matters for the decisionmaker's judgment.

Moreover, the pattern is in reality far more complicated than the standard exposition in which the analyst produces an *objective* study, and the decisionmaker's judgment enters at a later stage erected on the foundation of these objective results. That makes the analytical and judgmental stages seem clean-cut. Few studies are that pure. The decisionmaker's judgments quite typically are dumped in at an early stage in the form of guidance, assumptions, and terms of reference. The more political a study, the less likely is it to be pure. In fact, the process can be (and has been) far more corrupted, when questionable (phony) numbers are introduced. Since judgment and analysis are thoroughly intertwined in all but a few studies, the attempt of decisionmakers to shift roles by referring to fundamental analyses should be treated with some skepticism. The decisionmaker should not be permitted to escape the full burden of responsibility by the invocation of analysis.

The temptation for those who have introduced analytical techniques into the government to treat their own positions or careers as identical with analysis is understandable. No outsider should yield to the same temptation. The roles and even the temperaments of decisionmaker and analyst are quite distinct. The confusion tends to disguise the heavy personal burden borne by the decisionmaker. More important, if analysis is treated as synonymous with particular decisions or personalities, there is a risk that it will be throttled or abandoned after their departure. From the standpoint of public policy this would be a major loss.

Second, we should avoid the erroneous belief that the performance or potential power of analysis will be uniform in all contexts. If a town is considering building a bridge, a number of difficult analytical problems must be addressed: does demand warrant construction, where should the bridge be built, what should be its capacity, and so on. But once these questions are resolved the engineer falls back on a solid technical base. By contrast, for such goals as deterrence, assured destruction, controlled nuclear warfare, damage limiting, to say nothing of welfare benefits, we fall back, not on a firm technical base, but on what may be scientific mush. The distinction is not always appreciated. The difficulty is sometimes dealt with by referring euphemistically to *the model problem.* But our ability to formulate models depends upon our knowledge of the mechanics of the real world. For many problems our knowledge is meager, and the proffered models are misleading or downright erroneous. The lack of good models in many problem areas simultaneously limits the power of analysis, while increasing the burden placed on judgment. In treating analysis as a uniformly efficient problem-solving technique, the variability of analysis, which reflects the variability of the knowledge base, is ignored.

Though analysis is a powerful tool, specific analyses vary greatly in quality. Some are little more than trash. But we need to discriminate, rather than to reject analysis *in toto.* At the present time there is some risk that we will do the latter. In an address some years ago Secretary Enthoven observed: "My general impression is that the art of systems analysis is in about the same stage now as medicine during the latter half of the 19th century; that is, it has just reached the point at which it can do more good than harm." That was a frank and realistic, if somewhat pessimistic, assessment of the state of the *art.* Scientifically speaking, there are numerous blind spots in medicine. Yet, most of us ultimately are inclined to accept the doctor's diagnosis, if not his advice. Quite plainly at the present time Congress and the public are having second thoughts regarding how much trust to put in systems analysis. No doubt it is necessary to develop a greater ability to discriminate. Nonetheless, I suggest that policy will benefit substantially from the analysts' diagnoses.

Third, there is little doubt that analysis has been oversold. That strikes me as a rather standard result in matters political. But the reaction against the overselling could be more costly than the overselling itself. Analysis is a powerful instrument: with it our batting average has been far higher than without it. Analysis is also an adaptable instrument. The McNamara regime has in many respects been a highly personalized one. Its performance should not be taken as defining the limits of this flexible tool. Admittedly, analyses vary substantially in quality. Each should be taken with a large grain of salt. On the other hand, if one does not demand too much of it, analysis will prove to be a most serviceable instrument.

36

Policy Analysis: A Theoretic Framework and Some Basic Concepts

Yehezkel Dror

PREFACE

1. This paper is a preliminary attempt to appreciate the meanings and significance of policy analysis. Policy analysis will be presented within a broad theoretic framework, some basic concepts of policy analysis will be explored, and a few main implications of the development of policy analysis for political science and for politics will be indicated.

.   .   .   .   .

BACKGROUND

3. Policy sciences are the academic context of policy analysis. First proposed in 1951 by Harold D. Lasswell[1] and diligently espoused by him since,[2] no real progress in the development of policy sciences can be noted till the last few years. Only recently there seems to be an upsurge of interest in policy sciences—with or without the use of that term. This increasing interest is demonstrated, for instance, by: (a) establishment of new university programs in policy sciences; (b) publication of an increasing number of books in policy sciences; (c) a growing number of panels, symposia, and similar activities at various professional meetings, devoted in effect to policy sciences; and (d) establishment of a new professional periodical, called *Policy Sciences: Policy Analysis, Systems Approaches, and Decisionmaking,* with Dr. Edward Quade as Editor-in-Chief, published by American Elsevier starting in 1970.

4. Closely related to the upsurge of activities on applied social science and in futuristics, the new interest in policy sciences can, in part, be ex-

Prepared for delivery at the Sixty-Fifth Annual Meeting of The American Political Science Association, Commodore Hotel, New York City, September 2–6, 1969. This selection includes only pp. 1–15 of the paper.

The idea of policy analysis is further developed in Yehezkel Dror, *Design for Policy Sciences* and *Ventures in Policy Sciences* (New York: American Elsevier Publishing Co., 1971).

plained in the United States by the following variables: (a) increasing concern about concrete policy issues, such as race relations, Vietnam, and pollution; (b) intense pressures by students for more "relevant" teaching; (c) a desire to keep up with physical sciences to meet questions of the "They brought mankind to the moon. What can social sciences do?" type; and (d) accelerating confrontation with competitive pressures and cooperation demands by the fast entrance of defense-experience based systems analysis methods and organizations into the areas of social problems.

5. Despite these pressures and efforts, policy sciences are not only far from being operational, but cannot even be regarded as launched on their way. I think it is fair to say that at present the most promising approaches to social problems are related to systems analysis, which is based on normative economics, engineering, and decision theory—with no contribution whatsoever from the behavioral sciences, including political science.

6. If systems analysis were indeed a useful approach to social problems, this would be too bad for the behavioral sciences, but it would not matter from a broader social point of view. The trouble is that systems analysis in its present state-of-the-art—while being the most useful available approach —is still quite helpless in facing complex social issues. In particular, systems analysis is inadequate for treating complex social issues in eight main interdependent respects:

a. Systems analysis focuses on proposing preferable policies, neglecting the institutional contexts, both of the problems and of the policymaking and policy-implementation processes. Thus, "institution-building" is not within its domain of applicability.

b. Systems analysis does not take into account political needs, such as consensus maintaining and coalition building.

c. Systems analysis has difficulties in dealing with "irrational" phenomena, such as ideologies, charisma, high-risk commitments, martyr tendencies, and unconventional styles of life.

d. Systems analysis is unable to deal with basic value issues and often inadequately explicates the value assumptions of analysis.

e. Systems analysis deals with identifying preferable alternatives among available or easily synthesized areas. Invention of radically new alternatives is beyond its scope, though it can help by showing the inadequacy of available alternatives.

f. Systems analysis requires some predictability in respect to alternatives. Situations of fargoing qualitative uncertainty (when not only the probabilities of various outcomes, but the dimensions of the possible outcomes are unknown) cannot be handled by systems analysis.

g. Systems analysis requires significant quantification of main relevant variables.

h. Basic strategy choices—such as attitudes to risk and time—are not explicitly faced by systems analysis. Rather, maximin and discount of the future ("positive interest rates") are usually assumed.

7. These eight characteristics are not equally shared by all systems analysis studies. Indeed, the main pioneers of systems analysis will clearly label such characteristics as inadequate and diligently search for ways to overcome them. But if we look on available systems analysis studies of real issues rather than at professions of faith or introductory statements, then my list of inadequacies of present systems analysis may justly be criticized as overmild. It is these serious inadequacies of systems analysis combined with the even more fatal inadequacies in other available approaches to applications of knowledge and rationality to complex social issues which justify intense efforts to build up policy sciences, including policy analysis.

THEORETICAL FRAMEWORK

8. The main features of policy sciences, as shared by policy analysis, can be defined as follows:[3]

a. Policy sciences are an interdiscipline, focusing on public policymaking.
b. Policy sciences are based on behavioral sciences and analytical approaches, relying also on decision theory, general systems theory, management sciences, and similar modern areas of study.
c. Fusing pure and applied research, policy sciences are mainly concerned with improving policymaking on the basis of systematic knowledge and structural rationality.
d. Policy sciences, as all applied scientific knowledge, are in principle instrumental-normative, in the sense of being concerned with means and intermediate goals, rather than absolute values. But policy sciences are sensitive to the difficulties of achieving "value free sciences" and try to contribute to value choice by exploring value implications, value consistencies, value costs, and the behavioral foundations of value commitments.
e. Policy sciences emphasize meta-policies (i.e., policies on policies), including policymaking modes, policy analysis, policymaking systems, and policy strategies. While the main test of policy sciences is better achievement of considered goals through more effective and efficient policies, policy sciences as such does not deal with discrete policy problems, but provides improved methods and knowledge for doing so.

9. Policy analysis belongs to policy sciences, but is only one—though a very important—component of policy sciences. Focusing on policy choices, policy analysis is, for instance, distinct from policymaking–system redesign and novadesign, from evaluation and learning feedback, and from behavioral study of policymaking—all of which are other essential components of policy sciences. Nevertheless, one of the distinguishing features of policy analysis, as compared with systems analysis, is its embedment in policy sciences—which provides an integrating interdiscipline permitting close interconnections between policy analysis and other components of policy sciences. Thus, policy analysis and policymaking–system redesign should closely interact: For instance policy analysis providing some need-specifications to be met by policymaking–system redesign and policy analysis itself is applicable to choice between different redesign alternatives, on one hand; policymaking–system redesign providing the institutional conditions for policy analysis on the other hand.

10. The basic theoretic design of policy analysis is based on applied decision theory and systems analysis. Systems analysis is often presented in literature in terms of methods, techniques, and tools.[4] This is natural because it is the tools and techniques which are tangible, explicated and easily communicable. But what is much more important is systems analysis as an approach, an orientation and even—to use an apt phrase by Sir Geoffrey Vickers[5]—a "frame of appreciation."

Reduced to its essentials, systems analysis is an effort to apply structured rationality to problems of choice. In particular, systems analysis in its pure form involves three main elements:

a. Looking at problems and alternatives in a broad way, which tries to take account of many of the relevant variables and of the probable results—that is, taking a "systems" view.[6]

b. Searching for an "optimal," or at least clearly preferable, solution among available alternatives, without being limited to incremental changes.

c. Explicit and rational identification of the preferable alternative (or alternatives) through comparison of expected results in terms of operational goals; this is done with the help of a large set of technicians, ranging from mathematical models to human gaming and from sensitivity testing to canvassing of experts' opinions.

11. To this basic framework of systems analysis, policy analysis adds the following components:

a. Penetration into underlying values, assumptions and strategies. These include, in particular, (1) exploration of the basic values at which policies should be directed, (2) long-range goal research, and (3) explicit analysis of alternative policy strategies (see sections 16 to 19 following).

b. Consideration of political variables, including (1) political feasibility analysis; (2) evaluation of alternative political pathways for policy approval and implementation; (3) examination of social power implications of alternative policies; and (4) analysis of coalition needs and political consensus implications.

c. Treatment of broader and more complex systems, involving (1) lower and new scales of quantification (e.g., nominal and nonmetric); (2) necessity to satisfy multidimensional and diverse goals; (3) fargoing qualitative uncertainty; (4) institutional change as a main mode of policy change; and (5) acceptance of minimin avoidances (that is, avoidance of the worst of all bad alternatives), sensitization, and long-range impacts as main goals of policy analysis, together with "preferization."

d. Main emphasis on policy alternative innovation, involving (1) intense attention to creativity encouragement; (2) much reliance on sequential decisionmaking, learning feedback and social experimentation, instead of "models," simulation and detailed policy schemes (such as PERT); and (3) much attention to systems novadesign (i.e., design anew), in addition to systems redesign.

e. Much behavioral science sophistication and inputs involving (1) recognition of "irrationality," ideologies, mass phenomena, depth variables and similar nonrational phenomena as main variables, both of social behavior and of legitimate goal formation; (2) changes in the development of analysis professionals and the disciplinary composition of analysis teams; and (3) rejecting of "hard science" as an exclusive yardstick for analysis and for analysis-relevant knowledge.

f. Institutional self-awareness, for instance in respect to (1) the necessity for multiplicity and redundance of analysis and analysis units; (2) early involvement of politicians, community leaders, etc., in the analytical activities; and (3) the limits of analysis as a perceptive set for cognizing human reality and aspirations.

12. This is a formidable list, however incomplete by itself. When we add the requirement for embedding policy analysis in policy sciences, the dangers of overutopianism in my approach become obvious. Coming from Israel, I accept the label "utopian" as more of a compliment than a condemnation. Nevertheless, let me try to hold the ambitions of policy sciences, and policy analysis, within "reasonable" limits by stating that 10 percent progress in the directions pinpointed above will have transincremental results for the capacities of policy analysis, and policy sciences as a whole, to contribute to better policymaking. Having reached this point, I also claim

that more than 10 percent progress in the proposed direction is possible, though intense efforts are needed to realize this potential. But before taking up some issues involved in actually developing policy analysis, let me try to concretize the proposed theoretic framework by discussing a few policy analysis concepts at somewhat greater length.

SOME POLICY ANALYSIS CONCEPTS

13. Building up policy analysis, on the lines indicated above, requires construction of a conceptual set—borrowing from other disciplines, adjusting from available knowledge, and by invention. The conceptual set should be much more than an economic taxonomy; it must express the main dimensions of policy analysis, its unique sensors for dealing with policy problems, and its main modes for developing preferable policy alternatives. The concepts serve also as the main anchor points for tools and methods —which serve to make the concepts operational. Thus, the concepts stand between the basic design, approaches, and methodologies of policy analysis on one hand and the technology of policy analysis on the other hand, with close feedbacks and intense interconnections: Progress in policy analysis technology stimulating changes in concept and even design; changes in design resulting in new concepts and search for new technologies; and changes in concepts requiring revision in design and transformation of technology. Simultaneously, policy analysis as a whole—including design, concepts and technology—interacts closely with policy sciences as a whole and with the environment, both as an independent and as a dependent variable. Furthermore, all the involved elements and variables are dynamic in themselves, for instance through invention and discovery advancing the state-of-knowledge of policy analysis.

14. Because of the multiple relevant change-factors and their dynamics, any set of policy analysis concepts is of limited stability and sure to need early revision. This is particularly true at present, with policy analysis being in its first phases of emergence and starting, hopefully, on a steep learning curve. Any effort to provide a "complete" and elaborate set of policy analysis concepts is therefore misplaced. But, in order to advance, some starting points must be put forth. As already indicated, these starting-point concepts—while provisional and tentative—are, in my opinion, sufficiently operative and innovative to demonstrate the feasibility of developing a high-capacity policy analysis knowledge. They even indicate the present availability of sufficient policy analysis knowledge to make a difference for the quality of policymaking—if that knowledge is put carefully, but with determination, to work.

15. For the limited purposes of this paper, I have selected five policy analysis concepts for a closer look: policy strategies, value sensitivity, opera-

tional code assumptions, political feasibility, and policy analysis network. [Note that the last three concepts are not considered in this excerpt.] This is only a small subset of the complete—and open—set of policy analysis concepts. Thus, other interesting concepts include, for instance: value explorations, alternative futures and goals, policy alternative research patterns, leverage envelopes (not points!), unexpected occurrence considerations, sign monitoring and recognition (including "social indicators"), systems delimitation, and many more. But the five selected policy analysis concepts should serve to concretize my view of policy analysis sufficiently to permit the reader to judge my approach and to make a decision on his own future commitment to the challenges of policy analysis, and policy sciences as a whole.

Policy Strategies

16. Policy strategies involve determination of the postures, assumptions and main guidelines to be followed by specific policies. They are a kind of "master policy," clearly distinct from detailed discrete policies, though these two pure types are on a continuum with many in-between cases. Belonging to the level of meta-policies, policy strategies are a main focus of interest of policy sciences. Explicit attention to policy strategies is a major characteristic of policy analysis, differentiating policy analysis from contemporary systems analysis. It is indeed quite amazing to note how neglected the problems of policy strategies are. Even the few authors who treat them explicitly—such as Charles E. Lindblom—do deal only with a narrow range of policy strategy choices and tend to be overinfluenced by one or another a priori ideology or the socio-economic-political conditions of a particular country and period.

17. There are a number of policy strategy dimensions, forming a multidimensional matrix with a large number of cells, presenting the different mathematical combinations of various strategy dimensions. Leaving aside the problems of calibration of the different dimensions—some of which are continuous and some of which have only a few points—there is the possibility of mixed strategies, in which in a given area of policy, different strategies can be followed in various policy instances. Whether to follow a "pure" strategy combination (a real cell of the multidimensional matrix) or whether to adopt a strategy mix (picking different cells according to a predetermined pattern, including as one possibility a random pattern) is itself a main strategy decision. There also are empty cells, because of logical contradiction, and nonfeasible cells, because of behavioral conflict. When we consider all this together, the picture becomes very complex, but not prohibitively so. We certainly can build up the main outlines of a strategy matrix, identify essential conditions for each strategy, and find out at least some criteria for preference of different strategy combinations under various conditions.[7]

18. Such a policy strategy matrix, in addition to its instrumental-normative uses, can also serve as a basic tool for behavioral study of policymaking. In fact, analyzing actual policies in terms of their implicit strategies can be an important instrumental-normative activity, because it can increase the self-awareness of policymakers and sensitize them to additional possibilities —and this by itself is a major contribution of policy analysis to the improvement of policymaking.

19. To conclude exploration of the concept of policy strategy, let me mention five main dimensions of policy strategies:

a. Identical-mixed. This dimension deals with the choice as to how far concrete policies should be identical in their strategy or follow mixed strategies. Concerning mixed strategies, various subdimensions of consistency patterns, redundance possibilities, pluralistic choice, and random selection provide rich choice which can be explicated and analyzed.

b. Incremental-innovative. This dimension deals with the choice between various degrees of policy-change (defined in terms of extent of change, scope of change, and time), ranging from small incremental change in few policy details over a long period to far-going, comprehensive, and rapid policy innovation.

c. High risk–low risk. This dimension involves the degree of risk to be accepted by policies. Here, the pure choices are between maximax on one hand and maximin or minimax on the other hand. Also involved are preferences between "average expected value," "lottery value," and similar choice principles between different forms of risk parameters. Another very important element of this strategy is the principles to be followed in comparing uncertainties.

d. Comprehensive-shock. This dimension involves the choice between comprehensive and "balanced" policies, which try to move multiple variables simultaneously in an internally consistent way, and shock policies, aimed at breakthroughs at main leverage points and/or systems disequilibration.

e. Sequential-extended. This dimension deals with the extent to which policies should adopt a sequential-decision strategy or work out in advance an extended strategy in the theory-of-games sense. (This choice should not be mixed up with the rigid-elastic dichotomy: An extended strategy can be very elastic and well adjusted to different contingencies—if nothing completely unexpected happens.)

Value Sensitivity

20. A main problem-cluster of policy analysis involves value questions. This includes the quite well-recognized (though unsolved) problem of indi-

vidual multidimensional utility functions which can neither be aggregated nor compared. But also included are a number of even more complex value issues, which usually are ignored by contemporary welfare theory and decision analysis. These include, for instance:

    a. Time preferences. The common economic assumptions of positive interest rates and discounting of the future are of limited validity for more complex policy issues. Thus, because of ideological preference and/or need expectations, the future may often receive priority over the present. Policy analysis must therefore deal not only with issues in which "interest rates" are heterogeneous, but interest rates will also, in part, be negative and noncontinuous. Indeed, the very terms of "interest" and "discount" rates are quite inappropriate when we deal with future-directed ideologies, commitments to self-sacrifice, and similar phenomena.

    b. Unknown future values. In most more complex policy issues, the main results of a policy will occur in the future and sometimes in a quite distant (10 to 25 years) future. Therefore, such policies should often satisfy future values. But future values are very difficult to predict, adding a serious qualitative uncertainty to the uncertainties of predicting the results of different policy alternatives.

    c. Options and future capacities as a goal. Easier to handle, but still difficult and neglected, are options—or future capacities—as a goal. Here, we are faced with the choice between definite goals, a number of defined future options as a goal, and capacities perhaps better to achieve as yet undefined goals in the future.

    d. Compact ideologies. Much of contemporary U.S. welfare and value theory assumes trade-offs between different goals, permitting side payments and enabling some uses of "Pareto Optimum" as a choice criterion. But when compact ideologies exist, values assume more of a "either all or nothing" form, trade-offs within dogma-structured goals are difficult, and Pareto Optimum may become logically irrelevant (for instance, when an ideology requires someone else to be worse off).

21. These and similar complexities can be handled to some extent with explicit value sensitivity analysis; construction of different value futures; search for minimin-avoidance solutions based on agreement on the worst outcomes, the worst plus one outcome, and so on; continuous value judgment by policymakers during various phases of policy analysis; and other tools, techniques, and arrangements. These complexities also, I think, illuminate the inadequacies of contemporary economic welfare approaches for policy analysis and the need for new efforts to work out a political-social theory of values.

Notes

[1]In Daniel Lerner and Harold D. Lasswell (ed.), *The Policy Sciences: Recent Developments in Scope and Methods* (Stanford, Calif.: Stanford University Press, 1951).

[2]For a recent version, see Harold D. Lasswell, "Policy Sciences" in *International Encyclopedia of Social Sciences,* Vol. 12, pp. 181–89.

[3]For an extended treatment see my paper "Prolegomenon to Policy Sciences," Rand Corporation, Santa Monica, Calif., 1969. See also my book *Public Policymaking Reexamined* (San Francisco: Chandler Publishing Co., 1968), pp. 240–45.

[4]The best recent presentations of systems analysis are: E. S. Quade and W. I. Boucher (eds.), *Systems Analysis and Policy Planning: Application in Defense* (New York: American Elsevier Publishing Co., 1968) and C. West Churchman, *The Systems Approach* (New York: Delacorte Press, 1968).

Some of the problems of applying systems analysis to broad social issues are discussed in C. West Churchman, *Challenge to Reason* (New York: McGraw-Hill Book Co., 1968), and Robert Boguslaw, *The New Utopians: A Study of System Design and Social Change* (Englewood Cliffs, N.J.: Prentice-Hall, 1965).

[5]See Sir Geoffrey Vickers, *The Art of Judgment* (New York: Basic Books, 1965), chap. 4. In contrast to U.S. applied decision theory, including most of systems analysis, which approaches problem solution by decomposition and treatment of different decision components (such as goals, alternatives, and predictions), Vickers emphasizes the need for a holistic, Gestalt view of problems. See also his recent collection *Value Systems and Social Process* (New York: Basic Books, 1968).

[6]This is the meeting point of "systems analysis" and "general systems theory." Both share a desire to look at phenomena in terms of broad interrelated sets, called "systems." Otherwise, despite the similarities in names, there is amazingly little common ground between systems analysis and general systems theory, though there is much potential scope for mutual stimulation and perhaps even some integration.

General systems theory is well presented in the following recent books: Ludwig von Bertalanffy, *General Systems Theory: Foundations, Development, Application* (New York: George Braziller, 1968); F. Kenneth Berrien, *General and Social Systems* (New Brunswick, N.J.: Rutgers University Press, 1968); and Walter Buckley (ed.), *Modern Systems Research for the Behavioral Scientist* (Chicago: Aldine Publishing Co., 1968).

It is interesting to note that the item "systems analysis" in the new *International Encyclopedia of Social Sciences* deals nearly exclusively with the general systems approach.

[7]Some efforts in this direction are presented in my forthcoming paper *Policy Strategies* (Santa Monica, California: The RAND Corporation, 1970).

37

MBO Goes to Work in
the Public Sector

Rodney H. Brady

The nation's largest organization in terms of spending power—the United States Department of Health, Education, and Welfare (HEW)—has been called unmanageable. It may have been at one time, but an important step toward making HEW more manageable has been the development and implementation of one of the most far-reaching management by objectives (MBO) systems in operation anywhere.

Although MBO is a familiar management tool in the private business sector, it had been used sparingly in the public sector prior to being introduced at HEW. The department turned to MBO as a means of copying with a veritable explosion in the size and scope of its operations. HEW's budget authority for the 1973 fiscal year is $87 billion—an increase of 70% over its budget of just four years ago, and the first civilian-agency budget in modern U.S. history to eclipse that of the Department of Defense. More than one third of all the money dispensed by the federal government this fiscal year will flow through HEW.

Prior to becoming the chief administrative and management officer of HEW in late 1970, I had been a senior executive and a management consultant in the private business sector and had discovered firsthand the value of MBO as an effective tool for managing large, complex organizations. However, the imponderable question facing me and my staff as we sought to implement a departmentwide MBO system at HEW was whether this method of management, believed by many to depend on the discipline of a profit and loss statement for successful operation, could be adapted to an organization that must ultimately measure success in terms of improving the quality of life.

Now, after over two years of experience with MBO, we have learned not only that this technique will indeed work at HEW but also that it has

Reprinted from *Harvard Business Review,* Vol. 51 (March–April, 1973), pp. 65–74. © 1973 by the President and Fellows of Harvard College; all rights reserved.

applicability to many other large, public-sector organizations. It is the objective of this article to (a) explain some major differences in introducing MBO to a public, as opposed to a private, sector organization; (b) briefly describe the MBO approach that has evolved at HEW and summarize the lessons we have learned in applying it; and (c) provide guidelines for other public- and private-sector organizations that may wish to adopt this management tool.

PRIVATE AND PUBLIC MBO

In 1954, Peter F. Drucker gave form to the concept of MBO in his book, *The Practice of Management.*[1] Ten years later, in giving the concept substance, he could still complain that "the foundation for systematic, purposeful performance of the specific task and function of business enterprise is . . . still missing."[2] Today, however, MBO is installed in numerous private companies and its premises are familiar to many business managers.[3] The strength of these premises lies in their simplicity:

- The clearer the idea of what one wants to accomplish, the greater the chances of accomplishing it.
- Real progress can only be measured in relation to what one is trying to make progress toward.

In other words, if one knows where he is going, he finds it easier to get there, he can get there faster, and he will know it when he arrives.

Although the premises of MBO have been tested and proven in the private sector, it has taken the public sector considerably longer to effectively incorporate them. Executives in the federal government have long grasped the *need* for more effective management, but for the most part they have failed to develop and implement systems such as MBO. This is one reason why they are so often frustrated in their attempts to manage large federal departments.

As John Gardner, who spent three years at the helm of HEW, put it: "When you figure out how to hold a middle-level bureaucrat accountable, it'll be comparable to landing on the moon."[4]

Similarly, Senator Abraham Ribicoff, HEW Secretary in 1961, remarked that "no matter how brilliant he is, no Secretary can handle the job with distinction because of the enormity of the task of managing billions of dollars worth of programs spanning the wide range of social needs in the United States."[5]

Former Secretary Ribicoff would have been quite correct if he had added that no Secretary can manage HEW with distinction unless he is given the management tools required to do the job. I am convinced that MBO is foremost among these tools. But before it can be used effectively, some problems that are unique to the public sector must be overcome. These include (a) defining objectives, (b) measuring benefits, and (c) the operating cycle.

The Objectives Problem

In the private-sector organization, the primary objective traditionally has been defined by the stockholders and board of directors as maximizing return on investment. This main objective is often supplemented by subobjectives such as rate of growth, development of new products, provisions for executive succession, and contributions to society.[6] Except for the latter (and even that to a large extent), all of these subobjectives focus directly on the primary goal of maximizing return on investment. It is possible, therefore, to translate the overall objective and each of its subobjectives into consistent, measurable, and mathematically relatable components. Thus, a single management system can be implemented throughout the enterprise to create a model of goal congruence.

In the public sector organization, however, there is no such single return-on-investment objective to which subobjectives can easily be tied. Unanimity on an overall objective for HEW, for example, does not exist among the 209 million Americans who are the department's "stockholders" as well as its "customers." Nor is such agreement to be found among those who cast the proxy votes for these stockholders—the decision makers in the legislative and executive branches, and even the judicial branch, of the federal government.

Moreover, on the rare occasions when these parties agree on subobjectives for HEW, the subobjectives are usually nebulous, difficult to measure, and lacking in the summing qualities that characterize the return-on-investment subobjectives common to the private sector.

The Benefits Problem

Measuring cost/benefits in the public sector is also more difficult than in private industry. One can calculate the dollar cost of teaching a disadvantaged child to read, for example, but how does one measure the "profitability" of this service to society? There is no single criterion for success when the benefit gained is in terms of newly unleashed human potential.

Although the department is continuing to seek ways to measure a dollar's effectiveness in, say, rehabilitating handicapped workers or reducing juvenile delinquency, such measurement is still a very rough science. In most cases, it will be years before the real benefits toward which these objectives are aimed can be evaluated effectively.

The Operating-Cycle Problem

A necessarily short operating cycle is another limited factor when introducing MBO into a public-sector organization. Although federal agencies like HEW have their own long-range goals, these goals are more likely to be upset than those in private industry. There are three reasons for this:

1. Federal agencies are budgeted annually in a complex process that too frequently is unpredictable.
2. A high rate of turnover among top-level, decision-making personnel is characteristic of the federal government.
3. Objectives set by public-sector managers in today's political setting will likely be deemed inadequate in tomorrow's political setting.

The MBO process in HEW is based on a one-year operating cycle—the federal fiscal year. Even given this relatively short time frame, the department's objectives for the year are subject to change, based on new or altered legislative mandates and/or new executive initiatives.

Yet, despite these not unexpected difficulties in establishing objectives and the allied difficulties of measuring progress toward their achievement, MBO has proved to be extremely helpful in managing the affairs of HEW. In the next section, I shall discuss how MBO actually operates in the department; but first, a closer look at HEW may help explain why a rigorous, formalized management system is essential if such a large, politically sensitive organization is to be managed effectively. Accordingly, the HEW structure and mission are described in [Figure 37.1].

APPLICATION AT HEW

Before MBO was introduced, the HEW operating cycle failed in several ways to systematically control the implementation of policy and budget decisions. For example:

- There was no adequate provision for stating program objectives that were based on specific, measurable results. Consequently, program success often was measured on the wrong criteria (e.g., the number of grants awarded rather than the number of people served or problems solved).
- There was no effective formal mechanism to ensure a continuing dialogue, throughout the operating cycle, between policy makers and program managers regarding the problems and successes encountered during the implementation phase. Consequently, there was both a lack of information for policy developers and a lack of guidance for managers.

FIGURE 37.1
The Structure and the Mission of HEW

HEW is charged with the responsibility for administering federal programs in the fields of health, education, income security, and social services. The department has over 100,000 employees, and it administers some 300 programs, ranging from cancer research to vocational education to family planning. Owing in part to the shift of national priorities away from defense spending and toward human-resources spending, HEW has recently been caught in a stream of national debate. It has been forced to operate in an atmosphere characterized by such highly political issues as school desegregation, busing, and welfare reform.

HEW is divided into seven major agencies and ten regional offices located across the country from Boston to Seattle. The staff of the Office of the Secretary provides advise to the Secretary as well as centralized support to the agencies and regional offices. The seven agencies and their basic missions are:

1. *National Institutes of Health* (NIH), which conducts and sponsors biomedical research and health-education programs.
2. *Health Services and Mental Health Administration* (HSMHA), which provides and sponsors health services, and conducts and sponsors research in the field of mental health.
3. *Food and Drug Administration* (FDA), which is a regulatory agency charged with ensuring that food, drugs, and other substances and devices utilized by consumers are safe and effective.
4. *Office of Education* (OE), which promotes the establishment of an effective and efficient educational system throughout the nation.
5. *Social Security Administration* (SSA), which operates the nation's system of social insurance through receiving contributions, processing claims, and making payments to beneficiaries; it also administers the Medicare program.
6. *Social and Rehabilitation Service* (SRS), which manages the federal social service and assistance payments programs.
7. *Office of Child Development* (OCD), which acts as an advocate for children and coordinates federal programs specifically aimed at children, youth, and their families.

While each of these agencies administers assigned programs, many of these programs require the cooperation of two or more agencies. For example, drug abuse prevention requires significant participation by nearly every agency.

The ten regional offices, and the field staffs of each of the agencies, oversee the delivery of services at the local level and maintain close contact with states, local governments, and grantees receiving funds from HEW. In this regard, it is important to note that less than 10% of HEW's money is spent on direct operations. More than 90% goes to Social Security beneficiaries or is dispersed to some 40,000 grantees, including state and local governments and educational or other non-profit institutions.

Part A of Exhibit I shows the HEW operating cycle prior to the introduction of MBO; Part B of the exhibit shows the operating cycle after MBO was introduced. Accordingly, when the system was implemented at HEW, its major operational goals were:

EXHIBIT I
Comparison of HEW Operating Cycles

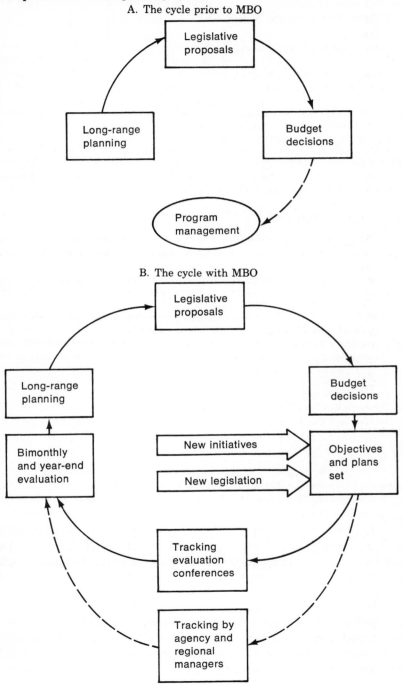

A. The cycle prior to MBO

Legislative proposals

Long-range planning

Budget decisions

Program management

B. The cycle with MBO

Legislative proposals

Long-range planning

Budget decisions

Bimonthly and year-end evaluation

New initiatives

New legislation

Objectives and plans set

Tracking evaluation conferences

Tracking by agency and regional managers

- To identify clear, measurable objectives.
- To monitor progress toward objectives that had been agreed on by both managers and policy makers.
- To effectively evaluate results.

Later I shall discuss how well the system met these goals. But first, let us take a closer look at how it actually works.

Setting Objectives

The annual MBO cycle begins when the department formulates its budget and makes the key resource and fund-allocation decisions for the coming fiscal year. Program managers are urged to accompany each request for funds with a list of measurable, results-oriented objectives.

By linking fund requests to the specific results the funds are intended to accomplish, HEW seeks to avoid awarding money on the basis of vague, projected activities. As mentioned earlier, this is a particularly acute problem in the public sector. To overcome it, HEW has instituted a six-stage, objective-setting procedure:

1. The Secretary employs the initial proposals as a starting point. He determines specifically what he wants the department to accomplish during the coming year and how the department's short-range goals will contribute to long-range objectives. He works closely with agency heads to refine their objectives and their requests for funds in the light of these goals. ([Figure 37.2] contains a typical dialogue between the Secretary and one of his managers as they attempt to formulate a results-oriented objective.)

2. The staff of the Secretary draws up the department's budget and then forwards it to the President and Congress for action.

3. The Secretary, who has determined priorities during the budgeting process, then formalizes them in a document that provides planning guidance to agency heads and regional managers.

4. These executives then review and alter their preliminary objectives to conform to changed budget priorities and overall department goals, typically selecting eight to ten objectives that represent the most important results expected of their respective programs.

5. Just prior to the start of the fiscal year, agency heads and regional managers submit these objectives, along with outlines of milestones that must be reached and resources that must be expended for their accomplishment, to the Office of the Secretary, where they are given careful analysis by his staff.

6. From this list of objectives, the Secretary selects those he will personally track. He also has the option of adding other objectives to the department's list (either at the start of the cycle or during the year), depending on his perception of HEW's changing mandate, the passage of new legislation, executive initiative, or other developments that affect the department's

role. Obviously, the Secretary cannot personally track all objectives. Many are tracked on a continuing basis by HEW agency leaders and managers at several organizational levels. In addition to the 70 objectives personally tracked by the Secretary last year, HEW agency heads and regional directors tracked approximately 300 objectives, and agency bureaus tracked about 1,500.

Monitoring Progress

The Office of the Secretary and the staff workers in each agency monitor progress in meeting objectives. The ongoing review process is facilitated by milestone charts that are prepared for each objective.

Of course, interim progress cannot always be expressed in terms of the final result. Yet by carefully selecting intermediate milestones that logic says must be achieved to accomplish the end result, one can in effect measure interim progress.

For example, one objective of the Health Services and Mental Health Administration (HSMHA) during 1971 was to increase the capacity of institutions receiving HSMHA support to provide family planning services for an additional 800,000 low-income patients. Exhibit II shows a detailed plan, including eight major milestones, that was outlined for accomplishing this objective. This was the status of the objective in October of 1971; since then, the other milestones have been reached and the objective has been completed.

The progress of objectives that are narrower in scope can usually be expressed more readily throughout the year in terms of final results. An example is the section of a HSMHA objective which called for providing immunizations to 8 million children. It was relatively easy to determine how many immunizations had been completed as the year progressed and to know by the end of the year that the objective had, in fact, been met.

Management conferences.   Managers are encouraged to maintain close contact with the Office of the Secretary and to seek advice or assistance in meeting their goals. In addition to this informal dialogue, the Secretary holds a bimonthly management conference with each agency head and regional director. These conferences, which are also attended by principal staff aides, are the keystone to the success of the entire MBO system.

It has been charged that the typical MBO system, characterized by such periodic appraisals, "perpetuates and intensifies hostility, resentment, and distrust between a manager and subordinates."[7] This may be the case in some instances, but it does not have to be. At HEW, for example, a publication entitled *Focus* is distributed to managers who are, or will be, participating in the bimonthly review conferences. It emphasizes that these are not "knuckle-rapping sessions" and states:

EXHIBIT II
Operating Plan for HSMHA Family Planning Objective

Resources committed: $88,815,000

Health priority — Family planning objective

Milestones	Completion date					
	July - Aug.	Sept. - Oct.	Nov. - Dec.	Jan. - Feb.	Mar. - Apr.	May - June
1. Expand and transfer OEO projects to increase capacity by 25,000 patients		▲				
2. Establish regional coordinating councils		▲				
3. Fund new projects, expand and transfer projects to increase capacity by 200,000 patients			△			
4. Report to Congress on five-year plan				△		
5. Fund new projects, expand and transfer projects to increase capacity by 250,000 patients					△	
6. Develop evaluation strategy for fiscal year 1973						△
7. Fund new projects, expand and transfer projects to increase capacity by 325,000 patients						△
8. Prepare final report						△

Key
▲ Completed
△ Not completed

"They are undertaken with the understanding that circumstances change; that, given the best will, spirit, and effort possible, *the things we do,* unfortunately, do not always *produce the results* intelligent men predict of them."[8]

Ten days prior to each management conference, an agency head or regional director submits to the Secretary a status report and evaluation on all objectives for which he is responsible. If a milestone has been accomplished on time and no problems are anticipated with future steps, the manager simply fills in the triangle representing the completion date of scheduled milestone (see Exhibit II). If, however, a milestone has not been completed on schedule or a future milestone is not likely to be completed on schedule, the agency head or regional director indicates the anticipated completion deadline by adding a triangle in the column which corresponds to the new planned month of accomplishment.

Managers also submit an evaluation of the status of each objective. This is based on a three-level classification system:

1. Satisfactory—no problem exists, nor is any anticipated, that will hinder the accomplishment of the objective on schedule.
2. Minor problem—although there is a problem, it does not presently jeopardize accomplishment of the objective.
3. Major problem—there is a distinct possibility that the objective will not be achieved in the absence of major corrective action.

The conference provides a dialogue between the Secretary and the manager, giving them a joint opportunity to identify and resolve management problems. Its agenda, planned jointly by the Secretary and the manager, centers on the objectives of the manager's agency. However, the conference is also used to familiarize both parties with changes inside or outside the agency that will affect its work. Even the objectives themselves may be changed to conform to new initiatives, thus resulting in a dynamic rather than a static process.

This ability to quickly change directions, even to the point of abandoning or drastically altering prior objectives, is a must in the public sector. Contrast this with the following statement on objectives by the former chairman of the board of Avis: "Once . . . objectives are agreed on, the leader must be merciless on himself and on his people. If an idea that pops into his head or out of their mouths is outside the objectives of the company, he kills it without a trial."[9]

Following each management conference, a detailed report is provided to the Secretary and other key participants. The report outlines the discussion items, decisions, and specific assignments. The status of each assignment is then reviewed at each succeeding conference until the action is completed.

Evaluating Results

In addition to the bimonthly reports just described, each manager submits a year-end evaluation to the Office of the Secretary which describes successes and failures in meeting objectives. The annual report details such things as revisions of objectives during the year, reasons for failure in fulfilling any objective, and steps taken to ensure that the same problems will not arise again. These evaluations are used in the long-range planning process to help make the department's future objectives more realistic as well as to help obviate potential problems.

PROBLEMS ALONG THE WAY

The cliché that old ways are not easily changed is particularly apt in the federal bureaucracy. This is true for a number of reasons, most of which are inherent in the nature of a system governed by a mixture of politically appointed personnel and professional personnel. In theory, the latter are subject to the policy decisions of the former. In reality, it is no secret that this is not always the case. Presidents and heads of departments come and go; yet the bureaucracy remains behind to keep the wheels of government turning.

The primary constraint to the success of MBO at HEW has been an attitude on the part of some managers that the regular attention required of them by such a system is either (a) not consistent with their roles or (b) not as effective a way to manage as some other approach. Some managers have viewed their roles as principally involving policy making, development of legislation, and defense of their budget requests. The intricacies of formalized management planning and control have taken a secondary role to these other functions. Too often, top-level managers have become preoccupied with handling crises in their agencies and have dealt with management issues on an ad hoc, rather than on an anticipatory, results-oriented basis.

Ironically, the fact that MBO gives managers access to the highest level of the department has been a hindrance, as well as a help, in gaining acceptance of the system. A common belief among managers in organizations of all types is that you have somehow failed if you have to bring your problems to the head of the organization. Thus, at HEW, some managers have proposed only those areas for control under MBO which would not prove a source of embarrassment in face-to-face dialogue at management conferences.

A related problem has been getting managers not only to adequately define problem areas but also to "stretch" in setting their objectives in those areas. In some cases, managers have established easily achievable objectives whose accomplishment is almost a foregone conclusion. Last year, for example, one HEW agency set a goal of decreasing by 2% the number of persons, in 13 selected geographical areas, who would need rehabilitative assistance of a certain type. By the end of the year, the goal had not only been met but had been exceeded ten times over.

Old ways can, however, be changed, as long as one can demonstrate good reasons for such change. Department leaders are satisfied that, in spite of the aforementioned obstacles, MBO has taken hold and is being genuinely accepted throughout the department.

BENEFITS OF THE SYSTEM

Although HEW still has significant problems, measurable results to date document some substantial benefits from the three-year-old MBO system. For example:

•During fiscal year 1972, the Food and Drug Administration (FDA) determined that, within existing resources, it would attempt to increase by 50% the number of import products inspected. This objective was met despite the delay and disruption to shipping caused by the Eastern Seaboard dock strike.

•In fiscal year 1971, the first full year of MBO in operation in the department, an objective of a program run by the Social and Rehabilitation Service (SRS) was to train and place 35,000 welfare recipients in meaningful jobs. SRS faced the need to convince the state agencies, which are the conduits for rehabilitation funds, that such concentration on public assistance recipients was warranted. It also faced the fact that the rehabilitation of welfare recipients is not an easy task. By establishing a results-oriented objective, carefully planning for its accomplishment, and communicating it to all levels of government, SRS actually exceeded its goal. It trained more than 40,000 welfare recipients and offered them a productive future by taking them off welfare rolls and putting them on payrolls.

Moreover, the rehabilitation objective in fiscal year 1973 is to move from a level of approximately 50,000 recipients per year to a level of 69,000. This planned 38% increase is approximately double the normally expected figure based on projected historical trend lines. Further, the department plans to achieve this objective with only a 14% increase in resources.

In addition to the short-term benefits from HEW's adaptation of MBO, there have been improvements in overall management. A key role the Secretary plays in regular management conferences is to ensure that the department is responding on an integrated basis to social problems, which rarely cut cleanly along jurisdictional lines of public agencies. In particular, he can use the conferences to communicate successes and problems identified elsewhere in HEW that have relevance to conferees.

FIGURE 37.2
An Objective-Setting Meeting at HEW

Here is a typical dialogue between former Secretary Elliot L. Richardson HEW and an agency head as they formulated an objective.

Agency head: One of our agency's most important initiatives this year will be to focus our efforts in the area of alcoholism and to treat an additional 10,000 alcoholics. Given last year's funding of 41 alcoholism treatment centers and the direction of other resources at the state and local level, we feel that this is an achievable objective.

Secretary: Are these 41 centers operating independently or are they linked to other service organizations in their communities? In other words, are we treating the whole problem of alcoholism, including its employment, mental health and welfare aspects, or are we just treating the *symptoms* of alcoholism?

Agency head: A program requirement for getting funds is that the services involved must be linked in an integrated fashion with these other resources.

Secretary: I am not interested in just looking at the number of alcoholics that are treated. Our goal ought to be the actual rehabilitation of these patients. Do you have data to enable you to restate the objective in terms of that goal?

Agency head: As a matter of fact, Mr. Secretary, we have developed a management information and evaluation system in which each grantee will be providing quarterly data on the number of alcoholics treated, as well as on the number of alcoholics who are actually rehabilitated.

Secretary: How do you define "rehabilitated"?

Agency head: If they are gainfully employed one year after treatment, we regard them as being rehabilitated.

Secretary: Please revise this objective, then, to enable us to track progress on how effective these programs really are in treating the disease of alcoholism and in rehabilitating alcoholics.

For example, in its initial presentation of proposed fiscal year 1973 objectives, the Office of Child Development (OCD) indicated it would establish a new category of day care worker. The new position, to be called "child development associate," will be filled by competent individuals who do not have special education or college degrees but who, nonetheless, are able to work well with children. The Secretary was able to receive assurances that this objective would be developed in such a way that it would provide a basis for similar categories of workers in other HEW programs.

CONCLUSION

MBO as a concept is simple—deceptively so. It is much easier to explain this technique than it is to introduce it to an organization, especially one as complex as HEW. Although the department is now in its third year of utilizing MBO as a primary management device, it is still building toward achieving a fully institutionalized, short-term management and control system that is used by all of its key managers.

Many lessons have been gleaned from HEW's experience with MBO that both add to the knowledge of the concept as used in the public sector and reinforce lessons already learned in the private sector. I shall conclude this discussion by grouping the lessons we have learned into four broad categories.

1. *Differences in public-sector approach:*

•While effective objectives can be established in public sector organizations, the process of developing the objectives is often more complex and requires broader coordination and participation of interested parties than in the private sector.

•Objectives in the public sector must take a different form from those in the private sector. In the former, the objectives must usually be stated in terms of interim results; in the latter, objectives can normally be stated in terms of the ultimate objective of "return on investment."

•Although progress toward achieving many public sector objectives is difficult to measure, few meaningful objectives are beyond effective measurement. Through utilization of milestone charts, which document accomplishments to be achieved by established dates, progress toward achieving almost any objective can be measured.

2. *Role of the top executive:*

•A chief executive officer who has both the will and the capacity to manage is essential to the effective utilization of an MBO system.

•MBO must be tailored to the chief executive's style of managing. One leader might take a decisive role in the operation of the system, while another leader might well have a different style of operating. Resistance to modifying the system to fit the style can destroy the MBO process.

•The chief executive officer must communicate clearly to other organizational components what he feels the general goals and priorities of the organization ought to be. Without such guidance, the subordinates' development of initial objectives for submission to the boss tends to be wasteful and counterproductive.

•The chief executive's attitude affects the spirit in which the system functions, and it will determine whether MBO encourages the defining and solving of problems or the hiding of problems. If MBO is perceived by a chief executive as a problem-solving and goal-reaching device (rather than as an opportunity to point an accusing finger at one of his subordinates), the subordinates themselves are likely to take this view.

3. *Managerial relationships:*

•The establishment of objectives must be a cooperative venture between subordinate and superior. Moreover, unless both parties feel that the objective is important, challenging, and achievable, even cooperative activity will become only a meaningless exercise.

•Managers must be persuaded that the primary function of MBO is to enable them to manage more effectively, not to use the management conference to reach the ear of the chief executive on random issues of particular momentary interest to the manager.

•To be effective, the MBO system must operate on a line manager-to-subordinate basis, not on a staff-to-staff basis. Although staff assistance is essential to keep the system functioning, staff must serve as a facilitator of the system and not its operator. To operate otherwise invites confusion in lines of authority and causes a breakdown in accountability.

•Unless the superior and subordinate have regular face-to-face reviews of interim progress, the importance of the system begins to be questioned, there is danger of misunderstanding, and much of the motivational value of the system is lost. Prior to such interim review meetings, it is essential that the superior's staff prepare him to ask the right questions and to avoid being "snowed" by the subordinate.

4. *General strategy considerations:*

•It is important to receive a detailed plan for accomplishing an objective at the same time the objective itself is submitted for approval. Otherwise, proposed objectives too often will not be well thought out in advance, and the possibility for eventual success will ultimately be decreased.

•A middle ground must be found between holding personnel too rigidly to their objectives and allowing them to alter the objectives at will. HEW's method has been to (a) have the Secretary himself approve all proposed changes and (b) ensure that such changes are evaluated in each agency's annual performance report.

•If an organization is consistently accomplishing 100% of its objectives, there is probably reason for concern rather than celebration. Objectives are not really effective unless an organization must "stretch" to reach them. During the last fiscal year, for example, approximately one fourth of HEW's objectives were only partially achieved and another one eighth fell far short of expectation. This is probably not an unhealthy balance.

•It is a mistake to try to make MBO so systematic and rigid that it precludes discussion of important matters not contained in formalized objectives. In fact, MBO should be expected to trigger ad hoc discussions of matters that are not included in stated objectives but are nonetheless vital to the success of the organization.

•MBO is perhaps better perceived as a muscle than as merely a tool. The more it is used, the stronger and more necessary it becomes. However, if MBO is merely a management system on paper and is not allowed to be exercised as an integral part of running an organization, it will atrophy and become useless.

Notes

[1] New York, Harper & Row, 1954.
[2] Peter F. Drucker, *Managing for Results* (New York, Harper & Row, 1964), Introduction, p. x.

[3]For more detail on both the theory behind MBO and its practical application in private companies, see "Managing by—and with—Objectives," *The Conference Board Record* (1968). Also see John B. Lasagna, "Make Your MBO Pragmatic," *Harvard Business Review,* November–December 1971, p. 64.

[4]Quoted in Robert Sherrill, "The Hatchetman and the Hatchetmyth," *Potomac* (Sunday Supplement to the Washington Post), February 6, 1972, pp. 13, 26.

[5]Quoted in Robert Sherrill, "The Real Robert Finch Stands Up," *The New York Times Magazine,* July 5, 1970, p. 19.

[6]For a discussion of social contributions in the private sector, see Raymond A. Bauer and Dan H. Fenn, Jr., "What *Is* a Corporate Social Audit?" *Harvard Business Review,* January–February 1973, p. 37.

[7]Harry Levinson, "Management by Whose Objectives?" *Harvard Business Review,* July–August 1970, p. 125.

[8]Department of Health, Education and Welfare, March 1972, Introduction, p. x.

[9]See Robert Townsend, *Up The Organization* (New York: Alfred A. Knopf, Inc., 1970), p. 130.

38
Management by Whose Objectives?

Harry Levinson

Despite the fact that the concept of management by objectives (MBO) has by this time become an integral part of the managerial process, the typical MBO effort perpetuates and intensifies hostility, resentment, and distrust between a manager and subordinates. As currently practiced, it is really just industrial engineering with a new name, applied to higher managerial levels, and with the same resistances.

Obviously, somewhere between the concept of MBO and its implementation, something has seriously gone wrong. Coupled with performance appraisal, the intent is to follow the Frederick Taylor tradition of a more rational management process. That is, which people are to do what, who is to have effective control over it, and how compensation is to be related directly to individual achievement. The MBO process, in its essence, is an effort to be fair and reasonable, to predict performance and judge it more carefully, and presumably to provide individuals with an opportunity to be self-motivating by setting their own objectives.

The intent of clarifying job obligations and measuring performance against a man's own goals seems reasonable enough. The concern for having both superior and subordinate consider the same matters in reviewing the performance of the latter is eminently sensible. The effort to come to common agreement on what constitutes the subordinate's job is highly desirable.

Yet, like most rationalizations in the Taylor tradition, MBO as a process is one of the greatest of managerial illusions because it fails to take adequately into account the deeper emotional components of motivation.

In this article, I shall indicate how I think management by objectives, as currently practiced in most organizations, is self-defeating, and serves simply to increase pressure on the individual. By doing so, I do not reject either MBO or performance appraisal out of hand.

Rather, by raising the basic question, "Whose objectives?" I propose to suggest how they might be made more constructive devices for effective management. The issues I shall raise have largely to do with psychological considerations, and particularly with the assumptions about motivation which underlie these techniques.

THE 'IDEAL' PROCESS*

Since management by objectives is closely related to performance appraisal and review, I shall consider these together as one practice which is intended:

- To measure and judge performance.
- To relate individual performance to organizational goals.
- To clarify both the job to be done and the expectations of accomplishment.
- To foster the increasing competence and growth of the subordinate.
- To enhance communications between superior and subordinate.
- To serve as a basis for judgments about salary and promotion.
- To stimulate the subordinate's motivation.
- To serve as a device for organizational control and integration.

Major Problems

According to contemporary thinking, the "ideal" process should proceed in five steps: (1) individual discussion with his superior of the subordinate's description of his own job, (2) establishment of short-term performance targets, (3) meeting with the superior to discuss progress toward targets, (4) establishment of checkpoints to measure progress, and (5) discussion between superior and subordinate at the end of a defined period to assess the results of the subordinate's efforts. In *ideal* practice, this process occurs against a background of more frequent, even day-to-day, contacts and is

---

*References for this section are given on p. 501.

separate from salary review. But, in *actual* practice, there are many problems. Consider:

No matter how detailed the job description, it is essentially static—that is, a series of statements.

However, the more complex the task and the more flexible a man must be in it, the less any fixed statement of job elements will fit what he does. Thus the higher a man rises in an organization and the more varied and subtle his work, the more difficult it is to pin down objectives that represent more than a fraction of his effort.

With preestablished goals and descriptions, little weight can be given to the areas of discretion open to the individual, but not incorporated into his job description or objectives.

I am referring here to those spontaneously creative activities an innovative executive might choose to do, or those tasks a responsible executive sees which need to be done. As we move more toward a service society, in which tasks are less well defined but spontaneity of service and self-assumed responsibility are crucial, this becomes pressing.

Most job descriptions are limited to what a man himself does in his work.

They do not adequately take into account the increasing interdependence of managerial work in organizations. This limitation becomes more important as the impact of social and organizational factors on individual performance becomes better understood. The more a man's effectiveness depends on what other people do, the less he himself can be held responsible for the outcome of his efforts.

If a primary concern in performance review is counseling the subordinate, appraisal should consider and take into account the total situation in which the superior and subordinate are operating.

In addition, this should take into account the relationship of the subordinate's job to other jobs, rather than to his alone. In counseling, much of the focus is in helping the subordinate learn to negotiate the system. There is no provision in most reviews and no place on appraisal forms with which I am familiar to report and record such discussion.

The setting and evolution of objectives is done over too brief a period of time to provide for adequate interaction among different levels of an organization.

This militates against opportunity for peers, both in the same work unit and in complementary units, to develop objectives together for maximum integration. Thus both the setting of objectives and the appraisal of performance make little contribution toward the development of teamwork and more effective organizational self-control.

Coupled with these problems is the difficulty superiors experience when they undertake appraisals.

Douglas McGregor complained that the major reason appraisal failed was that superiors disliked playing God by making judgments about another man's worth.[1] He likened the superior's experience to inspection of assembly line products and contended that his revulsion was against being inhuman. To cope with this problem, McGregor recommended that an individual should set his own goals, checking them out with his superior, and should use the appraisal session as a counseling device. Thus the superior would become one who helped the subordinate achieve his own goals instead of a dehumanized inspector of products.

Parenthetically, I doubt very much that the failure of appraisal stems from playing God or feeling inhuman. My own observation leads me to believe that managers experience their appraisal of others as a hostile, aggressive act that unconsciously is felt to be hurting or destroying the other person. The appraisal situation, therefore, gives rise to powerful, paralyzing feelings of guilt that make it extremely difficult for most executives to be constructively critical of subordinates.

Objectivity Plea

Be that as it may, the more complex and difficult the appraisal process and the setting and evaluation of objectives, the more pressing the cry for objectivity. This is a vain plea. Every organization is a social system, a network of interpersonal relationships. A man may do an excellent job by objective standards of measurement, but may fail miserably as a partner, subordinate, superior, or colleague. It is a commonplace that more people fail to be promoted for personal reasons than for technical inadequacy.

Furthermore, since every subordinate is a component of his superior's efforts to achieve his own goals, he will inevitably be appraised on how well he works with his superior and helps the latter meet his needs. A heavy subjective element necessarily enters into every appraisal and goal-setting experience.

The plea for objectivity is vain for another reason. The greater the emphasis on measurement and quantification, the more likely the subtle, nonmeasurable elements of the task will be sacrificed. Quality of performance frequently, therefore, loses out to quantification.

A case example. A manufacturing plant which produces high quality, high prestige products, backed by a reputation for customer consideration and service, has instituted an MBO program. It is well worked out and has done much to clarify both individual goals and organizational performance. It is an important component of the professional management style of that company which has resulted in commendable growth.

But an interesting, and ultimately destructive, process has been set in motion. The managers are beginning to worry because when they now ask why something has not been done, they hear from each other, "That isn't in my goals." They complain that customer service is deteriorating. The vague goal, "improve customer service," is almost impossible to measure.

There is therefore heavy concentration on those subgoals which can be measured. Thus time per customer, number of customer calls, and similar measures are used as guides in judging performance. The *less* time per customer and the *fewer* the calls, the better the customer service manager meets his objectives. He is cutting costs, increasing profit—and killing the business. Worse still, he hates himself.

Most of the managers in that organization joined it because of its reputation for high quality and good service. They want to make good products and earn the continued admiration of their customers, as well as the envy of their industry. When they are not operating at that high level, they feel guilty. They become angry with themselves and the company. They feel that they might just as well be working for someone else who admittedly does a sloppy job of quality control and could hardly care less about service.

The same problem exists with respect to the development of personnel, which is another vague goal that is hard to measure in comparison with subgoals that are measurable. If asked, each manager can name a younger man as his potential successor, particularly if his promotion depends on doing so; but no one has the time, or indeed feels that he is being paid, to thoroughly train the younger man. Nor can one have the time or be paid, for there is no way in that organization to measure how well a manager does in developing another.

THE MISSED POINT

All of the problems with objectives and appraisals outlined in the example discussed in the foregoing section indicate that MBO is not working well despite what some companies think about their programs. The underlying reason it is not working well is that it misses the whole human point.

To see how the point is being missed, let us follow the typical MBO process. Characteristically, top management sets its corporate goal for the coming year. This may be in terms of return on investment, sales, production, growth, or other measurable factors.

Within this frame of reference, reporting managers may then be asked how much their units intend to contribute toward meeting that goal, or they may be asked to set their own goals relatively independent of the corporate goal. If they are left free to set their own goals, these in any case are expected to be higher than those they had the previous year. Usually, each reporting manager's range of choices is limited to his option for a piece of the organizational action, or improvement of specific statistics. In some cases, it may also include obtaining specific training or skills.

Once a reporting manager decides on his unit's goals and has them approved by his superior, those become the manager's goals. Presumably, he has committed himself to what he wants to do. He has said it and he is responsible for it. He is thereafter subject to being hoisted on his own petard.

Now, let us reexamine this process closely: the whole method is based on a short-term, egocentrically oriented perspective and an underlying reward-punishment psychology. The typical MBO process puts the reporting manager in much the same position as a rat in a maze, who has choices between only two alternatives. The experimenter who puts the rat in the maze assumes that the rat wants the food reward; if he cannot presume that, he starves the rat to make sure he wants the food.

Management by objectives differs only in that it permits the man himself to determine his own bait from a limited range of choices. Having done so, the MBO process assumes that he will (a) work hard to get it, (b) be pushed internally by reason of his commitment, and (c) make himself responsible to his organization for doing so.

In fairness to most managers, they certainly try, but not without increasing resentment and complaint for feeling like rats in a maze, guilt for not paying attention to those parts of the job not in their objectives, and passive resistance to the mounting pressure for ever-higher goals.

Personal Goals

The MBO process leaves out the answers to such questions as: What are the manager's personal objectives? What does he need and want out of his work? How do his needs and wants change from year to year? What relevance do organizational objectives and his part in them have to such needs and wants?

Obviously, no objectives will have significant incentive power if they are forced choices unrelated to a man's underlying dreams, wishes, and personal aspirations. For example:

If a salesman relishes the pleasure of his relationships with his hard-earned but low-volume customers, this is a powerful need for him. Suppose his boss, who is concerned about increasing the volume of sales, urges him to concentrate on the larger quantity customers rather than the smaller ones, which will provide the necessary increase in volume, and then asks him how much of an increase he can achieve.

To work with the larger quantity customers means that he will be less likely to sell to the individuals with whom he has well-established relationships and be more likely to deal with purchasing agents, technical people, and staff specialists who will demand of him knowledge and information he may not have in sophisticated detail. Moreover, as a single salesman, his organization may fail to support him with technical help to meet these demands.

When this happens, not only may he lose his favorite way of operating, which has well served his own needs, but he may have demands put on him which cause him to feel inadequate. If he is being compelled to make a choice about the percent of sales volume increase he expects to attain, he may well do that, but now under great psychological pressure. No one has recognized the psychological realities he faces, let alone helped him to work with them. It is simply assumed that since his sales goal is a rational one, he will see its rationality and pursue it.

The problem may be further compounded if, as is not unusual, formal changes are made in the organizational structure. If sales territories are shifted, if modes of compensation are changed, if problems of delivery occur, or whatever, all of these are factors beyond the salesman's control. Nevertheless, even with certain allowances, he is still held responsible for meeting his sales goal.

Psychological Needs

Lest the reader think the example we have just seen is overdrawn or irrelevant, I know of a young sales manager who is about to resign his job, despite his success in it, because he chooses not to be expendable in an organization which he feels regards him only as an instrument for reaching a goal. Many young men are refusing to enter large organizations for just this reason.

Some may argue that my criticism is unfair, that many organizations start their planning and setting of objectives from below. Therefore, the company cannot be accused of putting the man in a maze. But it does so. In almost all cases, the only legitimate objectives to be set are those having to do with measurable increases in performance. This highlights, again, the question, "Whose objectives?" This question becomes more pressing in those circumstances where lower level people set their objectives, only to be questioned by higher level managers and told their targets are not high enough.

Here you may well ask, "What's the matter with that? Aren't we in business, and isn't the purpose of the man's work to serve the requirements of the business?" The answer to both questions is, "Obviously." But that is only part of the story.

If a man's most powerful driving force is comprised of his needs, wishes, and personal aspirations, combined with the compelling wish to look good in his own eyes for meeting those deeply held personal goals, then management by objectives should begin with *his* objectives. What does he want to do with his life? Where does he want to go? What will make him feel good about himself? What does he want to be able to look back on when he has expended his unrecoverable years?

At this point, some may say that those are his business. The company has other business, and it must assume that the man is interested in working in the company's business rather than his own. That kind of differentiation is impossible. Everyone is always working toward meeting his psychological needs. Anyone who thinks otherwise, and who believes such powerful internal forces can be successfully disregarded or bought off for long, is deluding himself.

THE MUTUAL TASK

The organizational task becomes one of first understanding the man's needs, and then, with him, assessing how well they can be met in this organization, doing what the organization needs to have done. Thus the highest point of self-motivation arises when there is a complementary conjunction of the man's needs and the organization's requirements. The requirements of both mesh, interrelate, and become synergistic. The energies of man and organization are pooled for mutual advantage.

If the two sets of needs do not mesh, then a man has to fight himself and his organization, in addition to the work which must be done and the targets which have been defined. In such a case, this requires of him and his boss that they evaluate together where he wants to go, where the organization is going, and how significant the discrepancy is. The man might well be better off somewhere else, and the organization would do better to have someone else in his place whose needs mesh better with organization requirements.

Long-Run Costs

The issue of meshed interests is particularly relevant for middle-aged, senior-level managers.[2] As men come into middle age, their values often begin to change, and they feel anew the pressure to accomplish many long-deferred dreams. When such wishes begin to stir, they begin to experience severe conflict.

Up to this point, they have committed themselves to the organization and have done sufficiently well in it to attain high rank. Usually, they are slated for even higher levels of responsibility. The organization has been good to them, and their superiors are depending on them to provide its leadership. They have been models for the younger men, whom they have urged to aspire to organizational heights. To think of leaving is to desert both their superiors and their subordinates.

Since there are few avenues within the organization to talk about such conflict, they try to suppress their wishes. The internal pressure continues to mount until they finally make an impulsive break, surprising and dismaying both themselves and their colleagues. I can think of three vice presidents who have done just that.

The issue is not so much that they decide to leave, but the cost of the way they depart. Early discussion with superiors of their personal goals would have enabled both to examine possible relocation alternatives within the organization. If there were none, then both the managers and their superiors might have come to an earlier, more comfortable decision about separation. The organization would have had more time to make satisfactory alternative plans, as well as to have taken steps to compensate for the manager's lagging enthusiasm. Lower level managers would then have seen the company as humane in its enlightened self-interest and would not have had to create fearful fantasies about what the top management conflicts were that had caused a good man to leave.

To place consideration of the managers' personal objectives first does not minimize the importance of the organization's goals. It does not mean there is anything wrong with the organization's need to increase its return on investment, its size, its productivity, or its other goals. However, I contend that it is ridiculous to make assumptions about the motivations of individuals, and then to set up means of increasing the pressures on people based on these often questionable assumptions. While there may be certain demonstrable short-run statistical gains, what are the long-run costs?

One cost is that people may leave; another, that they may fall back from competitive positions to plateaus. Why should an individual be expendable for someone else and sacrifice himself for something that is not part of his own cherished dreams? Still another cost may be the loss of the essence of the business, as happened in the case example we saw earlier of the manufacturing plant which had the problem of deteriorating customer service.

In that example, initially there was no dialogue. Nobody heard what the managers said, what they wanted, where they wanted to go, where they wanted the organization to go, and how they felt about the supposedly rational procedures that had been initiated. The underlying psychological assumption which management unconsciously made was that the managers *had to be made* more efficient; ergo, management by objectives.

Top management typically assumes that it alone has the prerogative to (a) set the objectives, (b) provide the rewards and targets, and (c) drive anyone who works for the organization. As long as this reward-punishment psychology exists in any organization, the MBO appraisal process is certain to fail.

Many organizations are making this issue worse by promising young people they will have challenges, since they assume these men will be challenged by management's objectives. Managements are having difficulty, even when they have high turnover rates, hearing these youngsters say they could hardly care less for management's unilaterally determined objectives. Managements then become angry, complain that the young people do not want to work, or that they want to become presidents overnight.

What the young people are asking is: What about me and my needs? Who will listen? How much will management help me meet my own requirements while also meeting its objectives?

The power of this force is reflected in the finding that the more the subordinate participates in the appraisal interview by presenting his own ideas and beliefs, the more likely he is to feel that (a) the superior is helpful and constructive, (b) some current job problems are being cleared up, and (c) reasonable future goals are being set.[3]

THE SUGGESTED STEPS

Given the validity of all the MBO problems I have been discussing to this point, there are a number of possibilities for coping with them. Here, I suggest three beginning steps to consider.

1. Motivational Assessment

Every management by objectives program and its accompanying performance appraisal system should be examined as to the extent to which it (1) expresses the conviction that people are patsies to be driven, urged, and manipulated, and (2) fosters a genuine partnership between men and organization, in which each has some influence over the other, as contrasted with a rat-in-maze relationship.

It is not easy for the nonpsychologist to answer such questions for himself, but there are clues to the answers. One clue is how decisions about compensation, particularly bonuses, are made. For example:

•A sales manager asked my judgment about an incentive plan for highly motivated salesmen who were in a seller's market. I asked why he needed one, and he responded, "To give them an incentive." When I pointed out that they were already highly motivated and apparently needed no incentive, he changed his rationale and said that the company wanted to share its success to keep the men identified with it, and to express its recognition of their contribution.

I asked, "Why not let them establish the reward related to performance?" The question startled him; obviously, if they were going to decide, who needed him? A fundamental aspect of his role, as he saw it, was to drive them ever onward, whether they needed it or not.

•A middle-management bonus plan tied to performance proved to be highly unsatisfactory in a plastic-fabricating company. Frustrated that its well-intentioned efforts were not working and determined to follow precepts of participative management, ranking executives involved many people in formulating a new one: personnel, control, marketing executives, and others —in fact, everyone but the managers who were to receive the bonuses. Top management is now dismayed that the new plan is as unsatisfactory as the old and is bitter that participation failed to work.

Another clue is the focus of company meetings. Some are devoted to intensifying the competition between units. Others lean heavily to exhortation and inspiration. Contrast these orientations with meetings in which people are apprised of problems and plan to cope with them.

2. Group Action

Every objectives and appraisal program should include group goal setting, group definition of both individual and group tasks, group appraisal of its accomplishments, group appraisal of each individual member's contribution to the group effort (without basing compensation on that appraisal), and shared compensation based on the relative success with which group goals are achieved. Objectives should include long-term as well as short-term goals.

The rationale is simple. Every managerial job is an interdependent task. Managers have responsibilities to each other as well as to their superiors. The reason for having an organization is to achieve more together than each could alone. Why, then, emphasize and reward individual performance alone, based on static job descriptions? That can only orient people to both incorrect and self-centered goals.

Therefore, where people are in complementary relationships, whether they report to the same superior or not, both horizontal and vertical goal formulation should be formalized, with regular, frequent opportunity for review of problems and progress. They should help each other define and describe their respective jobs, enhancing control and integration at the point of action.

In my judgment, for example, a group of managers (sales, promotion, advertising) reporting to a vice president of marketing should formulate their collective goals, and define ways both of helping each other and of assessing each others' effectiveness in the common task. The group assessment of each manager's work should be a means of providing each with constructive feedback, not for determining pay. However, in addition to his salary, each should receive, as part of whatever additional compensation is offered, a return based on the group effort.

The group's discussion among itself and with its superior should include examination of organizational and environmental obstacles to goal achievement, and particularly of what organizational and leadership supports are required to attain objectives. One important reason for this is that often people think there are barriers where none would exist if they initiated action. ("You mean the president really wants us to get together and solve this problem?")

Another reason is that frequently when higher management sets goals, it is unaware of significant barriers to achievement, leaving managers cynical. For example, if there is no comprehensive orientation and support program to help new employees adapt, then pressure on lower level managers to employ disadvantaged minority group members and to reduce their turnover can only be experienced by those managers as hollow mockery.

3. Appraisal of Appraisers

Every management by objectives and appraisal program should include regular appraisals of the manager by his subordinates, and be reviewed by the manager's superior. Every manager should be specifically compensated for how well he develops people, based on such appraisals. The very phrase "reporting to" reflects the fact that although a manager has a responsibility, his superior also has a responsibility for what he does and how he does it.

In fact, both common sense and research indicate that the single most significant influence outside himself on how a manager does his job is his superior. If that is the case, then the key environmental factor in task accomplishment and managerial growth is the relationship between the manager and his superior.

Therefore, objectives should include not only the individual manager's personal and occupational goals, but also the corporate goals he and his superior share in common. They should together appraise their relationship vis-à-vis both the manager's individual goals and their joint objectives, review what they have done together, and discuss its implication for their next joint steps.

A manager rarely is in a position to judge his superior's overall performance, but he can appraise him on the basis of how well the superior has helped him to do his job, how well he is helping him to increase his proficiency and visibility, what problems the supervisor poses for him, and what kinds of support he himself can use. Such feedback serves several purposes.

Most important, it offers the superior some guidance on his own managerial performance. In addition, and particularly when the manager is protected by higher level review of his appraisal, it provides the supervisor with direct feedback on his own behavior. This is much more constructive than behind-his-back complaint and vituperative terminal interviews, in which case he has no opportunity either to defend himself or correct his behavior. Every professional counselor has had recently fired executive clients who did not know why they had been discharged for being poor superiors when, according to their information, their subordinates thought so much of them. In his own self-interest, every manager should want appraisal by his subordinates.

THE BASIC CONSIDERATION

When the three organizational conditions we have just seen do in fact exist, then it is appropriate to think of starting management by objectives with a consideration of each man's personal objectives; if the underlying attitude in the organization toward him is that he is but an object, there is

certainly no point in starting with the man. Nor is there any point in trying
to establish his confidence in his superiors when he is not protected from
their rivalry with him, or when they are playing him off against his peers.
Anyone who expressed his fears and innermost wishes under these circumstances would be a damned fool.

For reasons I have already indicated, it should be entirely legitimate in
every business for these concerns to be the basis for individual objectives-
setting. This is because the fundamental managerial consideration necessarily must be focused on the question: "How do we meet both individual
and organizational purposes?" If a major intention of management by
objectives is to enlist the self-motivated commitment of the individual, then
that commitment must derive from the individual's powerful wishes to
support the organization's goals; otherwise the commitment will be merely
incidental to his personal wishes.

Having said that, the real difficulty begins. How can any superior know
what a subordinate's personal goals and wishes are if the subordinate himself—as most of us are—is not clear about them? How ethical is it for a
superior to pry into man's personal life? How can he keep himself from
forming a negative judgment about a man who, he knows, is losing interest
in his work, or is not altogether identified with the company? How can he
keep that knowledge from interfering with judgments he might otherwise
make, and opportunities he might otherwise offer? How often are the personal goals, particularly in middle age, temporary fantasies that are better
not discussed? Can a superior who is untrained in psychology handle such
information constructively? Will he perhaps do more harm than good?

These are critically important questions. They deserve careful thought.
My answers should be taken as no more than beginning steps.

Ego Concepts

Living is a process of constant adaptation. A man's personal goals,
wishes, and aspirations are continuously evolving, and being continuously
modified by his experiences. That is one reason why it is so difficult for an
individual to specify concrete personal objectives.

Nevertheless, each of us has a built-in road map, a picture of himself as
his future best. Psychologists speak of this as an *ego ideal,* which is comprised of a man's values, the expectations parents and others have held out
for him, his competences and skills, and his favorite ways of behaving. A
man's ego ideal is essentially the way he thinks he ought to be. Much of a
person's ego ideal is unconscious, which is another reason why it is not clear
to him.

Subordinate's self-examination.   Although a man cannot usually spell
out his ego ideal, he can talk about those experiences that have been highly
gratifying, even exhilarating, to him. He can specify those rare peak experi-

ences that made him feel very good about himself. When he has an opportunity to talk about what he has found especially gratifying and also what he thinks would be gratifying to him, he is touching on central elements of his ego ideal.

Given the opportunity to talk about such experiences and wishes on successive occasions, he can begin to spell out for himself the central thrust of his life. Reviewing all of the occupational choices he has made and the reasons for making them, he can begin to see the common threads in those choices and therefore the momentum of his personality. As these become clearer to him, he is in a better position to weigh alternatives against the mainstream of his personality.

For example, a man who has successively chosen occupational alternatives in which he was individually competitive, and whose most exhilarating experiences have come from defeating an opponent or single-handedly vanquishing a problem, would be unlikely to find a staff position exhilarating, no matter what it paid or what it was called. His ideal for himself is that of a vanquishing, competitive man.

The important concept here is that it is not necessary that a man spell out concrete goals at any one point; rather, it is helpful to him and his organization if he is able to examine and review aloud on a continuing basis his thoughts and feelings about himself in relation to his work. Such a process makes it legitimate for him to bring his own feelings to consciousness and talk about them in the business context as the basis for his relationship to the organization.

By listening, and helping him to spell out how and what he feels, the superior does not do anything to the man, and therefore by that self-appraisal process cannot hurt him. The information serves both the man and his superior as a criterion for examining the relationship of the man's feelings and his, however dimly perceived, personal goals or organizational goals. Even if some of his wishes and aspirations are mere fantasy and impossible to gratify, if it is legitimate to talk about them without being laughed at, he can compare them with the realities of his life and make more reasonable choices.

Even in the safest organizational atmosphere, for reasons already mentioned, it will not be easy for managers to talk about their goals. The best-intentioned supervisor is likely to be something less than a highly skilled interviewer. These two facts suggest that any effort to ascertain a subordinate's personal goals is futile; but I think not.

The important point is not the specificity of the statement that any man can make, but the nature of a superior-subordinate relationship that makes it safe to explore such feelings and gives first consideration to the man. In such a context, both subordinate and superior may come closer to evolving a man-organization fit than they might otherwise.

Superior's introspection.   A man-organization relationship requires the superior to do some introspection, too. Suppose he has prided himself on bringing along a bright young man who, he now learns, is thinking of moving into a different field. How can he keep from being angry and disappointed? How can he cope with the conflict he now has when it is time to make recommendations for advancement or a raise?

The superior cannot keep from being angry and disappointed. Such feelings are natural in that circumstance. He can express his feelings of disappointment to his protégé without being critical of the latter. But, if he continues to feel angry, then he needs to ask himself why another man's assertion of independence irritates him so. The issues of advancement and raises should continue to be based on the same realistic premises as they would have been before.

Of course, it now becomes appropriate to consider with the man whether —in view of his feelings—he wants to take on the burden of added responsibility and can reasonably discharge it. If he thinks he does, and can, he is likely to pursue the new responsibility with added determination. With his occupational choice conflict no longer hidden, and with fewer feelings of guilt about it, his commitment to his chosen alternative is likely to be more intense.

And if he has earned a raise, he should get it. To withhold it is to punish him, which puts the relationship back on a reward-punishment basis.

The question of how ethical it is to conduct such discussions as part of a business situation hinges on both the climate of the organization and on the sense of personal responsibility of each executive. Where the organization ethos is one of building trust and keeping confidences, there is no reason why executives cannot be as ethical as lawyers or physicians.

If the individual executive cannot be trusted in his relationships with his subordinates, then he cannot have their respect or confidence in any case, and the ordinary MBO appraisal process simply serves as a management pressure device. If the organization ethos is one of rapacious internal competition, backbiting, and distrust, there is little point in talking about self-motivation, human needs, or commitment.

CONCLUSION

Management by objectives and performance appraisal processes, as typically practiced, are inherently self-defeating over the long run because they are based on a reward-punishment psychology that serves to intensify the pressure on the individual while really giving him a very limited choice of objectives. Such processes can be improved by examining the psychological assumptions underlying them, by extending them to include group appraisal and appraisal of superiors by subordinates, and by considering the personal goals of the individual first. These practices require a high level of ethical standards and personal responsibility in the organization.

Such appraisal processes would diminish the feeling on the part of the superior that appraisal is a hostile, destructive act. While he and his subordinates would still have to judge the latter's individual performance, this judgment would occur in a context of continuing consideration for personal needs and reappraisal of organizational and environmental realities.

Not having to be continuously on the defensive and aware of the organization's genuine interest in having him meet his personal goals as well as the organization's goals, a manager would be freer to evaluate himself against what has to be done. Since he would have many additional frames of reference in both horizontal and vertical goal setting, he would need no longer to see himself under appraisal (attack, judgment) as an isolated individual against the system. Furthermore, he would have multiple modes for contributing his own ideas and a varied method for exerting influence upward and horizontally.

In these contexts, too, he could raise questions and concerns about qualitative aspects of performance. Then he, his colleagues, and his superiors could together act to cope with such issues without the barrier of having to consider only statistics. Thus a continuing process of interchange would counteract the problem of the static job description and provide multiple avenues for feedback on performance and joint action.

In such an organizational climate, work relationships would then become dynamic networks for both personal and organizational achievements. No incidental gain from such arrangements is that problems would more likely be solved spontaneously at the lowest possible levels, and free superiors simultaneously from the burden of the passed buck and the onus of being the purveyors of hostility.

Notes

[1]"An Uneasy Look at Performance Appraisal," *Harvard Business Review*, May–June 1957, p. 89.

[2]See my article, "On Being a Middle-Aged Manager," *Harvard Business Review*, July–August 1969, p. 51.

[3]Ronald J. Burke and Douglas S. Wilcox, "Characteristics of Effective Employee Performance Reviews and Developmental Interviews," *Personal Psychology*, Vol. 22, No. 3, 1969, p. 291.

References for Section on The 'Ideal' Process

*In this part of the article, which defines the ideal process and the major problems inherent in it,I draw heavily on the work of these authors, in sequence:

Alva F. Kindall and James Gatza, "Positive Program for Performance Appraisal," *Harvard Business Review*, November–December 1963, p. 153.

Herbert H. Meyer, Emanuel Kay, and John R. P. French, Jr., "Split Roles in Performance Appraisal," *Harvard Business Review,* January–February 1965, p. 123.

Ishwar Dayal, "Role Analysis Techniques in Job Description," *California Management Review,* Vol. XI, No. 4, 1969, p. 47.

Stanley Sloan and Alton C. Johnson, "Performance Appraisal . . . Where Are We Headed?" The *Personnel Administrator,* Vol. 14, No. 5, 1969, p. 12.

Philip R. Kelly, "Reappraisal of Appraisals," *Harvard Business Review,* May–June 1958, p. 59.

Robert A. Howell, "A Fresh Look at Management by Objectives," *Business Horizons,* Vol. 10, No. 3, 1967, p. 51.

Albert W. Schrader, "Let's Abolish the Annual Performance Review," *Management of Personnel Quarterly,* Fall 1969, p. 20.

George H. Labovitz, "In Defense of Subjective Executive Appraisal," *Academy of Management Journal,* Vol. 12, No. 3, 1969, p. 293.

Larry E. Greiner, D. Paul Leitch, and Louis B. Barnes, "Putting Judgment Back into Decisions," *Harvard Business Review,* March–April 1970, p. 59.

George Strauss and Leonard R. Sayles, *Personnel: The Human Problems of Management* (Englewood Cliffs, New Jersey: Prentice-Hall, Inc., 1967), p. 564.

Name Index

Subject Index

External auditing, 218-19

Factoring the budget, 373-79
Farm Credit Administration, 102
Federal Budget, preparation and execution of, 46-53
Fixed charges, 99-100, 107
in federal budget, 99
need for re-examination of, 107

Game Theory in operations research, 416
General Accounting Office, 180-84, 210
criteria for judging, 183
audit policy of, 210
General Services Administration, 189
Goal-setting as a function of budget, 277, 287
(SEE also BUDGET.)
Government corporations, or authorities, 93-95

Health, Education, and Welfare, Department of, 99, 103-4, 471-86
and management by objectives, 471-86
Hierarchy, 30-33, 327-39, 363 65
and OD programs, 363-65
and organization structure, 30-33, 327-39
in public agencies, 363-65
(SEE also ORGANIZATION DEVELOPMENT; and ORGANIZATIONAL STRUCTURE.)
Hoover Commissions, 290-91, 294, 388-89

Impounding, President's power of, 37
Incrementalism, 137-48, 161-75, 431-32
and Comprehensive approach, 135-37
and decision-making, 161-75
and PPBS, 431-32
characteristics of, 162

improvements in, 146-47
Information processing, 146-47
Information theory in operations research, 416
Institute of internal auditors, 231
Interest groups, 69-71
and political parties, 69
leaders of, 70-71
Internal auditing, 179-184, 209-19
and concepts for federal agencies, 209-22
relation to external auditing, 218-19
Internal reporting, 327-38
problems of, 331-34
procedures for, 329-30
purposes of, 327

Kestnbaum Commission, 77, 79-80

Land Management, Bureau of, 156
Legislation, 37-38, 62, 67-70
and decision-making, 96
role of committees in, 67-70
(SEE also CONGRESS; and COMMITTEES, and CONGRESSIONAL.)
Legislative-executive Relationships, 54-65
Linear programming in operations research, 412
Line-item budget, 378-82, 387-89, 429, 436
and performance budget, 388-93
and PPBS, 429, 436
and program budget, 388-89

Management and Budget, Office of, 57-65, 160-61, 178-93, 213-14
Management by Objectives (MBO), 241-42, 251-300, 379-84, 471-507
and chief executive role, 484
and personal goals, 491-92
criticisms of, 486-507

and PPBS, 429-433;41
(SEE also LINE-ITEM BUDG-
ET; and PERFORMANCE
BUDGET.)
Program Evaluation and Review
Technique (PERT), 375-76,
415-27
in accounting reports, 417-27
Programs, public, 120-23
different types of, 123
evaluation of, 120 22
sources of funding for, 122-23

Queueing Theory in operations research, 414

Reclamation, Bureau of, 118-19
Reform, budgetary, 4, 379-80

Search theory, in operations research,
416
Sensitivity training, 356
"Simulation" in public agencies, 376-
77
Staff units or officials, 302-39
activities of, 302
conflict associated with, 307-20
growth in number of, 313-15
in organization theory, 327-39
kinds of, 307-8
NII model of, 307-11, 330-34
(SEE also CENTRALIZATION;
and ORGANIZATIONAL
STRUCTURES.)

Standards for financial analysis,
acceptance of, 21-24
and accounting data, 16, 20-24
and budgets, 9-10
and costs, 8 9
(SEE also BUDGET; and CON-
TROL.)
Stress in budgeting and finance activities, 301-5
Symbolic logic in Operations Research, 416
Systems analysis, 447-65
and budgets, 454-57
and policy analysis, 464-65
definition of, 448
inadequacies of, 462-63
in governmental decision-making,
447-60
(SEE also COST-EFFECTIVE-
NESS ANALYSIS; PPBS; and
POLICY ANALYSIS.)

Taxes, 75, 90, 95
and expenditures, 90
and subsidies, 95
regressive, 75
Tension, nine sources of in staff activities, 309-20
(SEE also STAFF.)
Trust funds, 98, 106-7
and budget uncontrollability, 98
and needed review, 106-7

Value Theory in Operations Research, 416

THE BOOK MANUFACTURE

Public Budgeting and Finance: Readings in Theory and Practice, Second Edition, was typeset by Datagraphics of Phoenix, Arizona. Printing and binding were by Edwards Brothers of Ann Arbor, Michigan.. Dust jacket and cover designs were by Charles Kling and Associates. Cover material is Holliston Minitex.